Contents

PHILOSOPHICAL FOUNDATIONS
OF PROPERTY LAW

Philosophical Foundations of Property Law

Edited by
JAMES PENNER
and
HENRY E. SMITH

OXFORD
UNIVERSITY PRESS

OXFORD
UNIVERSITY PRESS

Great Clarendon Street, Oxford, OX2 6DP,
United Kingdom

Oxford University Press is a department of the University of Oxford.
It furthers the University's objective of excellence in research, scholarship,
and education by publishing worldwide. Oxford is a registered trade mark of
Oxford University Press in the UK and in certain other countries

Published in the United States of America by Oxford University Press
198 Madison Avenue, New York, NY 10016, United States of America

British Library Cataloguing in Publication Data
Data available

Library of Congress Control Number: 2013942281

ISBN 978-0-19-967358-2

Printed in Great Britain by
CPI Group (UK) Ltd, Croydon, CR0 4YY

Table of Cases

List of Contributors

Lisa M. Austin, Associate Professor of Law, University of Toronto

Alan Brudner, Professor Emeritus of Law and Political Science, University of Toronto

Eric R. Claeys, Professor of Law, George Mason University

Simon Douglas, CUF Lecturer in Law, University of Oxford, Peter Clarke Fellow and Tutor in Law, Jesus College, Oxford

Larissa Katz, Associate Professor of Law, University of Toronto

Dennis Klimchuk, Associate Professor of Philosophy, University of Western Ontario

Brian Angelo Lee, Associate Professor of Law, Brooklyn Law School

Ben McFarlane, Professor of Law, University College London

Stephen R. Munzer, Distinguished Professor of Law, University of California, Los Angeles

James Penner, Professor of Law, National University of Singapore

Arthur Ripstein, Professor of Law and of Philosophy at the University of Toronto

Carol M. Rose, Gordon Bradford Tweedy Professor of Law and Organization, Yale Law School, Emer. and Ashby Lohse Chair in Water & Natural Resource Law, University of Arizona, Rogers College of Law

Irit Samet, Senior Lecturer in the Dickson Poon School of Law, Kings College London

Henry E. Smith, Fessenden Professor of Law, Harvard University

Jeremy Waldron, University Professor, NYU Law School; Chichele Professor of Social and Political Theory, University of Oxford

Introduction

In 1992, in an article tellingly entitled 'Too Much Property',[1] Lawrence Becker told us that one of the things which property theorists might now avoid recapitulating at any great length was the 'now-standard conceptual apparatus of property theory: Hohfeld's analysis of rights, Honoré's analysis of ownership, and typologies of justificatory arguments'.[2] '[W]e can reasonably now refrain from publishing more than a swift, clear restatement of it.' This conceptual apparatus, essentially the idea that property is to be understood as a 'bundle of rights', such as the right to possess, the right to use, the right to sell, and so on, appeared to present a stable picture of the nature of property around which a consensus had formed. Individual 'sticks' in the bundle might draw differently on the different standard justifications. For example, the right to possess a chattel[3] might reflect a rights-based justification, extending the right to bodily security, or more generally, autonomy, into the world of tangible resources. On the other hand, the power to sell might better be justified on utilitarian grounds, for example by the claim that the power to sell allowed goods to move to their highest value user, thus enhancing allocative efficiency.

Becker also suggested that future work might 'dispense with the search for a deep justification of property rights (from metaphysics, moral psychology, natural rights, developmental psychology, sociobiology, or whatever) and focus on the behavioural surface: the observed, persistent, robust behavioural connections between various property arrangements and human well-being, broadly conceived.'[4] Whilst Becker did not himself use the analogy, his paper strongly suggested that property scholarship was approaching, if it had not already arrived at, a period of inquiry which in Kuhnian terms one would describe as one of 'normal science'.

In a somewhat different vein in 1993 Alan Brudner, commenting as editor of a special issue on property theory published in the *Canadian Journal of Law & Jurisprudence*, stated: 'skepticism about private property as a stable concept is shared by almost all of the . . . contributors. Some of them argue, while others assume, that property is intelligible only as a social construct, as a perfectly malleable category wholly at the service of collective goals.'[5]

Whilst superficially presenting different pictures of the discourse at the time, it is submitted that Becker's and Brudner's characterization of the contemporary state of play can be fruitfully assimilated. The 'standard conceptual apparatus', embracing

---

[1] Becker 1992. The piece is stated to be a review of Munzer 1990 and Waldron 1988, but is more a rumination on the state of property theorizing. Munzer 1990 is probably the *locus classicus* for what Becker calls the 'standard conceptual apparatus'.

[2] Becker 1992, 197. By 'typologies of justificatory arguments' Becker was referring to categories like Lockean labour-desert theory, utilitarian justifications of property, personality accounts like Hegel's, and so on.

[3] More accurately, the right to immediate, exclusive possession.

[4] Becker 1992, 206.   [5] Brudner 1993, 184–5.

the bundle of rights metaphor, is well known to be a reductionist or disintegrationist approach to understanding property, which had become the conventional wisdom in the United States in the latter half of the last century.[6] It would therefore not be surprising to find a majority of property theorists expressing a scepticism about property as anything other than a shifting and malleable assembly of norms whose content and character would change with changing social conditions which reflected changing collective goals.

At around the same time a similar 'settling down' appeared to occur in theoretical doctrinal analysis, particularly in North America. With the ascendancy of what might be termed the post-Realist consensus, including the increasing role of economic analysis in private law scholarship, legal scholars' and economists' characterization of property tended to converge on a very thin notion of property: roughly, property consisted in those entitlements which could be the subject of exchange under the law of contract and which were protected from the forced use or transfer by others. This perspective meshed nicely with the theoretical 'bundle of rights' picture, for under it the array of rights comprising property could naturally be treated one by one as the possible objects of contractual transfer or tortious interference. The important point to notice about this way of looking at things is that property itself, as simply the range of entitlements with which the law of contract and the law of torts engage, is intrinsically uninteresting—it is essentially a placeholder category. There is no little irony in this. Coase meant to argue against the obsession in mid-twentieth century economics with models of perfect competition.[7] But if transaction costs (broadly conceived) are important, the contours or nature of entitlements themselves might be susceptible to Coasean analysis.[8] Indeed, if the costs and benefits of institutions are truly put on the table, we have reason to question Coase's adoption of the bundle picture and its reception by law and economics.[9] If transaction costs point to the importance of entitlements, then this importance goes beyond their liability to be reallocated through market transactions or the different ways in which tortious interference with entitlements might be remedied, e.g. via damages (a 'liability rule'), or via an injunction (a 'property rule').[10]

If there ever was such a period of normal science it seems, perhaps unsurprisingly, to have had a very short duration. In a few short years following Becker's and Brudner's comments, works started appearing which began to undo any consensus in relation to the standard conceptual apparatus, whilst at the same time there was a renewal of interest in finding a coherent moral-political justification for property rights which was not merely a survey of different justificatory strategies. And following the seminal work of Merrill and Smith, in particular their paper 'What Happened to Property in Law and Economics?',[11] the importance of property as a doctrinal category could never again be ignored by private law theorists pursing an economic approach to the subject. It is beyond the scope of this introduction to

---

[6] Grey 1980.   [7] Coase 1960; Coase 1988, 14–15, 174.
[8] Merrill and Smith 2011.   [9] Coase 1988, 11; see generally Merrill and Smith 2001, 2011.
[10] Calabresi and Melamed 1972.   [11] Merrill and Smith 2001.

cover the rich array of developments that have taken place in the last 20 years, but we can look at some of the milestones along the way.

A few short years after Becker and Brudner wrote, the bundle of rights picture of property began to come under sustained attack. Schroeder's[12] and Penner's[13] attacks were particularly influential. Schroeder argued forcefully that Hohfeld and his intellectual successors had misrepresented or misconceived the Western intellectual tradition's understanding of property that culminated in the work of Blackstone: Blackstone did not naively think that property rights all related to *tangible* things; rather, the tradition in which Blackstone wrote appreciated, quite correctly, that the concept of property concerns those norms where something *external* to the subjects of law mediates their normative relations. She also launched a scathing attack on the idea that Hohfeld's paucital/multital rights distinction or the disaggregation of property into a bundle of incidents had found its way into modern property law, in particular modern commercial law. For his part Penner systematically assessed the standard category of incidents which were supposed to underlie the Hohfeld/Honoré intellectual nexus's characterization of property as an aggregation of norms, and showed that these could not properly be conceived without reliance on traditional notions of exclusive possession and powers of title which, as the standard conceptual apparatus was supposed to show, ought to be dispensed with. One of the things that both Schroeder's and Penner's work led to was a creeping realization that the bundle of rights picture of property might not only be the only game in town, but that it might not even be plausible when viewed with a sceptical eye. Worse, the standard conceptual apparatus of which the bundle of rights metaphor was a central component began to be seen as at best partial. The bundle picture is a tool for analysis and clarification of subsidiary issues such as the difference between a right and a liberty, but as Hohfeld himself probably realized, a theory of pieces needs to be supplemented or embedded within a theory of wholes. The radical bundle picture simply assumes that a person's property is no more than the sum of the Hohfeldian micro-relations making it up, and the property system is no greater than the set of rules creating these relations. Taken this way, the bundle picture is essentially *useless* as a tool of analysis, useless that is as a theoretical basis from which one might hope to generate some genuine insight into legal and philosophical issues raised by the phenomenon of property.

Shortly thereafter both Christman[14] and Harris[15] published book-length treatments of the subject whose main theoretical claims bore little relation to the standard conceptual apparatus. Prefiguring the distinction between norms concerning exclusion and norms which concern the powers of title to property which became a theme of Penner's 1997 *The Idea of Property in Law*, Christman sharply distinguished between what he called 'control rights' and 'income rights'. The former concerned rights such as the right to immediate exclusive possession of a chattel, securing the owner's use of what he owned. The latter concerned rights like the right to sell in the market, or to lease land for the profits it might generate.

---

[12] Schroeder 1994.   [13] Penner 1996a.   [14] Christman 1994.   [15] Harris 1996.

Christman forcefully argued that a system of property rights might justify the institution of the former but not the latter, and that in any case these different rights raised different moral concerns.

Harris's 1996 *Property and Justice* is, arguably, the *locus classicus* in modern property theory for an 'institutional' account of the phenomenon of property, that is, as a characteristic configuration of different kinds of rules, rather than the outworking of a 'right' to property. For Harris, any property institution comprises two distinct sorts of social rules. 'Trespassory rules', whether embodied in law or not, impose obligations on all members of the social group not to make use of a resource without the consent of an identified individual or group. In addition to this there are rules which comprise what Harris calls the 'ownership spectrum', the various uses of resources and the relationships to which they give rise that the trespassory rules presuppose and protect. Harris's picture of property is rich, complicated, and challenging and, along with Waldron's *The Right to Private Property*, Munzer's *A Theory of Property*, and Penner's *The Idea of Property in Law*, is now regarded as a central reference point for the subject.

Bringing up the rear is Penner's *The Idea of Property in Law*. This somewhat quirky work seems to have served in part as a pivot from the preceding work to the sort of work which populates this collection of essays. Whilst its central themes— that one needs to depart from Hohfeld in order to understand the structure of property norms, that both exclusion and the idea that property rights per se are those rights which might have been someone else's (the 'separability thesis') are equally important facets of property rights, that whilst a power to give is 'native' to property whilst a power to sell is not—remain controversial, the issues or problems that it set out are now generally regarded as ones which a philosophy of property must address.

Whether property has anything, conceptual or otherwise, holding it together has received a lot of attention of late in the United States as well, spreading outward from law and economics. Thomas Merrill and Henry Smith got things started with a theory of the *numerus clausus* in the common law.[16] Having diverse and idiosyncratic property rights might be of benefit, especially to those who create them, but each extra idiosyncrasy, especially in methods of fragmenting property rights, causes others to have more—more dimensions of variation even—to be on the lookout for. What combination of standardization and notice giving devices deals best with these informational externalities is an empirical question. But the rationale for property to send simple messages—based on exclusion strategies modified with governance strategies aimed at specific uses or activities—receives a functional explanation. Strikingly this functional explanation dovetails with deontic theories, and both are truer to property doctrine than the bundle picture can even promise to be.[17] Once one takes into account the cost of delineating individual uses and communicating entitlements to large and indefinite groups of duty bearers, as is the case with *in rem* rights, using exclusion strategies as a first cut makes some sense.

[16] Merrill and Smith 2000.   [17] Merrill and Smith 2007a.

Some would go so far as to label the right to exclude as the *sine qua non* of property, while others see exclusion as a necessary first approximation.[18] Perhaps an entitlement is more property-like the more it works outward from a thing subject to exclusion supplemented by rules and standards governing property use.[19] Indeed things themselves are a major source of property's ability to manage complexity through modularity: the legal system can be highly complex as long as the information is corralled—and partially hidden—in components like the things of property and rules like *nemo dat*, the unit rule in takings and the like.

If the philosophy of property is now more attentive to concepts lying between broad considerations of political philosophy and distributive justice on the one hand and individual rules on the other, the questions are what in the broad space that lies between needs explaining, and how we might justify what we find.

As might be expected, whatever the character of the work of those lawyer theorists interested in property and property law doctrines, philosophical scholarship on Locke, Hume, Grotius, Kant, and Hegel and their views of the nature of property never goes away, and they remain a continuing source of inspiration and puzzlement. This volume contains some of the most interesting work of those pursuing the philosophical issues raised by property law from these perspectives. One recent work deserves special mention, Arthur Ripstein's *Force and Freedom: Kant's Legal and Political Philosophy*. Though about much more than Kant's philosophy of property rights, property plays a central organizing role in Ripstein's account, and his account has re-inspired a generation of scholars to examine once again Kant's austere notion of private right and property's place within it.

In recent years scholarship in the philosophy of property law has flourished, as the bibliography to this volume attests. It is impossible to cover all of the ground here, except to say that the field is as productive and interesting as it has been for decades. The essays in this volume contribute to that scholarship under four broad themes. Waldron, Claeys, Klimchuk, and Brudner all revisit the work of a great philosopher, Hume, Locke, Grotius and Hegel, respectively, to assess different facets of the justification of the institution of property.

Waldron's chapter proposes that we should shift our attention, at least as a matter of inducting students into the theory of property, from Locke and Lockean-type theories of the foundation of property rights, to Hume. As Waldron sets out the Humean theory of the origin of property rights, it has one chief advantage over Locke: its historical realism. Difficulties with the 'realism' of Locke's theory are well known. As a straightforwardly moral theory of the foundations of property, it is easy to question whether any extant system of property and the distribution of property rights it protects could plausibly pass muster. Leaving aside obvious difficulties with the labour–desert account Locke proffers which have been extensively if not remorselessly elaborated in detail by generations of scholars, Waldron focuses on the stupendous information costs of the Nozickean scheme for the justification of holdings which covers both Locke and any other 'bottom-up'

---

[18] Compare Merrill 1998 with Smith 2002, 2004. [19] Smith 2012b.

justification of property rights of a similar kind. Such schemes rest upon two principles, one of 'justice in original acquisition' and one of 'justice in transfer'. As Waldron emphasizes, applying such a theory to determine the justice of any set of present-day holdings would require amounts of accurate historical information which would seem to be just impossible to obtain. Indeed, Waldron could have said more: the second principle, requiring justice in transfer, would seem unlikely to hold in any real-world system of property distribution, especially when the range of transfers are considered, from contractual exchange to regimes of inheritance to taxation, insolvency distribution, and much else. Whatever else might be said in favour of these modes of property distribution, it is unlikely that they would regularly uniformly deliver 'justice in transfer'. To take just two points: from the economist's perspective, information asymmetries and much else suggest that market transactions would regularly fail to deliver justice in exchange; and the history of taxation and eminent domain would not encourage one to think that there was much there to defend in the way of distributive justice in property holdings. The Humean account is innocent of these sorts of disadvantage. It is a bottom-up account because the extant, de jure system of property rights arises not from some state-imposed or social contractual convention, but arises rather as a salient solution to a coordination problem, the problem of best securing those de facto holdings individuals and groups have managed, in whatever ways, to acquire and defend. It is not the least romantic—it shares with 'last occupancy' theories of property the idea that the justice of instituting a system of de jure property rights is not a validation of the origins of the holdings it protects. This account is plausible and interesting, and yet Waldron points out its limitations, which might themselves point us to fruitful consideration of the nature of the institution of property. It will not allow us to regard property rights as the bulwark against state interference with individual liberty as some libertarians want to claim. There is no inviolable, morally justified, individual 'right to property' in defence of which people enter into a civil condition. Moreover, the Humean theory offers a minimal account of the very right in issue—it is a principle concerned to establish the de jure 'settling' of holdings—it does not determine the particular shape of the rights to those holdings. Thus such an account, on natural law terms, would suggest that our property institutions are short on *specificatio*, and long on *determinatio*, and it might well be theoretically liberating to think that every main interest in the *numerus clausus* need not be defended as an interest in property somehow ordained by the nature of private law or corrective justice or some other perspective on private right.

Claeys takes issue with the received wisdom on Locke. He shows how a reading of Locke resting on the value of productive labour deserves to make its way from recent work among philosophers into the philosophy of property and, how it does a better job of explaining and justifying property law. Rather than grounding property in the mixing of labour, which leads to the difficulties noted by Nozick and Waldron, Locke is best seen as assigning to property the purpose of protecting a natural right in people to work to provide for human necessities. This 'productive labour theory' answers the usual litany of hypotheticals about tomato juice and oceans and the like, and it provides a unified reason for the non-waste, enough-

and as good, and charity constraints. It provides a non conventional account of use rights. As for more robust rights of control, Claeys argues that these are justified by virtue theoretic and moral concerns about persons and consequentialist goals of the property system. Productive labour theory thus leaves plenty of room for other moral and prudential considerations in implementing property rights to secure the fruits of productive labour. In this way productive labour theory exemplifies the recent turn in property theory: it recognizes that there is a gap between the highest level values and the nitty-gritty of how property works and yet subjects the latter to the tools of philosophical analysis. Claeys follows through with applications to accession, capture, and prospective advantages in uncaptured resources. Interestingly, in leaving room for prudential—and one might even say consequentialist—considerations in this 'gap', the productive labour theory, like Waldron's Hume, can accommodate the law as it is and might well have a tendency to converge with economic theories.

Klimchuk's chapter explores a Grotian account of the right of necessity, that is, the right to trespass or make use of the property of another, first, to save life or limb, and secondly, to preserve one's own property. In contrast to an account (first elaborated in detail by Pufendorf) in which the right of necessity is a personal right which the necessitous trespasser has against the individual property owner that the latter allow the former to make use of the latter's property, for Grotius, the necessitous trespasser has a property right in the needed property. Grotius holds that prior to the advent of a regime of property rights, all resources are held in common, and this reflects the fundamental presumption of moral equality that obtains between all individuals. But property can be justified as providing us with a life of engagement with the material resources of the world which we want and cannot otherwise have. Yet any legitimate regime of property must depart as little as possible from the 'natural equity' of our common ownership. Thus, where life and limb are at stake, the property rights of the owner must cede to the necessitous trespasser; otherwise the regime of property would put the owner in the position of mastery over the very life or limb of the necessitous individual, and this would violate the fundamental presumption of moral equality. The application of this sort of reasoning is much less determinative of a right to trespass upon the property of others in order to preserve one's own property, but perhaps that is as it should be; as Klimchuk points out, neither our intuitions nor the law is straightforward on what the right answer is in such cases, and so perhaps that uncertainty strengthens the claim of the Grotian account to have captured the moral issues at stake. Beyond the specific case of necessity, there is a larger point of interest in the chapter. As Klimchuk elaborates the account, the right of necessity qua property right of the necessitous trespasser reflects, but does not exhaust, the force of the foundational principle of natural equality which limits any justifiable account of property. And this takes us to the larger question of the role of consent in political theory generally. Grotius does not hold that property regimes arise by any actual, historical consent; rather, they seem to arise as reasonable arrangements which provide us with something desirable which we could not have otherwise, and may be justifiably enforced so long as the constraints a property regime places on individuals with respect to the property that is owned by others does those individuals no wrong, that is, is not inconsistent with the equality they enjoyed in the original community of property. The 'may be justifiably enforced' qualification is there just because it remains contentious in political philosophy whether any authoritative arrangement which is coercively enforced is legitimate in the absence of some genuine, actual consent of those subject to it.

In a subtle exploration of the Hegelian characterization of a well-ordered polity, Brudner asks whether the paradox of the US Constitution's Fifth Amendment's 'takings' clause can be resolved in a way that other liberal theories, in particular Lockean and Kantian theories, seem incapable of. The paradox is this: to the extent that the law both allows the state to dispossess owners of their property, 'no questions asked', it would appear to undermine the independent right of owners—it would subvert their interests to those of the general welfare as represented by state action. On the other hand, the unqualified duty of the state to compensate an owner for a taking (in particular irrespective of any issues of distributive justice) would appear to sever the status of an owner's right from any connection with the political system that both guarantees that right and in which the owner forms part, as one of the objects of the common welfare that the state promotes. Brudner argues that, whilst Lockeans and Kantians can explain the paradox, they can only do so on the basis that there remains in liberal civil society a basic tension between the individual conceived of as independent atom whose moral status is inherently unconnected to the welfare of the polity (which comprises the welfare of its fellow citizens) that it inhabits, and the individual conceived of qua citizen, whose constitutive allegiance is to the common good. Brudner's conception of a mature polity as a 'dialogic community' promises to reveal this tension as escapable. Whilst the owner has no independent right of property that can be asserted against the state—property rights are only finally and fully determined as intelligible morally justified norms within the state—dialogic community does not reduce the individual to a means to the common welfare either—as a moral 'singularity' embedded in the mature polity the individual's property rights must receive the respect they are due, and so compensation for their value must be an unqualified duty of the state.

For their part Lee and Samet each examine a particular doctrine which, upon close inspection, reveals an illuminating aspect of the way in which property law respects the equality and autonomy of its subjects.

Lee's chapter tackles the large subject of the state regulation of property, as in the case of zoning or planning regulations, which do not dispossess owners of their land but which may impose large economic losses on some owners of land. One strand in the justification of the legitimacy of such regulation is the idea of 'average reciprocity of advantage', or implicit in-kind compensation. The claim is that the economically burdened owner may also benefit 'in-kind' by the regulation, and therefore, unlike in the case where the owner is physically dispossessed of his property, monetary compensation from the state may not justifiably be claimed. In the narrow economic sense of in-kind compensation, Lee compellingly shows that only in cases where a coordination problem amongst owners is solved—say where the state imposes a requirement on mine owners not to work their mines right up to the property line of an adjacent mine, with mutual benefit to both mine owners—does the principle of reciprocity of advantage actually work. In most other cases, from a requirement on all owners to remove snow from the pavements in front of their properties, to general zoning and planning restrictions, it is just fanciful to suggest that each individual owner burdened by the regulation, given the disparity of different owners' preferences and risk profiles, will genuinely be compensated in kind by that very regulation. However Lee argues that the idea underlying 'reciprocity of advantage' should not be discarded, but reconfigured to suit the 'moral economy' which underlies this sort of regulation. The in-kind compensation which every owner receives is the moral respect of being treated as a *civic equal* in those cases where the regulation is legitimate, that is, is not imposed by the state as a measure which benefits only one section of the public via the exploitation of another.

The justification of the doctrine of proprietary estoppel has been, to say the least, vexed. Samet argues that, properly understood, both from an interpretation of the cases and from a desire to bring moral coherence to this area of law, the obligation enforced in proprietary estoppel cases is one which lies between a fully-fledged promise and a representation giving rise to no obligation at all. Samet argues that many informal representations between individuals impose 'loss prevention assurance' or LPA obligations, under which the obligor is not bound to bring the represented state of affairs into being, as they would if the representation was made in a genuine promise, but is bound only to ensure that the representee does not suffer a loss owing to their reliance on the representation. LPA obligations serve a valuable social function, in Samet's view; there are many informal situations, she argues, where explicit promises are inappropriate, and the tentativeness of the relationship between the parties going forward makes it the case that some intentional ambiguity in their commitments, where some things are better left unsaid, is actually positive, for it reflects the less than full commitment of the parties to their future dealings. In such cases representations are not to be treated as promises, but nor are they morally innocuous. Representations in these circumstances generate LPA obligations. Samet elaborates the consequence of this view for property law. As she points out, the doctrine of proprietary estoppel, whereby the law enforces informal representations, threatens to undermine the good order of property law, under which transfers must normally be seen to be the intentional exercise of the owner's power to transfer. She argues that the normal remedy where someone has relied to their detriment on an LPA obligation should be personal as between the parties, rather than in general proprietary, e.g. by the transfer to the representee of the property that was promised to them. However Samet also acknowledges the appropriateness of such a transfer where in the eyes of the party the reliance could only be framed as a reliance on the transfer and nothing else, or where the reliance has been so extensive that the only way to remedy the loss consequent on it is the fulfilment of a representation that a transfer would be made.

Ripstein, Austin, Katz, Douglas and McFarlane, Penner, and Rose all produce essays which revolve around the central notions of possession, ownership, and title.

In a meticulous reappraisal of the owner's right to the immediate, exclusive use of a tangible property, Ripstein defends a 'deontic' justification of the basic rule of property: that non-owners must exclude themselves from tangibles that are not theirs. The basic claim is simple, yet subtle: the institution of the duty that non-owners not interfere with the property of others is not to be explained, on utilitarian or other instrumental grounds, as *a means* of implementing a policy favouring the productive use of tangible resources; rather, the authority relation created by the institution of the right is intrinsically linked to the nature of the right that it is. In the same way that my right to bodily security is a reflection of the value of my right to independent agency, i.e. that *as against others* I am entitled to determine how I shall act with the body that I have, property instantiates a similar 'value in the rule itself': the property is mine to use (productively, wastefully, wisely, foolishly, however) just because and insofar as it is *not yours*. It is only in the sense that, *as against others* it is mine to use, that the right to property is a 'right to use', and the essence of this right to use *as against others* reveals its intrinsically exclusionary nature. Whilst the institution of the right (or recognition of the right insofar as it is a universal, human right) is of value, in that it orders the interactions of private individuals, its value lies in the way of setting the terms of engagement under which values of whatever kind (autonomous pursuit of the good life, aesthetic endeavour, whatever)—insofar as they involve the use of tangible resources—are rightly to be realized. As a consequence, although the particular contours of the law may vary in order to shape the contours of the right of exclusion, these rules instantiating rights in tangibles cannot and do not create 'use-rights' in tangible objects.

For Austin, what replaces a normative account of possession is the concept of the rule of law. In previous accounts, the specific rule of first possession is tied directly to large questions of political morality, distributive justice, and the like. Instead, she shows how many of the contours of first possession can be shown to be required by the rule of law. She draws on Rawls to point out that we need not justify acts in a system by the rationale of the system. The opposite is not true either—particular rules sometimes do reflect systemic considerations—so the question usefully becomes whether aspects of the law that fall under the notion of possession reflect possessory norms or more general rule of law considerations. The law of possession could be otherwise, and it does reflect a basic need for something like first possession—or property—in the first place. Nevertheless, Austin argues that much of what goes under the heading of possession falls in the gap between the normative foundations of property and actual doctrine, and that the rule of law goes a long way to filling this gap. In any event, we must embed accounts in an overall theory of property. Austin has shown that providing an explanation for first possession is not something that previous substantively normative theories uniquely buy us.

For Katz, possession should not function as the linchpin of property at all. Instead, ownership combined with privity, force, and fraud get us what the relativity of title and its emphasis on possession are sometimes thought to provide. Interestingly, much of the two accounts—the one based on ownership and privity and the other based on possession and relativity—overlap, which calls into question the central place some give to possession in explaining (and justifying) property. The question remains whether there is a notion of entitlement that is not captured by ownership on the one hand and privity in connection with prohibitions on force and fraud on the other. The two accounts might not overlap completely in the domain of sequential possession. In light of Katz's arguments theorists need to ask whether there are moral or functional reasons for some role (perhaps a lesser one) for possession and why it takes us so far down the road to ownership (even if perhaps sometimes too far). More generally, Katz's chapter raises the question of whether previous theorizing about property is in effect too *in personam* after all.

Much of the new theorizing seeks to get beyond the Hohfeldian atomizing scheme as interpreted by the Realists. Douglas and McFarlane give a new and surprising twist on the Hohfeldian approach. Like the newer theorizing about property, they emphasize the content of the duty of non-owners. In their view this is truest to the Hohfeldian perspective. What is the content of the non-owner's duty? It is to refrain from deliberately or carelessly interfering with the owner's physical thing. Thus from Hohfeldian premises, they derive the importance of something very close if not identical to the 'right of exclusion' familiar from anti-Hohfeldian accounts. Further, they stress that their approach points to the centrality of a physical thing. Both are conventionally not associated with Hohfeld's approach—at least in its latter-day bundle of rights guise. And yet they derive this conclusion centring on exclusion and things from Hohfeldian premises, which are usually taken as antithetical to seriousness about non-reductionism in property theory.

Penner analyses what it means for a right to be transferred and thereby calls the Hohfeldian framework into question. In contrast to directional abandonment (A gives up X so that B can take it immediately thereafter) and novation, the transfer of a right presupposes that some notional entity moves from A to B (B acquires the very same right A had). For this to be true the personal aspects of the identity of A and B have to be irrelevant to the right, for otherwise the right would not be the same right post-transfer. Hohfeldian rights and duties are individuated by the right and duty holders that enter into the legal relation, making it impossible for the same right to persist through transfers. Harking back to his earlier work, Penner points out that the duty of C, D, and everyone else in the case of an *in rem* right likewise does not shift—it depends not at all upon the identity of the owner. Penner shows that far from requiring a robust notion of an 'office' of ownership, what transfer requires is the depersonalization of rights and duties, something that the atomizing Hohfeldian framework is ill-equipped to do. Likewise the power to transfer is a power to transfer to *someone*, not to *someone in particular*. And the fact that A and B switch right and duty and that the set of (*in rem*) duty holders fluctuates in general with births and deaths no longer requires us to deny the sameness of the right. Thus, rights that include the element of succession are those, whether *in personam* or *in rem*, whose identity is independent of the right bearer. Transmissible *in personam* rights do depend on the identity of the duty bearer(s), whereas transmissible *in rem* rights do not. With *in rem* rights, the duty is impersonal; the violation is of the right of the right holder, the one who is in the role of owner, who is allowed to sue. A duty can be impersonal and general without being *in personam* or public for that matter. Penner then goes on to show that the right to transfer can be grounded, not as a matter of convention, but in the human capability of responding to reasons, including the interests of others, not just our own.

At first glance, Rose's contribution would seem to be quite general, more so than much of the rest of recent theorizing. But this appearance is deceptive, because Rose gives us reason to focus on quite specific aspects of—again—the duty of non-owners. She asks: what is the psychology of ownership? She then distinguishes an inside and an outside perspective, that of the owner and the non-owner. We might, as she does, identify previous theorizing about property psychology with the inside perspective: the identity and incentives of owners. But she points to the importance of the non-owner's perspective in making property possible at all. And here is where human property is different from animal possession: non-owners are expected to and often do respect others' property rights even when the owner is not around. She notes that Merrill and Smith and Penner talk about information costs and the gross content of the non-owner's duty respectively, but this does not tell us that much about the psychology that makes non-owner forbearance possible. The Hawk/Dove game is another strand of theorizing from the non-owner's perspective, but not all respect for property comes from fear on the part of the non-owner. For one thing, property is more than possession and is respected even when fear—or reciprocity in a strict sense—does not counsel respect. Property's importance extends beyond possession, and the psychology of non-ownership needs to widen its focus further than the narrow version of the rational actor paradigm.

Our final two contributions, from Munzer and Smith, both step back from particular issues in the philosophy of property law and take penetrating looks at the shape of scholarship in property law theory itself.

Munzer takes up the differences between some of the new theorizing, especially the early work of Penner, and an elaboration of his approach to the bundle of rights. Munzer seeks to distinguish between verbal and substantive agreement and inquires into whether disagreements in this area can be dissolved, narrowed, or resolved. For Munzer the essence of his theory of property is that it is a set of legal relations with respect to things. By contrast, he sees variations on the exclusion thesis as being too monistic to capture the concept of property or its institutional manifestations. He also notes that Smith's work on modularity is not inconsistent with the bundle of rights and that the bundle picture need not be identified with legal realism—as witnessed by Douglas and McFarlane's contribution to this volume. All of which suggests that 'bundle of rights' itself might be a contested concept, one which is subject to a variety of verbal and substantive disagreements. Might it be the case that the 'bundle of rights' for Munzer is more of a framework or an analytical tool, as he professes here, and less of a *theory* of property, as the realists advertised? A theory should tell us which of the many 'sets' of legal relations do (or tend to)—fall under the notion of property—and why. Indeed, taking up Munzer's predilection for fuzzy concepts, might one say that exclusion is the 'formal essence' of property in that an entitlement or set of entitlements is more property-like to the extent that it does rely on exclusion (and separation) pertaining to a thing as the starting point for its delineation?

In his chapter Smith considers a particular reductionism to which property scholarship seems perpetually heir, that of a certain kind of anti-conceptualism under which property is not to be conceived of in terms of general concepts like the fee simple or the right to immediate, exclusive possession, but is rather to be understood and applied as a series of rules or norms to be applied on a case-by-case basis. Fruitfully borrowing from the philosophy of concepts the idea of an intension-extension distinction, Smith points out that certain ways of organizing our knowledge, certain ways of presenting our understanding to ourselves, make our access to that knowledge both more certain and less costly in terms of the information we require to make sense of an issue that knowledge is useful for resolving. It is the role of general concepts in law to do that for us, no less in property than elsewhere. Addressing in turn the realists and other modern anti-conceptualists, as well as 'trinitarians'—who conceive of property as a complex of the right to possess, use, and dispose of tangible resources—Smith points out the infelicities of this 'flattening out' of property doctrine. In particular it fails to appreciate the way in which rights and duties *in rem* allow us to deal with one of the hallmarks of property, that is the 'indefiniteness' of the identity of owners and duty bearers which significantly characterizes the relationship between an owner and all others who owe a duty not to interfere with an owner's property. Tying this analysis into his earlier work on the modular nature of property, Smith argues that rightly conceived, property law is both 'formalist', relying upon general concepts which, at low information costs, really do shape the doctrine of property law, but also 'functionalist', that is the doctrine is sensitive to bespoke fine-tuning (typically by statute but also by the exercise of powers of title and contract by individuals) where that, again on the information costs analysis, is feasible and permits worthwhile interactions between individuals in respect of resources. The welcome upshot is that this moderate formalism/functionalism is able to capture the 'emergent properties' of property. That is, such an analysis promises an ability to recognize how property doctrine as a whole serves the purposes which are normally thought of as native to private law, such as individual autonomy and interpersonal fairness.

These challenging chapters are certain to figure centrally in the philosophical discussion of property law in the years to come, and the editors wish the readers of this volume the same intellectual exhilaration as they make their way through the chapters as we have experienced in editing them, a privilege we have felt truly honoured to discharge.

The editors gratefully acknowledge the support that was provided by the Society of Legal Scholars, the UCL Faculty of Laws, and Oxford University Press for the Society of Legal Scholars Annual Seminar, 'The Philosophical Foundations of Property Law', held on 11 and 12 May 2012 at the UCL Faculty of Laws, at which the chapters in this volume were first presented, and thank the participants at the seminar for their extremely useful comments, suggestions, and criticisms.

JEP & HES

1

'To Bestow Stability upon Possession'

Hume's Alternative to Locke

Jeremy Waldron

1. Bottom-Up Theories

Against the view that property is wholly the creation of public law, some legal and political theorists have endeavoured to conceive of it as something grown and developed from the bottom up, independently of any sovereign or legislative determination.

Among modern theorists, Richard Epstein is a partisan of this conception. 'No system of property rights', says Epstein, 'rests on the premise that the state may bestow or deny rights in things to private persons on whatever terms it sees fit'. Rather, he says, 'the correct starting point is the Lockean position that property rights come from the bottom up.'[1] The modern democratic state, by contrast, defines itself in opposition to any theory positing these individual entitlements as 'pre-political', i.e. as existing prior to the creation of the state. Instead, in Epstein's account of the modern democratic view, 'property rights are arbitrary assemblages of rights that the state creates for its own instrumental purposes, and which it can undo almost at will for the same instrumental ends.'[2] Epstein thinks we should reject this top-down view. Property rights are not a gift of the state, he says; they have legal standing quite apart from human rule. To see matters aright, we have to be prepared to turn the tables on the modern state and go back to something like a Lockean account of the constraining force of property.

Does it have to be Lockean? I don't mean that 'Lockean' is a bad thing for a conception to be. I spent the best years of my life exploring and elaborating John Locke's theory of property and Locke's political theory generally.[3] And Locke's theory of property has proved attractive to generations since it was published in 1689. Locke saw property rights as rights that could be generated and sustained by individuals through their labour and exchange; and these rights, he thought, could be recognized in a human community without the benefit of any

---

[1] Epstein 2011, 99.   [2] Epstein 2011, 63.
[3] Waldron 1981; 1982; 1983; 1984; 1988, ch. 5; 2002; 2005.

edicts of positive law. In Locke's system, property was generated by the unilateral action of appropriators and cultivators approaching unowned resources without any authorization. The rights arose morally out of what they decided, on their own motion, to do. They were indeed generated, as Epstein puts it, from the bottom up. And all that people needed from positive law, on this account, when they set up a legal system to overcome certain difficulties in the state of nature, were principles of private law to recognize and accommodate the existence of property rights that were already well established and to facilitate their circulation.[4] 'The reason why men enter into society', says Locke, 'is the preservation of their Property', and that, as he said, presupposes that people already have property and that property is neither the work nor the plaything of public law.[5]

It is, as I said, an attractive theory, to a certain sort of mentality. What sort of mentality? Well, liberal, certainly, on account of its individualism and the orderly rights-structure that it generates. Capitalist, obviously, on account of its consecration of industry and markets and its acceptance of the resultant economic inequality. And above all, the Lockean account appeals to an anti-statist mentality—or rather, not anti-statist in any anarchist sense (though there have been Lockeans of that stripe as well), but to any political sensibility that is suspicious of state action, any political sensibility that wishes to regard property rights as a prior constraint on government, relegating the state to the status of a service-apparatus: the state doesn't invent property, it exists in order to sustain it.

For the preservation of property being the end of government, and that for which men enter into society, it necessarily supposes and requires that the people should have property, without which they must be supposed to lose that by entering into society which was the end for which they entered into it; too gross an absurdity for any man to own.[6]

All these features, all these facets of its appeal, are what have led many law professors to present the Lockean account in the early pages of their textbooks as the epitome of a bottom-up approach to the origin of property. It is easily understandable for their students; Locke's labour theory is a good way into the subject; and depending on the professor's own political predilections, it can be presented either as an unhelpful founding myth or as a reasonable (though no doubt still mythic) account of the origin of the system that their students are to study. So far so good.

Professor Epstein implies that the natural alternative to a top-down theory has to be Lockean.[7] Is that right? Should we designate Locke's theory as the only game in town, once we reject a top-down statist view of property?

Surely not, for even in Locke's own time, his theory that property was created by individual labour was controversial. Part of that controversy was admitted by Locke himself in his confrontation, early on in chapter 5 of the *Second Treatise*, with theories that based the origin of property on universal consent. Locke's response

---

[4] Locke 1689b, II, §222.   [5] Locke 1689b , II, §138.   [6] Locke 1689b, at II, §138.

[7] Of course there were lots of contemporary top-down theories: Hobbesian theories, Filmerian theories of the divine right of kings. And perhaps one can also put theories of universal consent in this category too, since although they are not necessarily statist, they presuppose something like a general will in the establishment of property rights.

was brusque: 'If such a consent as that was necessary, man had starved, notwith-standing the plenty God had given him.'[8] But that is, in effect, a controversy between Locke's bottom-up theory and a kind of top-down view, albeit one that looks to the consent of the whole community, rather than the action of the state. It has in common with the statist theory that it presents private property as a creation of the general will.

However, even if we restrict ourselves to bottom-up views, Locke's theory is still one among several, and admitted by him to be rather counter-intuitive.[9] What was particularly controversial was his claim that property in land was created unilaterally by individuals tilling and cultivating land—and doing so laboriously, mixing their labour with a portion of the earth itself. It was understood that this was one conception among many, that is, one conception among many others of this bottom-up kind. Its main rival was the theory of first occupancy, which claimed that men acquired property in some portion of the earth by occupying it, living on it, whether that occupancy involved physical cultivation or not.[10] This face-off, between Locke's labour theory and the theory (held by Samuel Pufendorf, for example)[11] that based property on occupancy, had considerable implications for how European incursions into America were regarded.[12] On the Lockean account, the Europeans found lands that native Americans roamed over and from time to time established fleeting settlements on, but not land which they had cultivated, not land that they had taken into their possession as property by labour, in the sense designated by Locke's philosophy. So that land was available for appropriation and cultivation by the European intruders. On the other side, it could be held that, even if there was no cultivation (and many denied the factual premiss of Locke's account), the Native Americans had taken possession of this land by occupancy, and their living upon it and their use of it as a hunting ground established for all practical and moral purposes that it was theirs.[13] The controversy about native

---

[8] Locke 1689b, II, §27.

[9] Locke 1689b, II, §40: 'Nor is it so strange as, perhaps, before consideration, it may appear...'

[10] Tully 1980.

[11] Von Pufendorf 1673, ch. 12. Note however that Pufendorf presents his theory of first-occupancy in a nominally top-down frame, namely as a principle establish by universal consent:

> at first, while the Human Race was but of a small Number, it was agreed, That whatever any one did first seize should be his, and not be taken from him by another; provided however, that he only possesses himself out of the common Store of what is sufficient for his private Service, but not so as to destroy the whole Fund, and so prevent a Stock for future Uses. But afterward, when Mankind was multiply'd, and they began to bestow Culture and Labour upon those Things which afforded them Food and Raiment; for the prevention of Quarrels; and for the sake of good Order, those Bodies or Things also, which produced such Necessaries, were divided among particular Men, and every one had his proper Share assign'd him, with this general Agreement, That whatsoever in this first Division of Things, was yet left unpossest, should for the future be the Property of the first Occupant. And thus, God so willing, with the previous Consent, or at least by a tacit Compact of Man, Property, or the Right to Things, was introduced into the World.

[12] See Tully 1993, 137.

[13] Note also that occupancy was often associated with tribal or collective ownership rather than individual ownership. I am inclined to think this doesn't make much difference, in a context where the claims of one collective stand (and have to be justified) against the claims of others. See Nozick

title was not the only arena where first occupancy and labour theories faced off, but it was a striking illustration of their opposition, and as such a helpful rebuttal of the view that Locke's theory, in its specificity, is the only bottom-up theory in town.

In 1974, Robert Nozick published *Anarchy, State and Utopia*, in which he set out and illuminated by discussion the logical frame common to theories of this sort. The logical frame includes, foundationally, a principle of unilateral acquisition—some principle of the form:

P_1:   *The first person, A, to do ϕ to a resource R under conditions C, gets to be the owner of R*

and a principle of justice-in-transfer, along the lines of

P_2:   *Any person, A, being the owner of resource R, may voluntarily, if he chooses, transfer that ownership to another person B, whereupon B gets to be owner of R.*

Nozick invited us to consider the possibility that principles like P_1 and P_2 were all one needed for the doing of justice in a modern society. In particular the state did not need to cultivate or act on any sense of the best distribution or of better-or-worse distributions of property: more or less unequal, for example, or more or less corresponding to desert or need. That a given array of property rights was the upshot of repeated applications of P_1 and P_2 was all one needed to know to judge it just, whatever distributive profile it presented.[14]

At the time, a lot of people criticized Nozick for failing to specify a value for ϕ in P_1. But Nozick was interested in theories *of this shape*, rather than any particular one of them. Both Locke's labour theory and the first occupancy theory are theories that fit this shape: according to Locke, ϕ = labouring upon; according to his adversaries, ϕ = occupying, seizing or taking possession of a resource. Nozick didn't need to commit himself to any particular value of ϕ in order to consider the challenge that any theory of this shape might pose (say) to a theory like Rawls's.

The point is that top-down theories, including the absolutist theories developed by Hobbes and Filmer in the generation before Locke wrote, and the general will theory elaborated by Rousseau 80 years later, *cannot* be adapted to the Nozickian template. It looks as though Nozick has done us the service of stating the essential *form* of a bottom-up theory, a form into which various contents—Lockean and non-Lockean—can be poured.

Before agreeing to this last proposition, however, we had better push our inquiry one step further, and ask whether bottom-up theories have to have this Nozickian shape. For it has to be admitted, even by aficionados of theories of this type, that it is a very demanding form. One has to be able to defend and justify P_1 and P_2. P_2

1974a, 179: 'We should note that it is not only persons favoring private property who need a theory of how property rights legitimately originate. Those believing in collective property, for example those believing that a group of persons living in an area jointly own the territory, or its mineral resources, also must provide a theory of how such property rights arise; they must show why the persons living there have rights to determine what is done with the land and resources there that persons living elsewhere don't have (with regard to the same land and resources).'

[14] Nozick 1974a, ch. 7.

may not be so difficult, for as Nozick observes it can be presented in terms of individual consent and Pareto-improvement; but P_1 presents a more demanding challenge. Given the Nozickian logic, whatever one's chosen value is for ϕ, one has to be able to justify putting all the weight of justice-in-distribution on this foundational variable. Who begins with what goods assigned as theirs makes an immense difference to the way subsequent actions and market transactions generate distributive outcomes. For example, Locke has to be able to show that labour, as the value of ϕ, can bear this burden: why should it make so much difference, especially so much subsequent difference, to who was the first to labour on a given piece of land?

Not only that, but any Nozickian conception is tremendously demanding of information. It is, as he calls it, a *historical* conception: one justifies Z's property in R now, not by the truth of any factual proposition dated in the present, but by a succession of factual propositions dating back into the more and more distant past, back all the way into the dawn of time when a human first confronted R, hopefully under the auspices of P_1. The morality of this is not particularly edifying: is first occupancy's petulant claim, 'I was here *first*' really a good way of rebutting present claims of need? And quite apart from the morality, establishing who was where when is awfully difficult, as the modern indigenous rights industry reveals. Who did what first, and under what conditions things were subsequently done to them—all this has to be untangled at a historical (and indeed pre-historical) level, if any theory of the Nozickian form is to be applied to legitimize indigenous holdings. This may be simple, say, for New Zealand, with only one wave of relatively recent indigenous settlement (though even there it is not at all simple as the Waitangi Tribunal has found); but try thinking about it for India. Or Kosovo.[15]

Does a bottom-up theory have to be this demanding, so far as empirical information and moral justification are concerned? I don't know whether you would call it a theory, exactly, but one view about the origin of property presents it as a matter largely of the successful use of force. The powerful and the cunning grab things, both from nature and from others who may already have the things in their possession, and the powerful and the cunning manage to hold on to the things they have grabbed and use their power, politically, to persuade the whole society to throw its force behind their depredations. This is a theory of occupancy, if you like, but it is not a theory of first occupancy; it is more like a theory of *last* occupancy. The group most recently in possession of land or resources at the time that a powerful state is established gets consecrated as the legal owner of that land, whether it was the first occupant or not.

Informationally, this is a much less demanding theory; no need for any inquiry going back, as Locke's and Pufendorf's accounts have to go back, to the dawn of time.

Morally, it is much less demanding also; in fact many would say it is morally bankrupt. (Indeed, it is not really a justificatory theory at all, or if it is, it rests on something as modest as a premiss of prescription: present possession, established

---

[15] See Waldron 2003.

Jeremy Waldron

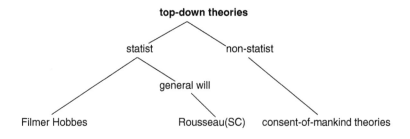

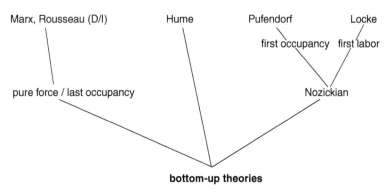

Figure 1

over a reasonable period of time, should be consecrated as legal property, presumably for reasons of stability and keeping the peace.)

Its logic is quite different from the Nozickian shape of Locke's theory. And many—quite rightly—find it plausible at least as a descriptive account of the (deplorable) way in which private property came into the world. It is roughly the theory referred to in Rousseau's *Discourse on Inequality* (as contrasted with his own more normative top-down theory in *The Social Contract*), and it is similar too to Marx's account in volume 1 of *Capital*.[16] This confirms the point about this really not being a justificatory theory: in the hands of its most distinguished proponents, its evaluative force is, if anything, negative.

Is there any space between these two broad types of bottom-up account? I mean between theories which have a Nozickian shape and theories of force or last occupancy?

There is, and it is occupied in my submission by the theory of David Hume, in *A Treatise on Human Nature*. (See Figure 1.) I have long had an interest in Hume's

---

[16] See the chapters on 'capitalist accumulation' in vol. 1 of *Capital* (Marx 1867). Needless to say, the reasons for sidelining Marx in a post-1989 world have nothing to do with the essential accuracy of his account of how capitalists acquired their property. That part of his theory survives, as more or less entirely convincing, even if for ideological reasons we are now happy to turn a blind eye to it.

theory and in its comparative advantages over Locke's account (or any Nozickian account).[17] Both are bottom-up theories. But Hume's, like the pure force/last occupancy theory, is much less morally demanding and much less demanding of historical information, than Nozickian theories are. Unlike the pure force/last occupancy theory, however, Hume's has some claim to offer a justificatory, even a moral account. It is morally less demanding than Locke's theory, but it is a moral account nonetheless. In the second part of the chapter I shall set out the main features of the Humean account.

2. The Humean Approach

The core of Hume's account of property is found in section 2 of Part ii of Book III of *A Treatise of Human Nature*.[18] That section contains two key passages on property, both justly famous.

The first establishes the human need for property. To survive and flourish people need to make use, not only of their own bodies, but of goods and resources that are external to them. But these goods are scarce, which means that—in the absence of limitless altruism—people are rivals for the use of these objects.[19] What's more, in contrast with the goods of body and mind, external goods are easily moveable from the possession and use of one person to the possession and use of another: depredation is a definite and profitable possibility; and anyone's possession and use of such a good is therefore vulnerable to other's depredations:

There are different species of goods, which we are possess'd of; the internal satisfaction of our minds, the external advantages of our body, and the enjoyment of such possessions as we have acquir'd by our industry and good fortune. We are perfectly secure in the enjoyment of the first. The second may be ravish'd from us, but can be of no advantage to him who deprives us of them. The last only are both expos'd to the violence of others, and may be transferr'd without suffering any loss or alteration; while at the same time, there is not a sufficient quantity of them to supply every one's desires and necessities. As the improvement, therefore, of these goods is the chief advantage of society, so the instability of their possession, along with their scarcity, is the chief impediment.

So there's a problem and clearly property rights are a solution:

the principal disturbance in society arises from those goods, which we call external, and from their looseness and easy transition from one person to another; [we] must seek for a remedy by putting these goods, as far as possible, on the same footing with the fix'd and constant advantages of the mind and body.

---

[17] See Waldron 1994.

[18] Almost all of the Hume quotations in this part of the chapter are from this section: *Treatise*, Bk. III, Part ii, section 2. (Hume 1739–40b).

[19] 'This avidity...of acquiring goods and possessions for ourselves and our nearest friends, is insatiable, perpetual, universal, and directly destructive of society. There scarce is any one, who is not actuated by it; and there is no one, who has not reason to fear from it, when it acts without any restraint, and gives way to its first and most natural movements.'

In this passage, what Hume is doing is sketching what H. L. A. Hart would call a general justifying aim for a property system.[20] But that is not the same as an account of how property might actually get under way. Particularly in the absence of a state or any other top-down decision mechanism, we need an account of how something which is a good idea in general can be parlayed into a set of rights established by individuals on a bottom-up basis.

Hume offers his solution in the second of the two famous passages I mentioned. It's a passage immediately following one about 'the instability of possession'. We need to put possession on a stable footing, he says. And he continues:

This can be done after no other manner, than by a convention enter'd into by all the members of the society to bestow stability on the possession of those external goods, and leave every one in the peaceable enjoyment of what he may acquire by his fortune and industry. By this means, every one knows what he may safely possess; and the passions are restrain'd in their partial and contradictory motions.... I observe, that it will be for my interest to leave another in the possession of his goods, provided he will act in the same manner with regard to me. He is sensible of a like interest in the regulation of his conduct. When this common sense of interest is mutually express'd, and is known to both, it produces a suitable resolution and behaviour.... After this convention, concerning abstinence from the possessions of others, is enter'd into, and every one has acquir'd a stability in his possessions, there immediately arise the ideas of justice and injustice; as also those of property, right, and obligation. The latter are altogether unintelligible without first understanding the former.

This is Hume's convention-based account of the origin of property rights. And I believe that it is a bottom-up theory and that it has a distinct non-Nozickian structure.

Before we go any further, two preliminary objections will spring to mind: (1) as set out above, the Humean account sounds much more like a top-down contractarian account; and (2) the Humean account already seems to presuppose the division of the world into individual possessions, which makes it kind of question-begging. Let's deal quickly with both of these objections.

(1) You will say: well, this account of Hume's looks like a top-down theory, with property based on social conventions, something like a social contract. It may not be a statist theory but it looks top-down nonetheless. But appearances can be misleading. And Hume is anxious to deny the apparent contractarian element in his account:

This convention is not of the nature of a promise.... It is only a general sense of common interest; which sense all the members of the society express to one another, and which induces them to regulate their conduct by certain rules. And this may properly enough be call'd a convention or agreement betwixt us, tho' without the interposition of a promise; since the actions of each of us have a reference to those of the other, and are perform'd upon the supposition, that something is to be perform'd on the other part.... In like manner are languages gradually establish'd by human conventions without any promise. In like manner

---

[20] Hart 1968, 4. See also the discussion of the logic of this distinction between general justifying and the allocation of particular burdens and benefits (duties and rights) in Waldron 1988, 330ff.

do gold and silver become the common measures of exchange, and are esteem'd sufficient payment for what is of a hundred times their value.

As these last examples indicate, what Hume has in mind is something like the emergent solution to a sort of coordination problem. There is a need for coordination, and it is answered by a shared sense of coordination on an option which comes to seem salient to us both. All this can happen without the interposition of any formal agreement or direction from on high.

(2) The second objection is that the theory seems to presuppose a world already divided up into individual possessions. After all, the convention is conceived as one which bestows stability *on people's individual possessions*, some of them appearing to have been consecrated already in Lockean terms—'a convention . . . to bestow stability on the possession of those external goods, and leave every one in the peaceable enjoyment of what he may acquire *by his fortune and industry*'. This has led some people to describe Hume's convention as a convention to respect the property of others[21]—which means it can hardly be offered as an account of the origin of property.

Well, I don't think that's the way to read it. The better reading, I think, is to construe 'possessions' in a literal de facto sense, as things that a person happens to have hold of, whether acquired by good fortune, honest industry, or other less estimable means. In this regard Hume's theory has something in common with the force/last occupancy account. It is uninterested in questions of who *first* had possession of a given resource; and it is certainly uninterested in the question which matters so much to Locke about *the means* by which first possession was acquired. Who has the resource *now*, when the opportunity for a convention to bestow stability on resources has arisen?—that is the crucial question from the point of view of Hume's theory.

A fuller elaboration of theories of this type is given by the modern economist James Buchanan in his book, *The Limits of Liberty*. According to Buchanan's model, we start from an assumption of conflict. Since time immemorial people have been seizing, using, and fighting over resources. Such conflict may be perpetual, leading as it does at any given time to essentially unstable outcomes, outcomes always likely to be disturbed and 'redistributed' in the next round of grabbing and fighting. But it is also possible that such volatility will die away:

as a result of the actual or potential conflict over the relative proportions of [resources] to be finally consumed, some 'natural distribution' will come to be established. . . . [T]he natural distribution may represent a conceptual equilibrium, in which each person extends his own behavior in securing (defending) shares in [resources] to the limit where marginal benefits from further effort are equal to the marginal costs that such effort requires.[22]

I find this a helpful account of the preconditions of the Humean approach. We begin from an assumption of conflict driven by possessive opportunism in the face

---

[21] Blackburn 2008.   [22] Buchanan 1975, 24.

of moderate scarcity and more or less unmitigated (perhaps intensified)[23] by such altruism as is natural to man. People grab things and use them; they argue and fight over them. Now things may settle down into something like a stable equilibrium, and that is what the Humean convention works on.

It is essential to recognize, according to this theory, that there is nothing moral about the possessions. Over time, the holdings determined in this way are going to be largely arbitrary. There is nothing moral or fitting or appropriate or—least of all—just about the natural distribution. It is simply an equilibrium in the arbitrary interplay of forces. We should not concern ourselves, Hume argues, with the distributive features of any possibly stable possessory regime that emerges from the era of conflict. Our aim should be to ratify any distribution that seems salient— that is, any distribution support for which promises to move us away from fighting over who should own what. The distribution might be equal or unequal, but the parties will already know that they cannot hope for a much better distribution by pitching their own strength yet again against that of others.

The idea is, in other words, that if any sort of stable pattern of de facto possession emerges, then something like a peace dividend may be available. It may be possible for everyone to gain by ceasing to fight any more over possessions. If each refrains from attacking the holdings of the others, then each gains (more or less automatically) an amount equal to the cost to himself of attacking others' holdings plus the cost to himself of defending against others' attacks plus the cost of the losses he would incur if his defences failed (times, of course, the probability of their failing). And each loses an amount equal to the amount by which he could augment his holding by attacking others' holdings (discounted, this time, by the probability of *their* defences failing). The Humean assumption is that the sum of these gains and losses is positive in the case of each person. I agree to respect what you have managed to hang on to, and you agree to respect what I have managed to hang on to: 'By this means, every one knows what he may safely possess.' Such an agreement, if it lasts, may amount over time to a conventional ratification of de facto holdings as de jure property.

On this account, even those who have been making a living in a Hobbesian way, preying on others, and taking and consuming things that other people have found, grown, or made, may be better off observing rules of property, along the lines indicated by the convention, than they would be in a world in which everything was up for grabs. I don't mean that such a 'natural distribution' will always emerge. Neither Hume or Buchanan is committed to the view that the conditions for a convention of this sort will always obtain, nor, when they do, that such a convention is always advantageous to everyone in a given territory. Certainly, neither of them provides grounds for supporting that view. As Jules Coleman has pointed out,

---

[23] Hume believes quite rightly that the fact that people have some altruistic feeling for their friends and family makes things worse not better so far as conflict is concerned: '[T]ho' this generosity must be acknowledg'd to the honour of human nature, we may at the same time remark, that so noble an affection, instead of fitting men for large societies, is almost as contrary to them, as the most narrow selfishness. For while each person loves himself better than any other single person, and in his love to others bears the greatest affection to his relations and acquaintance, this must necessarily produce an opposition of passions, and a consequent opposition of actions. . . .'

'cooperation that requires forgoing predation may not be a rational strategy for all agents'.[24] The gains that one can continue to expect from predation may, in certain circumstances, exceed the benefits one could expect from mutual restraint. If that is everyone's situation, no Humean convention is possible. If it is the situation of a few, then a Humean convention may be possible among the others, but it will also have to involve an element of self-defence against a rump of predators on whose allegiance the convention will have no claim whatsoever from either a moral or a rational choice point of view.

Notice, too, that Hume's account suggests realistically that any agreement will crystallize out, if it does, over a long period of time. It is not conceived as an instant promise, but as the gradual establishment of 'a general sense of common interest':

> Nor is the rule concerning the stability of possession the less deriv'd from human conventions, that it arises gradually, and acquires force by a slow progression, and by our repeated experience of the inconveniences of transgressing it. On the contrary, this experience assures us still more, that the sense of interest has become common to all our fellows, and gives us a confidence of the future regularity of their conduct: And 'tis only on the expectation of this, that our moderation and abstinence are founded.

Each person may be inclined to hold out and fight for a possible outcome in which he has more of the resources he wants or needs. But this may not be the outcome in the natural equilibrium. He may hold out for it a few times before becoming convinced that, even without securing that outcome, he will be better off with an outcome that is in the natural equilibrium than with a continuation of struggle. It may take time for us to become convinced of this—that is, for us to see that

> [i]nstead of departing from our own interest, or from that of our nearest friends, by abstaining from the possessions of others, we cannot better consult both those interests, than by such a convention; because it is by that means we maintain society, which is so necessary to their well-being and subsistence, as well as to our own.

So—to conclude our answer to objection (2), this is not a question-begging account of the origin of particular property rights. All it presupposes is that a pattern of distribution emerges which is steady enough—in the face of continual temptations to try and change it—to establish itself as a salient solution for the purposes of a Humean convention. 'I observe, that it will be for my interest to leave another in the possession of his goods, provided he will act in the same manner with regard to me. He is sensible of a like interest in the regulation of his conduct. When this common sense of interest is mutually express'd, and is known to both, it produces a suitable resolution and behavior.'

This is a bottom-up theory, quite different in character to the Nozickian style of theory (Lockean or first occupancy) that sits to its right in Figure 1. It does not have to make any argument concerning the independent desirability of the distribution of goods that is established. Nor does it have to make any moral argument about the moral appropriateness of the means—ϕ on p. 4—by which holdings were

---

[24] Coleman 2002, 57.

acquired. It is indifferent to that and tolerant both of considerable inequality and a range of moral diversity so far as the means of acquisition (from industry to violence) that were involved.

On the other hand it is not entirely amoral in the sense that the force/last occupancy theory is. It resembles that theory in certain respects—in particular, in its frank recognition of the likelihood of inequality and its complete lack of interest in first occupancy or first anything. But it does present a moral profile. Everyone is better off by the convention, on the Humean account, even given the lop-sided distributions that are likely to be characteristics of any natural equilibrium. Everyone is better off—that's the justification—which is different from the powerful just using their power to entrench a given distribution that they favour. (Of course, as Rousseau observes, it may sometimes be in the cunning interest of the powerful to represent a force/last occupancy strategy in Humean terms. But that's another story.)

As bottom-up theories of property go, the Humean story has one advantage over the Lockean story: it is much more realistic. It is not in denial about the elements of conflict and depredation at the origins of property. It recognizes modern property as something that emerges out of an era of conflict rather than something that presents itself to us with an impeccable pedigree. I think it would be a good idea if this theory were as widely studied, or as widely used as a template for the study of property, as the Lockean theory presently is.

In particular it probably generates a different sense of the relation between the property rights that emerge in this way, and the activities of state and law. Hume, like Locke, believes that property can get under way without the help of law. But he is not sure that it can get very far on its own. Maybe top-down supervision is necessary in order to maintain property rights against the constant temptation that people have to forget their medium- and long-term interest.[25] That is roughly analogous to Locke's view that we invent the state because it turns out that not everyone is a scrupulous respecter of morally established property. But Hume also hints, in several places, that his convention account—the account we have eluci-dated here—cannot really explain or characterize the emergence of complex forms of property appropriate for large societies. That may require genuine top-down creativity. Hume's theory, as I have explained, perhaps generates foundations for such a theory of property. But it cannot explain everything that is built on those foundations, and it is unlikely to generate a sense of strong entitlement whereby foundational claims of property can be used as points of resistance to more creative forms of state action. This means that the political advantages of bottom-up theories—the reason they are relished by people like Nozick and Epstein—may not accrue from the Humean account in the way they accrue from the Lockean account. That's a price of the Humean account's realism. It doesn't have the same capacity to generate libertarian fantasies as the Lockean account does. But just for that reason it may be a better—more respectable—foundational account for property professors to include in their textbooks.

---

[25] See Hume 1739–40b, III.ii.7.

2

Productive Use in Acquisition, Accession, and Labour Theory

Eric R. Claeys

1. Introduction

In 'Of Property', chapter 5 of his *Second Treatise of Government*, John Locke claims to supply '*the great Foundation of Property*' in man's '*Proprietor[ship] of his own Person*, and the Actions or *Labour* of it'.[1] Locke's account of labour seems intuitively persuasive to many readers, including many English and American judges. For example, the 1871 case *Haslem v Lockwood* required the Connecticut Supreme Court to decide who had appropriated manure scattered on a public road. Haslem spotted the manure first, directed servants to gather it into piles, and left the piles overnight intending to recover them the next morning when he returned with a cart. Before Haslem returned, Lockwood found the piles and carted them away. In the court's view, 'after the plaintiff [Haslem] had changed [the manure's] original condition and greatly enhanced its value by his labor, [defendant Lockwood] seized and appropriated to his own use the fruits of the plaintiff's outlay.'[2] The 'fruits of one's labour' metaphor all but decided the case.

In contemporary scholarship, however, labour arguments fare much, much worse. Labour theory is often portrayed as being incoherent. Lockean labour theory seems to appeal to two different modes of normative reasoning. On one hand, Locke grounds property in external assets in what seems to be an inalienable right: the '*Property*' 'every man has . . . in his own *Person*', which 'no Body has any Right to but himself'. On that ground, Haslem's manure-gathering seems to have given him an inalienable right to keep the manure. On the other hand, Locke also argues that labour-based property rights will generate value 100 times the intrinsic values of the resources covered by property.[3] This argument makes what seems to be a utilitarian prediction. On this ground, Haslem seems to deserve ownership of the manure because (and only to the extent that) his gathering benefits the community, by converting what had been a public nuisance into useful fertilizer. Even scholars

---

[1] Locke 1689b, Second Treatise, s. 44, pp. 298–9.
[2] *Haslem v Lockwood* 1871, 506.
[3] Locke 1689b, Second Treatise, s. 27, p. 287; see also Second Treatise, s. 40, p. 296.

generally sympathetic to Locke's political project assume that these two arguments try to 'square a legal circle'. Such scholars seek 'the reconciliation of these two divergent imperatives', often by jettisoning the rights-based foundations of labour theory.[4]

Separately, modern scholars assume that labour theory cannot supply an adequate foundation for property rights in practice. Scholars commonly raise three main adequacy objections. First, 'without a prior theory of ownership, it is not self-evident that one owns even the labour that is mixed with something else'. Thus, Haslem's gathering did not entitle him to own the manure unless he had property in the labour he or his servants performed while gathering the manure. Second, 'even if one does own the labour that one performs, the labour theory provides no guidance in determining the scope of the right that one establishes by mixing one's labour with something else.'[5] Did Haslem's gathering establish an entitlement only over the manure . . . or also over some or all of the highway? Last, in practice, more often than not property law refrains from grounding property claims in labour. Although the labourer acquired property in the *Haslem* case, far more often, property doctrines frequently ignore or disregard labour-based arguments. Doctrines associated with accession vest ownership of tangible resources in the owner of the land on which the resources reside (or, in which the resources are affixed). For example, if people discover a beehive on an owner's land after considerable effort and research but without the landowner's consent, the *ratione soli* doctrine gives the owner of the soil (*solum*) a decisive reason (*ratio*) to own the bees. Instead of praising the hive-finders' 'labor and skill', courts classify their conduct instead as a 'trespass, which can avail the [finders] nothing' and is 'injurious to the rights of property'.[6] The accession principles that settle acquisition claims in the bee dispute apply as well to soil, trees, domesticated animals, and minerals. If property law follows the principles at work in bee cases most of the time and labour theory only in odd cases involving cow manure, 'that discrepancy complicates the standard Lockean defence of private property'.[7]

In this chapter, I argue that these impressions reflect several major errors about the character and reach of labour theory. Labour-based principles have been out of fashion for at least half a century in scholarly discourse. As a result, contemporary property scholars have little feel how terms like 'labour' and 'use' relate to property doctrine. Indeed, each of the two sets of criticisms just recounted corresponds to a significant gap in property scholars' understanding.

To begin with, legal scholars are not as familiar as they should be with philosophical scholarship about labour theory. At least in American scholarship, most property scholars assume that a scholar can understand most of what needs to be known about Locke's labour theory by consulting Robert Nozick's *Anarchy, State, and Utopia* (1974)[8] and Jeremy Waldron's *The Right to Private Property* (1988).[9]

---

[4] Epstein 1998, 9; see also at 9–39.   [5] Rose 1985, 73.
[6] *Fisher v Steward* 1804, 61.   [7] Merrill 2010, 497.   [8] See Merrill 2010, 497–9.
[9] For three recent examples not otherwise considered extensively in this chapter, see Waldron's contribution to this volume; Dagan 2013, 260–1; Singer 2011, 14. Alexander and Peñalver 2012

The adequacy criticisms just recounted are informed by Nozick's and Waldron's critiques of Locke. Since these critiques were published, however, labour theory has been reconsidered at length in at least six books on legal or political philosophy.[10] Two of those works have converged on an alternative interpretation of labour, to which this chapter will refer as 'productive labour' theory. In this interpretation, 'labour' refers to 'purposeful activity, directed to useful ends, and which secures preservation in the primitive state and improves human life once basic necessities have been met'.[11] I call such labour *productive* to accentuate this interpretation's signature characteristic: ownership of an object is not morally justifiable unless the owner asserts it to deploy the object for 'productive use', understood as activity 'satisfying needs or supplying the conveniences of life'.[12] One of this chapter's two main goals is to familiarize legal scholars with the political-philosophy literature on productive labour and use.

Separately, labour theory suffers because of significant gaps between legal and philosophical scholarship. When scholars in political philosophy study moral rights, they tend to focus on the foundations for such rights. They may acknowledge that moral rights cannot be secured without being instituted, or implemented, or (Locke's term) 'settled' in law, customs, and government institutions.[13] Political-philosophy scholars assume that questions about how moral rights are implemented deserve to be studied in scholarship about law. Since legal scholars assume that it makes as little sense to 'implement' a 'right' as it does to square a circle, however, they have not followed up on political philosophers' suggestions how to fill their research agendas.[14] The second main contribution of this chapter is to fill this void between political philosophers and legal theorists. Using property doctrines, this chapter shows how a theory of labour, grounded in natural law and rights, may prescribe laws and policies appealing *both* to 'fairness' and 'welfare'[15]—reconciling each to the other and thus avoiding incoherence.[16]

To keep the following argument manageable, this chapter illustrates how productive labour theory applies to three related doctrines. This chapter focuses most closely on the doctrine of capture. Capture supplies the doctrine by which individuals appropriate unowned chattels, like the manure in *Haslem*. Locke's most

---

question Nozick's use of and fidelity to Locke, 53–6, but their critiques of Locke's justifications for exclusive private property, 46–9, are sceptical for reasons similar to Waldron's.

[10] See Kramer 1997; Sreenivasan 1995; Tully 1993, 96–136; Simmons 1992, 222–352; Buckle 1991, 125–90; Munzer 1990, 254–91. Two other, earlier books also deserve pride of place: Tully 1980; and MacPherson 1962.

[11] Buckle 1991, 150.   [12] Simmons 1998, 210.

[13] Locke 1689b, Second Treatise, s. 38, 45, pp. 295, 299.

[14] Consider for example Blackman 2011, which studies the capture case *Pierson v Post* (1805). Blackman recognizes that the judges relied on natural law labour theories in *Pierson*, and he seems quite open to such theories. When Blackman critiques the policy implications of *Pierson*'s holding, however, he relies exclusively on economic analysis. See also McDowell 2007.

[15] Kaplow and Shavell 2002.

[16] I thank Philip Hamburger, John Simmons, Joe Singer, Jeremy Waldron, and Tom West for convincing me to emphasize this contribution.

vivid illustrations of labour theory come from the acquisition of tangible articles—nuts, water, and animals.[17] Like capture doctrine itself, these examples raise a fundamental policy question: why *should* any individual be able to appropriate an otherwise-common resource, to the exclusion of all others? This chapter also studies 'lost capture' disputes, in which a plaintiff complains that a defendant wrongly deprived him of a rightful prospective advantage in finishing a capture. These cases clarify the precise limits of labour theory, because they highlight problems that arise when concurrent labourers compete to appropriate a single asset. Finally, this chapter examines the fixture and *ratione soli* rules to illustrate how accession takes disputes out of the coverage of acquisition principles.

In relation to these doctrines, this chapter proves the following two theses. First, productive labour theory justifies: why would-be owners should have limited legal liberty interests in pursuing opportunities to capture; why they should have broad property interests in appropriating unowned chattels; and why ownership of basic chattels should be vested in a landowner when those chattels sit on or are affixed to the owner's land. This justification may not be 'optimal' in the sense that it is superior to any other possible justification for property rights. In other words, the chapter does not prove that productive labour theory regulates acquisition and accession more convincingly than economic legal analysis,[18] Kantian normative theory,[19] or many other possible rivals. Yet this chapter does show that productive labour theory is 'permissible', i.e. that it is at least sufficient if not necessary to justify a legal system's enforcing the acquisition rules discussed here.[20]

---

[17] Locke 1689b, Second Treatise, ss. 28–30, pp. 288–90.

[18] Although this chapter cannot conduct an exhaustive contrast between labour theory and economic legal analysis, let me at least list the main differences that such a comparison would need to consider. Economic analyses of other property doctrines are inconsistent with black-letter law in important respects. Such analyses also prescribe that legal rules focus on facts that create overwhelming information problems for courts and other legal regulators. Claeys 2010a, 1388–94, 1437–45. Economic analysis often explains or justifies legal doctrine in relation to efficiency and utility when these criteria do not state normative reasons for action that any citizen regulated by a law would find binding. Many examples of such analysis misconceive of the 'rights' that the private law enforces, or underestimate the importance of property's multilateral structure. Claeys 2012, 134–40. Such analysis sometimes has trouble explaining whether certain and how to tally interpersonal utility, and sometimes it also founders trying to determine whether certain policy consequences should count as social 'costs' or 'benefits'. In addition, many examples of economic legal analysis are tone-deaf about the relation between law and social acculturation. See Claeys forthcoming.

[19] I believe and assume here that medieval natural law and early Enlightenment natural rights theories of politics justify law more convincingly than Kantian theories. The former ground legal obligations teleologically, in egoistic normative interests related to individual flourishing; the latter in deontological normative interests that make prescriptions from a priori conclusions about deonto-logical morality. In general, the former seem more satisfying because they are more attentive to human psychology than the latter. Claeys 2009b, 892–916. Among other things, because the obligations they prescribe are egoistic, natural-law and -rights theories are more likely than Kantian theories to prescribe rules likely to be obeyed and enforced stably in practice, with less hypocrisy or shirking. Again, however, one would need to compare how both approaches justify acquisition and accession doctrine to see whether my suspicions are correct. For a Kantian critique of labour theory and labour-based capture doctrine, see Drassinower 2006, 192–6. I thank Avihay Dorfman for encouraging me to discuss the objections I consider in this note and n. 18.

[20] Simmons 1994, 66–9.

Separately, because the judges who developed the doctrines studied in this chapter subscribed to labour theories quite like Locke's, these doctrines illustrate how legal doctrine may and should 'settle' the positive law of property.[21] In this chapter, I use acquisition and related doctrines to illustrate the relation between labour-based natural-rights morality and legal practice. Productive labour theory focuses acquisition-related doctrines while leaving lawyers a reasonable amount of flexibility about how those doctrines' contents should be specified.

This chapter's argument proceeds as follows. Sections 2–5 restate the foundations for labour-based property rights relying on productive labour theory, focusing specifically on the insights needed to apply those foundations to capture, lost capture, and *ratione soli* doctrines. Section 2 defines and justifies a natural-rights liberty interest in productive labour, and Section 3 extends that interest to property. Sections 4 and 5 show how labour-based property rights justify two legal principles related to accession: (in Section 4) exclusive control over land and chattels, and (in Section 5) accession principles. Sections 6–9 demonstrate my second thesis. Section 6 examines how property rights are settled in 'lost capture' disputes, Section 7 does the same in relation to capture doctrine and variations on it, and Section 8 does so for the fixture and *ratione soli* doctrines. Section 9 then makes some general observations about the relation between productive labour theory and legal practice.

2. The Moral Right to Labour Productively

2.1 The intellectual context for Lockean rights

Contemporary property scholarship has lost its feel for labour theory in large part because it has lost its feel for theories of natural law and rights that shaped Anglo-American law. During the 18th and 19th centuries, rights-based and utilitarian sources of obligation came to seem separate;[22] Locke's accounts of rights, morality, and political obligation precede that separation.[23] So let me begin by defining general terms important to Locke's accounts of rights, morality, and political obligation, and by restating a justification for a right to engage in productive labour. In case it needs saying, any such 'restatement' can only scratch the surface of Lockean property scholarship.[24]

---

[21] When I justify and examine particular acquisition or accession doctrines in this chapter, I will do so assuming that the officer responsible for the doctrine's content seeks conscientiously to make it conform as much as possible to the prescriptions of productive labour theory. That said, Locke himself doubted whether it was necessary or likely that most political communities would demand their officials to be this conscientious. In chapter 5 of the *Second Treatise*, Locke's justification for exclusive property rights works whether the citizens agree to secure natural rights or merely converge on a 'tacit and voluntary consent' around such rights and an economy with exchange and money. (See Locke 1689b, Second Treatise, s. 50, pp. 301–2.)

[22] MacIntyre 1984, 123–4.   [23] Olivecrona 1974. See Alexander and Peñalver 2012, 36–7.

[24] The following account relies substantially on Simmons 1992 and Buckle 1991 to describe productive labour theory and property rights. The account relies less on Simmons and Buckle and more on Myers 1999 and West 2012 to describe the (what West, Myers, and I believe to be the eudaimonistic and virtue-theoretic) normative foundations of such labour and rights. That said,

Like other medieval or early Enlightenment theories, Locke's account of natural rights is egoistic. Psychologically, humans are hardwired to pursue things that they believe to be good or happiness supplying and in which they believe themselves to be deficient.[25] Descriptively, humans are capable of reasoning deliberately how to judge and rank different apparent goods,[26] and of reasoning practically how to exercise dominion over inferior things to acquire those goods.[27] This background determines the character of normative obligations for Locke. People are obligated to pursue their goods, but they also have rights to engage in activity reasonably likely and necessary to acquire those goods. Because human goods ground both duties and rights, duties and rights have the character they have in interest (or benefit) theories of rights.[28] Locke confirms as much in an aside in the *Second Treatise*. Locke justifies law 'in its true Notion . . . not so much [as] the Limitation as *the direction of a free and intelligent Agent* to his proper Interest', and as 'prescrib[ing] no farther than is for the general Good of those under that Law'.[29]

When Locke refers to moral 'rights', he assumes a meaning for 'right' consistent with these egoistic, interest-based priors. For Locke, a moral 'right' consists of a strong normative interest[30] comprising two more specific interests. One of those interests is a claim-right, a negative right to exclude others from interfering with one's legitimate authority to make decisions in a particular field of choice. The other specific interest is a liberty, an affirmative capacity to pursue one's own gratification or well-being within the scope of that legitimate authority.[31] A moral right (back in the broader sense) is 'moral' if it has binding force and if its force is pre-political and non-conventional.[32]

Medieval and early Enlightenment natural law and rights theories portray individuals as being entitled to a sphere of free moral agency called the *suum* ('his own'),[33] encompassing the individual's rights to life, body, liberty, reputation, and other more specific rights. The moral right to labour is one of the rights included in the *suum*. The right to labour is the right to engage in activity reasonably likely and necessary to help the actor pursue 'prosperity'. Every person has a 'natural Inclination . . . to preserve his Being'. It is reasonable to infer that this inclination has a 'purpose, to . . . use . . . those things which were serviceable for his Subsistence, and given him as means of his Preservation'.[34] 'Prosperity' encompasses preservation

---

Simmons 1992, 58–9 is probably right that Locke's main rights-claims may be grounded on overlapping foundations.

[25] Locke 1700, II.xxi.31–69, pp. 250–81.   [26] Locke 1700, II.xxi.46, 262–3.
[27] Locke 1689b, First Treatise, s. 30, p. 162.   [28] See Simmons 1992, 92–4.
[29] Locke 1689b, Second Treatise, s. 57, p. 305.
[30] In this chapter, I use 'interest' in the sense in which it was used in Feinberg 1984, 33–4, unless context requires otherwise.
[31] When I speak of 'claim-rights' and 'liberties', I mean what Wesley Hohfeld called (respectively) 'claim-rights' and 'privileges'. Hohfeld 1913, 28–44. Simmons 1992, 92–3 (following Feinberg 1970) refers to the same incidents as 'rights' and 'moral powers'. I use the corresponding Hohfeldian terms because Simmons's terms are likely to seem idiosyncratic to many political-philosophy readers and most legal readers. See Kramer 1997, 15–23.
[32] Simmons 1992, 87–94.   [33] See Olivecrona 1974, 222–5.
[34] Locke 1689b, First Treatise, s. 86, p. 223.

and the other goods people may justifiably pursue.[35] Although 'prosperity' at least gestures toward human excellence,[36] most of the time it focuses on low common denominator 'civil goods': 'life, freedom, the wholeness of and freedom from pain in the body, and the possession of external things, such as a landed estate, money, equipment, et cetera'.[37] To capture these tensions in 'prosperity', I will in the rest of this chapter refer interchangeably to 'prosperity' and to 'self-preservation and-improvement'.

2.2. Labour as a moral right

The right to labour productively comes to mean the right to use one's person and planning faculties to pursue prosperity so specified. Labour includes a Hohfeldian liberty to engage in 'purposeful activity, directed to useful ends, and which secures preservation in the primitive state and improves human life once basic necessities have been met'.[38] Labour also entails a claim-right to be free all from interferences with the liberty except those resulting from exercises of the same liberty. Similarly, 'use' consists of the application of one's own person or other inputs to pursue prosperity in a manner consistent with other individuals' pursuing prosperity concurrently. That is why, for example, Locke contrasts the 'use of the Industrious and Rational' with the 'Fancy and Covetousness of the Quarrelsom and Conten-tious'.[39] In this sense, 'use' is inherently productive use. The moral right of labour is the right to 'use' persons and things only in the course of 'activity of improving for the benefit of life'.[40]

Labour's productive character answers the challenge (recounted in the Introduc-tion) to justify on what basis 'one owns even the labour that is mixed with something else'. When Locke says that 'every Man has a *Property* in his own *Person*', and that '[t]he *Labour* of his Body, and the *Work* of his Hands . . . are properly his', he may reasonably be understood to mean that men are entitled to be left alone to direct their purposive actions.[41] In the *Haslem* case, Haslem 'owned' a sphere of purposive action in which to search for resources useful to his farm because he had an inherent and inalienable moral faculty to direct and enjoy the benefits from his own moral agency.

---

[35] With one caveat—Locke deliberately avoided using the term 'prosperity' in the *Two Treatises*. Locke reported King James I to have said, in a 1603 speech to Parliament, that he 'acknowledge[d] himself to be ordained for the procuring of the Wealth and Property of his People'. In the original, the King had promised to procure the 'Wealth and *prosperitie*' of the people. Locke 1689b, Second Treatise, s. 200, p. 399 and nn. 4–11.

[36] I believe Locke de-emphasized perfection and excellence for fear that they would destabilize politics in Christian political communities. See Claeys 2009b, 916–34; Claeys 2008. Locke's deliberate avoidance of the term 'prosperity' confirms this interpretation.

[37] Locke 1689a, 66 (my translation). See Claeys 2008.

[38] Buckle 1991, 150. See Simmons 1992, 273.

[39] Locke 1689b, Second Treatise, s. 34, p. 291.   [40] Buckle 1991, 151.

[41] Locke 1689b, Second Treatise, s. 27, pp. 287–8; see also at s. 4, p. 269; Locke 1700, II.xxi.4, II.xxi.12, II.xxi.21, II.xxi.24, pp. 235–6, 239–40, 241–4.

To be sure, Locke was being hyperbolic when he referred to an inalienable sphere of liberty of action as 'property' capable of 'ownership'. Indeed, he almost certainly knew as much, for in the passage omitted by the ellipsis above, he only suggested that (my emphasis) 'we *may* say' that labour and work are 'properly his' who labours or works. In occasional context, the *Two Treatises* teach (the *First Treatise*) that no single person may assert over other men the dominion that people deservedly exercise over other animals and (the *Second Treatise*) that all men have equality 'in respect of...Dominion over one another'. The *Two Treatises* aim to embolden a citizenry to agree that a despot's absolute dominion creates a 'vile and miserable... Estate' for everyone else. To accomplish that goal, it helps to teach them that their rightful dominions over their own moral agencies are, if not property, at least a lot like property.[42]

3. Property Acquisition in Labour Theory

The institution of property extends the scope of labour (and the *suum*)—from actors to assets on which they hope to act. After all, 'the Condition of Humane Life, which requires Labour and Materials to work on, necessarily introduces *private Possessions*'.[43] Yet this extension requires considerable elaboration and qualification. If any person has an interest in labouring on an asset, then all do. As Locke acknowledges at the beginning of 'Of Property', it is reasonable to presume that the whole world has been 'given...to Mankind in common'. It then comes to 'seem[] a very great difficulty, how any one should ever come to have [an exclusive] *Property* in any thing'.[44]

3.1 Extending labour from the person to things

There are three basic limitations on the right and liberty to appropriate external assets.[45] One limit is internal—do not waste. This limitation distinguishes Locke's theory of property from Nozick's Lock*ean* theory. Nozick does not recognize the responsibility to use or the duty not to waste as limitations on appropriation.[46] Locke does. The priority to enjoy an external asset is limited by a condition 'well set, by the Extent of [the appropriator's] *Labour, and the Conveniency of Life*'.[47]

---

[42] Locke 1689b, Second Treatise, s. 54, p. 304; First Treatise, s. 1, p. 141; see also First Treatise, s. 30, p. 162; Second Treatise, s. 1.4, pp. 267, 269. I thank Robby George, George Kateb, and Paul Sigmund for helping me to clarify this point.

[43] Locke 1689b, Second Treatise, s. 35, p. 292. See also Locke 1689a, 124.

[44] Locke 1689b, Second Treatise, s. 25, p. 286.

[45] See Waldron 1988, 157–62.

[46] See Nozick 1974b, 175–82 (treating the sufficiency limitation but not discussing the use or non-waste limitation).

[47] Locke 1689b, Second Treatise, s. 36, p. 292.

Even if the first appropriator avoids waste, his property claim continues to be qualified by two external limitations.[48] One of these limitations requires that each gatherer leave 'enough, and as good left in common for others'.[49] (For ease of exposition, I refer to the 'enough and as good' limitation here as the 'sufficiency' limitation.[50]) The sufficiency limitation embodies the labour interests of all: because every member of a political community has the same right to exercise his moral agency, each deserves an equal opportunity to labour on external assets for his own personal prosperity. In addition, although appropriators ordinarily deserve to be left alone to use their own appropriations for their own personal uses, in an extreme case, one person's need to preserve his own life or safety can take priority over another's less-urgent needs. That extreme case gives rise to the charity proviso.[51]

3.2 The social character of productive appropriation

Many scholars assume that Lockean property rights are asocial or even anti-social. Although this assumption comes from sources too numerous to recount here,[52] Waldron deserves significant credit for reinforcing it. Waldron interprets Locke 'to derive the existence of special rights of private property from the general right to subsistence'. (Waldron means by a 'general right' a right that does not arise out of any particular relationship or transaction between individual persons, and by a 'special right' one that does.) When Waldron finds Locke's justification for special rights 'unsuccessful',[53] he holds Locke's justification for property to a standard that Locke himself did not try to meet. In Locke's account, property rights are general rights, subject to general qualifications and responsibilities.

Let me illustrate by applying productive labour theory to an example using Hohfeld's analytic vocabulary. Assume that Michael, Steve, and Nick inhabit an island, that the island does not belong to and is not governed by any organized political community, and that the only other inhabitants are deer.[54] Before any deer are caught, Nick, Steve, and Mike have Hohfeldian powers to appropriate the deer, each claiming deer caught as his own private property. The interest of each resident in unowned deer is correlatively subject to a Hohfeldian liability, of losing the opportunity to appropriate any deer captured first by one of the other inhabitants. Assume Mike appropriates six deer. When he does so, he acquires claim-rights and liberties against Nick and Steve, to repel them from interference with his use or

---

[48] Labour-grounded property rights have other external limitations—in particular, claims by children on support from parents. Locke 1689b, First Treatise, ss. 87–93, pp. 224–8; Kendrick 2011. I do not consider these limitations in text because they do not significantly shape the acquisition or accession doctrines to be discussed in Sections 6–8.

[49] Locke 1689b, Second Treatise, s. 27; s. 33, pp. 288, 291.

[50] See Waldron 1988, 209–18; MacPherson 1962, 208.

[51] Locke 1689b, First Treatise, s. 42, p. 170.

[52] See e.g. Austin this volume (criticizing state-of-nature accounts of property on the ground that they overemphasize 'the normative significance of a person-thing relation'); Kant 1797, 88 ('possession is nothing other than a relation of a person to persons').

[53] Waldron 1988, 106–7, 128.

[54] With acknowledgements (and apologies) to *The Deer Hunter* (1978).

enjoyment of the deer. Naturally, Steve and Nick are subject to duties and exposures correlative to any reasonable efforts Mike takes to protect his secure possession of the deer. These relations all seem unilateral because they flow from Mike's unilateral action on the deer.

Yet Mike's interests are qualified by the Lockean limitations. Obviously, if Mike kills the deer frivolously and lets their carcasses be 'putrified, before he could spend [them], . . . he invade[s]'[55] Steve and Nick's rights and they may take from him the deer he is wasting. Less obviously, Mike's power, claim-right, and liberty are all qualified by liabilities, duties, or exposures embodying the sufficiency limitation and the charity proviso. Assume that all the unowned deer on the island die as the result of a natural catastrophe. If Nick and Steve need deerskins for clothing, the sufficiency limitation entitles them to exercise a claim-right and power to take two of Mike's deer each, and it imposes on Mike a duty and liability to suffer their takings. If Nick and Steve each need one carcass's worth of venison to survive the upcoming winter, the charity proviso gives them similar powers and rights each to take one. If all three owners need three deer to survive, Nick, Steve, and Mike are all justified in fighting to acquire or protect three.

Contrary to Waldron's portrait of Locke's argument, none of the inhabitants establishes a special right in a deer by engaging in a personal transaction, i.e. killing or capturing a deer. Now, the inhabitants' conventional property rights may confer on them legal rights more exclusive and monopolistic than were suggested by the interlocking moral relations recounted in the previous two paragraphs. Nevertheless, at this point, we are focusing only on the foundations for those conventional rights. Non-conventional foundations set normative standards by which property laws and other conventions may be measured—but the latter need not embody the relations prescribed by the former in every detail.

Yet why allow appropriation that is unilateral or exclusive in any respect? The blunt answer: if people could not acquire property rights without prior social coordination, 'Man [would] have starved, notwithstanding the Plenty God had given him'.[56] The subtle answer: Labour and the limitations on property supply an 'effectual truth' that seem realistically likely to ground property rights on foundations as stable and humane as possible.[57] To use the terms on which Carol Rose relies in her contribution to this volume, Locke's theory of labour (like his understanding of politics generally) assumes that people can act as Hawks or as Doves, and that human reason can judge when different individuals should opt to act as Hawks or Doves in different repeat act-situations.[58] Owners may be predicted and should be expected to act as 'Hawks'—i.e. irascibly to repel threats to their property—when they have claimed that property for productive labour. Yet non-owners may also be predicted and should be expected to act as Hawks—i.e. irascibly to limit owners' property claims—when owners violate the waste and

[55] Locke 1689b, First Treatise, s. 37, p. 295.
[56] Locke 1689b, Second Treatise, s. 28.
[57] Zuckert 2005, 266; see Myers 1999, 194.
[58] See Rose, this volume (attributing Sugden 1986).

sufficiency limitations or the charity proviso. In all other situations, non-owners may be predicted and should be expected to suffer property appropriation like Doves. It is realistic to expect members of a political society to converge on practices and institutions that respect the strengths of these competing claims in different situations. Property rights then come to be socially obligatory because they are 'necessary for maintaining a harmonious social order. Since any withdrawal from private property would endanger society at large, withdrawal is contrary to the rational dictates of natural law'.[59]

3.3 Productive use as a limit on labour

Even if the right to labour generates social rights and obligations in relation to acquisitions, perhaps it provides 'no guidance in determining the scope of the right that one establishes by mixing one's labour with something else'.[60] In particular, as Waldron and Nozick have argued, perhaps labour provides no guidance because the idea of mixing labour creates category mistakes.[61] Nozick asked whether someone could claim ownership of the Atlantic Ocean by pouring tomato juice marked with traceable radioactive molecules in it, and Waldron hypothesized a ham sandwich dropped in cement.[62] True, the 'mixing' image[63] is somewhat hyperbolic. Even so, if understood as a metaphor, it clarifies how labour limits property rights while justifying them.

Productive labour theory does not confer property rights on any mere effort applied to an object. It justifies ownership over the object as it justifies labour—as a means reasonably necessary to effectuate some aspect of the actor's prosperity. When labour is understood as prosperity-producing activity, it provides far more guidance to property rights than the tomato-juice and ham-sandwich hypotheticals suggest.

First, productive labour theory does not establish property claims in mere exertion, only in activity that could contribute to some aspect of the actor's prosperity. Haslem was entitled to appropriate the highway manure if he intended to use it on his farm or to give or trade it to someone else who would use it similarly. By contrast, an actor does not feed anyone or accomplish any other productive use by burying a ham sandwich or pouring off tomato juice; the actor who does both has 'chosen foolishly to waste [his] tomato juice and ham sandwich'.[64]

Second (and somewhat contrary to the thrust of the mixing metaphor), moral rights to labour productively need not always justify rights of private property. In the tomato-juice hypothetical, the mismatch between pouring away and productiveness is not the only problem; the ocean ('that great and still remaining Common of Mankind'[65]) is also a bad candidate to be claimed as private property. Ocean

---

[59] Buckle 1991, 166.   [60] Rose 1985, 73.

[61] Waldron 1988, 185; Nozick 1974b, 174–5; see also Kramer 1997, 149–50.

[62] Nozick 1974b, 174–5; Waldron 1983, 43.

[63] Locke 1689b, Second Treatise, s. 27, p. 288.

[64] Mossoff 2002, 163. See Olivecrona 1974, 226.

[65] Locke 1689b, Second Treatise, s. 30, p. 289.

water has few or no private human uses; it has many common uses, especially fishing and travelling. Similarly, although manure may be used most productively when owned and consumed exclusively, a highway is used most productively when many people are granted rights to travel on it. That difference supplies one of several reasons why Haslem's manure-gathering did not entitle him to claim he had appropriated the highway.

3.4 The communicative function of productive labour

Separately, labour focuses the scope of property by virtue of having an equality component.[66] As A. John Simmons explains:

[T]he right of self-government...is...a right only to such freedom as is compatible with the equal freedom of others. To try to control for one's projects external goods that have already been incorporated into the legitimate plans of others, would be to deny to others that equal right. We may make property with our labour only in what is not already fairly taken as 'part of the labour' of another.[67]

Because 'productive use' is a normative interest held by political equals, productive labour theory stresses labour's communicative function much more than contemporary property scholars appreciate. 'Labor must show enough seriousness of purpose to "overbalance" the community of things' that exists because 'the World [was given] to *Adam* and his Posterity in common'.[68] For 'things of use', the best way to show that purpose is 'to use them'.[69]

This requirement highlights further problems with the tomato-juice hypothetical. Onlookers' social perceptions of things are keyed to their pre-political normative expectations. That which they expect to contribute to human prosperity, they perceive in entities and combinations whose uses lend themselves to human prosperity. People perceive manure as capable of being owned privately, but they perceive highways as commonses open to all travellers. Similarly, they perceive fish as good candidates for appropriation and ocean water as a bad one. (Note how the 'ocean' is a singular entity while 'fish' come in separate entities—even though in English the plural for 'fish' is identical to the singular.) On one hand, people's perceptions of ocean water accord with their expectations that the water be used as a common pathway; on the other hand, these perceptions accord with the fact that it would be extremely difficult, by labour or any other marker, to 'put a distinction between' a few water molecules and the ocean remaining in 'common'.[70] Radioactive carbon atoms do not adequately overcome these boundary-marking problems. Our intuitions suggest that the can owner abandons the juice by pouring it because it is impossible to keep the juice separate from a resource best left in common.

---

[66] Locke 1689b, Second Treatise, s. 4, p. 269.
[68] Locke 1689b, Second Treatise, s. 25, p. 286.
[70] Locke 1689b, Second Treatise, s. 28, p. 288.

[67] Simmons 1992, 275.
[69] Simmons 1992, 272.

4. Control Rights in Labour Theory

Even if an appropriator deserves property in the tangible objects he appropriates, the appropriations do not automatically determine what sort of property he acquires. Legal property rights differ considerably. One way to sort the differences is along a continuum ranging from 'usufructs' or 'use rights' to 'control rights'. As an ideal type, usufructs entitle proprietors only to consume or use an asset. The beneficiary of a usufruct must continue to use the object consistent with use patterns previously established, and his intended uses must be consistent with use claims of other would-be users. In temperate jurisdictions, traditional common law rights to river flow have many characteristics of usufructs.[71] By contrast, many assets are clothed with rights of exclusive control, possession, and disposition, to which I will here refer as 'control rights'. As an ideal type, control rights entitle an owner to determine near-absolutely how an asset may be used, by giving him the right to exclude others with few or no questions asked.[72] In political communities with well-developed money economies, land and chattels are protected by control rights.[73]

Locke's theory of labour declares a moral use right. The conditions on legal usufructs parallel and embody the moral responsibility not to waste (i.e. to use) acquired property and the sufficiency and charity limitations. Because Locke's theory is grounded in use, it does not justify control rights straightforwardly. Indeed, 'Of Property' focuses on that disjunction; the chapter answers how use-based property rights entitle any person to hold '*Property* ... exclusive of all the rest of [Adam's] Posterity'.[74] The answer: in theories of natural law or rights like Locke's, positive laws need not and often should not parallel strictly the moral principles they implement. Labour supplies a non-conventional 'Foundation' for property[75]—but it justifies and requires the exercise of prudent judgment to implement the foundations it lays. For some assets—say, riparian water in temperate climates—legal use rights appropriately secure labour-based moral use rights. Paradoxically, however, for land and chattels, legal rights of exclusive control secure labour better than usufructs.

The case for control rights rests on several overlapping arguments. Some of these arguments are virtue-theoretic. If people do not control the resources they need for their own self-preservation or -improvement, they grow to be not only spoiled but also child-like and psychologically dependent. By managing assets for his own

---

[71] Claeys 2013, 411–15.

[72] As I have explained elsewhere, Lockean property rights in land and chattels do institute many use-based priorities and exceptions: to name a few, adverse possession, Claeys forthcoming; nuisance, see Claeys 2010a, 1398–430, and a privilege to jostle a chattel accidentally as long as the jostling does not cause damage to the chattel, see Claeys 2010b, 398–401. When no such priorities or exceptions apply, however, land and chattel owners reserve residual authority to control their things' uses. 'Control' describes that residual authority.

[73] For a more comprehensive list, see Lueck 1995, 411 table 1.

[74] Locke 1689b, Second Treatise, s. 25, p. 286.

[75] Locke 1689b, Second Treatise, s. 44, p. 298.

long-range life plans, an owner comes to be 'rational', 'industrious', and 'Master of himself, and *Proprietor of his own Person*'.[76] Control rights also align property with deontological aspects of human morality. As Simmons explains, while '[s]elf-preservation requires only rights of use or access . . . , [s]elf-government is only possible . . . if the external things necessary for carrying out our plans can be kept, managed, exchanged (etc.) as the plans require'.[77] As the Introduction recognized, control rights also promote consequentialist goals; they encourage labourers to produce value truly useful to human preservation or improvement on the order of 100 times greater than could be extracted from tangible resources by correlative usufructs.[78]

Of course, these arguments provoke further objections. One states that it is impossible to endow owners with exclusive control over tangible resources without denying to non-owners equal access to those resources for their own self-preservation or -improvement.[79] Or, if a theory of labour justifies such denials, it must be incoherent, perhaps a utilitarian theory dressed in rights-talk. Here more than anywhere else, contemporary scholars misunderstand productive labour theory because they project anachronistic and inapposite philosophical distinctions onto the theory. Such objections assume that a right cannot count as a 'moral' right unless it has a characteristic that many non-philosophical legal scholars call 'absolute' and different philosophers call 'deontological', 'inviolable', or 'imprescriptible'.[80] All of these terms refer to a requirement according to which a person may not justly be deprived of a moral right without his prior consent. Many theories of natural law or rights justify moral rights coherently without being 'absolute' in this sense; productive labour theory is one of those theories. Because labour theory is part of a practical theory of politics, it justifies officials' reasoning practically, especially by making the best indirect-consequentialist forecasts they can in conditions of limited information.[81] Public officials may and should institute a system of conventional control rights if it seems practically more likely than alternatives to secure and enlarge citizens' non-conventional labour rights.

To be sure, when public officials make such practical determinations, they must respect a constraint that *resembles* the 'absoluteness' criterion discussed in the previous paragraph. In another usage, commonly associated with John Rawls, 'deontology' measures theories of politics by whether they make the Right lexically prior to the Good.[82] Although Locke's and Rawls's theories of politics differ in

---

[76] Locke 1689b, Second Treatise, ss. 34, 44, pp. 291, 298–9. See Myers 1999, 137–244; Locke 1693, ss. 33–39, 45, 75, 105, 110, pp. 25–30, 32, 53, 77, 81–2.
[77] Simmons 1992, 275.
[78] Locke 1689b, Second Treatise, s. 43 p. 298.   [79] See Singer 2011, 14.
[80] Kramer 1997, 128; Nagel 1995, 89–95; Waldron 1988, 13, 19, 158, 184.
[81] Munzer 1990, 273–4, suggests that labour–desert claims need to be limited by principles of utility and efficiency external to labour theory. Productive labour theory makes indirect-consequentialist arguments admissible, as economic and other utilitarian normative theories do. Yet productive labour theory requires lawgivers to use such arguments to determine how best to secure moral rights *internal* to the theory.
[82] Rawls 1971, 30–2.

many particulars, Locke's theory is deontological in the same limited, formal sense as Rawls's. For most practical purposes, Lockean politics makes '*the preservation of the Society*' and 'the publick good' coterminous with the preservation 'of every person in it' and 'the enjoyment of their properties in Peace and Safety'.[83] In Rawls's taxonomy, the preservation of every person's safety and property counts as the Right. In any case where the bare survival of the community does not demand otherwise, the securing of the safety and property of all citizens counts as the Good. In Rawls's sense, then, Locke's account of the Right is lexically prior to his account of the Good.[84]

This formal deontology criterion, however, does not prevent productive labour theory from using legal coercion to reorder property rights. The criterion institutes a burden of justification. For control rights to be justifiable, they must at least not diminish and should (preferably) enlarge citizens' concurrent moral powers to acquire assets and then labour on them. Here, 'citizens' refers to *all* citizens, not merely owners but also non-owners. Yet the burden of justification may be satisfied, as Locke illustrates by comparing the lot of a day labourer in England with that of an aboriginal king in North America.[85] As Buckle explains,

In the money economy, . . . subsistence, and even flourishing, becomes (for most people) no longer dependent on landed property, nor on the existence of an unappropriated common, but on deriving an income sufficient for life's purposes. So the purpose of the 'enough, and as good' clause, in the stage of the money economy, is satisfied if incomes provide a reasonable living.[86]

Of course, this justification fails if those who lack property cannot earn wages. It also fails if wages do not give non-owners opportunities at least as robust as the opportunities they would have in a community without property rights or exchange to acquire life-preserving or -improving goods. That said, I assume here that the English and American political systems satisfy these requirements tolerably well. Moreover, to the extent that these systems fall short of providing non-owners with the requisite opportunities to acquire the means of survival, their shortcomings may be addressed in fields separate from acquisition-related property law. In particular, public officials may limit the scope of control rights and recognize the sufficiency and charity limitations by instituting redistributive income taxation and public welfare programmes.[87]

---

[83] Locke 1689b, Second Treatise, s. 134, pp. 355–6. But see Myers 1999, 139–77 (suggesting that the Right and the Good are coterminous in Locke's general understanding of normative value, even if his theory of politics de-emphasizes the Good and focuses on the Right).

[84] See Zuckert 2005, 263–6; Myers 2005, 235.

[85] Locke 1689b, Second Treatise, s. 41, pp. 296–7.

[86] Buckle 1991, 159. G. A. Cohen argues that this response 'justifies private property only as long as appropriation generates an expanding common for the privately unendowed to forage on, and . . . therefore fails to justify actual private property in the real and fully appropriated world'. Cohen 1995, 188. Locke's argument, however, does not hinge on how many resources are available for appropriation from common property; the opportunity to purchase goods in market exchanges replaces the opportunity to appropriate from common-pool resources.

[87] Cf. Simmons 1992, 333–52.

Others criticize Locke's argument on the ground that Locke engages in an 'interesting exercise in armchair empiricism'[88] when he defends his contention that '['t]is *Labour* indeed that *puts the difference in value* on every thing'.[89] Perhaps the criticism here is that Locke makes a consequentialist argument in support of a broader moral argument. Yet not only Locke but also many contemporary moral theorists find it 'irrational, crazy',[90] to suggest that a moral theory could justify a claim that we have certain rights without considering the consequences the existence of such rights would entail. Perhaps the criticism is that Locke's consequentialism is informal or casual. If that is the objection, armchair empiricism often generates sensible prescriptions.[91] It takes considerable imagination, planning, practical intelligence, and effort to transform wild land into a productive farm; it is not unreasonable to judge that 99 per cent of the crops' value for human prosperity is attributable to the transformation and cultivation of the land.[92] As long as it seems practically likely that surplus crops will make their way to non-owners through exchange, the property system secures labour-based moral rights for all citizens by establishing and protecting the control rights of farmers.

5. Accession in Labour Theory

The justification for private property developed in the last two parts is ambiguous in an important respect: when someone appropriates an article and claims control rights over it, how far do the 'article' and the rights run? This is one of the problems raised by *Haslem*: is ownership over the manure settled somehow by ownership of the land on which the manure sits? Locke alludes to this problem. At one point, he states that 'whatsoever [an occupant] enclosed, and could feed, and make use of, the Cattle and Product was also his'.[93] Why does the landowner's occupancy of the land automatically entitle the occupant to claim ownership over the cow?

In property law, the policy issue here is often called one of 'accession'; because this term is used differently in different fields of law and scholarship, let me clarify how I will use the term in this chapter. In its earliest and narrowest usage, *accessio* refers to a situation in which an asset C, owned by A, is merged with asset D, owned by B, to create a new asset, E. In Roman law, *accessio* determines whether A or B owns E. This usage contrasts with *specificatio* (in which A transforms or improves D into E) and *confusio* (in which C and D are not merged but still commingled so that they cannot be sorted apart).[94] Black-letter English and American legal treatises[95] and seminal American cases[96] construe the term 'accession' to refer to

---

[88] Merrill 2010, 498.   [89] Locke 1689b, Second Treatise, s. 40, p. 296.

[90] Rawls 1971, 30.

[91] Indeed, as Section 9 explains, throughout his writings, Locke supplies many persuasive reasons why it is unreasonable to expect any more than armchair empiricism in practice.

[92] See Locke 1689b, Second Treatise, ss. 37–41, pp. 294–7.

[93] Locke 1689b, Second Treatise, s. 38, p. 295.   [94] See Arnold 1922.

[95] See e.g. Kent 1826, 2: 293–8; Blackstone 1765, 2: 405–6.

[96] *Lampton's Executors v Preston's Executors* 1829.

any situation in which ownership of C entitles A with a claim to own some other thing E as an accessory to C; in this usage, 'accession' encompasses not only *accessio* but also *confusio* and *specificatio*. Today, some scholars maintain that accession refers primarily to a principle for establishing ownership over property, distinct from and competing with acquisition or first possession.[97] (In this usage, a paradigm case of accession occurs when A's riparian land C grows to include accreted land.) Others maintain that accession 'doctrines about [allocating] newly discovered resources are really doctrines about defining the boundaries of already-owned ones'.[98] (Locke's newly occupied land and the cattle and crops on it provide a paradigm case for this view of accession.) In my opinion, all of these usages and examples raise a common problem: how properly to scale several individuals' claims of ownership in relation to one or more entities that are either owned or capable of ownership. If I were writing on a blank scholarly slate, I would call the policy issue a 'scaling' problem; since the term 'accession' has stuck in law and scholarship, I follow prevailing usage.

When understood as a scaling problem, accession renews the 'no guidance in determining the scope of the right' criticism against labour theory. Productive labour theory does not specify any particular scope to property rights on a one-size-fits-all basis. Yet it does have several responses that help focus property's proper scope. Let me explain by critiquing Simmons's response:

> The amount of property that we make by our labour is determined by the nature of the activity. We can take that which is necessary to our projects (and perhaps reasonable windfalls from those activities), but our property runs only to the boundaries of our implemented projects and not to just whatever we might envision): it is 'the spending [labour] on our uses' that 'bounds' our property.[99]

Simmons is surely right that labour limits the scope of any person's property claim in the strictest sense of 'claim'. Assume someone has laboured legitimately on an unowned asset (where 'legitimately' imports all the qualifications acknowledged in Section 3). As a matter of strict right, such a labourer deserves to continue using a thing on which he has laboured, only to the extent that, and as long as, the thing is reasonably necessary for him to produce plans for his prosperity. That limitation weakens fencers' claims to land not immediately under their fences, and land-owners' claims over manure.

Simmons is also right that appropriators may claim 'reasonable windfalls'—but his suggestion here requires considerable elaboration and qualification. Assume that unowned asset E has not yet been laboured on but is in close proximity to assets C and D, both of which *are* being laboured on by (respectively) owners A and B. Although neither A nor B's labour entitles them to claim E in the strictest sense of 'entitle', productive labour theory permits the law to assign ownership of E if

---

[97] See Merrill 2010, 460.   [98] See Newman 2011, 270 n. 70; see Smith 2007, 1766–7.
[99] Simmons 1992, 276 (quoting Locke 1689b, Second Treatise, s. 51, p. 302). I thank Henry Smith for encouraging me to develop the argument explained in this and the next two paragraphs.

such an assignment seems a convenient or prudent means to encourage labour by A, B, and others similarly situated. Since productive labour theory allows and encourages indirect-consequentialist reasoning, property law should deal with the relevant issues indirectly, by settling claims to resources in the class to which E belongs in all recurring disputes with the salient features of A and B's dispute. Indeed, Locke justifies private ownership with a similar argument. Locke argues that '*labour makes the far greatest part of the value* of things, we enjoy in this World'.[100] Strictly speaking, this argument entitles a labourer only to a lien on an external asset to the extent that he has laboured on it.[101] To expand the lien into absolute ownership, one needs an indirect-consequentialist argument as sketched in Section 4. Such an argument must explain why the lienholder is better positioned than anyone else to use the resource over which he holds a lien, most productively, to the general benefit of the entire community.

Moreover, productive labour theory also identifies the considerations that should inform a public official's sense of what assignments seem convenient or prudent in an accession dispute. Two factors loom large—the productive and communicative aspects of labour, as discussed above in Sections 3.3 and 3.4. As for labour's productive aspects, the public official should ask whether assets like C, D, and E will generate the greatest supply of benefits useful to human prosperity if assets in E's class are treated as standalone objects of ownership, accessories to assets in C's class, or accessories to assets in D's class. Separately, the prudent official should consider whether assets in E's class seems easily perceived as being 'part' of assets in C or D's class. Labour's productive and communicative aspects 'will usually— though not perfectly—tend to complement and reinforce each other, because the way in which human beings conceptually divide the material world into distinct "objects" is closely tied to the usefulness of the objects identified'.[102] So E is a 'reasonable windfall' to ownership of C or D depending on how these consider- ations apply in relation to particular assets, their relation to connected assets, and their likely intended uses.

Although these inquiries are not perfectly determinate, they are determinate enough to dispose of hard test cases. Some have wondered whether a king may appropriate an unowned continent—to the exclusion of the natives inhabiting it— when his explorer sets foot on it, or whether an astronaut may appropriate Mars for his country by clearing a place on it.[103] In both cases, certainly not. As an original matter, the explorer's and astronaut's claims of 'peculiar Right' are limited to '[w]hatsoever [they] tilled and reaped, laid up and made use of', or 'whatsoever [they] enclosed'.[104] The relevant inquiries are also determinate enough to provide useful guidance to common situations. In *Haslem*, the Connecticut supreme court

---

[100] Locke 1689b, Second Treatise, s. 42, p. 297.   [101] See Epstein 1979, 1226.

[102] Newman 2011, 271. Newman makes this generalization while relying on and interpreting the policy implications latent in Roman accession in law. Yet Roman property law is grounded in norms about 'use' considerably similar to 'use' as justified in productive labour theory.

[103] Rousseau 1762, I.ix, p. 197; Nozick 1974b, 174.

[104] Locke 1689b, Second Treatise, s. 38, p. 295.

rightly treated the manure as a entity separate from the public highway. Because highways are intended for human travel, the manure seemed 'a nuisance that affected public health and the appearance of the streets'. The manure would have made a much more natural accessory to farm land or other private land.[105] When a person encloses cattle in the course of fencing land, the fence communicates a clear intention to appropriate and manage the future use of both the cattle and the enclosed land. When a farmer plants corn, he entitles himself to the land reasonably 'necessary to... the activity of growing corn for the support of life'.[106] Because most people appreciate why that control is necessary,[107] they appreciate the motivations to fence and respect fences. Fencing comes to be understood as the prelude to productive use of land fenced in.

This justification for accession helps rebut a distributive criticism Merrill has made against accession doctrine:

[T]he principle of accession means that private property has built into its very operation a set of doctrines that mean the rich get richer... [I]t is disappointing but not surprising that Lockeans have ignored the principle of accession in their various accounts of why private property is justified. Accession can be powerfully efficient, but it is problematic on the grounds of individual desert favored by Lockeans.[108]

When Merrill refers to 'Lockeans', he really means 'Nozickeans', for by his citations his intended targets are really Nozick and Richard Epstein when Epstein followed Nozick closely.[109] Merrill's criticisms are inapplicable to productive labour theory, especially in land cases. To begin with, because accession presumes that land has already been distributed, even if accession makes the division of property slightly more unequal, the increases in inequality are bound to be minor at most. Next, as this section has explained, the moral interest in productive labour sets a ceiling on accession. Owner A of resource C may claim resource E as an accessory only to the extent that E is reasonably necessary to, or a reasonable windfall from, his likely intended uses of C.

In addition, as Merrill himself acknowledges, one of the main functions of accession doctrine is to assign control over a resource to a person who 'has the capacity to function as the owner of some prominently connected asset'.[110] That explanation states in utilitarian terms a labour-based point: the owner of prominently connected asset C is best-positioned '*put[] the difference of Value*' in accessory E.[111] Assume that C is a lot of land, that E is a meteor in or on C, and that E has uses for human prosperity. It is reasonable to presume that, in most cases, A is more likely than B or anyone else to find E simply because he and E are both in proximity to C. If that generalization is tolerably accurate, it would not be reasonable for B or any other non-owner to complain that they suffer harm by E's being declared an accessory to C.[112] (Nor may non-owners complain if someone else discovers E,

---

[105] *Haslem v Lockwood* 1871, 506.   [106] Simmons 1992, 276.
[107] Or, if they do not, they seem anti-social in that respect, and there is nothing morally wrong with holding them to a higher standard of sociability toward others' property.
[108] Merrill 2010, 499.   [109] See Merrill 2010, 497–9.   [110] Merrill 2010, 489.
[111] Locke 1689b, Second Treatise, s. 40, p. 296.
[112] Locke 1689b, Second Treatise, ss. 32–3, p. 291.

notifies A, and buys E from A; A 'uses' E for his own and others' prosperities if he sells it to someone who can use it more productively than he can.[113]) Perhaps non-owners may object that E should have been left as an unowned resource, where they could appropriate it to satisfy the needs the sufficiency limitation entitles them to pursue. As Section 4 explained, however, if the political community has secure property rights and a well-functioning market, A's discovery and use of E may be practically more likely to generate for non-owners jobs, incomes, or a wider range of useful products than they would get from usufructuary rights to search for, appropriate, and consume E.

6. Lost Opportunities to Capture in Doctrine

To this point, I have proved my first claim; in the rest of this chapter, I turn to my second, that Anglo-American capture, lost capture, and accession-related doctrines all illustrate how positive law may and should implement labour foundations. I begin with lost capture doctrine because it embodies the normative relations explained in Section 2. Consider a situation in which several claimants concurrently discover and race to appropriate the same tangible resource. The pursuer who actually appropriates the resource may harm the others by denying them access to a resource they had hoped to acquire for themselves. Morally, however, as long as all the pursuers pursue using ordinary means,[114] the appropriator's conduct does not wrong any of the other pursuers. All were labouring productively to attempt to appropriate the same resource; none wrongs the others by exercising the same liberty more successfully than they do.

Anglo-American tort law embodies that basic policy settlement, as is obvious from the seminal 1707 decision *Keeble v Hickeringill*. Keeble built large traps to lure ducks into ponds on his property. His (somewhat eccentric and perhaps mad) neighbour Hickeringill fired gunshots on his own property. Keeble alleged that Hickeringill shot not in the course of any beneficial activity but rather only 'intending to damnify the plaintiff in his vivary...and deprive him of his profit'. The jury found for Keeble and awarded him 20 pounds in damages. Chief Justice Holt concluded that Keeble had a valid action.[115]

Casebook authors intuit that *Keeble* is related to acquisition.[116] Holt's opinion explains why Keeble's complaint and judgment are exceptions to a general rule of free pursuit and acquisition. Keeble could not bring trespass to protect any proprietary interest in ducks he had not yet caught. Nor could he bring trespass to protect his interest in operating his trade completely free of unfair competition.

---

[113] See *Goddard v Winchell* 1892, 1125. The meteor example in text comes from this case.
[114] In text, 'ordinary means' refrain from attacking any of the other pursuers, and pursue the resource intending in good faith to use it for one's own prosperity.
[115] *Keeble v Hickeringill* 1707, 1127–8; see Solly 1949.
[116] See Merrill and Smith 2007b, 92–5.

Holt grounded this limitation in the fact that Keeble and Hickeringill both deserved equal moral liberties to catch ducks:

[E]very man that hath a property may employ it for his pleasure and profit, as for alluring and procuring decoy ducks to come to his pond. To learn the trade of seducing other ducks to come there in order to be taken is not prohibited either by the law of the land or the moral law; but it is as lawful to use art to seduce them, to catch them, and destroy them for the use of mankind, as to kill and destroy wildfowl or tame cattle.

Unfair competition scholars appreciate that *Keeble* announces seminal lessons about their field.[117] Holt's opinion portrayed 'unfair competition' as the residue of competitive activities not justified by legitimate exercise of the liberty to labour. Hickeringill's conduct toward Keeble was wrongful because it was malicious, but here 'malice' states a narrow exception to a strong presumption that most competition is legitimate. If unfair competition principles did not specify narrowly what means of competition are 'unfair', competitors would use the law to harass other competitors. One duck hunter might sue another solely on the ground that he suffered 'harm' from not catching as many ducks as he did before the latter started hunting; or the former might contrive a sophisticated economic argument why the local community could only support one decoy operation. Holt's reasoning created a strong presumption against these or other similar arguments. After all, 'if a man doth [a competitor] damage by using the same employment; as if Mr Hickeringill had set up another decoy on his own ground near the plaintiff's, and that had spoiled the custom of the plaintiff, no action would lie, because he had as much liberty to make and use a decoy as the plaintiff'. Holt confirmed as much when he compared the *Keeble* case to a precedent in which an older school sued a new competitor for building a better school and luring students to it.[118]

  Keeble's claim was not covered by the presumption in favour of competition because the presumption presupposes that efforts to appropriate resources must be *productive*—that is, likely to enlarge the labourer's legitimate prosperity. Holt suggested that the plaintiff in a case like Keeble's could prevail if he could show that the defendant performed 'a violent or malicious act' instead of competing in good faith. Here, 'malice' is best understood as a tendency to diminish the prosperity of the victim without significantly enhancing the prosperity of the actor. To illustrate, Holt contrasted the school case as decided with a hypothetical in which the school master of the established school assaulted students to scare them from going to the new school. Competitors had natural rights, Holt concluded, to be free from the latter but not the former. So specified, liberty interests in competing indirectly produced good social consequences: '[T]here is great reason to give encouragement thereunto', he explained, 'that the people who are so instrumental by their skill and industry so to furnish the markets should reap the benefit and have their action' against malicious disturbance of their trade.[119] Because Hickeringill's gun shooting

---

[117] See McKenna 2007, 1877–8.   [118] *Keeble v Hickeringill* 1707, 1129.
[119] *Keeble v Hickeringill* 1707, 1128, 1129.

interfered with and was found to be motivated solely by a desire to interfere with Keeble's trade, the shooting was wrongful and tortious.

7. Acquisition in Doctrine

7.1 The basic test for capture

Anglo-American law uses the capture rule to settle appropriation claims over chattels not yet owned, and not covered by any accession-related or other relevant doctrine. The manure in the *Haslem* case fits this profile because it lay on a public highway. So does the fox in the seminal American capture case *Pierson v Post*; that fox was susceptible to capture only because it had been chased onto 'a certain wild and uninhabited, unpossessed and waste land, called the beach'.[120]

It is at least permissible and in all likelihood quite prudent to employ the capture doctrine as the legal backstop for appropriation. Productive labour theory does not categorically require a society to make its acquisition rules track Locke's images of nut gathering, water scooping, or animal hunting. Yet Locke used these images because they illustrate powerfully the non-conventional expectations and moral interests by which citizens should judge their society's conventional property rules. These images' impressiveness make them a persuasive and stable template for legal acquisition rules.

Anglo-American property law builds on these images using principles of occupancy (for land) and capture (for chattels, our main focus here). According to Blackstone, these rules assign things to 'the first taker, which taking amounts to a declaration that he intends to appropriate the thing to his own use'.[121] Lawyers understand occupancy and capture rules to have two elements: an act of taking, and some declaration of intention to appropriate. These elements supply a first approximation. When an individual completes these elements in relation to an unowned tangible asset, it is reasonable to presume that he is using or is imminently about to use the asset to satisfy some aspect of his prosperity. A person may satisfy the 'act' requirement either by labouring on the asset (skinning a deer, or eating it) or by 'put[ting] a distinction between' the thing and the commons (netting the deer).[122] By definition, the eating deploys the thing to life-preserving or -improving use. Even if the skinning and netting do not automatically translate into present consumption or transformation, both 'increase[] the supply of goods available for human life, and thereby improve[] human life'.[123]

In addition, the occupancy and capture tests both make legal doctrine accomplish productive labour's communicative function. In both tests, the claimant's act must declare, or be accompanied by a statement declaring, an intention to establish dominion over the resource for future use. In the case of the deer, eating constitutes

---

[120] *Pierson v Post* 1805, 175.   [121] Blackstone 1765, 2: 9. See Blackstone 1765, 2: 258.
[122] Locke 1689b, Second Treatise, s. 28, p. 288.
[123] Buckle 1991, 150. See Locke 1689b, Second Treatise, s. 37, p. 294.

both present control and productive use. Skinning and netting claim control without making present use, but in both activities the control is universally understood as the prelude to future use. By contrast, consider another of Nozick's counter-examples, an attempt by an airplane pilot to appropriate land by flying over it and surveying it.[124] Although Nozick's survey does not defy non-conventional expectations about use and appropriation as blatantly as his tomato juice hypothetical does, the survey still fails to appropriate the land. The survey does not satisfy immediately any need related to human preservation or improvement. Nor are onlookers likely to construe it as the prelude to imminent preserving or improving activity, as they would understand fencing.[125] Socially, the survey seems to lack 'enough seriousness of purpose to "overbalance" the community of' virgin land.[126]

Still, Blackstone's tests for occupancy and capture accord with productive labour theory only presumptively. These tests do not expressly require that the appropriator use the land or chattel appropriated productively. For example, there is a disjunction between legal appropriation rights and the moral duty not to waste. Capture doctrine entitles Mike to claim exclusive ownership of a deer carcass even if he does not immediately eat or skin the carcass. Here, legal doctrine presumes that Mike has plenty of egoistic incentives to use the exclusive control the law gives him to use the carcass for his benefit. Because this presumption seems practically reasonable, property law may legitimately refrain from including an affirmative 'use' element in capture doctrine; it may instead reserve backstops only for exceptional cases. In particular, the doctrine of adverse possession entitles someone to dispossess an owner of his property if the dispossessor appropriates it and the owner neglects to reclaim the property for longer than the applicable statute of limitations.[127]

Blackstone's test creates another disjunction, for it does not incorporate any limits embodying the sufficiency limitation. Morally, Mike's legal right to appropriate deer under the common law test is defensible only as long as Nick and Steve continue to have ample opportunities to acquire deer and other resources for their legitimate life-preserving or -improving needs. Here, as Section 4 explained, public officials remain responsible for monitoring citizens' opportunities to labour for their own prosperities.[128]

7.2 Constructive capture

Separately, at the level of generality stated by Blackstone, the capture test seems structured consistent with an assumption that acquisition's labour-securing and -encouraging function always aligns with its claim-communicating function. This assumption is sensible as a starting presumption. In the absence of any more

---

[124] Nozick 1974b, 174.   [125] Locke 1689b, Second Treatise, s. 32, p. 290–1.
[126] Simmons 1992, 272.   [127] See *French v Pearce* 1831; Claeys forthcoming.
[128] The capture test does not embody Locke's charity proviso, either. But the test does not need to embody that doctrine, because the doctrine is embodied in the privilege of necessity. See *Vincent v Lake Erie Transportation Co.* 1910; *Ploof v Putnam* 1908.

information, 'those persons who, by their industry and labour, have used such means of apprehending' resources may reasonably be expected to use those resources to benefit themselves and others in the community.[129] Because this generalization is just a presumption, however, it may be rebutted as other facts come to light. As 'Of Property' itself suggests, Indians acquire property in deer by killing them, and a fisherman acquires property in fish and whales when he 'catches [them] in the Ocean', but perhaps the mere pursuit of a hare justly establishes a property over it.[130] Better to relax the strictness of property's claim-communicating function, Locke must have assumed, to encourage property's tendency to encourage labour to discover and pursue hares.

Ordinarily, lost capture and capture doctrines reward only the first clear capturer. In exceptional cases, however, property law may justifiably reward the first finder by entitling that finder to property. For an exception to be appropriate, officials must determine that there exists a bigger mismatch between the pursuit and successful capture of the resource than usually exists. They must also identify a proxy for successful capture that seems practically likely to preserve property law's claim-communicating function.

Consider *Haslem*. Haslem and his servants engaged in productive labour. By Haslem's intelligent direction and the servants' manual effort,[131] both 'increase[d] the value' of the manure; they transformed droppings that were 'comparatively worthless . . . owing to [their] scattered condition upon the highway' into a resource that could make someone's farm more productive.[132] Yet their labour did not satisfy the most literal understanding of capture doctrine's 'act' requirement. After Haslem and his servants left, it was at least plausible for passers-by to assume the manure piles had been left for the taking. Nevertheless, the organization of the manure into piles had at least some tendency to put passers-by on notice that someone was in the process of appropriating the manure. In the circumstances, the court instituted a reasonable compromise. By entitling Haslem to a 'reasonable time to procure the means to take [the manure] away', the court linked his acquisition right to his moral responsibility to complete his appropriation claim as quickly as he could (the court suggested one day). Ordinarily, the capture rule does not expressly require the capturer to labour immediately on the thing. In a case in which a court agrees to institute a constructive proxy for capture, however, the responsibility to labour helps determine the contours of and limits on the proxy the court adopts.

Similar exceptions justifiably apply to some kinds of whaling. For most fish and whales, fishermen abide by a 'fast-fish-loose-fish' norm—a norm of actual capture. However, this norm does not apply well to whales that sink to the bottom of the ocean when killed and resurface later. Without a variation from the fast-fish-loose-fish norm, whaling would 'necessarily cease, for no person would engage in it if the fruits of his labour could be appropriated by any chance finder'. In response, in the

---

[129] *Pierson v Post* 1805, 178.   [130] Locke 1689b, Second Treatise, s. 30, pp. 289–90.
[131] Both the direction and the effort count as labour. See Locke 1689b, Second Treatise, s. 28, p. 289.
[132] *Haslem v Lockwood* 1871, 507.

North Atlantic during the 19th century, whalers came to adopt an 'iron-holds-the-whale' custom. This custom awards property to the first whaler to sink his (marked) lance or harpoon firmly in the whale. To qualify, the whaler must continue in hot pursuit of the whale, and after the whale carcass is found the whaler must pay a reasonable finder's fee to the finder. The finder's fee encourages beachfront owners to labour to bring whale carcasses into commerce. But the main reward and encouragement—property over the whale—should go to the person who engages in the most labour-intensive activity—finding and killing the whales. Like the reasonable-time proviso in *Haslem*, the hot-pursuit requirement conditions a whaler's acquisition claim on converting his 'constructive' capture into actual capture as soon as he can. And the marked lance supplies a workable proxy for actual capture; it requires from the whaler 'the only act of appropriation that is possible in the nature of the case'.[133]

To be sure, it may not always be appropriate to institute a constructive-capture exception—or, it may be difficult to determine whether to institute an exception or instead abide by a bright-line rule. For example, many English or American judges would probably rule against Locke's hare chaser until he actually killed or confined the hare. New York judges departed from Locke's suggestion for hares in *Pierson*, the fox case. Post flushed out a fox, was in hot pursuit of it, and claimed to be close to catching it, but Pierson reached it first and clubbed it to death. Pierson argued for, and the New York Supreme Court decided the case with, a rule of actual capture: a fox hunter may not acquire legal possession over a fox without wounding it mortally, seizing it, or confining it in a net. Post argued for, and dissenting Judge Livingston would have decided the case using, a rule letting hot pursuit qualify as constructive capture.[134]

The choice between these two rules is not fully determined by labour norms or common-sense practical judgment. Some treatises suggested a hot pursuit rule was acceptable; many others required seizing or wounding.[135] In addition, the idea of 'labour' is indeterminate enough that both the majority and the minority opinions cited it in support of their positions. Writing for the court, Judge Tompkins concluded that 'encompassing and securing such animals with nets and toils ... may justly be deemed to give possession to those who, by their industry and labor, have used such means of apprehending them'. In dissent, Judge Livingston asked

---

[133] *Ghen v Rich* 1881, 162; see *Bartlett v Budd* 1868; *Taber v Jenny* 1856; Ellickson 1989. *Ghen* and similar cases teach another lesson: it may be reasonable for legal acquisition rules to track customs by which private parties voluntarily resolve acquisition disputes. That said, before relying on customs, officials should consider two questions. One is how well the custom seems to accord with the general prescriptions of labour theory—i.e. how well they help citizens enjoy or produce goods '*really useful* to the life of Man'. Locke 1689b, Second Treatise, s. 46, p. 317. Separately, where labour theory generates a range of permissible acquisition rules without requiring any single one, officials may choose to rely on a custom on the ground that the custom already 'settles' the dispute. Locke 1689b, Second Treatise, s. 38, p. 295.

[134] Compare *Pierson v Post* 1805, 175–6 (argument of Pierson's counsel), 177–8 (Tompkins's opinion for the court) with 176–7 (argument of Post's counsel), 181–2 (Livingston, J., dissenting).

[135] Tompkins relied primarily on Justinian, Fleta, and Bracton in support of the rule of actual capture, see *Pierson v Post* 1805, 176–8, while Livingston relied on Barbeyrac to defend constructive capture, see 181–2.

rhetorically (and not a little sarcastically): 'what gentleman . . . would . . . pursue the windings of this wily quadruped, if . . . a saucy intruder, who had not shared in the honors or labors of the chase, were permitted to come in at the death, and bear away in triumph the object of pursuit?' Ultimately, the majority decided the case focusing on labour's claim-communicating function; it preferred the killing, wounding, or confining rule 'for the sake of certainty, and preserving peace and order in society'.[136] This practical judgment is not unreasonable, but it is not beyond criticism. The judgment assumes premises that are implicitly empirical and may reasonably be disputed. If two or more individuals are in hot pursuit of the same fox, an actual-capture rule makes it more likely than a constructive-capture rule that one individual might shoot another accidentally in the course of trying to catch the fox. At a formal level, no one can say with certainty whether more people will be injured by the error costs of an actual-capture rule (accidental shootings) or the corresponding costs of the constructive-capture rule (quarrels that escalate into fights). Ideally, to settle the choice between those costs, judges would need empirical information. Yet that data is often unlikely to be available. How easy is it for a social scientist—let alone a judge—to forecast whether hunters will be provoked by a capture rule to duel farmers who kill foxes they are chasing? In the absence of such data, productive labour seems to frame the right questions, and it is not illegitimate to ask judges to rely on their practical judgment in the absence of thorough empirical data.[137]

The foregoing discussion of *Haslem, Pierson*, and the whale cases help correct another mistaken impression about labour theory—that 'notice to the world through a clear act' and 'reward to useful labour' are separate (note the plural) 'principles'.[138] If notice and capture-encouragement and -reward were two separate utilitarian principles, it might be hard to identify the utilitarian meta-principle that helps make them commensurable. By contrast, productive labour theory makes notice and capture-encouragement and -reward two corollaries of a single principle. Each goal deserves to be promoted only to the extent that it contributes to a state of affairs in which politically equal citizens have equal opportunities to labour concurrently on individually owned assets. In most cases in practice, reasonable officials should be able to determine whether an asset more resembles an ordinary animal or mineral on one hand or a whale on the other hand. Even if foxes and other animals

---

[136] *Pierson v Post* 1805, 178–9; also at 181 (Livingston, J., dissenting).

[137] *Pierson* is a hard case in another respect; it tests the boundaries between capture and lost capture doctrine. See McDowell 2007. Among other things, there may have been prior animosity between Pierson's (old money, farming) family and Post's (new money, wartime-equipment-supplying) family. Pierson may have appropriated the fox to spite Post and his family, and to send a message that local farmers did not approve of the sport of fox-hunting. Here, it was advisable to do what the New York courts did: decide the relevant issues in abstraction from complicating background social rivalries. As a matter of capture policy, better to let the first clear capturer decide how to 'use' the fox. If the case had been decided on using *lost* capture doctrine, it should have been dispositive that a substantial number of local residents would have found it 'productive' to have the fox killed and eliminated as a predator on their livestock. That possibility could and should have generated a per se presumption that Pierson did not act maliciously by killing the fox as soon as possible.

[138] Rose 1985, 77. My criticism in text follows Mossoff 2003, 412.

in hot pursuit create close cases for the capture doctrine, these close cases do not undermine the labour-based approach to capture generally.

7.3 Multiple proprietary claims

Ordinarily, black-letter doctrine holds that possession rights should be assigned in all-or-nothing fashion. The custom relied on in *Ghen* and other whaling cases, however, entitled whale finders to reasonable finder's fees. This custom makes sense in context. Because it is time and effort intensive to appropriate a whale into human commerce, it is justifiable to give two individuals rewards for doing so—the whaler, and the finder. The law of sunken ships and treasure provides another example. The legal system secures owners' control and future use by returning stolen or lost articles to owners; this general principle applies to sunken goods when it is feasible to find the owner of a sunken wreck or treasure. In such cases, finders and recoverers deserve restitution but not possession or ownership. When true owners are unavailable, however, productive labour theory recommends that triers of fact follow a series of presumptions. The first presumption is to award boats or treasures to the parties who actually recover—i.e. capture—them. First finders override the claims of actual recoverers only if and when they mark off their claims and then proceed in good faith and with reasonable diligence to recover the boats.[139] Yet both the first finder and the first recoverer contribute in different ways to the recovery of sunken goods. In the abstract, there is no way of saying whether the captain who finds a wreck or the one who salvages it successfully contributes more to the reintegration of the wreck into human commerce and use. In some circumstances, it may be reasonable to award the finder property and order restitution to the salvor; in others, the opposite assignments may be reasonable.

Here, productive labour theory justifies and encourages the same style of indirect-consequentialist reasoning as is used in the progression from actual capture to constructive capture. The law begins with a 'rule'-level presumption in favour of single acquisition and ownership, like the presumption in favour of a bright-line actual capture requirement. As the preference for actual capture is rebuttable, however, the one-owner presumption is also rebuttable, when the asset is unlikely to be discovered without rewarding different contributions to the discovery and recovery of the asset.[140]

8. Accession Policy and *Ratione Soli* Doctrine

Again, however, acquisition doctrine operates as something of a backstop, in *un*owned areas like beaches, highways, and oceans. Quite often, the most effective way to enlarge citizens' free exercise of their labour rights is to give them legal rights

---

[139] See *Treasure Salvors, Inc. v Unidentified Wrecked & Abandoned Sailing Vessel* 1981; *Brady v Steamship African Queen* 1960; *Eads v Brazelton* 1861.
[140] I thank Daphna Lewinsohn-Zamir for encouraging me to discuss this issue more fully.

that operate with little express reliance on the underlying moral rights. Chancellor Kent certainly appreciated as much. Although he justified civil property rights on natural rights grounds in his *Commentaries*, he acknowledged readily that acquisition had 'become almost extinct', and 'made to yield to the stronger claims of order and tranquility' associated with the alienation of property.[141] What Kent said of alienation is also true of accession. In most cases, the *ratione soli* rule and other related accession doctrines secure labour-based property rights more effectively than capture rules do. Productive labour theory can explain, just as well as other theories of property, why accession 'dominates first possession' in practice.[142]

Consider *Fisher v Steward*, the beehive case discussed in the Introduction. Fisher and several associates had found the beehive while trespassing on Steward's land, Steward had appropriated the hive, and the New Hampshire supreme court held that Steward's appropriation and possession were lawful. Although the court rejected the claim by Fisher et al. that their 'labor and skill' entitled them to the hive,[143] in so doing the court did not necessarily reject labour theory. It takes four separate practical judgments before it can be said that labour-based moral rights justify the positive-law holding in *Fisher*, and not all of these judgments are uncontroversial. Nevertheless, if a public official consulted simple and obvious observations about how people use land, trees, and bees, he might reasonably conclude that *Fisher*'s holding represents a reasonable way to secure in law property rights grounded in the moral right to labour. The first move is the move explained in Section 4: if Steward 'owns' his land, the best way to promote labour is to endow him as 'owner' not merely with a usufruct but rather with broad legal rights of exclusive control, use, and disposition over his land. Each of the next three judgments relates to a separate application of the accession policies discussed in Section 5.

Accession doctrines differ sharply in application, depending on how the proposed 'principal' and 'accessory' resources in question relate to one another. Legally, the most obvious difference is this: some accession-related doctrines apply as bright-line rules (say, the riparian doctrine of accretion[144]), while others apply as general standards varying in application to the totality of particular circumstances (say, the doctrines regulating the merger (*accessio*) or substantial transformation (*specificatio*) of goods[145]). To reconcile these and many other accession-related doctrines, however, leading early Anglo-American legal authorities justified accession in the same general terms identified in Section 5. According to Blackstone, accession applies when a 'given corporeal substance receive[s] afterwards an accession by natural or by artificial means, as by the growth of vegetables [or] the pregnancy of animals', but not in cases in which 'the thing itself... [is] changed *into a different species*'.[146] Blackstone stresses the perception-related aspect of accession doctrine. Entity B deserves to be treated as a legal accessory to entity A if it seems an outgrowth of or extension from A's 'corporeal substance', but not if it seems

[141] Kent 1826, 2: 290, 255–76.
[142] Merrill 2010, 460.
[143] *Fisher v Steward* 1804, 60–1.
[144] See *Nebraska v Iowa* 1892.
[145] See e.g. *Wetherbee v Green* 1871.
[146] Blackstone 1765, 2: 404 (emphasis added).

'a different species'. Kent explains accession in similar terms, but he also exempts cases in which B's poem is written on A's parchment, on the ground that the written manuscript belongs to the 'author[, who] has a higher, and, consequently, the *principal interest* in' it.[147] For Kent, the owner of entity A deserves to own entity B as an accessory if his labour to create A creates a normative interest in B; in this situation, accession focuses on the previous and likely future uses of A and B. In a similar vein, one early accession case acknowledged that it is 'very difficult to ascertain any principle of uniform and universal application, on which the [stand-ard] is itself founded', but then encouraged the law to identify the owner with 'the principal interest' in the asset or assets in question.[148]

To be sure, these legal tests are circular. One asks whether the proposed accessory is perceived so closely with the proposed principal asset that the former should be deemed an accessory to the latter; the other asks whether the former seems likely enough to be used beneficially as a package with the latter that it ought to be deemed a legal accessory to the latter. Notwithstanding this circularity, however, the tests provide enough guidance to focus legal inquiries into the issues needed to settle the *Fisher* case.

The first application runs from Steward's land to the trees on his land. Although there may not be perfect or irrefutable empirical information, it seems safe to rely on armchair empirics to conclude that trees are accessories to land. In doctrine, trees are deemed accessories because they are classified as fixtures and fixtures are automatically accessories.[149] To be sure, this per se classification could be chal-lenged. In human perception, trees seem less intertwined with land than soil seems. At the same time, because trees are rooted in ground, the law does no violence to human perception if it classifies a tree as part of the same *res* or 'entity' as land. In addition, it seems practically certain that trees and lands are used more productively if treated as a combined entity. If Fisher and friends could have appropriated trees on Steward's land, they would have deserved and received implied easements of access to tend and enjoy their trees. Such easements would require Steward and similarly situated landowners to monitor their boundaries. Such monitoring would make it more difficult for owners to enjoy their land to the fullest. In addition, a landowner may reasonably be expected to account for trees and how well they fit in with his plans for the long-range management of his land. No surprise, then, that in the *Fisher* case, Fisher and the other plaintiffs did not even contest Steward's ownership of the tree.[150]

So next, in a case like *Fisher*, the conscientious judge must determine whether Steward's exclusive control over the land and tree entitle him to corresponding control over the beehive. Doctrinally, that question presents another possible extension of the fixture doctrine. The answers to the two questions accession policy

---

[147] Kent 1826, 2: 296 (emphasis added). Here, Kent noted Roman law to the contrary, pro-nounced it 'absurd', and recommended that readers follow French principles in conformity with the principles explained in text.

[148] *Lampton's Executors v Preston's Executors* 1829, 459.

[149] See e.g. Brown 1975, ss. 16.1–2, pp. 514–22; Kent 1826, 2: 295.

[150] See *Fisher v Steward* 1804, 60.

makes relevant are not settled as decisively in relation to the beehive as they are in relation to the trees. That said, in *Fisher*, the court was almost certainly correct to conclude that the hive was an accessory to the land-and-tree. The court reasoned that it 'is much more consonant to our ideas of property to say, that the bees and honey in the [land owner's] trees belong to him in the same manner and for the same reason as all mines and minerals belong to the owner of the soil'. Since landowners are entitled to exclusive control over their land, and fixture doctrine entitles them to claim mines and minerals as accessories to their land, it is reasonable to presume that owners deserve ownership over lesser articles like beehives on the same grounds. The court then turned to the policies that might reverse the presumption created by the mine and mineral analogies: 'Will it be pretended that plaintiffs thereby acquired a right to the tree? If they acquired a title to the honey, they must necessarily have a right to take it away, to cut down the tree, to pass over the defendant's land for the purpose, &c'. In other words, the court forecast the consequences likely to follow if the hive (or the hive and tree together) were treated as an entity separate from the land. As the court understood, if the hive were a separate object of property, hive owners would be entitled to implied easements to traverse owners' land and service their hives—like the easements non-owners enjoy in rural communities to graze livestock or gather sticks.[151] Correctly, the court worried that such an easement would 'interfere[] with the rights and property clearly vested in defendant; [such an easement] is inconsistent with "the defendant's property; it lessens its value at least"'.[152] Behind the veil of ignorance, the 'interference' created by rights of access are much less justifiable for beehives than they are for grazing grass or sticks. The latter are far more urgent than the former to preserve the lives of inhabitants and their livestock.

The last extension runs from the land-and-tree-and-hive to the bees. Doctrinally, this extension involves not the fixture rule but the *ratione soli* rule. Anglo-American property law has long distinguished *domitae naturae* from *ferae naturae*, domesticated and wild species of animals. (Note that these presumptions are usually applied species by species, consistent with productive labour theory's indirect-consequentialist tendencies.) The *ratione soli* rule parallels the fixture rule; it assigns ownership over domesticated animals to the owner of the land in relation to which the animals have an *animus revertendi*, a habit of returning because their domicile is located on that land. By contrast, for wild animals, property law entitles landowners only to the exclusive opportunities to catch such animals on their own lots. If a hunter manages to lure a duck off a landowner's land before catching it (as Keeble did to ducks on Hickeringill's land), the hunter captures the animal.[153]

Here, too, none of these rules are strictly required by labour theory or the information and judgment that theory makes relevant. Nor do these sources require that or settle whether accession policies should be applied animal by animal, species by species, or using Blackstone's two-track distinction between domestication and

---

[151] Blackstone 1765, 2: 35.   [152] *Fisher v Steward* 1804, 61.
[153] See Brown 1975, s. 2.4, p. 17.

wild disposition. Even so, the common law settlements of these issues are not unreasonable. By making domesticated animals accessories of land, the *ratione soli* rule folds ownership of animals likely to be used in a manner that complements the use of land into ownership of the more-valuable land. And Blackstone's two-track distinction settles ownership of the most common and valuable animals (horses, dogs, and livestock) while providing a tolerably clear and easy-to-apply rule for other species.

9. On the Relation between Legal Property and Moral Rights to Labour

As applied in Sections 6–8, productive labour theory may seem to many readers an unusual moral theory. A theory of legal rights cannot really be 'moral', such readers may assume, unless it requires legal doctrine to embody or declare its prescriptions expressly. A few of the doctrines or cases just recounted appeal expressly to labour: *Haslem*, the whale cases, Holt's opinion in the duck case *Keeble*, and (at least in some respects) the fox case *Pierson*. Yet many more cases and doctrines seem not to rely on labour theory. In *Pierson*, the court declined to encourage labour in the pursuit of foxes as the whale cases did later for whales. In *Fisher*, the court expressly rejected the claim by Fisher and his associates to own the beehive by virtue of their 'labor and skill';[154] *Fisher* is representative of many other applications of the fixture and *ratione soli* rules. Similarly, many readers may lodge the squaring-the-legal-circle objection: labour theory seems to prescribe a 'specific structure of ownership whereby people [are] entitled to nothing more and nothing less than the concrete fruits of their labour', and that such prescriptions are inconsistent with 'consequentialist skeins of argument'.[155] The rules of decision in *Pierson*, any trespass case, and (especially) accession-driven decisions are inconsistent with that expected structure.

Some renditions of labour theory may have one or both of these characteristics; productive labour theory has neither. Productive labour theory supplies the foundations for the acquisition and ownership of property. The theory then permits public officials to secure those foundations reasoning practically and indirect-consequentially. Quite often, the theory encourages officials to institute a formal legal rule as a first approximation, but then to relax that approximate rule as more facts come to light. In lost capture disputes, courts presume that most pursuits of resources are legitimate and not wrongful, but then leave a plaintiff-pursuer free to prove that a defendant-pursuer acted 'maliciously' in the specialized sense explained in Section 6. In capture disputes, courts presume that manual capture is a workable proxy for appropriation; they relax and revise the concept of 'capture' as appropriate to encourage the beneficial gathering of resources that are cost or labour intensive to appropriate. In fixture and *ratione soli* disputes, courts build on presumptions about

---

[154] *Fisher v Steward* 1804, 61.   [155] Kramer 1997, 128.

exclusive control and immovable resources, to presume that fixtures and tame animal species are best controlled by the owner managing land.

In such reasoning, labour rights and consequential reasoning are not inconsistent. Different legal presumptions, forms, and variations are all judged by how well they secure concurrent labour rights to all interested parties. Moreover, in such reasoning, there is nothing inconsistent or paradoxical about rejecting appeals to labour in specific cases. *Fisher* confirms this lesson. As Section 3.4 explained, productive labour theory requires that labourers mark off the resources on which they mean to labour. When citizens so labour, it follows that others 'ought not to meddle with what was already improved by another's Labour'. But since labour interests are social, and since property rights can vary widely in character, non-conventional property rights must be 'settled' in law or other conventional authorities.[156] That background helps explain why the New Hampshire Supreme Court treated Fisher and his associates not as labourers but as trespassers. The boundary rules demarking Steward's land were justified by their tendency to encourage the productive use of land and to settle property disputes; Fisher and his associates violated those boundaries.

When productive labour theory is portrayed in this practical light, some readers may raise other objections.[157] In easy cases, settled by the capture rule or specific accession doctrines, perhaps ideas about 'natural rights' or 'labour' seem to contribute little or not at all to the substantive rules of decision. In hard cases, although public officials may cite 'natural rights' or 'labour' as policy goals, perhaps these terms contribute less to the legal rules finally adopted than pragmatic policy analysis seems to contribute. So portrayed, productive labour theory may seem indeterminate. Or, perhaps the 'rights' grounded by labour norms are too weak or tentative to serve as strong trumps against private aggression or unjust government action.

Although these objections raise issues too far-ranging to be settled decisively here, a few responses are in order. To begin with, it is unrealistic to expect a theory of rights to apply directly and concretely to practice. Locke justifies labour as '[t]he measure', the 'great Foundation', and the '*begin[ning of] title of property*'—but when justified on labour-based foundations property claims must still be 'settled' in conventional sources.[158] Labour-based claims need settlement especially because they structure property rights in accordance with correlative social obligations. Nozick's account of property rights may generate clearer starting prescriptions than productive labour theory does. But that account can be clearer because in it property is subject to fewer correlative obligations than it is in productive labour theory.[159] And it is worth sacrificing considerable clarity to accommodate property's social character. A stable system of property must accomplish two functions: not only must it order property rights in accordance with labour theory, it must also

---

[156] Locke 1689b, Second Treatise, ss. 31, 45, pp. 291, 299.
[157] I thank James Penner and Greg Keating for raising the following objections.
[158] Locke 1689b, Second Treatise, ss. 36, 44, 51, 45, pp. 292, 298, 299, 302.
[159] See Nozick 1974b, 151 ('A person who acquires a holding in accordance with the principle of justice in acquisition is entitled to that holding').

make that ordering popular and durable. Because productive labour theory states a social theory of property, it gives every citizen a stake in the political order's property laws. If the political process is tolerably well ordered, property laws will accommodate both the labour claims of owners and the non-waste, sufficiency, and charity claims of prospective owners and non-owners. Precisely because productive labour theory leaves the exact boundaries of positive acquisition and accession rules open-ended for settlement, it leaves the laws free to accommodate these competing claims in the manner that seems to the citizenry likely to strike the best balance of being just and politically sustainable.

Last, these objections make unrealistic epistemological assumptions about how determinate a moral theory of rights may be. Productive labour theory identifies an ideal state. Although judges and other officials must reason about practical consequences how best to actualize that ideal state, it is no small accomplishment to identify that ideal state. If readers find indeterminate the practical reasoning needed to implement productive labour theory, they are holding not only Lockean theory but also most political and legal practice to unrealistic expectations. When Locke theorizes about human practical action, he stresses that humans operate in a 'State of *Mediocrity*'. In this state, it is realistic for theorists to aspire only to 'Judgment and Opinion, not Knowledge and Certainty'.[160] This epistemological mediocrity is an obstacle for even the best observers on human life; ordinary public officials suffer from many more limitations. Different individuals have different dispositions, needs, and life circumstances.[161] In the best cases, those differences make it difficult for most public officials to understand most citizens' interests disinterestedly and sympathetically—and in practice those officials' capacities for judgment are clouded anyway by 'Passion or Interest'.[162] Take all these limitations together, and a political leader is 'wise', even 'godlike', if he manages 'by established laws of liberty to secure protection and incouragement to the honest Industry of mankind'.[163]

It is reasonable and just for a system of law to secure labour first through simple legal forms and to appeal back to moral foundations only in extreme cases. If most men reason as badly as often the last paragraph suggested, '[h]earing plain commands, is the sure and only course to bring [most men] to obedience and practice' and is 'likelier to enlighten the bulk of mankind, and set them right in their duties, and bring them to do them, than by reasoning with them from general notions and principles of human reason'.[164] At least in the first instance, then, property rights should be structured with forms that embody commands.

---

[160] Locke 1700, IV.xii.10, p. 645.
[161] See Locke 1700, II.xxi.55, pp. 269–70; West 2012, 33–5.
[162] Locke 1689b, Second Treatise, ss. 38, 45, 136, pp. 295, 299, 358–9.
[163] Locke 1689b, Second Treatise, s. 42, p. 298.
[164] Locke 1695, s. 243, pp. 178–9. The commands to which Locke refers here are scriptural commands about individual ethics. Yet what Locke says about scriptural commands applies equally persuasively to legal and other political commands. See Locke 1700, II.xxviii.8–9, pp. 352–3.

If people associate property with the image of capture, or with Blackstone's paean to property as 'sole and despotic dominion',[165] conventional property rights should be attractive and vivid enough that citizens may assert them vigorously against unjust action by neighbours or the government. Only in the cases in which legal forms stray considerably from labour foundations—whale-hunting, or treasure-salvaging—does it become appropriate for public officials to recalibrate the forms more closely to fit their foundations.

10. Conclusion

When Lockean labour theory is grounded in productive use, it grounds ownership of property in each person's non-conventional right to acquire and deploy external assets to satisfy some aspect of his self-preservation or -improvement. In acquisition doctrines, productive labour theory focuses laws on securing to all citizens concurrent equal opportunities to acquire and use assets, each to labour for his own distinct though productive goals. This productive rendition of labour theory is more persuasive and internally coherent than the interpretations of Lockean labour theory most influential in American legal scholarship on property—those presented by Nozick and Waldron a generation ago.

Although this productive account of labour does not totally determine the content of property doctrine, it strikes a sensible balance between focus and flexibility. At the deepest level beneath practice, productive labour theory supplies property regulation with an overriding focus. One level beneath practice, the theory justifies officials' instituting useful indirect-consequentialist presumptions and working paradigms. At the level closest to practice, productive labour theory supplies focused practical goals on which officials may focus as they apply or refine those intermediate presumptions.

This account of labour also answers what legal scholars assume to be the most devastating adequacy objection against theories of labour—that such theories apply only to highway manure, foxes on beaches, and other stray resources. Property rights should be scaled in whatever manner makes it most likely that the resources will be laboured on productively. So should the contents of the 'resources' themselves. Paradoxically, far more often than not, conventional bundles of resources and rights are established without direct or explicit expectations relating to labour. But since conventional property rights are always bounded implicitly by background legal accession principles, all conventional property rights should always be grounded in, and may always be critiqued by, productive labour theory.

Although this style of practical reasoning is far from determinate, if acquisition disputes are a reliable guide it is good enough for government work. And if Locke's theory of labour is good enough for government work, it deserves much more respect that it enjoys among contemporary property scholars.

---

[165] Blackstone 1765, 2: 2.

3

Property and Necessity

Dennis Klimchuk*

In this chapter I want to explore the prospects of the idea that, in one of its instances, the doctrine of necessity is best understood to be a consequence of the foundation and scope of rights in property. The instance I have in mind is one sort of case in which a plaintiff would invoke the private law defence of private necessity, namely when she uses or consumes another's property to save herself from peril. The idea that her right to do so is in effect a kind of property right has its roots in medieval political philosophy.[1] Aquinas, for example, held that in cases of extreme need it is not strictly speaking theft for one to take another's property because in those circumstances that property becomes one's own.[2] The version of the view I will defend here, however, is one I claim to find in Grotius. I put the attribution guardedly because my interpretation of Grotius is contestable at a few points. I will not dedicate much space to defending the claim that I've understood him correctly.[3] My aim here is to the defend the view, not the claim that it was Grotius's.

1. Some Conceptual Preliminaries

I am for the greater part of this chapter limiting its *justificandum* along two axes; in Section 5 I will suspend these limitations. First, I will consider private but not public necessity. The distinction between the two is, we will see in Section 5, quite complex. To start I'll adopt the line drawn in the *Restatement (Second) of Torts*:[4] private necessity is invoked by an individual seeking to protect her interests or the interests of another (s. 197); public necessity is invoked by an individual seeking to prevent a 'public disaster' (s. 196). By a public disaster the drafters seem to have

---

* This and a linked paper, cited in the chapter, descend from presentations I've made at the departments of philosophy at the Universities of Ottawa and Western Ontario, at the faculties of law at the Universities of Toronto and Western Ontario, at workshops on property theory at McGill and at NYU and at a workshop on private law theory at the University of Toronto. This chapter was first presented at the conference from which this volume proceeds. I have benefited a great deal from the many comments and questions I've received. I am particularly indebted to Sarah Bittman, Alan Brudner, James Penner, Arthur Ripstein, Henry Smith, and Ernie Weinrib.

[1] For an excellent brief overview see Mäkinen 2011.
[2] Aquinas 1265–74 vol. 38, 81, 83 (2a 2æ Q. 66 Art. 7).
[3] I do that in another paper. Klimchuk (ms.).   [4] American Law Institute 1965.

meant a disaster that will affect many people. Below we will see that 'public' sometimes bears another sense in this context. I'll postpone consideration of the complexities and work for now with the simplest case: a plaintiff trespasses on another's property to protect an interest of hers. The doctrine of private necessity holds that she has a right to do so—I'll call this the *right of necessity*—but is subject to what I will call the *duty of repair*: she must compensate the owner for any damage she might thereby cause. According to common law a second mark of public necessity is that persons acting under its authority are not subject to the duty of repair.

Secondly, unless I say otherwise, we should imagine that the sort of case we are considering is one in which what is at stake is life or limb. The *Restatement* and the common law[5] allow that private necessity also applies when what is at stake is the plaintiff's realty or chattels, at least when their value exceeds—perhaps only when significantly—the cost of the damage she may reasonably foresee will be caused to the property on which she trespasses or that she uses. It is a nice question whether the justification for the life and limb cases and property cases is the same. I will suggest that though he did not address the question, for Grotius the answer would likely be that it is not and that he would be right in saying so.

I adopt these limitations in part just to simplify. The case of a person saving her life by using another's property is I think the simplest in the sense that it is the one for which the least disagreement as to the justness of the doctrine is likely to arise. But in part the limitations reflect the kind of account I will defend. On some approaches to necessity the question of what sort of interest is at stake is arguably secondary. This might be so if one held, for example, that the normative significance of necessity is that it compromises the voluntariness of the plaintiff's actions (a thought more common in the criminal context). On the Thomistic-Grotian approach, however, necessity shares conceptual space with limits on property imposed by poverty. As for the distinction between private and public necessity, I will argue that the Grotian account can explain some public necessity cases and that the others are cases of necessity in a very different sense than in the private necessity cases.

Finally, a point of terminology. What I call the right of necessity is often, perhaps most commonly, referred to as a privilege.[6] One has a privilege to *x*, on the standard Hohfeldian analysis, when one is not under a duty not to *x*. Certainly a plaintiff invoking private necessity has a privilege to trespass on another's land in this sense. By using 'right' I want only to highlight that she has more than that. She has more than that because she also has a right that the owner not interfere with her doing so. The owner is thus under a duty to refrain from interfering.[7] On this basis it seems apt to promote the plaintiff's entitlement to the status of a right. Perhaps this is objectionable on other grounds. Let me emphasize that all I hope to indicate by the choice of 'right' is this feature of the plaintiff's entitlement. (It is also, for what it's worth, Grotius's language.)

---

[5] *Vincent v Lake Erie Transportation Co.* 1910.

[6] This language was introduced by Bohlen 1926, adopted by the *Restatement*, and supported recently by, for example, Stevens 2007.

[7] See comment k to s. 197 of the *Restatement*, *Ploof v Putnam* 1910.

2. Winstanley's Challenge

Grotius's account of the doctrine of necessity is set in his account of property generally. Here I want to set that account in the context of what I think is a central question in early modern treatments of property. I will frame that question as a challenge posed by the Digger Gerrard Winstanley in his early writings.[8] As a way of setting the stage, I will outline two other answers to that challenge, both found in Locke's account of original acquisition. Let me emphasize that my claim isn't that Grotius and Locke were as a matter of fact responding to Winstanley. Locke may have known about Winstanley,[9] but he did not discuss him, and Grotius wrote several years before him. Nor even is my claim that the question animating Winstanley's challenge is expressly addressed by Grotius or Locke. It is rather that the issue frames part of the background of their treatments of property and it is illuminating to ask how each answers the challenge.

The Diggers were radical egalitarians and communists who, in mid-17th-century England, occupied and cultivated a number of small tracts of waste land. They expressed in their actions the growing sentiment that it was unjust (and inefficient) that land could be held unused by the wealthy while the poor grew in number and desperation.[10] The Diggers' most prolific and celebrated spokesperson was Gerrard Winstanley. Among his writings were a series of pamphlets published as the first group of Diggers settled on a plot of land at St George's Hill (or George Hill, as Winstanley called it) in 1649.

What I will call Winstanley's challenge is expressed in an argument he makes in the first of these pamphlets, 'The True Levellers' Standard Advanced'.[11] There Winstanley argues that God is 'mightily dishonoured' by the state of affairs in which the world is held by a few who buy and sell it amongst themselves, 'as if he were a respecter of persons, delighting in the comfortable livelihood of some, and rejoicing in the miserable poverty and straits of others'.[12] (He continues: 'From the beginning it was not so'; I'll turn to that part of Winstanley's view in a moment.) A 'respecter' is one who is partial.[13] God is dishonoured because this inequitable state of material affairs is inconsistent with our moral equality. But the problem isn't just with the sort of material inequality that private property makes possible. It is with the

---

[8] I would like to thank three of my students for helping me understand Winstanley and the challenge his view poses: Sarah Bittman, Michael Cuffaro, and Bo Luan.

[9] See Ashcraft 1986, 165 n. 145 for a review and assessment of the circumstantial evidence.

[10] On the Diggers and their place in the broader context of similar movements see chapter 7 of Hill 1991.

[11] Subtitled: 'A declaration to the powers of England, and to all the powers of the world, shewing the cause why the common people of England have begun and gives consent to dig up, manure and sow corn upon George Hill in Surrey; by those that have subscribed, and thousands more that gives consent'. 'The True Levellers' Standard Advanced' was signed by many Diggers, but we understand Winstanley to have been its author.

[12] Hill ed. 1983, 78.

[13] Hobbes characterizes an arbitrator who does not deal equally between the parties to a dispute before her as guilty of 'respecting' one of them, conduct which is forbidden by equity. Hobbes 1642, 3.15. In Section 3 we'll see a similar link between equity and equality in Grotius.

institution of private property itself. On Winstanley's account, private property is
bound up essentially with relations of domination rather than their being a contingent effect of it. 'In the beginning of time', Winstanley says,

the great creator Reason, made the earth to be a common treasury, to preserve beasts, birds,
fishes, and man, the lord that was to govern this Creation; for man had domination given to
him, over the beasts, birds, and fishes; but not one word was spoken in the beginning, that
one branch of mankind should rule over another.[14]

On Winstanley's account, then, it follows from each of us having been created as a
'teacher and ruler within himself', that is, not naturally subject to anyone else's
authority, that the world is held in common.

Winstanley's critique of private properly is expressed through a set of robustly
theological and teleological claims: the world is the way it is and we are the way we
are because of ends instilled by its and our Creator; the inequality that is the fated
consequence of private property is unjust because it dishonours the Creator by
implying that he is partial to some and indifferent to others in creation. But I think
we can extract from Winstanley's account a metaphysically neutral challenge to
private ownership, one that we may fairly ask any account of the foundations of
private property to answer. The challenge is that equality, understood in a particular way, is arguably inconsistent with private property. For Winstanley our equality
consists in a kind of moral independence: we are equals in the sense that no one is
naturally subject to another's authority. This sense of equality is shared by Locke
and, I will argue, Grotius (and others in the early modern period, for example
Kant). So they also share the foundation that forces the challenge as Winstanley
understands it. The prima facie tension with equality and private property consists
in the fact that in claiming ownership of, say, a bit of realty I unilaterally claim a
right to exclude others from it even when I am not using it—that is, to unilaterally
subject them, in this way, to my authority. But that seems inconsistent with our
being equals. That is Winstanley's challenge.[15]

On Winstanley's view, this challenge cannot be met. No one can show that, or
better, why, *she* has a special claim to a particular part of the world, to the exclusion
of all others.[16] One way out of the dilemma, cast this way, is to hold that title to
realty doesn't really amount to a claim *to* a piece of the earth. It is rather a claim
against others, pursuant to an arrangement we make amongst ourselves, to have
exclusive rights to use a part of our common world, under conditions and subject to
limitations we all recognize. This, we will see, is part of Grotius's view. Winstanley
would reject it. We might say that on his account each of us has an inalienable right
that the world be held in common.

---

[14] Hill ed. 1983, 77.

[15] Note that, understood this way, the claim that the world is a common treasury is not the anchor
of the argument. For Winstanley this claim is a representation or perhaps consequence of our equality.
In Section 3 I will argue that this is the structure of Grotius's view as well.

[16] I am generalizing a point made by Winstanley in 'An Appeal to the House of Commons': Hill ed.
1983, 120.

Locke, too, would have rejected the idea that private property rights arise merely as a matter of a convention, but on different grounds. For Locke the point follows from his view that as soon as I use the world in a way that excludes another's use of it—I eat an apple, say—I have made a claim of ownership. If the consent of all others was necessary before I could consume anything then 'Man had starved, notwithstanding the Plenty God had given him'.[17] And so Locke seeks a non-conventional account of the right of original acquisition. We can find two such accounts in the fifth chapter of the second volume of *Two Treatises of Government*. Because in the second chapter of that volume Locke argues that we are all equal in that we are subject only to the law of nature and not, by nature, to anyone else's authority[18] I think that we can regard these two accounts as attempts to answer Winstanley's challenge on its own terms.[19]

Locke's first answer is in the account for which chapter five of the second *Treatise of Government* is most famous: anyone may gain ownership over something in the commons by mixing her labour with it, subject to the limitations that enough and as good is left for others[20] and that what she takes does not spoil before she uses it.[21] We can divide this into two components: an account of the *basis* of original acquisition and an account of its *limits*. The basis of original acquisition is the mixing of one's labour with the object of ownership. This makes an unowned thing one's own because each of us already has property in our persons and so, Locke argues, in our labour and (therefore?) in the work of our hands. The limits are the rules that one leave enough and as good for others and that what one takes does not spoil before one uses it. This answers Winstanley's challenge[22] by anchoring the right of acquisition in a capacity each of us has and in limiting its exercise in a way that respects others' equal entitlement to the world and its resources: we must leave others' options, measured in a particular way,[23] as they were before we appropriated and we cannot appropriate in a way that merely puts some of the world beyond anyone's use.

Locke's second answer[24] promotes what counts as a limit to original acquisition in the first to a free-standing basis for it. '[H]e that leaves as much as another can make use of', Locke argues (we could add on his behalf 'and as good'), 'does as good as taking nothing at all'.[25] When it does not affect anyone's access to the world and its resources, acquisition is permissible precisely because it does not affect anyone's

---

[17] Locke 1689b, Bk. II ch. 5 § 28.   [18] Locke 1689b, Bk. II ch. 2 § 4.

[19] This might seem a contrivance, but I don't think it is, because I think we can see much of the *Two Treatises* as defending this conception of equality and working out its institutional consequences. So though Locke did not explicitly frame his discussion of property in the state of nature explicitly as an answer to the question how private property is consistent with equality, it's fair to say that in the broader context he represented it as being so.

[20] Locke 1689b, Bk. II ch. 5 § 27.   [21] Locke 1689b, Bk. II ch. 5 § 31.

[22] How well, I will not consider here.

[23] Just how they are to be measured is, of course, a tricky question.

[24] Locke does not explicitly offer this as an alternative account of the basis of original acquisition. I borrow the idea that we can treat it that way from Sreenivasan 1995, 47–50.

[25] Locke 1689b, Bk. II ch. 5 § 33.

access to the world and its resources. Having left the world, in effect, as it was before I claimed a part of it, I am neither subjecting you to my will nor denying you an opportunity I enjoyed, and in this way I treat you as an equal.

3. Grotius on Property and Necessity

We can divide Grotius's account, as Locke's first, into two components: the *ground* and the *limits* of rights in property. The ground on Grotius's account is consent, either express or tacit. We start[26] in a state of common ownership in the limited sense that each of us has a right to the resources of the world and (really the same point) no one has a right to prevent us from using them. We move from this state to a regime of private property by agreement. For Grotius the problem that Locke found with consent—that if it was necessary to secure consent before consuming any resources 'Man had starved, notwithstanding the Plenty God had given him'— does not arise, for two reasons. The first is that for Grotius the concept of private property is required to do less work than it is on Locke's account. What it does is explain how I can be wronged by another's interference with land or a thing though I am not currently in its possession. But it is not (and need not be) invoked when I exercise the right to use the world's resources prior to the adoption of a regime of private property. In exercising the original use right we have a model for private property, because in, say, consuming something I have excluded others from its use. But we don't yet have private property. The second reason Locke's problem is not Grotius's is that Grotius allows that tacit consent is sufficient to put a regime of private property in place; and, in fact, that is how he believes it arose. Reasoning out from the exclusion implicit in use we came to recognize a right to exclude free of the requirement of actual, present possession.[27]

While we needn't think that an explicit, dated agreement lies at the foundation of the regime of private property it doesn't follow that we have come to adopt it for no particular reason.[28] As Grotius tells it, private property makes materially possible a life we want and cannot otherwise have. But in a sense this point is inessential to his account. The theory of property, as Grotius develops it, does not bear the burden of justifying the adoption of private property. What it does rather is explain how it is possible and set the conditions under which it is permissible. Put another way, for Grotius the question whether we ought to adopt private property is a

---

[26] I consider how historical this sense of starting is in Section 4.

[27] See Grotius 1609, 22 and Grotius 1604, 317.

[28] Perhaps there is a helpful parallel here to Hume's account of convention: '[T]wo men pull the oars of a boat by common convention, for common interest, without any promise or contract; thus gold and silver are made the measures of exchange: Thus speech and words and language are fixed by human convention and agreement.' Hume 1777, 306. Property, on Hume's account, is conventional in this sense. See Hume 1739–40c, 484–501 (3.2.2). In his contribution to this volume, Jeremy Waldron sorts accounts of the foundations of private property in a way that suggests that the parallel I propose to draw between Grotius and Hume on this point might be misleading.

question about the good and the theory of property, strictly speaking, concerns the right but not the good.

This brings us to the second component of Grotius's account, the limits of property rights. While private property exists as a convention, there are constraints on the forms it may take. Some consist in first-order substantive rules, such as the law against theft. The right of necessity derives from a more abstract, second-order principle that I will call the foundational presumption: '[W]e must consider what was the intention of those who introduced private property: which we must suppose to have been, to recede as little as possible from natural equity.'[29] Two aspects of the fundamental presumption need to be clarified. First: in what does natural equity consist? On what I believe to be the best interpretation of the text—and, in any case, the view I will defend here—'natural equity' refers not to the original use right directly but rather to the equality to which it gave expression. In holding that neither you nor I need the other's permission to use the world's resources before the institution of private property, Grotius represents the idea that we enjoy the kind of moral independence from one another that I suggested prompted Winstanley's challenge. It is from this state that we must suppose that those who introduced private property intended to recede as little as possible.

Second: what is the force of this 'must'? Grotius answers questions about human institutions by asking what we must suppose of those who introduced them more than once. The modality varies along a continuum. At one end the claim is that certain features of an institution are conceptually necessary elements of it. An example is the presumption that a state cannot recognize what Grotius calls the 'promiscuous Right of resisting' because 'it [the state] cannot otherwise attain its end. If this prohibition does not exist, there is no State, but a multitude with the tie of society.'[30] On the other end is the principle that, in the absence of evidence to the contrary, a people ought to be presumed to have retained more rather than less liberty in establishing a state.[31] The foundational presumption is, I think, between the two but closer to the first. It is not analytic, but it is more than an interpretive presumption. The claim is that consistency with natural equity so far as is possible is a condition of the acceptability of a regime of private property. Thus the foundational presumption is normative and objective in the sense that it does not depend on facts about what happened in the past—and so, though Grotius introduces it in a way that might be taken to suggest otherwise, it does not depend on there having been a datable event that marked the adoption of private property.[32]

The idea, then, is that natural equity is a baseline from which only such departures as are necessary are permissible. This is very abstract. It will help to get clear on what's at stake. The adoption of private property confers on persons the

---

[29] Grotius 1625, Bk. II, ch. 2, para. 6.1. The language here might seem to be at odds with the fact that, as I've claimed, for Grotius we needn't think that the regime of private property was adopted by an explicit, dated agreement. I address this herein.

[30] Grotius 1625, Bk. I, ch. 4, para. 2.1.   [31] Grotius 1625, Bk. I, ch. 3, para. 8.1.

[32] Indeed, this would also be at odds with his account of our gradual and tacit adoption of the convention.

right to exclude others from parts of the world and things in it that they are not using or otherwise possessing. What's at stake is how this right can be made consistent with our starting point. The foundational presumption directs us to depart from that starting point as little as possible.

So as a first step—we will see a second is necessary—this yields the following principle: the right to exclude may extend only so far as is necessary to realize the ends for the sake of which we adopt private property. This entails the right of necessity because we can achieve the material benefits private ownership makes possible without enjoying a right to exclude that makes into trespasses others' life-saving uses of our property.

This is only a first step because the account so far is vulnerable to the problem that whether it yields the results Grotius thinks it does depends on what one thinks the ends for which sake we adopt private property are. The point is especially well made if we consider the account of necessity defended (against Grotius) by Pufendorf.[33] On Pufendorf's account the right of necessity is a right one has against another that she allow one to use her property, rather than a right directly to the property. The owner's right to exclude extends farther on Pufendorf's account than it does on Grotius's. But one's duty to others requires that one not exercise it in certain circumstances. The right extends as far as it does precisely so that one has the opportunity to waive it. Following Aristotle, for Pufendorf one of the ends for which sake we adopt private property is that it provides opportunities for the cultivation of certain virtues (here beneficence). So as I read him, Pufendorf adopts the principle that the right to exclude may extend only so far as is necessary to realize the ends for the sake of which we adopt private property. He has, however, a different list of those ends than does Grotius, a list which yields a stronger right of exclusion.

Grotius did not address this issue. We could essay two sorts of answers on his behalf. The first weighs in on the question what ends ought we to seek to realize through the institution of property and rejects the cultivation of virtue from that list on, say, the grounds that its inclusion would be illiberal. That's a sound argument, and sufficient to the point. But it is inconsistent with my claim that for Grotius the theory of property explains how and on what conditions we may adopt private property, but does not itself bear the burden of justifying its adoption, and in this sense concerns the right but not the good. The second answer to the challenge posed by Pufendorf's view accepts this. The thought is that in setting the boundary of the right to exclude at the point that makes the life-saving trespass a wrong so as to provide for the property owner a virtue-cultivating opportunity to waive that right is to not merely recede from but rather negate natural equity. It is in effect to assign to the property owner qua property owner arbitrary control over the would-be trespasser's life.

So in its more complete exposition, we can say that the fundamental presumption not only entails the principle that the right to exclude may extend only so far as

---

[33] See Pufendorf 1672, Bk. II, ch. 6.

is necessary to realize the ends for the sake of which we adopt private property but also rules out the pursuit of certain ends. It does so not on the grounds that they are insufficiently valuable but rather on the grounds that they are inconsistent with the formal conception of equality with which the regime of private property must be consistent. So the more complete justification of the right of necessity is that those ends it is permissible to seek to realize through the adoption of private property can be realized without granting to owners a right to exclude that makes into trespasses others' life-saving uses of their property.

To tie things up to this point: Grotius's answer to Winstanley's objection to consent—that one cannot consent to adopting a regime of private property because one cannot consent to an institution of domination—comes in the limits component of his account of property rights. It is that when the institution of private property respects the foundational presumption it makes that institution consistent with our equality in the sense that Winstanley thought made the right to treat the world as a common treasury inalienable.

That is Grotius's account of the right of necessity. What remains is his account of the duty of repair. Grotius explains it in two ways. First he argues that:

There are some who think...that, as the man used his own Right, he is not bound to restitution. But it is more true that this Right was not plenary, but limited by the burthen of restoring what was taken, when the necessity was over: for such a Right suffices to preserve the natural equity of the case against the rigour of ownership.[34]

This in effect deploys the foundational presumption but runs it in the opposite direction. The structural symmetry of the justification of the right of necessity and this articulation of the justification of the duty of repair might seem in itself to count in the latter's favour. However it also brings into relief a concern that might be raised about the argument. So articulated, the justification of the duty to repair supposes that in adopting private property we necessarily adopt as a baseline a particular, and particularly exclusionary, version of the rights of ownership. One might object, however, that if private property exists by convention, then no particular version that convention may take can exert the sort of normative force as a baseline as does the state of natural equity.

One answer to this objection is that, as we have seen, Grotius (and others in the tradition in which he wrote, for example Aquinas) holds that while private property exists by convention it is subject to non-conventional constraints. And sometimes he writes as though the default *is* the adoption of a particular, and particularly exclusionary version of the rights of ownership, for example implying at one point that to be an owner of something is to be able to use it as one chooses.[35]

The better answer to the concern is to interpret the passage quoted above in light of a justification of the duty of repair Grotius offers in a summary of his account of necessity in a later passage. There he argues: 'more is not to be taken than it [the necessity] requires; that is, if keeping the thing is sufficient, it is not to be used; if using it is sufficient, it is not to be destroyed; if destroying it is requisite, the price is

---

[34] Grotius 1625, Bk. II, ch. 2, para. 9.   [35] Grotius 1625, Bk. II, ch. 7, para. 2.1.

to be repaid'.[36] There are two ideas here. The first is that refraining from repairing the costs one imposes is just like destroying another's property when merely using it would suffice. Each is an instance of taking more than one needs. The second is that what imposes the duty of repair is not the principle that one ought to depart from a default of a particularly robust interpretation of the right to exclude as little as possible, but, rather, that the right of necessity only permits one to take what one needs to extricate oneself from the perilous situation. To take more, indeed, would arguably violate natural equity because it in effect and at least in part would allow someone to arbitrarily determine how another's property should be used, contrary to the independence at the heart of the sense of equality upheld by natural equity.[37]

4. Three Important Objections

Three important objections can be raised to this account.

1. The first questions its justificatory structure, that is, its accounting for what makes the adoption of private property possible and setting the conditions under which it is permissible by considering how we might move into such a regime from an original condition of common ownership. This might be thought to be objectionable on a number of grounds: that the original community of property is probably a fiction and in any case prehistoric; that even if it were a matter of historical record, nothing would come of it because facts don't entail values; and that even if—indeed especially if—it is not meant to represent a period of history but is rather a kind of construct, it is justificatorily unhelpful because it builds the conclusion into the premises. Finally, one might argue that the move from a world of unowned things to a world of property is not the right place to begin a theory of property, on the grounds either that a theory of property ought to begin with articulating the structure of ownership rather than its acquisition or that, because our world is a world in which all acquisition is derivative, if the structure of ownership can be explained by an analysis of acquisition it would not be *original* acquisition that would bear that normative weight.

The first step of the answer to these challenges is that they suppose that the idea of the original community bears a different sort of weight in Grotius's account than it

---

[36] Grotius 1625, Bk. III, ch. 17, para. 1.1.

[37] James Penner raised the following important objection to this account of the duty to repair. If the guiding principle is that we depart from the regime of ownership as little as possible, it arguably follows that what necessity does, at most, is force sales. The point is most sharply made in a case where the defendant consumes rather than merely uses the plaintiff's property. (While holed up in his cabin during a storm, say, she eats some of the food she finds there.) Penner's thought is that the owner's title is better respected by compelling him to sell his property than it is by compelling him to make a gift of it; that the former marks a more modest departure from the regime of property. That seems right. But the objection takes as a starting point what Grotius denies, namely that the imperilled trespasser's consumption of the food is an infringement (however well justified) of another's property right. In a way I will elaborate in the conclusion, for Grotius the right of necessity is in a sense a property right, rather than a right that another allow one to use her property.

does. It is really a representation of a conception of equality, conjoined with some non-controversial facts. The non-controversial facts are that we cannot but occupy parts of the world and consume its resources. The normative work is done by the claim that until we choose to organize ourselves around a regime of private property, no one can by right exclude another from a part of the world she is not possessing. And this, in turn, is a claim about our equal standing with respect to our common world. This claim is not a claim about a period in history; nor, because it is not itself a claim about the structure or content of private property, does it smuggle the conclusion of Grotius's argument into the premises.

My suggestion is that the original community is a representation of these claims, as is, I would argue, the state of nature in early modern contract theories. For example, Hobbes's account of the state of nature[38] in the end comes down to the claim that we are equally vulnerable to one another and under no duty to defer to others' judgments when we come into conflict. Similarly, the original position in Rawls's theory of justice[39] is a representation of a conception of equality, one that rests on a view about what is morally arbitrary from the point of view of distributive justice.

There is a second point of parallel with Hobbes and Rawls. Each takes the relevant position of equality as a baseline, departures from which need to be justified, and are justified only to the extent that they are necessary to realize the ends of the arrangement into which parties are represented as contemplating entering and only in terms acceptable from the perspective of the baseline. This structure is reflected in what Susanne Sreedhar calls 'the necessity principle' in Hobbes,[40] and in what Rawls calls the difference principle. The necessity principle is the basis of what Hobbes calls the true rights of the subject, 'those things, which though commanded by the sovereign, he may nevertheless, without injustice, refuse to do'.[41] These rights are those that either we cannot give up or that it would be unnecessary to abandon to secure the benefits of the commonwealth.[42] Rawls asks what departures from an equal distribution of basic material goods could be justified to those subject to an unequal distribution and concludes that it is only such inequality that would improve the condition of the worst off, and no more.[43]

What I called the foundational presumption in Grotius's account has the same structure as the necessity and difference principles. The original community of property, the state of nature and the original position each represent the baseline in which the principles governing departures from them are anchored.

Finally, this explains why, prior to working out an account of the structure of property rights, and even in a world in which all acquisitions are derivative, it makes sense to ask on what terms we could move from a world of common ownership to a world of private property. That question just is a way to represent the question what the structure of property rights are, because it is a way to ask what structure is consistent with the normative constraints to which private property is subject.

---

[38] See Hobbes 1651b, ch. 13.   [39] See Rawls 1999, chs. 3–4.   [40] Sreedhar 2010, 49.
[41] Hobbes 1651b, 21.10.
[42] 'Nor doth the law of nature command any divesting of other rights, than of those only which cannot be retained without the loss of peace'. Hobbes 1640, 93–4 (17.2).
[43] Rawls 1999, 55.

2. The second objection concerns the place of consent in the account. What answer does Grotius have to the late-comer who does not sign on to the convention of private property?

One response is that this is not an objection to Grotius's account of necessity. That account finds the right of necessity in a limit to the right to exclude in any acceptable regime of private property that we might establish. The doctrine of necessity is a constraint on what we might consent to, but its justification does not itself rest on our consent.

This answer is sound, I think, but I realize it is a bit unsatisfactory. So let's pose the objection to Grotius's account of private property generally. There are two possible answers. The first is to accept that if private property exists as matter of consent, there is at some point no answer to someone we might call the principled property anarchist, just as, if the authority of the state rests in the end on the consent of the governed, there is at some point no answer to the principled political anarchist. This answer might be unavoidable. But it is hard to accept. It is hard to accept, that, for example, no wrong would be done to me by someone who sets up camp in my backyard and defends herself by claiming that she does not recognize the institution of private property, however truthful and principled her claim.

One response to the principled property anarchist is to deny that she has not already consented to the regime of private property. It is impossible not to participate in the institution as it now exists and so to realize whatever benefits it brings. One might argue that this constitutes a kind of tacit consent, which is consent enough to deny the principled property anarchist the right to build on my property. The response to this, in turn, is to say that consent that is impossible to withhold is no consent at all. Accepting this we might say that, while living in a world of private property might not all but per force bring about each participant's consent to it, it does not follow that the world is fairly up for grabs. We do not need to follow Locke and hold that I have a natural property right in the fruits of my labour, I think, to say that the modern day Digger in my backyard would be taking a kind of advantage of me.

An alternative approach to the objection considers the idea that there is a second account of private property in Grotius, related to the first in the same way as what I counted as Locke's second is related to his first. Recall that Locke's second account promoted what was in the first a limit on the right of original acquisition—that one leave as much and as good for others—to a basis for it: leaving as much and as good for others is like taking nothing at all, so there is no basis on which others could claim to be wronged. Similarly, one might promote the condition that the regime of private property depart from natural equity as little as possible to a basis for private property rights. In a system that respected the condition we could answer the principled property anarchist by insisting that our right to exclude her does not wrong her because it is consistent with the constraint that the equality she enjoyed in the original community of property be respected in the regime of private property.[44]

---

[44] This may be Kant's view. At the least it purports to find in Grotius a view about the role of consent in the foundation of property akin to the role Kant gives to consent in his explanation of how

This is not Grotius's express view. One might argue, however, that this is where his view ends up, if one begins by arguing that the sort of tacit, incremental consent that he claims accompanied the development of private property is not consent of the sort that does independent justificatory work. I won't weigh in on this question here, except to note that we are on the edge of a basic question in political philosophy, namely whether actual consent to a set of political institutions is a necessary condition for their legitimacy, in particular for institutions that claim title to coerce or to authorize coercion. Answering yes leaves open the problem of the principled anarchist. The alternative is the claim that so long as that state does not deprive anyone of something to which they have a right, then no one has grounds on which to base principled resistance to or rejection of its authority. But this too seems unsatisfactory. It is one thing to say that I am not wronged by anyone whose actions are in conformity with what each of us is entitled to and another to say that anyone in particular, or any institution, has thereby been authorized to uphold those entitlements with force.

This doesn't need to be settled here, where our interest is in the doctrine of necessity. But we might draw the lesson that, in this way, the theory of property invariably weighs in on a core issue in political philosophy.

3. The final objection concerns the foundational presumption. The worry is that it is indeterminate and—or perhaps 'and therefore'—threatens to require the reshaping of a significant bit of property law and of doctrines in adjacent areas of private law that support the law of property (for example nuisance).

As with the second objection, there is a quick and arguably dispositive answer to this objection, but one that is admittedly unsatisfying. That answer is that this objection is strictly speaking not a worry here, where the claim is only that the foundational presumption yields the right of necessity. But of course if it does so at the expense of demanding an unacceptable revision of the laws of property and tort on pain of inconsistency then this response is too quick. So let's dig more deeply.

A look back to Grotius will initially deepen but then, I will argue, answer the concern. What deepens the concern is Grotius's argument that a second limit on the right to exclude is what he calls the Right of Harmless Use, the right that I may use another's property if my use causes her no harm and if it is of benefit—in one formulation Grotius says great benefit—to me. Now he does not explicitly cast this right as an implication of the foundational presumption, but he does characterize it as sharing with the right of necessity two properties, namely that each is a non-conventional limit on private property and that we can suppose that the reservation of both was intended by those who introduced private property. And one might plausibly argue that the right of harmless use is entailed by the principle that in

we should understand the social contract in 'On the common saying: that may be true in theory but is of no use in practice'. There Kant argues that the social contract is not a fact but rather '*only an idea* of reason, which, however, has undoubted practical reality, namely to bind every legislator to give his laws in such a way that they *could* have arisen from the united will of a whole people and to regard each subject . . . as if he has joined in voting for such a will': Gregor ed. 1996, 296–7 (8: 297). One of the kinds of law to which a people could not have consented is one inconsistent with their legal equality.

setting the scope of rights in private property we recede as little as possible from natural equity.

Part of the objection is that it is hard to say whether this is so, and this illustrates how indeterminate the foundational presumption is. I'm not sure this worry *simpliciter* is that troubling. The necessity principle in Hobbes and the difference principle in Rawls are each, it seems to me, no less indeterminate. It may be tricky to determine when the right to exclude goes beyond the point at which it serves the permissible ends for the sake of which private property is adopted, but, I'd say, no less so than it is to determine the point at which retaining the right of nature imperils the peace secured by the commonwealth (as the necessity principle in Hobbes requires) or to determine the point at which material inequality no longer serves to benefit the worst off (as Rawls's difference principle requires). The more troubling part of the objection is that, to the extent that something like the right of harmless use is entailed by the foundational presumption, this shows that it is at odds with what many would argue is the core of private ownership, which consists most importantly in the authority to determine how and by whom one's property is used.

Now, as we saw above, Grotius himself implies at one point that to be an owner of something is to be able to use it as one chooses.[45] How can the right of harmless use be made consistent with this? Perhaps it cannot, quite. Perhaps, then, we cannot take either or both the right of harmless use and this characterization of ownership at face value, unqualified. But let's give Grotius the benefit of the doubt and see how far they can be reconciled.

Grotius's illustrations of the right of harmless use show that he understood it in a way that defuses at least some of the apparent tension. First he cites with approval Seneca's claim that no one has a right to prevent another from lighting a fire at hers. It is hard to see how your merely taking a light from my fire is inconsistent with my right to use it as I choose. A second set of examples, which he borrows from Plutarch, has a different structure. We may not destroy food we will not eat, or conceal or muddy a spring of water when we have used it. Here the principle is that others have a right that I not simply make things unusable for no reason.

Each of these is a case of a restriction of an owner's right that is modest in two senses. It does not deprive her materially of anything she would otherwise have, and to the extent that it prevents her from using her property the uses it prevents are difficult to justify. The first owner excludes others for the sake of doing so; the second and third deny others a benefit they have no intention to enjoy.

Of course, again, one could argue that the point of property rights is that one needn't answer for the ends for which one exercises them. A third set of examples of the application of the right of harmless use, the one in which Grotius had the most interest, is not vulnerable to this response and I think reveals what is really at issue here:

---

[45] Grotius 1625, Bk. II, ch. 7, para. 2.1.

[L]and, and rivers, and any part of the sea which is become the property of any people, ought not to be shut against those who have need of transit for just cause; say, because being expelled from their own country they seek a place to settle; or because they seek traffic with a remote nation.[46]

The idea is this: by introducing private property we make possible the enjoyment of rights no one had before and allow persons to impose on others duties to which no one was subject before. Persons in the first of the two categories in Grotius's example are, like homeless citizens, in a situation in which they bear only the new duties and enjoy none of the new rights.[47] The right of harmless use, here, serves to limit the right to exclude so that it does not leave anyone with literally nowhere to go. My point in emphasizing this example isn't just that it shows that the burden of the right is arguably modest. It is rather that it shows that it, and the foundational presumption more generally, do not serve to subordinate owners' authority to the contingent interests of others. They serve instead to limit property rights in a way that respects the fact that in introducing private property we introduce a normative mechanism by which persons can be made vulnerable to, and by virtue of, the actions of others in a way that they were not before.

5. Saving Property and Public Necessity

I've worked throughout this chapter with the example of someone saving her life by trespassing on or damaging another's property. In this section I will ask whether and if so how the Grotian account I've defended applies in cases in which what is defended is property and in cases of public rather than private necessity.

1. Grotius does not address the question whether life and limb cases and property cases rest on the same grounds. When he introduces the right of necessity he does so with a list of examples that are ambiguous on this point (stopping the spread of a fire, freeing a ship caught up in nets), though elsewhere he seems to treat cases of poverty as paradigmatic.

I think the answer most consonant with his account is that property cases are in ways akin to but not in all respects the same as life and limb cases. The conceptual tools necessary to account for the property cases, I'd suggest, are deployed by Grotius in his account of the duties of finders. He says:

[A]s in the state of community of things, a certain equality came to be observed, so that one might be able to use those common things not less than another; so when ownership is introduced, there is a sort of association established among owners, that he who has it in his power a thing belonging to another, is to restore it to the owner. For if ownership were only

---

[46] Grotius 1625, Bk. II, ch. 2, para. 13.1. He adds 'or because they seek their own in a just war'. I omit that from the discussion above because it adds complications unnecessary to the point at hand.

[47] I borrow this characterization of the situation of the homeless from Waldron 2009, 166. Waldron argues that the institution of private property must be justifiable to persons in such a situation, and that this entails a right to the use of public spaces. I think Grotius anticipates this sort of argument.

so far effective, that the thing is to be restored to the owner if he asks for it, ownership would be too feeble, and custody too expensive.[48]

In the original community our equality expresses itself in our each having a right to use common things no less than any other. Once ownership is introduced it requires us to regard ourselves as part of a kind of association that insures owners, in a limited way, against the costs of accidental dispossession. It does so by imposing modest duties on finders. One way to think about this argument is as holding that a kind of formal equality is constant between the two regimes, but is articulated in different duties in each. Another—perhaps just a way of filling out the first—starts with the observation that by introducing private property we make possible kinds of vulnerability that would not have obtained in the original community. The person who has lost something cannot simply replenish her stocks from the commons, so the regime of private property would be an unduly burdensome one for her if finders were in fact keepers, at least in cases in which the duties on the finder are lightly borne.

Now suppose that luck arbitrarily selects my property for destruction and I can save it by damaging yours. We might argue that the same equality-respecting association among owners that imposes duties on finders grants rights of self-help to the imperilled property owner. This seems clearest in cases where the stakes are high and the costs low: where say, my property is priceless and the damage I'd cause to your property minor and easily repairable. But, arguably, the balance is irrelevant in light of the duty to repair.

I say 'arguably' because whether that is so depends on how we think of the relationship between the right of necessity and the duty of repair. When he introduces the duty of repair Grotius says, 'when it is possible, restitution [must] be made'.[49] This implies that one has the right unqualified, and then the duty independently, which duty is defeasible under some unspecified conditions of impossibility. Restitution might be impossible because the property damaged was priceless but I think Grotius had a different kind of case in mind. The idea that the right of necessity and the duty of repair are independent is most plausible in life-preserving cases, for example one in which an impecunious and starving person steals food.[50] On this view of the relationship between the right of necessity and the duty of repair, we can understand the intuition that property cases be subject to a condition that requires that the value of the property saved be greater (perhaps substantially greater) than the costs imposed on the other property owner. But even this can't be right: I can't be insured against my losses, free of charge, by everyone whose property happens to be of lesser value. This suggests, I think, that the association-among-owners rationale requires us to understand the relationship

---

[48] Grotius 1625, Bk. II, ch. 10, para. 1.2.   [49] Grotius 1625, Bk. II, ch. 2, para. 9.

[50] Alan Brudner pointed out to me that on Grotius's account of the duty of repair as I've reconstructed it we would say of an impecunious imperilled trespasser not that she had a defence to the property owner's claim or (merely) that she was judgment-proof, but rather that she was not under a duty to repair, because in her case by leaving costs where they fall she would not be taking any more than she needed.

between the right of necessity and the duty to repair to be different in property-saving cases. When property is at stake, one's right is conditional on one's having the means to discharge the duty of repair.

I'm not sure even that interpretation answers a more basic worry about property cases. How could anyone's property interests, we might ask, license them to determine how my property ought to be used? There might not be an answer to that challenge, but I think the account drawn by analogy from Grotius's account of the duty of finders makes as strong a case in favour of the application of the doctrine of necessity to property cases as can be made.

2. According to the *Restatement*, public necessity is invoked by an individual seeking to prevent a 'public disaster' (s. 196). What does 'public' mean here? As I stated above, the drafters seem to mean by a public disaster one that affects many people (floods, fires, etc.). But I think some cases reflect another sense of public (sometimes as well), and arguably more than one sense of necessity. Let's consider three cases that will illustrate the distinctions I mean to draw.

> *Mouse's Case.*[51] In a storm on a river one person's goods are thrown overboard by others to save them all. Had the goods not been thrown overboard the barge would have sunk and all would have been lost. The owner's claim to recover the costs from other passengers fails.

> *The King's Prerogative in Saltpetre.*[52] The King's agents may dig for saltpetre, a component of gunpowder, on anyone's land, and owe no compensation. But they must be respectful in a number of ways: they must dig where it is least obtrusive, only during the day, not come back often, etc.

> *Dwyer v Staunton.*[53] A number of persons cross onto the plaintiff's land when a storm renders the highway impassable. The plaintiff's claim in trespass fails. The court holds that private citizens may drive on others' property—and, in fact, may enter it forcibly—when the roads are blocked owing to sudden and temporary causes, such as snowstorms. They must take other routes if possible, and cause no more damage than is necessary. But they need not be in a state of emergency themselves, and need not compensate the owner for unavoidable damage brought about by the exercise of this right.

Though sharing the property of departing from the paradigmatic cases of private necessity on one or more points, these comprise a conceptually heterogeneous class.[54] There are two principal points of complexity.

---

[51] 1608.   [52] 1606.   [53] 1947.

[54] These three cases are collected under public necessity by Baudouin and Linden 2010, 467. While *Mouse's Case* and *Saltpetre* are commonly classified as cases in public necessity, the inclusion of *Dwyer* is a bit controversial. One point of controversy is whether the right of trespass in such cases is a species of the right of necessity. The court in *Dwyer* represented necessity as one of two justificatorily sufficient grounds to deny recovery. (The other is the principle *salus populi suprema lex*.) Sissons DCJ cites an earlier American case, *Morey v Fitzgerald* 1884, that unequivocally rests the traveller's right to trespass in circumstances on necessity, as does the court in *Cambell v Race* 1851, to which the court in *Morey* refers. But the *Restatement* excludes such cases from the category of public necessity, covering them instead in an adjacent section, 195 ('Deviation from Public Highway'). Of course the fine-grained

The first is what counts as public. *Mouse's Case* illustrates the simpler version of one of two senses of public at work here, what we might call its aggregate sense. Necessity is public, in this sense, when it involves many people. In *Mouse's Case* the imperilled group included the plaintiff. Let's stick for now with that factual structure; later in this section I'll ask what the impact on the analysis is if the owner is not among the group of persons who save themselves by using her property.

The classic case of pulling down a house to stop the spread of fire and so to save a town is, at one level, like *Mouse's Case* so far as the nature of public is concerned,[55] but it introduces a complexity. A town is a corporate and legal entity. So there is an institutional sense of public engaged by such a case. The same is true in *Saltpetre*. On the one hand, there the court emphasizes that the property owner from whom the saltpetre is taken is a member of a group that shares in the overall benefit realized by the imposition of the cost, as Mouse was. But they also emphasize that this right is importantly and inalienably the King's. It is in the name of the defence of *the realm* that it may be exercised. Let's call this the political sense of public. This is the only sense at issue in *Dwyer*. There trespassers claim a right against a property owner in the name of a public right secured by the state, namely the right to travel through the realm.

While the sense of necessity in *Mouse's Case* is just like that in the sort of case we have been considering throughout this chapter, it is different in *Dwyer*, and the point is complex in *Saltpetre*. In *Dwyer*, recall, the trespassers themselves were not in a state of necessity, at least not a dire one: they just wanted to go home, and there was no other way to do so. The 'necessity' in such cases derives, we might say, from the unqualified nature of the public right in whose name the defendants claim the right to trespass. What about *Saltpetre*? To the extent that the King's agents take private persons' property on the grounds that otherwise everyone's life or at least well-being is at stake they act subject to the sort of necessity that characterizes private necessity cases. To the extent that they act under the particular authority of the King, in defence of everyone not qua group of individuals but *qua* subjects of the realm, they arguably don't act under the same sort of necessity; nor under the necessity in *Dwyer*. Arguably, in this sense, they don't act under necessity at all, at least no more than we would say a state does in, for example, imposing conscription.

---

sorting is not necessarily dispositive of the conceptual question of the foundations of the right. More significant is that s. 195 imposes a duty of repair on the trespasser, suggesting that if anything the reporters regarded such cases as instances of private necessity. Notwithstanding these complexities I include *Dwyer* and like cases in the category for three reasons. The first is just that they are sometimes so regarded. The second is that, as I will argue in this section, elements of the structure of the claim in *Dwyer* and like cases are found in cases that are undeniably cases of public necessity, and it is helpful to consider cases in which those elements are closer to the surface. Finally, my question here is to what sort of cases does the right of necessity on the Grotian account extend, and so it seems right to begin with an inclusive sense of the category of public necessity.

[55] And, I think, in factual structure as well. It's hard to imagine a situation in which the spread of fire could be stopped by pulling down a house and that house not be in the path of the fire and so fated to be lost.

What I want to suggest is that in cases in which the necessity is like that in private necessity cases and the sense of public is aggregate, public necessity cases fall under the same account as private ones. There is nothing in the fact that many individuals' lives are at stake that affects the foundation of the right of necessity. What needs to be explained is why in such cases compensation is not owned. First, here is a twist. *Mouse's Case* was decided as it was because it happened on a river. Had it happened at sea, Mouse would have had the benefit of the law of general average, which would have required those whose cargo was spared to collectively make up his loss. The coexistence of the two rules in one system is explicable by the fact that the law of general average has its own, very long history.[56] If we were starting from scratch, however, arguably we would not have different rules for cases at sea and cases occurring elsewhere. So let's ask: which rule, if either, does the Grotian account prefer?

The way to answer that question is to ask whether the justification for the duty of repair applies in the facts of *Mouse's Case*. That justification, again, rests on the principle that damaging without compensation is an instance of taking more than one needs, as one would if one kept property when all that was necessary was borrowing it, or destroyed it when merely using it would have sufficed. Now: would the defendants in *Mouse's Case* be taking more than they needed if they did not compensate Mouse for his loss? It's at first not clear how to answer that. Here is a suggestion. Recall that Mouse's goods would have been lost anyway, and that Mouse is a beneficiary of their having been lost as they were. So if he were compensated, he would be better off than had his goods not been thrown overboard. It seems to me that we can say that if the plaintiff is left better off relative to the *status quo ante* after being compensated then the defendant has been asked to do *more* than take only what is necessary. And if we can say that, then we can explain why the defendants need not compensate in cases like *Mouse's Case* on the same grounds that they must in the sort of case we have been considering to this point.

But that's a bit quick, on textual and on conceptual grounds. The textual point is that Grotius endorses the law of general average in the context of cases of goods thrown overboard at sea. Let's consider the rationale he provides. He says:

the owners of goods which are thrown overboard to lighten the ship, recover a part from the others whose good are saved by that proceeding; for a person who preserves, by any step, his property which was in danger of perishing, is by [doing so] so much the richer.[57]

In other words (I think we can say): we might conclude that in fact those whose goods survive *do* take more than was necessary if they do not compensate, in just the way that anyone who saves his property at the expense of another would.[58]

---

[56] On which see Cooke and Cornah 2008, 1–19. On the evolving rationales for the rule see in particular Cooke and Cornah 2008, 9–15 and Rose 2005, 6–14.

[57] Grotius 1625, Bk. II, ch. 10, para. 9.2. My addition.

[58] The argument here has the feel of a claim in unjust enrichment. I have argued elsewhere that, while it seems promising for many reasons, the view that the duty to repair bears the structure of a claim in unjust enrichment does not bear careful scrutiny. The main stumbling block is that sense cannot be made of measuring the defendant's gain by the plaintiff's loss in such cases, as the unjust

So which answer is right? That depends, it seems, on what the right baseline is. Do we measure the plaintiff's post-jettisoning position against the state of affairs in which she would have been had no cargo been tossed overboard, or against the position of her fellow passengers, whose property was preserved? I don't think the principle underlying the duty to repair in the private necessity cases can by itself answer this question. To this extent the Grotian account reproduces the common law's ambivalence.[59]

Note that the Grotian account does unambiguously assign significance to the distinction between cases in which the plaintiff is a member of the group that benefits from the invasion of her property rights and those in which she is not. The case in favour of interpreting the principle underlying the duty to repair in private necessity in the way that denies the plaintiff's recovery rests on her sharing in the benefit realized through the use or destruction of her property. Compensation would leave her better off than she would have been and so imposing the duty to repair would arguably burden defendants with a greater obligation than merely taking no more than they need. It follows that on the Grotian account if the plaintiff was not among the beneficiaries of the use or destruction of her property there is no basis to deny her compensation. If it is analytic that no compensation is due in public necessity then let's call such cases multi-party private necessity cases. The claim of *Mouse's Case* to a place in the category of *public* necessity rests on Mouse's having been among the beneficiaries of his goods being lost, because it is only in virtue of that property that a case in support of the court's denial of his claim for compensation can be made out.

Let's wrap things up by considering *Saltpetre* and *Dwyer*. At one level *Saltpetre* continues to be like *Mouse's Case*. Understood as resting on the aggregate sense of public, this is a public necessity case in the sense I just specified, and carries with it the same rationale for relieving the trespassers of the duty to repair. The property owner is among the beneficiaries of the realm's defence. To the extent, however, that the right in *Saltpetre* rests on its being an exercise by the King's agent of an inalienable right and duty of the crown the conceptual basis for denying compensation must be found elsewhere, in principles distinctive of public law.[60] This seems to me to be true of cases such as *Dwyer*, which involve private citizens using other private citizens' property in the name of a distinctively public right.

So in sum: for one particular subset of the category, the Grotian account extends to, or at least illuminates, cases of public necessity, and the ones to which it does not

---

enrichment account requires. See Klimchuk 2001. I made the case in the context of private necessity but it seems to me to carry over into public necessity cases.

[59] This ambivalence is expressed by the drafters of the *Restatement* who reserve judgment on the question whether compensation ought to be due in public necessity cases, arguing that on the one hand morality requires it but acknowledging on the other the right of states to immunize those acting on their behalf from liability.

[60] Though maybe these levels of analysis come together. They might for Kant. This is suggested by analogy with his claim that, as beneficiaries of a rightful condition, the wealthy have an obligation to the poor that the state may uphold through taxation. See *The Metaphysics of Morals* in Gregor 1996, 468 (6: 326).

extend are cases of necessity in a very different sense than in the cases on which I have focused in this chapter.

6. Is the Right of Necessity a Property Right?

In conclusion I would like to defend the claim I made at the outset of this chapter that one might put the upshot of the account of the private law doctrine of necessity I've defended here as holding that the right of necessity is in effect a property right. By this I mean to highlight three elements of that account.

The first is that necessity is on Grotius's account a property right in the sense that it is not a personal right in the way that, for example, Pufendorf has it. On Pufendorf's account, recall, the right of necessity is a right that another use her property in a particular way (i.e. for one's benefit). On Grotius's account, by contrast, the right is just a right to use the property. Second, there is a sense in which for Grotius necessity is not a defence. It is just the exercise of a right, under certain limitations, to use a bit of the world. It is like a kind of easement imposed by law.

Finally, in claiming that on this account the right of necessity is a property right I mean to highlight the fact that it anchors the justification of the doctrine of necessity in a view about our relationship to our common world. The world is each of ours, according to Grotius, and there is a sense in which it remains so even if and after we choose to divide it up. This sense limits the ways in which, and degrees to which, we can exclude others from the parts we have claimed as our own.

4

Private Property and Public Welfare

Alan Brudner

'...The property of subjects is under the eminent domain of the state, so that the state or he who acts for it may use and even alienate and destroy such property, not only in the case of extreme necessity, in which even private persons have a right over the property of others, but for ends of public utility, to which ends those who founded civil society must be supposed to have intended that private ends should give way. But it is to be added that when this is done the state is bound to make good the loss to those who lose their property...Nor will the state, though unable to repair the losses for the present, be finally released from the debt, but whenever it possesses the means of repairing the damages, the dormant claim and obligation will be revived.'

Grotius, *De Jure Belli ac Pacis*, Bk. III, ch. 20.

1. The Fifth Amendment Paradox

The law governing public takings of private property is as simple to state as it is difficult to fathom. The common-law rule is that government takings of private holdings without the owner's consent are permissible provided the taking serves a public purpose and the owner is compensated at market value.[1] The public purpose need not be extraordinary, nor need the taking be uniquely capable of achieving it. It is enough that the taking reasonably furthers a public end. Where no constitutional protection for property exists, a court presumes a duty to compensate, but the legislature may displace the presumption by stating clearly its will to do so. Where the right to property is constitutionally entrenched, the common-law rule is binding on legislatures.

Grotius's facile '[b]ut it is to be added' attests to the facial incoherence of this rule. The duty to compensate suggests a property prior to the public interest, one established by direct acquisition—whether original or through contract—independently of the general welfare, common good, or democratic process. But if such a property exists, why should the owner's consent be unnecessary for the

---

[1] *Manitoba Fisheries Ltd v The Queen* 1979.

state's acquiring his holding for an ordinary public end?[2] Is it that the private right 'give[s] way' to the public interest when respecting its full force would permit the owner unilaterally to veto a public measure or to extract a disproportionate share of its public benefit—that is, when exercising the right would be inconsistent with membership in a civic body? But then why should it be irrelevant that the public benefit might be obtainable without the expropriation or that the subjective cost to the owner is disproportionate to the state's marginal gain in choosing against the next best beneficial option? If property preceded the state, respecting it to the point of inconsistency with civic membership would require that the expropriation be shown to be necessary for a significant public gain; yet no such requirement exists.

Let us then try out the opposite possibility. The state's permission forcibly to take a directly acquired holding for an ordinary public end whether or not the taking is necessary to achieve the end suggests that property in specific things is mediated by the public interest—that there is no property outside it. But then why should it be necessary for the state to compensate the erstwhile holder for an 'expropriation'? Is it that the owner would otherwise be forced to bear the entire cost of a benefit redounding to all? But distributive justice cannot explain the common-law duty to compensate, because that duty exists even if the owner would be commercially favoured by a public easement to an extent that offset his special burden and even if the owner's *ex ante* holdings exceeded his fair allotment by the amount taken from him. How can distributive justice explain a compensation requirement that might very well create or perpetuate a distributive *in*justice? It would seem that a distribution-blind duty to compensate must reflect a property preceding any collective distribution. But then why is consent not required for a discretionary public use of someone's resources?

In sum, the common-law takings rule is facially paradoxical in that it seems to view property as a hybrid concept—neither purely private nor purely public but somehow both in combination. The rule reflects the state's eminent domain—its sovereign lordship over all things within its territory—but then qualifies its

---

[2] By an 'ordinary public end' I mean an end of political association that is distinct from collective self-preservation at one extreme and the upkeep of government at the other. In a case of public necessity, expropriation with compensation is compatible with private property given that secure property presupposes a state. At the other extreme, government may not expropriate for its buildings, desks, stationery, and whatnot because the obligation to defray the cost of government falls on the citizenry as a collective body, not on anyone singly. Even if compensation at market value were paid, that would not remove the special burden from the owner, whose interest in secure possession has been uniquely harmed. Here distributive fairness (the requirement that burdens be reciprocal) bars a taking even absent a private right of property. However, for the ends for the sake of which government is instituted, a choice may arise whether to purchase in the market at the expense of the citizen body or to expropriate and place a special burden on a private individual. Here distributive fairness does not determine the former course because the specially burdened individual might be reciprocally advantaged by the government project in a way that makes the taking ultimately fair. So any bar or fixed constraint on takings for public ends of this sort must come from a private right of property somehow conceived. The question is whether the constraint embodied in the Fifth Amendment (expropriation is permissible with no questions asked about necessity or proportionality but subject to an absolute duty to compensate the owner) reflects a coherent conception of property.

eminence. Neither consent nor necessity is required for a public taking, but compensation is. Eminent domain with something 'added'.

I concede that a welfarist understanding of political justice can make sense of a prima facie duty to compensate someone for a public taking of his holdings. For one who believes that the just is whatever maximizes social utility or promotes human well-being, the legal right to hold something as one's own must be justified by the general happiness or common good. So, private property might be understood as promoting the efficient employment of resources or as protecting a human interest in a sphere of individual sovereignty—one wherein the individual's choices regarding the use and disposition of things need consider no wish, preference, or need of others. No doubt, the interest in *dominium* may occasionally have to yield to the more inclusive (or greater) good of which it is an ingredient (unit); but on those occasions, public takings must be carried out with the least harm to the interest secured by the property right and with the least impact on economic incentives—hence the presumed duty to compensate the owner. Moreover, the welfarist would say, the presumptive duty ought not to be lightly set aside. In particular, it ought not to be displaceable by everyday calculations of cost and benefit, because the political ruler's judgment that the benefit of an uncompensated taking would outweigh its cost is fallible and presumptively self-serving; it is always inclined to overestimate the benefits to those to whom its rule is beholden and to underestimate the costs to the owner. Still, circumstances might arise in which the net gain from an uncompensated taking exceeds the threshold required to allay concerns about mistake and bias. In those circumstances, the welfarist will say, the state may take without compensating. Thus, the welfarist can explain not only the prima facie duty to compensate but also its displaceability by legislation a court interprets as clearly overriding the presumption.

Imagine, however, that the common-law rule is constitutionally entrenched such that, while the right to hold something as one's own is defeasible, the duty to compensate for a public taking is not. Not even a national emergency can permanently override it. It is doubtful that any welfarist conception of political justice could accept that configuration of property norms; for it is simply dogmatic to claim that no exception to the duty to compensate could ever be justified by the common good. The welfarist cannot have it both ways. He cannot assert at once that there is a threshold of net gain, the surpassing of which justifies an uncompensated taking, and that there is no such threshold.[3]

More surprising than the welfarist's inability to explain the state's permission to expropriate for ordinary public ends combined with an unqualified duty to compensate the owner is that the natural right theories of Locke and Kant cannot accept that combination either, though they have different reasons for rejecting it. No

---

[3] The welfarist might label as 'takings' only those limitations on ownership not reciprocally beneficial to the owner and say that there is an absolute duty to compensate for takings so defined. But that is to finesse the absolute duty, not to explain it. A limitation on ownership serving a special interest is prohibited by the common-law rule, not allowed if compensation is paid. The compensation requirement for an exercise of eminent domain presupposes a taking in the public interest.

doubt Locke can explain a state power to tax individuals as members of a collective body in order to sustain the civil society that perfects their natural rights to liberty and property.[4] The same social contract by which they collectively institute a civil condition authorizes the sovereign to tax them collectively to support it; while consent by a majority of their representatives suffices to validate a specific tax as levied for a public purpose. Perhaps Locke could also accept a state power to expropriate with compensation when the preservation of the civil order requires it, for then the property right would be yielding (to the extent necessary) to the logical conditions of its own existence. However, Locke cannot accept a state power to single out an individual from the collective body and, for an ordinary public end, deprive him of something he has laboured to acquire and that meets the conditions for rightful acquisition: that nothing unconsumed be spoiled and that enough and as good be left for others. Since acquisition meeting those conditions confers (for Locke) a valid right prior to public authority, and since public authority is justified only as protecting natural rights, unconsented-to takings for ordinary ends are impermissible even if compensation is paid.[5] Spreading the monetary loss does not transform a singling out into a collective tax, because no one else has suffered a transgression of his private property. Accordingly, it is difficult to see how Locke could understand the state's eminent domain.

By contrast, Kant can explain the state's permission to take directly acquired holdings without consent (eminent domain), but he cannot account for an indefeasible duty to compensate. For Kant, the right to own *simpliciter* is indefeasible, for it is required by the right to the maximum scope for liberty consistent with equal liberty. Without ownership, no one could use land from which he was physically absent, and yet such use is compatible with the equal user rights of all under a general law.[6] However, the right to own the *specific* things one has peaceably acquired in a state of nature is (for Kant) only provisional, for that right is established by unilateral actions pursuant to an arbitrary choice to claim something specific as one's own; and no one may, consistently with his innate right to be his own master, acknowledge a coercive obligation unilaterally imposed on him by another.[7] For Kant, conclusive rights over specific things can be established only omnilaterally through the general will; and so the state's non-consensual taking of unilaterally acquired holdings for a public purpose infringes no prior right. Such a taking is permissible, not because valid property rights in specific things are defeasible, but because there are no valid property rights in specific things outside public law.[8] For that reason, however, there can be no unqualified duty to compensate the provisional owner either; there is only a duty optimally to balance the interest in secure possession with other public interests.

To be sure, there is for Kant a *presumptive* duty to compensate someone whose holding was peaceably acquired, for the provisional right has force unless explicitly disconfirmed by the general will's representative. But this is so only because

---

[4] Locke 1689b, Second Treatise, para. 140.
[5] Locke 1689b, Second Treatise, para. 138–9. [6] Kant 1797, 168–9.
[7] Kant 1797, 77, 82, 85, 87. [8] Kant 1797, 124.

holdings peaceably acquired *can* be confirmed by the general will, whereas those acquired by dispossession cannot be, for the general will cannot recognize an acquisition inconsistent with the right to own.[9] The state's presumptive duty to compensate merely reflects this comparative advantage enjoyed by those whose possession was original, prescriptive, or derived through a voluntary exchange. Without that advantage, rightful possessors would be on a par with dispossessors, contrary to the right to own that the civil condition is supposed to perfect. Because, however, the provisional right's force reflects a possible validity rather than an existing one, the provisional owner cannot complain if the general will erases his right.[10]

The question, then, is whether *any* theory of the relation between property and the state can generate the combination of rules we imagined: that forcible expropriations for an ordinary public end are permissible subject to an *indefeasible* duty to compensate the owner. Of course, our question would lack importance if that configuration were merely imagined—why dream up a conceptual monstrosity and then seek a logical explanation for it? But we need not have imagined the rule, for it is in the American Constitution.

In the United States, an owner's right to compensation for a public expropriation is guaranteed by the Fifth Amendment in absolute terms. The Amendment's taking clause states: '. . . nor shall private property be taken for public use without just compensation'.[11] In *Pennsylvania Coal v Mahon*, Justice Holmes doubted that the guarantee admitted any exceptions. True, the state may prohibit without compensation uses of holdings that exceed the bounds of rightful use—that are legal nuisances. That is the police power to regulate private property in a manner not amounting to an expropriation. It is not this chapter's concern. The state may also act for the public welfare in a way that injuriously affects an owner's economic interests but without interfering with his ownership.[12] In such cases, the state may or may not incur a duty of distributive justice to compensate the injured party depending on whether that party is reciprocally advantaged by the public measure to an extent that offsets his loss. That too falls within the police power and outside this chapter's concern. My focus here is on state *expropriation*, which I take to mean something distinct from unfair disadvantaging.[13] When the state wishes to

---

[9] Kant 1797, 78. But long possession can convert a wrongful possessor into a rightful one, for the alternative would be a perpetual inconclusiveness of title inconsistent with the right to own; see Kant 1797, 108–9.

[10] John Rawls's position is Lockean with respect to personal property and Kantian with respect to means of production and natural resources. For Rawls, the right to the exclusive use of personal property is one of the basic liberties, the priority of which would seem to rule out expropriations short of public necessity. Because, however, his theory of justice is indifferent as between public or private ownership of the means of production and natural resources, there can be no right in his political liberalism to compensation for a nationalization of holdings of that kind; see Rawls 1993, 298.

[11] The same guarantee has been read into the Fourteenth Amendment applying to the several states (*Hairston v Danville and Western Ry. Co.* 1908).

[12] For example, it might construct a major highway diverting traffic from a gas station on a county road.

[13] Yet, one branch of the takings jurisprudence of the United States Supreme Court assimilates expropriations to economic harms that are compensable only if the owner has been burdened for the

dispossess an individual (singled out from the collective body) of his rightful holding ('private property') or to prohibit a use that lies within the owner's right to use, it must rely on its power of eminent domain. And the exception-less limit of that power, said Holmes, is the duty to compensate the erstwhile owner.[14]

Holmes provided no theoretical argument for an absolute duty to compensate for a public taking. To the extent that an argument can be gleaned from his judgment, it is that it would be distributively unfair for the state to lay the whole cost of a public benefit on the shoulders of one. Compensating from the public purse transforms an expropriation of one to the taxation of all. We saw, however, that the argument from distributive justice cannot explain an unconditional duty, for it holds only if the distribution of holdings was *ex ante* fair and compensation is required to preserve the fair distribution. So, if A's peaceably acquired holdings cannot be justified under any scheme of distributive fairness, then distributive justice could not object to an uncompensated conversion of A's excess holdings to a public use. And yet the takings clause would (I say without fear of contradiction) still prohibit such an uncompensated taking. So an absolute duty to compensate for a public taking cannot be explained by the state's duty to distribute public burdens fairly. It must be explained by the idea of a private property independent of the public interest that the public authority must respect. But then the puzzle with which we began resurfaces: why are non-consensual takings for ordinary public ends (that might be achievable by other means) permissible?

The issue is whether there is a coherent theoretical account of the Fifth Amendment's takings clause. In what follows I argue that Hegel's theory of the relation between property and the state understands the takings clause. Indeed, I argue that, relative to a company of philosophers including a welfarist (of whatever hue), Locke, and Kant, Hegel is *uniquely* able to understand the takings clause. That thesis might seem to leave open the question whether an absolute duty to compensate is truer to political liberalism than the presumptive duty explained by Kant and so whether an entrenched guarantee of compensation is, in Rawls's phrase, a constitutional essential for liberalism. Not so. One cannot demonstrate Hegel's capacity to explain an absolute duty to compensate for a public expropriation without also showing that such a duty is entailed by the liberal idea (shared by Kant) that the separate human individual is an end-in-itself. So I shall also make that argument.

The chapter proceeds as follows. In Sections 2 and 3, I expound Hegel's derivation of an inherently valid (though still inchoate) property in specific things prior to the idea of a civil authority. In Section 4, I set forth Hegel's account of the necessity for the transition to a rule of law within which the pre-civil right to private

---

benefit of others; *Penn Central Transp. Co. v New York* 1978. Perhaps the most influential article on takings law in the last fifty years also dissolves the distinction between expropriating and unfair disadvantaging; see Michelman 1967. For an approach to the takings clause that respects this distinction, see *Loretto v Teleprompter Manhattan CATV Corp.* 1982.

[14] Justice Brandeis, dissenting in *Pennsylvania Coal Co. v Mahon* 1922 did not dispute this. He simply characterized the Kohler Act (prohibiting the mining of coal adjacent to buildings) as an exercise of the police power.

property is apparently solidified but in which are also generated positive rights to welfare that upset the assumptions underlying the derivation of private property. The result is a 'civil society' (*bürgerliche Gesellschaft*) marked by a tension between the public welfare and private property, where each claims a self-contradictory absolutism requiring illogical accommodations and concessions. While it is possible to view the takings clause as reflecting this tension, it is also possible (I argue) to view it as belonging to the constitution of a well-ordered political community. In Section 5, I set forth Hegel's account of the state as a holistic entity of which a public sphere aimed at the common welfare and a private sphere ordered to the singular (atomistic, separate) person are distinct and mutually complementary parts. The idea of a property that is established inside the state but outside the public sphere yields the configuration of norms contained in the takings clause. It also removes the appearance of paradox in that combination.

2. Why Acquisition?

In the justice paradigm Hegel calls Abstract Right, the human individual claims to be an unconditioned end solely by virtue of its inborn capacity for free choice. An unconditioned end is one that is neither relative to a subject (it is objective) nor valuable for the sake of some further end (it is final). The capacity for free choice is plausibly such an end, because it is the original purposiveness that is universally and necessarily expressed in positing the particular, contingent ends toward which action is directed. A bearer of the capacity for positing ends is called a person, and the capacity itself is called personhood.

The person's capacity for free choice makes possible its rejecting as motives for action all ends given by life. For the person, all such ends are optional and their value relative to the chooser. Accordingly, for the justice paradigm built on the supposed unconditioned end-status of free will, everything but the free will is consigned to the sphere of contingency and relativity. The human individual is pictured as a bifurcated being: on one side, a generic person stripped of individuating features; on the other, a particular individual rich in such features.[15] Yet only the generic person counts for the public reason of right and wrong; and so any property right must be derived solely from it, without regard to physical needs or the satisfaction of wants. Because, moreover, the individual qua person is here regarded as morally self-sufficient—as owing its end-status to nothing beyond its free will—Hegel begins with a solitary person, from whose project to validate end-status he derives a private property.

It would be a mistake, however, to view Abstract Right as a state of nature of the kind deployed by contractarian theories of civil authority. This is so because, unlike Hobbes, Locke, and Kant, Hegel does not think that persons really are morally self-sufficient—that they have natural rights outside all association; and so he does

---

[15] Hegel 1820b, para. 35.

not think that they are *by nature* dissociated from each other. Hegel's own standpoint is distanced from that of Abstract Right, which will in the end be integrated into an ethical system ordered to his own conception of an unconditioned end. Hegel begins with a stateless condition, not in order to show why already dignified human beings must institute a state, but rather to show how their *quest* for dignity conceptually impels them to a state of a certain kind. Like Aristotle, Hegel begins with a stateless condition in order to demonstrate that a political community sufficient for dignity is the human being's *telos* or natural end. So, while his account of the state begins from the atomistic person, it is not (as Locke's and Kant's accounts are) *based* on this person. Considered on its own, Abstract Right will turn out to be an untenable abstraction from the political community to which it in truth belongs. A framework of justice ordered to a person who claims to be morally self-sufficient will turn out to be embedded in a political community that requires such an adversary for the confirmation of its own natural authority.

In detaching itself from everything empirically given, the person juxtaposes itself to a world of particular things. A 'thing' is whatever is not a person or part of a living person—whatever lacks a capacity for free choice and is not bound up with that capacity in a free nature.[16] Lacking free will, a thing has no side that is unconditioned, and so it can place no other being under an obligation not to use or destroy it. Not being an end, it may be used solely as a means. Correlatively, the person is permitted to subdue all things to its ends.[17] This permission is unlimited by the survival needs of others, for, as we have just seen, such needs are for persons' subjective wants with no standing to put an absolute end under an obligation to accommodate them. Thus, there is no proviso on permissible acquisition that no one be disadvantaged by it with respect to life's needs. The Lockean proviso is unknown to Abstract Right just as it is unknown to the common law.

The question, however, is why one end must respect another's acquisition. A thing offers no moral resistance to its use by an absolute end, but why should one absolute end respect the dominion over a thing of one who is not his superior? The fact that the empirical individual needs things for biological survival cannot provide a reason for respect, for if another's chosen attachment to life cannot limit an end's permission to acquire unoccupied things, neither can it place an end under an obligation not to acquire things already taken into possession. Acquisition by one end could command the respect of equal ends only if it were required by ends qua ends, for only then would respect be necessarily reciprocal and therefore not servile. But why should an absolute end have need of anything?

Hegel's justification of a private property in things is perhaps best illuminated by a contrast with Kant's, since both begin from the end-status involved in free will. Kant derives property from the person's innate right to the maximum liberty consistent with equal liberty. To own something distinct from one's person, he argues, is to have a right to stop someone else from using it even though one's

---

[16] Hegel 1820b, para. 42.   [17] Hegel 1820b, para. 44.

physical possession of the thing has been discontinued. If it were impermissible to do this, then one's liberty to use usable things would be arbitrarily curtailed, for ownership is consistent with everyone's equal liberty under law. But an arbitrary limitation of liberty is wrong, and so property must be possible for free wills.[18]

Though elegant, this argument is incomplete. While it justifies the practice of owning in general, it does not justify a person's ownership of the particular things it directly (without the mediation of a public authority) acquires, and in fact Kant provides no such justification. On the contrary, he regards a property in things directly acquired (whether by first occupation or through voluntary transfer) as provisional, pending omnilateral review by a citizen legislature in a civil condition. For Kant, only holdings mediated by the general will are conclusively one's property, if one can call a revocable licence to use state-owned things 'property'. By contrast, Hegel provides a justification for a person's property in the specific things it acquires directly—independently of any approval by a public authority. That justification is the subject of this and the following sections. It begins as follows.

The person claims to be an unconditioned end, and yet it is in fact conditioned as a void by the luxuriant world of contingent beings from which it abstracts. As that which is *not*-contingent, personality depends for its identity on the world of contingent things. This dependence confers on contingent things the appearance of an independence that challenges the person's claim to unconditioned end-status. That status is something merely claimed and asserted. But this means that the person is an unconditioned end only in its own estimation, which is to say that it is not an unconditioned end after all. A disparity thus opens between the person's subjective conviction of end-status and the reality of its dependent existence. Insofar, therefore, as the person remains aloof from things, it is self-contradictory as an unconditioned end. This internal contradiction implies that the person *lacks* the world as that whose subordination to its ends validates the person's claim of final worth. Because it lacks the world, the person also desires it. This is not an appetite given by nature from which personality can detach itself but an intellectual desire of personality for validation as an end. To satisfy this desire, the person must step out of its self-relation and perform actions of a type that realize or make good its claim of authority over things.[19] Specifically, it must perform actions that put objects into a relation of subservience to it. These actions will constitute a property because they will (partially or perfectly) *validate* a claim of end-status vis-à-vis a thing. The question for discussion is: can there be an objective validation of this claim outside the framework of public law?

3. The Validation Scale and Grades of Ownership

If property in an object is a person's validated claim to end-status vis-à-vis that object, then we understand property when we understand what types of action

---

[18] Kant 1797, 69.   [19] Hegel 1820b, para. 41.

validate the claim and with what grade of perfection. If a kind of action (say, taking physical possession) validates the claim to some degree, then performing that action generates a right, having a corresponding grade of force, to be master of the object to the exclusion of all but those whose actions have produced better validations. So, an action partially validating end-status produces a right *in personam*; it implies a correlative obligation to respect the claim on those who have taken no self-validating action with respect to the object. Grades of ownership based on superior and inferior validations of end-status must be distinguished from better and worse claims to possession based on temporal priority of possession. A first possessor and a squatter have the same grade of ownership based on the degree of self-validation produced by physical possession. What resolves their rival claims is the first possessor's temporal priority. But what resolves the rival claims of a mere possessor and a long user (as we'll see) is the better validation of end-status produced by use.

Action-types that validate a claim of end-status to different grades of perfection generate ownerships that stand to each other as gradations of a vertical scale. Those whose actions on a thing have validated a claim of end-status better than the actions of others have stronger claims to be master of the thing than those whose validation was inferior, and those whose actions have validated the claim perfectly have claims inferior to none. Theirs is an unqualified ownership—a right *in rem* or against the world.[20] Accordingly, by virtue of the validation scale, it will be possible to distinguish (as the common law does) between inferior and superior titles to things and between relative titles held against some and absolute titles held against all. Each grade of ownership on the scale contains the exclusive power to perform all mastery-displaying actions of which the object admits, limited only by the remainder, reversion, or right to recovery of those with superior claims. The question on which we must focus is this: is an unqualified ownership or right *in rem* available outside public law and if so, how can private property still be subordinate to the public welfare such that non-consensual takings for ordinary public ends are permissible?

3.1 Physical possession[21]

To begin with, the person proves its end-status by physically bringing unoccupied things under its control—that is, by possessing them.[22] First possession confers a (relative) right to possess, use, and alienate a thing to the exclusion of all non-possessors even if possession is interrupted because it (partially) validates a normative claim—that this person is the thing's end until the person chooses to relinquish it. Possession is, however, the weakest form of self-validation because it leaves the thing with an independent existence over against the person. The thing is brought under a person's control but is not yet subsumed to its free choice of ends. Thus,

---

[20] In this chapter, a right *in rem* means a right to be master of something that is valid against all. A right *in personam* is a right to be master of something that is valid against some but not all.
[21] This and the following subsection take material from Brudner 1995, 45–57.
[22] Hegel 1820b, paras. 54–58.

the right conferred by first possession is only a better claim than can be made by those who have established no control at all; it is not yet unqualified ownership. In possession, moreover, the person's self-proving activity is hemmed in by physical constraints, for there are narrow limits to what one can manually grasp or surround with a fence. The possessive personality desires the world (universe), but there is only so much a body can do.[23]

Because physical possession is right-generating only as giving reality to the person's claimed end-status, not every act of possession counts as creating a possessory right. There must have been an intention to control the object to the exclusion of others, for otherwise possession is not the validation of a claim to end-status. Second, there must have been a physical occupation normally adequate for control and observable by others, for if possession is clearly indefensible or merely intended, then end-status is not objectively validated.[24] Accordingly, the common-law prerequisites for the enforcement of possession are just the conditions for the person's validation as an end prior to enforcement. The common law does not bestow property rights pursuant to some socially desired goal. It *certifies* a property already implicitly accomplished by actions on the ground of a kind that validate end-status.

William Blackstone thought that first possession confers a right against the world—that it is the first ownership legitimating all subsequent transfers.[25] Were that true, the doctrine of eminent domain would be false, for there cannot be separate sovereigns over the same undivided parcel of land. Against Blackstone stands Kant, for whom all directly acquired title is relative (better than the dispossessor's) and provisional (pending public review) and for whom rights *in rem* (having force even against the state) are therefore impossible—a view that renders the compensation requirement of the takings clause incomprehensible. Liberals seem faced with a choice between extreme proprietary individualism and collective ownership. We'll see, however, that a *via media* exists.

The equation of first possession with unqualified ownership engenders well-known problems. First, why should one person's choice unilaterally to possess a specific object place all other persons under an obligation to respect his exclusive possession of that object? Here one must distinguish two reasons why unilateral acquisition might fail to create obligations in others. One is that the equality of persons might rule out unilaterally imposed obligations even if there were no competition for objects and so even if acquisition by one disadvantaged no one else. That is Kant's reason for denying that first possession creates a right *in rem*, but it is not Hegel's. Kant denies that direct acquisition can produce a right *in rem* because he sees acquisition as permitted but not necessary. If there is no rational necessity for acquisition, then it is indeed inconceivable that one person's arbitrary

---

[23] Hegel does not airbrush Abstract Right. It is the normative framework based on the possessive personality for whom dignity consists solely in dominion over things. Hegel looks this paradigm in the face, observes its downfall, and then integrates it into the total public life sufficient for dignity, wherein its excesses are tamed.

[24] *Pierson v Post* 1805.   [25] Blackstone 1765, 258.

choice to possess something could bind non-consenting equals. But Hegel, we saw, explains acquisition as essential to an end-status self-contradictory without it, and so the obligation to respect acquisition by unilateral actions can be a priori reciprocal. If there is an a priori reciprocal obligation to respect persons as ends, then there is an a priori reciprocal obligation to respect the possession in which end-status becomes real.

Another reason why first possession might fail to create a right *in rem* is one that Hegel recognizes. It has to do with interpersonal competition for scarce means of self-validation. The problem is that, in gaining proof of his end-status through the object, the first occupier also makes the object unavailable for the self-validation of others. Why should they accept this? Unilateral possession could confer a valid right to exclusive possession only if that right were somehow reconciled with the freedom of acquisition of competitors for the object; and so far it has not been. I'll return to this.

A further problem with equating first possession with first ownership was noticed by Holmes.[26] If first possession suffices to confer unqualified ownership—a right against the world—then whatever other powers come with ownership, the right to possess must be what ownership is. Someone who divested himself of the right to possess could not be an owner, while someone who acknowledged ownership in another would also acknowledge legal possession in that person and so could assert no possessory right against him. Yet tenants have possessory rights against persons they acknowledge as owners, and owners temporarily divest themselves of possessory rights without ceasing to be owners. If first possession is first ownership, how can possessory right and ownership come apart?

These problems become soluble if we regard the claim that first possession is first ownership as mistakenly seeking a right *in rem* at the beginning of property's development rather than at its end. The grain of truth in this claim is that, because it leaves the object with an appearance of independence, possession is the least satisfactory validation of end-status; and so (assuming the competition problem solved) it confers on the first possessor a title relative only to those who have yet to establish even this minimal connection with the object. True, the 'only' here is 'all', but the possessory right is not yet a right *in rem* because it is contingent on no other person's gaining a better validation in the object by annulling its independence; to the one who does, the possessory right will yield. Possession, in other words, confers a relative or imperfect property, better only than no connection to the thing at all. That is why the first occupier has a right to exclude all other would-be possessors, and it is why no trespasser can defeat a possessory title (even that of a thief) by appealing to the right of the true owner.[27] Yet because possession is an imperfect property, it will end up being subordinate to a non-possessory ground of title that represents a fully adequate realization of personality as an unconditioned end. Thus, someone with the best possessory title (e.g. a tenant) may be distinct from the absolute owner; while, conversely, ownership based on actions that confirm

---

[26] Holmes 1881, 163–7.   [27] *Costello v Chief Constable of Derbyshire* 2001.

end-status perfectly can serenely cede finite rights of possession to another, even as possession continues to confer relative (including temporally finite) rights.

3.2 Use

That first possession confers no right *in rem* is attested to by the common law itself. Suppose P takes possession of a pristine tract of land by enclosing it with a fence on which he posts signs warning off trespassers. While P takes an extended holiday, S squats on the land and puts it to intensive use for 12 years. If P takes no action to oust S, his title will be extinguished in favour of S's.[28] What is the ground of S's title? Against everyone but P, S can point to his possessory actions, because no one else but P has established a possessory connection with the land. Against P, however, S cannot appeal to his physical possession, because there is no reason why S's possessory acts should displace P's. On the contrary, since P's acts occurred first, they should withstand any subsequent acts of possession as those of a mere trespasser. To be sure, we say that P has been dispossessed or that his possession has been discontinued, leaving S alone in possession of the land. However, the discontinuance of P's possession is not a precondition of S's possessory right but a legal conclusion thereof. What we mean is that S's occupation was of such a kind as to oust P's, to deprive it of juridical force. If S had merely replaced P's signs with his own, P would not have been dispossessed. Similarly, if P had made the slightest use of a portion of the fenced-in area, no acts of S would have succeeded in dispossessing him.[29] Accordingly, P is dispossessed not because S performed actions amounting to mere possession, but because he performed actions that were superior to possessory ones as validations of end-status. What are these actions?

We saw that possession fell short as a validation of end-status because it left the thing with an appearance of independence. Use is a better validation because using something as one pleases subdues it to the person's free choice of ends. Also, use transforms the thing's physical character, consumes its use value, and in that way reduces it to the finality of the person.[30] Accordingly, use is a better property—a better validation of end-status vis-à-vis the thing—than possession without use. Possession is 'adverse' to that of the previous occupier and sufficient to dispossess him only if it consists in public acts of use (with an intention to control) where the previous occupier is making no use of the land. Thus, time will not run in favour of a trespasser, because the intentional possession of the first occupier confers a title good against non-possessors and hence invincible against subsequent acts that are merely possessory. Yet it will run in favour of someone whose use has the potential (needing only a certain longevity to ripen into a mastery of the object) to override the bare possession of the previous occupier and whose property in the thing is thus potentially superior. The user's property is superior, however, not because the law decrees it to be so for public ends, but because use is superior to possession as a

---

[28] *Buckinghamshire County Council v Moran* 1989.
[29] *Re St Clair Beach Estates Ltd and MacDonald* 1974. [30] Hegel 1820b, paras. 59–64.

validation of end-status. Once again, the common law merely recognizes a pre-existing relation of dominion.

Nevertheless, use is not a complete property. As so far constituted, property is inadequate as a validation of end-status in several respects. In possession and use, first of all, the person proves its end-status in a self-contradictory way, for it finds itself dependent on external things for the confirmation of its mastery of them. Therefore, the same possessive and usufructuary actions that cancel the object's independence also perpetually reinstate it. The person's satisfaction is necessarily ephemeral because each satisfaction produces a new lack *ad infinitum*.[31]

Second, taking possession and using are physical actions that purport to ground an *intellectual* right to own something to the exclusion of others—a right whose validity is independent of the contingency of continuous physical possession. Yet the intellectual right is thus far limited by the requirement that the thing should have been at one time physically possessed. While struggling to free itself from its contingent origins, the right continues to be anchored to them, and this dependency contradicts the *unconditioned* end-status that personality seeks.

Third, we have not yet bridged the gulf between fact and right. Possessing and using are contingent happenings that purport unilaterally to exclude other persons from control of the object. If excluding were not disadvantaging in a normatively relevant sense, the claim of right to exclusive possession could be validated a priori; for, acquisition being necessary for end-status, the obligation to respect de facto acquisition could be notionally reciprocal, hence acceptable by equal ends. The property unilaterally established by possession and use would then suffice for a right *in rem*, for the laws of first and adverse possession would reconcile the free acquisition of each with that of all, and no person would be deprived in a way that is normatively significant for Abstract Right. However, if someone is so deprived, then unilateral acquisition could not confer a property, for it could not then be freely recognized by those it purports to bind.

On Hegel's account of acquisition, unilateral acquisition must deprive others in a normatively significant way. That is, it must deprive others, not only of the things they might biologically need or subjectively fancy, but also of the things they require for the confirmation of their end-status. We have seen that acquisition confers rights insofar as it stems from a contradiction between the person's claim to end-status and the apparent independence of objects. This contradiction generates an urge of the will to cancel that independence and to validate its own finality. Understood as a desire of the will rather than an appetite of the body, the acquisitive project is inherently one of infinite accumulation. If (as for the ancients) acquisition is understood as required for the body, its limits can be set by the body's subordination to the final end of living well. When, however, acquisition is viewed as essential to the validation of a final end, all previous restraints are off. No doubt, new (freedom-generated) restraints will emerge once Abstract Right is integrated into the political life sufficient for end-status; but at this stage, there are none.

---

[31] Hegel 1807, paras. 173–5.

Personality claims a right to subdue the totality of things and cannot in principle rest satisfied until it has done so. Furthermore, because personality is at this stage the singular personality of the atomistic individual, the presumed right of personality to infinite accumulation is the equal right of *each separate* personality to such acquisition. We have, therefore, competitive claims of right to an infinite accumulation. Under these conditions, any unilateral acquisition by one necessarily frustrates the project of another, for it makes him worse off in terms of his self-validation as an end. Because a right based on unilateral acquisition would preclude the self-validation of all other persons, it cannot be valid in an unqualified sense.

Accordingly, if private property is to exist prior to a public scheme of distributive justice, it must somehow reconcile one person's right to exclusive possession with the freedom of acquisition of all others. A unilateral acquisition can generate property if and only if it is made consistent with the right of others to an unlimited accumulation.

3.3 Exchange

Exchange remedies the three defects in unilateral acquisition.[32] First, in alienating my possession, I resolve the contradiction between my claimed mastery of the object and my actual dependence on it for validation. That is so because, on the one hand, I demonstrate my independence of the object by letting it go; but, on the other, I remain the recognized owner of the object's exchange value. As the product of an agreement of free wills, exchange value is the same metaphysical identity of qualitatively different particulars that personhood is. Therefore, the person can depend on it without contradicting its end-status vis-à-vis material things; what it depends on is an intellectual object that is just the reflection of itself. No doubt this object has a physical token that may be possessed and used (say, for melting into a substance convertible to a tooth). But the fact that money is a token shows that what is owned in owning money is something intellectual—that a coin's use value as a physical object is something ancillary and insignificant. In any case, once property in exchange value can be realized without the mediation of physical currency, its emancipation from materiality is complete. While a banknote may still have some incidental use value as a piece of paper, the number debited from the purchaser's bank balance to the credit of the seller's has no material or useful properties whatsoever.

Second, when exchange takes the form of an executory contract—of an exchange of promises to deliver equivalents in the future—ownership has freed itself entirely from the contingency of empirical possession. It is no longer the case that I must possess something empirically in order to have the right to possess it even when I am away from it. By virtue of contract, I have the right to possess something even though I have never possessed it and whether or not I actually possess it. In this way, contract turns acquisition by original possession on its head. Whereas before,

---

[32] In this subsection I read Hegel's extremely condensed text (1820b, paras. 71–4) in a way that should be regarded as Hegelian in inspiration rather than textually determined.

empirical possession preceded intellectual possession (a right to possess) and was needed for it, now intellectual possession precedes empirical possession, which is not needed for it. Indeed, the intellectual possession is not even of the material object bargained for; it is rather ownership of a certain monetary value of the object, for this is what the promisor guarantees irrespective of whether the promisee purchases a substitute matter on breach. In the executory contract, then, owner-ship's independence of matter and contingency is complete and so too, therefore, is ownership. We can say that end-status is best embodied, not in the intellectual possession of a material object, but in the intellectual possession of an intelligible object—exchange value.

Third, exchange solves the competition problem. To isolate the property-valid-ating role of exchange, assume that the object offered for sale has never been sold before, that the holder has it through first or adverse possession. Now, in purchas-ing the object, I recognize the other's ownership by awaiting his decision to alienate it and by giving him an equal value in return. Yet I do not thereby foreclose my opportunities for unlimited acquisition, because I recognize his ownership of the thing only insofar as it becomes available to me, and he recognizes my ownership under the same condition.[33] But not only does my contractual partner recognize my ownership. Because (assuming perfect information) all other persons have passed on the opportunity to acquire something offered for sale in a public market, indeed have registered the cost of their disappointment in the value I must relinquish to own it, recognition for holdings acquired through open exchange is omnilateral rather than simply bilateral. That is to say, my contractual partner is a conduit for a mutual recognition between the all and the individual even prior to the existence of a public authority. The market recognizes something as mine only insofar as I reciprocally acknowledge others' interest in the object by paying the social cost of their going without it. As a consequence, contracts manufacture rights *in rem*; relative rights go in and absolute rights come out.[34]

The upshot is that our final properties are not in the physical things we possess in isolation but in their metaphysical values realized in exchange. What I own without qualification is not the thing I unilaterally possessed, but only the equivalent value allotted to me by the market when I relinquish my possession—a value reflecting everyone else's frustration in letting me have it. Inversely, the one who owns something as a pure commodity abstracted from its material and useful properties is its absolute owner, for his ownership is recognized by all in return for his acknowledging (by paying) its social cost. To him alone belongs a right *in rem*.

---

[33] Hegel 1820b, paras. 72–4.

[34] David Hume's 'social convention' theory of property explains property as originating in a common interest in the secure possession of what people already hold or might acquire through fortune and industry. But according to Hume's account of human nature, our avidity is 'insatiable, perpetual [and] universal', while external goods are scarce relative to our limitless wants; Hume 1739–40a, 492. Why then would we, especially the stronger among us, tacitly agree to an arrangement that perpetually excludes us from what we desire? The market exchange theory of property unites the convention theory with what is missing from it—namely, an account of how a convention of respect for exclusive possession can be made compatible with freedom of acquisition.

Thus, the best validation of end-status with respect to an object is a paper title indicating receipt through a market transaction from someone qualified to relinquish an ownership that is best so far—that no one else can trump. The ownership conferred by that paper requires no physical possession, trumps ownership by prior possession (for example, a squatter's), and, once certified against prior claims, cannot be extinguished by adverse possession.[35] Indeed, it can even stand serenely aloof from a tenant's temporally finite right to exclusive possession. It is timeless, metaphysical ownership—the kind of ownership that alone fulfils a claim of end-status raised above all finitude, relativity, and contingency.

That contract is the perfection of property is reflected in the law of property. At common law, ownership by possession and use yields to ownership by deed or contract. Thus, before its first sale, no one but a prior possessor may eject a squatter from Blackacre. But if a prior possessor with best relative title conveys Blackacre to a buyer, the buyer may eject the squatter though the squatter's possession preceded his. Is this because the buyer received and now asserts the seller's best relative title? That cannot be, because the seller's title was relative to those who had established no connection with Blackacre, whereas the buyer's title is good also against the seller by virtue of the latter's having consented to it by a voluntary transfer. So the buyer has more than the seller had thanks to the seller's recognition. But recognition, we saw, is not simply bilateral. The buyer's title is also good against those who either passed on Blackacre or bid unsuccessfully for it and for whose disappointment the buyer paid. Let us say this group comprises all. So the buyer's right against all is now based on an action in which all were involved and reciprocally considered rather than (like the first possessor's) on a unilateral doing exclusive of all. This means that the buyer may eject the squatter, not because he asserts the seller's prior possessory right, but because he wields a new right against the world that is derived from a market exchange and that trumps the squatter's relative title based on possession.

Now suppose that buyer (B) sells Blackacre to C, who is dispossessed by D, who purports to sell the fee simple to E, who, unaware of D's defective title, sells the 'fee simple' to F, and so on for a hundred years. Notwithstanding that he took in an open market, the last buyer lacks a right *in rem*, for his right is provisional on no one's (in this case none of C's heirs) showing up with a better claim from the distant past. Even if there were no better claim, no one could know this, and so all property would be provisional—infected with contingency—leaving the person's claim of unconditioned end-status unrealized. Knowledge of title, it thus turns out, is not an end of policy that public law adds to the pre-civil derivation of property—something

---

[35] On the surface, the ousting of adverse possession by certification of title has an instrumental explanation. The quieting purpose of certification would be defeated if a squatter could oust the registered title holder by long use. But there is a deeper reason. Without certification, ownership acquired through exchange is provisional on no one's showing up with a prior claim, and in that sense it is still relative or *in personam*. That is why adverse possession can still defeat it. Once certified, however, ownership via exchange is truly absolute or *in rem*; and the relative property conferred by the unilateral action of using cannot trump *in rem* ownership recognized by all.

external to the person's self-validation in ownership of things; it is rather intrinsic to the fulfilment of that project.

Accordingly, whereas unilateral possession confers a relative property, acquisition in an open market confers a right *in rem*—or would if not for the fog obscuring the chain of title. At this point, natural property requires an artifice to resolve that uncertainty in a way that reconciles the last buyer's property with a dispossessed owner's. So, market actors might set up a public record of transactions and accept a registered deed of sale with patently unbroken pedigree as valid against the world; and, obversely, they might tacitly deem an open market exchange to pass absolute title to a good faith purchaser who buys without public notice of a dispossessed owner's title.[36] By means of such a convention, market society completes the saga of the person insofar as a pre-civil condition can do so. It establishes a valid right *in rem* and so (but for the egocentricity of Abstract Right, about which more presently) fulfils personality's project of self-validation in things.[37]

The foregoing account of property reveals the conceptual link between property and contract.[38] It shows that contract is not the arbitrary transfer of a property juridically complete prior to exchange but rather itself the perfection and legitim-ation of private property. Perhaps it is not a complete legitimation. After all, if the rightfulness of exclusive possession depends on there being an equal opportunity to bid for commodities, then it would seem to depend on everyone's having the wherewithal to bid, for otherwise equal opportunity is formal. Yet Abstract Right is indifferent to how buying power is distributed. Because it sees end-status as reposing solely on free will, Abstract Right is content if every person is formally at liberty to bid for objects and to enter into exchanges to acquire them, and if every object is available at a price. Having or not having the means to bid is a peculiarity of the individual having no interpersonal salience; only persons count for Abstract Right, and they are neither rich nor poor.

---

[36] Indeed, market actors could also cooperate in setting up a title registry, and they could mutually guarantee title by voluntarily paying into an insurance fund from which compensation is paid to anyone aggrieved. Thus a public authority is not needed for publicly recognized and certified title; it is needed only to compel compliance with the public system already in place. Rather than creating property, the public authority puts the finishing touches on it.

[37] What if, as with chattels, there is no public record of transactions? In that case, another custom is required to bolster the market's fulfilment of the right *in rem*. It must be generally accepted that, if the thief (T) cannot be found, the *bona fide* purchaser (BFP) may elect either to restore the object to the owner (O) in return for the price he (BFP) paid or keep the object and compensate O. If T is known, reconciling O's and BFP's rights *in rem* would seem to require that BFP retain the object, leaving O to seek compensation from T. The law of market overt (one-sidedly favouring the BFP) was abolished in the UK by the Sale of Goods (Amendment) Act, 1994, ch. 32. This effectively means that there are no *in rem* rights to chattels in Britain, that all property in chattels is provisional there.

[38] James Penner denies this link, arguing that property is sufficiently explained as an exclusive right to determine the uses of a thing; see Penner 1997, 91–2. However, Penner's argument seems to be a *petitio principi*. He first stipulates that the concept of property is individuated by the interest in determining the uses of things and then, finding nothing in the concept so defined that entails a right to make binding agreements, he concludes that property and contract are separate concepts. They are indeed distinct concepts, but it doesn't follow that they are unconnected. If property is understood as a valid claim to be master of an object, then the social validation that comes through contract may be seen as the fulfilment of property.

Still, complaints about formalism are out of place here, for they come from outside a framework that is unabashedly formalistic. Abstract Right has not yet revealed itself as inadequate on its own terms; hence its principled formalism cannot be effectively criticized simply by calling it formalistic. Unless Abstract Right collapses irretrievably from within, we must grant that it has, all on its own, a legitimation story for exclusive possession that is at least plausible in that it can point to a form of omnilateral approval for omnilaterally binding proprietary obligations. Crucially, moreover, this framework can point to an omnilateral approval for directly acquired holdings that is given prior to public law and distributive justice. For such an approval one need not await the deliberate ratification of private holdings by a democratic public authority; it is already given by the market. Even if inadequate on its own, the omnilateral recognition of private property through market exchange might be worthy of some respect, and whatever measure of respect is owed might be owed unconditionally.

4. Property in Civil Society

Thus far, Hegel (with some interpolations of our own) has derived a private property prior to the rule of law—one that is independent of distributive fairness or the public interest. This explains a stringent duty to compensate an owner for a public taking but leaves unexplained the public authority's permission to take for ordinary ends without consent. To understand this permission, we must understand the necessity for a public authority as well as the revisions this necessity forces to the previous account of property.

The objective reality of the person's mastery of things was not fully attained until the person relinquished its de facto possession to another in return for the other's (and society's) recognition of its ownership. Thus the person's realized end-status is embedded in a common will wherein each recognizes and confirms the other as an owner. However, the person who at this stage claims to be an absolute end also claims that its end-status is innate in its singular free will and so independent of any relation to another. We who are observing the person's development can see that end-status is realized only in a relation of mutual recognition, but the person we are observing claims to be morally self-sufficient; and so it treats the common will materialized in exchange as a conventional pact subordinate to the self-related person for whose sake it came into being. At this point, therefore, the common will has no explicit normative authority. That valid rights issue only from mutual respect is a proposition whose truth has not yet been demonstrated to the person whose education to right we are following. For this person, right consists in a permission to reduce all things to its singular self. Each person claims a permission to realize its *separate* end-status and so to flout the common will—the framework for joint end-status—whenever it suits.[39] No one can wrong another.

---

[39] Hegel 1820b, paras. 81–2.

Accordingly, the social realization of personality's unconditioned worth turns out to be its vulnerability to the unbridled liberty of its egocentric associates. The completion of property demands that the person transfer its possession to someone who claims a permission to disregard his contract if he chooses. In this way, the self-related person's worth-claim is refuted by the very anarchic character of the social interactions to which this view of the person's worth gives rise. If each solitary person thinks of itself as an absolute end, then no one is an end, for each may use the other as he or she pleases. Faced with this self-contradictory result, the person must abandon the claim that its end-status depends on itself alone—that it rests sufficiently on its singular free will. The self-destructiveness of this claim reveals the common will as a better ground for the person's unconditioned worth and as a more coherent foundation of ownership rights.[40] Hitherto something derivative from the self-related person to which it remained inferior, the common will is now recognized as authoritative law.

Accordingly, we have passed to a condition in which mutual recognition is the sole ground of valid right-claims, not only for us the observers (inherently), but also for the person whose self-realization qua end we are observing (actually). In this way, the property rights in acquired things that were formerly implicit but contradicted by the claimed supremacy of the singular will become explicit. Property rights are thus perfected by the rule of law, but they are not created thereby, because there was already a social validation of property in things directly acquired prior to public authority. The latter has simply given explicit normative force to that prior validation.

4.1 The origin of welfare entitlements

It looks like the derivation of private property can end there, in which case there could be no state power of eminent domain. As with Locke, the justifying reason for civil authority would be to perfect the 'natural' rights to freedom of movement and to the grade of property attained by one's action on an object. Were the civil authority to interfere with rightful possession or use for an ordinary public end, it would violate the right it was instituted to perfect even if it compensated the owner. Expropriations would be *ultra vires*.

However, the derivation of private property cannot end there. This is so because the very transition to a rule of law brings to sight a common good that contradicts the atomistic premise of the derivation. The argument for private property began from the individual person's claim to moral self-sufficiency based on the end-status involved in its singular free will. Property in a thing was justified as the validation of an isolated person's claim of final worth. Yet the perfection of that property has contradicted its starting point, for it has revealed the person's moral dependence both on a market and on the public authority that enforces the market's *imprimatur* on holdings. Because, moreover, the justification of private property assumed

---

[40] Hegel 1820b, para. 104.

naturally dissociated free wills, it also assumed that the free will is the only public thing, that all needs and goods were the subjective addictions and preferences of discrete individuals. That is why the inchoate duties of Abstract Right were only negative obligations not to interfere with freedom of movement or with the grade of property a person had acquired. There could be no positive duty of concern for another's welfare, for the end-status realized in the common will inhered in a capacity for free choice that turned every animal need into an optional attachment and that, being innate, had no needs of its own. There was thus no public conception of welfare that free and equal ends could be coercively required to promote.

All these assumptions are overturned with the transition to a rule of law. This is so because the common will's normative authority implies a changed conception of what is unconditionally true about agents and a correspondingly enlarged understanding of their potential for freedom. If the common will is authoritative for persons, then authoritative law is law that is immanent in the agent's reasonable will rather than law that is given by a natural teleology external to the will. Therefore, agents are inherently autonomous—capable of acting from principles (universalizable maxims) rather than immediate inclination and subject only to laws they can give themselves. This means that law is normative only insofar as it can be self-imposed by ends, while persons are respected as ends only insofar as they are subject to laws to which ends can assent. Accordingly, the transition to a rule of law brings in its train a new conception of what is essential to agents and therefore a new conception of what is necessarily public: not only the agent's capacity for free choice but also its potential for self-determination. Moreover, this transition also brings to sight the link between normativity and autonomy. Law is authoritative only as an expression of a common will each agent can regard as its own. Therefore, agents have a positive right to autonomy correlative to the duty on authority-claimants to rule solely as ministers of the common will.

The problem these developments pose for the previous account of property is plain. That account presupposed morally self-sufficient, hence atomistic ends whose end-status reposed solely on their capacity for freely choosing among subjective inclinations. The account's climax, however, reveals persons as potentially self-determining moral subjects and citizens who necessarily share a common good—namely, the realization of that potential. Whereas, moreover, the persons of Abstract Right had (inchoately) only negative rights against interference with liberty and property, moral subjects have a positive right to autonomy correlative to the duty on authority-claimants to rule in the name of what all citizens can rationally will for themselves.

Now, it might seem that this positive right to autonomy is satisfied if authority-claimants rule *solely* as ministers of the common will, specifying and enforcing the duty to respect the negative rights hitherto unfolded and nothing more. Not so. The very elevation of the common will from a derivative embodiment of the singular will to an authoritative law involves an expansion in the content of rights. This is so because the exclusively negative form of the right to freedom was tied to a conception of freedom identified with the capacity for choosing among subjective ends. The transition to the rule of law, however, has revealed that conception of freedom as too thin. By virtue of their capacity for undetermined choice, agents can act from respect for the law guaranteeing equal rights, and the realization of that potential for autonomy is a public good. So, if the rights of agents are connected to a public conception of freedom (to what equal ends can reciprocally demand from each other), then there is no non-arbitrary basis for limiting rights of freedom to the negative ones dictated by the thin conception that has been revealed as partial. Those rights must be generalized without regard to any restriction imposed by the superseded conception. But a generalized right to freedom includes positive rights to the conditions of autonomy in addition to negative rights against interference. Let us see what revisions to property theory these new developments require.

A positive right to the conditions of autonomy is specified in the following ways. It implies, first, what Hegel calls a right of insight.[41] This is a right to the procedures and practices by which law's impartiality may be validated through the participating reason and assent of those subject to it. This right generates the requirements of publicity and systematicity in the law, of reasoned decisions, as well as the rules of due process in court (another clause of the Fifth Amendment). Second, the right of autonomy implies what Hegel calls a right of intention. This is a right to see in the adverse legal consequences of one's actions only the traces of one's own choices—hence a right (for example) against strict liability for penal consequences. Third, the right of autonomy implies a right of welfare.[42] This is a right, not to the satisfaction of one's personal aims, but to the minimum level of resources needed to liberate the mind for the pursuit of self-authored projects and to guarantee independence from those who would otherwise control the means of subsistence. Accordingly, the common will has undergone a metamorphosis just in becoming recognized as authoritative. It has become the common welfare.

A positive right to welfare is a right to the material and cultural preconditions of an autonomous life. Although some speak of this right to resources as property, I eschew this terminology for two reasons: one, because it blurs a distinction between private ownership and citizen entitlements that I wish to vindicate; two, because, in doing so, it smuggles into language a contestable position—namely, that property is nothing more than a right to a certain allocation of social wealth.[43] Instead, I will reserve the name 'property' for a person's (relatively or fully) valid claim based on its own actions to be master of an object (the property of Abstract Right), and I will refer to positive rights to resources as 'entitlements' to social wealth.

Nevertheless, the distinction between private property and entitlements to social wealth leaves room for the idea of a positive right to the exclusive control, use, and trading of the resources to which one is entitled from the common store. Although this looks like a positive right to property, it is not. It is rather a positive right to property-like powers and remedies as a condition of autonomy. A property-like power or remedy is one extracted from the direct relation between a person and a

---

[41] Hegel 1820b, paras. 132, 215, 224.   [42] Hegel 1820b, paras. 128–30, 230.
[43] See Reich 1964.

thing of which it is an integral part in order to enjoy and protect holdings allocated by the common welfare. The power is property-*like* because, while the exclusive rights to control, use, and alienate are integral to property understood as a person's valid claim to mastery of a thing, they are only accidentally joined to an entitlement to a resource. My entitlement to a plot of land could be satisfied even if I were given it on condition that I leave it for the use of others every seven years. I could enjoy the *x* loaves of bread I receive from the common store even were I prohibited from trading any for a quantity of eggs. Likewise, an injunctive remedy against trespass is conceptually connected to a person's exclusive mastery of a thing; it is not so joined to an entitlement to a resource from the common store, for that entitlement could be protected by a liability rule requiring takers to pay court-determined damages. So a property-like rule is one borrowed from its conceptual home in the direct relation between person and thing for employment in a public allocation to which it is only contingently connected.

Property-like rules are conditions of living autonomously. This is so partly because the secure (i.e. intellectual) possession of necessities liberates the moral subject for the pursuit of ends other than subsistence and partly because property-like rules protect a sphere wherein the person's autonomy may find expression through its exclusive use, management, and alienation of things according to its own will and its own goals. At this stage, therefore, it is appropriate to speak of a quasi-property (held from the common welfare) in resources as a condition of autonomy and so as a legally cognizable need of the human individual. In Abstract Right, the individual's needs were juridically insignificant, since all need signified a natural 'necessity' from which the free will could detach itself, hence really an optional value having no normative force for other persons. At this stage, however, needs are freedom's needs—agency goods, as we might call them. Understood as objective requirements for acting from self-authored ends, they now come within the purview of right.

4.2 Civil society as a bifurcated entity

Once the material conditions of self-determination are acknowledged as something to which subjects are entitled from rulers as a condition of their valid authority, the negative right against intrusions to property generated by Abstract Right cannot remain unaltered; for that right is now shaped by what citizens owe each other as members of a civic body ordered to the common welfare. I say 'shaped' because the rights paradigm ordered to the self-related person has been superseded by one ordered to the autonomous citizen, and no logic has yet come forward to redeem it as part of a whole. Recall that the market recognition relied upon by Abstract Right as validating exclusive possession took no account of disparities of buying power, for those disparities reflected peculiar features of the individual having no bearing on what persons owed each other as abstract ends. Yet disparities in buying power are obviously relevant to what citizens owe each other as members of a collective body ordered to the common welfare. Since Abstract Right (we can now say) erred in treating these inequalities as irrelevant to the justice of private spheres of sovereignty over resources, it is superseded by a new, welfarist paradigm in whose entitlements the negative rights of Abstract Right are *merged*. As a consequence, there is now no property independent of the common welfare. Rather, a right against interferences with historically acquired holdings is now inwardly limited by the equal right of all moral subjects to the material conditions of self-determined action. Thus historically acquired holdings may be forcibly redistributed by the public authority without violating rights, provided that the redistribution is for the common welfare. No compensation is owed in any stringent sense, for there was no right to holdings that could not be justified by the collective welfare. Accordingly, whether compensation is paid depends solely on what conduces to the common welfare—on whether the benefits of compensation (e.g. alleviating anxiety, avoiding the frustration of expectations on which investments were based) outweigh its administrative costs, or as to how far compensation is fiscally consistent with achieving the positive ends of government. Previously inexplicable, the state power of eminent domain is now eminently intelligible; what is now mysterious is an absolute duty to compensate the 'owner'.

Still, the human agent's quest for validation cannot end there, for, far from being confirmed, its claimed end-status has come to naught. The elevation of autonomy to the fundamental end of civil union has generated a theoretical momentum whose end-point is the negation of autonomy. The systematic realization of the right to self-determination turns out to be the thoroughgoing submersion of a sphere of private sovereignty in the absolutism of the common welfare. Persons do not own what they possess and use; rather, they hold licences from the state that are revocable at will, perhaps with compensation, perhaps without. Property thus reflects the end-status, not of the individual agent, but of a collectivity in which the individual's separate end-status is submerged.

Given the self-contradictoriness of this result, the common welfare cannot coherently be pursued to its logical end-point. Its logical momentum is curtailed by an equally logical recoil, leaving space for the self-related person of Abstract Right to reassert its priority and lordship over things. Civil society is just this restless oscillation between opposite poles—between the priority of welfare and the priority of the person—neither of which offers repose. On the one hand, the person's claim of unconditioned worth finds no reality outside a common welfare inwardly constitutive of ownership; on the other, this realization of the person is its obliteration, requiring a return to the beginning—and so on endlessly. This is why Hegel calls the public sector of civil society an 'external state'. In civil society, the state is one side of a split entity of which the other is the market. As such, it is one particularism juxtaposed to many others—a powerful sovereign pitted against a multitude of petty ones interacting through exchange. Neither sovereignty can abide the other, yet neither can conquer the other without subverting itself.

Now, the Fifth Amendment paradox might be understood as reflecting this basic tension in liberal civil society—as a kind of neurotic accommodation of mutually ambivalent opposites in a divided soul writ large. So, forcible takings for ordinary public goals (whether or not the taking is necessary for the goal) are permitted because the person is an end only within a civic body ordered to the common welfare; but compensation is unconditionally owed because that terminus annihilates the person, whose end-status depends on separateness and self-relation.[44] On this critical view, the paradox of the takings clause is not simply apparent or facial; it is a real incoherence symptomatic of a deeper one in the bifurcated structure of a civil order at once derived from, and hostile to, the stateless person.

Though plausible, a critical view of the takings clause is not uniquely explanatory. Another explanation is available—one that reveals the takings clause as coherent. The general idea is that the contradiction inherent in civil society is logically surmounted in the political community (what Hegel calls the 'State') and that a takings law of the kind found in the Fifth Amendment reflects that solution. If this is correct, then the takings clause belongs to the law of a well-ordered political community. Even if, historically speaking, that clause reflects the conflict in civil society between state and person, its intelligibility is not relative to civil society; it is part of the constitutional law of a whole entity reconciling the public and private sides of the human individual. This would imply that the takings clause is a durable element of liberal constitutionalism even if civil society is an ephemeral form of political association.

5. Property in the Political Community

The conflict in civil society between state and person stems from the atomistic premiss from which civil authority was derived. Like the rights paradigm, the welfarist one presupposes a person that regards itself as morally self-sufficient—as depending for its dignity on its free will alone—and so as naturally solitary. No doubt, the welfarist framework rejects that conception of the human being in favour of one that regards the individual as a moral subject who comes to dignity only through equal membership in a civic body. Nevertheless, that framework is thoroughly shaped by the view of the person it rejects.

Recall that the welfarist paradigm was attained by elevating to normative authority a common will of dissociated and (putatively) self-sufficient ends—a common will that morphed into a common welfare just in acquiring normative force. The anti-individualism of the welfarist paradigm is determined by this atomistic starting point. Because the person's claim to *separate* end-status is equated with its claim of permission to a *welfare-blind* dominion over the world of objects, the common welfare had to come forward as an end hostile to the person's separate end-status as such. Yet the common welfare's rational authority depended, we saw, on its fulfilling an individual end-status that was self-contradictory in isolation. Thus, the welfarist paradigm's atomistic foundations assured its hostility to the very individual end-status its authority depended on perfecting. Inevitably, this latent flaw surfaced when the collective welfare asserted its authority. That authority

---

[44] For a discussion of how this tension is reflected in the public takings jurisprudence of the US Supreme Court, see Radin 1988.

entailed the disappearance of spheres of individual sovereignty, hence the inversion of the collective welfare into something partisan and tyrannical. The individual's recoiling from that outcome produced the tension between individualism and collectivism that civil society involves.

We can see, however, that this tension is not primordial but consequent, not an ineluctable feature of civil life but the result of a certain conception of the human individual's final worth. Specifically, civil society's fragmentation is the disillusionment of atomism—of the human individual's claim to moral self-sufficiency based on its innate capacity for free choice. The human individual's end-status, it has turned out, depends on its acknowledgement of a public authority that reciprocally takes the individual's realized end-status for its aim. But if that is so, we must now turn against our atomistic starting point as denying the human being's political nature and as twisting the natural bond between state and person into mutual hostility. We must instead regard the human being as standing *ab initio* within a relationship of mutual recognition between itself and a public authority—one wherein each respects the end-status of the other as a condition of its own confirmation as an end.

I call this relationship dialogic community. Its political manifestations are two—one undeveloped and inadequate to its dialogical structure, the other fully adequate thereto. We begin with the inferior manifestation. It will take us far from anything recognizable as liberalism or private property; still, it is a logical step we must take in order to win our way back.

5.1 Property in the totalitarian state

Dialogic community unites explicitly the poles whose interdependence was revealed in the mutual ambivalence of state and person in civil society. Because the public authority and the person are valid ends only in being freely recognized by the other, each supports the other's independence for the sake of its own realized worth. Instead of subduing the other to its own primacy, each defers to the end-status of the other. Each renounces its claim to exclusive end-status and becomes a means for the other's validation. Thus, the political community defers to the individual's free agency and moral self-determination as to that which spontaneously confirms political membership as the human good; and it thereby shows that individual agency first comes to its rational importance—hence dignity—within a political community. From its side, the individual agent renounces its claim to moral self-sufficiency and, through devoted public service, recognizes its political unit as the ground of its dignity. Because each defers to the other, each is preserved (and indeed validated) as an end though allowing itself to be a means. Each depends for confirmation on the other; yet this dependence is consonant with the end-status of both, for the other is no indifferent object but one that has the other's end-status for its aim.[45]

---

[45] Hegel 1820b, para. 152.

At its first appearance, however, dialogic community is a polity one may call 'totalitarian', for it allows no independent existence to a sphere of private acquisition aimed at validating the individual person. Rather, private acquisition is respected only as a material support for service to the collective body, in free devotion to which the individual's honour is alone thought to rest. There is no public recognition for acquisition directed to the end-status of persons conceived as standing outside the collective unit, for the separate person is equated with the apolitical person grounding 'bourgeois' civil society. Hence there is no place for private law in the strict sense—that is, for a transactional law developed for the occasional interactions of otherwise dissociated persons by judges who take no account of common ends and who are independent of political masters. We have come to this because the common welfare's collapse as public reason—its inversion into a particularism opposed to many others—has discredited the atomistic starting point that caused it; and nothing has occurred yet to redeem atomism as a position required by the common good itself—as one established *within* dialogic community. Because the self-related person's worth is now denied, there is no respect for a property valid outside public life or for a private law for hypothetically dissociated persons. True, private (direct) acquisition is permitted, but only because the subordination of privately acquired wealth to politics and war is the ever-repeated nullification of the atomistic self that proves the latter's destiny in the united people. The true import of private acquisition is that it reflects the end-status of the political community in what is distinct from community—a truth made explicit in the commandeering of the compatriots' private holdings to support the people's wars and in the confiscation of the holdings of outsiders.

Yet the totalitarian polity's realization as an end is simultaneously its negation as such. In order to gain confirmation as the human individual's good, the polity must defer to individual free choice and moral self-determination, reciprocally recogniz-ing the independent worth of individual agency and conscience. Yet the polity here defers only to an agent who surrenders its independence; it does not respect the one who does not. The agent who seeks its rational importance solely in public service cannot truly possess an independent worth; for it then attains its dignity as a patriot and soldier, as a member of a collective unit, but not as an end in its own individual right—not as a *separate* end. Hence this agent lacks the qualification objectively to confirm the political unit as the human individual's end. By contrast, the agent who possesses this qualification stands outside the polity as an isolated atom—as one whose worth-claim challenges the polity's end-status and so cannot be recognized by it. Nevertheless, this agent is entitled to stand outside, for it is the independent end that dialogic community requires for its validation, yet (in its totalitarian phase) has no room for. Because the agent who claims end-status on its own contradicts the polity's natural authority, the polity must reduce to a means—to slavery—the outsider whose independence its authority simultaneously requires. In this way, the activity meant to validate the polity's natural authority reveals it as an arbitrary and violent power.

5.2 Property in the dialogical state

The totalitarian polity's downfall as the common good points the way forward. That downfall reveals the necessity to the political community's confirmed end-status of recognition by an adversarial agent—one who initially claims worth on its own, apart from community. This means that the agent's refusal of the one-sidedly collective unit as its natural end must be respected by the dialogical polity in order that this polity may in turn be independently acknowledged by the singular person as its end—as the solid ground of its separate worth. Put succinctly, the totalitarian state's self-contradictory realization shows that the atomistic person is itself inherently embedded in a dialogical relation with the political community. Each requires the other's recognition for perfected rights and valid authority, respectively. Civil society exhibited this latent connection, but in the deformed (bifurcated) shape that it takes for persons who are unaware of it—who regard themselves as morally self-sufficient and therefore apolitical. When (through the logical process Hegel has traced) they become aware of it, they can submit to the polity's authority without loss to their separate worth; for the polity now reciprocally defers to the atomistic agent, whose path of self-discovery is the means by which the polity is objectively confirmed as the good. With this mutual recognition, the dialogical polity implicit in civil society comes into explicit existence.

The dialogical polity is structurally different from both civil society and the totalitarian state. It is not an entity bifurcated into mutually external and particularistic sectors—state and market—each unilaterally (but half-heartedly) seeking to subordinate the other. But neither is it a holistic body of patriots opposed to a subordinated market of atomistic owners. Rather, the dialogical polity is a holistic entity that encompasses both a public administration (of formal justice and welfare) and a free market of atomistic owners as particular instances of its own archetypal form of mutual recognition—as reflecting media by which that form is independently validated (in the conative action of supposedly self-sufficient agents) as the form of all valid worth-claims. It is thus a One inwardly articulated into public and private sectors, which are now equal and mutually limiting parts of a whole. Each part acknowledges the other as an end without self-sacrifice because each recognizes the other through the mediating whole that preserves both as equally necessary types of its dialogical structure. Thus, private property instantiates dialogic community, for objective ownership was established only through a mutual recognition between de facto possessors who are also conduits for a mutual recognition between the 'all' and the individual, the former conceding exclusive ownership, the latter paying the market price of that concession. The public welfare paradigm also manifests mutual recognition, for the moral subject submitted to authority on condition that authority submit its laws to the test of self-imposability by self-respecting ends. Both paradigms are necessary, for both are logical stepping-stones toward the dialogical polity's confirmation as an end in the spontaneous worth-seeking of the singular agent.

The dialogical polity is the entity that Hegel designates by the term 'State'. Whereas civil society was an 'external' state, the dialogical polity is the state *sans phrase*—the state that conforms to the idea of the state as an impartial whole. The dialogical polity is also the entity on which Hegel lavishes the praise that liberal champions of civil society have found servile and idolatrous. 'The State', he writes in language that Aristotle reserved for the divine mind, 'is an absolute unmoved end-in-itself . . . [It] has supreme right against the individual, whose supreme duty is to be a member of the state.'[46] Yet, once read against Hegel's analysis of the totalitarian *polis*, these statements lose their illiberal tenor. Hegel's state is a final end for the individual only because, unlike the *polis*, it contains all that is required for the satisfied end-status of the separate individual; and it is the separate, not (necessarily) the apolitical, individual who is the darling of liberalism. Qua final end, the state has supreme right against the individual considered in his or her natural immediacy or apart from belonging; but all the institutions reflecting the end-status the individual claimed apart from belonging (for example, private property, the market, due process) are received back from the whole (so purified of immediacy) as examples of the form of mutual recognition reflecting that form's natural authority in the juristic achievements of its other. So nothing is lost to the individual but the husk of immediacy. We can say that the individual surrenders to the state its isolated singularity (the claimed self-sufficiency of which is the root of civil society's internal conflict and the cause of totalitarianism's destruction of the singular as such) but receives back official respect and concern for its embedded singularity.

Now, the idea that the singular person's property in specific things is first stabilized inside the dialogical state but outside the latter's public sector lends coherence to the takings clause of the Fifth Amendment. Recall that a right *in rem* was inchoate in a stateless condition, incoherent in civil society, and non-existent in the totalitarian state. Because a right *in rem* first stabilizes as one determination among others of the dialogical state, the latter has eminent domain in the sense that property is intelligible only within it. As there is no coherent property outside the state, no one can assert a property *against* the state. To do so is to adopt the position of moral self-sufficiency that the foregoing logical development has refuted. Inasmuch as no one may assert a property as an external constraint on state authority, the latter may take for ordinary public ends without consent and without having to show necessity or cost–benefit proportionality. Because, however, property exists in the state as the private property approved in a free market and not as a product of the public welfare, the public authority has an unqualified duty to respect it both as legitimated by a mutual recognition and as part of the life sufficient for dignity. For the public authority to respect private property as an internal determination of the state rather than as an external limit, it is enough to compensate the owner at a value judicially determined as fair rather than at a price he negotiates.

---

[46] Hegel 1820b, para. 258.

6. Conclusion

For Hegel, natural right consists in the ensemble of instances of mutual recognition organized within the body of the mutual recognition state. Private property exists because it is one of these instances; it exists subject to limitation because it is *only* one. And the same may be said for the rulers' duty to promote the welfare of those duty-bound to obey them. That idea of reciprocal limitation within a whole explains the otherwise incomprehensible paradox of the Fifth Amendment: a state authority to expropriate for ordinary public ends subject to an unqualified duty to provide just compensation to the owner. It also shows why a liberal should prefer the constitutional guarantee of compensation understood by Hegel to the presumptive right explained by Kant. The separate end-status of the individual person is fulfilled, not in the general-will state in whose sovereignty the individual can stand only as a citizen, but in the dialogical state, within which the individual can stand both as a citizen and an owner.

The argument for a constitutional duty to compensate for a public expropriation goes with a certain understanding of what an expropriation is. It is not any sort of discriminatory harm to economic interests nor does it depend on a taking's imposing a financial burden without promising a compensatory benefit. Someone may be expropriated even if he would end up no worse off in welfare terms. Setting aside citizen obligations (to pay taxes, not to harm common goods), an expropriation is an interference with a thing's subjection to the control, non-nuisance use, and alienating power of someone the validation scale identifies as its relative or absolute owner. So, any legal limitation on exclusive possession, socially ordinary use, or the freedom to alienate non-harmful things is an expropriation unless attached to something allotted from the common store.

It is doubtful, finally, whether any non-Hegelian conception of natural right can resolve the Fifth Amendment paradox. If natural right is equated with an unbounded liberty, then there is, as Hobbes taught, no natural right to own capable of limiting the sovereign. As the origin of the distinction between mine and thine, sovereignty is unlimited by the concept 'mine'; hence it does no wrong in taking without compensating, not even presumptively.[47] If, as Kant thought, there is a natural right to own but no natural, conclusive right to own anything in particular, then there is a presumptive but not absolute right to compensation for a public taking of one's (peaceably acquired) particular holding. If, as Locke claimed, there is a conditional natural right to own the particular thing into which one has infused one's labour, then, absent necessity, the state's forcible taking of an acquisition meeting the condition is robbery with or without compensation. And if the basis of right is the common welfare, then one's property is defined by the sum of the laws embodying distributive justice; and whether compensation is due for the suffering caused by a public taking depends on whether the benefits accruing to the 'owner'

---

[47] Hobbes 1651a, 83, 117.

from the public project will offset his loss. Only if private property and the public welfare are particular instances of an encompassing idea requiring both can they coherently acknowledge each other as an unconditional limit. Thus, only dialogic community explains an authority to expropriate for the public welfare limited by a right of compensation indefeasible by the public welfare.

Though no other theory of natural right can reveal the Fifth Amendment's takings clause as coherent, another line of thought can shed light on the puzzle it contains. A permission in the state forcibly to take someone's holdings for the public welfare combined with an indefeasible duty to compensate the owner might be understood as reflecting the tension in a civil society built on morally self-sufficient atoms. I mean the tension between a public authority justified as actualizing the stateless person's welfare-blind property rights, on the one hand, and the authority of a public welfare hostile to those rights, on the other. Thus a critical theory of atomism yields a critical theory of the takings clause. However, if explanations of legal doctrine that reveal it as coherent are superior to those that criticize it as incoherent, then the Hegelian explanation is better than the critical one. Moreover, viewing it so might change even the way we regard the takings clause from the standpoint of our historical situated-ness within civil society. If that clause belongs to the law of a well-ordered political community, then there is no reason to view it merely as a symptom of the present disorder. We might just as well see the takings clause as the glinting of the well-ordered community *in* the present disorder.

5

Average Reciprocity of Advantage

*Brian Angelo Lee**

1. Introduction

Compensation plays an integral role in the system of practices which constitute the institution of property. This role is most obvious in legal requirements that people or organizations who engage in certain activities that adversely affect other people's property must compensate the owners of the affected property.[1] Compensation requirements therefore provide a lens through which one can obtain a clearer view of the scope and nature of property entitlements and obligations.[2]

In situations where the law says that compensation is owed, three questions immediately arise. One is who should determine the amount of compensation required. Guido Calabresi and Douglas Melamed (1972) famously addressed that issue by distinguishing between 'property rule' protection and 'liability rule' protection for entitlements, and the later literature on this question, much of it inspired by Calabresi and Melamed, is now vast.[3] A second question is what amount of compensation is required. Because the practical outcome of a given case will often depend significantly on specific assessments of the amount of compensation owed, this second question is one which courts and litigants must grapple with routinely.[4]

* I wish to thank James Penner, Henry Smith, and participants in the 2012 Philosophical Foundations of Property Law conference at University College London for their helpful comments on an earlier draft of this chapter. Any errors are my own. The Brooklyn Law School Dean's Summer Research Stipend provided financial support for this project.

[1] These requirements may not be solely legal. There is an extensive literature on the relationship between informal social norms and the institutions of property, and compensation requirements may play a prominent role in those norms. See e.g. Ellickson 1991. Although my discussion here will focus solely on explicitly legal requirements, there may also be connections to these more informal systems of property regulation. Exploring that possibility will have to wait until another day.

[2] This clarity is possible even if one does not necessarily subscribe to the stronger claim that '[o]f course, the so-called remedy defines the nature of the right'. Calabresi 1997, 2205. See also Coleman and Kraus 1986, 1342–3.

[3] Note that Calabresi and Melamed's choice of the term 'property rule' was not intended to imply that property entitlements necessarily receive protection of that sort, but rather that such protection, when found at all, is typically found in property contexts. Property entitlements often receive only 'liability rule' protection. Indeed, that was one of the main focuses of their discussion.

[4] Answering this question in any given case may require considering a variety of perspectives, including the game-theoretic, the economic, and the moral.

However, a third basic question has drawn much less sustained attention: what form should that compensation take? The two basic alternatives are monetary compensation and non-monetary compensation. The latter alternative can be further divided into compensation that is of a form essentially similar to the loss for which compensation is being provided—'in-kind' compensation—and compensation which lacks that essential similarity. Meanwhile, both monetary and non-monetary compensation can be either explicit or implicit.

Some of these possible forms of compensation are, at least on their face, readily understandable. Explicit monetary compensation, for example, is a familiar part of ordinary life. Other options, however, are less straightforward. Of these, implicit in-kind compensation both has played a prominent role in attempts to justify various governmentally imposed burdens on property owners and is particularly theoretically challenging.[5]

The basic notion of implicit in-kind compensation goes by various names: 'average reciprocity of advantage', 'reciprocity of advantage', and 'implicit in-kind compensation' are the most common. Although the terms are frequently used, there has been little close analysis of their meanings, and it is not evident that any significant difference exists among the concepts to which they refer. In this chapter, I shall treat them as essentially interchangeable, but I shall typically use the term that first appeared historically, 'average reciprocity of advantage'.

Although the notion of reciprocal advantage potentially has application in a wide range of contexts, in the United States it typically arises in analyses of the law of eminent domain and of 'regulatory takings'. When the government exercises its power of eminent domain to confiscate privately owned property for use in some public endeavour, a familiar legal principle requires the government to pay compensation to the owners of the taken property. In the United States, this requirement has been elevated to a constitutional mandate. The Fifth Amendment to the US Constitution explicitly provides, 'nor shall private property be taken for public use, without just compensation'.[6]

At first glance, the law governing compensation for physical taking of real property might seem relatively straightforward. Questions quickly arise, however, when property owners assert that a government regulation which affects the use of their property is so restrictive that the regulation's imposition should be treated as equivalent to a physical confiscation and the government should therefore be required to compensate the owners for the inconvenience caused by that regulation. These claims of alleged 'regulatory takings' naturally give rise to two questions: first, whether the governmental action constitutes a 'taking',

---

[5] The phrase 'implicit in-kind compensation' appears to have been first coined by Richard Epstein (1985). Although I shall borrow the term, I do not wish to imply that what I mean here by that term and what Epstein meant are necessarily identical.

[6] US Const. amend. V. In 1897 the US Supreme Court held that this amendment is binding on state governments as well as the federal government, by virtue of having been 'incorporated' in the Fourteenth Amendment. *Chicago, B. & Q. R. Co. v Chicago* 1897, 236–8. State constitutions themselves typically contain similar language.

and, second, if it does, what amount of compensation would be 'just' for a taking of this sort.[7]

Judicial and academic discussions of these two questions have often appealed to the concept of average reciprocity of advantage. However, these appeals have frequently been cursory, leaving the concept unanalysed and consequently failing to understand its limitations. This chapter aims to rectify that situation. Its discussion shall proceed as follows. First, a brief survey of prominent examples from judicial opinions and academic commentary will give us a basic idea of what work the concept is intended to accomplish and how it is thought to achieve those ends. I then shall argue that the classic paradigm of average reciprocity of advantage is best understood as arising from a regulation's having solved a coordination problem, and that the specific conditions necessary for regulatory burdens to reliably provide a genuine reciprocal advantage are likely to be satisfied only infrequently. Hence, when we closely examine attempts to justify various property regulations on the grounds that the owners burdened by those regulations have been made whole by receiving in-kind compensation, we see the implausibility of such justifications. Nevertheless, I argue, we should not conclude that average reciprocity of advantage therefore has no role to play in justifying property regulations, since such a conclusion would itself have implausible implications inconsistent with broadly and deeply held convictions about the legitimate scope of such regulations. Instead, I shall suggest, the proper conclusion is that when government regulations burden property owners, the presence of reciprocal advantages benefiting those owners derives its importance, in significant part, not from an illusory potential to make property owners whole but rather from the role that such reciprocity plays in preserving the respect due to civic equals.

2. Background

The basic notion of in-kind compensation or average reciprocity of advantage has been invoked to justify several central features of property law, including states' power of eminent domain, the permissibility of zoning, and more generally the power to regulate property uses under certain circumstances without owing monetary compensation (i.e. without committing a 'regulatory taking'). Although these justifications follow a similar general strategy of arguing that the presence of a reciprocal advantage remedies any deficiencies left behind by incomplete or wholly absent monetary compensation, the details of those justifications vary depending on context. Hence, before we attempt to analyse the concept of average reciprocity of advantage, it will be helpful to begin with a brief survey of these varied applications, in order to acquire a clearer sense of what work the concept typically is intended to do.

---

[7] Although these questions are conceptually distinct, in practice they are sometimes conflated, with the answer to the first question about whether a regulatory taking has occurred hingeing upon whether the property owner has received sufficient 'in-kind' compensation to balance out the burdens imposed by the restriction.

2.1 Judicial opinions

The case generally credited with introducing 'average reciprocity of advantage' into the American legal lexicon is *Pennsylvania Coal Co. v Mahon*, decided by the US Supreme Court in 1922.[8] At issue was the constitutionality of the Kohler Act, a Pennsylvania statute which prohibited mining for coal in ways which would cause the subsidence of residences located above the mine shafts. The Pennsylvania Coal Company had earlier sold the surface rights to certain land to Mahon (or Mahon's predecessor in interest), but the contract had reserved the right to extract all of the coal under the surface and had explicitly allocated any risk of subsidence to the owners of the surface rights.[9] Despite those express contractual provisions, Mahon sought an injunction to prohibit the company from removing coal that provided support for the land's surface, arguing that the Kohler Act prohibited such removal. The trial court denied the injunction, finding the Act to be unconstitutional; the Pennsylvania Supreme Court reversed, and a subsequent appeal brought the case before the US Supreme Court.

Justice Oliver Wendell Holmes, Jr, writing for the majority, began his analysis of the case by noting that '[g]overnment hardly could go on if to some extent values incident to property could not be diminished without paying for every such change in the general law'.[10] However, once the diminishment 'reaches a certain magnitude, in most if not in all cases there must be an exercise of eminent domain and compensation to sustain the act'.[11] The court ultimately concluded that this particular regulation did go 'too far' and therefore constituted a 'taking' for constitutional purposes. However, in reaching that conclusion, the court had to distinguish an earlier case, *Plymouth Coal Co. v Pennsylvania*, which had upheld another regulation limiting the amount of coal that could be removed from a mine. That regulation had required 'the owners of adjoining coal properties to cause boundary pillars of coal to be left of sufficient width to safeguard the employees of either mine in case the other should be abandoned and allowed to fill with water'.[12]

Holmes distinguished *Plymouth Coal* on two grounds. First, the regulation in that case was necessary to protect third parties—it 'was a requirement for the safety of employees invited into the mine'—rather than merely a means of restoring

---

[8] The court actually had already used the phrase in *Jackman v Rosenbaum Co.*, decided seven weeks before the decision in *Mahon*. Although both opinions were written by Justice Oliver Wendell Holmes, Jr, *Jackman* never attained the prominence that *Mahon* has enjoyed in recent decades. For an analytical overview of the development of the concept of average reciprocity of advantage in US Supreme Court jurisprudence, see Oswald 1997, 1489–522.

[9] Whether the contract was with Mahon or Mahon's predecessor in interest is unclear from the court's discussion. All that matters legally, however, is that during the relevant period a covenant bound Mahon and the coal company.

[10] *Pennsylvania Coal Co. v Mahon* 1922, 413.

[11] *Pennsylvania Coal Co. v Mahon* 1922, 413.

[12] *Plymouth Coal Co. v Pennsylvania* 1914, 540. The *Plymouth Coal* court noted that neither party questioned the constitutionality of the regulation which was the focus of that decision. The issue under dispute concerned the proper method for determining how large the required pillars would have to be.

landowners' subsidence rights which they had freely bargained away.[13] Second, the regulation in *Plymouth Coal* 'secured an average reciprocity of advantage that has been recognised as a justification of various laws'.[14] The latter explanation became the principle for which this case is remembered.

Justice Brandeis, however, offered a vigorous dissent. He conceded that average reciprocity of advantage, conceived as Holmes did, was 'an important consideration, and may even be an essential [*sic*]' when the state was exercising its power 'for the purposes of conferring benefits' on others, but when the goal was 'to protect the public from detriment and danger', average reciprocity of advantage was irrelevant. Brandeis reached this conclusion on the basis of previous Supreme Court cases which had upheld the constitutionality of harm-preventing regulations, contending that in each case the owner who suffered the restriction enjoyed 'no reciprocal advantage . . . unless it be the advantage of living and doing business in a civilized community'.[15]

As a matter of interpreting the Fifth Amendment's constraints on the scope of governmental power, later US Supreme Court decisions declined fully to embrace the potentially sweeping implications of Justice Holmes's analysis. Nevertheless, the notion of reciprocal advantage continued to play a role both implicitly and explicitly in Supreme Court opinions.[16]

The most prominent explicit invocation of the principle came decades later in Justice William Rehnquist's dissent in *Penn Central Transportation Co. v New York City*. At issue in *Penn Central* was New York City's Landmarks Preservation Law, which had been enacted in the wake of the 1965 destruction of Manhattan's stately Pennsylvania Station and was now being challenged for its prohibition of alterations to Grand Central Terminal.[17] Explicitly invoking Holmes's language in *Mahon*, Rehnquist argued that because the buildings protected as 'landmarks' were scattered throughout the city rather than concentrated together in zoning units, the owners of those landmarked buildings received no average reciprocity of advantage from the existence of the restriction. Therefore the regulation should be deemed a taking, because it sharply reduced Grand Central's economic value 'with no comparable reciprocal benefits'.[18]

The majority, however, held that the regulation was not a taking under the Fifth Amendment. Justice William Brennan's majority opinion conceded that '[i]t is, of course, true that the Landmarks Law has a more severe impact on some landowners than on others', but asserted that this fact 'in itself, does not mean that the law

---

[13] Holmes asserted that the third parties in *Mahon*, who had chosen explicitly to sell their right to surface support, could be protected simply by being warned in advance that subsidence was likely.

[14] *Pennsylvania Coal Co. v Mahon* 1922, 415. Holmes did not indicate whether either of these two bases for distinguishing the cases would have been sufficient to do so on their own. Nor did he indicate the relative weight of these two considerations.

[15] *Pennsylvania Coal Co. v Mahon* 1922, 422.

[16] See generally Coletta 1990, 304–45; Oswald 1997, 1489–520.

[17] *Penn Central Transportation Co. v New York City* 1978.

[18] *Penn Central Transportation Co. v New York City* 1978, 140 (Rehnquist, J., dissenting). Chief Justice Warren Burger and Justice John Paul Stevens joined in the dissent.

effects a "taking"'.[19] Invoking past cases which had upheld regulations restricting landowners' ability to engage in activities harmful to their neighbours, Brennan noted that '[l]egislation designed to promote the general welfare commonly burdens some more than others.... Similarly, zoning laws often affect some property owners more severely than others, but have not been held to be invalid on that account'.[20]

Nevertheless, even Brennan felt the pull of the reciprocal advantage intuition, and he hastened to argue that the owners of Grand Central received at least partial compensation from the landmark law's operation: 'Unless we are to reject the judgment of the New York City Council that the preservation of landmarks benefits all New York citizens and all structures, both economically and by improving the quality of life in the city as a whole—which we are unwilling to do—we cannot conclude that the owners of the Terminal have in no sense been benefited by the Landmarks Law'.[21] Thus, although full reciprocity clearly wasn't required as a constitutional matter, the presence of at least partial reciprocity continued to be important.

In *Keystone Bituminous Coal Ass'n v DeBenedictis*, the US Supreme Court suggested that average reciprocity of advantage is the justification even for the state's police power (while adopting a very generous accounting of reciprocal advantage to uphold the constitutionality of the regulation in question).[22] Writing for the majority, Justice John Paul Stevens, who had joined Rehnquist's dissent in *Penn Central*, cited that dissent as he asserted that '[t]he Court's hesitance to find a taking when the State merely restrains uses of property that are tantamount to public nuisances is consistent with the notion of "reciprocity of advantage" that Justice Holmes referred to in Pennsylvania Coal. Under our system of government, one of the State's primary ways of preserving the public weal is restricting the uses individuals can make of their property. While each of us is burdened somewhat by such restrictions, we, in turn, benefit greatly from the restrictions that are placed on others. These restrictions are properly treated as part of the burden of common citizenship.'[23]

---

[19] *Penn Central Transportation Co. v New York City* 1978, 133.

[20] *Penn Central Transportation Co. v New York City* 1978, 133–4. The fact that Brennan relied on cases which involved activities harmful to neighbours left his argument potentially open to the objection, modelled on Brandeis's dissent in *Mahon*, that even if average reciprocity of advantage was irrelevant for regulation of harmful activities, it still remained a relevant requirement for property regulations which were designed to produce a public benefit rather than to prevent a public harm. However, Brennan could have two available lines of reply. First, he might have argued that landmark preservation law was in fact a harm-prevention measure. (The harm in question was the loss of aesthetic value imposed by the planned alterations to Grand Central.) Second, he might have invoked the academic literature which has argued that there is no principled way to distinguish between imposing harm and ceasing to provide benefits.

[21] *Penn Central Transportation Co. v New York City* 1978, 134–5.

[22] *Keystone Bituminous Coal Ass'n v DeBenedictis* 1987.

[23] *Keystone Bituminous Coal Ass'n v DeBenedictis* 1987, 491 (internal citations, quotation marks, and footnote reference marks omitted). Justice Stevens's argument that the regulation in *Keystone* complied with the requirements endorsed by the *Penn Central* dissenters did not sway Justice Rehnquist, who remained a dissenter in *Keystone* as well.

2.2 Academic commentators

Academic commentary has also made appeal to average reciprocity of advantage. We can briefly catalogue some prominent examples.

Lee Anne Fennell has invoked the idea as a general justification for the eminent domain power.[24] Fennell starts from the assertion that the ordinary practice (in the United States) of providing compensation equal to the assessed fair market value of the taken property systematically shortchanges the owners of that property, leaving a substantial 'uncompensated increment' between the value which owners of taken property place on that property and the fair market value that they receive in compensation.[25] Therefore, Fennell argues, an important question is whether receiving reciprocal advantages—or 'in-kind' compensation—might close the compensation gap sufficiently to justify the existing eminent domain system.[26] The key issue for Fennell is whether 'this exercise of eminent domain [is] of a type that, if universalized, would provide back to the burdened landowner enough benefits to induce a reasonable landowner's willing participation in the overall scheme'. The answer matters, because '[i]f the overall system delivers results that are both efficient and distributively acceptable, then we might hypothesize that landowners are receiving back from the system enough in-kind benefits to make up for the burdens that the system imposes on them'.[27]

Frank Michelman's classic discussion of utilitarian justifications for eminent domain suggests that to the extent that 'demoralization costs' are a significant source of disutility, condemnees' perceptions of receiving reciprocal advantages from the overall system of eminent domain could help tilt the utilitarian calculus in favour of permitting condemnation. The relevant questions, then, are: first, whether 'there [is] implicit in the measure some reciprocity of burdens coupled with benefits (as, for example, in a measure restricting a large area to residential development) or does it channel benefits and burdens to different persons?' And,

---

[24] Fennell 2004, 987–9.

[25] Fennell is not alone in making that assertion. Indeed, today it appears to be generally accepted in the academic takings literature. See e.g. *Coniston Corp. v Village of Hoffman Estates* 1988, 464 (Posner, J.); Merrill 1986, 83. I have argued elsewhere that there is good reason to question that assertion. See Lee 2013. However, determining that assertion's ultimate accuracy is unnecessary for the purposes of our inquiry.

[26] James Krier and Christopher Serkin have offered a similar justification for states' power of eminent domain, at least when that power is exercised for genuinely public uses: 'Over time... imbalances should even out as those whose property is taken in one round for one public use are later benefited by other public uses subsidized by condemnation of other private property.' Krier and Serkin 2004, 866.

[27] Fennell 2004, 987. There is a potential circularity problem lurking in Fennell's argument, because our judgments about whether a legal system is distributively acceptable themselves depend upon our judgments about what sorts of compensation, including implicit in-kind compensation, are paid to burdened parties. It is no surprise that if we start by assuming that the overall system is in fact distributively acceptable, then we might naturally hypothesize that landowners are receiving adequate in-kind benefits, since the truth of that hypothesis was already included in the initial assumption: unless we already believe that landowners are receiving adequate benefits in compensation for the burdens imposed upon them, we cannot confidently assert that the system indeed is distributively acceptable.

second, how likely is it that the 'members of the class burdened by the measure' were able to influence the decision to impose the measure sufficiently 'to have extracted some compensatory concession "in kind"'?[28]

Michelman himself seems rather sceptical about the possibility of genuine reciprocity in such circumstances, describing these sorts of reciprocity considerations as serving 'a utilitarian purpose to cater to the sense of security by preserving an illusion of long-run indiscriminateness in the distribution of social burdens and benefits'.[29] However, Michelman later returns to the justificatory potential of reciprocal advantage when he presents a Rawlsian 'fairness'-based account of permissible uses of eminent domain. Michelman focuses on a probability-based interpretation of reciprocal advantage: 'A decision not to compensate is not unfair as long as the disappointed claimant ought to be able to appreciate how such decisions might fit into a consistent practice which holds forth a lesser long-run risk to people like him than would any consistent practice which is naturally suggested by the opposite decision'.[30]

Lynda Oswald has developed the idea that average reciprocity of advantage may be relevant in zoning contexts.[31] Such reciprocity, she suggests, provides a justification for the subset of zoning ordinances that prohibit non-hazardous activities, such as 'height or minimum-yard regulations'.[32] These restrictions

confer benefits upon similarly situated property owners by holding each of them to a uniform standard. Although each property owner may find use of his or her land restricted by the regulation, each is benefited by having similar burdens imposed upon his or her neighbors. Thus, although a property owner might be limited to residential use, he or she is secure in the knowledge that neighboring properties are also so limited, and that a factory will not be erected in the midst of the residential area, where it would greatly diminish the value of his or her residential property.[33]

Richard Epstein makes extensive use of average reciprocity of advantage, under the name 'implicit in-kind compensation', in his broad account of when the state may impose restrictions that burden property owners without paying those owners monetary compensation. Such restrictions are justified, Epstein argues, only if they either are imposed under the state's 'police power' to regulate nuisances and similar harmful activities or are accompanied by implicit in-kind compensation sufficient to leave the burdened property owner at least as well off as he was before the

---

[28] Michelman 1967, 1218.   [29] Michelman 1967, 1218.   [30] Michelman 1967, 1223.
[31] Oswald 1997, 1510.
[32] She asserts that zoning ordinances prohibiting hazardous activities 'are more properly grounded in the state's nuisance-prevention power'. Oswald 1997, 1510. However, some people would decline to draw this distinction, and would instead suggest that even the police power itself derives from the presence of reciprocal advantage. Justice Holmes's opinion in *Jackman* provides one example. Holmes asserted that the 'exercise of [the police power] has been held warranted in some cases by what we may call the average reciprocity of advantage, although the advantages may not be equal in the particular case'. *Jackman v Rosenbaum Co.* 1922, 30. (I am not certain that the cases which Holmes cites to support this assertion actually do what Holmes claims. However, resolving such details is unnecessary for our present topic.) I take up this suggestion below, in discussing the US Supreme Court's decision in *L'Hote v New Orleans* 1900.
[33] Oswald 1997, 1510.

regulation was imposed.[34] (In a footnote, Epstein argues that the principle even can explain the rules governing judicial bias.[35])

One common thread running through these academic discussions is use of the concept of reciprocal advantage to justify governmental restrictions on property owners—either through regulation or physically taking the property—by asserting that because average reciprocity of advantage has provided the burdened owners with sufficient compensation, those owners have no just grounds for complaint (and thus no claim for additional monetary compensation). The question that naturally arises then is exactly how 'average reciprocity of advantage' provides that compensation, and whether that sort of compensation can do the justificatory work that has been asked of it.

3. Sources of Average Reciprocity of Advantage

Addressing that question requires first identifying exactly what average reciprocity of advantage is, and how it arises. Justice Holmes's seminal *Mahon* opinion offers no elaboration of the concept of 'average reciprocity of advantage' or of its role in justifying regulations.[36] What it does offer is a reference to *Plymouth Coal* as a paradigm situation in which average reciprocity of advantage is present. Hence, identifying exactly how average reciprocity arises in that case will help us to identify more generally when such reciprocity will be available to provide compensation for the burdens of government action, and, I shall argue, will also reveal that this availability is likely to be infrequent. The key first step in this inquiry is to see that

---

[34] Epstein 1985, 195–215.

[35] Epstein 1985, 196 n. 2. Epstein's argument in brief: 'When the state resolves a dispute between A and B, it wrongfully takes property if it makes the incorrect judgment. Forcing A to pay B $100 for a debt not owed takes $100 from A. Not making A pay the $100 when it is owed takes it from B. The demand for unbiased judges therefore translates into a demand that the probability of error be symmetrically distributed, so that each side receives, in the form of erroneous judgments in its favor, ex ante compensation for those erroneous judgments entered against it' (internal citations omitted). Thus, Epstein concludes, requirements that judges be unbiased ensure that litigants receive sufficient in-kind compensation for the rule that bars litigants from suing judges for allegedly erroneous judgments. Unfortunately, this argument suffers from a fatal flaw, springing from its tacit reliance on an assumption of repeated trips through the legal system. If a particular litigant appears in court only once, there is zero chance that any error will offset. If a litigant appears only a few times, the chances that errors will perfectly offset are poor. Only if a litigant appears so often that the Law of Large Numbers applies will Epstein's result reliably occur. Outside of that extreme situation, all that one could say is that each litigant has an equal *ex ante* subjective probability of coming out ahead or coming out behind. However, that probability cannot plausibly be advanced as a form of compensation. If Jones suffers a loss as a result of an erroneous judgment, no one would say that she is made whole by the fact that there had been a chance that she might not have suffered the loss, or even by the fact that there had been a chance that she might enjoy an erroneous gain. Thus, whatever the justification is for judicial immunity for erroneous judgments, implicit in-kind compensation cannot be it.

[36] With respect to the purely constitutional question, the 'reciprocity of advantage' which a regulation offered appears to be relevant for calculating the net amount of burden that the regulated landowner suffers and therefore whether the regulation went 'too far'. However, Holmes's language was not entirely clear, and he does not indicate how 'average reciprocity of advantage' is distinct from simple 'reciprocity of advantage'.

the reason why the regulation in *Plymouth Coal* produced an average reciprocity of advantage was because the regulation had the effect of solving a coordination problem.

Suppose that two owners of adjacent parcels are both engaged in mining coal. Both owners have a straightforward economic incentive to dig out as much coal as possible in order to maximize their profit. However, both owners also realize that the other owner may be the first to exhaust the mine on his property, at which point the abandoned mine may be flooded.[37] If the amount of coal remaining between the two mines at that time is small, then it will not be able to withstand the pressure applied by the influx of water from a flood in a neighbouring mine, and if that coal barrier gives way, the dry mine will be flooded as well.

From the perspective of the owner of the still-operational mine, the flooding is economically costly in several potential ways. First, it may make remaining coal deposits wholly inaccessible. Second, even if access to some of the remaining coal can be restored by means of pumping, draining those areas will be quite expensive. Third, the cost of rescuing miners trapped by the flooding and of compensating the families of miners who were killed will further decrease profits. (Even a mine owner who is bereft of any compassion for his miners cannot abandon trapped miners or the families of fallen miners without cost, since such behaviour would make it difficult or impossible to find people who would be willing to work in his mines. And without miners, a mine has no economic value.) As a result, a profit-maximizing owner has strong self-interested reasons to avoid premature flooding of his mine.[38]

Now a coordination problem becomes evident. Suppose that the two adjacent miners are Jones and Smith, and that C is the number of feet of coal which must remain in order to provide an adequate barrier against flooding. Jones has three options. If she is cautious she can cease mining when the mine shaft reaches a point C feet from the property line. Unless Smith has trespassed on her property, Jones then can be sure that her mine will not flood even if Smith floods his mine. However, by leaving C feet of coal unextracted, Jones foregoes considerable

---

[37] Accidental flooding of coal mines was an ever-present danger. For a brief survey of the problem, written a few years after the ruling in *Mahon*, see Ash 1941. For a catalogue of major US coal mine disasters involving inundations, see Keenan 1963, 66–78.

[38] My reading of *Plymouth Coal* here diverges from Abraham Bell's. Bell (2009) takes the 'reciprocity' in this case to be protection of the mineworkers. Bell's reading seems incompatible both with the text of Holmes's opinion—which explicitly distinguished between protecting workers' safety and average reciprocity of advantage—and with the logic of the argument. It is not at all clear that diminishing the risk to the workers' health would necessarily provide as much value *to the mine owner* as the unextracted coal did. Moreover, the Pennsylvania Supreme Court's decision, which the US Supreme Court was reviewing, made it clear that providing an advantage to mine owners was an important aspect of the statute. Thus, in finding the statute to be justified, the Pennsylvania court quoted from its judgment in an earlier state case involving a similar regulation: 'This rib of solid coal not to be mined into by either of the adjoining owners was to be contributed by each in equal parts for the mutual benefit of each, for the protection of the surface, to secure independent systems of ventilation, drainage and workings, and in aid of an industry so great and widely diffused that the State as a whole is interested therein.... This regulation works no hardship on one for the benefit of another, but is impartial, just and reasonable, imposing a common burden for the benefit of all such owners'. *Commonwealth v Plymouth Coal Co.* 1911, 149 (quoting *Mapel v John* 1896).

potential profit. So if Jones is daring or thinks she has accurate information that Smith is cautious, Jones might extend her mine all the way to the property line, in the hope that Smith will have chosen to leave C feet of coal unextracted on his property.

Either of these two options is potentially less than optimal both for society and for the individual owners. If Jones is daring but guessed wrong about what Smith would do, the barrier between the two mines will be thin, and Jones's mine will flood when Smith's does. In the likely event that the costs of a prematurely flooded mine are considerably greater than the market value of C feet of coal, Jones will have suffered a large loss (and total social wealth will have suffered to the same extent, since no one gained from Jones's loss). On the other hand, if Jones acted cautiously but Smith was equally cautious, then both will have stopped excavating when C feet of coal remained on their property, leaving unextracted twice as much coal as necessary. Jones suffers a loss of profit from the needlessly unextracted coal, and again this is a deadweight social loss since no one gains from Jones's loss.[39]

Either way, a third option is preferable: ideally, Jones and Smith would each mine up to C/2 feet from the property line. This would provide a total barrier of C feet to prevent flooding, while halving the amount of foregone profit that each would suffer as a result of leaving unextracted coal. The social product would be maximized, and both Smith and Jones would be better off compared to either scenarios noted above. This advantage would not necessarily be reciprocal in every circumstance; Jones would still personally be better off if she extracted coal all the way to the property line and Smith turned out to have acted cautiously. In those circumstances, she would maximize her profit from the coal near the border and would still enjoy safety from flooding. However, if Jones cannot be certain in advance which strategy Smith will follow and if she has multiple mines (as is likely for a mining company) and therefore will be engaging in this game many times, the expected payoff of following that strategy is likely to be less than the payoff from splitting the costs of safety, assuming that the costs of one or more prematurely flooded mines outweigh the profit obtainable from an extra C/2 feet of coal in the relevant mineshafts. Thus, on average both Jones's mining company and Smith's will enjoy a reciprocal advantage if they both reliably leave C/2 feet of coal on each side of the property line.

This is, of course, precisely the outcome which the regulation in *Plymouth Coal* produces.[40] The regulation then is a permissible restriction on mine owners' property rights because it in fact enhances the practical scope of those rights.

---

[39] This cost could be substantial. In *Plymouth Coal*, the counsel for the coal company stated that the amount of coal which the lower court had required be left unmined in that case 'amounted to 734,147 tons, which could be mined at a net profit of about $300,000'. *Plymouth Coal Co. v Pennsylvania* 1914. Using the US Consumer Price Index to adjust for inflation, that sum would be equivalent to approximately $6.9 million in 2012 dollars.

[40] Because the effect of the regulation is mutually advantageous, in an ideal world private bargaining might have produced the same outcome without government intervention. However, the importance of many potential impediments to private bargaining has been thoroughly established since at least as far back as Coase 1960. When such impediments are significant, government regulation may accomplish what private bargaining cannot.

They are now free to mine to within C/2 feet of the property line rather than having to choose between stopping C feet from the property line or running a significant risk of a catastrophic loss. Thus, considered in its application over many mines, the regulation limits the amount of coal that might permissibly be extracted in any individual instance but increases the total amount of coal that the mines' owner can extract in the aggregate. The 'average reciprocity of advantage' which the regulation provides removes any rational grounds for the burdened owners to complain about it.[41]

Once we turn our attention to the facts in *Mahon*, however, the picture looks quite different. The regulation prohibiting mining activities which cause subsidence protects owners of surface rights from harm (either economic or physical) but provides no benefit to mining companies that own the subsurface rights. The amount of coal that those companies are physically capable of extracting is not lessened by surface subsidence, nor does such subsidence impose any extra costs on the miners. Hence the regulation provides no advantage at all to the mining companies, for whom its imposition is a net loss. Their objections to the regulation cannot be dismissed as irrational.

Two important features of average reciprocity of advantage should now be evident. First, it arises in situations in which there is a commensurability between the burden and the benefit, and the benefit is at least as large as the burden. In *Plymouth Coal*, the burden and benefit were both measured in extractable amounts of coal, and the regulation had the effect of increasing the amount of coal that mine owners could practically expect to acquire over time. Since the burden and benefit were in the same currency, and they both are tangible and measurable, we can be confident that the regulation in fact does leave everyone better off, except perhaps in extraordinary circumstances. Hence, the parties 'burdened' by the regulation would be objectively irrational to object to it.[42] Second, this net positive result was possible because the regulation in question solved a coordination problem.

---

[41] This is slightly overstated. If the burdened owner will not be a repeat player—perhaps because she owns only one mine, intends to close it in the near future, and leave the mining business forever—then the owner will not necessarily enjoy the long-term benefits of coordination. (If mining is the most valuable use for that property, she will still be able to benefit financially from the regulation by selling the property, since the regulation's beneficial effect on the profitability of mining will be included in the property's market price. However, if mining is not the property's highest-value use, or if she happens to have a high personal value in using the property for some other purpose, then the regulation will not benefit her.) However, there is little that lawmakers can do about such a case when setting general rules. If this owner's idiosyncratic preferences were to determine the general permissibility of regulations that serve a generally valuable coordinating function, then the law would let this owner impose her idiosyncratic preferences in a way that decreased the value of every other mining company's property. As the basic law of nuisance demonstrates, property law in general does not recognize any such right (or, perhaps better stated, recognizes a duty not to impose too much on others). Thus uses which are idiosyncratic in a given area and unreasonably interfere with others' use and enjoyment of their property can be abated as nuisances, while owners who suffer inconvenience as a result of their hypersensitivity to uses which are reasonable and ordinary in a given area have no remedy under nuisance. See e.g. American Law Institute 1979, § 821F; *Walter v Selfe* 1851 64 ER 849, 852 (Ch.); 4 De G & Sm 315, 322.

[42] Of course, a mine owner did care to challenge the regulation in *Plymouth Coal*, despite the advantage. The motivation for that challenge, however, was not any objection to the requirement that

4. The Limits of 'In-Kind' Compensation

Coordination problems are only one type of bargaining problem. Other types exist, and governments sometimes impose regulations to address them.[43] The most prominent sort of problem in property theory is the problem of open-access resources, which potentially gives rise to 'tragedy of the commons' situations.[44] Hence, a form of 'average reciprocity of advantage' argument might seem a promising choice to provide the basic elements for a justification of property systems at a very general level.[45] However, the regulations which address these other types of problem do not necessarily generate a similar reciprocity of advantage, and in fact commonly will not. The conditions that we have observed produce an average reciprocity of advantage for the regulated parties are sufficiently stringent—benefits provided in the same currency as the costs of the regulation, in an amount greater than the loss, with the result that objecting to the regulation would ordinarily be irrational—that the presence of genuine reciprocity of this sort is likely to be infrequent.

---

some coal be left in place as a barrier, but rather disapproval of the procedures used to determine the specific amount of coal that would have to be left in place. The coal company's counsel stated: 'The complaint of plaintiff in error is made solely on the ground that the manner and method of fixing the width of a barrier pillar between adjoining coal properties described in the act is unconstitutional, and if allowed to stand, will be productive of much injustice and consequent litigation.' *Plymouth Coal Co. v. Pennsylvania* 1914.

[43] I use the term 'bargaining problem' to refer generically to situations in which private negotiation cannot be relied upon to produce the optimal outcome. Such problems can arise for many reasons, including lack of perfect information or the presence of significant transaction costs. Moreover, disagreement may exist about what outcomes are 'optimal'. Sorting through those large issues is unnecessary for present purposes. The term 'bargaining problem' here is merely a loose and convenient shorthand.

[44] The problem addressed in *Plymouth Coal* bears some obvious similarities to the classic 'tragedy of the commons' scenario, but the two are not identical. Obviously, if the resource in question is just coal in general, large amounts of coal extraction will continue, even over the long run, with or without the regulation. Even if we define the relevant resource more narrowly, as the amount of coal that potentially could be mined if the regulation exists but which will not be available absent the regulation if both mining companies pursue the same strategy (either risky or risk avoiding), the coal problem still differs, because one possible outcome is *under*-extraction of the resource (if both parties are risk averse) rather than overuse. In such cases, a subsequent reallocation of property rights, so that both parcels were owned by the same party, would permit safe extraction of the remaining excess coal. By contrast, in ordinary common-pool open-access problems, once the inefficient rush to extract has run its course, there is no way to recover any of the lost potential resources imposed by the inefficiency. Once oil has been brought up from the ground inefficiently quickly, producing excessive storage costs and damaging the geological structure of the oilfield in a way that limits the total amount of oil available for extraction, there is no way to recapture those losses by reallocating rights to the oilfield. One cannot simply pump the oil back into the ground. The famous boom and bust of the Lucas oilfield at Spindletop in the early 20th century is a classic example of this phenomenon. See e.g. Craft 1995, 701.

[45] Joseph Raz 1990, 6–11, offers a coordination-based theory of law's authority in general. Raz's focus is much broader than the topic of our discussion, which assumes that law can be authoritative and focuses instead on issues concerning the normative adequacy of particular sorts of laws. Although there may be interesting interactions between coordination-based accounts of the authority of all law and coordination-based justifications for specific laws, space does not permit exploring that possibility here.

An example may help make this point clear. Some cities in cold-weather climates have laws requiring that building owners shovel the sidewalks in front of their buildings after a snowfall.[46] Although building owners do not own those sidewalks, the regulation imposes upon them an affirmative duty to keep those sidewalks clear of snow. The regulation's benefit to society is obvious. Sidewalks laden with snow are at best inconvenient to pedestrians, and at worst dangerous. Because sidewalks are linear, travelling from a point in front of one building to a point in front of another building requires travelling along the sidewalk in front of each intervening building. Thus, snow in front of one building harms not only those people who walk to or from that particular building, but also anyone who wishes to walk between locations located on opposite sides of that building.[47] For sidewalks on a given block to perform their function, every segment of the sidewalk needs to be clear.

This is a garden-variety assembly problem, with the accompanying customary concerns about holdouts. In the eminent domain context, the solution to the possibility that holdouts may impede completion of public projects requiring the assembly of large numbers of parcels is to permit the government to compel owners to sell the necessary parcels. In the sidewalk context, the solution is to require owners to keep the sidewalks free from snow.

At first glance, this scenario might seem similar to the *Plymouth Coal* scenario: because the passableness of the sidewalk in total depends upon the passableness of each of the sidewalk's segments, the payoff to any one building owner of shovelling snow depends upon the actions of other building owners. Moreover, considered from one perspective, the particular cost imposed upon each owner, namely a duty to keep a segment of sidewalk free of snow, receives compensation of exactly the same sort—other owners' having a duty to keep adjoining segments free of snow.

There is, however, one pivotal difference between the two. Coal mining companies necessarily care about extracting more coal. That is the very fact that creates the problem which the *Plymouth Coal* regulation addresses, namely excessive extraction of coal in the short run. The payment provided by average reciprocity in *Plymouth Coal* then is not only in the same currency—extracted coal—as the burden imposed by the regulation, but is also a payment that we can be certain that the recipient cares to receive. In the sidewalk case, by contrast, although the compensation could once again be thought of as in the same currency as the cost—clean stretches of sidewalk—there is no certainty that the burdened party

---

[46] Larissa Katz has written about these laws in some detail (Katz 2012). Arthur Ripstein (2009) also touches upon them in the course of offering a Kantian analysis of the state's authority to establish public roads and enforce traffic laws. Ripstein's account explicitly foregoes any assumptions of a balance between individual burdens and benefits, appealing instead to 'the systematic requirements of individual freedom, which depend on distinctively public spaces'. Ripstein 2009, 233.

[47] The inconveniences include getting one's pants dirty, ruining dress shoes, soaking one's socks, and not being able to walk or wheel across the section that is covered in snow. Note that these inconveniences are largely binary—pants that are dirty have to be laundered, no matter how dirty they are, damaged dress shoes either must be repaired or discarded, even if only slightly damaged, and a patch of snow that is too deep to travel through is an insuperable obstacle whether it is 10 feet across or 100 (just as a deep unbridged river stops all land travel, no matter how wide the river is).

cares to receive that particular currency. Whether the sidewalk is buried in snow may be a matter of complete indifference to some building owners. For example, people who travel in cars can easily enter or exit the building's driveway no matter how much snow is located elsewhere. Other owners might prefer a snow-free sidewalk but not enough to outweigh the cost to them of cleaning their own sidewalk—for example, aged shut-ins who rarely venture outside. For these groups of people, the value of the 'compensation' received is less than the cost of the burden which the regulation has imposed upon them. The advantage isn't really 'reciprocal', because the net utility of the regulation differs across burdened persons.

Although the regulation requiring the shovelling of sidewalks imposes an affirmative duty, the same problem arises in regulations that impose negative duties as well. Richard Epstein has suggested that 'implicit in-kind compensation' can justify a significant range of negative regulations—for example, regulations prohibiting large signs—by ensuring that the parties affected by the regulation are no worse off than they would have been without the regulation: 'The landowner who cannot erect a large sign is assured that his neighbor cannot put up a sign that will block his own.'[48]

The problems with this example are illuminating. Suppose that X owns commercial real estate and that a major road runs along that parcel's northern edge. Further suppose that Y owns a parcel immediately south of X's property. (X's property is thus located between Y's property and the road.) A regulation prohibiting large signs may be quite burdensome to X, who is hampered in attracting travellers to his business. The fact that Y suffers a similar limitation is little consolation to X, since even if Y erected a large sign which blocked the view of X's sign from certain angles, X's sign would still be visible from the road, the one angle that really matters. Moreover, Y may have no interest in having a large sign at all, in which case X has received literally zero benefit from the regulation. Or X might enjoy the art of sign painting and would be happy to have his large sign be visible only from vantage points inside his own property. In all of these situations, X has received no 'in-kind compensation' from the regulation. There is no average reciprocity of advantage.

These problems intensify when one of the purposes of the regulation is to address the interests of future generations. Rules which require environmental remediation, ecological conservation, or architectural preservation are obvious examples of rules that are enacted in significant part because of their very long-term benefits. Such rules may be wise, but they necessarily lack reciprocity of advantage. Although we who are alive today can do much to benefit or burden the future, time's arrow prevents future generations from returning the favour (or exacting revenge). Future generations may be grateful for regulations which required that the present generation plant trees which will reach maturity decades in the future, but there is no way for those future generations to reciprocate by increasing the amount of greenery available today.

---

[48] Epstein 1985, 196.

There is no avoiding this problem by appealing to future generations' ability to make sacrifices themselves to benefit still later generations. Although such future sacrifices could plausibly forestall any claims of unjust enrichment by our descendants, they do not in fact provide compensation to the present.[49] Indeed, only those people who care much about the fate of later generations in this specific regard would even find those future sacrifices appealing, and those people likely would already have voluntarily made the sort of sacrifices which the regulation demands. The regulation exists precisely because not everyone is in that category, and those who are not but feel the regulation's burden receive no benefit from the possibility of other people's making sacrifices to promote a result which is a matter of complete indifference to the landowner who must today bear the burden of the government's action.[50]

Whenever the government limits private owners' property rights, either through regulation or exercises of eminent domain, this lack of true reciprocal benefit is likely to be common, and perhaps even typical. Given the diversity of human interests and circumstances, any assumption that general restrictions on property will reliably provide burdened property owners with specific benefits that equal or exceed their specific losses is heroically optimistic, except in unusual circumstances where the regulation in question overcomes coordination problems, as in *Plymouth Coal*.

This problem is especially obvious in the context of physical takings. Owners of land that has been taken for some public project may have no interest at all in the fruits of that project—for example, a jazz devotee whose land is taken to build an opera house, or a childless couple whose land is taken to build a school. This is particularly true when the taken property is a residence and the displaced owners end up having to move far away from the neighbourhood that benefits from the project.[51] However, it is equally applicable in the context of regulations. Thus, for example, in *Penn Central* the US Supreme Court noted that 'the property owner in [*Euclid v Ambler*] who wished to use its property for industrial purposes was affected far more severely by the [zoning] ordinance [limiting industrial uses]

---

[49] An additional problem is the lack of any guarantee that the future generations will themselves choose to accept a parallel burden with respect to subsequent generations. There is inherently no way for an earlier generation to determine what obligations future generations will voluntarily choose to accept.

[50] If there is any doubt about that, considering a closely analogous situation may make the difficulty here obvious. If we focus only on people who are all alive at some specific time, no one would contend that if A is burdened to provide some benefit to B, that loss receives compensation if B is burdened to provide a benefit to C. A's loss obviously has not diminished merely because B too has suffered a loss. Now note that the same holds true if we allow for the possibility that A, B, and C exist at different times.

[51] Krier and Serkin 2004, 868–9 suggest one way that this might happen: if the public project increases property values to such an extent that the owner of the taken property, who received compensation based on the pre-project market value of that property, no longer can afford the post-project cost of housing in that neighbourhood, then that owner will be compelled to relocate to a less expensive neighbourhood that may be too far away from the project to enjoy its benefits. However, an effect on market prices is not necessary for this result to occur. If vacancies in the neighbourhood are few, and the taken property was one of the few inexpensive properties in that neighbourhood, then the unfortunate owner may simply have no available affordable options to buy or rent.

than its neighbors who wished to use their land for residences'.[52] And there is no reason to think that the zoning regulation in *Euclid* necessarily provided the frustrated industrialist a benefit commensurate to the burden it imposed. The benefit might have equalled the loss, but if so that would be seen to be more a fortunate accident than any inherent feature of the zoning ordinance's operation.

Recognizing that regulations burdening property owners will not reliably provide specific reciprocal advantages sufficient to make those owners whole naturally leads to the alternative suggestion that even when adequate amounts of specific reciprocity are absent, the burdened property owner nevertheless receives benefits from the existence of the more general system which created those government actions, and those benefits provide the required reciprocity of advantage. However, as we shall see next, appeals to general reciprocity of advantage provide no sanctuary from the basic problems faced by appeals to specific reciprocity.[53]

4.1 General reciprocity

The broadest potential formulation of an argument from general reciprocity of advantage would be very broad indeed. It would assert that although the costs of any one specific regulation fall unequally upon members of the community promulgating the regulation, that community will promulgate many regulations, and there will be considerable variation in the people who are burdened by each regulation. As a result, although the effects of any given regulation will be more costly than beneficial to some people, and more beneficial than costly to others, the people who suffer a net loss from any particular regulation may enjoy a net gain from other regulations, with the effect that on average they are no worse off than they would have been had there been no governmental regulation at all.

The chief appeal of this sort of argument is its ability to justify a wide range of regulations even when burdened owners receive no monetary compensation for their losses. However, that ability is also its fatal defect: the argument proves too much, because the universe of property restrictions that would pass this test is not only wide, but completely unbounded.

The problem here springs from the argument's assumption that when calculating the total benefits and burdens which the affected landowner has experienced, the relevant comparison class (the baseline) is a world without legal regulation at all. But in fact the question isn't whether the landowner is owed compensation for the mere fact of being subject to some legal regulations, but rather whether the

---

[52] *Penn Central Transportation Co. v New York City* 1978, 134.

[53] Hanoch Dagan offers what he calls an 'intermediate conception of long-term reciprocity'. On this view, monetary compensation for regulatory burdens is not required 'if, and only if, the disproportionate burden of the public action in question is not overly extreme and is offset, or is likely in all probability to be offset, by benefits of similar magnitude to the landowner's current injury that she gains from other—past, present, or future—public actions (which harm neighboring properties)'. Dagan 1999, 769–70. To the extent that my criticisms of the 'specific' and 'general' varieties of average reciprocity of advantage are persuasive, they should have equal force against Dagan's 'intermediate' formulation, because it is merely a hybrid of the other two, lacking any additional feature which would make it immune to the particular difficulties discussed in this chapter.

landowner is owed compensation for being subject to a specific regulation. Hence, the relevant comparison is to a world without *that* regulation, not a world bereft of regulation altogether.

Consequently, appeals to general reciprocity of advantage are typically narrower: although a specific application of the legal rule in question may be burdensome to a particular landowner, over time the continued operation of that specific rule also confers benefits upon that landowner, and the total benefits are large enough to match or exceed the burden.

The US Supreme Court's decision in *L'Hote v New Orleans* (1900) offers a simple example of this sort of argument at work. New Orleans had enacted a law restricting houses of ill repute to a specific area of the city. Owners of nearby property who did not welcome having such establishments concentrated in their neighbourhood challenged the regulation's constitutionality. The Supreme Court upheld the regulation as falling within state governments' 'police power', and went on to quote approvingly a treatise's justification of the exercise of that power: 'If [a landowner] suffers injury [from a regulation intended to protect the general welfare], it is either *damnum absque injuria*, or in the theory of the law, he is compensated for it by sharing in the general benefits which the regulations are intended and calculated to secure.'[54]

One difficulty inherent in arguments of this sort is specifying the appropriate level of generality with which to categorize the regulation. In the *L'Hote* case, is the regulation best categorized as a restriction on the location of prostitution? Is it better categorized as a restriction on the location of disreputable businesses in general, including brothels, saloons, and pool halls? Is it a restriction on the location of businesses of any sort? Is it a restriction on the location of uses of any sort?

Suggesting that the regulation should be understood broadly makes it easier to imagine that owners burdened by an application of the regulation today might receive benefits from later applications of the regulation on others, but such suggestions also invite suspicions of disingenuousness and questions about relevance. The plaintiffs in *L'Hote* weren't objecting to regulations about the location of businesses in general; they were objecting to regulations about brothels.

Embracing a narrower understanding of the regulation avoids those relevance problems but, by the same token, also decreases the plausibility of assertions that those burdened by the regulation received a compensating reciprocal advantage. In *L'Hote*, the purpose of the regulation was to keep prostitution away from the rest of the city's residents. The plaintiff's complaint was that concentrating brothels in designated red-light districts had the effect of bringing prostitution next door to his property. There is no coherent way to assert that the regulation's general benefit of keeping prostitution at a distance has compensated the plaintiff for the specific burden of having prostitution brought nearby. Prostitution has been kept at a distance only from others; it has been made proximate to the plaintiffs.

---

[54] *L'Hote v New Orleans* 1900, 599.

There is no obvious principled way to identify the appropriate level of generality at which to evaluate regulations' provision of reciprocal benefits. That fact alone may be enough to call this sort of argument into question. Moreover, the argument faces an additional difficulty. Even on a broad interpretation of the relevant regulation, there is no inherent reason to be confident that every particular burdened individual will ultimately receive compensation equal to the loss that he or she has suffered. In a multi-dimensional world with complex and dynamic circumstances and diverse preferences, there is no certainty that a regulation's total benefits to any particular individual will match or exceed the burdens felt by the individual. If the general effect of the regulation is to increase total social wealth, and that increase in wealth is fairly widely distributed, then we might hope that many burdened owners, perhaps even most burdened owners, will end up better off as a result of the regulation's existence.[55] However, that is little comfort to those owners who do not receive such compensation. Those owners have still suffered a net loss, and pointing to others' net gains as justification for the system which imposed that loss abandons the basic premise of the 'average reciprocity of advantage' justification, namely that the regulation is justified (and requires no payment of compensation) because those who are burdened receive benefits commensurate to their burden. The 'average reciprocity of advantage' test is whether those whom a legal rule harms in one respect are overall made whole, not merely whether society is in general better off with such a rule than without it.[56] The latter approach may have some merit, but adopting it is to abandon 'average reciprocity of advantage' in all but name.

4.2 Probabilistic compensation

A more sophisticated version of the general reciprocity argument attempts to address these sorts of problems by invoking probability. Lee Anne Fennell's discussion of eminent domain offers a convenient example of this style of argument. After arguing that the standard used to determine the amount of compensation paid to owners of

---

[55] These assumptions are quite optimistic. Extensive public choice literature has argued that the benefits of legal rules accrue disproportionately to those people and organizations who are best situated to exert influence on lawmakers, and the burdens of those legal rules fall disproportionately on those who lack such influence. Stigler 1971 offers a classic statement of this sort of argument. In recent decades, however, public choice theory has developed considerably. See e.g. Farber and O'Connell 2010 for a recent overview of the field. Whatever the merits of public choice analyses in general, common sense and even a slight acquaintance with history suggest that there is some plausibility to this basic concern.

[56] Justice Brennan's discussion of average reciprocity of advantage in *Penn Central* falls into this latter category. Brennan asserts that an architectural preservation regulation which burdened the Penn Central Railroad provided an average reciprocity of advantage, because the regulation made New York in general better off. This reasoning, of course, reduces the concept of reciprocal advantage to an empty shell and twists its employment into something close to the opposite of its original intent. Where once the concept was designed to illuminate which rules went 'too far' in burdening individual owners despite being generally beneficial to the public, the *Penn Central* court construes it as a justification for any publicly beneficial legal rule, no matter how far that rule goes. The court would have done better simply not to have mentioned reciprocal advantage at all, or to have declared that the concept was irrelevant to interpreting the US Constitution.

property taken through eminent domain systematically undercompensates those owners, Fennell asks how the use of that standard could nonetheless be justified. She concedes the implausibility of claims that specific reciprocity of advantage will make up the difference between full compensation and the compensation that actually is paid: '[I]t is unrealistic to expect that those who are *in fact* burdened by eminent domain will receive back benefits that make up for their own loss—at least in that particular instance.'[57] And she criticizes the simplest form of appeal to general reciprocity of advantage on the grounds that '[i]t seems disingenuous to suggest that an increase in the expected value of one's holdings through generalized society-wide eminent domain practices can satisfy [eminent domain's just compensation] requirement, where different individuals suffer greatly divergent outcomes'.[58] A general advantage that is enough to make whole an owner who suffers only slightly from a particular exercise of eminent domain may well be insufficient to make whole someone who suffers greatly.

However, Fennell finds more promise in what we might categorize as a form of *ex ante* probabilistic analysis (the inspiration for which she attributes to Frank Michelman's discussion of Rawls): 'Under this approach, before knowing whether one's own land will be condemned, one asks whether this is the *sort* of eminent domain arrangement that will tend to make one better off over the run of cases, given the range of possible distributive outcomes.'[59]

The general idea with probabilistic arguments of this type is that it is possible to compensate for a *chance* of loss (e.g. a chance that one's property will be taken through eminent domain without full compensation for all of one's subjective value in the property) by offering a *chance* of gain (e.g. a chance that one will enjoy the public projects that will be possible if the state has a power of eminent domain). If the chance of gain is large enough to counterbalance the chance of loss—i.e. if the expected value of the outcome of accepting the regulation is non-negative—then we might say that the regulation provides an average reciprocity of advantage, and therefore is justified, even if occasionally the actual outcome is a net loss for specific unlucky landowners.

This sort of argument has the advantage of avoiding the basic problem, noted earlier in other versions of average reciprocity arguments, that the diverse nature of the world makes it highly unlikely that generally applicable regulations could avoid creating some net losers except in relatively rare instances involving coordination problems. The probabilistic approach accepts the existence of actual net losers, but contends that even they enjoyed an average reciprocity of advantage from the rule that created the loss, because *ex ante* the most likely result over time for those owners had been a net benefit.

Nevertheless, even this version of reciprocal advantage is unpersuasive, because there is no way to know that the burdened landowner would have agreed *ex ante* that the 'bet' inherent in accepting the regulation was attractive. Even if most people would have found that bet to be attractive, risk preferences vary from person

---

[57] Fennell 2004, 978.   [58] Fennell 2004, 987–8.   [59] Fennell 2004, 988.

to person, and some landowners might be risk-averse enough that they would not have found the bet attractive. Compounding this problem is the fact that different landowners will place different values on the payoffs offered by the various scenarios. Some owners might greatly enjoy civic goods which the relevant governmental actions promote—e.g. the sorts of public works which require the exercise of eminent domain—while others might be largely indifferent to those benefits. As a result, different landowners would likely differ in their assessment of the bet offered by any given regulation, and there is no guarantee that each landowner who suffers an actual net loss was one who *ex ante* would in fact have found the bet attractive.[60] Thus, even on the probabilistic account, there is still no assurance that those burdened by the contested legal rule have in fact enjoyed an average reciprocity of advantage with respect to it.

4.3 Basic structural problems

Moreover, there is an inherent problem with the logical structure of general reciprocity justifications for imposing restrictions without compensation. One way to approach the difficulty is by observing a peculiar difference between these justifications and the ordinary way of thinking about physical takings. Ordinarily, under the law of physical takings, the amount of monetary compensation which the owner of taken property receives is not reduced by the amount of value which the owner receives from the general effect of public project for which the condemnation occurred.[61] This makes sense, because everyone else receives the same benefit without having to surrender their property. Thus, deducting the project's benefit from the compensation paid would effectively make the condemnee worse off relative to everyone else.[62] One might therefore expect a similar approach in the regulatory takings context. However, the opposite is true when general reciprocity of advantage is invoked to justify denying monetary compensation to burdened landowners: the general benefit received from the system is counted as diminishing claims for compensation.

The puzzle deepens when we consider how the law treats compensation for partial takings. When the government condemns only a portion of a privately owned parcel rather than the entire parcel, it may reduce the compensation that it pays for the taken portion if the portion that was not taken benefits from the public

---

[60] These sorts of probabilistic argument have the additional curious feature of entailing that even those owners who enjoyed net *benefits* from the application of a legal rule could have a claim for compensation (or at least a justified complaint about the rule) if their risk preferences and personal valuations of potential payoffs would have led them *ex ante* to reject the bet which good fortune happened to allow them to win. Thus, although this sort of argument would, if successful, potentially allow regulations to evade objections from people who had ended up net losers as a result of the regulation's application, it would open those regulations to objections from people who had in fact profited from the regulations but who would not have wished *ex ante* to chance that outcome.

[61] See e.g. Sackman et al. 2012, vol. 3, s. 8A.03[2].

[62] See e.g. Krier and Serkin 2004, 866 ('To be sure, condemnees are still worse off relative to all the rest of the public who realize the benefits of the same government project but retain their property as well').

project that the taking enabled. However, this deduction occurs only to the extent that the remaining portion receives an idiosyncratic, 'special' benefit from the project. Merely receiving the same 'general' benefit as everyone else in the community receives from the project does not produce an offsetting reduction in compensation for the taken portion.[63]

Again, the intuition behind this doctrine seems straightforward: if the landowner receives a special benefit from the project, then that benefit diminishes the extent to which the taking has left the landowner worse off than everyone else in the community. However, as just noted, generally shared benefits do not have that effect. Hence, sharing in a general benefit does not diminish the amount of monetary compensation owed.

So the law governing partial physical takings is clear and consistent. But note that it is common in American law today to think of property ownership as a 'bundle of rights', and of property regulations as merely removing one element, or a few elements, from the bundle.[64] On that view, a regulation seems to have an effect quite similar to a partial taking, which also removes a portion of the entitlements which a property owner had formerly enjoyed. That structural similarity might naturally lead us to expect that the rules for compensation would be the same in both cases—monetary compensation would be decreased only for special benefits that the owner received from the government action, not for general advantages received. Yet once again the opposite is true when general reciprocity of advantage is invoked to justify denying monetary compensation to burdened landowners. Such a stark inconsistency begs for a justification, but no obvious candidate is available.

5. Reciprocity and Respect

Since 'general' reciprocity does not provide a coherent justification for the permissibility of imposing restrictions on property owners without paying monetary compensation, and the requirements for 'specific' average reciprocity of advantage are likely to be satisfied only rarely, appeals to average reciprocity of advantage seem, at least at first glance, unable to justify the sorts of property restrictions for which they are invoked.

The question then is what we should conclude from this inability. There are three possibilities. We might conclude that these property restrictions must be illegitimate, since they do not provide the required average reciprocity of advantage. Alternatively, we might conclude that we should reject the presence or absence of average reciprocity of advantage as a test for the permissibility of property

---

[63] See Sackman et al. 2012, vol. 8A, s. G16.04[1].

[64] An influential minority of commentators has challenged this assumption in recent years. See e.g. Merrill and Smith 2000 and Penner 1997. However, they remain a distinct minority, and for our purposes it is not necessary to decide whether the 'bundle of rights' conception is in fact the best way to understand the nature of property. We need merely note that the conception is widely held.

restrictions. According to this view, outside of regulations which address coordination problems, attempts to justify governmental imposition of burdens on property owners by appealing to average reciprocity of advantage (and related concepts) are simply mistaken; the concept cannot do the justificatory work that is asked of it. Finally, we might instead conclude that the concept of average reciprocity of advantage has been misunderstood and needs to be reconceived, but that a properly understood version of the concept in fact can justify those governmental impositions. Let us examine each of those possibilities in turn.

5.1 Accepting the conclusion

One possible response to the recognition that average reciprocity of advantage will not reliably compensate owners of property burdened by government restrictions is to conclude that those restrictions are therefore illegitimate unless the government pays monetary compensation to make the burdened property owners whole. This is the most straightforward conclusion to draw from average reciprocity's problems, and one which might appeal to people who are generally averse to government restrictions on property.

However, it faces an important difficulty: the number of restrictions that are likely to prove impermissible by this standard is so large—and so much larger than existing legal practices currently assume—that embracing this conclusion would call into question the plausibility of the entire approach which had led to such sweepingly revisionist consequences. The relevance of average reciprocity of advantage to questions about the legitimacy of government actions is not a logically necessary truth, like the truths of arithmetic. It rests on certain assumptions, and, as with any argument, if the conclusions that follow from these assumptions seem too implausible, the proper lesson may well be that we should reject some or all of those assumptions rather than that we should accept a host of counter-intuitive conclusions.[65]

Of course, someone who has independent grounds for welcoming those conclusions—someone who finds those conclusions completely plausible—would have good reason to embrace the assumptions which lead to them. In this case, some libertarians of a particularly austere sort might fall into that category. But even this sort of person would then have to provide some explanation of why so many

---

[65] Avoiding this very problem is in fact the role that appeals to implicit in-kind compensation play in Richard Epstein's theory of the property rights. Epstein begins with strong assumptions about the rights of property owners, including a requirement that regulations must be accompanied by compensation which makes regulated parties whole except when the regulation either prohibits a nuisance (which Epstein further limits to interferences involving physical invasions) or is justified 'by the doctrines of consent and assumption of risk'. Epstein 1985, 198. This set of assumptions, taken alone, would entail that a vast array of common government regulations, such as zoning, would be constitutionally impermissible. Therefore, Epstein's theory needs some mechanism for explaining how regulations which do not fall within his exceptions but which are widely accepted as legitimate can be justified within his theory. The notion of 'implicit in-kind compensation' fills this role. Recognizing the limited frequency of actual reciprocity of advantage therefore poses a significant challenge to Epstein's argumentative strategy.

other people over extended periods of time have been mistaken in their assessment of those conclusions' plausibility. Meanwhile, everyone who lacks an independent commitment to those conclusions has good reason to compare the relative plausibility of the conclusions to the relative plausibility of the assumptions and to reject whichever is less plausible. In this case, long-standing public and judicial beliefs about the permissible scope of government regulation and the legitimacy of eminent domain are likely to prevail over relatively novel and arcane theoretical analyses, if we are asked to choose between them.

5.2 Rejecting the premisses

This recognition naturally leads us to the second possible option, rejecting one or more of the theoretical assumptions which led to analysing the permissibility of property restrictions in terms of average reciprocity of advantage. Two main assumptions are the likely candidates here. One is the assumption that if a restriction on property is justified, then unless the restriction fell within the 'police power' the owner who is burdened by that restriction must have received full compensation for the costs of that burden, i.e. must have been 'made whole'. The second assumption is that average reciprocity of advantage has some role to play in justifying property restrictions at all.

Rejecting this second assumption might initially seem to be the most natural response. After all, if a concept (such as average reciprocity of advantage) has been introduced to solve a particular problem (such as the assumed need for payment of full compensation to justify government-imposed burdens on property owners) and the concept fails to solve that problem (such as by failing to provide reliable compensation), then a straightforward reaction simply is to discard the inadequate solution.

However, we should not be too quick to choose this option, for two reasons. The first is that if we do reject the relevance of average reciprocity of advantage, and thus retain the assumption that non-police-power restrictions on property are permissible only to the extent that burdened property owners are made whole, then we still face the basic problem of justifying the imposition of regulations unaccompanied by monetary compensation, since there is no obvious alternative source of compensation to make owners whole. Hence, rejecting the second assumption would once again require denying the legitimacy of a vast range of regulations that are widely accepted as legitimate, and as we noted above, that conclusion comes at a heavy cost in plausibility.

Moreover, there is a second reason to hesitate before consigning average reciprocity of advantage to the dustbin of irrelevance: as we saw earlier, both courts and commentators have found the concept sufficiently compelling that they have often invoked it in this context. Thus, it is reasonable to suspect that there must be something to the idea, even if it has typically been misunderstood.

If so, then the more plausible approach is to reject the assumption that burdened property owners necessarily must be 'made whole' if restrictions on their property are to be permissible. (Again, assuming that exercise of the 'police power' is not involved.) This approach would assert that the real mistake of standard average reciprocity of arguments lies not in their appeal to reciprocal advantage as a solution to a compensation problem but rather in their identification of the specific problem that reciprocal advantage is required to help solve.

In fact, there is good reason to think that the intuitive plausibility of appeals to average reciprocity of advantage do not depend on convictions that such reciprocity will necessarily make burdened property owners whole. Discussions of the possibility of compensation by means of average reciprocity of advantage are striking in their lack of concern about measuring the exact (or even approximate) amounts of the losses that burdened property owners suffer and the reciprocal benefits that they are said to receive. The suggestion is, at most, that the burdens and benefits might even out over time. As a practical matter, this apparent indifference to the specific quantities of burden and benefit involved is unsurprising, since measuring either with any reliability would be extremely difficult. But those practical difficulties merely accentuate the implausibility of justifications that would rely upon assertions that these benefits 'make whole' the owners who bear these burdens. And the ease with which discussions of reciprocal advantage gloss over these measurement questions suggests that, at heart, they are not particularly relevant to the justifications being offered. Explicitly, such justifications may be about whether burdened owners have been made whole, but implicitly they likely are about something else.

The question then is what work reciprocal advantage actually does in justifying the government's burdening property owners with restrictions for which they do not receive monetary compensation. A plausible answer is that such reciprocity provides a form of compensation sufficient to show the burdened landowner the respect due among civic equals.

5.3 Partial, 'objective' compensation

In Section 4 we saw that concerns about variations among property owners' subjective valuations and risk preferences undermine claims that reciprocal advantages made burdened property owners whole. A natural response to courts' and commentators' continued invocation of average reciprocity of advantage despite this difficulty is to conclude that what really matters must not be eliminating owners' subjective feelings of loss, but rather providing an objectively adequate form of compensation.

At first glance, this approach may seem similar to substituting a notion of 'constructive' compensation for actual compensation. However, that similarity is not exact. Appeals to 'constructive' satisfaction of some legal requirement are common when the party against whom the appeal is levied has acted in some deficient way—negligently, perhaps, or in bad faith. In such circumstances, the actions of a reasonable and well-intentioned actor are attributed to the actual actor for purposes of satisfying the legal requirement which otherwise would stand in the way of a judgment against that actor.[66] Resort to 'constructive' compensation in the

---

[66] See e.g. *Sanborn v McLean* 1925, holding that a property owner was bound by a predecessor's agreement about which he had good reason to inquire, even though the owner claimed to have lacked actual knowledge of that agreement.

takings context, however, does not easily fit that paradigm, since the burdened owner will often have done nothing wrong. That certainly is true in the case of ordinary physical takings or zoning, and may well be true in the case of other regulations. (Regulations which are merely the exercise of some 'police power' will straightforwardly fit the paradigm, but, as we have seen, justifications of those regulations typically do not make appeal to average reciprocity of advantage in the first place.) The only 'wrong' that these owners have done is to have preferences or risk tolerances that differ from many other property owners', and that is no wrong at all.

The question then is why merely partial subjective compensation may sometimes be appropriate, even when the burdened owner has done nothing wrong.[67] Fully developing a general account of how the interaction of chance with the web of civic duties within which the institution of property sits may justly result in the government's imposing burdens upon landowners without also providing a sub-jectively equal measure of compensating benefits is a large task necessarily beyond the scope of this chapter. However, it is possible here for us to see how the presence of reciprocal advantages can contribute to such a general account.

5.4 Reciprocity and shared sacrifice

To see how the presence of reciprocal advantage, even subjectively partial reciprocal advantage, can help justify imposing restrictions on property owners, we must broaden the focus of our discussion to include not only the owner who is burdened by some restriction but also the other members of society who benefit from that restriction. Consider a touchstone principle of American constitutional law gov-erning compensation for physical takings, described in the oft-quoted words of Justice Hugo Black's opinion in *Armstrong v United States*: 'The Fifth Amend-ment's guarantee that private property shall not be taken for a public use without just compensation was designed to bar Government from forcing some people alone to bear public burdens which, in all fairness and justice, should be borne by the public as a whole.'[68] Note that the principle's emphasis is not on leaving those burdened by takings at least as well off as they were before the taking—the principle says nothing about making them whole. Instead, the court focused on ensuring that burdens are shared, that is, on ensuring that the community participates in bearing the burdens of public life.

---

[67] I have argued elsewhere (Lee 2013) that governments that take property through eminent domain may sometimes justly pay merely partial compensation for the subjective losses suffered by owners of the taken property, even when considerations of practicality or administrability do not require paying less than full compensation.

[68] *Armstrong v United States* 1960, 49. William Treanor has traced the considerable influence of the '*Armstrong* principle', noting that it has 'received a remarkable degree of assent across the spectrum of opinion'. Treanor 1997, 1153; see also at 1153 nn. 17–22 and accompanying text. The basic idea was not original with the *Armstrong* court. For one historical antecedent, see *Vanhorne's Lessee v Dorrance* 1795, 310 ('[N]o one can be called upon to surrender or sacrifice his whole property, real and personal, for the good of the community, without receiving a recompence in value. This would be laying a burden upon an individual, which ought to be sustained by society at large').

The bearing of reciprocal burdens is important for its role in preserving the respect due to civic equals. To this end, a key purpose of requiring that the government compensate owners for the burdens placed upon them by that government is not to make the burdened property owners whole, but rather to avoid exploitation of individual members of the community in ways that fail to respect their dignity and status as civic equals. Involuntary imposition of restrictions on property owners for the benefit of others has an inherent risk of being exploitative and thus disrespectful of those owners' status as civic equals. However, disrespect will arise only if the restriction is not accompanied by an appropriate amount of compensation either from the beneficiaries of the restriction or from those authorized to act on their behalf.

Two features of respect are important to recognize here.

First, unlike the monetary economy of 'making whole', the moral economy of paying respect does not always require full compensation, because compensation payments have a symbolic dimension in addition to their material effects. As a result of that symbolic dimension, payment of money under some circumstances can convey disrespect, by commodifying the good for which payment is offered.[69] However, under other circumstances, such as leaving a large tip for a waiter who has provided unusually good service or paying money to purchase a music album which the musician has made freely available for downloading, monetary payments can be a positive sign of respect. In compensation contexts, monetary payments can convey respect when they are tangible, costly acknowledgements of the loss which the payment's recipient has suffered and of the recipient's equal moral standing to the person making the payment.

Because the necessary acknowledgement occurs when the amount of compensation paid is large enough to have the required symbolic effect, there is no inherent reason why the amount of compensation must necessarily equal the amount of the loss. An amount equal to the loss suffered is a natural candidate for the appropriate amount, but in fact may not always be correct, because duties of respect are themselves reciprocal. Thus, those duties bind burdened property owners in their relationship to society just as much as they bind society in its relationship with those property owners. One consequence of this reciprocity is that burdened property owners have a duty not to impose too much on everyone else. Since it would be disrespectful to the other members of the community to demand full compensation for the burdens of property restrictions when paying such compensation would impose enormous costs on society, there is no requirement to meet such demands, and thus no disrespect from declining to do so.

In general, actions which might be disrespectful under some circumstances are not disrespectful at all if they are compelled by necessity. Intentionally shoving me out of the way in a crowded plaza would be disrespectful under many circumstances, but not if you did so in order to rush to the aid of a choking child. In the property context, likewise, there is no disrespect involved in the imposition of

---

[69] Proffering an unsolicited bribe or offering to pay for sex are two standard examples. For some prominent discussions of commodification see Radin 1987, 1905–6; Radin 1996a.

regulations such as zoning that have large overall social benefits but which affect so many different people that there would be stratospheric transaction costs involved in paying monetary compensation to ensure that each burdened party is made whole.[70] In such cases, the land-use burdens accepted by the wider community under the regulation may be sufficient to ensure that their imposition on any given member of the community is not exploitative or disrespectful, even if that particular member suffers a net loss as a result of the regulation.

Recognizing the operation of reciprocal duties of respect in the context of legitimating state action enables us now to see why justifications involving the notion of reciprocal advantages or in-kind compensation have considerable intuitive appeal: to the extent that the compensation and the burden share a common currency—that is, to the extent that it is the same burdens that are shared—the connection between the regulated owner's burden and everyone else's burden will be sufficiently tight that equality of civic status will be easy to recognize.

Moreover, a second important feature of respect is that involuntary restrictions on people can be less exploitative if the burdened individuals themselves benefit from the general imposition of those restrictions. Being compelled to benefit others is less disrespectful if the system which imposes that compulsion simultaneously is benefiting the party who suffers the compulsion. Under such circumstances, the imposed burdens are more easily understood as participation in a shared project of civic governance rather than a naked imposition of power for the benefit of others.[71] Therefore, to the extent that a burdened property owner enjoys a reciprocal advantage from the general rule which imposes the burden, the risk of exploitation and disrespect diminishes. Because the presence or absence of average reciprocity of advantage can consequently serve as a proxy for the risk of exploitation and thus the amount of potential disrespect, attentiveness to that presence or absence can indeed play a valuable role in ensuring that regulatory burdens do not go beyond the bounds permitted by the requirements of civic equality, even when average reciprocity of advantage is insufficient to make each burdened party whole.

6. Conclusion

We can now briefly recapitulate the course of this chapter's argument. The paradigm case of average reciprocity of advantage is one in which a restriction on property serves to solve a coordination problem, thereby leaving all of the affected

---

[70] The sensitivity of respect to considerations of necessity cuts both ways. Even large demands placed on a wide range of people to benefit only a few (or even one) may not be disrespectful if the demand reflects some vital necessity on the demander's part. Space does not permit the development here of a detailed investigation of the functioning of the moral economy of respect, or of the normative foundations of that economy. Sufficient for present purposes is simply to recognize how a plausible account based on respect for civic equals can coherently make sense both of key elements of property law's takings compensation practices and of the intuition that reciprocal advantage has a role to play in justifying those practices.

[71] Nicole Garnett has observed that a lack of in-kind compensation in the context of physical takings increases dignitary harms. Garnett 2006, 137.

parties better off by their own lights. One party may be burdened with a short-term loss, but it receives a longer-term gain that is at least as large, and in the very same currency as the loss. Under such circumstances, no rational person would object to the regulation, and consequently it is easy to see that the parties who are burdened by the regulation have no legitimate claim to monetary compensation. However, those circumstances are likely to be quite rare. When a restriction on property does not serve to solve a coordination problem, the diversity of personal interests and risk tolerances among property owners makes it likely that appreciable numbers of the owners who are burdened by the restriction will not be made whole by the benefits which the restriction provides. Thus to the extent that average reciprocity of advantage is intended to justify regulations on the grounds that those burdened by the regulations have been made whole and therefore have no cause to complain, the concept is unable to do the work asked of it. However, that fact does not compel us to conclude that vast numbers of common restrictions on property are therefore illegitimate, nor that courts and commentators have widely been mistaken in thinking that average reciprocity of advantage is relevant to justifying government's imposition of burdens on property owners. Rather, the proper conclusion is that average reciprocity of advantage's role is not to make burdened property owners whole, but, instead, to ensure that each property owner's status as a civic equal is accorded proper respect.

6

Some Strings Attached: The Morality of Proprietary Estoppel

Irit Samet*

1. Introduction

Proprietary estoppel is a concept in flux. Within a span of two years two major House of Lords cases expressed significantly different views about its nature and scope.[1] Academic views about its role and proper place within the law of property are just as diverse: for some, proprietary estoppel (hereafter PE) is a black horse threatening to introduce chaos and subjectivity into areas of law where clarity and objectivity are *sine qua non*. Others see it as an indispensible part of the property lawyer's toolkit, a necessary mitigating device which enables the court to strike the right balance between the requirements of formality and interpersonal justice. Even if your sympathies, like mine, lie with the latter camp, you must still take seriously the concerns raised by the sceptical position. I believe that getting a clearer view of the justifying principle which underlies PE will help us to delineate the borders of the doctrine more accurately, get a better idea of the remedy it offers, and achieve a more informed balance between what it offers to a successful claimant and the formal requirements typical of property law. In this chapter I therefore set off to find what Lord Hoffmann once called 'the moral values which underlie the private law concept of estoppel'.[2]

The argument is partly descriptive and partly normative in the following sense: whereas the justifying principle I suggest can be reconciled with the *results* in the majority of the case law and the court's focus on 'detrimental reliance' as a constitutive element of the liability, it challenges the tacit assumption that when a PE claim is accepted the court enforces a promise made by the defendant. The function of PE, I will argue, is to enforce a different, less stringent kind of moral

* I am very grateful to Ben McFarlane, John Mee, James Penner, Prince Saprai, Andrew Robertson, Henry Smith, Rachael Walsh and the participants of the Philosophical Foundations of Property Law conference at UCL, and the Society of Legal Scholar (2012) Conference for their helpful comments. The usual caveat applies.

[1] *Cobbe v Yeoman's Row Management Ltd* 2008; *Thorner v Major* 2009. On the pendulum movement between the two cases see McFarlane and Robertson 2009.

[2] *R v East Sussex County Council, ex parte Reprotech (Pebsham) Ltd* 2003, 35.

obligation, which is to compensate another person for the way in which he changed his position to his detriment in reliance on your representation, or to give him a timely warning not to rely on it (henceforth LPA obligations, for Loss Prevention Assurance). That is not to say that the court should expand the range of cases in which a PE claim is accepted. My quibble is with the present analysis of the commitment which the owners came under, not with the threshold beyond which the owner's statements or conduct are considered as implying it. The practical effect of the interpretation suggested here will therefore be largely limited to the remedial aspect of the doctrine, and the range of situations in which it applies will be left intact.

To make a successful PE claim, the claimant must prove the following:

1. A statement or action (which can include silence or inaction) by the defendant, who ought to appreciate that the claimant is likely to rely on it;

2. An act by the claimant in the reasonable belief that he has or will get an interest in land, induced by that statement or action;

3. Consequent detriment to the claimant if the defendant is entitled to resile from her statement or action.[3]

The three necessary elements for PE are therefore *representation* by owner of property (O), on which another person reasonably *relies* (R) to his *detriment*. But, as the multiple caveats and disjunctives of the definition immediately reveal, PE is a legal umbrella that covers a wide range of factual scenarios. Still, I want to argue that in spite of the considerable differences between them, all the typical cases of PE in which the owner's words or conduct induced reliance can be analysed as enforcing on the defendant her moral obligation to abide by her LPA, not a duty to fulfil a promise.[4]

The chapter proceeds as follows: I start in Section 2 with a discussion of the nature of the LPA obligation, and the way in which the ability to assume it is valuable for representor as well as representee. In Section 3 I am arguing that the state should enforce LPA obligations which are assumed by sellers of property rights in the pre-contractual period. This is because a legal rule that forces compliance with one's moral duty in these circumstances will foster and encourage the socially valuable practice of efficient pre-contractual reliance. Private arrangements between the parties cannot do the work all on their own, and a default rule for allocating responsibility for pre-contractual reliance must be in place.

In Section 4 I want to show that proprietary estoppel sets out this rule. A careful reading of the case law shows, I believe, that the owners communicated willingness

---

[3] As defined by Neuberger 2009. The limitation of PE to one kind of property, namely, to land, has been criticized. All that is said in this chapter can be equally applied to other forms of property. An extension of doctrine may be at hand: in *Fisher v Brooker* 2009, which dealt with intellectual property the PE claim failed on the facts and not for the reason that the subject was not land [11].

[4] This definition is meant to exclude the 'acquiescence' group of cases where the owner's obligation arises out of her failure to correct R's mistake about her property rights. I believe that these cases feature a wholly different justifying principle which I discuss in my 'Proprietary Estoppel and Responsibility for Omissions' (Samet forthcoming).

to take responsibility over the effects which their representation had over R's investment decisions, but not a commitment to make the representation itself good. The way in which PE forces the owner to comply with that duty serves the social goals that were laid down in Section 3. I will argue as well, that PE should be read as enforcing LPA obligations even where it operates in situations of promises to give a gift which fail on formality requirements. I then want to show how this interpretation of the obligation that lies at the heart of PE can help us to understand the most unique, and contentious aspect of the doctrine, namely, the remedy which successful claimants in PE can expect to get.

2. Between Promise and Detachment

2.1 The moral principle

Let us start with a small-scale example. Imagine that on Monday morning you phone up a fellow parent (P) and offer to pick up his daughter from school tomorrow for a play date with your son. He happily accepts. But as Monday evening comes to a close you realize that your son hasn't finished his homework due on Wednesday, nor did he have enough time to practise sufficiently his solo flute part for the coming school concert. You want to cancel the play date. On what terms can you do so without breaking your duty towards P? This depends of course on the level of your commitment to the representation 'I will have your son tomorrow after school'. If your offer is a promise, in cancelling you will have broken your obligation unless P releases you from it. For, the whole point of promise is that the promisor is taking on a duty to do as she promised even if she is now reluctant to do so. But it seems to me that in the circumstances, the obligation you have taken upon yourself does not feature this high stringency level of 'make the representation good or breach your duty'.

The better interpretation of the situation (though it is hard to say for sure without more details) is that you will be breaking your moral obligation to P only if he incurs some *harm* as a result of you backtracking. Thus, if P booked a doctor's appointment or car service thinking that childcare for Tuesday afternoon was sorted out, you will have a duty to take his son from school after all, help him to find an alternative, or make it up for him some other way.[5] But it would seem overly moralistic to say that unless you stick to the original plan, you have wronged P. Promises no doubt come with an 'emergency rule' which stipulates that if very serious reasons for retracting come up—say if your grandma was run over by a bus—the duty to fulfil them will be annulled (leaving perhaps a trace in the form of some other weak obligation to try and rearrange). But what our little story was meant show is that some obligations have a very different set of opt-out clauses built

---

[5] Strictly speaking, you have to cover P's babysitter costs, but this is probably impractical in an amicable relationship. It may well be a case where making up for the reliance damage is not really possible—a problem that will resurface in section 4.2.

into them. The reasons that legitimize retraction from these obligations are of a much less serious nature than those cited by the 'emergency rule'. Thus, depending on the circumstances, your representation that 'X will obtain' can commit you either to do all that you can to make it come true, unless an emergency distracts you, or merely to make sure that the representee is not harmed if you no longer wish that X obtains. I call this relaxed obligation LPA.[6]

Here is another example. Take O, a busy CFO, who cheerfully says to his friend R 'no need to fix a formal meeting, just drop by any Wednesday'. It would seem odd if R accuses O of wronging him when O later asks him to come between 15.00 and 16.00 if he wishes to see her on a particular Wednesday. But R will have a reason to complain, and the CFO should feel guilty, if R has already arranged his schedule based on her proclaimed flexibility. This is because the commitment that arises out of R's statement is probably an LPA obligation, not a promise. In this and other LPA situations, the stance which O is taking towards her representation is fundamentally different from that of a promisor: whereas the promisor vows to make good the representation itself, O only assumes responsibility for the (reasonable) effect it had over R.

In my view, LPA and promise are not instantiations of the same obligation albeit with a different content (namely, to make the representation good vs. compensate for reliance).[7] There is an important analytical distinction between them which reflects the intricacies of interpersonal relationships. To be sure, it is possible to make a promise to 'either make my representation good or compensate you for your reliance losses'. But in the situations I discuss here and in the rest of the chapter, the obligators do not do that. They simply make a representation that 'X will obtain' ('let's have dinner next week', 'I'll see you tomorrow', 'we'll sign the contract soon'), but the duty which they thereby acquire is not to make the representation good. Rather, what these representations entail is a low-key commitment and a partial responsibility over the representation—to its effects on others not to its content. In the spontaneous flow of interpersonal relationship we are often not explicit about the level of commitment at which we aim, and that may lead to friction—what the representor understood to be the lighter kind of obligation, the representee can take to be a promise. But it seems to me that most people are equipped with enough subtlety and emotional intelligence to discern on a regular basis the level of commitment at which the representor aims—a promise or a mere LPA. This social skill to sort out LPAs from promises enables us to evaluate the behaviour of a person who retracts from a representation (should we be angry with her?) as well as to assess whether we can change our mind about a

---

[6] Many of the scenarios which Southwood and Friedrich describe as 'less than a promise' (like the 'dinner party' (p. 266) and 'job offer' (p. 268)) are in fact examples of LPA obligation (Southwood and Friedrich 2009); the same is true for the scenario discussed in Deigh 2002, 497–8.

[7] For the view that voluntary moral obligations can be of different kinds (not only with different content) see Shiffrin 2008, 285. Raz 1982, 931, 936: 'promises are but an extreme case of voluntary obligations'.

representation we made to other people (should I stick to it even if I have a cold, or will only a broken leg discharge me from this commitment?).[8]

You could insist that what I call LPA obligation is just a unique kind of promise, in which the opt-out clause is much more relaxed (so that you need not do as you promised as long as you make sure that the promise does not suffer any harm as a result). In fact, nothing in the following analysis of the moral or legal obligation will change if you call this kind of obligation, say, L-promise. As long as you accept that representations can give rise to either 'normal' or 'L' promises, we can proceed together. I do believe however, that the difference between a representor who takes it upon herself to fulfil the representation, and a representor that leaves the door wide open for withdrawal, as long as no harm is caused, is material and deep enough to justify the stipulation of a separate category of voluntary obligations.[9]

Now that we are clear, I hope, about the nature of the LPA obligation we can explore its moral grounding. Let us start with what Thomas Scanlon calls Principle L (for Loss prevention):

If one has intentionally or negligently led someone to expect that one is going to follow a certain course of action, X, and one has good reason to believe that that person will suffer a significant loss as a result of this expectation if one does not follow X then one must take reasonable steps to prevent that loss.[10]

These 'reasonable steps', says Scanlon, can take three forms: doing X, giving timely warning that one is not going to do X, or compensating the other person for the loss.[11] Principle L is not dependent for its validity on any social convention, says Scanlon. It is a moral principle that finds its justification like all other moral principles, i.e. by showing that it cannot be reasonably rejected. Since it is not unreasonable to refuse to grant others the freedom to ignore the losses caused by the expectations they intentionally or negligently lead us to form, principle L embodies a valid moral norm.[12]

---

[8] Note also, that since promises are not routinely prefaced by a locution such as 'I promise', unclarity about whether the representor has taken an obligation upon herself can arise in the context of any odd promise. Such ambiguity is inescapable if you accept Scanlon's view that neither the language, nor even the concept, of promise is necessary for promise relationship (see Scanlon 1998, 297). Subtle social skills are also required in order to decipher the precise ambit of a promise, see Raz 1982, 932.

[9] I appeal here to the pragmatist argument that 'concepts prove their worth in how cost effectively they allow one to pick out useful categories': Henry Smith: 'Emergent Property' in this volume.

[10] Scanlon 1998, 300; for an earlier version of the loss prevention principle see MacCormick 1972: 'if one man acts in a potentially detrimental way in reliance upon beliefs about another's future conduct, and if the other person by some act of his intentionally or knowingly induced the former to rely upon him, then the latter has an obligation not to act in a manner which will disappoint the other's reliance' (p. 69). In support of the principle MacCormick indeed invokes some famous estoppel cases (pp. 64–6). However, his argument for the principle and the way it supports a general account of promising lack the ingenuity of Scanlon's analysis (Raz 1972 and Pratt 2002, 93).

[11] O incurs a duty to make the representation good only when she makes a promise, and if O's communication to R is to be considered as one, much more has to happen: the principle on which the obligation to keep a promise is based (which Scanlon calls F for Fidelity) requires that A acts with intention to provide an assurance that he or she will do X, B knows this and A knows that B knows (see Scanlon 1998, 304).

[12] Scanlon 1998, 301.

One worry is that principle L is placing on O too much responsibility for the free choices of people who came to develop all kinds of expectations on the basis of her behaviour. To borrow an example from Charles Fried: if R decides to renew the lease over his flat because he derives much pleasure from listening to the members of the quartet who meet next door to practise, does the violinist owe him any compensation when they decide to practise at the cellist's home instead? 'Why should my liberty be constrained by the harm you would suffer from the disappointment of the expectations you choose to entertain about my choices?'[13] This is a serious concern, and we will come back to it when we discuss the 'reasonableness' condition for the legal enforcement of principle L. But in the next section I want to focus on the way in which Scanlon's accounts for principle L is missing an important aspect of the LPA obligation, namely, its voluntary modus.

2.2 The value of LPA

In the general framework of Scanlon's project, principle L occupies a specific (and crucial) place: it is one of the stepping stones on the way to establishing the moral obligation to keep promises on principles that 'no one can reasonably reject as a basis for informed unenforced general agreement'.[14] By revealing the roots of the duty to keep a promise in more basic moral principles like principle L, Scanlon hopes to refute the widely accepted Humean view of the promissory obligation as deriving from the prohibition to abuse a useful social convention. Scanlon's move has been the subject of lively debate, but for our purposes only the free standing status of principle L as a valid moral principle is important.

Principle L, says Scanlon, must be a valid moral principle because it is 'not unreasonable to refuse to grant others the freedom to ignore the losses caused by the expectations they intentionally or negligently lead others to form'.[15] But the noble end of protecting the Rs of this world from harm is only one part of the story. Perhaps no less important for the justification of principle L is the great value of the relationships that can form around the obligation that it encompasses. Scanlon's Principle L is framed as a tort-like duty to take care not to induce in others unrealistic expectations about representations that we make. But as should be clear from my examples, I believe that the LPA obligation can also behave as a contract-like duty when it embodies a specific stance that O can choose to adopt towards a representation she made: namely, refusing to commit to the *content* of the representation but willing to ensure that it does not have a detrimental *effect* on others.

LPA, in other words, has a voluntary mode. A 'voluntary' obligation is one that binds the obligor because she intended to be bound in that way. In the way Scanlon depicts the obligation in principle L, the duty to compensate R (or give timely warning) is only a *by-product* of O's representation, and her behaviour afterwards.

---

[13] Fried 1981, 10.   [14] Scanlon 1998, 153.   [15] Scanlon 1998, 31.

But here I want to highlight the way in which coming under an LPA obligation can be *purposeful*—similar to the way in which making a promise is an intentional assumption of a duty to keep it.[16] In its voluntary mode, the great value of the LPA obligation derives from the interest we have in being able to take on duties towards other people, assume responsibility over representations we make, and invite trust. The ability to commit facilitates cooperation, and allows people to engage in projects that require much more than a wise guess about the other party's intentions.[17] The way in which the LPA obligation is valuable not only to the representee, but also to the representor will play a crucial role once we turn to look at the legal enforcement of these moral obligations. I will argue that the *modus operandi* of this enforcement, namely PE, cannot be understood without reference to the value of the LPA obligation to both parties, R and O.

The ability to communicate to others that we take on an LPA obligation in regards to some representation of ours allows you to reap the benefits of commitment even when you are not (yet) willing to fully bind yourself to the content of the representation. This intermediate level of commitment facilitates a flexible spontaneous flow of societal and personal relationship. It allows you to indicate your intentions about a certain state of affairs X, and invite the cooperation of others in regards to it, before you have fully made up your mind about it. Crucially, it allows you to do so in a subtle way, without explicitly mentioning the possibility that the state of affairs mentioned in the representation may never materialize. The representor's hope is that the representee is socially adept in a way that will enable him to discern her low level of commitment on this occasion. This mutual understanding will enable both parties to look forward to the cooperation without the embarrassment of having to put on the table the chance that it will fail. For being explicit about the possibility of failure will many times hasten the end of the project (see further Section 3.2). Thus, the ability to communicate to others that we are willing to take on LPA obligations adds another string to the bow with which we orchestrate the intricate building of interpersonal trust.

In the babysitting story, for example, if 'I will have your daughter around tomorrow' could only be interpreted as a promise, you would have to wait until you can be absolutely sure that the play date suits you, or add to the representation a caveat that you may change your mind, but will stick to the plan if the other parent relies on it. But by the time you can firmly make up your mind it may be too late (she will have had other plans), and sometimes the moment for full blown commitment indeed never arrives. And the caveat that you may change your mind would sound odd, if not offensive—the other parent should be able to understand from the circumstances at which level of commitment the representation is pitched—promise or a mere LPA. And it seems to me that there is something

---

[16] This is the core of the distinction between my reading of proprietary estoppel and the interpretation suggested by Spence (1999)—see n. 44.

[17] As Fried explains in the context of promises: 'if [cooperation with others] is my purpose ... it is essential that I be able to deliver myself into their hands more firmly than where they simply predict my future course' (Fried 1981, 13); see also Raz 1977a, 227–8.

awkward and overly direct in the demand that we always have to be upfront and explicit about the precise nature of the commitment we take. In the spontaneous flow of social interaction there is an important place for subtle understandings and intentional ambiguity, and occasional misunderstandings is a worthwhile price to pay for that. Our ability to initiate LPA-based relationships surely exemplifies the way in which 'the power to make binding promises, as well as to forge a variety of other related forms of commitment, is an integral part of the ability to engage in special relationships in a morally good way under conditions of equal respect'.[18]

3. Legal Enforcement

In this section I argue that people often assume LPA obligations during the course of negotiating for contract, and that the state is justified in enforcing these obligations on parties who refuse to abide by them. In Section 4 I will argue that contrary to the language of promise in which it is cast, the job of PE is to enforce these LPA obligations. As a general framework for the discussion I assume the liberal 'harm principle' as interpreted by Joseph Raz. The harm principle stipulates that the coercive power of the state can only be used to prevent people from causing harm. But according to Raz, the state is also under a duty to help citizens lead an autonomous life. For that purpose, the state should promote autonomy-enhancing practices and create valuable opportunities for the citizens. One important way of achieving this purpose is to outlaw actions which undermine worthwhile practices even when it is impossible to identify harm to any particular person.[19] Thus, when a valuable practice is likely to come under too much strain if the moral obligations on which it is based are disregarded, the state is entitled to coerce people to oblige in order to protect the said practice.

In light of that, I want to show that the legal enforcement of LPA obligations is justified for two reasons: as a protection of an important autonomy-enhancing social practice, and as preventing harm to individuals. Although the first justification may seem more tenuous, I will argue in Section 4 that it is crucial for understanding the unusual operation of the legal device that enforces LPAs in the context of transactions in property, namely, PE. And as this first line of reasoning is under-explored it will be the main focus of this section. More specifically, I want to show that the state is correct in compelling people to abide by LPA obligations which they assumed in the course of negotiating an agreement to transfer property rights.[20]

---

[18] Shiffrin 2008, 285. Note that like any relationship of trust, LPA can have an intrinsic value over and above the projects that are facilitated by it (see Kimel 2003, 28–9).

[19] Raz 1986, 412–19. Put in that way, the harm principle is wider than Mill's classical rendition in an important way: the definition of harm is here extended to include the 'impairment of institutional *practices* that are in the public interest' (Feinberg 1973, 33, my emphasis). In his classical formulation, J. S. Mill talks only about 'harm to others' (Mill 1993, ch. 1 para. 9).

[20] In the text, I examine the enforcement of LPA obligation in the context of commercial relationship because of the general context of the chapter, i.e. proprietary estoppel. Parallel problems

3.1. Encouraging pre-contractual Investment

Our starting point would be the observation that 'there are economic gains from negotiating contracts over an extended period of time'.[21] The respective duties of the parties at this preliminary but crucial stage, in which they take the necessary time to shape their future relationship, have been the subject of intensive debate. One such controversy revolves around the fact that 'in most exchanges, the parties have opportunities to make investments that can make the bargain more valuable, and such investments are cheaper and more valuable when made in advance [i.e. before an agreement is signed]'.[22] A classic case is one in which R, who is negotiating an agreement to procure a neighbouring piece of land from O, can make investments that will help him utilize the larger space in more efficient way. For example, R may purchase the advanced machinery for which he requires the extra space, train his workers to handle it, and secure customers' reservations for the new product. All this will enable R to start production much sooner after completion, and the early stream of cash will not only benefit R, but also highly increase O's chances of being paid a good price on time. The surplus from the deal can be significantly increased.[23] R's expenditure can also take the form of inaction, as when R forgoes business opportunities that compete with his contemplated relationship with O (e.g. to purchase an alternative lot from R's other neighbour).[24] Choices of that kind made in anticipation of a contract have a key role in building up R's commitment to the deal. Both R and O stand to gain from them.[25]

These and many other examples lead to the pretty uncontroversial conclusion that it is a 'social goal at this stage . . . to induce surplus-maximising investment'.[26] But the question what should the law do, if anything at all, to promote this admirable goal is highly contentious. You could think that if and when pre-contractual investment is likely to increase the surplus from the deal the parties will go on to make it without any intervention from the outside; the common good in the form of efficient pre-contractual investments will be taken care of by the free market. But this is not so. There is a serious obstacle on the way to ideal investment decisions at this stage of the

---

on the domestic setting are often approached with a different, albeit related, legal tool: the Common Intention Constructive Trust. The current tendency is to view PE and CICT as running in close but different streams (for a helpful comparison between them see Dixon 2008, 372–4). In the commercial setting 'P.E. has usually been considered a more reliable and certain instrument for remedying unconscionable conduct than the rather fluid concept of the constructive trust' (Etherton 2009, 125).

[21] Katz 1996, 1267.

[22] Katz 1996, 1267; on the 'beneficial aspect of reliance', see Goetz and Scott 1980, 1267–70.

[23] For many more examples of efficient pre-contractual investment see Craswell 1996, 490–1; Katz 1996, 1254–6, 1267–8. For example from English cases on PE, see my discussion in Section 4.1.

[24] Another common situation is one in which O is bidding for a contract for which he needs to employ a sub-contractor—R. For sophisticated products and services R will oftentimes have to make an investment in research and maybe production before the results of the bid are known. This can be highly relevant for property development joint ventures, see the facts of *Cobbe v Yeoman's Row Management Ltd* 2008 and discussion n. 52.

[25] There could also be a problem of 'over-investment' here: see discussion of the 'reasonableness' condition in PE in text to n. 51.

[26] Ben-Shahar 2004, 1848.

relationship, which the specialists nickname the 'holdup' trap: a party who has an opportunity to invest will face the following dilemma—if the deal is eventually aborted he will have to bear the costs all by himself, and if the negotiations proceed, the other party can exploit his relative weakness as the one who is more deeply invested in the prospective deal, make extra demands, and draw all the surplus benefit from the investment to herself.[27] Obviously, unless the potential investor can somehow be assured that he will enjoy at least part of any surplus created by the investment, and that he will not have to bear its costs all on his own, he will not invest. Thus, if we just leave the parties to their own devices, many opportunities will be lost.

How can the potential investor be reassured? One way is for R to ask, or for O to offer, that they enter a preliminary contract about the question of who will bear the costs of the pre-contractual investment. When the parties explicitly agree on this question, this contract should govern their relationship in regards to the matter. But for reasons I shall discuss in Section 3.2, the solution of a collateral contract is unfeasible in many situations in which such potential surplus-maximizing investment can be thwarted by the 'holdup' problem. The law must therefore provide a default arrangement for the numerous instances in which parties who enter contractual negotiations fail to reach a private arrangement which allocates their respective responsibility for pre-contractual investment. The default rule must take into account the need for clarity in the arrangements between the parties, as well as the need to facilitate efficient pre-contractual investments.[28] In the absence of an explicit invitation to invest by the other party (backed by a promise to cover the expenses over it in case she withdraws from the negotiations for no fault of R's), what will often trigger the investment is a representation of O that a contract is around the corner. Relying on this representation, the other party may spend money or forgo opportunities that he would otherwise take.

Here is an example: a farmer who applied for a mortgage to purchase a field did not hear from the bank for a long time. As the season for planting approached fast, he asked the bank what to do. Their answer was 'you go ahead and farm the property'.[29] How should the law treat reliance on such representations? From an economic point of view, it has been shown by Bebchuk and Ben-Shahar that 'A rule that assigns liability to any party who retracts from a preliminary representation he has made during the negotiations, for the reliance expenses incurred by the other party after the representation, [will ensure that] the other party will make the optimal reliance investment during the pre-contractual stage.'[30] This optimal outcome is a result of the way in which this rule shields the investing party from the 'holdup' problem: the representor will hesitate to make demands that aim at

---

[27] Craswell 1996, 492.   [28] Bebchuk and Ben-Shahar 2001, 427. Craswell 1996, 485–6.

[29] Facts of *Bixler v First National Bank of Oregon* 1980, in Craswell 1996, 534.

[30] Bebchuk and Ben-Shahar 2001, 447. Or as Goetz and Scott put it: 'legal rules that encourage self-protective adaptation by the [representee, i.e. encourage him to wait for a concrete offer] achieve desired reductions in detrimental reliance, only at the cost of concomitant reductions in beneficial reliance' (Goetz and Scott 1980, 1271).

seizing an unfair share of the surplus generated by the investment lest the negotiations break down and she will have to bear the costs of R's reliance. Other writers
who approach this issue from an economic efficiency perspective concur with this
suggestion.[31] It has also been shown that the benefits of the investment-friendly
environment that such a rule creates are so great that they can overcome any
'chilling' effect that the liability might have on one's willingness to enter negotiations, or make representations.[32]

Moving beyond considerations of efficiency, a rule which ascribes responsibility
for the result of a pre-contractual representation better reflects 'the different "tones"
of the "understandings" and commitments that the parties wish to express throughout the negotiations'.[33] A bipolar position according to which the parties are either
within the contractual realm—where the parties have to make their representations
good, or fall outside this realm—where only marginal tort-like norms govern the
failed relationship is unfaithful to the natural evolution of the relationship between
the parties. As Ben-Shahar observes, when the parties move along the path towards
an agreement, they typically go through different stages of 'intermediate species of
liability'.[34] This same reflection led Lon Fuller to call for the introduction of
nuanced 'scale of enforceability' in contracts, i.e. a continuum of remedies that
tackle the other party's wish to withdraw which spans from restitution through
covering reliance expenses and up to the award of the expectation value.[35]

Unfortunately, Ben-Shahar's own solution to this normative gap between what
the parties commit to in the pre-contractual stage, and the minimal legal duties
that govern their relationship does not reflect properly the idea that the *measure* of
the liability should mirror the deepening commitment.[36] But his discussion does
bring to the fore the fact that commitment to a joint project and responsibility for
one's representations come in stages. The fully-fledged commitment to the deal, in
the form of a promise to go ahead with it, is embodied in the contract itself. But
before we get to this final phase, a negotiating party will often come under lesser
obligation to take responsibility over the effect which her representations had over
the other party. She will, in other words, come under a duty to either warn the
other party that any pre-contractual investments that he makes on the basis of these
representations will be his own risk, or bear the costs of any (reasonable) reliance
which her representation(s) to him induced.

Such gradual build-up of trust which is accompanied, and propped up, by
intensifying levels of commitment is particularly important in the context of

---

[31] Goetz and Scott 1980, 1287; Craswell 1960, 487–97, 531–6.

[32] As shown by Bebchuk and Ben-Shahar in section VI of their paper (2001); see also Ben-Shahar
2004, 17 and 31.

[33] Ben-Shahar 2004, 1830.   [34] Ben-Shahar 2004, 1871.

[35] Letter from Lon L. Fuller to Karl Llewellyn cited in Ben-Shahar 2004, 1831.

[36] Ben-Shahar (2004) suggests that a party to fairly advanced negotiations should be able to enforce
the negotiated-for contract in terms to which the other party agreed to, which, presumably, would be
the most favourite terms for that party. The remedy therefore remains the same: O has to make her
representation good, only the content of the representation changes as the parties get closer to seal the
deal (see Markovits 2004, 1918).

transactions in property rights. For here, a sealed commitment would mean that O has to part with a highly valuable asset that cannot be replaced by purchasing an identical item in the market. The last stage of a contractual duty is therefore final in a particularly rigorous sense. For that reason, we can expect owners to be especially keen on going through a prolonged period of discussions in which the various aspects of the deal are carefully considered. In this extended period of negotiations many opportunities for surplus-enhancing investments may arise. When the parties are not in a position to reach a collateral contract on who will bear the costs of these investments, R will hesitate to rely on the future contract unless he can be reassured that O will not exploit his position to extract extra benefits for herself. The unique nature of the subject matter in these transactions render R even more vulnerable to the holdup trap, as O knows that R cannot find an exactly similar commodity anywhere else.

Without pre-contractual investment the final deal may well be less lucrative for both parties, or fail completely if an over-careful R chooses to take whatever alternatives he can find. O would therefore want to encourage R to invest while she takes the necessary time to fully make up her mind whether she is willing to transfer her property right to him. It is therefore in the interest of both O and R if she can assume an informal obligation to take responsibility over the reliance which her representations to R induced.[37] Like the examples we looked at in the first section of this chapter, this is another context where the ability to assume LPA obligations is highly valuable for the representor, as means of inviting trust and cooperation before taking full responsibility to make her representation good. However, the fact that O has a moral obligation to compensate R if she retracts from her representation would hardly ever be enough to reassure R that no holdup trap awaits him if he relies on it. Given the scale of the investment that can be expected when it comes to the purchase of property rights, it is improbable that R will count on O's moral integrity, or rely on unofficial sanctions, such as harm to her reputation to motivate her sufficiently to fulfil her obligation.

If the required investment is substantial, R will probably only go ahead with it if he can rest assured that a recalcitrant O will be coerced by the state to comply with her obligations. And the state in this case would be justified in enforcing on O her moral duties not only in order to prevent harm to R but also as means to encourage efficient pre-contractual investments.[38] For the state, recall, is under a duty to promote autonomy-enhancing practices, and to do that, it can and should employ the law to preserve the environment in which these practices thrive.[39] As we saw, many efficient pre-contractual investments will only go ahead if people abide by

---

[37] For more examples of the way in which the representor can benefit from a pre-contractual reliance on her representation, and hence from a rule that encourages R to make them, see Craswell 1996, 495.

[38] For a justification of legal enforcement of promises along the same lines see Raz 1982, 934–7. Even those who reject Raz's account of the source of obligation to keep promises can agree with him that the *state* has a good reason to enforce promises because of their special value to relationships, see Pratt 2007, 567. Raz himself would probably endorse the extension of his argument to LPA relationship as he says there that 'whatever reason there is for the law to protect promising practice requires it to protect the wider practice of undertaking to protect voluntary obligations of any kind' (Raz 1982, 936).

[39] It is an interesting question whether legal enforcement of the moral obligation which stands at its basis can indeed influence the practice. I do not have the space to discuss this issue, but see Raz's positive answer to this question (Raz 1982, 934), and Avery Katz's argument that if the rules encourage

their moral duty to compensate the investing party for relying on a representation from which they wish to retreat. A legal rule according to which O has to comply with her LPA, will help to foster an environment where efficient pre-contractual reliance thrives, and valuable transactions in property rights can prosper.[40]

3.2 Building up trust: the role of LPA

This leads us back to an important question which was left open: why can't we expect of the parties to negotiate and agree on the question of reliance expenditure and thus save themselves (and us) the doubts, the arguments and the litigation that follows? As you surely have noticed by now, I believe that by making a representation that 'I will do X' or that 'X will happen' we do not necessarily come under the obligation to make this representation good; rather, depending on the circumstances, we may only have a duty to make sure that the representee is not harmed if he relied on our representation to his detriment. But even if you accept that parties who make informal representations at the pre-contractual stage may come under an LPA obligation to the other party, you can still argue that the *law* should only enforce explicit promises, or agreements. The law, so the arguments goes, should not intervene where people refuse to fulfil some vague casual assurances which they (allegedly) gave to others, as we want to encourage people to be clear and unequivocal about the obligations they assume. If we insist that only recipients of explicit promises can expect the assistance of the court in getting them fulfilled, we will save ourselves a lot of judicial headache as people will learn to ask for explicit guarantees before they rely to their detriment.

Accordingly, unless R was promised by O that his pre-contractual investment will be covered (in part at least) if she withdraws from the negotiations, he will have to bear their costs on his own. The way out of the 'holdup' trap is only by means of explicit agreement. This approach, however, while it would add clarity to the parties' legal obligations at the pre-contractual stage, is likely to nip in the bud many efficient pre-contractual investments as such preliminary agreements can hardly be expected to be the norm. The reasons for that are many and varied. It has been argued that such agreements will many times be inefficient as they increase the transaction costs, are dependent on the costly-to-verify extent of R's reliance, and may encourage overinvestment.[41] But here I would like to focus on a different reason that militates against a rule according to which a party who wishes to guard himself against the perils of the holdup trap must insist on an agreement in which the responsibility for pre-contractual investments is expressly allocated between the parties.

reliance rational players will rely and this will become the convention (Katz 1996, 1253–6, 1264). For a more sceptical view in the context of PE see Mee 2011, 192.

[40] See Goetz and Scott on this point: 'when the mutual interests of both parties are furthered by more assured promises, the promisor will voluntarily look for legal mechanisms for providing additional reassurance . . . especially when extra-legal sanctions are relatively ineffective' (Goetz and Scott 1980, 1278).

[41] See more in Schwartz and Scott 2007; Katz 1996, 1306; and Ben-Shahar 2004, n. 37 and sources cited there. For criticism of these arguments (but not of this position) see McFarlane 2010, 100.

The point is that many relationships go through a sensitive phase in which there is no place for the explicit and earnest nature of requesting and offering promises. In many cases asking for guarantees against the holdup trap will undermine the very thing which the parties strive to build, namely, trust. For in asking for an agreement, R will effectively be saying to O 'I do not really trust your representation enough to rely on it, and/or I suspect that you may exploit my decision to invest to gain an unfair advantage'—hardly a trust-building message. From the other direction, when O vows to R that she will compensate him for relying on her representation in case she chooses to withdraw from it, she is putting the option of withdrawal on the table. Surely, while the negotiations go on, the possibility that O will retreat is always in the background. But as it happens in the context of many interpersonal relationships, being explicit about the possibility of breakdown can be fatal. Some possibilities are better left unmentioned, even when the chances of them materializing is not negligible. If the law is to encourage the practice of pre-contractual investment it must help the parties create that 'space for trust which [they] seek to establish', and to do that it must enable them to solicit and offer reliance without being forced to discuss the eventuality of relationship breakdown.[42] The default rule must therefore be that the party who withdraws from her representation has to compensate the other party for his reasonable reliance on it.

State enforcement of LPA obligations can also be justified as a direct application of the harm principle, that is, as a legitimate intervention in O's affairs in order to prevent her from harming R.[43] A contractarian would say that the legal enforcement of principle L is justified as it cannot be reasonably objected to. The ensuing liability would be similar to that which can be found in other tort doctrines such as fraudulent misrepresentation and deceit. In Section 4, I argue that PE can, and should be interpreted as the legal enforcement of LPA obligations which owners come under as a result of representations they make in regards to their property. The double justification for using the state coercive power to force O to oblige, namely, to facilitate efficient reliance as well as to protect unfortunate Rs, will play an important role in this interpretation; most importantly, it will help us to understand the proprietary (rather than tort-like) nature of the doctrine and the unusual care taken by the courts in making sure that R is fully compensated for his loss.

4. Proprietary Estoppel

In this section I argue that PE can be justified as the legal enforcement of LPA obligations which people come under in the context of property rights transfers.[44]

---

[42] Quote from McFarlane 2010, 103.

[43] See Scanlon 2001, 101, citing one of the landmark American cases in estoppel: *Hoffman v Red Owl Stores Inc.* 1965.

[44] In his book on estoppel, Michael Spence suggests that the Australian doctrine of estoppel can be 'given a satisfactory basis in principle' as the enforcement of a duty 'to ensure the reliability of induced assumptions' (pp. 1, 2) (Spence 1999). Relying on MacCormick's work (see n. 10) Spence emphasizes the protective function of the principle, seeing it as a species of the general duty 'not to cause

In terms of the *results* in the relevant case law this is mostly an interpretive claim; namely, it is a claim about the principle that underlies the recent case law, and not a suggestion for major reform. That said, understanding PE in this light would have a profound influence on the way in which PE claims are made by R and discussed by the courts. This understanding of PE as enforcing LPA obligations would greatly help us to clear away some major ambiguities and incoherences that afflict the doctrine, and thus enhance its usefulness as an arbitrator of disputes over property.[45]

PE, by nature, works to disrupt the good order of property law. When a successful PE claim is made, the court may respond by transferring, changing the nature of, or altogether abolishing proprietary rights. This they do without requiring first that the parties abide by the strict formality rules that govern transactions in property rights. The doctrine also seems to fly in the face of another sacred principle of property law, namely, that interests in property should only be transferred in a consensual manner. The idea being that the function of the law of property is to protect individual property rights and that, in applying it, the court must not engage in distributive justice issues, as these should be left to the legislator.[46] For some, this is a reason to embrace PE as breaking away from an obsolete perception of property law, and as one way in which equity allows the court to redistribute property rights without the consent of the owner.[47] Others are alarmed by the unruly doctrine and call to limit its operation, claiming that 'where the parties can reasonably be expected to regulate their relationship by a binding contract, if they want to do so, equity should fear to tread'.[48]

---

preventable harm' (Spence 1999, 4). I certainly agree with him that estoppel and the remedy for it should be tailored to compensate reliance losses, but the justifying principle he suggests is partial. As this paper makes clear, I believe that an important part of the value, and hence the justification, of the moral obligation which is enforced by PE is the way it benefits both parties to the transaction. In portraying it as a duty not to cause harm Spence misses the voluntary mode of the duty, which, I argue, is crucial to understanding the way in which the doctrine is applied by the courts.

[45] In his 1999 paper on the subject, Michael Pratt rejects what he calls the 'reliance theory' of PE, and argues instead that 'estoppel gives effect to a duty not to disappoint certain induced expectations that have been relied on'. But when he comes to explain the harm done to R he says that 'by omitting to perform the defendant defeats the plaintiff's expectations that his loss will be made good or worthwhile by performance of the promise' (Pratt 1999, 214). This confuses expectations with hopes—R can indeed expect that his loss 'will be made good', but he can only hope that the promise will be fulfilled. Otherwise it is not clear how reliance can elevate an informal, and hence unenforceable, promise to a legally binding one. Pratt's answer to this question is that 'where a promisor's conduct justifies an entitlement to rely on an expectation, it will also justify an entitlement to the expectation itself' (Pratt 1999, 218). This is a questionable move, and is hard to reconcile with the growing demand for 'proportionality' between reliance and expectation (see Section 4.2). On the interpretation suggested here, O's 'conduct' lends itself to be interpreted by R as inviting reliance but *not* as a commitment to make R's expectations true (Pratt 1999).

[46] For a critical exposition of this idea and its strong influence on the common law see Rotherham 2002, ch. 2.

[47] E.g. Rotherham 2002, 291–7.

[48] Neuberger 2009, 544, and sources cited there. The most dramatic attempt yet to limit the boundaries of PE is made by Lord Scott in his leading speech in *Cobbe v Yeoman's Row Management Ltd* 2008. The supreme court has, however, reinstated much of PE's power in *Thorner v Major* 2009, see McFarlane and Robertson 2009.

PE is indeed not in the business of enforcing agreements to transfer property rights. This is the turf of contract law and the carefully tailored formal requirements of land law. But on the interpretation suggested here, PE can hardly be described as a tool for non-consensual transfer of property. True, to fulfil her duties, O may, and often does, have to part with a proprietary right (see Section 4.2). But the circumstances in which PE claims are embedded will be such that O communicated to R her willingness to take responsibility for his reliance on her representation. As we shall see, it may well be the case that a full compensation for the loss will indeed entail transfer of property rights to R, but this is a risk which O has taken once she pushed, or allowed, her relationship with him to go this far down the road towards a fully-fledged promise. Certainly, since the test for taking on the obligation is objective, some Os who never meant to assume an LPA obligation towards R, but behaved as if they did, will be caught by the net of PE against their will. This, however, can be readily justified as a necessary step to protect the valuable practice in which reliance is solicited in informal manner—R can hardly be expected to rely on O's representation if she is allowed to claim that her intentions were different from what her words or conduct communicated.[49]

Importantly, this careful guard of R's rights is accompanied by vigilance of no lesser degree not to enforce LPA obligations on O when her behaviour did not take her into its normative remit. To kick-off his PE claim, R must prove that his changed position was a response to O's representation and not something he would have done anyway.[50] R must then show that O's representation could have reasonably be interpreted as inviting reliance. Indeed, '[i]t is not enough to hope, or even to have a confident expectation, that the person who has given assurances will eventually do the proper thing', and R who works on the basis of hope or prediction, rather than a reasonable interpretation of O's representation, is taking a risk.[51] Yet, sometimes, this caution is overdone. Thus, one of the many highly

---

[49] For one of many examples see *Thorner v Major* 2009, at [5]). But that does not change the voluntary nature of the obligation PE is enforcing in principle (see Raz 1982, 935).

[50] Since it is of course impossible to bring direct evidence for such mental link (apart from the claimant's testimony), once R proves that O has made a representation that could reasonably be interpreted as inducing reliance, there is a presumption that R's response to it was indeed in reliance on the representation (*Greasley v Cooke* 1980, 1311). Thus in *Haq v Island Homes Housing Association and another* 2011 (CA) the defendant managed to show that R's actions were not in reliance on O's representation (from whom the defendant bought the land): R was allowed to enter the premises and carry out substantial building works prior to the final conclusion of an agreement for a new lease. Before the agreement in principle was duly signed O sold the land. The Court of Appeal found that the claimants did not rely on what they (unreasonably) perceived as O's representation about the agreement in principle. This can be gleaned from the fact that they committed themselves to the building contract *before* the parties arrived at the agreement in principle, and before they obtained from O the keys that allowed them access to the new premises (82).

[51] *Cobbe v Yeoman's Row Management Ltd* 2008, 66. See also *Attorney General of Hong Kong v Humphreys Estate (Queen's Gardens) Ltd* 1987 PC: 'there is no doubt that the government [R] acted in the confident and not unreasonable hope that the agreement in principle would come into effect... But... HKL [O] did not encourage or allow a belief or expectation on the part of the government that HKL would not withdraw [from the negotiations]', at 124; and *Parker v Parker* 2003 (Ch) HC: 'Put shortly, it seems to me that the highest that Lord Macclesfield's case can be put is that when he moved to the castle he believed that he might acquire the right to a life occupancy, not that he would obtain it.

controversial restrictions on the scope of PE in *Cobbe* was Lord Walker's require-ment that R must believe that O has made a legally binding promise to him.[52] This condition is surely in contradiction with the interpretation of PE as governed by LPA obligations and not by promises.

But Lord Walker's condition can hardly be reconciled with much of the case law, especially with the numerous cases in which claimants who were expecting to inherit from the representor knew very well that wills are revocable (see discussion of 'gifts' below).[53] And so in the subsequent HL case of *Thorner v Major* no evidence was adduced that R ever believed O to be making a legally binding promise to him, and it seems therefore that Lord Walker's condition was not accepted as a statement of the law.[54] The restriction is not really necessary to explain the result of Cobbe itself; instead, it can be understood as a paradigmatic case of a representation that was not meant, and should not have been interpreted as, implying that R can rely upon it. In the relationship between this particular O and R, it was legitimate (if not very kind) of O to have expected that R would bear the risk all on his own.[55]

Another aspect of the reasonableness requirement relates to the reasonableness of the action taken by the representee—was it reasonable of him to give up the alternative, to buy such expensive machines, or to invest in a training programme that would be worthless if the deal fails? This requirement is crucial for the proper function of the doctrine, as without it, R, who knows that O will be liable for his expenses if she withdraws her representation, may be tempted to make a big investment for whatever small chance of getting a benefit from it. As shown by Craswell and others, this moral hazard problem can be solved if the 'courts can evaluate [R's] reliance decisions and refuse to infer a commitment, whenever [R] has chosen an inefficiently high level of reliance'.[56] Conditions of 'reasonableness' in tort, as well as here, enable the court to do that job, and protect the representor against this unfairness.[57] Let us see then how the individual categories of PE cases can be successfully interpreted as enforcing LPAs.

In my judgment that is not enough.' Lewison J at 218; and *Crossco No. 4 Unlimited and others v Jolan Ltd and others* 2011, 114.

[52] *Cobbe v Yeoman's Row Management Ltd* 2008, 66, 68. In this case, Mr Cobbe, an experienced property developer orally agreed with a director of a management company which owned a block of flats that Cobbe would apply for planning permission to demolish the existing block of flats and to erect, in its place, a terrace of six houses. Upon the grant of planning permission, the property would be sold to Cobbe who would then develop the property, sell the six houses, and share the profits with the management company equally. Cobbe spent the next 18 months, engaging architects and other professionals, in applying for planning permission which was then duly granted; the defendants immediately withdrew from the agreement. In a controversial decision, the HL found that Cobbe had taken the risk that the joint venture would not materialize, and hence rejected Cobbe's PE claim.

[53] A point that applies to various other CA cases as well, see Etherton 2009, 119–20.

[54] McFarlane and Robertson 2009, 538.

[55] *Cobbe v Yeoman's Row Management Ltd* 2008: 'the fact is that he ran a commercial risk, with his eyes open, and the outcome has proved unfortunate for him', at 91. See also Neuberger 2009, 543 and Matthews 2010, 44.

[56] Craswell 1996, 494.

[57] Goetz and Scott 1980; Craswell 1996, 531–6. I do not have enough space here to detail the way in which the reasonableness requirement is applied in practice. For such an account see Robertson 2000.

4.1 Varieties of PE

PE claims have been accepted in situations that are very different from each other, both in terms of O's behaviour, and in terms of the relationship between O and R. In what follows I want to show that, while the court enforces LPA obligations in all these different cases, the reasons *why* O is called upon to take *that* level of responsibility over her representation can be very different. The factual scenarios that typically give rise to a PE claim are traditionally divided into three groups: 'common expectation', 'imperfect gift', and 'acquiescence'.[58] I believe that liability in the acquiescence cases is based on a different principle, and I therefore leave the cases in this category aside for now. As for the other two categories, in which O made a representation in words or conducts, I prefer to classify them according to what R seeks to secure from O: bargain/joint venture or gift.

a) Bargain

The dual goal of PE to reinforce a valuable practice and protect R from harm is most prominent in bargain or joint venture situations. Here, R and O embarked on a way to start a new collaboration, like land development in *Cobbe* or a new pub in *Pridean*; or they may wish to give their existing relationship a new direction—like upgrading a lease in order to build up R's business as planned by R in *Haq v Island Homes*; or they may just work towards extending their proprietary relationship, e.g. by renewing a lease as in *Keewalk Proceedings Ltd v Waller*.[59] In situations of that kind, we saw, it would be good for both parties to have recourse to a buffer zone between the no-return point of enforceable promise, i.e. formal contract, and an (almost) obligations-less stage. In this buffer zone we can find the right conditions for R to make investments that promote the envisaged cooperation while leaving O more time to decide whether she wants to part with an irreplaceable property interest.[60]

When R is in court claiming PE, the hope for cooperation has already been thwarted. The point of contention between the parties is whether O communicated to R a commitment to the envisaged deal that could reasonably have led O to

---

[58] See for instance Gray and Gray 2009 para. 10.189.

[59] Respectively: *Cobbe v Yeoman's Row Management Ltd* 2008; *Pridean Ltd v Forest Taverns Ltd* 1996; *Haq v Island Homes Housing Association and another* 2011; *Keewalk Proceedings Ltd v Waller* 2002.

[60] In *Haq v Island Homes Housing Association and another* 2011, for example, R started works to build the new supermarket before the sluggish lawyers finalized the agreement. Her diligence would have enabled her to open the store sooner and pay the higher rent as set in the proposed deal (on the facts, the CA found that there was no reliance on O as the encouraging representation was made by R's lawyers rather than by O). Similarly, in *Cobbe v Yeoman's Row Management Ltd* 2008 without the major work done by the survivor the development would not have gone ahead. In a controversial decision, the HL found that the representation was not one that R can reasonably rely on, and awarded him only quid pro quo monetary remedy. On my interpretation of PE, even if Cobbe's PE claim were accepted, he could not get what he wanted, i.e. his share of the profit from the development as orally agreed with O (unless, on the facts, that was the only way to compensate him for his reliance, see Section 4.2).

believe that he could safely start working to promote it (for instance, invest in the premises he is about to lease, take a risk in mortgaging his own house, or even start operating from the site and begin to build a brand for himself).[61] Many times, especially when R is advised by lawyers, he would know that if O wanted to make a promise, i.e. take on herself a full commitment to the deal, she would come up with a formalized agreement ready for him to sign. But that does not mean that before the deal is sealed O cannot assume a smaller-scale obligation to encourage the advancement of the cooperation. Thus, R may still legitimately understand O as indicating that he can act in reliance on the prospective deal, and rest assured that she will bear the costs of such actions even if she eventually chooses not to transfer the coveted proprietary right(s) to him. He will argue, in other words, that O communicated to him a commitment that falls short of a promise, but goes well beyond the minimum that is required of a negotiating party by tort and contract law.

O, on her part, will deny that the relationship between R and herself has ever entered such a normative zone, and claim that in acting in the hope that the deal will go ahead, R has taken upon himself the risk that it will never materialize.[62] In that spirit, we can interpret the courts' insistence that a 'gentlemen's agreement' cannot form the basis for PE as saying that where O makes it clear that R can only rely on 'her word of honour', she expresses a reluctance to take any obligations upon herself, be it a promise or LPA.[63] If she wishes to change her mind, the consequences will be limited to the way such U-turns injure one's honour or reputation. Thus, in spite of the language often used by the courts, the undertaking which is enforced by PE in bargain situations is of an LPA kind, not a promissory kind. In the pre-contractual stage representations ought to be read as inviting reliance, not as commitment to make them true. In addition, the suggested analysis of R's claim reflects much better the essence of the remedy which the courts award to successful PE claimants. For, as we shall see in Section 4.2, the remedy for PE in fact features requirements and limitations that clearly set it apart from the standard remedy for enforceable promises.

b) Gifts

Another popular setting for PE claims is that of failed gifts. In these cases, the moral duty of O is indeed to keep a promise she made, but the law only enforces on her a more basic kind of moral obligation, i.e. LPA; and justly so. In the gift situation, we

---

[61] As R did in, respectively, *Brewer Street Investments Ltd v Barclays Woollen Co.* 1954; *van Laethem v Brooker & Caradoc Estates* 2005; *Gonthier v Orange Contract Scaffolding Ltd* 2003.

[62] In *Pridean Ltd v Forest Taverns Ltd* 1996, for example, Aldous LJ said that 'the pertinent question to ask is—what was the expectation that the appellants were allowed or encouraged by the respondent to assume?' On the facts, he accepted O's answer, namely 'an expectation that the negotiations would lead to the joint venture company or it would be purchased if the parties could agree terms'. O, in other words, committed to negotiate seriously, but nothing more.

[63] See *Jorden v Money* 1854, 221–3; *Ramsden v Dyson* 1866; *Thorner v Major* 2009, 53; Matthews 2010, 33

typically find an R who laboured under the assumption that O will keep a promise she made to leave him some property in her will. R's expectation often leads him to spend many years in the service and company of O, where it is clear from the circumstances that the promise was, at least, a major component of his motivation for doing so. Alas for R, O refuses to fulfil her promise, or dies without complying with the strict rules of testamentary gifts that govern the legal enforcement of the moral obligation to keep it. To decide R's PE claim, the court needs to ascertain whether it was reasonable of R to 'place trust and confidence in [O]'s unwritten oblique promises and indications'.[64] In situations of this kind it would be totally unrealistic to expect R to ask for a guarantee that his reliance will be compensated for if the promise is not fulfilled. As the Lord Neuberger notes in the context of *Thorner*: 'formal contractual rights and obligations were simply not the stuff of the relationship between Peter [the uncle—O] and David [the nephew—R]'. It only seems natural that equity will provide a solution for people who have reasonably relied on a promise (or a series of them) in circumstances where they cannot be expected to use the legal tool that normally ensures the enforceability of the obligation to fulfil it.

A good example can be found in the recent PC case of *Henry and Mitchell v Henry*: Geraldine Pierre (O), a wealthy landowner from the Caribbean island of St Lucia, allowed Calixtus's grandmother to build a house on her land and live there. Calixtus (R) was born in the house and continues to live there to this day. O visited R's plot daily and treated him like her son. R testified that O 'stated many times to me . . . that she would leave the land for those that worked the land and for those that cared for her in her home country'. The plot provided food for R and his family, as well as for O. Upon her death O left the plot to her niece Theresa, and Calixtus claimed that PE arose in his favour. The question before the Privy Council was whether R had indeed acted to his detriment. Sir Jonathan Parker thought that he did. R remained working on the land (unlike other farmers who left for the big city), cared for O and provided food for her, and thus he effectively deprived himself of the opportunity for a better life elsewhere; that was enough to establish a detriment and usher in the equity of PE.[65]

The gift cases, then, deal with situations that are very different in kind from the bargain/joint venture ones. Although R is expecting to receive property rights in return for his loyalty, assistance, and company, there is no deal in which goods are exchanged for services.[66] What R has is an explicit but merely oral promise to give

---

[64] Neuberger 2009, 542.

[65] *Henry and Mitchell v Henry* 2010, 62; cf. *Cook v Thomas and another* 2010 where Lloyd LJ rejected the PE claim of R who moved in with her mother when she lost her previous accommodation, even though she and her partner kept the mother company and did some work in the house ([74], [103]).

[66] The arrangements are mostly a species of what James Penner called 'mutual agreements' under which parties to personal relationship promote their mutual interests, to distinguish from 'bargain' agreements in which each party is supposed to serve his or her own interest by complying with the agreement (see Penner 1996b, 335–8). However, as you would expect from an attempt to arrange human affairs in neat categories, there are cases around that fit neither, or both, categories. In some PE gift cases, for example, a personal arrangement between the parties comes close to an exchange of

him a gift upon O's death. PE is sometimes denigrated as a doctrine which allows the claimant to circumvent the formalities requirements just because he happened to rely on the promise. But this need not be the case. In Section 4.2 we will see that in fact the courts do not really enforce the promise as if it were properly formalized. Crucially, in PE cases the court looks to see whether the reliance was proportionate to the promised benefit. I suggest that if we want to bring out the difference between formal and informal promises, we can analyse the remedy for the latter as falling short of enforcing on O the full force of her moral duty to R. Instead of tracking the moral obligation(s) of O, namely to keep her promise, the remedy offered by PE should be seen as the legal enforcement of a *different*, narrower, kind of obligation: LPA.

If you are happy with Scanlon's account of the duty to keep promises you can interpret the function of PE in the gift category as enforcing on O (the promisor) only the core obligation that lies at the heart of her promise. For, according to Scanlon, the obligation to keep a promise is an extension of the moral duty laid down by principle L (which requires you to compensate other people for reasonable reliance on your representation unless you warned them not to do so). By enforcing on O only the more basic duty that is implied by her promise, we give the requirements of formality their due respect. Thus, while we prevent at least an important part of the harm which broken promises cause the promisee, we acknowledge the utmost importance of formality as attesting to the true intentions of the donor. This way of balancing R's interests against policy considerations can work well, albeit with less conceptual elegance, even for those who do not accept Scanlon's account of promises (e.g. because they believe that the duty to keep a promise is *sui generis*, or is based on an independent social norm). On these accounts PE will be seen as forcing O to fulfil, not her promise, but a different, yet closely linked, kind of obligation towards people she induced to trust her.[67]

4.2 The remedy

If the interpretation of PE I suggest is accepted by the courts, this should change the point of departure, if not the end result, of their decisions in regards to the remedy. In a nutshell, when a successful PE claim is made against O, she should be enforced to compensate R for his reliance loss, not to make her representation good.[68] PE as

---

benefits (see Lord Walker's discussion of *Dillwyn v Llewelyn* 1862 in *Cobbe v Yeoman's Row Management Ltd* 2008, [50]). Similarly, in some cases that are firmly set in commercial relationship, O has arguably made a promise to R that does not seem to have any potential to benefit O, see for example the life tenancy promised to the Earl in *Parker v Parker* 2003.

[67] And see Raz 1982 where he says that in principle the liberal state can enforce only reliance-based duties for *any* promise/contract (Raz 1982, 937).

[68] Richard Craswell has made a powerful argument according to which Fuller and Purdue's classification of the remedial interests to expectation, reliance, and restitution is not a useful starting point for normative or instrumental analysis of contract remedies. This is because remedies can be defended only with reference to the purpose or policy which they are meant to serve (Craswell 1996, 11). His suggestion, however, is not to eschew the idea of a baseline for measuring contract damages (Craswell 1996, 80). Rather, when we come to analyse the different remedies in this field, we should

we know it today is a fairly recent phenomenon. But over this short period, an interesting shift has already registered in the case law from an almost automatic award of the expectation value to a great emphasis on the proportionality between the remedy and the claimant's reliance loss.[69] The result is a gap between the way the courts respond to a legally enforceable promise (i.e. contract), and the way they treat successful PE claims. This gap is readily understood if the function of PE is to enforce a different kind of obligation, the discharge of which does not require O to make her representation good (unless this is the only way to compensate R for his reliance loss).

In *Jennings v Rice* for example, the claimant, Mr Jennings, worked many years for free for Ms Royle, a wealthy widow. The lady encouraged J to believe that he would receive property worth at least £435,000 under her will, but eventually passed away intestate. At first instance, J was awarded £200,000 calculated by reference to the market price of the care he had given her. J appealed on the basis that the promises made to him reasonably led him to expect a more generous share of her estate. The CA dismissed the appeal, rejected the view that the equity of PE is principally satisfied by awarding the expectation value, and stated that 'the most essential requirement is that there must be proportionality between the expectation and the detriment'.[70] This and other recent CA cases which highlight the requirement of proportionality between the claimant's reliance and the remedy support the view, detailed below, that the essential remedy of PE is tailored to cover R's reliance loss, not to fulfil his expectations.

The interpretation of the basic remedy for PE as a compensation for reliance losses has some clear advantages. From a conceptual point of view, it marks a significant improvement in the internal coherence of the doctrine. Many commentators accept that the defendant's responsibility is anchored in the claimant's detrimental reliance.[71] Hence, it is only natural to expect that 'hand in hand with reliance-based enforcement [there would come] reliance-based relief'.[72] Moreover, even in breach of contract cases it is far from clear why we should take the expectation value (rather than the reliance loss) as the standard measure for remedy. The strongest conceptual (to distinguish from practical) arguments in favour of that rule are based on the unique structure of contracts as bilateral

---

ask not which of the three interests they serve, but to what extent they strive to fulfil the claimant's expectations and hence the promise he was given (Craswell 1996, 83). My analysis of the remedies for PE goes along very similar lines: since the commitment which is enforced by the doctrine is to cover reliance losses, the reliance interest serves as the baseline, where the value of the remedy is highly flexible and can climb up to the expectation measure when this is necessary for achieving the aim of the remedy (i.e. to encourage optimal reliance).

[69] As Matthews shows, the proportionality requirement does not sit well with the historical origins of PE (Matthews 2010, 53).

[70] *Jennings v Rice* 2002, 36; *Sledmore v Dalby* 1996, 208–9; *Ottey v Grundy* 2003; in Australia see *Commonwealth of Australia v Verwayen* 1990, per Mason CJ 208–9; *Giumelli v Giumelli* 1999, 123.

[71] See Cooke 2000, 7–13 and sources cited there.

[72] Cooke 2000, 167. Cooke herself does not accept this view of the estoppel remedy even in proprietary estoppel cases, but her view on this point is based on conservative instinct rather than specific arguments (Cooke 2000, 168, and see criticism in Neyers 2003, 35).

agreements which involve consideration.[73] This is of course not the place to examine this issue, but it is obvious that the relationship between R and O in estoppel cases cannot support a *principled* award of the expectation value. From this point of view then, O should only be made to compensate R for his reliance loss, not for his frustrated expectations.[74]

Taking the reliance value as the base point of the PE remedy would also serve another major concern of property law, namely, 'to contain the situations in which property rights arise'.[75] A happy side-benefit of reducing the basic measure of the remedy from expectation to reliance would be the inevitable reduction in the economic value of property rights that are passed via PE, as the reliance value is very often lower than the expectations one. But the containment goes deeper than that: if we take the reliance value as a base point for remedy, it would be reasonable to limit the recourse to proprietary, to distinguish from monetary, remedies to a minimum. We could, in other words, expect that as a rule property rights would be transferred (or otherwise changed) only where a personal remedy cannot achieve the goal of compensating the claimant's reliance loss (see more on this point later in this section).

The problem is of course that in many, if not most, of the recent cases in which PE was successfully argued, the claimant ended up getting the value of his or her expectation. O, in other words, was often forced to make her representation good. One way to proceed when a fissure opens between a suggested interpretation of a doctrine and the current practice is to urge the legislator, or the Supreme Court, to introduce a sea-change in the way the cases are decided. That, however, will not be necessary here. For, as Bright, McFarlane, and Robertson show, the *results* of PE cases do not reflect the view that the expectation value is the standard measure of the remedy. On the contrary: the courts emphasize again and again that the remedy must be in tune with the claimant's reliance. The reason why it appears that the remedy is tailored to cover the claimant's expectation is that in the knotty circumstances typical of PE this is the only way to ensure that the reliance loss is adequately compensated for.

The contrast between the relative ease with which the value of expectation can be determined and the complex task of calculating reliance losses is well known.[76] If

---

[73] See Benson 2001, 175; Penner 1996b, 352. The classical challenge to the expectation measure of damages for breach of contract has been laid down in Fuller and Perdue 1936, and has been taken seriously by contract theorists ever since (see n. 35).

[74] A liability rule that awards R the value of his expectation will also exacerbate the 'over-reliance' problem—see Craswell 1996, 494.

[75] Bright and McFarlane 2005b, 449.

[76] For some writers this gap even explains why the standard remedy for a breach of contract is based on the expectation (and not reliance) value, as Fuller and Perdue explain: 'granting the value of the expectancy . . . offers the measure of recovery most likely to reimburse the plaintiff for the (often very numerous and very difficult to prove) individual acts and forbearances which make up this total reliance on the contract (Fuller and Perdue 1936, 60). According to the authors, the prevailing practice of bargain contracts actually makes it the case that expectation interest is swallowed by the reliance interest as the expectation of profit becomes a legitimate reliance; this, however, is a highly implausible analysis, see Penner 1996b, 350; Raz, in contrast, keeps the expectation and reliance interests separate, and argues that the former should be satisfied for practical reasons similar to those put forward by Robertson et al., see Raz 1982, 938.

you want to make absolutely sure that the claimant's reasonable reliance loss is recompensed, give him his expectation value. As Robertson shows, in the typical cases of PE, quantifying the reliance loss is often so complicated that satisfying the expectation remains the only way to ensure that R does not suffer the harm from which PE is supposed to protect him.[77] Following a careful survey of the latest English and Australian cases, he concludes that the reasons why in most cases of successful PE claims the court ends up awarding the expectation value are therefore a matter of practice not of principle.

According to Bright and McFarlane, the only set of circumstances in which the courts automatically award the expectation value are those where (1) O and R have reached a complete, albeit informal agreement, (2) O does something that convinces R that she will honour the agreement, and (3) R fulfils his part. But the reason *why* the remedy is fashioned in that way is that the parties are (deemed to) have settled the question what is the value of *reliance* in their eyes, namely, the (value of) the property right that is the subject of the agreement.[78] But in all other situations, they conclude, 'there is no default rule in favour of protecting [R]'s expectations'.[79] Indeed, there are many other cases in which the court grants R the value of his expectations. But this attests only to the difficulty of quantifying a reliance loss that comprises of personal services, opportunities missed out, life-changing decisions, or all of the above, and is, therefore very hard to quantify.[80]

Where the reliance loss is clearly slight in comparison with the expectation, the courts often order O to compensate R for his reliance loss and no more. For example, in *Campbell v Griffin*, a classical 'gift' case, the Court of Appeal awarded R only a monetary charge over the house in which he was claiming to have a life interest.[81] And in other cases, even as the award approximates the expectation value, the courts make adjustments that clearly differentiate the enforcement of what Lord Walker defined as R's 'moral. . . . claim on the property', from the way in which promises are enforced by contract law.[82] In *Malik v Kalyan* for example, the Court of Appeal awarded R half of the house he was promised (the other half he inherited anyway), but charged against it half of the legacies which O intended to leave to his daughters.[83]

It seems therefore that the courts, even as they recognize that the reliance loss is the focal point of PE, are so careful to protect R that they tend to treat him almost

---

[77] Robertson 2008, 303–15; Spence 1999, 7.　　[78] Bright and McFarlane 2005a, 458–62.

[79] Bright and McFarlane 2005a, 462.

[80] See Robertson 2008, 305–15 and cases cited there. Robertson suggests that 'the court is, in effect, holding the representor responsible for the factual uncertainty brought about by his or her inconsistent conduct. . . . the onus is properly cast on the representor to show that there is a disproportion between the claimant's expectation loss and the detriment' (317). However, this suggestion is quite problematic from the point of view of civil litigation principles where it is up to the claimant to prove all the elements of his claim, including the precise scale of his damage. It also seems that it many cases the loss value is unquantifiable in principle, and there is hence no burden of proof that anyone could lift.

[81] *Campbell v Griffin* 2001, 36. See also *Beale v Harvey* 2003; *Ottey v Grundy* 2003; *Burrows v Sharp* 1991.

[82] *Campbell v Griffin* 2001, 34.　　[83] *Malik v Kalyan* 2010, 32.

as if he approached them with a duly formalized contract in his belt. The result is a troubling mismatch between the defendant's responsibility and what she (very often) has to do in order to discharge it. Yet, I want to argue, that this friction between the liability and remedy can be readily dissolved if we bear in mind the dual justification of the doctrine, as suggested in this chapter. For the point of PE as enforcing LPA obligations is not merely the prevention of reliance loss to R; PE is not merely a tort-like doctrine that aims to compensate R for foreseeable harm. Rather, as we saw, it is a unique legal device whose purpose is to facilitate and encourage efficient pre-contractual reliance. And if the law is to do its job properly in this area, a particularly rigorous enforcement of O's LPA duty is essential.

A rule according to which R's claim is subject to the limitations that apply to any odd claim for compensation for harm in tort will undermine the doctrine's purpose. For, if R knows that in case of dispute he will have to bear the high costs of proving the precise value of his reliance, and will miss on those investments that cannot be measured with precision (especially prone would be missed opportunities), his investment decision will be overcautious.[84] If we want to encourage efficient reliance we must formulate the liability rule in such a way that would reassure R that all his reasonable reliance costs will be covered, even if the loss which they embody cannot be measured in any exact way, and that any doubts about its measure will be resolved in his favour. This rule, while it can be harsh on the representor, would still serve her interests best, as the surplus from efficient reliance will be enjoyed by both parties. Given the limitations of reasonableness and proportionality, the burden on O, should she wish to withdraw from her representation, ought not to be too heavy, even with such pro-representor rule of liability in place.

Under the interpretation of PE as enforcing LPA obligations the principle for remedy should therefore be as follows: the claimant—R—is entitled to have all his reasonable reliance loss covered by O. In a case where the only way to ensure that the reliance value is covered in full is to award the claimant the value of his expectation the court should do so. This rule is still different from the standard practice in that it calls on the court to take the reliance loss, rather the expectation, as the baseline of the remedy. But since it encourages the judge to award the expectation value whenever he or she is concerned lest the reliance loss cannot otherwise be fully compensated, and since the courts anyway require proportionality between the reliance and the loss, no major revolution is needed. Such conservative result (in terms of the practice) is highly desirable in a field like property law where the acute importance of stability and predictability requires that we take extra care not to thwart people's expectations about the state of the law.

A clear understanding of PE as compelling O to abide by her LPA obligation will also help us to be more precise about the boundaries of the court's discretion with regards to the remedy. One of the famous characteristics of PE—admired by some but highly dubious according to others—is the extraordinary flexibility with which the remedy for it is fashioned by the courts. But even wide discretion can and

---

[84] And see Katz on that point: 'if reliance is less than fully protected, then parties who cannot capture its benefits will underrely' (Katz 1996, 1308).

should be based on principles, especially so in property law where clarity and predictability are of particular importance. For parties to a dispute on a unique and (often) precious right can expect to know what they need to do in order to prove their claim and what are the chances of success. Some appellate judges have suggested that when deciding the remedy for PE the court ought to take into account a wide range of considerations, from the level of indecency that can be attributed to O, to the parties' relative needs, or even any 'alterations in the benefactor's assets and circumstances'.[85]

Yet, if the justifying principle behind the doctrine is as suggested in this chapter the judge should not take such considerations into account. Future changes in O's circumstances should matter only inasmuch as foreseeing them influenced her (perceivable) commitment to the state of affairs envisaged in her representation. Similarly, the general moral standard of O's behaviour should not affect the measure of remedy, as the only issue on the table is whether her behaviour gave rise to an LPA obligation—other morally relevant aspects of her conduct are beside the point. The parties' relative needs lie even further beyond the boundaries of the relationship that is relevant for a PE claim. Indeed, the influence which such factors seem to have exerted on the results of some cases can sometimes be explained as stemming from principles that are external to PE or, more often, on the basis of the conventional elements of the PE claim.[86]

A related problem is the allusive role of the 'unconscionability' element of PE. The fear is of course that the 'unconscionability' element will tempt the court to use equity as a 'sort of moral U.S. fifth cavalry riding to the rescue every time a claimant is left worse off than he anticipated as a result of the defendant behaving badly'.[87] Peter Birks for example, dismissed unconscionability as a 'fifth wheel on the coach' of estoppel.[88] Lord Walker, in contrast, glorifies it as 'unifying and confirming, as it were, the other elements' of the PE claim.[89] The interpretation of PE advanced here supports Lord Walker's view. At the bottom of PE lies a moral wrong that taints the defendant's conscience: inviting R to trust and rely on her, or carelessly making R believe so, and turning her back on him later.[90] This, as we saw, is not to say that the point of PE is to make people obey their moral obligations (and it is highly doubtful anyway whether this is possible at all). But it does mean that we see O's behaviour as morally wrong and that it is a legitimate interest of society to curb this kind of behaviour in order to foster a socially valuable

---

[85] See respectively *Crabb v Arun District Council* 1975; *Sledmore v Dalby* 1996; *Jennings v Rice* 2002, 52. For a critical exposition of the way in which O's behaviour influenced the courts' decision see Robertson 2010, s. B.

[86] Robertson 2010, 421.

[87] Neuberger 2009, 543. As an example one can perhaps point at Rotherham's view of the function of PE in cases of unilateral mistake as tackling 'unconscionable opportunism' (Rotherham 2002, 294).

[88] Birks 1996, 63s.

[89] *Cobbe v Yeoman's Row Management Ltd* 2008, 92. See also Spence (1999, 14) who sees 'unconscionability' as relating to the strength of the moral duty that lies at the heart of estoppel according to his interpretation, and the criteria for unconscionability he offers at pp. 59–66.

[90] I am here using 'unconscionability' to denote an action that is contrary to objective moral norms—on equity as employing the consciability standard in that sense see Samet 2012.

practice and protect people from certain harms. Unconscionability turns out to be the hub of the doctrine, in the sense that the other elements should function to eliminate it.

One of the main reasons why we want to be as clear as possible on the nature of the unconscionability that underlies PE is the potential effect which the remedy for it may have on third parties. PE is once more in a muddle: authorities and scholars disagree about the position of third parties in a way that leaves this aspect of the doctrine in an unacceptably volatile state. Here, again, a solid view about the justifying principle behind PE can, I believe, help us to resolve the difficulties. Thus, if PE is designed to enforce LPA obligations the remedy it offers should, wherever possible, remain within the relationship of O and R and not spill over to other players.[91] In other words, the remedy for PE should in principle be of a *personal* nature, like monetary compensation or licence, rather than a proprietary right.

This is because transfer of property rights was only expected by the parties to take place at the final stage when a full promise is being delivered and fulfilled. The LPA obligation, in contrast, looks backwards, and aims to ensure that R occupies the same position he did before the representation was made. At this stage, he had, of course, no property right of O's. A proprietary right should therefore only be awarded where it is impossible to devise a personal remedy that adequately covers R's reliance loss.[92] As Bright and McFarlane show, this property-thin approach, even if it is not explicit in the case law, reflects the results in most of the cases.[93] Moreover, in many of the decisions in which a property right has been transferred it was actually possible to take a more imaginative approach and devise a personal remedy that would have answered R's predicament without affecting third parties.[94] This interpretation of proper remedy for PE turns out to be no more, and no less, radical than is proper for reforms in property law.

5. Conclusion

'Equitable estoppel' Lord Walker said once, 'is a flexible doctrine which the court can use, in appropriate circumstances, to prevent injustice caused by the vagaries and inconstancy of human nature'.[95] In this chapter I argued that the inconstancy which PE sets to amend is not that of retreating from a representation one made, but rather that of denying one's responsibility for the way in which the retreat affected other people. The core moral obligation which is enforced by PE does not require O to stick to her representation. On the contrary—the obligation's

---

[91] See also Spence 1999, 34.

[92] A classical example would be the (somewhat unusual) *Crabb v Arun District Council* 1975 where R's reliance consisted in leaving his property landlocked, so that only by granting an easement the detriment could be removed.

[93] Bright and McFarlane 2005a, 466–76.

[94] The authors criticize these cases as 'proprietary overkill' (Bright and McFarlane 2005a, 473–5).

[95] *Cobbe v Yeoman's Row Management Ltd* 2008, 46.

uniqueness and value lie exactly in the way in which it allows the representor to retract from her representation, subject only to a responsibility she must take for R's reasonable reliance upon it.

O, we saw, may assume this LPA obligation intentionally in order to encourage R to make investments to promote a joint project even before she can fully commit to it. She may also be reasonably understood by R to take this obligation on. On either case, the state is justified in enforcing the LPA obligation as an exercise of its duty to foster autonomy-enhancing practices. For the formation of such LPA-based relationships enable parties to make optimal investment decisions at the pre-contractual period, and a frequent refusal to abide by the LPA duties which the relationships imply will collapse the practice of making such investments at a heavy cost to social good. We saw how the circumstances typical of negotiations towards a transfer of property rights exacerbate R's difficulties on the way to an optimal investment decision: the uniqueness and high value of the subject matter of these transactions raise the stakes for both seller and buyer, and as a result the seller is likely to require a longer negotiation period, the necessary investments by the buyer are likely to be substantial, and the risks of the 'holdup' trap will soar in tandem. By reassuring R that the moral obligations that arise out of O's representations will be fulfilled, PE facilitates efficient pre-contractual reliance in the many cases where the parties cannot be expected to agree on how to meet the reliance loss if the deal is aborted.

In that, the doctrine of PE goes well beyond ordinary tort doctrines that seek to protect representees from faulty representors. For the harm that PE is set to prevent, namely, the collapse of the efficient pre-contractual reliance practice, is detrimental to everyone—representees, as well as representors. It is in the interest of O, in other words, to protect the interests of R. As a result, we should not be surprised to find that the balance between the parties' interests in a PE claim is different from that of ordinary tort claims—since it is in O's interest to give R the maximum encouragement to pitch his investment at the optimal level, it makes sense to formulate a rule that makes it relatively easy for him to recover his losses if O retreats. And thus, when the courts enforce on O her LPA obligation, they rightfully go to a great length to ensure that R is fully compensated, so much so that O is many times ordered to make her representation good. This result, I argued, does not reflect the view that O's representation embodied a promise to R that she is now ordered to fulfil. Rather, it reveals the complex justification for enforcing the LPA obligation which O's representation gave rise to—not only as a protection from misrepresentation, but also as a means to support and boost high-surplus transactions in property right.

7

Possession and Use

Arthur Ripstein*

My aim in this chapter is to examine the relation between possession and use in the concept of property.[1] Many writers find it difficult to see how property could be of any interest or importance if it was not related in a fundamental way to an owner's use of the property. At the same time, doctrinally speaking, the right to exclude is often said to be the fundamental or even the sole organizing norm of property law. In what follows, I will develop a conceptual argument for the priority of exclusion—which I will refer to by the term 'possession'—over use. Possession, as I shall articulate it here, is the formal precondition of use, but does not depend upon the particularities or actuality of use. But I shall go further, and argue that the sense in which possession, and so use, both figures in the law and matters cannot be explained except by reference to the concept of exclusion. Rather than having the right to exclude others so that you may use your property, your property is useful to you because it is exclusively yours. The only interest in use that the law of property protects is specific to the owner and explicitly contrastive: it protects the owner's interest in being the one to determine the use of the object, as against others. That is just to say it protects an interest in exclusive use.

Versions of the thesis which I will defend have been defended by others. In *The Idea of Property in Law* James Penner writes:

It is my contention that the law of property is driven by an analysis which takes the perspective of exclusion, rather than one which elaborates a right to use. In other words, in order to understand property, we must look to the way that the law contours the duties it imposes on people to exclude themselves from the property of others, rather than regarding the law as instituting a series of positive liberties or powers to use particular things.[2]

* I am grateful to Lisa Austin for exacting comments on an early draft, to participants in the workshop 'Philosophical Foundations of Property Law' for their comments and questions, and especially to James Penner and Henry Smith, both for including me in their conference and volume, and for their extremely helpful comments on the post-conference draft.

[1] I will say nothing here about intellectual property. Nor shall I even comment on whether it is usefully characterized as property at all, or whether any unification of property and intellectual property is to be sought. Instead, I will focus exclusively on property in land and chattels.

[2] Penner 1997, 71.

My way of framing the issue differs from Penner's however, because I do not endorse or defend his subsequent claim that 'This can be expressed as follows, in what I shall call the *exclusion thesis: the right to property is a right to exclude others from things which is grounded by the interest we have in the use of things.*' Or rather, the claim can be taken in two ways, one of which I reject, and the other of which I endorse. The claim I reject is that property protects a general interest in use, without attending to the specifics of the way in which it is exercised on particular occasions. On this first interpretation of Penner's subsequent claim, the fact that it 'is difficult in the extreme to quantify the many different uses one can make of one's property, so as to give a workable outline of what the "right to use" property actually is,' is an unfortunate limitation, and the law's focus on exclusion is 'simply a matter of what is most practical'.[3] On the second interpretation, which I do endorse, the 'interest we have in the use of things' to which the law gives effect cannot be specified except by reference to the norm of exclusion itself. It is not that actual or likely use is too complicated to express in a norm, necessitating a retreat to a more manageable norm of possible use as a proxy; possible use is itself only a value when qualified by 'rightful' or 'exclusive'. Rather than the right to property protecting an interest by imposing duties on others, the relevant interest is itself an implication of the right; your interest in using your property is a matter of the relations you stand in to others. I do not mean to deny that a person who uses something typically derives a benefit from so doing, or that it is a good thing in general that human beings get to use things. The 'value' of use in either of these senses is not part of any explanation because serving it is not part of the doctrine or its rationale.

My argument is organized into three parts. First, I will make some general remarks about the formal nature of possessory rights in property. In the second and third sections of the chapter, I will argue for the priority of possession over use both directly, by showing how the concept of a property right is necessarily formal, and indirectly, by showing that attempts to generate a formal right as an over-inclusive version of an interest in use must fail. I cannot exhaustively catalogue all such attempts. Instead, I will focus on two familiar strategies, and suggest that each presupposes the priority of possession, and so cannot treat it as an overinclusive proxy for something else.

In the past, under the influence of legal realism and the 'bundle theory' of property, the point of an interest based account was to unmask property, and to show that current aspects of property law could be changed so as to address other interests, or the same interests more effectively. The accounts I will consider, by contrast, are interest based but seek to explain, and to some degree to vindicate, property as it currently is. At the same time, they concede that the details of doctrine do not fit its justification perfectly. They remain instrumental, because they suppose that the purpose of exclusion is to advance a purpose that is contingently connected to exclusion. Where the first account grants this power to

---

[3] Penner 1997, 71.

the owner because she is a human being capable of *benefiting* from control over resources, the second, autonomy-based account grants the power to the owner as a way of enabling her to *exercise* her own autonomy. Neither is capable of making sense of the priority of possession, and this inability, in turn, prevents either from making sense of a basic right to use. Both treat the generality of the right to exclude as a response to epistemic limitations; because non-users and non-agenda setters cannot typically know who is using the item in question, or the agenda user has set for it, a simple 'keep out' rule protects the use-based interest as effectively as possible. I will contend, however, that both accounts actually presuppose a more robust concept of possession. I will conclude with some more general remarks about the relation between rights and interests.

1. Possession

The most familiar doctrinal feature of property law (in tangibles) is the right to exclude. Despite its familiarity, it raises the question for many contemporary theories of property: to what end? There is plenty of controversy about the nature of rights in general, and property rights in particular. What is not controversial, however, is the thought that, once someone has a right to do something, the right holder is thereby permitted to exercise the right foolishly, imprudently, and, at least within limits, immorally. If you have a right to freedom of expression, you are allowed to say things that you should not say. And if you have a right to private property, you are allowed to exercise that right in stupid, pointless, and unhelpful ways. Although there is moral and occasionally legal controversy about whether you need to make your property available to another person to save his or her life, there is no controversy about whether you need to make your property available to someone who could put it to better use than you can. You do not. Utilitarian theories of property argue that in general, systems of private property increase overall welfare. They do not, and could not, argue that in every instance every exercise of property rights does so. Instead, they treat rights as generalizations which must be honoured because of the benefits generated by general conformity to them. Thus they must be respected *even when* they fail to provide the goods they are supposed to. I will argue that the only real alternative to this instrumental view is to suppose that rights have a different type of generality, which cannot be reduced to the sort of empirical generalization on which all overinclusive rationales must depend.

The structural features of the right to exclude are simple and familiar: outside of certain qualifications, an owner gets to decide what will happen with her property and, most fundamentally, gets to decide the terms on which *anyone else* may use that property for any purpose. There are, to be sure, various restrictions and qualifications imposed on the rights of owners by other areas of the law. So, for example, common carriers must take everyone on their vehicles or vessels, business establishments may not discriminate on the basis of race, and public officials may commandeer property in an emergency. These are all nonetheless exceptions, restrictions, and qualifications on a structure that normally leaves the decision entirely to the owner. If you are not a common carrier, you get to decide who rides in your car or boat, and you are allowed to decide who comes into your home; no question of grounds even comes up. Nor may you ordinarily commandeer any other person's property.

The right to exclude is not, on its face, a protection against harm or loss. Harmless trespasses against land are actionable, and although in common law jurisdictions trespasses against chattels ordinarily require that some damage be established, the threshold does not depend on any sort of interruption in the owner's use of or plans for the object. And even with chattels, if no harm is suffered but the non-owner gains an advantage, the owner is entitled to recover damages which are measured by the defendant's gain.[4] The basic structure of the wrong consists in using something that belongs to somebody else.

The basic action-guiding norm of property reflects the constitutive role of possession: that norm speaks to non-owners and says 'do not use or interfere with anything that is not yours'. It formulates this norm in distinctively second-personal terms: 'is not yours' rather than 'belongs to owner [insert name here]' precisely because the basic action-guiding norm does not require anyone to know about title; it only requires that people know that something does not belong to them. Henry Smith has noted this is an epistemically undemanding rule, which requires almost no information to apply; such information as it does require is autobiographical, and so typically available to each person. It is, at the same time, morally very demanding, as it requires people to abstain from the property of others pretty much no matter what, and so restricts many other things they might wish to do with it, including very worthwhile things. These familiar features can be explained in two ways. One attaches priority to the epistemic, and says that we make the morally demanding rule because it is easy to implement. The other view goes in the opposite direction: the morally demanding rule requires an epistemically easy implementation; our moral situation is not, in the first instance, a matter of ignorance.

But even putting it in these terms understates the significance of possession. It is trite law, though puzzling to some writers, that you can commit a trespass even if you are in no position to know who the owner is. If you take another's coat, innocently mistaking it for your own, you have a full defence to any criminal charge, but still commit a trespass against chattels; if, through no fault of your own, you are confused about where your land ends and your neighbour's begins you commit a trespass. In such cases, there may be a question about the seriousness of the wrong. But it is uncontroversial that you commit a legal wrong.

---

[4] There is an ongoing controversy as to whether such damages are properly characterized as gain based, or rather that the measure of the damages is tied to the invasion of the right. I defend the version of the former position in Ripstein 2007; for a defence of the latter position, see Stevens 2007. The difference between our positions is not important to the question addressed here, which is just that damages can be awarded even if the owner suffers no actual harm or consequential loss.

These familiar markers of property doctrine reveal that the right to exclude is purely formal. It does not matter how you are using your land or chattels; others wrong you if they use it. If you leave land unoccupied, because you are hoping to sell it when the real estate market turns around, or because you simply never get around to developing it, others who enter your land commit a legal wrong against you. Although someone might propose an extended sense of 'use' in which even such things qualify,[5] perhaps modelled on Sartre's famous claim that to fail to decide is to decide against deciding, to do so would empty the claim that property protects use of any content. Instead, such examples show the nub of a property right is that the owner *rather than others* gets to determine how the thing will be used. Indeed, the person who uses or interferes with land for which you have made no plans commits exactly the same legal wrong as the person who enters your land in a way that interferes with your use of it. The damages you get for the loss of your use are, for reasons to be explained in Section 3, predicated upon a trespass. The difference between the case where your land is unused and the case in which you are using it is just in the claim to damages for consequential loss. The basis of those damages is the same wrong as in the case where you are not using it. If you suffer the same disadvantage with respect to something that you do not own (or with respect to which you have no other possessory rights) you have no claim to have those losses made up. Your original right is the right to exclusive possession; consequential loss does not give rise to an independent cause of action.

As a matter of property doctrine, then, your basic right is a right, as against other private persons, to restrict their use of what belongs to you. Because you have a right to determine how your property will be used, you have other, concomitant rights also. If someone uses your property without your authorization, you have the entitlement to have your title to it vindicated through nominal damages, and are entitled to whatever benefit that person gains through the use of your property. Further, if someone damages your property, whether in the process of using it or through carelessness, you are entitled to have your property restored to its original state. The right against damage is just the right that the question of what is done with your property is yours to answer.

In characterizing the right to exclude as basic, I do not mean to suggest that it is not subject to all of the familiar public law limitations. As James Harris describes them, these are of two forms, 'property limitation rules' and 'expropriation rules'. Much libertarian writing about property supposes that the fundamental nature of the right to exclude must render these public law doctrines morally suspect. On the view I am defending, however, the right to exclude is a right as against other private persons (including public bodies acting in private capacities). The public law limitations and permissions to expropriate are instances of the 'vertical' relation between the state and citizens, rather than of the 'horizontal' relations between private persons. It is precisely because the right to exclude is basic to horizontal relations that such doctrines are required, and take on the distinctive form that they

---

[5] Penner 1997.

do. If property were organized around use in general, or the particularities of use, why should expropriation and limitation of property rights be so restricted, rather than being available whenever property could be used more effectively by someone other than the owner? If property were organized around use in general, the horizontal/vertical distinction would be also puzzling; why should expropriation and limitation be the exclusive province of a public authority?[6]

I hope what I have said so far is in no way controversial as a description of the doctrinal situation. To describe the broad contours of doctrine is not the same as explaining its rationale, or even its deep structure. In Section 2, I will argue that this surface structure of property rights is also its deep structure.

2. The Priority of Exclusion

These commonplaces of property doctrine can be made to seem puzzling. The combined impact of John Stuart Mill's 'harm principle' and American Legal Realism has made many writers wonder whether property doctrine could mean what it says. It protects against harmless loss, and so, many have wondered whether it has some other purpose, some way of relating it more directly to the prevention of harm and loss. But the puzzle is older. In the High Middle Ages, writers also puzzled over the nature of private power. For Aquinas, the puzzle came up because he was convinced that property could not be a natural feature of the moral world, since it was plainly permissible for religious orders to do away with it, and hold everything in common. His solution was to characterize it in terms of a sort of stewardship of resources. The basic idea, which remains prominent in discussions of property up to this day, was that an asset is likely to be preserved better and used more fruitfully if a single person is responsible for it. That argument can only be made to work on the assumption that the person responsible for the asset also gets to claim its benefits. Hence the right to exclude is understood as a sort of steward's stipend, a way of channelling benefits to increase their overall amount.

A different version of the same line of thought contends that it is good for people to be able to make decisions and plan and order their own lives. Giving them exclusive control over resources better enables them to do so, and makes them less dependent on natural circumstances and the whims of others.

Beyond the specifics of these accounts, there is an underlying intuitive idea also. The right to exclude entitles an owner to prevent other people from using his or her property. The power that an owner has in relation to others can be understood either as a disadvantage to them or, alternatively, as a restriction on their autonomy.

---

[6] Even in cases where the power to expropriate is exercised to transfer property from one person to another, as in the controversial *Kelo* (2005) case decided by the US Supreme Court, the stated rationale for the expropriation and transfer of land to a developer was that the development would increase the municipal tax base, which is, in turn, an uncontroversial public purpose. As Merrill and Smith (2007a, 1880) have noted, most property law professors regard *Kelo* as unsurprising, but most ordinary Americans consider it appalling. Yet even in such a case the fact that the land is used more effectively does not enter into the rationale for expropriation, except indirectly.

My right to exclude you from my backyard either disadvantages you or stops you from doing what you would otherwise like to do. The two versions of the interest theory seek to show that any such restrictions are justified on the grounds that they protect either advantage or choice for the owner. But the only way to make those things relevant, it would seem, is to understand those benefits in terms of the possibility of use. The owner is not entitled to exclude others just for the benefit of so doing, which would either be no benefit at all, or, at worst, a distasteful benefit consisting of the power to lord over others for the sake of lordship. As Penner puts it, 'The right to property is grounded by the interest we have in using things in the broader sense. No one has any interest in merely excluding others from things, for any reason or no reason at all. The interest that underpins the right to property is the interest we have in purposefully dealing with things.'[7]

The natural place to look for a genuine benefit or exercise of freedom on the part of the owner is in the owner's actual use of the thing. An interest in controlling something could only be significant (so this line of thought goes) in relation to the possibility of its use.

In criticizing this line of thought, I do not mean to suggest that ownership can be decoupled entirely from use. However, I want to suggest instead that the key to understanding the doctrinal structure of property law focuses not on actual use, nor even directly on its formal possibility. Instead, it focuses on relational independence, which can only be characterized formally, and so generates a protection of the formal possibility of use. The protection of actual use follows from the protection of its formal possibility, but the protection of its formal possibility follows from each owner's entitlement as against others, that owner, rather than any other person, determines how the object is used. Thus the relevant concept of use presupposes the concept of the right to exclude.

I should perhaps reiterate that in characterizing use as presupposing exclusion, I do not mean to deny that we can think about use in other senses. In some sense, the right to exclusive use can only be conceived in relation to the possibility of its violation, that is, of somebody using an object despite it belonging to another. More generally, it might be thought to be a good thing that usable things be used by someone. My claim is only that these senses of use do not enter into the justification of property rights or the explanation of property doctrine. The first is expressly prohibited by property doctrine under the headings of trespass and conversion; the second includes uses to which the user has no right, such as the use I make of your neighbouring building as a source of shade. The law of property is sometimes thought to require a philosophical foundation precisely in order to explain this distinction. A concept of use that includes both poles is an especially unpromising foundation for the distinction between them.

I appreciate that this claim may seem backwards or even circular. In order to motivate and situate it, I will frame it in relation to a powerful recent defence of an

---

[7] Penner 1997, 71.

interest theory, and show why the interest theory cannot make sense of the right to exclude that is at the heart of property doctrine.

Henry Smith's characterization of the relation between exclusion and use provides a clear and forceful articulation of the issue. In the process of developing an alternative to the still-dominant 'bundle theory' of property, Smith suggests that the elements of property are not as independent and contingent as bundle theorists maintain. To the contrary, they have what he characterizes as a unifying 'architecture', a structure whereby the various parts interlock and interact, rather than simply being held together by some external twine. Smith distances himself from the bundle theory by seeking unity, but the unity that he seeks is still, like the bundle theory, to be found in understanding property as a strategy for solving a problem posed in terms that are entirely foreign to its doctrine.

Now there is one sense in which this strategy of seeing property as the solution to a problem has to be correct. If they are to have any normative significance, property rights must solve some sort of problem that somebody could somehow think required a solution.

The difficulty comes with the characterization of the problem and its solution. Despite repudiating the bundle theory, Smith remains committed to its underlying structure, because he regards property rights as instruments for solving a problem that can be characterized without reference to any concepts of either property or right. Instead, he argues that power is 'delegated to owners',[8] that is, the powers that owners have as against other persons are to be traced to the advantages of giving them those powers. Once more, this suggestion admits of a thin and unproblematic reading, but also of a more robust and controversial one. On the thin reading, the powers of ownership are not inexplicable, but rather form part of a system of norms; on the more controversial reading, the powers of ownership are granted to owners because under certain familiar and recurring circumstances, they are an effective way of securing purposes that make no reference to them. I take it that Smith intends the more controversial interpretation, although I do not suppose he intends it to be controversial. As I understand it, his proposal is that the grant of power is itself a tool for achieving a result, the nature and desirability of which can be specified without any reference to the instrument being used to achieve it. The result in question is the satisfaction of an interest, and the strategy for satisfying/advancing/protecting that interest is selected based upon its efficacy in relation to that interest and other conflicting purposes. That is why he characterizes the exclusion strategy as a 'default' that works well much of the time, and so something from which departures must be explained or rationalized. The exclusion strategy itself is, in turn, one of what he identifies as two dominant strategies in property, the other of which is governance, that is, top-down control of resources. The resulting architecture can be adjusted in order to accommodate a variety of further purposes.

Here is how Smith puts the point:

---

[8] Smith 2012b, 1724.

The architecture of property emerges from solving the problem of serving use interests in a roughly cost-effective way. In modern societies this usually involves a first cut through a more use-neutral exclusion strategy and refinement with governance in the form of contracts, regulations, common law doctrine, and norms. At the core of this architecture is exclusion because it is a default, a convenient starting point. It does not mean that exclusion is the most important or 'core' value because it is *not a value at all*. Thinking so usually reflects the confusion of means and ends in property law: exclusion is a rough first cut—and only that—at serving the purposes of property... But the point here is that the exclusion-governance architecture is compatible with a wide range of purposes for property.[9]

I will say very little about what Smith calls the 'governance' strategy. I will note here, without defending, my view that legislative approaches to the allocation of resources must also be conceptualized in less instrumental terms than Smith appears to be proposing here. My focus here will be on the exclusion strategy. I will argue that it cannot be understood as a sort of tool, generally available for whatever purposes lawmakers happen to consider important. Instead, the use-related 'purposes' served by the exclusion strategy cannot be characterized except in terms of the concept of exclusion or its cognates.

Smith is correct to say that progress can only be made in understanding the law if we distinguish between means and ends. The importance of that insight, however, can be lost if it is brought to an issue with the wrong preconception of the kinds of things that can be a means and the kinds of things that can be an end. The difficulty with Smith's analysis, which is common to recent attempts to get beyond the bundle theory, comes in the assumption that the values underlying property are themselves characterizable without reference to property-like concepts. Smith's characterization of the centrality of exclusion bears repeating here. 'It does not mean that exclusion is the most important or "core" value because it is *not a value at all.*' At one level, such a claim seems difficult, indeed impossible and pointless, to deny. It is not as though anyone thinks that it is a good thing, all other things being equal, for one person to exclude another. Indeed, it is even difficult to see how it could be a good thing in its own right that one person has the legal power to exclude another. These difficulties lead, naturally enough, to the thought that the point or purpose of exclusion must be something else, to be found outside it. Use presents itself as a plausible, even obvious candidate.

The difficulty with the chain of reasoning that I have just characterized is that it starts with an assumption about what it would be for something to be of value, and the assumption is, roughly, that something is a value if it is a good-making feature of states of affairs. The question of whether a value is being promoted effectively then becomes a question about the most appropriate means for its promotion. Applied to the case at hand, since exclusion is not a good-making feature of states of affairs—the world is in no way better simply because of some particular act of exclusion—it is represented instead as a means for bringing about something that is such a good-making feature. Use of resources, or use combined with appropriate

---

[9] Smith 2012b, 1705 (italics in original).

allocation, is thought to be the value served by adopting such a strategy; the means of achieving it are then evaluated exclusively in terms of their efficacy.

This strategy for thinking about means and ends generates two difficulties. The first is that frequently moral principles, including some of the most basic ones, do not appear to be about value or its production at all. If talk of value is required here, value does not attach to ends, but rather to means. The basic negative morality that prohibits wrongs against persons and property does not focus on what a person accomplishes, is likely to accomplish, or is seeking to accomplish, but rather on the means that he or she uses in pursuit of whatever purposes. On this familiar understanding, the moral problem with acts of theft and violence is not that the wrongdoer is trying to accomplish the wrong thing, or brings about bad results. Instead, the problem is in the means the wrongdoer uses to achieve those results, a problem that can be articulated without any reference to the ends being pursued.[10] The point here is not that you can only commit a wrong by using prohibited means to commit. Instead, it is that the wrong itself consists in doing certain things to achieve your purposes that are themselves wrongful. To take a familiar example, murder is not wrongful because it involves (say) the use of illegal weapons; murder is wrongful because taking another person's life in order to achieve whatever purpose you hope to achieve is wrongful.

This first difficulty with Smith's strategy for relating means and ends is an instance of a second, more general difficulty. It is a familiar feature of practical thought, and indeed, a familiar feature of thought more generally, that some types of reasoning cannot be reduced to any other type. Perhaps the most familiar instance of this is that simple arithmetic concepts such as counting cannot be formulated without reference to the concept of succession. I do not mean here to prejudge future developments in logic; my point is simply that neither the legitimacy nor the intelligibility of arithmetic is hostage to the possibility of reducing it to some form of logic that does not include the concept of succession. Again, discussion of the nature of spatial relations has in recent centuries focused on the question of whether they must be understood in non-conceptual terms. Whatever the final answer to that question might be—if it makes sense to speak of finality here—the starting point for such debates is the recognition that relations such as 'to the left of' are different from relations such as 'taller than'. The former require the characterization of the items in purely relational terms; nothing is left or right to any degree except in relation to some other location; the latter merely compares things that have whatever height they do and would have that height even if there was nothing else in the world. Neither the legitimacy nor the intelligibility of familiar spatial concepts, and other concepts that present themselves as irreducibly relational—such as 'uncle' and 'nephew'—requires reduction to something non-relational. In the same way, neither the legitimacy nor the intelligibility of the familiar morality of prohibited means depends on showing it to be in the service of something that can be characterized in terms of outcomes without any reference to

---

[10] Ordinarily, people.

means.[11] Instead, the idea that one person wrongs another by using prohibited means—in this case, the other's property—is basic to the morality of property. The thought that I wrong you by using your property relates us to each other, but applies in the same formal way apart from any question of how or even whether you are using your property. You get to decide how to use it because it is yours.

The second difficulty is related to the first but not identical with it. This time the problem is that focusing on what a legal rule is likely to produce diverts attention from the question of what that rule is. In so doing, it also leads to a truncated conception of what the rule could be. By looking at the function of the adoption of a rule, understood in terms of its expected effects, attention is drawn away from the type of reasoning in which the rule figures. The change in focus to effects instead of mode of reasoning, in turn, makes rules stand in a problematic (not to say mysterious) relation to reasons or values. The generality of the rule appears to be a convenience, captured by Smith's characterization of the exclusion strategy as a 'default' rather than a fundamental feature of the type of reasoning in which rules figure.

It is open to Smith to object at this point that his analysis does not apply to particular acts, but instead to general rules, and that the value of the general rule is to be found in what it produces, even though individual acts are to be assessed in light of the general rule. So exclusion is not a value, but violation of the owner's exclusive right is objectionable because it is the violation of a rule designed to produce more value. I mention this possible rejoinder only to set it aside as irrelevant to the current issue. Whether raised at the level of particulars or at the level of general rules, the same dilemma arises: the justification of an obligation to support a worthwhile activity is either one that tells you that you should act in ways that will have certain effects with respect to the activity—an empirical justification—in which case it is an open question whether conformity to the activity's rules is the best way to do so. Alternatively, if it does tell you to abide by the rules, then it seems that the rules have, after all, entered into their own justification, either in a direct and completely circular way or, alternatively, indirectly through an ever so slightly larger circle, in which some meta-rule governs not merely whether you contribute but *how* you contribute. If you are supposed to be supporting a practice or activity, the question immediately arises whether you should support it by acting in accordance with its rules, or in some indirect way without following them. That is, any rule that tells you to follow the rules simply displaces the dilemma to a new level. That rule, in turn, is subject to the same

---

[11] Admittedly, the analogy with counting is imperfect because any conceivable reduction of arithmetic to logic would need to be entirely without remainder if it is to have any intellectual interest. By contrast, the attempt to explain moral concepts involving the use of means in terms of their results does not aspire to a perfect fit; in the hands of its most distinguished practitioners, such as Sidgwick, moral reductionism is thought to be required because the 'morality of common sense' is not precise, and so it must be vindicated in terms of something else that is, at least in principle, precise. Such reliance on the distinction between what is and is not precise entails that a reductive project in practical philosophy will inevitably be revisionary. The conceptual problems noted in the text reflect the tension between a pure reduction of one set of concepts to another and the revisionary exercise of replacing one set of concepts with another.

dilemma. There may be very good moral grounds for supporting all manner of worthwhile activities and practices, but it is a contingent empirical matter about who is best situated to support them, and which acts various people should do to support them.

Smith's characterization in terms of a useful structure in circumstances of imperfect information also draws attention away from the structure of property and focuses instead on its ease of application. The fact that something is generally easy to apply does not entail that its point is to be easy to apply. The ease of application reflects the fact that the rule itself consists in one person—'the owner'—having authority over others with respect to the object in the sense of being in charge of it. In order to provide guidance with respect to any particular object, you first have to answer the threshold question of whether you are the owner of that object. Because property rights are acquired, that threshold question can be answered simply by determining whether you have acquired the object or not. But the simplicity follows from the fact that it does not concern itself with use, but only with exclusion, because the rule constitutes only two possible roles in relation to a given object of ownership. Either you are the owner, in which case you are entitled to determine how the thing is used, or you are not, in which case you may not determine how it is used except with permission of the owner. On this understanding, the exclusion is basic.

The same point can be made more generally: Smith's denial that exclusion is of value at all arises within a framework according to which value must attach exclusively to states of affairs. Putting someone in charge of something is, on his view, an expedient that is useful in conditions of limited information; assigning the role of 'owner' to particular persons with respect to particular things enables people to coordinate more effectively in their shared task of seeing to it that things are used appropriately. The difficulties with this way of framing the issue emerge once the supposed contrast comes into view: supposing perfect information, what would the terms of use for the object be? Since Coase,[12] economists have insisted that with perfect information, the parties will bargain to the same result regardless of how initial entitlements are assigned. However, if entitlements do not consist in the right to exclude, the parties are not in a position to set out the terms for their negotiations. Unless some things are up to some people, bargaining cannot even get started, even with perfect information.[13]

I should also note in passing that the ease of application of the basic action-guiding norm of property does not exhaust the norm. You can commit a trespass

---

[12] Coase 1960.

[13] Indeed, in a world without information costs, parties would also still need the concept of exclusion to govern the side effects of their own use of their own property. Only if one person is in charge of a piece of property does it make sense to ask about the side effects of one person's use on another. The concept of 'use and enjoyment of land' that figures in the law of nuisance supposes that it is up to a landowner to determine how to use his or her land, restricted only by the entitlement of other landowners to use theirs. The distinction between nonfeasance and misfeasance organizes the entire law of nuisance: it is not up to your neighbour how you use your land, nor up to you how your neighbour uses his or her land. The 'not up to' aspect of this is ineliminable.

against land even if you are in no position to know where the boundary is, and so unable to answer the simple question of whether you are the owner or not. Legal norms are supposed to guide action; many legal norms give formal guidance even if the particulars of their application are not known or even knowable. The law of negligence is action-guiding even though it imposes objective standards the content of which may be opaque to some people; the law of contract creates binding arrangements even if the parties were not fully aware of what they were getting themselves into. These limitations on the full availability of relevant legal facts are not an exception to the publicity requirement; they are the direct implication of it, as applied to private rights. Public legal rules enable people to arrange their own affairs, but can only do so legitimately provided that they enable each of a plurality of persons to do so. As such, the rules have to be objective, in the sense that your right to your property does not depend on what you or I, in particular think about it, or what either of us is in a position to learn about it. At the same time, public rules must be such that they can provide guidance in general.

My point in drawing attention to the ways in which courts need to know more is not to divert attention from the action-guiding rules of property law to the activities of courts, but rather to pave the way for a different explanation of the role of publicly available standards in the law of property. It is a general requirement of the rule of law that people know where they stand as against both the government and as against other private individuals. I do not want to overplay this feature of the rule of law, because the existence and structure of the legal profession depends in no small part on the fact that it is often quite difficult to figure out exactly where you stand. Of course you do know what you are not allowed to do, namely use something that is not yours. And that is certainly an easier legal rule than one that would require you to figure out who the owner was first. But the rule is really just a reflex of the idea that the owner has exclusive use of what he or she owns, which is in turn simply the priority of possession over use. If use is facilitated by a rule in which people know what they are not allowed to use, it presupposes the formal notion of use outlined above, which is itself subordinated to possession, rather than antecedent to it. Any non-exclusive conception of use is as much frustrated by the rule as enabled by it.

Smith suggests that his modular approach to property has advantages over the realist 'bundle of sticks' characterization of property, analogous to the advantages of modern formal linguistics over traditional taxonomic linguistics, which took its cue exclusively from the classification of Latin forms. I agree that the modular model has those advantages, but, at the same time, it shares with the realist a concern with content and particularity; Smith concedes that if there were no information costs, the law of property would work pretty much the way that the realists say that it does.[14] Linguistics and cognitive science are more profitably used as drawing our attention to formal features of property, rather than treating them as proxies for other, content-based features. To do that engages a project that Smith says he seeks

---

[14] Smith 2012b, 1705.

to avoid, namely a return to earlier versions of formalism, and indeed, ultimately to Latin categories, though in this case juridical rather than linguistic ones.

Bringing these two difficulties together points the way to a different approach entirely: the 'value' served by exclusion is one that cannot be characterized without reference to the very same family of concepts of which exclusion is itself a member. The concept of authority, understood as someone being in charge of how others may deal with some matter, arguably belongs in the same family of concepts.[15] When one person has authority over another with respect to some matter, then the person in authority is entitled to change the normative situation of the other with respect to that matter. The owner alone determines whether it is permissible for others to use or interfere with the object. The owner's authority is present even when the owner is absent; another person's title tells you that the use of the object in question is not up to you.

Property has an authority structure; the right to exclude is generally exercised by the owner, in relation to all non-owners; ownership both empowers the owner with respect to the thing and restricts others. Non-owners must defer to the owner's authority, even if the owner is not present to exercise it, and even if the owner is incapable of exercising it; how the thing is used is up to the owner *as against all others*. Before working through this analysis in detail, however, it is worth noticing the grounds for supposing that such obligations are irreducible in an analytically illuminating sense. In order to establish this, the appropriate approach is not to try to show irreducibility directly—that is likely to make things seem unduly mysterious—but instead to articulate just what would be involved in a successful reduction of such ideas.

The nub of the difficulty is that a reductive account would need to identify values served by second-personal rules without surreptitiously either recasting the rules so that they don't fit the values to which they are supposedly reduced, or recasting the values so that they actually presuppose the rules. The rules would be recast if they demand or forbid superficially similar but fundamentally different classes of actions. The values would be recast if it turned out that the interest protected was an interest in exclusive use that could not even be specified except by reference to the concept of exclusion.

Much realist writing about property self-consciously sought to recast the rules, by showing that they lacked sufficient structure, and to urge replacement of them. More recent doctrinal reductionism seeks to explain the rules without recasting them, but cannot escape the difficulties that the realists faced. Richard Posner's attempt to reduce the law of negligence to economic efficiency is an example of this sort of recasting that interferes with a successful reduction. The concept of efficiency does not contain resources for drawing the law of negligence's fundamental distinction between nonfeasance and misfeasance, and so can offer only an ad hoc

---

[15] Some might insist that this isn't really authority, that authority must somehow be instituted and assigned to someone based on the benefits of so doing. To so insist, however, amounts to defining authority so that it necessarily has an instrumental basis. My point is that the familiar idea of 'being in charge of' does not presuppose that it must be assigned by some collective.

explanation of the distinction between failures to confer benefits and wrongful injury. It also fails to capture the law's requirement of objective standards. On Posner's interpretation of the Hand test, a court must also consider the expected extent of injury in determining whether precautions are required, and so require greater precautions in the presence of high income earners than in the presence of low income earners. In both of these respects, the rule that he characterizes as efficient is different from the rule in the law of negligence. Posner's account also adopts the means-end structure endorsed by Smith; it characterizes a state of affairs—optimal investment in safety—as the objective, and the rule as a means for achieving it. The aggrieved plaintiff figures only incidentally and instrumentally in the analysis of the wrong. Whatever the interest or value of such an exercise, it does not provide a successful reduction of rule concepts to instrumental ones. Instead, it urges their replacement with different concepts. It is not surprising that recent writers in Posner's tradition have been expressly concerned with what the law should be, and openly indifferent or even hostile to the law's own distinctions.[16] This is not the place to take up the possibility that other economic analyses might provide a better fit for the existing law of negligence; I mention Posner's analysis here only to illustrate the type of failure of a reductive enterprise that it exemplifies.

The opposite difficulty is that of recasting the values. If the value that is served by the adoption of a legal rule turns out, on closer inspection, to actually presuppose the rule, then the reduction has failed because the thing to which the rule was to be reduced turns out to be identical with the rule itself. To illustrate, consider the proposal that the prohibition on unauthorized touching is to be explained in terms of the harm that such touchings are likely to do. The difficulty is that such a rationale would seem to support only a prohibition of harmful or dangerous touchings. A familiar response to this thought is to suggest that the relevant harm is that of *being touched without your permission*. Although few would deny that it is harmful to you to be touched without your permission, the analytical structure of this move merits comment. The harm which a prohibition on unauthorized touchings serves to prevent is the harm of unauthorized touching. It cannot be identified as harm except by reference to its own wrongfulness.[17] As Joel Feinberg has pointed out, the 'harm principle' defended by John Stuart Mill has no analytical power unless harms are identified without reference to the very actions that bring them about. If the action itself figures in the characterization of the harm, the concept of harm simply becomes a format in which any proposed prohibition of a class of actions can be stated. Applied to the case at hand, if your right to your own body, to the exclusion of others, is understood relationally, the claim that you are

---

[16] Posner 1995. See also Kaplow and Shavell 2002.

[17] In their standard hornbook on torts, Prosser and Keeton contrast torts with crimes, noting that unlike a criminal case a tort action is brought at the initiative of the aggrieved party and that 'its primary purpose is to compensate for the damaged suffered, at the expense of the wrongdoer'. Keeton et al eds. 1984, 7. Talk about a 'purpose' in terms of 'compensation' makes it look as though the purpose of the tort action is something that can be specified without reference to the concept of a tort action, but in fact the purpose is simply to instantiate a rule: wrongdoers must compensate those whom they have wronged.

harmed when it is violated simply reiterates the wrong of the violation, and adds nothing.

In characterizing this as an example of a value that actually presupposes a rule, I do not mean to deny the fundamental role of positive law in making the underlying moral idea more determinate in its application to particulars. Nor would I deny that in making such determinations, legal officials appropriately take account of the ease or difficulty with which particular formulations can be followed. I reject only the claim that the *value* can be characterized without reference to its expression through a rule, and the concomitant suggestion that the rule itself is required only on epistemic grounds.

In drawing attention to the parallel between your right to your own body and property rights, I do not mean to suggest that property rights are the same as bodily rights, either in their stringency or in their importance. Instead, the point of the parallel is to suggest that the right to determine what others do to your own body provides a formal model of the right to exclude, and that the value of the right cannot be characterized except in relation to the right to exclude. The same point is true, I shall argue, of the right to property: it is an entitlement to stand in relations to others, and it is as that entitlement that it has its moral significance.

I now want to generalize this point and apply it to Smith's characterization of the right to exclude as being in the service of use. How are we to understand the concept of use, such that it is the value served by the right to exclude, but is not equivalent to it? I will suggest that there is no such concept. Instead, the concept of use as it figures in the law of property is a concept that subordinates actual, particular use to possible use, and understands possible use, in turn, in a contrastive/second personal way. Possession takes priority over use. As a result, either the right to exclude is replaced with a different, superficially similar right or, alternatively, the value served by exclusion turns out to be the value of exclusion, and instrumental talk about rules serving values turns out to be a wheel that is not part of the mechanism.

To bring the point into focus, consider first the most familiar feature of the morality of means rather than ends. If the use of certain means is prohibited, the wrong is against someone in particular, and the prohibition applies independently of the ends in whose service those means are being used. The standard prohibitions on the use of means are themselves relational; if I take, use, or damage your property, I wrong you in particular, and you in particular have standing to hold me to account for doing so, and to demand the object in question or its equivalent. The inquiry concerns what I have done to you; my motives do not enter. Nor do the overall consequences of my act. There are, to be sure, exceptional cases in which extreme circumstances make the use of otherwise prohibited means acceptable, particularly with regard to criminal prohibitions. But even these do not change the legal relations between the parties.

I now want to suggest that Smith's focus on use as a value that is served by exclusion is unable to capture these familiar features of property. Smith's characterization of property as modular goes some distance towards explaining the particular wrong against property. The advantages of exclusion as a strategy—foremost among which are simplicity and publicity—would be lost if the merits in a particular case needed to be assessed every time. Instead, Smith suggests, usable things are much more useful if those to whom use has been assigned are also delegated the power to determine how the thing will be used. That way, others are in a position to know that they are not allowed to use or interfere with the thing, and owners are in a position to make plans about how best to use the thing, without worrying that another person will have a more valuable use or pressing need for it.

In order for the argument for exclusion as a strategy to work, however, a further premiss is required, according to which long-term planning is a prerequisite to the preservation of a thing or to its effective use. Otherwise the value of making usable things useful would not be served by modularity and exclusion. If things could be used best by being held in common, or through a system of usufruct, the value of use would say nothing in favour of exclusion or modularity. Despite the venerable lineage of this supplementary premiss—it figures explicitly in a long line of thinkers, from Thomas Aquinas through to John Rawls—it is fatally ambiguous between an empirical claim that is irrelevant to the point at hand and a normative claim that actually presupposes the concept of exclusion.[18]

The factual version of the claim is that if someone is in charge of an asset, and gets the benefit from the asset, they are more likely to take care of it. This idea receives its pithiest statement in Larry Summers's quip that 'in the history of the world, nobody has ever washed a rented car'. Only if you are in a position to reap the long-term benefits of taking care of something will you take care of it. It is not my purpose here to question the truth of this claim, but only its relevance. The difficulty comes with characterizing the concept of the usefulness of an asset at an appropriate level of generality. The rental car getting dirty, the land eroding, and the fruit rotting on the tree are all examples of assets deteriorating because proper care is not taken of them. To characterize these as deterioration, however, presumes that the relevant uses of the object in question have already been specified. It also supposes that the other resources required in order to preserve the asset in question are appropriately used for that preservation. Thus the proper stewardship of water is presumed to be the cleaning of cars; the proper use of effort the harvesting of fruit; and the proper state of cars as clean and fruit as non-rotten. All of these are fine and good, but themselves presuppose not that things be useful, but rather that things be used in particular ways. Usefulness is not actually a part of the analysis. To focus instead on particular use would only make matters worse, because it would make it even more difficult to establish the relevant generality; others do not gain a licence to interfere with the owner's property just because the particular use has shifted.

Nor can exclusion be justified by focusing on its role in seeing to it that things are used in the ways in which they are most highly valued; putting to one side the question of whether the fact that someone decides to use something a certain way shows that it is 'highly valued', ownership sees to it that things are used in ways that

---

[18] Just to be clear, I would not presume to accuse either Rawls or Aquinas of equivocation or even ambiguity. Both are resolutely non-reductive in their approaches, and both are committed to a broadly Aristotelian understanding of the relation between the factual and the normative.

they are valued[19] by their owners, that is, those who are entitled to determine how they are used. It is difficult to deny that exclusion serves use in this sense, but only because this sense of use collapses into the idea that whatever is being done with the property has been determined by the owner.

The difficulty, then, is that the concept of use that figures in the law of property has two features that resist reduction. First, it is the owner's use, rather than use in general that is protected. Although there are other ways of thinking about use, they do not figure in the law of property. Second, the owner's use is sufficiently weighty to constrain others from interfering with the thing, sufficient to override whatever competing interests those others might have, but it does not impose any require-ments on others to protect or improve the thing, or to cooperate in any way in seeing to it that the owner can use the thing effectively. Nor are others constrained to take steps to ensure that the thing is preserved for future use. If use, or even use-by-the-owner were important, these restrictions are difficult to characterize as unfortunate results of an easy to apply but sometimes overinclusive rule. Yet they apply systematically. A rule that enjoined non-owners to preserve property that was in peril, or to take low cost or even costless steps to aid and abet others' use of their property would encourage use. The law imposes no such burdens, because it does not value use per se, but only the owner's use, and even the owner's 'use' only to the extent that use concerns the free exercise of the powers of exclusive title to the property in question. It has nothing to do with the social value of his use, or whether the owner himself manages to realize any subjective value from the exercise of those rights and powers. Indeed, the only sense in which the owner benefits from using presupposes the right to exclude: the owner gets to decide how the things will be used, by whom, and on what terms.

Perhaps I am reading Smith too literally here, and a more charitable interpret-ation would focus instead on the ways in which planning is made possible by the exclusion strategy. If you know that others will not pre-empt or interfere with your use of the thing, you are in a better position to decide how best to use it; if you know that another person is in charge of an object, you will know to check with that person before incorporating it into your plan. All of this seems plainly right. Indeed, it is a very good characterization of the right to exclude. The difficulty comes in characterizing it in terms of an idea of use that can be itself articulated without reference to the concept of exclusion that it was supposed to explain. You need to keep off the property of others even if they are not currently using it; the you/other contrast cannot be reduced to any combination of monadic or compara-tive features of particular users or even users in general. The difficulty, finally, is that once the modality shifts from actual use to possible use, that is, usefulness, the question of usefulness is subordinated to the question of right, that is, of who is entitled to determine how the thing will be used. The person who is entitled to determine how it is used gets to do so, *as against others*. That is the only interest in

---

[19] In the sense of 'value' in which markets are said to move resources to their most highly valued use. I do not mean to say that property owners always use their property in the ways that they subjectively value most highly or from which they expect the most benefit.

use that the law of property promotes. Not only does it not protect use; it only protects your agency as against other people. It does not secure your agency against the ravages of nature, and it only protects it against others with respect to how the thing in question will be used. So your agency, like your use of your property, cannot be specified except in terms of proprietary concepts.

I have focused on the irreducibility of the you/other contrast as it shapes the right to exclude, and limits the relevance of use. In so doing, I do not mean to deny that people may be pleased that property enables them to plan through consistent and predictable rules. Nor do I mean to deny that it is a good thing to know where you stand. My point instead is that the right to exclude is exclusively about where you stand as against others. It is only if the obstacles to successful planning are already assumed to be choices made by other people, people wanting to use the same thing that you want to use, or wanting to use their things in a way that interferes with your use of what is yours, that exclusion begins to look like the solution to a problem about use, rather than about authority. Instead, the problem to which exclusion is a solution is one of determining who has authority over what. In order for people to be able to determine for themselves what they will do, to the exclusion of all others, it had better be the case that everybody knows where he or she stands, as against each of those others. But it does not follow from this that the purpose of having rights to exclude, of people having authority over things, is to be found in the sort of notice that it gives. To the contrary, the purpose of notice is that it is notice with respect to authority. The value of planning is not, in fact, the value of something that can be understood without reference to the right to exclude.

Still, it might be wondered whether the account that I am pressing has discharged its burden of justification, or has simply refused to accept it. It seems to make perfectly good sense to ask whether it is a good for people to have this form of authority over others, to ask what is served by so doing, and so on. Asking such questions is the mark of the 'critical reflective attitude' that H. L. A. Hart insisted was required in thinking about legal doctrines and practices, and to avoid the pathologies that he saw in the identification of legal with moral obligation, what Hart calls 'old confusions between law and the standards appropriate to the criticism of law'.[20] The claim that the appropriate standards of criticism must be sufficiently distant from the rules opens up a gap between standards and rules, one that makes the claim of the rules to be binding always look suspect.[21]

---

[20] Hart 1983, 11.

[21] Joseph Raz's 'normal justification thesis' is a particularly clear case of this sort of approach (Raz 1985). Raz thinks that the obligation to act in accordance with a rule (or conception of a rule) is philosophically in need of explanation, and so must be addressed in terms of the advantages that that rule provides in enabling people to do what they have reason to do, independently of the rule itself. Yet the puzzle is itself an artefact of Raz's way of setting things up. He regards it is a truism that a person has reason to act in conformity with the reasons that apply to him or her. As a result, the special obligations of institutional roles, respecting the property of others, and any form of interpersonal authority needs to be explained because each permits or requires a person to ignore reasons that would otherwise apply to him. But the sense in which the truism is a truism generates no such puzzle. Unless relational deontic concepts are excluded in advance from the category of possible reasons, there is no mystery as to how they are possible.

However, the critical reflective attitude is not proprietary to instrumental accounts of law in general, or of property in particular. Indeed, just as property provides the form of authority, so, too, each person's right against unauthorized interference with his or her own body can be understood as a form of authority. As Penner has pointed out, the right to your own person is *in rem*, rather than *in personam*. But if we ask why what others do with or to your body is up to you, there seems to be only two possible types of answers: one says that you have such authority because giving people authority in this way is likely to promote happiness, autonomy, or something else in the long run. The other type of answer says that you are not available for other people to use; the reason what others do to or with your body is up to you is because it is not up to them. That is the 'value' served by your right to your own person. To even talk about a value being served here is highly misleading, because there is no conceptual space between the value and what serves it. There is no way to ask whether a prohibition on touching others without their permission is the most effective way to protect one person's independence from another, but lack of efficacy towards an external end is not the only, or even the most interesting way in which practices can be defective from a standpoint capable of triggering a 'critical reflective attitude'. Human history is littered with examples in which it has not been adequately honoured, in which human beings have been treated as property or worse.

In pointing to the parallel between rights to person and rights to property I do not mean to make the hysterical suggestion that the two are the same. My claim is only that in looking for the point or purpose of 'giving' someone the right to exclude others from their property, the form of the answer can be the same, just as the form of the right is the same. It is up to the owner to decide what happens because it is not up to any other person—the owner is entitled to be independent of others with respect to the use of the things in question. This is not to say that an unauthorized touching is no worse than a trespass to land; it is to say instead only that the owner's independence, understood relationally and contrastively, is the reason that the owner gets to decide. The owner's right to independence as against others is the reason that the basic action guiding norm of property says that if it is not yours you are not allowed to use or interfere with it. It doesn't matter who the owner is; the owner's independence is a constraint on your conduct.

Still, it might be thought that more needs to be said; why does the owner get to constrain the conduct of others? The fact that it is your body sounds like a sufficient reason for others to need to keep off; the fact that it is your property seems to be less so. Your body is you; but your property is merely yours. That is why any suggestion of a parallel between the justification of your right to your own person and of your right to property is apt to strike some as hysterical. So something further that could matter to me, or to the law, might be thought to be needed here, and the general benefit attaching to the usefulness of useful things might be thought to fit the bill.

It is worth noticing, however, the structure of this challenge: what is thought to call out for some form of justification is one person's authority over another, and the demand for justification arises precisely from the thought that one person is *not* the master of another. That thought runs up against its natural and internal limit when it comes to each person's body. You are master of your own body, but not of mine, and I am master of mine but not yours. Taken together, these thoughts turn out to be equivalent to the more general thought that each of us is *sui juris* as against the other, that is, the normative structure is relational. In the case of property, each property owner is master of his or her property, as against others. That is the justification of the rule in property. The justification is not that protecting property protects individual agency, either in particular cases or overall, if agency is understood as something apart from each person's standing as against others. The relevant value is not something separate, which the rules try to achieve or even instantiate, such that the rules can be improved by making them realize the value better, because the value exists in the rule; it is the form of interaction that has moral significance.

Again, to assert that the independence of the owner's choice from that of others is not to assert that nothing else has moral significance, and so has no bearing on the question of when or how public law might justifiably limit property rights. The idea that the value at issue in property cannot be characterized except by reference to authority and exclusion does not bear such a burden any more than theoretical attempts to justify the rule of exclusion in terms of use must suppose that usefulness is the only thing of moral importance. It means only that the justification of the right to exclude presupposes the concept of exclusion. Rather than being entitled to exclude others because you have an interest in using what is yours, what is yours is useful to you because you have a right to it, as against others.

Treating the justification of the basic rule of property as something that cannot be expressed except with proprietary concepts may give rise to a different set of concerns, about the distribution of property, and so to the thought that perhaps the unjustified justifier is the idea that everyone should have some set of holdings so as to have a sphere of independence from others. But if that is what is meant by the requirement of a justification of private property, it is not a justification of the rule of exclusion, because it presupposes it. It may well provide reasons for a public authority exercising the powers discussed by Harris to redistribute property, to take things from some people, and give them to others, but any such justification is the justification for distributing those things *as property*, that is, presupposes that property is already about relations of exclusion. Any other way of thinking about the importance of people having things would fail to generate the norms of property law at all, because it would be indifferent between one person interfering with another's property and the first failing to provide property to, or increase the usefulness of the property of the second.

To sum up, the value isn't something separate, which the rules try to achieve or even instantiate, such that the rules can be improved by making them realize the value better, because the value exists in the rule; it is a form of interaction that has moral significance.

With this in mind, I now want to return to Smith's emphasis on publicity. It is, of course, of the first importance that a system in which some people have authority over others with regard to things be one in which people can, as a general matter, know where they stand as against each other. That way, an owner can exercise authority even while physically absent; notice that the thing in question is not yours allows you to bring your conduct into conformity with the owner's authority over you without knowing anything more. The fact that something is not yours does not give you notice that you cannot benefit from it, or even use it, if use is understood in an expansive non-relational sense. You can use my fence as a windbreak; you can use my garden as a backdrop for your photographs; as we ride along the highway you can use my bicycle as a draught to ease your ride. You can do each of those things, even though you are fully aware that my fence, garden, and bicycle are mine rather than yours. You can also do things that end up changing what is mine, for example, taking down your fence and exposing my house to ultraviolet light. The basic rule of property, then, does not give you notice that you cannot change a thing or take advantage of its empirical features. It tells you only that you cannot determine how it will be used to the exclusion of others. Your use of my fence does not constrain me from taking it down; your use of my garden does not preclude my fencing it in; the advantage you get from my draught does not require me to continue riding ahead of you.

It emerges from these examples that the role of information goes in the opposite direction of the one suggested by Smith. 'Not yours' is the basic normative concept; what you know on the straightforward way is whether or not you have authority with respect to the useful thing in question. The epistemically undemanding rule lets you know where you stand in relation to others, not in relation to the overall benefits of things being used.

Once the priority of possession is properly understood, the places in which use explicitly figures in the law of property can be understood in a new way. Here I limit myself to gesturing towards the form of an account without specifying its details. First, consider nuisance. The plaintiff in a nuisance action must establish that the defendant interfered with his or her quiet use and enjoyment of land. Even here, however, use is subordinated to possession. The normal remedy for a nuisance is an injunction,[22] to which the plaintiff is entitled only if there is a conflict between uses; no injunction will be granted if there is no conflict, because in such a situation the defendant's activity does not interfere with the plaintiff's exclusive use of land. Conversely, the traditional law of nuisance does not allow a defence of 'coming to the nuisance'. If a landowner starts to use land in a new way, he or she is entitled to an injunction that shuts down a neighbour's long-standing activity that interferes with the new use, precisely because it is exclusively up to the owner to decide what takes place on his or her land.[23] A court will look at the nature of the interference in light of the locality in which the land is situated; at no point does it compare the importance or usefulness of competing uses.[24] You are only permitted to change your neighbour's land in the ways that are the inevitable results of each of you deciding how to use what is yours. Moreover, an activity that takes place entirely on

---

[22] *Shelfer v City of London Electrical Lighting Co.* 1895 (CA).
[23] *Sturges v Bridgman* 1879 (CA).
[24] As Henry Smith puts it, 'although evidence of courts actually engaging in cost-benefit analysis is surprisingly slight'. Smith 2004, 995.

the defendant's land in not actionable in nuisance, no matter how severely it diminishes the usefulness of the plaintiff's land. Building a tower that blocks the path of sunlight to your neighbour's land is not only not a nuisance but does not so much as raise an issue of nuisance, even though it raises obvious issues about restricting use.[25] There is an important difference between trespass and nuisance, but the difference is not marked by a shift from a focus on exclusion for focus on use or usefulness.

Another place where the law might be thought to focus on use rather than exclusion is in the law of adverse possession. Adverse possession looks puzzling because the previous owner had good title. A trespasser comes along, and acquires good title in land, without acquiring it from the previous owner. As soon as the question of how that title arose is introduced, however, the puzzle begins to disintegrate. The previous owner's good title is a matter of the owner having acquired it from someone, who must, in turn have had good title. That earlier title, however, must have been acquired simply from some previous owner having acquired something through taking possession of it. That is, good title presupposes that possession can be acquired simply through following normal procedures for acquisition. That, in turn, is only possible provided that the title can really be good, that is, not subject to challenge based on some documentation from the past. Far from giving priority to active users of land over those who possess land without using it, adverse possession regards use merely as a mark of acquisition, as the manner of taking possession.[26]

3. Bringing Actual Use Back In

I have argued so far that possible use takes priority over actual use in the law of property, and that the right to possible use takes priority over the possibility of use. In this penultimate section, I want to come back to actual use, and explain how it figures in the operation of the law of property.

In noting the difficulty that Smith's approach has with the information demands on courts, I drew attention to their inevitably knowing the identity of a property owner in processing any sort of proprietary dispute. In many disputes about property they also need to know something else, namely the way in which the owner was using the property in question. In the nuisance cases, information about the plaintiff's use of her land is required in order to identify an interference with it. If the plaintiff's use and the defendant's use do not come into conflict, then there is no claim; if there is no claim, there could be no easement.[27] In a claim for damages when property is damaged or destroyed, the damage to the property, understood as a 'thing' and the particularities of its use are relevant. So, too, in a claim for damages

---

[25] *Fontainebleau Hotel Corp. v Forty-Five-Twenty-Five, Inc.* 1959.

[26] I develop this argument in more detail in Ripstein forthcoming.

[27] This is the central holding of *Sturges v Bridgman*, despite the attempts by Coase and those following him to characterize it as a case about the development of residential housing.

predicated upon a trespass to land or chattels. The ground of the claim is that the defendant entered the plaintiff's land or used the plaintiff's chattels without authorization. But the measure of the damages depends upon the way in which the plaintiff was using or would have used the land or cattle in question, that is, it depends on the use with which the defendant interfered.

The ways in which particularity figures in the law's processing of property disputes might be thought to open up space for a middle ground between the austerely formal model of exclusion I have put forward here, and the more substantive idea of usefulness that I have characterized as irrelevant.

In a series of recent articles, Larissa Katz has proposed such a model, which seeks to relate particular use to the interpersonal dimension of freedom.[28] Her account emphasizes choosing rather than using, arguing that the law of property is organized around what Katz usefully calls an owner's entitlement to 'set the agenda' for the thing that is owned. Katz's strategy is to focus on the particular use that the owner is making of the resource, and to suggest that the law properly protects only that. So the law is not interested in use in general, but rather in how *this* owner is using *this* object, and its interest in that question is purely relational, assigning priority to owner's choices over those of others.

The owner's role is not to make every decision about a thing, which would indeed require the protection of a right to exclude. The owner's role is rather to make authoritative decisions about things—to set the agenda for the thing—and so to regulate the kinds of use that others can make of it. This requires the protection of a different kind of constraint on the conduct of others. It requires that others defer to her authority every time.[29]

Katz's strategy, then, is to account for the formality of property entirely in terms of the owner/non-owner distinction, while assigning priority to actual uses (via agendas) rather than possible ones.

Exclusion enters her account only indirectly, in a manner similar to the way it enters Smith's account. Since you cannot tell another person's agenda for an object, you use the fact that you do not own it as a proxy. An unoccupied field might be lying fallow, awaiting planting, or serving as a firebreak. As a non-owner, it may be possible for you to check with the owner, but it often will not be. As such, the simplest and most straightforward rule to give effect to a norm of protecting the owner's agenda would be the one that abstracts from information about both the owner and her agenda, and focuses exclusively on information that will be readily available. So the way to protect use, on this understanding, is to protect possession. Possession, as such, has no independent significance.

Katz is certainly right that the owner is the one who gets to set the agenda for an object. However, the idea of an agenda here is sufficiently abstract that it might be taken in more than one way. On the most concrete reading, an owner's agenda is the specific plan for an object's use over an extended period. On the most abstract, the owner's agenda might be one of simply keeping his or her options open as against others. The difficulty with the most abstract reading is not that it does not

---

[28] See Katz 2008, Katz 2010a, Katz 2011b.   [29] Katz 2011b, 21.

fit the way in which the law typically thinks about property, but rather that it fits too well, that is, *possible use* is typically the agenda that an owner has. The more abstract reading fits better, because somebody can own something and want it as an investment, or acquire something without having yet determined how he or she plans to use it, or even determine how long he or she expects to own it.

The more concrete interpretation of the concept of an agenda also fails to fit some of the familiar landmarks of property law, and does so in cases in which a simple and easy to follow rule could fit the agenda model much better. If the owner has no current agenda for an object, why is a harmless trespass actionable?[30] Conversely, the priority of ongoing agendas should make room for a defence of coming to the nuisance, since the latecomer's agenda is less established.[31]

None of this is to deny that if a property right has been violated, the remedy will take account of the particularities of the plaintiff's use of the thing. If it is up to the owner to decide how the thing is used, then, if the owner has made a decision, interfering with that right in a way that prevents the owner from using something is itself an interference with the owner's exclusive right. The fact of the wrong turns on the owner's exclusive right; the extent of the wrong sometimes turns on the particularities of the way in which the owner has exercised that right.

4. Conclusion

I have argued that the right to exclude cannot be explained in terms of an interest in use. The justificatory relation goes in the opposite direction: your interest in using the thing is protected not only *to the extent* to which you have exclusive right to it, but also *because* you have exclusive right to it. Property rights are interpersonal and relational, and the benefits that they provide two owners reflect their interpersonal and relational status.

In this concluding section, I want to briefly draw attention to the way in which property rights stand as a case study for a more general way of thinking about private rights. Instead of rights being grounded in interests, as the interest theory of rights maintains, I want to suggest instead that the proper direction of analysis yields what we might call a rights theory of interests. The interests protected by the law are always legal interests, which is to say that they are vulnerable to wrongdoing, but not to other things that might set them back in the same way. Private rights are also exclusively negative, that is, they reflect the distinction between nonfeasance and misfeasance. Even if the usability of your property could be improved dramatically if I was required to confer a small benefit on you, the law does not require me to do so. It does, however, require me to refrain from using or interfering with your property, even if doing so imposes a significant burden on me and allowing me to use your property would impose no disadvantage on you.

---

[30] In 'Exclusion and Exclusivity in Property Law' (Katz 2008) at 303, Katz suggests that *Jacque* (1997) may have been wrongly decided.

[31] This is the approach of Lord Denning MR in *Miller v Jackson* 1977 (CA).

In emphasizing the priority of exclusion over use, I do not mean to deny that many things are more useful, or used more effectively, under a system of private property, any more than I would deny more generally that upholding rights makes life better in many ways. My claim has only been the concept of a right is not an instrument through which a public authority decides whether to delegate the decision to a private agent based on the goods expected to accrue from doing so. The law of property is not the solution to a problem about usefulness. It is the solution to a problem about authority, and the basic norm of that solution is that nobody has authority over anyone else.

8

Possession and the Distractions of Philosophy

*Lisa M. Austin**

1. Introduction: The Puzzle

Possession is puzzling.

In property law, it is one of the core doctrinal ideas. Moreover, it has multiple aspects.[1] It can refer to the relationship between a person and a thing (such as when we inquire into the facts concerning whether a person is in physical control); it can refer to the rights that follow from that relationship (such as the right of possession); and it can refer to the question of *to whom* these rights can be attributed (the question of title). Sometimes these different aspects are not clearly separated in a particular case, and which facts are decisive in meeting the test for possession in different legal contexts varies widely. Indeed, its perceived fluidity has often led to charges of being simply a vehicle for judicial policy making.[2]

That possession is both central to the law of property and doctrinally puzzling makes it an attractive focus for legal theorists. But this theoretical attention introduces another set of puzzles. One of the predominant trends in theoretical reflection upon possession is to focus on the idea of *first* possession as the key to understanding possession generally, and to claim that the key to unlocking the mystery of first possession is to look to the underlying justification for property rights. In this chapter I claim that these two moves are mistaken. Before I outline my claim, let me provide several examples.

In Richard Epstein's well-known article on possession, he argues that the question of possession is: 'What principles decide *which* individuals have ownership rights (whatever they precisely entail) over *what* things.'[3] This is what I have labelled above as the question of title. It is distinct from questions regarding the nature of ownership rights and justifications for ownership. However, in examining the common law rule that first possession of an unowned thing can support a claim to ownership, Epstein in fact looks to various theories regarding the nature of, and

* I would like to thank the participants of The Private Law Theory Workshop (University of Toronto, April 2012), the participants of The Philosophical Foundations of Property Law (UCL, May 2012), Christopher Essert, Amnon Lehavi, and the editors of this volume for their helpful comments on earlier versions of this chapter.
[1] Dias 1956, 247.   [2] Dias 1956, 239.   [3] Epstein 1979, 1221.

justification for, property (for e.g. the labour theory, custom).[4] The central problem, he claims, is that '[t]here is no way that any individual act can account for a
claim of right against the rest of the world.'[5] In the end, he defends first possession
as providing a better system of property rights—largely because this is the system
we have inherited. As he states:

It may be an unresolved intellectual mystery of how a mere assertion of right can, if often
repeated and acknowledged, be sufficient to generate the right in question. As an institutional matter, however, it is difficult in the extreme to conceive of any other system.[6]

What is interesting is the arc of this argument. He begins by announcing a focus on
the question of title but in seeking to answer this question becomes tied up in the
seeming unilateral nature of the claim and, from there, at least some of the
questions regarding the nature of, and justification for, ownership.

Something similar occurs in Carol Rose's now canonical article about possession.
Her focus, as her title suggests, is on the question '[h]ow do things come to be
owned?'[7] In particular, she points to the common law maxim that 'first possession
is the root of title'.[8] She argues that in trying to answer the question of why
possession is the basis for title, we 'hit on some fundamental views about the nature
and purposes of a property regime'.[9] Cases like *Pierson v Post*, according to Rose,
indicate an apparent tension between two principles—the clear-act and the reward-
to-labour principles.[10] However, this tension can be reconciled if we understand
the clear-act principle to require individuals to speak 'clearly and distinctly' about
their property claims, which turns out to be useful labour from the perspective of
economic theory: '[w]e will all be richer when property claims are unequivocal,
because that unequivocal status enables property to be traded and used at its highest
value.'[11] The question of title, therefore, ultimately is resolved (or made less
mysterious) by looking at the functions of property.

This theoretical attention to *first* possession, along with the strategy of looking to
the justifications and functions of property for clarification are consistent with a
much older tradition of philosophical reflection. As J. W. Harris points out, '[f]rom
classical times there has been a juristic tendency to cloth the law's reliance on first
occupancy as a root of title with the dress of natural right.'[12] The natural law

---

[4] Epstein 1979, 1225 ff.

[5] Epstein 1979, 1230. Even if we posit an original community where all property rights are held in
common, a parallel problem arises: 'there is nothing which says that those who prefer common
ownership should prevail over those who do not. Equality of rights could be achieved by treating
each individual as having the equal entitlement to convert unowned things to his ownership, or by
treating all as equal co-owners of resources in the common pool. Neither is easily justified, and the
latter has no obvious superiority over the former.' (Epstein 1979, 1238.)

[6] Epstein 1979, 1242.   [7] Rose 1985, 73.   [8] Rose 1985, 75.

[9] Rose 1985, 76.   [10] Rose 1985, 77.

[11] Rose 1985, 82. She also, in her careful and insightful manner, warns that there are always
'ambiguous subtexts' and points to the role of audience in determining which kinds of communica-
tions count: 'the audience presupposed by the common law of first possession is an agrarian or a
commercial people' which has largely left out property claims based on aboriginal practices of land use
(Rose 1985, 87).

[12] Harris 1996, 214.

tradition, with its state-of-nature stories, gives a central position to first possession in accounts of property. But these strategies are also consistent with interpretive theories of law, such as Ronald Dworkin's, that argue that what the law *is* is not simply a matter of description but is always also a matter of justification. For Dworkin, 'Lawyers are always philosophers, because jurisprudence is part of any lawyer's account of what the law is.'[13] Therefore an interpretive account of the law of possession would insist that what possession is is bound up with its justification.

My claim in this chapter is that theoretical accounts of possession that take this question of justification as central are mistaken. We can unravel what it means for the law to recognize a right to possession, and in doing so account for the main features of the law, without having to also say something about why we have private property and why it is valuable. This claim rests upon two interrelated points. The first point is that justifying a particular element of a practice (like possession) is different from justifying the practice as a whole (like property law, or even law more generally). Answering questions regarding the elements of a practice requires reference to the practice itself but not the reasons for the practice. The second point is that the relevant practice that can illuminate the nature of possession is the practice of law itself. By this I mean the particular ideas of the rule of law and the omnilateral structure that is distinctive of legal relations. I argue that these constitutive elements of law provide the central organizing principles of possession and the idea of private ownership in the common law. This is why justificatory strategies that rely on extra-legal ideas—whether by imagining a pre-legal state of nature or by passing quickly through law to weightier ideas of substantive justice— distract us from seeing the centrality of law to a proper understanding of possession.

2. Legal Justification

In this section I want to offer a different view of legal justification. In order to outline what I mean by legal justification, I draw upon a distinction made by Rawls in an early essay entitled 'Two Concepts of Rules'. In it Rawls claims that there is an important difference 'between justifying a practice and justifying a particular action falling under it'.[14] After outlining what this distinction is for Rawls, and why he thinks it important, I show how it can help us distinguish between what are very different types of justification.

By 'practice' Rawls means 'any form of activity specified by a system of rules which defines offices, roles, moves, penalties, defences, and so on, and which gives

---

[13] Dworkin 1986, 380.

[14] Rawls 1955, 3. This distinction is not unique to Rawls. He himself was influenced by Hart's understanding of rules and social practices, although I will not take up the question of their relationship here except to say that Hart does not make ideas of the rule of law as central to his account of law as a social practice as I do here. Rawls was specifically concerned in this article to defend a version of rule utilitarianism. This, and his particular example regarding promising, has given rise to a large literature that I cannot discuss here, much of it about utilitarian accounts of promising.

the activity its structure'.[15] One could substitute for 'practice' some other terms like 'institution' or 'system of rules' and Rawls does this at various points. The main point of Rawls's invocation of the distinction between justifying a practice and justifying a particular action that falls under that practice is that different types of arguments are appropriate for the different questions. When we justify a practice, we ask whether that practice is valuable on grounds that themselves are independent of the practice; when we justify a particular action that falls under a practice, we remain within the terms of the practice itself and seek to explain that particular action as part of the practice.[16]

Rawls argues that the neglect of the distinction between justifying a practice and justifying a particular action that falls under the practice is connected to 'misconceiving the logical status of the rules of practices'.[17] One conception of rules, he argues, is the 'summary view' and this conceals the importance of the distinction. Although Rawls is concerned with the summary view in the context of utilitarian claims, several things are important to note about its features. On the summary account, rules are 'reports that cases of a certain sort have been found on *other* grounds to be properly decided in a certain way'.[18] Individual cases are decided on grounds such as direct utilitarian calculations and the rules that develop are 'summaries' of this, and function as helpful guides for rational decision. One element of this is that '[t]he performance of the action to which the rule refers doesn't require the stage-setting of a practice of which this rule is a part'.[19] Although Rawls frames his distinction in terms of utilitarianism, his central point is more general—one view of rules sees them as able to be articulated on grounds that do not themselves rely upon the practice.

Rawls contrasts this with what he calls the 'practice conception' of rules. In contrast with the summary view, where rules summarize individual cases, the rules *define* a practice. It is the practice that is logically prior to particular cases and is what provides the definition of the individual action:

given any rule which specifies a form of action (a move), a particular action which would be taken as falling under this rule given that there is the practice would not be *described* as that sort of action unless there was the practice. In the case of actions specified by practices it is logically impossible to perform them outside the stage-setting provided by those practices, for unless there is the practice, and unless the requisite proprieties are fulfilled, whatever one does, whatever movements one makes, will fail to count as a form of action which the practice specifies. What one does will be described in some *other* way.[20]

Rawls provides the example of baseball: one can only steal a base in a game of baseball. From this Rawls draws a number of important implications. He argues

---

[15] Rawls 1955, 3.

[16] Rawls also argues that within a particular practice there are different arguments open to individuals who hold different offices within that practice and which are themselves defined by that practice (Rawls 1955, 28). This point regarding the different kinds of arguments open to individuals in different offices is what Dworkin resists with his claim that legal philosophy is essentially the same as what judges or citizens do when interpreting the law. See e.g. Dworkin 2004, 2: 'a legal philosopher's theory of law is not different in character from, though it is of course much more abstract than, the ordinary legal claims that lawyers make from case to case.'

[17] Rawls 1955, 19. [18] Rawls 1955, 19. [19] Rawls 1955, 22.

[20] Rawls 1955, 25.

that '[i]f one wants to perform an action specified by a practice, the only legitimate question concerns the nature of the practice itself ("How do I go about making a will?")'.[21] Justification of one's particular actions are better understood as explanations that show these actions accord with the practice.[22]

We can map these two conceptions of rules onto two conceptions of legal justification in relation to possession. If we adopt the summary view then we would seek to understand possession in light of its desirability in relation to external factors that are not themselves part of the practice of private property or even law. This is, as I have already outlined, the dominant theoretical strategy. If we instead adopt the practice conception of rules then we would seek to understand possession in relation to the practice that provides its possibility. The justificatory question, on this latter view, is not concerned with accounting for the desirability of the doctrine of possession but with explaining why it is an aspect of a larger social practice. It is like stealing a base in baseball: only possible because of a particular practice and therefore only intelligible in relation to that practice.

What I want to further suggest is that the relevant social practice that makes possession intelligible is law itself. Even more strongly, the claim is that certain constitutive elements of the practice of law form the *organizing principles* of the law of possession, and indeed of private ownership.

But what does it mean for law to be a practice? Most accounts of the nature of law, despite important differences, include some acknowledgement that the rule of law is a constitutive element. It is the rule of law that I want to invoke as providing a set of ideas about the practice of law in relation to which possession can be understood and explained. There are many different views regarding the rule of law, involving its formal aspects, its procedural elements, and its substantive demands. There are also many different views regarding its basic nature, in particular whether it is a moral or prudential ideal. While it is beyond the scope of this chapter to provide a full account of where I stand in relation to all these debates, I do want to outline a number of formal elements of the rule of law that are fairly uncontroversial and then say a few general things that are likely more controversial but, I hope to show in the following sections, helpful when applied to the task of rendering possession intelligible in relation to the practice of law.

Most accounts of the rule of law agree that its core elements include what Lon Fuller called the 'principles of legality': generality, publicity, non-retroactivity, clarity, non-contradiction, ability to comply, stability, and congruence between rule and enforcement.[23] Although there might be different accounts of how we should understand these principles to cohere, these features are usually understood to support two general ideas regarding the rule of law: (1) that it constrains the exercise of state power (whether by judges or other officials); (2) that it permits individuals to plan in light of the legal consequences of their actions.[24]

---

[21] Rawls 1955, 26.   [22] Rawls 1955, 27.
[23] Fuller 1969. There are also procedural aspects which I do not discuss here.
[24] Waldron 2008.

Fuller also claimed that the principles of legality formed the 'inner morality' of the law, a view contested by many, most notably Raz.[25] Although I do not think it is necessary to refer to the principles of legality as 'moral' I take the position here that they are indeed a constitutive part of the *practice* of law.[26] This does not mean that a particular law—e.g. statute X—must itself conform to the principles of legality in order to be considered an authoritative law. Consider the analogy with friendship. I might think that one of the constitutive elements of a relationship of friendship is that friends take each others' interests into account. However, that I do not do so on a particular occasion is not determinative of whether the *relationship* itself may nonetheless be considered to be one of friendship. Similarly, we can evaluate specific actions in relation to another person whom we have identified as a 'friend' in light of the criteria of friendship—in doing X, were you acting as a good friend? We can also dispute what some of these criteria for friendship are. All of this is possible without calling into question the basic idea that the criteria of friendship are understood to be what *constitutes* this as the unique form of human relationship called friendship. These formal aspects of the rule of law function in a similar way and help to constitute the practice of law as the distinctive practice that it is.

Other accounts of the rule of law have stressed its role in expressing a form of community. For example, Oakeshott describes it in terms of 'human beings joined in an exclusive, specifiable mode of relationship'.[27] This association is not about achieving certain ends but about 'procedural conditions imposed upon doing', or non-instrumental rules.[28] Without taking up Oakeshott's views in detail here, either for elaboration or critique, I want to simply point to the importance of viewing the rule of law as a mode of human relationship. Others have noted that the rule of law can be understood as a mode of governance.[29] Although the difference might be merely semantic, governance connotes a distinction between those who govern (and are constrained in their governance by the rule of law) and those who are governed. Such language is at home in the traditional 'public law' discussion of the rule of law and its emphasis on the constraints it places on public power. To use the language of relationship is to also see how the rule of law can bind individuals together in a particular mode of association and this is helpful for seeing how such ideas operate within the realm of 'private law' ideas. Whatever else might fill in the content of private law norms, these norms are situated within a practice that seeks to relate individuals *to each other* in a particular way.

This relationship between individuals is what Kant referred to as an 'omnilateral' relation. An omnilateral relationship is one that holds equally between each individual and every other individual. In this it sounds much like E. P. Thompson's famous description of the universality and equality that characterize the rule of law,

[25] Raz 1977b.

[26] I have argued elsewhere that they are routinely adverted to in common law reasoning. See Austin forthcoming.

[27] Oakeshott 1983, 119. Oakeshott considers this a 'moral association' but he primarily uses 'moral' as a term contrasting with 'prudential' and 'instrumental'.

[28] Oakeshott 1983, 148.   [29] See e.g. Waldron 2008, 36.

making it an 'unqualified human good'.[30] Weinrib has recently described omni-laterality and its role in private law in the following terms, in which he emphasizes its public nature:

> The relationship between the litigating parties is bilateral, linking the plaintiff to the defendant; the relationship among members of the state is omnilateral, linking everyone to everyone else. Both the bilateral relationship between the parties and the omnilateral relationship among members of the state have their respective normative dimensions. For the bilateral relationship, the normative dimension consists in the parties' subjection to the correlatively structured bases of liability. For the omnilateral relationship, the normative dimension consists in every member's subjection to the state's lawful authority as it acts in the name of the citizenry as a whole. In adjudication, a court combines these two dimensions by projecting its own omnilateral authority onto the parties' bilateral relationship. The court thereby extends the significance of its decision beyond the specific dispute, making it a norm for all members of the state.[31]

Although the idea of omnilaterality may be an important aspect of an account of state authority and state institutions, we should not be so quick to equate it with either: the state does not create omnilaterality but some conceptions of the state and its legitimacy presuppose its possibility. The conception of omnilaterality that is normatively independent of particular institutions is of a relationship between persons marked by the qualities that characterize the rule of law.[32]

In what follows, I will show that omnilaterality and the rule of law illuminate how possession is at its core an idea of legal order with respect to 'objects' (places and things). Possession can be understood in these terms quite independently of justification stories, of either the state-of-nature or Dworkinian variety.

3. Possession and Title

Let me begin with a claim of C. B. Macpherson, which I take to be uncontroversial. He argues that '[a]s soon as any society, by custom or convention or law, makes a distinction between property and mere physical possession it has in effect defined property as a right'.[33] If I am holding an apple, then I have physical possession of it. I have a property right when I put the apple down and it still remains 'mine' in some sense. I take this as the starting point for what follows. As outlined earlier, there are three basic aspects of possession in property law: what Macpherson calls 'mere physical possession', a right to possession, and possessory title. A right to

---

[30] Thompson 1975, 266. He used the term 'equity,' by which he meant equality rather than what lawyers mean by equity. To avoid confusion, I have substituted equality. Thompson was also quite sensitive to the horizontal dimensions of law. See 267 ff.

[31] Weinrib 2011, 196.

[32] It might be that the rule of law requires institutions in order for society to coherently implement its demands. Many accounts have stressed, for example, the importance of courts and an independent judiciary (Waldron 2008, 20). My point is simply that we can separate the idea of omnilaterality from the question of particular institutions.

[33] Macpherson 1978, 3.

possession is the form of 'property as a right' that I am concerned with here. I argue in this section that possessory *title* is the result of seeking to maintain the distinction between physical possession and a right to possession within a system of property that is part of a legal practice as outlined in Section 2. In other words, possessory title is about ensuring that a right to possession is consistent with the rule of law. We do not need to search for pre-legal origins to understand possessory title, we just need to understand the defining role of the rule of law.

Suppose that I have a possessory right to the apple that I have picked and I want to put it down and save it for later use in a pie. This ability to put it down—to no longer have to be in physical possession of it—is at the heart of what we mean by property rights but it also generates a problem for a system of law. The problem is that, even though I have a right of possession, once I put it down it is no longer clear *to others* who is entitled to the apple. A system of property needs title conditions, or rules that indicate to all who the person with a right of possession is. For the sake of simplicity I will refer to this person as the owner, for in Section 4 I will show how the idea of a right of exclusive control is connected to ideas of use and alienability that are often thought to constitute the core elements of private ownership.[34]

Title conditions are one of the ways that the legal system keeps ownership consistent with the requirements of legality, including the requirements of publicity and the ability to comply with the law. If the legal system recognizes a right of possession—and this is the starting assumption of this discussion—then this right needs to conform to these constitutive elements of the practice of law. Everyone subject to the law needs to be able to ascertain that something is owned and who the owner is if they are to avoid liability as well as make use of their own legal powers, such as powers of contracting; if I know that something is owned then I will not interfere with it, if I know who owns it then I can negotiate with the owner for permission to use it.[35]

In the absence of the state creating a public system of title, such as when it sets up a land registry system of some sort, common law courts developed the idea of possessory title. What possessory title rules say, in general, is that you should consider as owner the person who is *acting* as owner; the person acting as owner is the person acting as if she is the rightful possessor by exercising control over the thing in question.[36] Now, of course, the person *acting* as owner is not necessarily

---

[34] Section 4 outlines the relationship of the right of possession to ideas of use and alienability, as well as to the fragmentation of ownership. With these ideas in place, we can make a distinction between an owner and a rightful possessor—such as in the relationship of bailor/bailee or licensor/licensee.

[35] I am drawing here on a distinction made by H. L. A. Hart, that some laws impose obligations (let's call these liability rules) and some provide facilities for individuals to realize their wishes (let's call these power-conferring rules). Ownership involves both liability rules and power-conferring rules, and intersects with other areas of private law that involve both liability and power-conferring rules (like contract law) and the requirements of the rule of law must be understood in relation to both. See Hart 1961, 27–8.

[36] The test for possessory title is actual control and intent to control; what counts as fulfilling this test varies according to factual context.

the person who *is* the owner. In fact, in solving the problem of title through relying upon possession another problem is introduced. Ownership allows me to put down my apple but title requirements seem to require that I keep holding it.

What is important to keep in mind is that possessory title rules do not say: the person holding the apple *is* the owner. They are rules addressed to third parties who need to know that things are owned and by whom if they are to follow the law. Numerous discussions in the case law confirm this view, with their emphasis on needing clear rules to avoid disputes[37] and needing to avoid a free-for-all where the strongest win over the weakest.[38] These are not ideas of ownership but ideas of legal order. Ownership is not forgotten, but preserved in a particular way, through the idea of the relativity of title. For example, the rest of the world is entitled to treat a finder as owner, but the owner's claim to the thing found remains superior.[39] I may put 'my' apple down and somebody else might pick it up and have their possession protected as against others, but it remains 'mine' and the court will assist me in its return.

Although this idea of the relativity of title preserves both the idea that ownership allows me to put my apple down and the need to create a public system of title, it introduces another systemic issue. We can see the possibility that the person in actual possession of the apple is not the owner but to make out this claim in court the owner has to prove that they are the owner—in other words, they have to prove their prior and superior title to the finder. The owner will have to show prior possession. Moreover, since there is always the possibility of other prior claims, there is scope for a great deal of uncertainty in this system of title, which undermines the rule of law values it is meant to express. This is why all legal systems of property have some means of cutting off prior claims. These methods get more complicated, and sometimes are rendered obsolete, as the state steps in to provide systems of title that do not rely upon possession.[40]

There are many details that could be filled in but I want instead to point to the key differences between this account of possessory title and the accounts that I started out discussing. On my account, possession gives someone a title claim not because possession justifies ownership in some manner—as useful labour, as a reward, etc.—but because a system of property must conform to the rule of law and this requires a public system of title. In this way possessory title does not point to justification stories for ownership but towards the requirements of the practice of law. Seeking to understand the law of possession through state-of-nature inspired stories of first possession is a mistaken strategy for it supposes that the question of why we want a practice like property law is the best, or even a good, way to tell us what the practice is. Moreover, its very strategy is to seek what is normative about property independently of the practice of law. For similar reasons, this account departs from a Dworkian approach to interpretation insofar as that approach

---

[37] *Pierson v Post* 1805.   [38] *Parker v British Airways Board* 1982.

[39] *Parker v British Airways Board* 1982.

[40] For example, many states that embrace a Torrens system do away with the doctrine of adverse possession or retain it only to deal with a narrow range of disputes.

suggests that the strategy for understanding possessory title is to seek the underlying moral principles that justify it. The salient idea of justification, I suggest, is much more modest and limited to an explanation of how it is a part of the practice of law.

4. The Right of Possession and its Omnilateral Structure

The argument so far is that a number of the questions of possession can be understood as working out what a right to possession means within a system of law. But, one might now object, surely we need to ask more substantive justificatory questions if we are to get much further in understanding possession. Even if we can make sense of the possessory title cases, there are other important questions regarding how we are to understand the nature of the *right* of possession—a right that was assumed, rather than explained, in the discussion of title. This question of the nature of the right becomes particularly important in relation to other questions regarding property rights, such as the relation between possession and 'ownership' or the relation between possession and other property rights traditionally 'bundled' into ownership such as alienability and use. In other words, what about the idea of ownership? Surely there we need to return to more original justificatory questions, or at least some understanding of the types of interests served by possession?

My answer is no and I will provide this answer in a very counter-intuitive way. I want to return now to the state of nature, and the one that I want to return to is Kant's. Kant, like many theorists, was preoccupied by the question of how a unilateral act—individual appropriation—could lead to a right of possession binding on others. His answer was that possession is not about unilateral actions but omnilateral relations. As I have already discussed, omnilaterality is an idea of law— sometimes associated with its 'public' nature but best understood as involving a relationship that holds equally between each individual and every other individual.

Kant introduced this idea in the service of the kind of justificatory story I have been arguing is unnecessary—and even unhelpful—for understanding possession. For Kant, because the right of possession is omnilateral, it is not possible in the state of nature; external objects can only be 'mine' in a civil condition.[41] However, in a state of nature we can have *provisionally* rightful possession.[42] What this means is that when I pick an apple from a tree, place it in a basket and proceed to build a fence around the tree and the basket, I do not violate the freedom of another. The important point, however, is that it is also the case that you do not violate my freedom when you climb my fence and take my apple (so long as I am not holding the apple, for that is an interference analogous to assault). For the apple, or the apple tree, to be 'mine', it must also be the case that you wrong me (violate my freedom) when you interfere with my possession of it.[43] And this requires the

---

[41] Kant 1797, 257.   [42] Kant 1797, 257.

[43] If another person deliberately takes the apple and destroys it simply for the reason of harming the interests of the person who picked it then an individual can, as a matter of right, resist such treatment. For Kant, one of the duties of right is the duty of rightful honour: 'Do not make yourself a mere means

omnilateral perspective, which for Kant implies the civil condition. Since the right of possession is only possible in a civil condition, this provides a reason to enter into a civil condition and even to compel others to do so. Provisional rightful possession (in a state of nature) therefore serves as a bridge connecting the idea of freedom and the rightful condition. Because of this it also plays a role in determining the boundaries of legitimate political authority, which for Kant is rooted in the requirements of a rightful condition.[44]

However, we can accept Kant's insight regarding omnilaterality and not follow him in his particular justificatory story. As I outlined earlier, omnilaterality is not simply a way of characterizing the public perspective of law and its institutions. Importantly, it implies an understanding of horizontal relations between individuals that are characterized by the universality and equality that many have argued is bound up in our most basic—and formal—understandings of the rule of law. Rawls's argument regarding the practice conception of rules tells us that to ask whether possession is justified is simply to ask whether it can be explained through reference to the practice of which it is a part. To say that the right of possession is omnilateral is therefore to say that we can understand it in relation to the practice of law. Indeed, as I will now outline, the concept of omnilaterality provides us with the formal structure of the right of possession.

To illustrate this structure, consider the following three examples. First, suppose that we accepted the idea that my possession of an apple created an obligation that you refrain from interfering with my possession. This would mean that my act, which is unilateral, imposes an obligation on you. It is true that we get a kind of correlative right and duty through this, whereby my right to possession is correlated with your obligation to refrain from interference. However, I would not be under a *reciprocal* obligation to anyone else simply in virtue of my unilateral act. Your possession of an apple could, in such a system, impose an obligation on me to refrain from interference with this possession. Now we would both be under obligations to respect each other's possession. This does not, however, transform these obligations into reciprocal obligations—they are simply two unilaterally imposed obligations that as a matter of fact, but not necessity, mirror one another. The relation can be represented through the diagram in Figure 8.1.

Suppose now that we instead posit that everyone enters into a series of bilateral agreements whereby A agrees to forbear from encroaching on B's possession in exchange for B's promise to forbear from encroaching on A's possession. A and B would then do the same with C, and so on. This relation can be represented through the diagram in Figure 8.2. The result of this is that A has a right of possession as against B and C and both B and C have obligations to forbear from

---

for others but be at the same time an end for them' (Kant 1797, 237). However, the right to resist being treated as a means does not itself transform the act of treating someone as a means from a violation of virtue into a violation of right. Therefore this does not establish a Kantian right of possession in the state of nature, simply an individual privilege to resists some kinds of interference with possession.

[44] See Ripstein 2009, chs. 8 and 9.

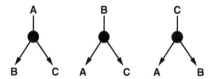

Figure 8.1. Unilateral Structure

Figure 8.2. Bilateral Structure

encroaching on A's possession. However, this is not a correlative right and duty in *property* because there is nothing about A's possession that is the ground of B and C's obligation to forbear from interference with it. The fact that A has a right and both B and C a duty is simply the incidental effect of the various agreements, the normative force of which lies in contract. To get an idea of possession as a right good against the world one has to then create the further fiction of notional contracts, unless one supposes that one can contract with everyone in the world.

Both the unilateral structure and bilateral structure of a right of possession are different from the idea of an omnilateral structure. Instead of a collection of unilateral relations running in parallel, or a collection of bilateral agreements binding particular people together, an omnilateral relation would take the form: *everyone's* power to possess is the ground of the liability that *everyone* has to fall under an obligation to refrain from interference with those things acquired by other's exercise of that power. We can represent this in a diagram as in Figure 8.3. In this way, you get the correlative right and obligation but there is a general and systematic quality to it precisely because it is not a series of bilateral agreements involving particular individuals. It is also important to note that in this structure non-owners are not related to one another as non-owners, nor are owners related to one another as owners. Instead, each person is related equally to each other in a very particular way: through a correlative relation involving a power to possess and a liability to falling under an obligation. It is this omnilateral structure of an otherwise bilateral relation that creates the generality and impersonality that characterizes ownership. The logical result of this structure is a correlative relation between owner (who could in principle be A or B or C...) and non-owner (who could in principle be A or B or C...). What omnilaterality shows us is how people may be directly related (whoever is the owner is related to whoever is the non-owner) yet in a thoroughly general way (who the owner is and who the non-owner is can change yet the relation remains the same).

Figure 8.3. Omnilateral Structure

An omnilateral relation sounds a lot like Hohfeld's 'multital' rights.[45] However, it is distinct in at least two important respects. Consider Hohfeld's characterization of possession as a multital right: 'If A owns and occupies Whiteacre, not only B but also a great many other persons—not necessarily all persons—are under a duty, e.g., not to enter on A's land. A's right against B is a multital rights, or right *in rem*, for it is simply one of A's class of *similar, though separate*, rights, actual and potential, against very many persons.'[46] The first distinction between multital and omnilateral lies in the characterization of multital rights as a 'class of similar, though separate, rights'. The second distinction between multital and omnilateral lies in the characterization of multital rights as being held against a large and indefinite group of people. For Hohfeld, A as owner holds multiple rights against multiple people. Possession as an omnilateral relation has a different structure that provides a way of seeing that there is just one right at issue, not multiple rights, and this right is not held against multiple particular others but rather a general other. The owner holds a right as against anyone who is a non-owner, whoever that might be. It is one correlative relation, but a relation marked by the generality and impersonality of owner and non-owner.[47]

This account of omnilaterality also differs from more recent accounts of the structure of property rights. I will take two here to illustrate the differences. James Penner argues that we need to focus on the nature of the duty to not interfere with the property of others. This duty is not specific to particular owners. As Penner outlines, even if the owner of Blackacre changes, '[e]very one else maintains exactly the same duty, which is not to interfere with the use and control of Blackacre. It matters not one whit to the content of this duty in respect of Blackacre that B now owns it instead of A.'[48] Penner argues that Hohfeld went wrong in accepting that there should be symmetry between rights and duties. Instead, we need to see that the *duty in rem* is primary.[49] In contrast, my account of possession as an omnilateral relation maintains the symmetry between rights and duties while agreeing with Penner that there is no specific duty owed to specific owners. The key is not to eschew this symmetry but to understand the generality of the rights and duties at issue. The owner who holds the right holds that right *as owner* and not as a specific person—it is like a role that one steps into but which others may also occupy in

---

[45] Hohfeld 1917b.   [46] Hohfeld 1917b, 719, emphasis mine.
[47] In this I agree with Kocourek who argues, on different grounds, that the distinctive feature of *in rem* rights is not that they are held against a large and indefinite class of people but that there is no need to identify the person who holds the duty. Kocourek 1920 and 1921.
[48] Penner 2000, 23.   [49] Penner 2000, 27.

one's place.[50] This is why it makes no difference if the owner sells her property to someone else—all this means is that someone steps into her shoes and is now the owner while the right, as the right of the owner, remains identical. Similarly, the duty is owed by another who is *not-the-owner*. There is nothing about my particular identity that informs this duty, nothing that is specific to me. I have the duty to not interfere because I am not the owner. It is simple, and, in its generality, does indeed correlate with the right.[51]

Others have defended a conception of ownership as an 'office'.[52] This is helpful as a way of illustrating the fact that who the owner is does not matter—different particular individuals may hold the office of ownership.[53] However, the idea of an office has more difficulty in helping us to understand the role of non-owners. To say that various individuals can hold the 'office' of non-owner is a strange use of the idea of an office. Office usually connotes the conferral of authority whereas non-ownership is characterized by liabilities and obligations that require explanation. If the idea of office is simply used to illustrate the idea of impersonality then it is unclear what it adds, analytically, to our understanding of ownership. In contrast, the idea of omnilaterality provides a way of understanding how it is logically possible to have a correlative relation between owner and non-owner that is nonetheless general and impersonal. Perhaps more importantly, it connects the structure of possession with the idea of law.

5. Possession and the Incidents of Ownership

The argument so far is that possessory title can be understood through ideas of legality and the right of possession can be understood in formal terms as an omnilateral relation. Both are legal ideas, part of our understanding of the rule of law, and therefore show how possession can be understood in relation to the practice of law rather than through reference to extra-legal norms. I do not mean to suggest that we can understand the law of property simply by looking at the logical structure of an omnilateral relation, and I will say more about its limits in Section 6. But I do mean to argue that this provides us with the core analytic form of private ownership that can illuminate the relationship between possession, use, and alienability without necessitating a return to the justification of property.

Let me start with use. Accounts of ownership that include possession as a core right often ground this in some idea of use and the interests served by exclusive use.

---

[50] Others also note this generality as a distinctive feature of property rights. See e.g. Merrill and Smith 2001a, 788.

[51] Because this account of the omnilateral structure of possession preserves the correlativity between right and duty, it is not susceptible to the critique launched against Penner that he cannot account for the fact that this plaintiff has a claim against this defendant. See Dorfman 2010, 12 and Dorfman 2012.

[52] Essert 2013; Katz 2012.

[53] Although it does potentially carry the further connotations of involving a delegation of authority that is then exercised on behalf of the body who delegated it, which does not easily map onto an account of private property.

At the same time, as Harris has pointed out, it is more accurate to characterize 'use' in terms of open-ended use 'privileges' rather than 'rights'.[54] Possession as a right of exclusive control protects one's ability to use something but there are no separate rights to particular uses or even a general 'right' to use one's property that can be understood independently from the right of exclusive control. My use of my property is a privilege because in using something that is within *my* exclusive control, I wrong no one.

But consider the idea of use more closely in relation to the apple example. I can pick an apple and put it into a basket and we can consider this a kind of use. Suppose, however, that I want to save this apple until I have a full basket so that I can bake several apple pies. In a world without a right of possession, saving the apple in a basket is not a cognizable 'use' because once I put the apple down I have no entitlement to it. I might do a number of things to protect my ability to use the apples in the future. But none of these things is a present 'use' of the apples—it is a present use of other things in order to protect a hoped-for future use of the apples. Keeping the apples in the basket only counts as a use in a world of property rights. Just like stealing a base is only intelligible as an action within the practice of baseball, the use of things that one no longer physically possesses (such as when I put the apple down) is only intelligible as a use within a practice of law that recognizes a right of possession. The right of possession does not protect uses that we can understand in non-legal terms, in relation to natural abilities. What it does is legally secure an ability to use an object of property in ways that are otherwise not possible.

How does possession relate to alienability? I contend that the possibility of alienability is implied by the omnilateral structure of the right of possession. A 'transfer' is really just a substitution of one owner for another. Someone steps into my shoes as owner. This is possible because of the general form of the right of possession—the structure of the right and its correlative duty is general in nature, between the owner and non-owner. This generality already implies that it does not matter who the owner or the non-owner is. The particular person who happens to be the owner may change and the particular people within the set of 'non-owner' may change but the nature of the correlative right and duty remains the same.[55] Whether I, as the particular owner, want to transfer my rights to you, so that you become owner, is a matter between the two of us with one caveat. That caveat is that there is still a separate question of the rules regarding when title passes. This is a separate question because it is governed by different concerns regarding legality, as outlined earlier. Non-owners need to know who the particular owner is so that they can take steps to avoid liability or plan their affairs through negotiating with the owner for particular uses, etc. A system of property, if it is to function in a manner

---

[54] Harris 1996, 214.

[55] In this way, cases of the assignment of property rights are the logical implications of the omnilateral structure of the right of possession. For an alternative account that seeks to make cases of assignment a kind of intermediate case between *in rem* and *in personam* rights, see Merrill and Smith 2001.

consistent with the rule of law, cannot leave the question of how title passes to the determination of the particular parties involved in the transaction.

To illustrate this point, take the example of gifts. This is, in essence, a unilateral transfer of rights. In addition to my intention to transfer these rights and your acceptance of this transfer, the law adds a 'delivery' requirement. What the delivery requirement amounts to is a requirement that the original owner no longer has possession of the object and the intended owner has possession. In other words, it is a variant of the test for possessory title and its function should be understood in relation to the general functions of rules of title.

What about the alleged fragmentation of ownership? There are a number of ways in which this set of ideas can come apart. For example, an owner can alienate a right of possession for a period of time, through a lease. But notice what then happens. The landlord and tenant have a relationship. It is not characterized by the neighbour test of negligence law, or the consensual regime of contract. Instead, it is characterized by the fact of the law needing to make sense of the idea that together the landlord and tenant hold the fee simple absolute and that there has been a temporal division in relation to the right of possession. It is not the case that the landlord has retained the right to alienate and the tenant has the right of possession. The tenant has a right to alienate the estate that the tenant has—and can assign her interest or enter into a sublease. The landlord has a right of possession, but it is a future interest. To say that they have been unbundled is inaccurate. The estate has been divided in a very particular way—temporally—that gives rise to different portions that themselves are temporal slices of the right to possession and the concomitant ability to alienate. These different temporal slices are themselves related within the analytic framework of ownership.

The structure of an omnilateral relation can also give us a better way of thinking about non-possessory rights. I want to illustrate this through a consideration of a particular example drawn from the law regarding servitudes—restrictive covenants. A covenant is simply an agreement between two individuals and is enforceable as a contract. It becomes a question for property law when the agreement is between two owners and one (or both) sell their estate: is the successor in title bound by the terms of the agreement? The traditional common law answer has been that benefits (both positive and negative) can run with the land, but not burdens. The traditional answer in equity is that a negative burden can run but not a positive one.[56] The resulting property interests are classified as non-possessory rights in land owned by someone else. My claim here is that understanding the right of possession as an omnilateral relation can illuminate these interests and their doctrinal features. Take the example of a negative burden. For a negative burden to run, equity has insisted on the requirements of a Dominant Tenement (land to be benefited), a Servient Tenement (land to be burdened), and a burden that 'touches and concerns' the land. We can understand these requirements as seeking to determine which obligations are ones that can be construed as obligations between owners qua

---

[56] *Tulk v Moxhay* 1848; *Austerberry v Oldham Corporation* 1885; *Rhone v Stephens* 1994.

owners rather than the particular individuals who happen to be the owners. If they are agreements between owners, then it makes sense that they could 'run with the land'. All this means is that whoever the particular owner happens to be is obligated because they are the owner.[57]

6. A Principled Practice of Property?

It is important to underscore the fact that there is nothing in the account I have offered of possession that says it *must* be this way, that a society must recognize private ownership. The entire thrust of my argument has been to claim that possession is intelligible without any commitment or reference to why we might think it is valuable or justified generally. It may be consistent with quite a number of different justificatory accounts and it may be critiqued from quite a number of different justificatory accounts. Moreover, there is nothing in this account that suggests a particular role for the state in relation to property rights—for example, that the state protect private property. All of these are important debates but, as I have tried to claim here, debates that are not part of what the courts do when they engage in legal justification or the elaboration of the legal idea of possession.

Therefore this argument is quite consistent with the view that we can collectively change aspects of the law of possession in order to pursue substantive social goals. For example, most jurisdictions have, to a large extent, moved away from reliance upon possessory title in relation to land and instead created various state-sanctioned systems of title. In doing so it is plausible to argue that substantive social goals, including economic goals, have been integrated into these systems.[58] We can also choose to adopt hybrid forms of private ownership, changing the basic structure to reflect social goals. Arguably, jurisdictions that have embraced landlord-tenant reform for residential tenancies have done just that.

However, there is a deeper challenge to the view of justification that I have offered here. The challenge goes like this. Suppose that we adopt an interpretive account of the law which, following Dworkin, means that the ideas of 'fit' and 'justification' are always part of legal interpretation. Dworkin has recently refined his account to include ideas of legality as 'the nerve of the dimension of fit'.[59] Although he was referring to ideas of procedural fairness, a more robust account of the rule of law could be developed as an aspect of this dimension. Dworkin could therefore argue that the fact that possession can be made intelligible within an account of the rule of law in no way undermines his general argument regarding the nature of legal interpretation—it simply confirms the importance of the dimension of 'fit'. Considerations of substantive justice remain potentially involved in any question of interpretation.

---

[57] See Essert 2013 and Austin 2013.
[58] See also Lueck 2003, for arguments as to when, from an economic perspective, common property is better than first possession for determining control over a particular resource.
[59] Dworkin 2004, 25.

I want to respond to this challenge by examining Dworkin's general claim that the principles of substantive morality are already a part of the common law tradition, which for him is why what the law is always also involves the question of the law's moral justification. Although in this chapter I cannot respond to all possible claims regarding the role that morality might play in common law reasoning, I do want to resist Dworkin's account by showing that the principles that he calls 'moral' are better understood as specific examples of the principles of legality. The need to apply the rules of property in light of the demands of the principles of legality can indeed affect the substance of property law but it does so by remaining within an analytic framework defined by the rule of law and not broader ideas of political morality.

Consider Dworkin's famous example of *Riggs v Palmer*, and its reliance on the principle that wrongdoers should not profit from their wrong.[60] Although not a case about possession, it is important because Dworkin takes this as one of his central examples of a 'principle' operating within the common law, a principle that illustrates the deep link between common law reasoning and broader understandings of morality. The Supreme Court of Canada recently discussed this principle but in quite different terms and this discussion shows how we can view such principles as examples of legality considerations rather than principles of morality.

Hall v Hebert concerned the doctrine of *ex turpi causa non oritur actio* and its use in barring recovery in tort.[61] Justice McLachlin argued that many of the cases of 'accepted application of the maxim' were cases that illustrated the 'narrow principle' that 'a plaintiff will not be allowed to profit from his or her wrongdoing'.[62] However, she went on to state that a better understanding of the basis of the maxim is that it prevents introducing 'an inconsistency in the law' by forcing the court to say that the same act is both legal and illegal.[63]

Can this account of illegality and wrongdoing account for *Riggs v Palmer*? There are two main threads to the decision in *Riggs v Palmer*: a discussion of the equitable construction of the statute and a discussion of common law maxims regarding wrongdoing.[64] What is interesting is that both involve, in broad contours, a similar set of considerations to those outlined by Justice McLachlin in *Hall v Hebert*. With respect to the statutory interpretation point, the court framed its concerns in terms of contradiction with common reason,[65] and with the very point of laws pertaining to wills—to secure the 'orderly, peaceable and just devolution of property'.[66] In relation to the common law maxims, the court pointed to the direct relationship between the murder and the inheritance. The grandson murdered his grandfather so that he could inherit before his grandfather could change his will. In permitting

---

[60] *Riggs v Palmer* 1889.
[61] *Hall v Hebert* 1993. The court extensively cites Weinrib 1976, although Weinrib did not explicitly endorse the integrity of the legal system rationale.
[62] *Hall v Hebert* 1993, para. 17.   [63] *Hall v Hebert* 1993, para. 17.
[64] For a discussion of this case in terms of equity, see Klimchuk forthcoming and Smith forthcoming.
[65] *Riggs v Palmer* 1889, 510.   [66] *Riggs v Palmer* 1889, 511.

this, the court would sanction murder as a means of acquiring title, which, in turn, would contradict the very idea of the legal acquisition of title.

Even if I deny the significance of morality in common law reasoning in Dworkin's framework of Herculean justification, this does not mean that it does not arise in other ways. My claim, however, is that these other ways should also be understood within a framework of legality, or the rule of law, and not as a set of additional considerations whose significance is to be understood independently of this framework. Let me provide two examples.

The first is the idea of consistency within the law. Dworkin refers to this as the dimension of 'fit' and argues that its central 'political' concept is procedural fairness.[67] But consistency in the law is one of Fuller's principles of legality[68] and is not necessarily best classified as 'procedural' but certainly as part of the formal and structural elements of the practice of law as outlined previously. In mature liberal democratic legal systems, law is never a matter of only common law decisions, even in areas of 'private' law like property. Instead, there is a mixture of common law and statutes and the two must be interpreted in a manner that maintains consistency in the system as a whole. Moreover, there is nothing in my account here that suggests that a legislature cannot take into account general ideas of justice in determining the norms of legislation. If we put these two ideas together, we can see that what I have been calling extra-legal ideas can enter into legal reasoning even when the question is not about the direct application of a particular statute. One example of this would be contemporary discussions of 'public policy' in cases where the courts must determine whether to invalidate a particular provision on the grounds of being contrary to public policy.[69] In determining what public policy amounts to, courts look to statutes and constitutional texts.[70]

A second way in which extra-legal considerations, including morality, enter into legal reasoning within a framework of legality is in relation to the idea of followability. Laws must be followable. This connects with other ideas of legality such as publicity and non-retroactivity as aspects of the core rule of law idea that law should guide individuals and permit them to plan their activities in light of their legal liabilities and legal powers. The common law has always been concerned with how the law operates on the ground, in light of the actual social practices and expectations of communities. There is no reason why the judges cannot take such considerations into account, in order to ensure the actual conditions of followability. However, it would be a mistake to think that such considerations import broader ideas of justification into common law reasoning for their normative significance lies in their service to the values of legality.

---

[67] Dworkin 2004, 25.
[68] Fuller put the point narrowly, in terms of avoiding contradictions in the law.
[69] The provision could be a condition, a covenant, a term of a trust, etc.
[70] See e.g. *Canada Trust Co. v Ontario Human Rights Commission* 1990.

7. Conclusion

My argument in this chapter has been that unlocking the mysteries of possession by starting with first possession and then seeking to account for first possession by asking broad justificatory questions regarding the function and desirability of ownership is mistaken. State of nature stories, in focusing on pre-legal relationships, and interpretive accounts of law, in focusing on law's place within a broader account of political morality, both ignore the importance of law. I have instead invoked Rawls's practice conception of rules to show how we can understand justification in relation to constitutive elements of a practice quite apart from any account of the desirability of that practice. Possession, I have claimed, is best understood in light of the legal practice of which it is a part. The constitutive elements of this practice, as presented here, are the formal aspects of the rule of law. Possessory title shows us how the right of possession can be made consistent with the systemic demands of the principles of legality; the formal structure of the right of possession is omnilateral, itself an idea of equality and universality.

To justify possession, on my account, we need to explain it in relation to the rule of law. In contrast, to understand why we might want the rule of law, or how its features should relate to social goals or particular social institutions, raises another set of questions. My goal here has not been to answer these other questions but to pull them apart from an account of possession.

Let me conclude, however, by stepping outside this account of possession and legal justification in order to offer one reason for the general desirability of such an approach. Freeing possession from any particular external justificatory story means that it can be consistent with a variety of such stories.[71] These need not overlap or agree in any way for possession itself to be explained or elaborated upon. And in contemporary pluralist societies, marked by deep divisions over basic values, this is no small advantage.[72]

---

[71] For disagreement on this point, see Ripstein this volume.   [72] See also Smith 2009.

9

The Relativity of Title and *Causa Possessionis*

*Larissa Katz**

It is often said nowadays that to any dispute between those who claim possessory rights in a thing, the common law proposes a clear and simple answer: 'first in time, stronger in right'.[1] Whether the dispute is between a 'true owner' and a finder;[2] between two finders; between a bailee and a thief; between two thieves; or between any other putative possessors, the same simple rule claims to tell us whose right is superior. This rule is attractive in its simplicity—temporal priority is all that matters when deciding these disputes—but it is also surprising in its disregard for all other possible considerations. Shouldn't the law care about the *type* of possessory claims we are concerned with? Doesn't it matter (for reasons going beyond the temporal priority of his claim) that one party is in possession *as the true owner*, or only as a thief, etc.? And don't the prior interactions between the parties matter to the law, as well? For instance, shouldn't it matter to the law whether or not one party put the other party into possession in the first place? All these considerations seem to have moral salience when considering who should be entitled to possess a thing. It would be odd if the law took no notice of them.

The reason why the 'first in time, stronger in right' maxim seems so appealing to many contemporary property lawyers, I argue, is that it is entirely consistent with their understanding of ownership and rights to possess more generally. On the view that currently dominates property law and theory, ownership is simply the right to exclude all others from the owned thing. In this way, it is different only in degree (and not in kind) from other possessory interests.[3] For bailees, finders, and even thieves have the right to exclude some others from the things in their possession;

* This chapter was begun while I was an HLA Hart Visiting Fellow in Law & Philosophy, Oxford Centre for Ethics & the Philosophy of Law, Oxford University. I am grateful to CEPL for funding and support. I am grateful too for comments from participants at the Property-Works-in-Progress workshop at Fordham Law School, the Philosophical Foundations of Property Law conference at University College London and the Private Law Theory workshop at the University of Edinburgh. I am especially grateful to Simon Douglas, Robin Hickey, Ben McFarlane, James Penner, Henry Smith, Lionel Smith, and Malcolm Thorburn for their comments. Ted Brook provided excellent research assistance.
  [1] 'Qui prior est tempore, potior est jure'.
  [2] *Parker v British Airways Board* 1982, 1019.
  [3] See Pollock and Wright 1888, 93 stating that possession gives rise to a 'right in the nature of property'; McFarlane 2008, 144 arguing that possessors' rights to exclude are identical to those of owners; Holmes 1872, see n. 7.

the only difference is that they may not exclude quite *as many* people as the true owner. Accordingly, if all possessors have claims of the same type, it seems that the only available criterion by which we can distinguish their claims is their temporal priority. Although it is not a strict entailment relationship, then, the connection between the conception of ownership as a right to exclude and the rule of 'first in time, stronger in right' is very close indeed.

In this chapter, I argue that for many years the common law embraced a richer conception of ownership than a mere right to exclude, and partly as a consequence of this, it also expounded a subtler and more complex understanding of the relativity of title than the simple 'first in time, stronger in right' rule. Although more recent case law and scholarship has tended to overlook many of these matters, the common law has traditionally analysed disputes among putative possessors in terms of their '*causa possessionis*'—the normative ground of their claims to possession—and not merely in terms of the temporal priority of their claims. First, this means that first in time is not always stronger in right, for these other considerations may sometimes trump temporal priority. But second, it also means that even when the 'first in time' rule generates the right answer, it does so in a way that obscures the larger normative framework that explains *why* that is the right answer. Although the primary aim of this chapter is the intellectual recovery of this buried tradition, my secondary purpose is to revive interest in this tradition as a living doctrine. For a possessor's *causa possessionis* is clearly morally salient to disputes among possessors, so there is good reason for the law to recognize it, as well.

***

This chapter is in two parts. In Section 1, I consider the special importance of the role of true owners in possessory disputes. As I have argued elsewhere,[4] the role of true owner at common law has been traditionally understood to encompass a good deal more than just the right to exclude others from one's property. Rather, it has been thought of as a position of exclusive authority over the thing, empowering owners not only to decide who may be excluded from it, but also to create dependent property rights in the thing, to determine the use to which the thing shall be put, and much else besides. Accordingly, any account of the possessory interests of non-owners should do so in a way that leaves in place the owner's exclusive claim of authority over the thing. That is why when the law recognizes the right of bailees or finders to exclude others from a thing, it does not put them on the same footing as the true owner. Rather, it recognizes that in the absence of the true owner, bailees and finders may act as what I will call 'owners *pro tem*', stewards of the office of ownership in the absence of its titular head. Finders are finders, and owners are owners, with their own special place in a system of property. Although the maxim 'first in time, stronger in right' will generate the right answers in most disputes between true owners and bailees and finders, it fails to capture the important difference in the kind of right that each claims. The concept of

---

[4] See Katz 2008. For the centrality of the idea of ownership in a system of property, see also Katz 2011a; see also Merrill 2012.

ownership *pro tem* is significant: it preserves the authority of owners by enabling a finder to slot herself into a role that is protective of the office of ownership.

This concept of ownership *pro tem* does not, however, explain all the variety of rights to possess in the common law. Not all holders of rights to possess are owners *pro tem*. Someone who mistakenly assumes something is hers and someone who knows it is not but who asserts dominion over it anyway—i.e. a thief—both possess without deference to the authority of the true owner.[5] What explains this other variety of right to possess, that of the wrongdoer? In Section 2, I argue that there is a second and distinct normative nexus that exists between a wrongdoer and a later possessor in some contexts.[6] The ancient concept of privity explains this normative nexus. Privity is an under-theorized but widely used concept in the private law.[7] It describes the relationship that exists where two or more people share the same foundation of right or interest, whether that means they partake of the same office, the same blood, the same transaction,[8] or the same right.[9] Privity in effect creates a double-blind situation: privies cannot stand outside their relationship to take an external perspective on the rights and obligations that they owe one another. And from the outside looking in, privies rise and fall together with respect to the right or interest that they share, whatever the arrangements are that they have made internal to that relationship.[10] Privity explains one very limited kind of right to possess that is available even to wrongdoers: if a wrongdoer in bare possession of a thing puts another in possession of it, then there is a shared foundation to both possessors'

---

[5] Someone who mistakenly assumes ownership of someone else's thing at least commits trespass and is not able to claim the role of a finder, which would account for her taking possession of a thing in a manner consistent with the true owner's retained rights. See n. 21.

[6] Of course privity does not exist just in the context of wrongdoers. It is rather that wrongdoers depend on privity for their right to possess.

[7] See Holmes 1872, 7; Tettenborn 1982. Rastell 1721, Privity: 'Because of what has passed between these parties, they are called privies in respect of strangers, between whom no such convey-ances have been made.' Privity in estate, privity in deed (reversion to X): Holmes 1872, 46.

[8] Privity of contract was a late addition. See Palmer 1992, 10–11. Other privities include the privity of tenure, deed, title, estate, possession, and blood. Ballantine 1919 (privity of possession creates continuity of possession by mutual consent. Other privities discussed include: ancestor-heir, lessor-lessee, judgment debtor-execution purchaser).

[9] A form of privity arises where there is a shared foundation of some purely negative normative position, for instance, where adverse possessors join forces against a true owner through privity of possession. 'Recent Case Notes' (1929) 29 *Yale Law Journal* 795 at 806 (describing privity of possession between adverse possessors); *Brown v Gobble* 1996; *Illinois Steel Co. v Paczocha* 1909 ('It is said that there must be privity between the successive occupants, but this does not at all mean that there must be a privity of title. . . . The privity between successive occupants required for the statute of limitations is privity merely of that physical possession, and is not dependent upon any claim, or attempted transfer, of any other interest or title in the land'). See also *Kepley v Scully* 1900 (no writing requirement for 'conveyance' between AP1 and AP2: really the deed itself is just evidence of privity. It is this privity that enables tacking not the transfer of property rights.). See 'Notes of Cases' (1900) *Virginia Law Register* 490 at 491, 'the parol transfer by the first to the second possessor of property held adversely, with succession of occupancy, is held, in *Illinois Steel Co v Budzisz* 1909, to be sufficient to unite the two possessions into one for the purpose of acquiring title by adverse possession.'

[10] *Beverley's Case* 1603 (issue estoppel extended to your privies); Coke 1628, 1: 71 (estoppel of lessor-lessee); *Laverty v Snethen* 1877 (privity of bailment means bailee stands on bailor's title and so any determination of the bailee's rights vis-à-vis outsider, resolving the question of ownership, is also binding on bailor). Bailor has duty to protect bailee who is sued in relation to title/possession.

claims to possess the thing. The second possessor is estopped from denying the right to possess of the wrongdoer insofar as his own claim to be legitimately in possession of the thing depends on it too. This leaves an earlier possessor, though a wrongdoer, in a position to maintain a right to possess at least *inter se*.[11] Once again, the relative merits of claimants in this kind of a contest attests to the importance of the *causa possessionis*, the ground on which a person came into possession of a thing.

1. Finders and Ownership *Pro Tem*

1.1 Owners and finders

When the true owner comes out of possession of his property, either by granting a bailment to another or by losing it, it is not difficult to determine who as between the true owner and the bailee or finder, has the superior right to possess it. Of course, it is the true owner, who also happens to have the chronologically prior possessory claim, as well. In a way, then, disputes between true owners and bailees or finders are clear cases where 'first in time, stronger in right' consistently generates the right answer to the question of whose possessory right should prevail. But although it consistently generates the right answers here, it does so in a way that is highly misleading. For it suggests that such disputes are just a species of a more general principle of 'first in time, stronger in right', where the relevant normative considerations are the same. But, as I shall endeavour to show in this section, they are not. Ownership is a unique position of authority over the thing, and the owner's position is always different in kind from that of any other possessor.

By declaring someone to be the owner of a thing, a system of property settles the important question of who among us has supreme decision-making authority with respect to that thing (subject of course to public law regulation). And yet, in any system of property, things may get lost, stolen, or otherwise separated from their owner. Is the business of ownership on hold until the thing is back in the hands of the true owner or can the office of ownership function even in the absence of its chief officer? The relativity of title is, on my account, the mechanism by which the common law deputizes someone to stand in for the owner until the owner is found. In a sense, things are never lost; owners are. The thing itself remains in the system of property, within the jurisdiction of the office of ownership. What is missing is the owner, and what is called for is someone to act in her stead.

A person who comes into possession as a 'finder' acquires a special position within our system of property, a position I will call 'ownership *pro tem*'.[12] A finder

---

[11] This normative nexus, built on relationships of privity, may exist between a finder/bailor and her bailee. My point is just that this is the only normative nexus on which a true bare possessor, someone who does not own or take possession as a finder, can depend. See e.g. Palmer 2000, 12: 'If the finder bails the chattel to another, the estoppel which applies at common law between bailor and bailee will prevent the recipient from pleading that the finder is not the owner.'

[12] Many jurists have struggled to explain the nature of finders, often resorting to ideas of quasi-bailment to explain their relationship to the true owner while they are in possession of the thing. There are many problems with this analogy of finders to bailees: they are there unilaterally, without any

occupies the office of ownership temporarily while the owner is missing but merely as the steward of the position itself.[13] A finder's right to possess is not identical in kind to an owner's on this account:[14] it is fundamentally a duty-based position, the possibility of which the law preserves *through* a special right to possess.[15] The finder has a basic responsibility to the owner when she undertakes to serve as owner *pro tem*, and it is arguably the discharge of this responsibility that the law protects against interference by third parties.[16]

A finder must know her place: she lacks the authority to assert total dominion of a thing that someone else owns.[17] She is commissioned to assume the office of ownership only temporarily and indeed only partially, on an emergency basis.[18] A finder thus bears many of the burdens of ownership but lacks the full set of beneficial privileges or powers that characterize ownership: she lacks absolute rights to use, sell, consume for her own gain. If she does use the thing, she is liable for any

---

transfer of rights from the owner, and possess only insofar as they are unable to put the thing back into the hands of the true owner. The concept of ownership *pro tem* better accounts for the position of finders in relation to an office of ownership. See Palmer 2009, para. 26-001, for further discussion of the problems with treating finders as bailees.

[13] If finders are able to escape their role as owner *pro tem*, it is because of statutory interventions that extinguish the right of an owner to sue for wrongful interference. When is there a conversion? *Sovern v Yoran* 1888 (no 'right' if not made a bailee); *South Staffordshire Water Co. v Sharman* 1896; *Hannah v Peel* 1945. Note that there is some controversy in the law about whether the finder's obligations survive the loss of the thing itself. See Fox 2006, 343: 'special' property as a rule depends on having the goods in possession. But see discussion in Douglas 2008: confusion in the law on the liability of finders for careless loss.

[14] Contrast this with the widespread push in the common law since the late 19th century to see owners and finders as holders of the same generic right. Consider e.g. Holmes 1881, 187–8: 'The common law should go so far as to deal with possession in the same way as title and should hold that when it has once been acquired rights are acquired which should continue to prevail against all the world but one until something has happened sufficient to divest ownership.' See also *The Winkfield* 1902, 60: 'as between bailee and stranger, possession gives title—that is, not a limited interest, but absolute and complete ownership . . . '.

[15] Foremost among these are the duties to seek out the true owner, and to take reasonable care of the goods. See *Parker v British Airways* 1982, per Donaldson LJ, 1017, 1018: 'a person having a finder's ["very limited"] rights has an obligation to . . . acquaint the true owner of the finding and present whereabouts of the chattel and to care for it meanwhile'.

[16] A finder, in the absence of an owner, has a right to sue in conversion as in the absence of the owner she will always have responsibility to steward the position of owner. The common law tradition once clearly linked responsibility to the true owner and the right to sue for interferences with possession in the context of bailments. See e.g. Bacon and Gwillim (1798, 6: 685) in a comment on *Armory v Delamirie* 1722: 'Because, as the finder is answerable for the jewel to the person in whom the general property is, he has a special property therein'. There are difficulties with this interpretation, pointed to in Clerk 1891: pointing out that this was not explicitly decided on this basis. See also Blackstone 1765, 2: 395; and *Rooth v Wilson* 1817, and especially *Claridge v South Staffordshire Tramway Co.* 1892: (consistent with the view that possession is the basis of a generic form of right to possess in the nature of property). This line of reasoning is in disfavour. See *The Winkfield* 1902 (expressly overturning *Claridge*).

[17] See *R v Watts* 1953, 7 (evidence of ownership throws burden on finder to show he had come into possession lawfully. Under the *Forest Act*, marks on logs prima facie evidence of ownership. Not theft in that case because no mens rea: accused reasonably believed they had permission to salvage as had done so for those owners before).

[18] See *R v Thurborn* 1849: finders are not guilty of larceny where they have the intention to take just a partial and temporary right.

loss or destruction that results.[19] Nor does the finder have one of the most characteristic powers of ownership, the power to create *independent* property rights in that thing, e.g. liens.[20] A finder in effect does nothing more than keep the seat warm for the true owner (which some finders forget, to their great disadvantage, when they assume the position of owner without being in a position to escape the bonds of finding, for instance, by establishing that the thing was abandoned).[21] It follows then that the finder must step down where the true owner is located—not because the owner's right is the *earlier* right but rather because the finder, as deputy, is not required once someone higher up the chain of command appears. This explains why the finder must yield to whoever has dominion over the thing, even someone who becomes owner *after* the finder's own right to possess is acquired.[22]

Finders and owners are not simply prior and later holders of otherwise identical rights to exclude, with the result that temporal priority does not fully account for their relative merits. The relationship between finders and owners has a hierarchical structure: a finder has a position within the office of ownership, and her special right to possess depends on the authority of that office. The subordinate nature of a finder's 'special property' was clearly expressed in the old common law crime of larceny: a person was guilty of larceny at common law if he appropriated a thing 'with the intent to take the entire dominion over them, knowing or having a reasonable belief at the time he found the goods the true owner thereof'.[23] The basis on which a person takes possession thus matters to their status in our system of property.[24] A person is a finder, with a finder's right to possess, only if he took possession on that basis. This explains why in the early history of the common law,

---

[19] Palmer 2009, para. 26-090: 'conversion is committed whenever the finder uses the goods for his own benefit, or hires them to a third party, or intercepts and consumes the profits of them, or seriously mishandles them'. See also Palmer 2000: a finder will herself be bound by such rights (*in personam*).

[20] A finder cannot create a lien that will be binding on the owner, either in herself or in someone else. Palmer 2009, para. 36-036, citing *Pegasus Leasing ltd v Confini* 1991 unreported, 13 November 1991, Sup Ct NSW Eq Div. The American case law suggests the same. Apart from statute, a finder who returns lost property is not entitled to a reward unless publicly offered: *Automobile Ins. Co. of Hartford Conn. v Kirby* 1932. However, when a specific reward is offered, a finder may be held to have a lien against the owner for the amount of the reward: *Everman v Hyman* 1892. In contrast, there is no situation in which a finder could create binding subordinate rights in another via pledging (pawning) the goods. At common law, a pledgor must either be the owner of the goods at the time of the pledge, or show that he enjoyed the owner's authority to pledge them: *Cole v North Western Bank* 1875, 362–3. The unauthorized pledgor commits conversion against the true owner *Advanced Industrial Technology Corp Ltd v Bond Street Jewellers Ltd* 2006, para. 3.

[21] A finder may have the power to require that other claimants prove first that they are the true owner (using interpleader). See Clashfern 2008, para. 489.

[22] Palmer 2009 para. 26-002: a finder's obligations move with title to the goods as the title shifts from original owner to new owner.

[23] *R v Thurborn* 1849. *Causa possessionis* also matters to the distinction in the common law between mere trespass and conversion: see *Foulds v Willoughby* 1841 (removal of a horse, with no intention to take dominion of it, is a mere trespass not a conversion). A possessor without a good *causa possessionis* is especially vulnerable with respect to the true owner—even more so than a finder. Thus, in *R v Riley* 1853, a man drove his neighbour's lamb out with his own by mistake and then sold it. As he took possession by mistake—and not as a finder—his initial taking was trespassory.

[24] This does not mean that a wrongdoer never receives any protection in law against a subsequent possessor: they sometimes do but for reasons to do with relations of privity rather than property.

finders typically called witnesses, generally their neighbours, to attest to the found nature of the goods and so the basis of their possession as finders.[25]

The concept of ownership *pro tem* is a feature of a system of property rights organized around ownership as sovereignty. There are examples of its use elsewhere in the common law, to protect the position of owner. For example, the common law anciently held that *strangers* could set themselves up as essentially a trustee of a dispossessed owner of land by retaking possession of it in the name of and for the use of the true owner.[26] The self-proclaimed champion assumed a kind of owner-ship position through this intervention that was both temporary and partial: the possession was meant to be entirely for the benefit of the owner. Taking position like this in the name of the true owner, even without the permission or the knowledge of the true owner, had the effect of establishing the intervenor as *owner pro tem*. If the dispossessor brought an action essentially to quiet title, the *owner pro tem* had at that point to get the backing of the true owner within five years.[27] This historical example illustrates the notion of *owner pro tem*, someone whom the law treats as stewarding office of owner on behalf of the true owner, without the full benefits of that position.

The concept of *ownership pro tem*, I readily concede, suggests a highly restrictive and perhaps even servile position for finders: a finder does not enjoy the very same right to exclude as an owner would, restricted only by the extent of excludability. Rather, the finder, like a rescuer, takes on a position of voluntary servitude to another for which there is no entitlement to promotion or reward for service.[28] A finder's right to possess is grounded not just in the fact of her possession but in her role in service of the owner. Why then *would* anyone take this on? That is of course an empirical matter that is outside my account of the structure of the role within our system of property: finders might hope that the true owner never shows up and so that they are able to convert the thing to their own use with impunity; they may count on being able later to show that the thing was abandoned all along. And of course modern finders' statutes give finders at least a shot at gaining absolute possession of the thing, by extinguishing an owner's right to recovery after a certain amount of time has passed.[29]

---

[25] Hickey 2010, 10, citing Pollock and Maitland 1898, 175.

[26] This is described in Coke 1628, s. 258a: 'If an infant or any man of full age have any right of entrie into any lands any stranger in the name and to the use of the infant or man of full age may enter into the land and this regularly shall vest the lands in them without any commandement, precedent or agreement subsequent.' The intervenor would have to get assent within five years or lose the right if the disseisor sought to bar the right through levying fines with proclamations in royal courts.

[27] Coke 1628, s. 258a.

[28] Many states and territories have implemented statutory rewards for finders. At common law, however, finders are not entitled to rewards. See Palmer 2009, para. 26-094. If a reward has been offered, the finder generally has a contractual right to the reward.

[29] See e.g. British Columbia's Unclaimed Property Act SBC 1999, C 48. The act outlines a range of limitations periods based on the value of the lost item. Generally, limitation periods range from 6 years (the limitation period for conversion in some jurisdictions) to a few months in others, when combined with other steps (such as a reasonable search for the true owner, turning the thing over to the police).

1.2 Finders versus finders

The law does not rely on a single, uniform metric, first in time, stronger in right, for comparing the relative merits of all rights to possess. Temporal priority *does* matter, but not because rights to possess are just so many identical rights to exclude. Indeed, within a system of property that is organized hierarchically around the concept of ownership as sovereignty, there *are* certain kinds of conflicts that are easily sorted out through a temporal ordering, precisely because they involve identical but independent rights. This is true of competing claims of finders, where one finder loses the thing and someone else subsequently takes possession of it *qua finder*.[30] There is in these cases no deep normative nexus between finder one and finder two: there is no privity between them, and it would be absurd to treat finder number two as possessing in the name of the first finder. When a thing is lost, it is presumed to have an owner, but we cannot well say that it ought also be presumed to have had prior finders. In a contest between finder one and finder two, we are not dealing with rights that relate to one another hierarchically. The second finder, rather, asserts the same ground of possession that the first finder did: he takes as a finder, which is to say he takes on the responsibility of owner *pro tem*. We are thus are dealing with two claims of precisely the same kind.[31] This is where a 'first in time, stronger in right' principle makes sense because we are then in the situation that exclusion theorists think we are always in: a situation where we have to decide as between identical and *independent* rights to possess who will prevail.[32] Thus, finder number one prevails over finder number two because he has secured the position of owner *pro tem* first: his superior right emerges from the earlier finding of the thing and the prior assumption of responsibility to the true owner.[33]

2. Privity, Estoppel, and Rights to Possess outside of Ownership

The concept of ownership *pro tem* explains the relative merits of the rights of owners and finders and informs also the relative merits of the rights of finders and later possessors of the thing. But finders are not the only possessors who garner the

---

[30] We would have no reason to compare the relative merits of these two claims if the first right is extinguished for independent reasons. Of course if a finder voluntarily divests herself of possession, she ceases to be a finder: *R v Harding* 1807. If the finder loses the thing, there is some authority for continuing to treat her as responsible, qua finder, for the goods. See Douglas 2008 (discussing controversy). In that case, she remains an owner *pro tem* and the question is properly her relative priority vis-à-vis a later finder.

[31] Both finders, it is assumed, claim to have 'special property' in the goods derived from the true owner's 'absolute property'. See Chitty 1844, 1: 169. See also *Bridges v Hawkesworth* 1851.

[32] In *Cumming v Cumming* 1847, 18 the Supreme Court of Georgia stated in dicta that finder-finder disputes exemplify *qui prior est in tempore, potior est in jure*.

[33] *Deaderick v Oulds* 1887, 489. Of course, this is not to deny the special powers that finder 1 derives from the true owner—the power to maintain an action of trover, for example. And as the Superior Court of Delaware stated in *Clark v Maloney* 1840, the rightful owner's absolute power is not affected by any subsequent loss, meaning that the first finder's 'special property' does not change either.

law's protection. A thief and a person who assumes dominion of someone else's thing by mistake are not in the same position as a finder.[34] They are wrongdoers whose possession is irreconcilable with the owner's position of authority.[35] And yet the common law appears to protect such bare possessors[36] against later comers.

What accounts for the protection of wrongdoers in these cases? Temporal priority predicts the winner in many cases involving wrongdoers, without, however, accounting for the normative relation between them. For that we need to look to other normative concerns, namely the state's monopoly on the use of force and the protection of privity.

The law's general prohibition against force explains (without controversy) some of the circumstances in which a wrongdoer can maintain a limited right to possess: there is reason to protect even wrongdoers against forcible dispossession. In our legal system, as in others, force is not limited to battery: it means the use of a forbidden personal power to overwhelm another's agency, e.g. threats, intimidation as well as armed force, etc.[37] There are not only private law reasons for banning forcible dispossession (unjustified interferences with our person) but public law ones as well (the state's monopoly on the use of force even in the protection of *rights*, a basis for limiting even the use of force in self-help, e.g. by an owner against his own dispossessor).[38] Courts put a wrongdoer back in possession not because of

---

[34] *R v Riley* 1853. P1 will be liable in conversion to the person with an immediate right to possession (usually the owner, but not always) regardless of whether she took the object in good faith and without negligence. *Cochrane v Rymill* 1879; *Consolidated Co. v Curtis* 1892. There are cases where someone assumes dominion mistakenly believing that they are entitled to do so: *Wilson v New Brighton Panelbeaters Ltd* 1989. However, mere appropriation without any denial of the plaintiff's right to possession and enjoyment generally does not amount to more than a trespass. *Fouldes v Willoughby* 1841. The kind of possession matters in these cases: if a person takes possession as a mere bailee for a thief or a finder, he generally escapes liability for conversion: *Hollins v Fowler* 1872, 23 ('Any person who, however innocently, obtains possession of the goods of a person who has been fraudulently deprived of them, and disposes of them, whether for his own benefit of that of another person, is guilty of a conversion, unless the possession was obtained by him *as a finder or as bailee*, or by purchase in market overt . . .'). See also, *Mackenzie v Blindman Valley Co-operative Association* 1947.

[35] Although merely finding something is not a conversion, 'the law of theft will bite' where the finder appropriates the goods dishonestly: Sheehan 2011, 283. A mere finder who appropriates something honestly but without the intention of restoring it to the owner may be held liable in trespass: Pollock and Wright 1888, 18, 172. A person who appropriates lost goods dishonestly will certainly be held liable in trespass: Pollock and Wright 1888, 184, 206; *Merry v Green* 1841; *Hibbert v McKiernan* 1948.

[36] Clerk 1891; *Buckley v Gross* 1863 (bare naked possession, possession without interest). Finders are also said to be in 'bare possession', but this obscures the special role finders have to play. When I talk about bare possessors I deliberately leave finders out.

[37] Rastell 1721, 39: assault, 'a kind of injury to a man's person of a more large extent than battery, for it may be committed by offering a blow or by a terrifying speech'; *Bürgerliches Gesetzbuch* (Civil Code), s. 863 (Ger.) (forcible taking is a forbidden personal power). Stoljar 1984b (true ouster, where you orchestrate a coup d'état, may not involve armed force or even threats, but the takeover itself can be seen as a battle of wills in which the adverse possessor unilaterally overwhelms the owner's will with her own). See also Getzler 2005.

[38] Even the owner is limited in what she can do to regain possession: the owner has the right to enter and repossess her land only before the statutory period expires and only without violence. See Oosterhoff and Rayner 1985. See also Merrill and Smith 2007b, 198; Dukeminier and Krier 2002, 125–6. The owner cannot force the squatter but, if she meets resistance, must bring an action to eject. See La Forest 2006 (the right to enter and retake possession independent of court action but any

the temporal priority of a right to possess (although a wrongdoer must necessarily have *possessed* first to have been dispossessed by force) but because of this ban on the use of unauthorized force.[39] Indeed, normative concerns about force displace more measured consideration of the relative merits of *property* rights. As Bracton said, 'Force must be dealt with before property.'[40]

Temporal priority similarly predicts the outcome in cases between wrongdoers and those whom they put in possession of a thing; however, once again, it does not account fully for the legal concepts and normative concerns that determine the relative merits of these rights. For this, we need to look to the concept of privity and principles of estoppel.[41] Privity, as I explained above, arises where two or more people share the same foundation of right, whether that is a shared transaction, a shared estate, shared blood, or shared possession.[42] Principles of estoppel follow from the shared nature of this foundation: a privy cannot deny the other's right without at the same time undermining his own.[43] A form of privity arises between a wrongdoer and someone he puts in possession: the foundation of any interest either has in the thing is the wrongdoer's original possession of it. When a wrongdoer bails a thing to a second possessor, that second possessor grounds his own possession on the prior possession of the wrongdoer.

Why cannot a second possessor make out or rely on any *independent* foundation for his right to possess? Why for instance cannot a P2 simply point to the bare fact that he is currently in possession as the reason why he ought to be left in possession? Put another way: can a P2 not change his *causa possessionis* midway (from bailee of P1 to a bare possessor)? The answer is, simply, no.[44] The salient normative concerns here are closely connected to the law's protection of even bare possession against forcible interference. P2 must answer for his possession in a manner that satisfies the prior question of how he came to acquire it from P1 (the wrongdoer) without force and fraud. Any story that P2 can tell about how he came to be in

---

violence might amount to assault). See also *Powell v McFarlane* 1979, 476 citing Coke: 'Until the possession of land has actually passed to the trespasser, the owner may exercise the remedy of self-help against him. Once possession has actually passed to the trespasser, this remedy is not available to the owner.' Narrow exceptions carved out for resisting a disseisor who is in the process of dispossessing you. The prohibition on forcible dispossession is familiar to us at least from the great 19th-century debate between the German jurists, Savigny and Jhering.

[39] This gives rise to the apparent paradox of adverse possession. For an account of adverse possession that makes sense of the law's ultimate recognition of squatters who usurp ownership authority, see Katz 2010a.

[40] de Bracton 1250, vol. 3. A disseisor/intruder must be restored where Owner takes the thing back by force. 'Prius enim cognoscendum est de vi quam de ipsa proprietate.' ['Though the [owner] puts himself in seisen rightfully from the point of view of right, he does so wrongfully since without judgment'.]

[41] Coke 1628, 461, 271; Viner 1742, 534–5 ('privity'); *Lampet's Case* 1613; *Woodhouse v Jenkins* 1832; Wingate 1658.

[42] Privity of contract, estate, blood, and possession, respectively.

[43] Only once you have effectively severed the privity by terminating the relationship in fact or in law can you ask courts to consider the true grounds of P1's possession. Rastell 1721, 330–1 (estoppel, privity).

[44] This is what the Romans thought too: Salkowski 1886, 420 (discussing the 'common dictum' that no one can change the ground of his possession).

possession of the thing thus necessarily takes as its starting point P1's own right to possess. This means that P2, once put in possession by P1, cannot claim a new basis for his possession that is independent of P1's. So P2 cannot raise questions about ownership (his own or another's) in answer to P1's claim to possession of the thing if he has not first resolved the mystery of how he acquired it *from* P1 without force or fraud.[45] P2 cannot say someone else owns the thing for this is to change the subject entirely—from the question of how P2 came to be in possession of the thing to the question of who owns the thing. A *jus tertii* defence, that shows that a third party has a stronger right to possess, does not answer the question of how P2 obtained the thing from P1. It is not even enough to say that P2 himself is really the owner. Ownership is not in and of itself an adequate answer to the question of how a person acquires possession from another legitimately. The fact that P2 owns the thing may of course have been a reason for P1 to have given the thing to P2. But, where P1 did not relinquish possession to P2 on this basis, P2 is not able to avoid the problem of legitimate acquisition. That would require us, I think, to infer an authority on the part of an owner to enforce the legal obligations of others, which no owner in fact has.[46]

Thus, a wrongdoer ought to be able to maintain a right to possess on grounds of privity even as against a later possessor who turns out to be the true owner. This sounds scandalous, but it has deep roots in our common law tradition. Thus, in an entry under estoppel in the ancient law dictionary, *Termes de la ley*,[47] it was taken for granted that a person had to play out the role of privy even if it turns out that he was himself the owner with a supreme right to the thing:

Also if a man seised of land in fee simple will take a lease for years of the same land of a stranger by deed indented; this is an estoppel during the term of years and the lessee is thereby barred to say the truth, which is that he that leased the land has nothing in it at the time of the lease made and that the fee simple was in the lessee: But this he shall not be received to say til after the years are determined because it appears that he hath an estate of years and it was his folly to take a lease of his own lands and therefore shall thus be punished for his folly.[48]

It is only once privity is severed, once P2 is no longer in possession through P1, that he can then ask the courts to address the question of ownership. In a more recent

---

[45] It is uncontroversial that a P1 is protected against forcible dispossession.

[46] Thus, an owners' right to self-help does not extend to the use of force to regain property, once lost. See Blackstone 1776, 3: 4; *Davis v Whitridge* 1848; Brantly 1890, 'Where a recaption has been affected violently, the party is liable criminally or civilly, but the circumstance that force was used does not . . . oblige the owner to restore the thing to the possessor', citing *Scribner v Beach* 1847.

[47] *Termes de la ley* (Rastell 1721) continues to hold sway over the common law: *Meering v Graham White Aviation Company ltd* 1918–19, 1502–3.

[48] Rastell 1721, 331. For a more recent application, see *Doe d. Bullen v Mills* 1834 (P3 buys possession for £20 from P2 and claims, as against the plaintiff Bullen to be the owner. In fact P2 is the real owner but had entered into a lease with Bullen. P3 is treated as an assignee of the lease in privity with Bullen (the landlord) and so is estopped from challenging Bullen's title). See also *Clarke v Adie* 1876, 435 per Lord Blackburn: a licensee working under a patent owned by another 'is very analogous indeed to the position of a tenant of lands who has taken a lease of those lands from another. So long as the lease remains in force . . . he is estopped from denying that his lessor had a title to that land.'

case of a tenant who turned out to be the owner of property he had leased, that means surrendering the lease, if that is indeed possible under its terms, or waiting for it to run, before challenging his landlord's right.[49]

In summary, if P2 is content to play the role of privy, he can account for how he acquired the thing from P1 legitimately. But, by the same token, P2 cannot cast off his role as P1's privy because that would deprive him of the ability to account for how he came into possession from P1 without force or fraud.[50] Any right to possess that P2 has thus necessarily takes as its foundation P1's right to possess. Now that is not reason for anyone else to take P1 to have a right to possess in fact; it is just reason for P2 to act as though P1 does.

This analysis makes sense of a case like *Armory v Delamirie*.[51] In that case, a chimney sweep boy took a ring for appraisal to a jeweller,[52] who removed the stone and refused to return it. The court ruled in favour of the boy, even though, had he been put to the task of establishing ownership, he almost certainly would not have been able to do so. The crucial point to take from this is that the jeweller could not put the boy to the task of proving ownership because the fact of the jeweller's possession outside of privity is not something the law could recognize. The only thing the jeweller could be doing, in taking possession of the jewel, is to stand on the boy's own right to possess, as his bailee. For the jeweller had acquired the stone *from* the boy without any intervening gap in possession. The only legitimate basis for the jeweller's having acquired the thing from the boy (P1) was as his privy. And a privy cannot attack the foundation of his own right.

With this in mind, we can see even the famous case of *Asher v Whitlock*—*locus classicus* for the standard approach to the relativity of title with respect to land—in a different light, as a case concerned with a web of privity. In that case, a squatter (P1) drew up a will purporting to leave his personal interest in the land to his wife but if she should remarry to his daughter. His wife remarried the defendant (P2), who then came to live with her and her daughter on the land. The daughter subsequently died, leaving a will, in turn, in which she named the plaintiff as her heir. The case seems to highlight the crucial role of the concept of privity in safeguarding a P1 and those standing on his possession against the claim that, *in pari delicto*, the last in possession wins.[53] The question was whether the defendant P2 was in possession independently of P1's heirs or in privity with them, such that he

---

[49] The law takes an analogous approach to appeals to the fact of ownership to justify the use of force. Nicholls 1865, 1: 116: 'And if he pleads that the horse was his own, and that he took him as his own and as his chattel lost out of his possession, and can prove it, the appeal shall be changed from felony to the nature of trespass. In this case let it be awarded that the defendant [the owner] lose his horse for ever; and the like of all usurpations in similar cases, because our will is that every one proceed rather by course of law than by force.' See, however, Radin 1923, 262, calling into question the veracity of claims made by Britton, 'the anonymous manipulator of Bracton'.

[50] The estoppel of P2 leaves us free to infer a conversion following a demand for a thing previously in possession of P1. 'The ordinary presumptive proof of a conversion consists in evidence of a demand of the goods by the plaintiff and a refusal to deliver them by the defendant': Chitty 1883, 2: 619.

[51] *Armory v Delamirie* 1722.

[52] The apprentice actually was the one who took the jewel but the relationship between the jeweller and his apprentice does not matter to me here so I will simply refer to the latter as the jeweller.

[53] Mellor acknowledges specifically that the law was that the last in possession wins.

could not challenge the basis of their right by raising a *jus tertii*. Here was a web of privity with at least two strands to it: if P2 entered into possession as a *licensee* of the daughter, he takes as her privy and so would then be estopped from challenging the basis of her heir's good title (that is P1's own right) by raising a *jus tertii*.[54] And secondly, in law, there was a nexus of privity between the testator P1 and his daughter and her heir, which means that the daughter and the plaintiff stood on the same footing as P1 with respect to the land, even though the plaintiff had never in fact occupied the land: privity of blood supplied the necessary connection.[55] The potential for this case to be analysed in terms of privity rather than property seems to have been well understood by the courts. Thus, most of the discussion concerned whether the defendant was a trespasser adverse to the daughter or as a licensee of the daughter and so in privity then with her and her heirs, and so estopped from challenging the possession in which he himself shared by raising the matter of *jus tertii*.[56] Of course, there are some very famous statements in Asher by Justice Cockburn on the nature of a right to possess as an inheritable and devisable form of property. But it is worth pointing out that even Cockburn J. had already suggested an alternative ground for denying the defendant the right to challenge P1's title as owner: that P2 while not in privity with the daughter (and so her heirs) and so estopped for that reason, yet could not be heard on the question of ownership because as a trespasser he must be seen as taking by force. Indeed, if we recall that the daughter was *in possession* with her mother when the defendant P2 joined them, this is not such an outlandish claim: there was no intervening gap in possession that would enable him to explain that he got possession independently of the daughter.

2.1 A public law problem?

In cases of force and privity, there are limits on the ability of a later possessor to raise challenges to a wrongdoer's title that would not make sense if courts were just concerned with administering a system of property rights. But if we recognize that force and privity form the basis of rights to possess rather than temporal priority of property rights, the puzzle is solved.

---

[54] Mr Merewhether took this position, finding that the defendant could not dispute validity of the will, because he was the daughter's invitee.

[55] Ancestors/heirs are in privity of blood and so death of one operates like a release, putting the heir in the ancestor's position. Privity then between the daughter and the testator, privity too between daughter and her invitees. See Ballantine 1919 (on privity between ancestor/heirs invitor/invitees). Only heirs can continue adverse possessor's title (only heirs, not devisees, are in privity) and need privity because otherwise there is no power of appointment. So there is no privity between the widow and the testator. But there is privity between the daughter and testator, explaining how she gets to continue his possession. There is privity between her and her heirs, and privity between her and the stepfather, explaining why he cannot challenge the title of her or her privies. A web of privity!

[56] Defendant entered by permission of the daughter so cannot dispute title by her or her privies. See also *Doe v Birchmore* 1839. There was a debate between Cockburn J. and others about whether the defendant's possession was adverse—he claimed it was—which is just to say that he is trying to escape being treated as in possession as a privy. Implication is that had the defendant come in adversely he might have been able to show title and possession in someone else prior to the Testator.

The way that privity works outside of the law of property to shape our relations with respect to things seems to raise a public law problem: if there is some truth of the matter in the law of property about our status vis-à-vis others with respect to a thing, how can we justify the intervention of privity to bind us to serve in altogether different roles? Jeremy Bentham seems to have been concerned with an analogous question in the context of the common law's approach to personal identity. The common law approach, he thought, gives a sloppy answer to the problem of identity—'who are you with whom I have to deal?' Instead of a law of names that attached a fixed label to each person, the common law allowed people to acquire identities based on usage.[57] Thus, a single person could have multiple names in use in different contexts and times. Bentham thought this was deeply problematic for law enforcement: people could not properly be held to account to the state and others if they can have more than one name. But at least one aspect of the common law approach to identity can be seen as a solution to (different) public law problem, rather than a symptom of lazy government. The common law's insistence that a person stand by whatever identity he has assumed, even if that means sticking to a 'false' name or position, is not the result of a failure to develop laws and mechanisms for fixing and ascertaining a person's identity or true position in law.[58] It reflects, rather, the law's response to a separate and prior public concern, prior to any question of who a person really is or what status they really have in a system of rights: the use of force or fraud to dominate others (and so what passes for 'relativity' of rights or identity is just as important in a system that *does* have official registries of names and property rights, as most common law countries now do). We can see this prior concern with force or fraud in cases where courts refuse to allow someone to correct a misstatement about their name or status where that identity is the basis for their relationship with someone else.[59] Where a person denies their true identity or status in dealing with others they may then be estopped from correcting their own falsehood or mistake.[60] A person cannot go back on his own deed or statement, even if it is to assert the truth, where the objectively untrue

---

[57] Bentham 1843, 557 (the problem of identification: names are matters of public concern because the state has an interest in identifying individuals in a fixed and stable manner).

[58] Rastell 1721, 330: 'Estoppel is when one is concluded and forbidden in laws to speak against his own act or deed, yea though it be to say the truth.'

[59] Rastell 1721, 330 gives the example of a man, J.S., who entered into a contract with another under an assumed identity (T.S.). J.S. was estopped from asserting his true identity because T.S. was the name he had given the obligee in that transaction.

[60] Take *Horn v Cole* (1868): the owner of goods denied ownership publicly in order to evade his own creditors. (Thanks to Ben McFarlane for raising this case with me in conversation.) The court held he was estopped from later correcting himself even though he had not specifically intended to deceive the defendant in that case. Estoppel is justified here because the only story he can tell about how it happened that he denied ownership involves the scheme to defraud his own creditors. He cannot himself acknowledge that he has dealt with his creditors in a way that denies or undermines their rights (i.e. their rights to attach property in his estate). This does not mean, of course that his property really was outside the reach of his creditors but just that he is estopped from denying or going back on his prior statement. See *Gale v Lindo* 1687 (Ch) (where fake gift is meant to make a bride seem richer than she is and so more marriageable but fake donor cannot enforce the promise to return the thing by showing that the arrangement was a sham and he in fact continued to own it). But see *Freeman v Cooke* 1848, holding that A is not estopped.

position he occupies or identity he assumes is part of the only coherent narrative he can give a court about his relations with another.

2.2 Privity: the missing link between property and person

The concept of privity suggests that there is an intermediate stage between our rights to our person, grounding a ban on forcible dispossession, and property rights, protecting the office of ownership and the rights derived from it. Privity thus enables a mode of relating to one another that is in addition to contract and property. Privity enables us to share an aspect of ourself—our bare possession of a thing, sheltered behind our right to our person—with others. It thus expands the scope of control we have over things just in virtue of our right to our person, even in the absence of full-blown property rights in that thing. The precariousness of control over things based on possession alone are well known and often cited as the reason why property rights are so important if we are to do anything other than consume things (hurriedly) ourselves. Arthur Ripstein makes this point with the story of a man who, without the benefit of property rights, cannot establish the freedom to drink without interference from a cup in his possession. Our man P1 may fondly imagine that he will have the drink all to himself so long as he holds on to the cup. He may think that mere possession affords at least that much control over the thing. So imagine P1's dismay when 'straw-man' comes along, slips a very long, flexible straw carefully into the cup and sucks the drink up without touching him or anything he was actually holding on to—consuming the drink but without force. P1 has no basis for demanding that straw-man recognize his superior claim to the drink nor defer to the agenda he has set for it. A system of property rights, of course, would sort out the problem by allocating exclusive agenda-setting authority to an owner.

Now let's assume we don't have a concept of property but we do have law and courts. The concept of privity would extend P1's control over the drink by enabling him to bring straw-man into possession as his privy. Here is how. What if instead of being taken by surprise, P1 had *invited* straw-man to share his drink. Imagine that this invitation had been extended *before* the drink was accessible to the man with the straw (do whatever mental contortions you need to—imagine he was curled in a fetal position over the top of the cup, unable to drink it but able at least to keep it from others). The power to form relationships of privity enables us to bring others in to partake of something, interest, or aspect of ourselves that is otherwise out of others' reach, protected initially behind our rights to our person.[61] Once straw-man gains possession of the drink in privity with drinking-man, principles of estoppel arise to prevent him from shedding the guise of privy and claiming possession independently of the first possessor. We do not need to posit property rights in that drink in order to explain the constraints on straw-man that arise in a relationship of privity: the internal logic of privity does that for us (and I will say more about that in a moment).

We can situate privity and the control it enables us to exert over others with respect to things somewhere between the right to the person (giving us minimal

---

[61] Clashfern 2008.

control only over things actually in our possession), on the one hand, and property rights (conferring authority over things even when they are out of our possession), on the other. Privity extends the circumstances in which a non-owner can control a thing just in virtue of his right to his person to situations where the thing is out of his possession so long as it is in the possession of his privy. For so long as the thing is in the possession of me or my privy, the terms of our particular relationship of privity (which may take the form of a bailment, licence, or lease) continues to govern us. But privity imposes constraints just on my privies and not on the world at large, which is why, once my privies too are out of possession, I have no further control of the thing. Where P1 and P2 are in privity but P2 loses possession to P3, P3 is not estopped, as P2 would be, from challenging P1's right to possess the thing (unless P3 is bound as P2's privy to stand and fall on the same foundation of right as P2). Privity thus falls far short of ownership, which enables us to maintain decision-making authority (or noumenal possession) even without phenomenal possession.

2.3 Let the chips fall where they may

'First in time, stronger in right' has some appeal as a heuristic for the relativity of title. But even as a heuristic, it is lacking and has the potential to mislead us. When there is simply no normative nexus between possessors, the law's default position is quite the opposite of what the standard position on temporal priority suggests: it is to favour the position of the *last* to possess. Because of principles of estoppel, a wrongdoer has an enforceable right to possess in a contest with his privies and (a fortiori, against someone who forcibly dispossesses him).[62] But that same wrongdoer has no right to possess if he is out of possession and P2 comes into possession independently. In these cases, the matter properly ends with a judicial shrug: *in pari delicto, potior est conditio defendentis*— effectively, 'let the chips fall where they may'.[63]

A wrongdoer may have a right to possess but her ability to maintain the trappings of ownership depends on the cover of privity (it is otherwise in the case of finders, as I have discussed, who claim owner *pro tem* status).[64] Thus, a wrongdoer is in a

---

[62] *Anderson v Gouldberg* 1892, 296: 'One who has acquired the possession of property, whether by finding, bailment, or by mere tort, has a right to retain that possession against a mere wrongdoer who is a stranger to the property. Any other rule would lead to an endless series of unlawful seizures and reprisals in every case where property had once passed out of the possession of the rightful owner.'

[63] In equal wrong better is the position of the defending party.

[64] Actions for conversion have more to do, it seems, with the usurpation of authority than the mere fact of the taking of the thing. *England v Cowley* 1873 (tenant left in possession of goods so there was no conversion). *Rly v McNicholl* 1918, 605: 'It appears to me plain that dealing with goods in a manner inconsistent with the right of the true owner amounts to a conversion, provided that it is also established that there is also an intention on the part of the defendant in so doing to deny the owner's right or to assert a right which is inconsistent with the owner's right. That intention is conclusively proved if the defendant has taken the goods as his own or used the goods as his own.' A good example of the sort of assertion of rights by someone not in possession which will amount to conversion is the decision of McNair J in *Douglas Valley Finance v S Hughes (Hirers) Ltd* 1969. In *Douglas*, the defendant had purported to buy two lorries from a third party to whom the plaintiff had let the lorries on hire purchase. The defendant then caused the valuable 'A' haulage licences relating to the vehicles to be transferred to other vehicles and purported to sell them back to the third party. The learned judge held that although the defendant never had possession of the vehicles, this series of transactions constituted a 'wrongful assumption of ownership by the defendants and a denial of the plaintiffs' right'.

position to complain about someone else's assertion of dominion over a thing where that person is in effect his privy.[65] Free of the constraints of privity, however, a P2 can in effect maintain that the dispute is outside the system of property rights that courts are meant to administer and that the court should leave P1 and P2 as it finds them (with P2 in possession of the thing). It is here, in those cases where the concepts of privity and force are not engaged, that *jus tertii* defences may have a role to play in the common law.[66]

Something like this is in effect the position that was taken in *Buckley v Gross*.[67] There the plaintiff was in possession of tallow that the police suspected was stolen. The plaintiff was arrested and the police seized the tallow. Eventually the charges were dismissed, and the plaintiff, released but the tallow was not returned to him. Instead, the police sold the tallow to the defendants. The plaintiff sued the defendants for conversion. The plaintiff lost: bare possession does not ground a right to possess that endures beyond the fact of possession.[68] Nor was this a case of either force or privity. The police, having lawfully taken the tallow, were not put into possession as the plaintiff's privies and, at the same time, had a justification for the use of force (it was an authorized taking).[69]

3. Conclusion

Our common law approach is not nearly as reductionist as the standard approach to the relativity of title suggests: the relative merits of rights to possess tracks to some extent their *causa possessionis*. While to a large extent our property system appears to function as a 'first in time, stronger in right', it thus does so for very different reasons than the standard approach to the relativity of title suggests. The best case for the 'first in time, stronger in right' model is that it predicts outcomes in most cases between possessors: our common law rules about the relativity of title determine who as between A and B is entitled to exclude whom, without deciding whether either of them would be able to exclude C. But even this virtue—fidelity to the actual workings of the legal machinery of property—is overstated.

---

[65] There is a debate about whether a conversion is an assertion of dominion or just the exclusion of someone with a better right to possess. See Douglas 2009. The question is not settled across the common law world. See *Canada Colors & Chemicals Ltd v Shea Brothers* 1945 (Ont HCJ), para. 4 (taking the view that conversion is the exercise of dominion). *The Winkfield* 1902 (CA); See *Moorgate Mercantile v Finch* 1962: the use of a borrowed car for the purposes of smuggling was a conversion. This makes sense only of the basis that the decision to put the car to an *illegal* use was clearly a usurpation of the owner's agenda-setting authority.

[66] A return to an older view, widely seen as discredited by Asher: *Doe d Carter v Barnard* 1849 (proof of title in another defeats the claims of the prior possessor).

[67] *Buckley v Gross* 1863.

[68] Hickey 2010, 119. Hickey argues that the plaintiff did not have sufficient possession because of the statutory divestment rather than the possessory facts.

[69] See *Field v Sullivan* 1923 (Supreme Court of Victoria) (suggesting that a wrongdoer (P1) could sue a third party (P3) who derives rights from a P2 who unlawfully took possession from P1). See discussion in Fox 2006, 346 (contrasting this with cases where the third party does not derive right from P2 and so is not liable to our wrongdoer).

10

Defining Property Rights

*Simon Douglas and Ben McFarlane**

1. Introduction

In order to consider the philosophical foundations of property law, it is first necessary to consider the nature and content of property law. In particular, we need to ask what, if anything, is special about it. Writing in 1996, Penner noted that some then recent works had assumed that the 'actual nature' of property had been 'satisfactorily explained by the Hohfeld-Honoré bundle of rights analysis'.[1] No one writing such a work today could make such an assumption: partly thanks to Penner's contribution, and also those of Merrill and Smith,[2] the 'bundle of rights' analysis has come under sustained critical pressure.[3] In particular, it has been contrasted with a competing model which places the 'right to exclude' at the core of property law.[4] This chapter focuses on the contested question of the 'actual nature' of property law, taking as its focus case law bearing on the definition of property rights.

In Section 2.1, we examine the scope of property rights by looking at the duties imposed on the rest of the world in cases where A has an undoubted property right, such as a freehold of land or ownership of a chattel. In Section 2.2, we again examine the scope of property rights, this time by considering how, in more peripheral cases, the courts have determined if A's right has the effect of a property right. Our conclusion accords with that of Penner in his 1996 paper: the 'bundle of rights' analysis provides us with no assistance in determining what is special about property rights. Further, along with Penner, as well as (for example) Merrill and Smith, we conclude that the distinctiveness of proprietary rights lies in what, in loose terms, might be called the right of exclusion. More precisely, as far as the structure of the law is concerned, the special feature of a property right lies not in any liberties it affords A to make use of a resource, but rather in the duty, owed to

* We are grateful to John Mee for comments on an earlier version of the chapter. Ben McFarlane is also grateful for the support provided by a Philip Leverhulme Prize.
[1] Penner 1996a.
[2] See e.g. Merrill 1998; Merrill and Smith 2007b, I-28 ff.; Smith 2002; Smith 2012b.
[3] For recent contributions to the debate, see e.g. Claeys 2009a; Munzer 2011.
[4] See e.g. Merrill 1998. See also Cohen 1954, 371.

A, that it imposes on the rest of the world. Our core argument, then, is that the distinctiveness of property rights is best understood, not by looking at the positive uses available to A, but rather at the negative duties owed to A by the rest of the world. The novelty of this chapter lies not so much in the nature of its conclusion but rather in the means by which that conclusion is reached, and the implications drawn from it. For we reach the conclusion by employing a Hohfeldian analysis, and we argue that it compels us to give a narrow definition to property rights, limiting such rights to cases where the rest of the world is under a prima facie duty to A not to deliberately or carelessly interfere with a physical thing.

It may seem surprising that a Hohfeldian analysis can be used both to argue against the bundle of rights perspective and to support a requirement that a property right must relate to a physical thing. As to the first point, it is clear that, as a matter of intellectual history, the adoption of the bundle of rights model was, in many cases, supported by reference to Hohfeld's insistence on breaking down rights such as a freehold or ownership into a more complex set of distinct legal relations.[5] As to the second point, it has been suggested that 'Hohfeld could not have been more insistent in his view that rights in rem are not properly conceived as rights to things'.[6] As will be seen, however, neither of these observations is inconsistent with the analysis proposed here. That analysis will be developed in Section 2 through discussion of case law, but it will be useful to set out its basic form in this introduction.

First, consider the case in which A has an undoubted property right, such as a freehold of land or ownership of a chattel. To determine the nature of A's right, it is useful to contrast A's position with that of X, a party without any such property right. It may be natural to think of A's right as a right to the 'use, fruits and abuse' of the thing to which A's right relates; or as consisting of those rights of A (such as to take and retain possession; to use, manage, and take the income from the thing, etc.) that feature on Honoré's list of the incidents of ownership;[7] or, to use Harris's term, as an 'open-ended set of use-privileges'.[8] From a Hohfeldian perspective, however, two points must be remembered when considering the effect of a property right on A's legal relations: first, any right of A's must be a right against a particular person;[9] second, there is a crucial distinction between liberties and claim-rights.[10]

Consider the case where A has ownership of a car. If we say that A has a right to use the car, we may mean that A has a liberty as against B to use the car: this means that A does not owe a duty to B not to use the car and thus will not commit a wrong against B simply by using the car. This liberty is clearly recognized by the law: of

---

[5] For an example, see Corbin 1922, 429: 'Our concept of property has shifted... "property" has ceased to describe any res, or object of sense, at all, and has become merely a bundle of legal relations—rights, powers, privileges, immunities.' This is not to say that the bundle model would not have gained prominence without Hohfeld; the metaphor was known before 1913 (see e.g. Lewis 1888, 43: 'The dullest individual among the *people* knows and understands that his *property* in anything is a bundle of rights'). Nonetheless, as Penner (1996a, 731) notes, the Hohfeldian analysis permitted a 'revolutionary refocusing; henceforth, property will be characterized as a complex aggregate of jural relations, not as a particular relation between owner and object.'

[6] Penner 1996a, 725.   [7] Honoré 1961.   [8] See Harris 1996 at e.g. 30 and 45.

[9] See e.g. Hohfeld 1919, 76.   [10] Hohfeld 1919, 38 ff.

course, it does not mean that A is under no duties to B in relation to A's use of the car (A has a duty to B, for example, not to physically injure B by driving the car carelessly); but it does mean that A's deliberate use of the car is not, by itself, a wrong against B. Prima facie,[11] A has a similar liberty not just against B, but against the rest of the world. We now need to compare A's position with that of X, a party without any property right in the car. Crucially, X also has a liberty against B to use the car, which is evident from the fact that if X does use the car he commits no legal wrong against B.[12] In its content, X's liberty against B is identical to A's liberty against B. Moreover, as is the case with A's liberty, X's liberty against B does not depend on, to use Honoré's phrase,[13] any particular title: X, prima facie, has the same liberty as against C, D, E etc. As far as use of the car is concerned, then, the difference between A's position and X's position lies in the fact that A has a liberty as against X to use the car, whereas X has no such liberty against A. In Hohfeldian terms, of course, the fact that X does not have this liberty against A is the result of X's owing a particular duty to A. In other words, in distinguishing A's position, and thus determining the distinctiveness of a property right, we need to focus on the fact that X (and, prima facie, everyone else) owes a specific duty to A in relation to X's use of the car.

To understand what is special about a property right, then, we need to focus on X's duty to A, and to discover its precise content. At this point, we can consider another possible meaning of the statement that A has a right to use the car: the possibility that A has a claim-right against X to use the car. We now need to bear in mind a third point about Hohfeld's scheme, one eloquently elucidated by Finnis:[14] a claim-right 'can never be to do or omit something: it always is a claim that somebody else do or omit something'.[15] As Finnis notes, this flows from the correlativity of the Hohfeldian scheme: what content could X's duty have if A were to have a claim-right to act (or not act) in a specific way? It is possible for A to have a claim-right against X correlating to X's duty to A not to interfere with A's use of the car. It is important to note, as Finnis does, that A's holding of a liberty as against X to use the car does not have any necessary bearing on the separate question of whether X has such a duty to A not to interfere with A's use of the car.[16] For example, if A and X are each present at an academic conference where a buffet lunch is served each has a prima facie liberty against the other to take and eat a chocolate mousse; this liberty remains even if there is only one such mousse remaining, and X (or A's) exercise of their liberty will leave A (or X) with only fruit for dessert. The point is that A's prima facie liberty against X to perform a particular activity (here, to take and eat the mousse) can exist without X's also being under a duty to A not to interfere with that activity of A: here, this means that it is possible for X to have a liberty against A to take the last mousse, and thus prevent A's doing

[11] Prima facie because, for example, A may have made a contract to hire the car out to C for a period, such contract imposing a contractual duty on A to C not to use the car for that period.
[12] For an example see *Hill v Tupper* 1863, discussed in Section 2.2(a).
[13] Honoré 1960, 456.   [14] Finnis 1972.   [15] Finnis 1972, 380.
[16] In fact, this is the chief fallacy (apparent in the work of Professor Stone) that Finnis sought to expose in his essay.

so. So, to establish if X's duty to A includes a general duty not to interfere with A's use of the car, we need to analyse the relevant case-law. As will be seen in Section 2.1, with the possible exceptions of a very small number of isolated cases, no such general duty has been recognized.

The first point is thus a methodological one. A Hohfeldian perspective forces us to direct our attention not on the positive uses A may wish to make of a thing, such as A's car, but rather on the content of the prima facie duty owed to A by X, and thus also owed to A by the rest of the world. This duty, as will be seen in Section 2.1, consists of a duty not to deliberately or carelessly interfere with A's physical thing. The Hohfeldian approach thus directs us away from the bundle of rights model and towards one based on those duties of the rest of the world that may be said, somewhat imprecisely, to make up A's 'right of exclusion'. The second point is a substantive one: when we conduct our inquiry into the nature of X's duty, we will discover that the prima facie duty is defined by reference to the physical thing to which A's right relates: to the car. X's duty is not so broad as to be a duty not to interfere with A's use of the car; it is rather a duty not to deliberately or carelessly interfere with the car itself.[17] The Hohfeldian analysis, when applied to the case law, thus leads us to emphasize the role of physical things in defining the content of property rights. Whilst surprising, this conclusion is perfectly consistent with Hohfeld's own work: that work made clear that A's property right cannot usefully be understood as a right to a thing; instead, to understand the claim-rights involved in a property right, we must look to the duties owed to A. This, however, does not preclude the possibility that the content of those duties may be defined by reference to a thing. Indeed, when briefly considering possible particular species of the generic multital rights, Hohfeld first isolated '[m]ultital rights, or claims, relating to a definite tangible object: e.g. a landowner's right that any ordinary person shall not enter on his land, or a chattel owner's right that any ordinary person shall not physically harm the object involved—be it horse, watch, book, etc.'[18] That category—which, in our view, presents the only definition of property rights that excludes irreducibly dissimilar rights from the set—is organized by the nature of the particular things to which the prima facie duty of the rest of the world (the 'ordinary person') relates.

Our view, then, is that Hohfeld's insights into the nature of legal relations are of great importance in revealing the distinct role of property rights within the legal system. At the level of legal relations, we conclude, the distinctiveness of property rights lies not in their allocation of particular valuable uses to A but rather in the duties such rights impose on the rest of the world. This analysis supports the claim of Merrill and Smith that property, in its core instances at least, uses an 'exclusion' strategy rather than a 'governance' strategy.[19] The latter strategy, like many economic analyses of property law, focuses on particular uses of resources and thus on

---

[17] For two recent and striking examples of this point, see *Club Cruise Entertainment and Travelling Services Europe BV v Department for Transport (The Van Gogh)* 2008 and *D Pride & Partners (a firm) v Institute for Animal Health* 2009. These two cases are discussed in Section 2.1(b)(i).

[18] Hohfeld 1919, 85.   [19] See e.g. Merrill and Smith 2007b, 1–28 ff.; Smith 2002.

particular activities of the parties. On the model proposed in this chapter, by contrast, decisions as to property rights do not involve the allocation of particular uses or the distribution of particular sticks in a bundle of rights. Indeed, the structure of property law can be understood without examining the positive uses that A may make of A's thing. In this sense, property law operates in a 'low cost' way: it does not identify and allocate particular uses of a resource.[20] It has no need to undertake such a complex process as A's liberties in relation to a particular thing derive simply from the general proposition, broader than and prior to property law, that any action of A (or X) is permitted if it is not wrongful. Property law takes advantage of that proposition in a very efficient way: when complemented by the existence of a prima facie duty, owed to A by the rest of the world, not to interfere deliberately or carelessly with a physical thing, it ensures that A has, in Harris's words, an 'open-ended set of use privileges' in relation to that thing. Any analysis which assumes that property law seeks to allocate particular sticks in a bundle of rights therefore misses a key point noted by Merrill and Smith,[21] and buttressed by a Hohfeldian approach: the varied physical uses that an owner may make of a thing are not protected directly by claim-rights against the right of the world. The potential for A's physical enjoyment of the thing would exist independently of property law;[22] property law need only provide a prima facie duty owed to A by the rest of the world.

2. Setting the Limits of Property Rights

2.1 Where A has an undoubted property right

We have seen that, on a Hohfeldian approach to property rights, it is vital to establish the precise nature of the prima facie duty owed by the rest of the world to A, a party with a property right. In this section, we will consider the scope of that duty in cases where A has a clear property right, such as a freehold of land or ownership of a chattel. The argument made in this section is that the duty, which correlates, in somewhat loose terms, to A's 'right of exclusion', consists only of a duty not to deliberately or carelessly interfere with A's physical thing. It does not extend to a duty not to interfere with particular positive uses that A may wish to make of A's thing.

a) The 'right to exclude'

An owner of a thing, whether it is a chattel or land, has a 'right to exclude' others from the thing. Some scholars have singled out this right as the most significant

---

[20] See too Smith 2012b.　　[21] See e.g. Merrill and Smith 2007b, I-28 ff.; Smith 2002.

[22] This seems to be the point that Penner 1996a has in mind when noting at 766 that: 'owning property provides an owner with no powers that he did not have before. An owner's "use rights" in property turn on whatever natural capacities an owner or his licensees have to exploit "things" that can be objects of property, such capacities being protected by the right of exclusive use for those things he owns.'

right held by an owner. Merrill, for instance, writes 'Give someone the right to exclude others from a valued resource...and you give them property. Deny someone the exclusion right and they do not have property.'[23] Some refinements are required before this 'right to exclude' can be translated into Hohfeldian terms. Exclusion, on its face, relates to a particular activity which A may carry out in relation to his thing. As noted above, it is impossible for A to have a Hohfeldian claim-right which refers solely to an activity of A. The right to exclude could be understood as a Hohfeldian liberty physically to keep others away from A's thing, but it would be difficult to argue that such a liberty is a necessary component of the concept of property.[24] To understand the 'right to exclude' as a claim-right, we need to focus not on A's activities in relation to the thing, but rather on those of the rest of the world. The 'right to exclude', as a claim-right prima facie binding on the rest of the world, correlates to duties owed by the rest of the world to A. This legal duty can be readily inferred from tort law. A tort, which is a type of civil wrong, involves the breach of a legal duty.[25] This means that if a third party, let us say B, is held to have committed a tort by physically interfering with A's chattel or land, we can infer from B's liability in tort law that he is under a legal duty to A (as are all other third parties: C, D, E etc.) not to physically interfere with A's thing. It is the law of torts, therefore, which recognizes that the holder of a clear property right in a thing is owed a legal duty by all others not to physically interfere with the thing.

Beginning with moveable things, or chattels, it is the three torts of conversion, trespass, and negligence that recognize that an owner of a chattel is owed such a legal duty. A simple illustration can be found in the case of *Vine v Waltham Forest Council* where the claimant was an owner of a car that was clamped by the defendant local council and was charged £108 to have it removed. Because the clamp warning sign was not properly visible the claimant had not consented to the interference with her car and she successfully sued for trespass to goods. This straightforward claim demonstrates that the defendant was under a legal duty to the claimant (as were all other third parties) not to physically interfere with her car. When the defendant did physically interfere with the claimant's car, in the form of clamping it, this was a breach of a legal duty and hence a 'tort'.

The duty not to physically interfere with an owner's chattel is not an absolute duty because the torts which recognize this duty also have requisite mental states. In the torts of conversion and trespass it must be shown that the defendant's physical interference with the claimant's chattel was deliberate,[26] whereas in the tort of negligence it must be shown that the interference was brought about negligently. Where the physical interference is neither deliberate nor negligent, therefore, the defendant will not be in breach of this duty. An example is the case of *Overseas Tankship (UK) Ltd v Morts Dock and Engineering Co Ltd (The Wagon Mound No 1)*

---

[23] Merrill 1998; Cohen 1954, 371.

[24] See Penner 1996a, 743–4: 'The fact that we may not have the right to throw trespassers off our land, and must call the police to do so instead, for instance, does not mean that we do not have a right to the land, but only that our means of effecting the right are circumscribed.' Penner therefore prefers the term 'right of exclusion'.

[25] Birks 1995.   [26] *BMW Financial Services (GB) Ltd v Bhagwanani* 2007.

where the defendant causally contributed to the partial physical destruction of the claimant's wharf (in the form of fire damage) by releasing bunkering oil into a harbour. However, because the fire had not been reasonably foreseeable, it was held that the defendant had not been negligent in respect of the fire damage and so was not liable in tort law. The duty owed to an owner of a chattel not to physically interfere with his chattel is not an absolute one: it is therefore most accurately described as a duty not to deliberately or carelessly interfere with the chattel.

Turning to land, the principal torts protecting land, trespass, negligence and nuisance, reflect a similar duty. Again, to give a simple illustration, in *Ellis v Loftus* the defendant's horse put its head through the railings that separated the defendant's land from the claimant's and bit the claimant's horse. This crossing of the boundary, albeit by a very short distance, was held to be a trespass, Lord Coleridge saying: ' . . . if the defendant place a part of his foot on the plaintiff's land unlawfully, it is in law as much a trespass as if he had walked half a mile on it . . . '[27] The defendant's liability in tort for this physical intrusion demonstrates that he is under a legal duty to the claimant, as are all other third parties, not physically to intrude upon the claimant's land. Again, this duty is not absolute as the torts have requisite mental states, namely that the interference be deliberate or negligent.[28]

What constitutes a 'physical interference' with land is usually slightly different to a physical interference with a chattel. In the context of chattels, a physical interference typically takes the form of physical contact with the chattel or causing physical damage to it: touching the surface of a painting, punching a hole in it, slashing it with a knife etc. are all clear forms of physical interference. In the context of land, however, the physical 'interference' usually takes the form of an intrusion, a physical crossing over the boundary of the claimant's land. This is due to the *ad coelum* principle that a freeholder's right does not just relate to the surface of his land, but to a vertical column extending both upwards and downwards. Take, for instance, *Anchor Brewhouse Developments Ltd v Berkley House (Docklands Developments) Ltd*,[29] where the top of the defendant's crane, elevated at a great height, oversailed the claimant's land and this was held to be sufficient for liability in trespass. It cannot really be said that the defendant's crane made 'physical contact' with the claimant's land. Rather, the physical interference consisted of the defendant's crossing of the claimant's boundary. The notion of physically interfering with a claimant's land by crossing its boundary has been developed and extended by the tort of nuisance. It is difficult to draw a clear distinction between the actions of trespass and nuisance,[30] but, broadly speaking, when the thing crossing the boundary of the claimant's land has, in Merrill's words, 'physical dimensions',

---

[27] *Ellis v Loftus* 1874, 12. See also *Lawrence v Obee* 1815, *Gregory v Piper* 1829, and *Kynoch v Rowlands* 1912.

[28] *Goldman v Hargrave* 1967. Although, it is not clear if the defendant need be at fault if he has an ultra-hazardous risk on his land: *Rylands v Fletcher* 1868, cf. *Cambridge Water Co. Ltd v Eastern Counties Leather Plc* 1994.

[29] 1987. See also *Star Energy Weald Basin Limited and another (Respondents) v Bocardo SA (Appellant)* 2010.

[30] See Nolan 2012.

so that it can be seen to the naked eye, such as crane, car, person, rock etc., then the physical interference will be a trespass.[31] When the thing crossing the boundary does not have this 'dimensional' characteristic, such as odour, fumes, light, sound waves etc., then the physical interference will be a nuisance.[32]

This extremely brief account of the torts of conversion, trespass, negligence, and nuisance demonstrates that, subject to the requisite mental states being satisfied, if a defendant physically interferes with a claimant's chattel or land he will be held to have committed a tort. This tells us that A, an owner of thing, is owed a legal duty by B, C, D ... etc., not to physically interfere with the thing deliberately or carelessly. It is this legal duty which is being described when A asserts that he has a 'right to exclude' others from his thing.

b) The 'right to use'

The second often emphasized stick in the 'bundle of rights' is the 'right to use': Honoré called this right a 'cardinal'[33] feature of ownership.[34] Whilst it is clear, as will be seen below, that an owner of a chattel or land does have a 'right to use', this right is of an entirely different nature to his 'right to exclude'. We saw in the last section that an owner's 'right to exclude' has the status of a 'claim-right' because it denotes a legal duty on others to behave in a certain way: A's 'right to exclude' is a shorthand description of the legal duty imposed on B, C, D ... etc not to physically interfere deliberately or carelessly with A's chattel or land. In contrast, when an owner claims that he has a 'right to use' his thing, he is not normally asserting that others owe him a legal duty to behave in a certain way; rather, he is asserting that he himself is permitted to behave in a certain way, i.e. to use his chattel or his land. Put a little differently, when A claims that he has a 'right to use' his thing, he is asserting that he is under no legal duty to B, C, D ... etc. not to use his thing and, in the absence of such a duty, his use is permitted. When an owner asserts a 'right' in this sense, the better word is 'privilege' or 'liberty', as Cave J. said in *Allen v Flood*:

> it was said that a man has a perfect *right* to fire off a gun, when all that was meant, apparently, was that a man has a freedom or *liberty* to fire off a gun so long as he does not violate or infringe anyone's rights in doing so, which is a very different thing from a right the violation or disturbance of which can be remedied or prevented by legal process.[35]

As Cave J. thus noted, an owner's 'right to use' his thing, being no more than an assertion that his use is legally permitted, is more accurately described as a 'liberty to use'.

'Liberties to use' can be readily observed in everyday life. We are all free to ride our bicycles, write with our pens, toss our coins, walk in our gardens ... etc. However,

---

[31] Merrill 1985, 28–9.   [32] e.g. *Rapier v London Tramways Co.* 1893.

[33] Honoré 1961, 116. As James Penner reminds us, the 'incidents' of ownership Honoré identifies are a mixture of the genuinely legal, i.e. legal norms that actually go with ownership (e.g. the right to possess, the power to alienate), and the functional (e.g. the right to use, to manage, and to income, the 'right to capital'). In view of this it is not clear whether Honoré himself would dispute our central claim that there is no genuinely legal norm which can be identified as a right to use.

[34] See also Clarke 2005, 241–2.   [35] *Allen v Flood* 1898, 29, emphasis added.

such liberties are infrequently the subject of judicial notice, as they come to the fore only when someone challenges an owner's specific use of his chattel or land.[36] An example of this is the case of *Bradford v Pickles*.[37] The defendant acquired title to a parcel of land overlooking the city of Bradford and proceeded to sink a borehole into a natural reservoir under his land. The claimants sought an injunction to prevent the defendant taking water from this reservoir, as it would have the effect of drying up natural springs used by the city. Further, it was alleged that the defendant's only motive in sinking this borehole was to force the claimants to purchase the land at an inflated price. The House of Lords, rejecting the claim, held that the claimants could not challenge the defendant's use of his land, Lord Halsbury saying, 'If it was a lawful act, however ill the motive might be, [the defendant] had a right to do it.'[38] The defendant's 'right' to take water from his land, mentioned by Lord Halsbury in this sentence, is a 'liberty', not a 'claim-right'. The reason for this is that the defendant's 'right' to take water from his land does not denote a legal duty on others to behave in a certain way (what could be the content of such a duty?). Rather, the 'right' denotes the fact that the defendant himself was under no legal duty to the claimant (or anyone else) not to take water from his land and, in the absence of such a duty, that specific use was permitted.

An owner's liberty to use his chattel or land is obviously important as there is not much point in owning something that you are not permitted to use. However, the value of one's liberty depends largely upon whether or not the liberty is accompanied by claim-rights. The best example of this from the case law is *Allen v Flood* where the claimant, a shipwright, had been employed on a rolling contract by a shipowner. The defendant, a union representative, threatened to call a strike if the shipowner continued to renew the claimant's contract, at which point the shipowner stopped employing the claimant. The court held that although the defendant had deprived the claimant of a clear liberty (the claimant's liberty to enter a contract of service with the shipowner) the defendant had not committed a tort in so doing because, as a majority of the House of Lords found, the defendant was under no legal duty to the claimant not to behave in this way. One's liberty to do an act, therefore, is only protected if the law is also willing to impose duties on others.[39] Returning to property rights, the important question is whether an owner's 'liberty to use' his chattel or land is protected by the imposition of a duty on others that extends beyond the basic duty not to physically interfere, deliberately or carelessly, with A's thing.

It is certainly true that an owner's 'liberty to use' is indirectly protected by the basic duty of non-interference. If A, for example, wishes to build a house on his land, he would find it difficult to exercise this liberty if third parties, B, C, D..., could walk across or occupy his land with impunity. The fact that B, C, D... are under a legal duty not to physically interfere with the land leaves A free to pursue his building plans unhindered. However, this protection of A's liberty is achieved

---

[36] Harris 2004, 434.   [37] See also *Tapling v Jones* 1865.
[38] *Bradford v Pickles* 1895, 594–5.
[39] Harris refers to these as 'fencing' duties, protecting a sphere of permitted action: 2004, 434.

indirectly, in the sense that the duty upon B, C, D . . . not to physically interfere with A's land does not correlate with A's liberty to use his land.[40] To give an example, in the well-known case of *Spartan Steel & Alloys Ltd v Martin & Co. Ltd* the defendant carelessly damaged a power cable whilst carrying out road mainten-ance and cut off power to the claimant's factory. The power loss prevented the claimant from processing a number of its metal ingots and offering them for sale. The defendant, therefore, had deprived the claimant of its 'liberty to use' its chattels. Despite this it was held that the defendant committed no tort because, by merely preventing electricity from coming into the factory, it had not physically interfered with the ingots.

Spartan Steel is an illustration of the fact that it is possible to deprive an owner of his liberty to use his thing without breaching a duty not to physically interfere with the thing. It is in this sense that an owner's 'liberty to use' his thing does not correlate with the duty imposed on others not to physically interfere with it. The only way in which this liberty can be protected directly, therefore, is if the law were to impose a correlative duty on others, i.e. a duty not to impair an owner's ability to use his chattel or his land. The next question is whether there is any evidence that such a duty has been recognized. This is an important question as it informs us of the status of an owner's 'right to use' his thing. So far we have seen that this right describes the owner's permission, or 'liberty', to use his thing. What we are essentially asking now is whether it also describes a legal duty on others, i.e. a duty not to impair the owner's ability to use his thing. We will consider the evidence for such a duty in cases involving chattels and land separately.

i. Chattels

Whilst it is clear that an owner of a chattel, A, is owed a legal duty by B, C, D . . . not to physically interfere with A's chattel, the question posed in this section is whether B, C, D . . . also owe A an additional duty, namely a duty not to impair A's ability to use his chattel. There is some slight evidence in the law of torts for the recognition of such a duty. One case is the conversion claim in *Douglas Valley Finance Co. Ltd v S Hughes (Hirers) Ltd* where the claimant owned two lorries which had valuable licences that permitted them to be used for commercial haulage. The defendant wanted these licences for its own vehicles and, acting fraudulently, persuaded the licensing authority to transfer the licences to its vehicles. Finding the defendant liable, McNair J. said that the result of the defendant's conduct was that the claimant's lorries 'had lost the function of being capable of use for their only designed and contemplated purpose, just as much as if the wheels of the lorries had been permanently removed'.[41] What is interesting about this case is that the defendant could not have been in breach of its duty not to physically interfere with the claimant's lorries because no physical contact was ever made with them. The defendant's liability in conversion, therefore, suggests that it was under an additional duty to the claimant, namely a duty not to impair the

---

[40] Harris 2004, 434 and Hohfeld 1919, 77.
[41] *Douglas Valley Finance Co. Ltd v S Hughes (Hirers) Ltd* 1969, 754.

claimant's ability to use its lorries. Another possible line of cases that may support the recognition of this duty can be found under the action called 'slander of title'. One example is the case of *Western Counties Manure Co. v The Lawes Chemical Manure Co.*[42] The claimant had produced a large quantity of manure that it was offering for sale and the defendant published a notice stating (falsely) that the claimant's manure was of a very low quality. This notice was designed, as Pollock B said, 'to injure the plaintiffs in their business',[43] and the defendant was found liable. Again, the defendant had not physically interfered with the claimant's manure in this case, but had merely damaged the claimant's prospects of selling it. It may be possible to analyse this case on the basis that the defendant was under a further duty to the claimant not to impair the claimant's ability to use its manure.

There is much more substantial evidence, however, for the contrary view that there is no legal duty not to impair an owner's ability to use his chattel. In the two recent cases of *Club Cruise Entertainment and Travelling Services Europe BV v Department for Transport (The Van Gogh)*[44] and *D Pride & Partners (a firm) v Institute for Animal Health* the courts refused to recognize such a duty. In the first case the claimant was an owner of a ship that was scheduled to cruise from Harwich to Norway but, due to an outbreak of norovirus on the ship, the defendant issued a detention notice to the claimant under the Merchant Shipping Act 1995.[45] It later transpired that this had been done improperly, there being no statutory basis for the detention notice, and the claimant sued in conversion. The court held that the defendant's conduct, which consisted of no more than handing a sheet of paper to the claimant with the details of the detention notice on it, did not amount to a tort. In a telling passage Flaux J. said that 'if there had been actual physical restraint of the ship by chaining it to the quayside, that would have constituted the tort of trespass to goods'.[46] In other words, had there been a physical interference with the claimant's ship, this would have amounted to a tort, but merely impairing use was not actionable. Whilst the defendant, therefore, was under a duty not to physically interfere with the ship, it was not under a further duty not to impair the claimant's ability to use it. The second case, *D Pride*, reached a similar conclusion. The defendant carelessly caused an outbreak of the foot and mouth disease close to the claimant's land and whilst this did not infect any of the claimant's pigs, a quarantine zone was imposed which prevented the claimant from sending its pigs to the abattoir. Tugendhat J. held that if physical damage could be shown to the pigs then that would have been actionable, but merely impairing the claimant's ability to use the pigs did not give rise to any liability in tort law.[47] The defendant was not under a legal duty to the claimant not to impair the claimant's ability to use its pigs.

---

[42] See also *De Beers Abrasive Products Ltd v International General Electric of New York Ltd* 1975.
[43] *De Beers Abrasive Products Ltd v International General Electric of New York Ltd* 1975, 223.
[44] See also *Mogul Steamship Co. Ltd v McGregor, Gow & Co.* 1892 and *Perre v Apand Pty Ltd* 1999.
[45] s. 95.
[46] *Club Cruise Entertainment and Travelling Services Europe BV v Department for Transport (The Van Gogh)* 2008, [50].
[47] *D Pride & Partners (a firm) v Institute for Animal Health* 2009, [83].

ii. Land

Turning to land, there is again a small number of cases that may be used to support the view that A, a freeholder, is owed a legal duty by B, C, D . . . not to impair A's ability to use his land. The early economic tort case of *Keeble v Hickeringill* is such a case. The claimant, who had freehold title to land, set up nets and decoys around a pond on his land in order to catch wildfowl. The defendant, a neighbour, disrupted this by setting off a gun on his own land to scare the birds away. No physical interference with the claimant's land was pleaded and Holt CJ characterized the claim as one of impairment of use: 'The plaintiff in this case brings his action for the apparent injury done him in the use of that employment of his freehold, his art, and skill, that he uses thereby.'[48] The claim, brought in an action on the case, succeeded. Because the defendant could not have breached his duty not to phys-ically interfere with the claimant's land, his liability in this action suggests that he was under a further duty to the claimant not to impair the claimant's ability to use his land. It is not clear if *Keeble v Hickeringill* survived the economic torts case, discussed in Section 2.1(b), of *Allen v Flood*, where it was stated that *Keeble* was no more than a straightforward nuisance claim.[49]

Of course, re-characterizing *Keeble* as a nuisance claim does not answer the problem, but merely pushes it within the tort of nuisance: if it is a typical nuisance claim, then does this demonstrate that the tort of nuisance recognizes that a freeholder, A, is owed a legal duty by B, C, D . . . not to impair A's ability to use his land? There is some evidence for this. To give one recent example, in the case of *Birmingham Development Company Ltd v Tyler* the claimant, a freeholder, was in the process of erecting new buildings on its land when it had to stop works due to the presence of a poorly constructed building on the defendant's neighbouring land which the claimant thought was in danger of collapsing. The claim did not succeed on the facts, as it was found that the claimant's fears were unfounded. However, the Court of Appeal held that if there had been a real danger of collapse, then that danger in itself could constitute a nuisance. This is important in the present context because the presence of such a danger does not (until it materializes) involve any form of physical interference with the claimant's land. The only effect it would have had is that the claimant would have been unable to build on his land, i.e. it would have deprived the claimant of a liberty to use his land. Rimer LJ held that such an impairment of use could form the basis of a claim in nuisance, saying: 'to live in the shadow of such a danger will obviously be to interfere with his enjoyment of his property. It may prevent him from using part of it for fear of what will happen if there is a collapse.'[50] This may be read as the recognition of a duty on the defendant not to impair the claimant's ability to use his land.

Nonetheless, each of *Keeble* and *Birmingham Development* can be interpreted as consistent with the absence of duty not to interfere with the use of another's land. As for the former case, it is clear that noise can constitute a nuisance, and this is

---

[48] *Keeble v Hickeringill* 1707, 1129.
[49] See the comments of Lord Herschell: *Allen v Flood* 1898, 133.
[50] *Birmingham Development Company Ltd v Tyler* 2008, [52].

consistent with the model of nuisance set out above, as the passing of sound waves onto or over the claimant's land constitutes a form of physical interference. As to the latter case, it should be no surprise that the threat of physical interference, in the form of debris from a collapsing building entering the claimant's land, will suffice for the grant of a *quia timet* injunction, as such an injunction may be available where the 'earlier actions of the defendant may lead to future causes of action'.[51]

Moreover, as was the case with chattels, there is much evidence for the contrary view that there is no general duty not to interfere with the use of another's land. Nuisance cases such as *Birmingham Development Company Ltd v Tyler* have been described as 'exceptional'[52] because in the standard nuisance case there is something, such as smoke, fumes, or noise, emanating onto the claimant's land. It was explained above that a physical interference with land typically consists of some form of 'boundary crossing', and in the normal nuisance case this is satisfied by the smoke, fumes, noise, etc., moving across the claimant's boundary. There are a number of nuisance claims that have been rejected because they did not involve this form of physical interference.[53] For example, in *Bryant v Lefever*,[54] the defendants, by building a taller house and using the roof to store timber, prevented smoke from escaping from the claimant's neighbouring chimneys. In the absence of any easement held by the claimant to the flow of air, the defendant's conduct was found not to be a nuisance: as nothing produced by the defendant had crossed onto the claimant's land, the defendant could not be held responsible for difficulties caused to the claimant by the smoke. Coase, in his seminal discussion of nuisance, applied the reciprocal causation approach to his analysis of the case and argued that the judges failed to take proper account of the costs imposed on the claimant by the defendant's activities. The court's approach is, however, consistent with the model proposed in this chapter as it focused not on the uses to which the claimant wished to put his land but rather on whether the defendant could be said to have physically interfered with that land.[55]

The best recent example of such an approach comes from the leading case of *Hunter v Canary Wharf* where the defendant, by erecting the Canary Wharf tower, had prevented television signals from reaching the claimant's land. Although this had deprived the affected freeholders of a liberty, as they were no longer able to watch television in their homes, the claim was rejected because the defendant had in no way physically interfered with their land. Lord Goff said:

---

[51] See per Lord Upjohn in *Redland Bricks v Morris* 1970, 665. Note too the valuable discussion of Bagshaw 2012, 416–21.

[52] *Anglian Water Services v Crawshaw Robbins & Co. Ltd* 2001, [54].

[53] E.g. *D Pride & Partners (a firm) v Institute for Animal Health* 2009, *Anglian Water Services v Crawshaw Robbins & Co. Ltd* 2001, *Perre v Apand Pty Ltd* 1999, and *Tapling v Jones* 1865; cf. *Thompson-Schwab v Costaki* 1956 and *Laws v Florinplace Ltd* 1981.

[54] 1879. See Smith 2004, 1004–5 for a useful discussion of the decision.

[55] See Coase 1960.

for an action in private nuisance to lie in respect of interference with the plaintiff's enjoyment of his land, it will generally arise from something emanating from the defendant's land. Such an emanation may take many forms—noise, dirt, fumes, a noxious smell, vibrations, and suchlike.[56]

Lord Goff is here clearly asserting that, generally, a defendant will be liable only if he is responsible for something crossing the boundary of the claimant's land. Without this form of physical interference there is, generally, no liability in nuisance. Lord Goff went on to point out that, in 'relatively rare' cases, activities carried out on the defendant's land may be 'in themselves so offensive to neighbours as to constitute an actionable nuisance'.[57] The example given by his Lordship was of *Thompson-Schwab v Costaki*,[58] in which the nuisance consisted of the use of land for prostitution. Interestingly, Lord Goff described the nuisance as consisting of the 'sight of prostitutes and their clients entering and leaving neighbouring premises': this focus on sight, which necessarily requires the passing of light rays over the claimant's land, means even that rare case can in fact be reconciled to the general model of nuisance, in which a defendant will only be liable if he is responsible for something crossing the boundary of the claimant's land.[59] Whatever one's view as to whether conduct that is offensive in this sense ought to constitute a nuisance, it is important to note that the courts approach that question without conducting an examination of the particular uses that A may wish to make of his land.

It thus seems that A, a freeholder of land, is owed no legal duty by B, C, D ... not to impair A's ability to use his land. Rather, A is merely owed a duty by B, C, D ... not to physically interfere with his land. This conclusion mirrors that drawn in respect of chattels. The purpose of this section has been to determine the status of an owner's so-called 'right to use' his thing. What we have seen is that whilst this means that he has a 'liberty to use' his thing, in the sense that his use is permitted, it does not denote a legal duty upon others not to impair his ability to use it. A 'right to use', therefore, is a mere liberty, not a claim-right.

c) Conclusion

Proponents of the 'bundle of rights' view typically describe an owner of a thing as having both a 'right to use' the thing and a 'right to exclude' others from the thing. Whilst this is not entirely inaccurate, we have seen in this section that they are very different types of right. An owner's 'right to exclude' is a 'claim-right' because it denotes a legal duty upon others not to physically interfere with the thing. A 'right to use', on the other hand, does not denote a legal duty, but merely expresses the owner's liberty to use his thing.

---

[56] *Hunter v Canary Wharf* 1997, 686.   [57] *Hunter v Canary Wharf* 1997, 686.
[58] 1956.
[59] See too *Bank of New Zealand v Greenwood* 1984 (discussed by Lord Goff in *Hunter v Canary Wharf* 1997, 686) in which the prima facie nuisance consisted of the reflection of dazzling light from the glass roof of the defendant's veranda onto the claimant's land.

2.2 Determining if B's right counts as a property right

So far we have seen that in cases where A has an undoubted property right, A is owed a duty by the rest of the world not to physically interfere with A's thing. This duty is the key difference between A's position and that of X, who does not have a property right: X, unlike A, is not owed a duty by the rest of the world not to interfere with A's thing. This duty, therefore, which correlates with A's 'right to exclude', is how we define A's property right. In this section, we will consider how this concept of a property right may assist in determining if B's right counts as a property right.

a) Physical things

It was argued in Section 2.1 that A's holding of an undoubted property right, such as a freehold of land or ownership of a chattel, does not entail the rest of the world's being under a duty to A not to interfere with particular uses A may wish to make of A's thing. In that sense, A's potential use of the thing is not crucial when distinguishing the position of A from that of X, a party without a property right. The converse point can be seen when considering the Court of Appeal's decision in *Jonathan Yearworth & Ors v North Bristol NHS Trust*. The case concerned the defendant's admittedly careless storage of semen samples provided by claimants prior to undergoing treatment that might affect their fertility, on the basis that a hospital, for which the defendant was responsible, would store those samples so as to permit possible future use of the sperm. The question was whether the claimants had any cause of action as a result of the defendant's carelessness. The storage of the semen was regulated by the Human Fertilisation and Embryology Act 1990. As noted by the court, the scheme of the Act is 'to confine the provision of human reproductive treatment services to persons licensed under the Act'.[60] As the claimants, unlike the defendant, held no such licence there was no positive use that they could make of the stored material: for example, no claimant could have insisted on the return of his sample, nor on storing it in his own freezer. Indeed, the Act prevented any claimant from directing the hospital to make a particular use of the sample: for example, the court noted that no claimant had the power to insist that sperm from the sample be implanted into the uterus of his willing wife or partner.[61] As a result, the defendant argued that no claimant could be seen as the owner of any sample and, as a result, the defendant's carelessness was not a breach of the duty not to carelessly interfere with another's property. The court did refer[62] to Honoré's elaboration of the incidents of ownership, emphasizing in particular the 'right (liberty) to use at one's discretion';[63] yet the relevant legislative provisions

---

[60] *Jonathan Yearworth & Ors v North Bristol NHS Trust* 2009, [42].
[61] *Jonathan Yearworth & Ors v North Bristol NHS Trust* 2009, [43]. The men could have made such a request, but the hospital would then have had a statutory duty to consider a range of relevant factors, including the welfare of the prospective child, before deciding whether to accede to such a request.
[62] *Jonathan Yearworth & Ors v North Bristol NHS Trust* 2009, [28].
[63] Honoré 1961, 116.

made clear that the claimants did not have a set of open-ended liberties to use the material. Due to the special nature of the physical thing in question, the 'bundle of rights' that may be held in a standard case of ownership of a physical thing was clearly absent.

The claimants were, however, successful. Whilst it was true that the legislation 'effected a compulsory interposition of professional judgment between the wishes of the men and the use of the sperm', the court also held that 'the absence of their ability to "direct" its use does not in our view derogate from their ownership.'[64] A crucial factor in this conclusion was that 'the Act assiduously preserves the ability of the men to direct that the sperm be *not* used in a certain way: their negative control over its use remains absolute.'[65] The legislation specified, for example, that, in the absence of consent from a specific claimant, the defendant could not store his material, nor use it for the treatment of anyone other than the claimant. It seems that these limits on the defendant's ability to use the sperm did not give rise to a direct statutory duty to the claimant: the claim-right recognized by the court was not deduced directly from the terms of the legislation. Rather, the court reasoned that each claimant had a common law claim-right that the defendant not carelessly interfere with a physical thing (the sample) because the regulatory scheme laid down by the statute left the claimant in a position sufficiently analogous to that of A, a party with an undoubted property right, such as ownership of a car. In reaching that conclusion, the crucial feature of A's position was not seen to be A's liberty to use the thing at A's discretion—after all, the claimants had no such liberty in *Yearworth*—rather, the crucial feature was seen to be the 'negative control' that flows from the fact that the rest of the world has a prima facie duty to A not to deliberately or carelessly interfere with A's thing.

Yearworth is an unusual case as it was plausible for the defendant to argue that a physical thing was not capable of being the subject matter of a property right. In general, of course, any discrete physical thing may be the subject of ownership: in other words, the rest of the world may come under a prima facie duty to A not to deliberately or carelessly interfere with that thing. Where physical things are concerned, then, the question of whether or not B's right counts as a property right is more likely to arise in a case where B claims a right that differs from ownership. This chapter is not the place for a full discussion of the *numerus clausus* principle.[66] It is, however, worth noting that the existence and operation of the principle is more obviously consistent with an approach that focuses not on allocating and protecting particular uses of property, but rather with one that emphasizes the duties imposed by property rights on the rest of the world. For example, in *Hill v Tupper*, A, a company, held an estate in the Basingstoke Canal. A made a contractual promise to B that he would have the exclusive right to put pleasure boats on the canal, and to hire out those boats. X, the landlord of an inn

---

[64] *Jonathan Yearworth & Ors v North Bristol NHS Trust* 2009, [45].
[65] *Jonathan Yearworth & Ors v North Bristol NHS Trust* 2009, [45].
[66] See e.g. Rudden 1987 and Merrill and Smith 2000, which sparked an ongoing academic interest in the principle. For a recent survey see e.g. Davidson 2008. See too McFarlane 2011.

adjoining the canal, then started to compete with B by also hiring out pleasure boats on the canal. B claimed that X had thereby committed a wrong against B: X had 'wrongfully and unjustly disturbed... [B] in his possession, use and enjoyment' of the 'right and liberty' granted to B by A. The Exchequer Chamber rejected B's claim. It was held that, whilst the contract between A and B gave B a right against A, it gave B 'no right of action in his own name for any infringement of the supposed exclusive right'.[67] So, whilst X had interfered with A's right to exclusive possession of the canal, and had thus committed a wrong against A, X had committed no wrong against B.

In *Hill*, then, A's dealings with B did not amount to A's having transferred one of his proprietary bundle of rights, a 'right to put pleasure boats on the canal', to B. After all, A had no such claim-right; A simply had a liberty, as against X, to use the canal in that way. And B, both before and after his dealing with A, had that same liberty against X. It could be claimed that A had a claim-right to hire out pleasure boats on the canal; yet, as we saw in Section 1 above, it is not possible for anyone to have a claim-right that refers only to his or her own behaviour. A could then assert a claim right that no one interfere with his ability to use the canal for the hiring out of pleasure boats. As we saw in Section 2.1, however, no such claim-right exists: A's protection for such activities is indirect, as it comes from X's general duty not to physically interfere, deliberately or carelessly, with A's land. For example, if A itself had intended to start up a business hiring out pleasure boats, and X had interfered with this by buying or hiring all the available pleasure boats in the area, X would commit no wrong against A. It would therefore be very difficult, and one might reasonably think impossible, for A to give B a claim-right against X that A itself did not hold.

It may be objected that this analysis proves too much: it would suggest that if A has a freehold of land, A should never be able to confer a lesser property right on B. Of course, as recognized by the court in *Hill*, this is not the case: the difficulty for B was not that he was claiming a lesser property right, but rather that, due to its content, his right was not on the recognized list of such rights.[68] The analysis here does not seek to deny the existence of this list; rather, it suggests a particular way of understanding what occurs when such a lesser property right is created. Consider the effect on X, a stranger, in a case where A grants B a legal easement, such as a right of way across A's land.[69] There is no transfer of a particular proprietary stick from A to B; both before and after A's grant, X, along with the rest of the world, is under a prima facie duty to A not to physically interfere, deliberately or carelessly, with A's land. As a result of the grant, X does come under a new duty: a duty to B. We need to be precise in describing this duty: it is very commonly said that X's duty is not to interfere with B's easement, but this formulation is either pointless or misleading. It is pointless if it is an attempt to describe B's right by referring to the

---

[67] *Hill v Tupper* 1863, 127. See McFarlane 2013.

[68] See *Hill v Tupper* 1863 per Pollock CB at 127–8.

[69] For a Hohfeldian analysis of the effect of the grant of an easement, see Hohfeld 1917a and Smith 2004, 1003 ff.

right itself: how do we know what it means to 'interfere with an easement' if we have not yet defined the easement? It is misleading if it means that X has a duty not to interfere with B's exercise of his right of way: if, for example, X blockades a local petrol station and so prevents B, who has no petrol for his car, from exercising a vehicular right of way, X commits no wrong against B.

In his influential 1987 discussion of the *numerus clausus* principle, Rudden refers to the 'cloning' of claims that occurs where a lesser property right is created: this is probably the best way to understand the effect on X of A's grant of an easement to B. Whereas X previously had a duty to A not to physically interfere, deliberately or carelessly, with A's land, X now owes a similar (but not identical) duty to B. X's duty to B is more limited than X's duty to A: the interference with A's land will only be a wrong against B if it interferes with the part of the land over which the easement is exercised, and in such a way as to impede B's right of way. Crucially, for our purposes, the duty to B cannot be more extensive than the previous duty to A. So, whilst we do need to bring in reference to the use of land when considering the easement, it is not the case of A creating a lesser use right from A's bundle of rights to use the land. Rather, it is the case of A's imposing a new duty on X, owed to B, with the content of that duty modelled on X's general duty to A, but *reduced* by the limit placed on B's use of the land.[70]

On one view, the *numerus clausus* principle can be seen simply as a product of the general rule that A, by means of his unilateral conduct or his dealings with B, cannot impose a new duty on X.[71] Of course, in certain situations (such as A's taking possession of a physical thing), exceptions are made to that rule. In such cases, it seems that an assessment of B's liberty to use A's land (or, in the case of restrictive covenants, B's claim-right that A not make a particular use of A's land) must be undertaken, to determine if that liberty or claim-right is of a kind that is sufficiently important to warrant the imposition of an additional duty (or, in the case of a restrictive covenant, a liability) on X, now owed to B.[72] This attention is required because the creation of a lesser property right does not redistribute existing rights in a zero sum game, taking from A and giving to B, but rather creates new duties on X. These duties exist in addition to the duties owed to A: in this way, A's property right retains its unity even as lesser property rights are created.[73] In one way, however, the general approach of property law is reversed: a specific type of use (or non-use) of land is evaluated and its significance assessed, as a decision is made (sometimes by the courts,[74] more usually by the legislature) as to whether the *specific* use (or non-use) allocated to B is of sufficient importance to warrant the

[70] It is of course possible for the agreement between A and B to impose additional contractual duties on A alone not to interfere with B's use of the easement. The mere grant of an easement from A to B does not, however, impose such additional duties on A.

[71] See McFarlane 2011.

[72] For a discussion of this point in relation to restrictive covenants see McFarlane 2012.

[73] This point may be captured by Honoré's analysis of the 'residuarity' of ownership: see Honoré 1961, 120.

[74] So, for example, in the period following the decision in *Tulk v Moxhay* 1848, the courts carefully defined the content required of A's promise to B before such promise could be capable of binding not just A but also A's successor in title: the process is discussed in detail in McFarlane 2012.

imposition of an additional general duty on the rest of the world. This explains the striking contrast between, on the one hand, the precise requirements, often seemingly over-technical in their nature,[75] placed on the content of lesser property rights and, on the other hand, the open-ended nature of the uses available to an owner.[76]

b) Non-physical things

If property is understood as chiefly consisting of rights to use, then there is no difficulty in extending the scope of property rights to cover any potentially useful or valuable resource. Indeed, from a Hohfeldian perspective, if B has a contractual right to be paid £100 by A, or even a bare licence to make some use of A's land, it is possible to think of B having a 'bundle of rights', consisting of the different legal relations B has not just with A but also with the rest of the world. Yet, both from that Hohfeldian perspective and as a matter of current law, it is clear that a distinction is made between those two examples and cases in which A has an undoubted property right, such as a freehold of land or ownership of a car.

In *OBG v Allan*, for example, the claimant company had a valuable contractual claim-right against Z. The defendants, having been improperly appointed as the claimant's receivers, took charge of the claimant's land and chattels, as well as of the contractual right. There was no doubt that, lacking the authority conferred by a proper appointment, the defendants had breached their duty not to deliberately interfere with the claimant's land and chattels. The defendants had also purported to settle the claimant's contractual claim against Z. The claimants, unhappy with the terms of that settlement, argued that the defendants had also converted that contractual right. The trial judge accepted that the purported settlement did not reflect the true value of the right, and this finding was not disturbed on appeal. The argument that it is possible to convert a purely contractual right has some academic support[77] and, indeed, was accepted by a minority of the House of Lords. Baroness Hale, for example, took the view that a contractual right qualifies as property as '[t]he essential feature of property is that it has an existence independent of a particular person: it can be bought and sold, given and received, bequeathed and inherited, pledged or seized to secure debts, acquired (in the olden days) by a husband on marrying its owner' and that '[o]nce the law recognises something as property, the law should extend a proprietary remedy to protect it'.[78] In both her Ladyship's speech and that of Lord Nicholls (the other member of the minority) this analysis was buttressed by reference to the value and commercial importance of intangible rights.[79]

---

[75] See, for example, the requirement that an easement for the flow of air relate to a flow through a defined channel: this requirement is viewed as overly technical by Coase 1960, 14, but is defended, on the grounds of lowering information costs, by Smith 2004, 42–4.

[76] For a good demonstration of this point see *Copeland v Greenhalf* 1952: B's right could not count as an easement as it did not consist of a liberty to make a defined use of A's land, but rather amounted to a claim to exclusive possession of that land.

[77] See e.g. Green and Randall 2009, 128–39.   [78] *OBG v Allan* 2008, [309].

[79] See e.g. *per* Baroness Hale at *OBG v Allan* 2008, [311].

The majority of the House of Lords, however, refused to extend the tort of conversion to a case of interference with a contractual right.[80] The key point was forcefully made by Lord Hoffmann:[81]

By contrast with the approving attitude of Cleasby J[82] to the protection of rights of property in chattels, it is a commonplace that the law has always been wary of imposing any kind of liability for purely economic loss. The economic torts which I have discussed at length are highly restricted in their application by the requirement of an intention to procure a breach of contract or to cause loss by unlawful means. Even liability for causing economic loss by negligence is very limited. Against this background, I suggest to your Lordships that it would be an extraordinary step suddenly to extend the old tort of conversion to impose strict liability for pure economic loss on receivers who were appointed and acted in good faith.

In *OBG* then, as in *Spartan Steel* (discussed in Section 2.1),[83] the court's characterization of a particular form of loss as 'purely economic' was decisive. In *Spartan Steel*, the defendant contractors were liable for the economic loss suffered by the claimants as a result of the damage to those ingots which, at the time of the power cut, were in the process of being melted. This consequential loss was recoverable as it flowed from the defendant's breach of their duty not carelessly to physically interfere with the claimants' physical things. In contrast, the economic loss flowing from the claimants' admitted inability to melt further ingots was characterized as non-recoverable 'purely' economic loss: such loss did not flow from a breach of duty as there is no general duty not to interfere with a particular use of another's things. In *OBG*, the defendant receivers were liable for any economic loss suffered by the claimants as a result of their taking over of the claimant's land and goods, as such loss flowed from a breach of the defendants' duty not deliberately to physically interfere with the claimant's things. In contrast, the economic loss supposedly flowing from the purported settlement of the contractual claim was characterized as non-recoverable 'purely' economic loss. This characterization was based on the fact that there is no general duty not to interfere with another's contractual rights.

As was made clear in Lord Hoffmann's speech, the effect of a contract between A and B on a stranger's duties to B has been worked out through the economic torts and the position has been reached that such duties are limited to a duty to B not to intentionally procure a breach by A of A's contract with B and a duty to B not to cause B loss by the use of unlawful means. Lord Nicholls, in his dissenting judgment, readily accepted that the economic torts have this narrow compass[84]

---

[80] In *OBG Ltd and ors v United Kingdom* 2011, [96] the European Court of Human Rights (Fourth Section) dismissed OBG's application that United Kingdom had failed to provide adequate protection for OBG's contractual right (a possession protected by Article 1 of Protocol 1 to the European Convention of Human Rights) as 'manifestly ill-founded'.

[81] *OBG v Allan* 2008, [99].

[82] [Those comments were made in *Fowler v Hollins* 1872, 639, explaining the strict liability in conversion as 'founded upon what has been regarded as a salutary rule for the protection of property, namely, that persons deal with the property in chattels or exercise acts of ownership over them at their peril.']

[83] *Spartan Steel & Alloys Ltd v Martin & Co. Ltd* 1973.

[84] *OBG v Allan* 2008, [174]–[195].

and yet, rather surprisingly, went on to find that the defendants could be strictly liable in conversion for their deliberate interference with B's contractual right. Such an analysis overlooks the important reason why liability in the economic torts is so limited. A strict, general duty not to interfere with another's contractual rights would be unduly burdensome on strangers to a contract—in Merrill and Smith's terms, it would impose unduly high information costs on such parties—as it would be a duty to B not to interfere with an activity of A (the performance of A's contractual duty to B) when there is no a priori limit to the possible activities of A to which the duty relates (as A's contractual promise to B may take almost any form) and no obvious means for a stranger to discover the content of A's contractual promise to B. In contrast, compliance with the strict general duty not to deliberately interfere with a physical thing is much easier, as the tangible thing itself sets the boundaries of the stranger's duty.[85] Indeed, the facts of *OBG* itself provide a good example of the complications that would flow from a duty not to interfere with a contractual right. The defendant receivers' settlement of the contractual claim was only a purported settlement: its payment to an incorrectly appointed receiver could not remove Z's contractual duty to the claimant. That duty remained intact[86] and there was thus no interference with any right of the claimant.[87]

It can therefore be argued that if B's right does not relate to a physical thing, it should not be seen as a core case of a property right, as the right does not correlate to a general duty, prima facie binding on the rest of the world, not to physically interfere, carelessly or deliberately, with a particular thing. Indeed, it could further be argued that, if instances of the concept are not to be irreducibly dissimilar, a conceptual definition of property rights[88] should exclude rights that do not relate to a physical thing, such as choses in action and intellectual property rights.[89] This argument cannot be fully explored here, but one point is worth noting. It relates to the recent and powerful argument of Smith in favour of the 'modularity' of property rights.[90] The module, on this view, consists of a particular thing, from which A has a 'right to exclude' others. A key benefit of this approach, Smith argues, is that complexity is reduced: the only concern of outsiders is to stay off another's thing. Any of the specific and varied uses that A may make of A's thing are thus internalized within the owner's 'module'. The argument is presented as a contrast to the bundle of rights theory, which is said to hark 'back to Hohfeld and before, in attempts to analyze legal relations into their smallest atoms'.[91]

---

[85] See e.g. Smith 2012b.

[86] At least until OBG's own liquidators, acting as OBG's agents, consented to the purported settlement. As noted by Lord Hoffmann *OBG v Allan* 2008, [89], [107] it was therefore not the case that the actions of the defendant had caused any loss to the claimant, which was in any case inevitably headed for liquidation: see too the judgment of the European Court of Human Rights (Fourth Section) *OBG Ltd and ors v United Kingdom* 2011, [93].

[87] See Douglas 2011b.

[88] Such a conceptual definition should be distinguished, for example, from the question of what meaning should be given to the term 'property' or 'property right' in the context of a particular statute, such as Insolvency Act 1986, s. 11(3).

[89] This argument has been made, for example, by McFarlane 2008, 132–53.

[90] Smith 2012b.   [91] Smith 2012b, 6.

The present chapter, however, has arrived at a position very similar to that of Smith, but by the express application of a Hohfeldian analysis. The 'right to exclude' is of interest to outsiders precisely because it consists of a general prima facie duty not to physically interfere, deliberately or carelessly, with A's thing. Further, Hohfeld explains why the owner's varied and specific uses of a thing are of no concern to outsiders: the owner's 'right to use' is a 'liberty', meaning that it does not denote a legal duty on outsiders to behave in a certain way, but merely expresses the owner's freedom to use the thing. In other words, the 'lumpiness' of property rights can be seen to depend on the fact that such rights are defined not by focusing on the individual and varied uses that A may make of a resource, but on the general duty of the rest of the world not to interfere with a physical thing. This leads to a point worth noting here: when we move away from physical things, and into the realm of choses in action or intellectual property, this 'lumpiness' disappears, as there is no physical thing around which the general duty owed by the rest of the world can coalesce. A copyright, for example, can be seen to consist in a series of general duties, owed to a copyright holder by the rest of the world, to refrain from particular activities (such as the reproduction of a copyrighted work). In sharp contrast to the core property model, however, the precise content of these duties has to be specified, generally by legislation, and the duties cannot be explained as simply a duty not to physically interfere, deliberately or carelessly, with a particular physical thing. This may help to explain why, as recently noted by Mulligan,[92] the *numerus clausus* principle currently plays no part in intellectual property law: as there is no physical thing around which an intellectual property right can be coherently defined, there is no reason why the varied specific duties imposed on the rest of the world cannot be fractured and disaggregated.

c) *Equitable property rights*

There is, of course, a long-standing and continuing debate as to whether equitable property rights, such as the right held by a beneficiary of a trust, can usefully be seen as property rights.[93] That debate cannot be fully explored here. Nonetheless, two points are worth making. First, the bundle of rights approach may contribute to the view that the establishment of a trust is a means for A, an owner of property, to separate out a right to use or benefit from A's thing, and to confer that right on B, the beneficiary of the trust. On this view, B's right must be seen as proprietary as it comprises that 'cardinal' feature of ownership: the right to use and benefit from a resource. A Hohfeldian perspective, however, helps us to see that this analysis involves a significant misunderstanding of the effects of a trust. When A sets up a trust, A comes under particular duties to B. The duties owed to A by a stranger such as X do not change; nor does X come under any immediate duty to B. The establishment of a trust is best seen as a 'process of cumulation, and not division'.[94]

---

[92] Mulligan 2013.

[93] For recent contributions to this debate see e.g. Nolan 2006; McFarlane 2008, 23–32 and 206–66; McFarlane and Stevens 2010; Edelman 2013.

[94] Jones 1998.

As a judge of the High Court of Australia put it: 'an equitable interest is not carved out a legal estate but impressed upon it'.[95]

For example, consider the case in which A, without authority, makes a gift of a right held on trust to X, and X then disposes of that right without retaining any traceable proceeds of it, and before having acquired knowledge of the initial trust. In such a case, B can make no claim against X.[96] This is the case even though X is *not* a bona fide purchaser for value without notice of the trust, and even though X, by his deliberate action, has clearly interfered with the use and benefit derived by B from the trust asset. Similarly, in cases where the trust relates to a physical thing, the courts have not recognized a duty of X to B not to interfere with the physical thing; such duties, both before and after the creation of the trust, are owed to A.[97] This state of affairs is perfectly consistent with the fact that A can establish a trust in B's favour without any objective signs (such as writing or even the provision of consideration) that might alert X to the existence of the trust; and that the particular use or benefit that a trust allocates to B (where B is one of a number of trust beneficiaries) can take almost any form: in other words, there is no *numerus clausus* of trust rights.

On this view, then, in a case where A holds a property right in a physical thing on trust for B, the establishment of a trust does not affect the modularity of that right: strangers still owe the same general duty of non-interference to A, not to B. Smith has argued that, in its functioning, the trust does take advantage of a modular strategy.[98] This analysis may be correct; but only if we recognize that the organizing module in relation to a trust is not a physical thing (as in the core case of property rights) but is rather another right. For example, if A has ownership of a car, and sets up a trust in B's favour, it is clearly not the car itself that A holds on trust for B: it is A's right to the car. It is for this reason that a trust can exist in relation to any right, even if that right is purely personal (such as a bank account), and even if it is non-assignable.[99] A trust, however, must relate to the whole of a distinct right held by A:[100] if, for example, A simply promises that B can share occupation of A's land for a period,[101] or that A will not make a particular use of A's chattel, B acquires no equitable property right.[102] This is because A has not come under a duty to B in relation to the whole of any distinct right held by A. Equitable property rights thus resemble legal property rights insofar as their content is not focused on particular

---

[95] Per Brennan J. in *DKLR Holding Co. (No. 2) Pty Ltd v Commissioner of Stamp Duties* 1982.

[96] See e.g. *re Montagu's Settlement Trusts* 1987; *Bank of Credit and Commerce International (Overseas) Ltd v Akindele* 2001; *Farah Constructions Pty Ltd v Say-Dee Pty Ltd* 2007.

[97] For authorities denying the existence of such a duty see e.g. *Earl of Worcester v Finch* 1600; *Lord Compton's Case* 1580; *Leigh & Sillavan Ltd v Aliakmon Shipping Co. Ltd (The Aliakmon)* 1986; *MCC Proceeds Inc. v Lehman Bros.* 1998.

[98] See Smith 2012b, 1713.

[99] See e.g. *Don King Productions Inc. v Warren* 2000; *Barbados Trust Co. Ltd v Bank of Zambia* 2007.

[100] See McFarlane and Stevens 2010, 11–12.

[101] See e.g. *King v David Allen & Sons Billposting Ltd* 1916; *National Provincial Bank v Ainsworth* 1965; *Ashburn Anstalt v Arnold* 1989.

[102] See e.g. *Taddy & Co. v Sterious & Co.* 1904; *Barker v Stickney* 1919.

activities (such as particular uses of a physical thing) of the right holder. They differ, however, from legal property rights as the organizing module in the case of equitable property rights—setting the limits of the duties and liabilities of strangers—is not a physical thing, but is rather a right held by A. So, where A holds a right on trust for B, Z can come under the core trust duty to B (a duty not to use a right for Z's own benefit) but only if Z has acquired either the same right that A held on trust for B, or a right that counts as a product of that right.[103]

This analysis can explain what Smith has called the recursiveness of rights under a trust:[104] if A holds on trust for B, B can then set up a trust of B's right in favour of B2. This is due to the fact that the establishment of the initial trust creates a new right, which itself can be made the subject matter of a trust. It should not be assumed that property rights must have that same potential for recursiveness: if, for example, A grants B an easement, it is difficult to see how B might grant B2 an easement of that easement. Perhaps most importantly, the organization of trust rights around a primary right (the subject matter of the trust)[105] can explain why, as is true where B has a purely contractual right against A, the rest of the world is not under a general duty, owed to B, of non-interference. It is because the grounds on which B establishes his or her right cannot depend on an unmediated relationship to a physical thing; rather B's right necessarily depends on another person (in this case, the trustee) being under a particular duty to B.

It is therefore unfortunate that, in the recent case of *Shell UK Ltd v Total UK Ltd*, the Court of Appeal equated the position of a trust beneficiary with that of A, an owner of a physical thing. It did so when holding that, where the defendant had breached its duty not carelessly to physically interfere with A's land, and A's property right in the land was held on trust for B, the defendant was also liable for consequential economic loss suffered by B (and not A), at least if A was joined in any action brought by B against the defendant. The decision has been widely criticized[106] and is contrary to previous case law that denies that, where A holds A's right to a physical thing on trust for B, X is under a duty to B not to interfere with that physical thing.[107] A central problem is the assumption that, B, rather than A, has the right to benefit from the land and so B, rather than A, is the 'real owner' of that land.[108] This assumption is consistent with the model in which the creation of a trust transfers a proprietary 'right to use' from A to B, but ignores two key points, clear from a Hohfeldian perspective: first, the existence of the trust depends on A's duty to B to use A's property right in the land for B's benefit; second, there is no

---

[103] See McFarlane and Stevens 2010. Z is under an immediate duty to A not to dishonestly assist A to breach any of A's duties as trustee to B, but the presence of this general ancillary duty (like the general ancillary duty to B not to procure a breach by A of A's contract with B) does not distinguish B's right under the trust from a non-proprietary right: see McFarlane 2008.

[104] Smith 2012b, 21–2.

[105] In the term used by Gretton 2007 at 839, the right of the beneficiary is a 'daughter' right as its subject matter is another right.

[106] See e.g. Edelman 2013; Rushworth and Scott 2010; Turner 2010; Low 2010.

[107] See the cases cited at n. 97. See too Douglas 2011a, 39–47.

[108] *Shell UK Ltd v Total UK Ltd* 2010, [132].

reason why that duty, owed by A to B, need have any effect on the question of whether X has a duty to B (as well as to A) not to physically interfere with A's thing.

3. Conclusion

This chapter does not purport to provide a complete Hohfeldian analysis of the nature of property rights. We have concentrated on the distinctive claim-rights held by A, a party with a property right, against the rest of the world. We have not examined the particular duties and liabilities which A may be under in relation to the property; nor have we considered the possible powers that A may hold as part of his property right. Nonetheless, even this partial analysis provides a useful insight: a Hohfeldian analysis of the distinctive claim-rights held by A can be used to support not the view that property consists of an atomized bundle of rights, but rather the contrasting view that a property right is a coherent whole, defined around the concept of a general prima facie duty of the rest of the world not to physically interfere with a physical thing. In this way, the chapter supports Smith's claim that property law is distinctively 'modular' or 'lumpy'. If we accept that any individual property right has this coherence, we then need to ask if property law as a whole is similarly unified. In particular, if B's right does *not* impose the characteristic general duty of non-interference with a physical thing, is that right merely beyond the core of property law, or should it instead be seen as conceptually non-proprietary? It has often, and accurately, been said that Hohfeld made no sustained attempt to differentiate property rights from other multital rights, but we can nonetheless be drawn back to his *en passant* comment that multital rights can be distinguished on the basis that 'some rights in rem, or multital rights, relate fairly directly to physical objects; some fairly directly to persons; and some fairly directly neither to tangible objects nor to persons'.[109] It may be that, as the distinctive features of a property right depend on the existence of duties not to interfere with a physical thing, the coherence of property law depends on its limitation to that first category of multital rights.

[109] Hohfeld 1919, 86.

11

On the Very Idea of Transmissible Rights

*James Penner**

In order to understand transmissible rights, rights which can be transferred by way of gift or contract, and which may pass from one person to another by operation of law, for example on death or bankruptcy, we need to address two questions. The first question is conceptual. How are we to conceive of an ideational entity like a right being the subject of a transfer? The second is moral. How should we go about justifying an owner's power to transfer the right he holds: in particular, can such a power be justified in a 'state of nature'—more precisely, on moral grounds which would apply universally—or do owners have such a power only because of the institution of a convention? Before pursuing these questions, however, a brief word on why this matters.

1. Title and Succession

Lawyers distinguish between the case where a person acquires land as a successor in title from a previous owner, say by a conveyance pursuant to a contract of sale, and the case where a person acquires a title to land merely by taking possession of it, which (adverse) title may, by virtue of a limitation act, become the best or only title to the land following the extinction of the prior owner's title. In the first case, we say the title holder in question is the transferee of the title or the right to the land from the transferor. In the second case, the adverse possessor acquires an entirely new title in the land (which he can, of course, transfer to another). It is not necessary to cloak the distinction in the common law doctrine of relativity of title to make sense of this. All one needs is the distinction between rights that are acquired by transfer and rights originating in the taking of possession. So, for example, one might hold that following 12 years of disuse—evidenced, perhaps, by the use of the adverse possessor whose possession itself does not give rise to any title—an owner's title is deemed to be abandoned, with the result that the owner's

* I must thank participants at the PFPL conference for their very helpful comments, and also, for theirs, George Letsas, Arthur Ripstein, Irit Samet, Prince Saprai, Jeremy Waldron, and Charlie Webb. I owe particular thanks to Rob Chambers, Miguel Lopez-Lorenzo (who suggested the final title), Nick Sage, and Henry Smith, all of whom read several drafts. None bears any liability for this final version.

property is once again *res nullius* with the consequence that the next possessor acquires a good, new title.[1]

A second example of the distinction is provided by assignable personal rights, like debts, or company shares. Again, there are two alternatives which, whilst not coinciding precisely with the distinction between the acquisition of title by transfer and the acquisition of title by possession, turn on distinguishing between a right acquired via a transfer and a new right arising in consequence of a different sort of event. Debts can be assigned, i.e. transferred, under s. 136 Law of Property Act 1925, which requires the assignment to be in writing and the debtor notified. As a debt is intangible, there is no parallel to the case of land by which a third party could acquire such a right by possession. But in such cases *novations* can occur. That is, the debtor could agree to undertake the same obligation that he has to his creditor in favour of a third party in consideration of the creditor's releasing him from that debt. In the case of company shares, for example, on this view of things the company would agree to cancel the shares of the 'transferor', at the same time issuing shares in favour of the 'transferee'. The parallel with abandonment, which extinguishes the prior right, and the originating of a new right is obvious. And a novation no more links the two rights together to give rise to a genuine transfer than does the case of adverse possession of land. Indeed, in the case of a novation, the very term indicates that the second right is a new one. What is most pressing about the case of assignable personal rights, if we take their assignability seriously, is that they force us squarely to confront the idea that an intangible, ideational entity, i.e. a right, can be transferred, though one should note here that common law rights of ownership in land are also, in fact, ideational. An owner of land has an *estate* in the land, an abstract title determined by the length of the right to possession (or seisin).

Whilst in these examples I have contrasted cases of transfer with cases where a new (though similar) right arises on the occurrence of another event (adverse possession and novation), it is important to remember that transfer is only one example of succession to property rights in the law. Lawyers also understand that X's rights might become Y's rights in other ways, principally by operation of law. Death and insolvency are obvious cases. On death, X's title to all of his tangible and intangible property either passes directly to his heirs by way of inheritance,[2] as remains the case in most civilian legal systems, or to his personal representative, as is the case in modern common law jurisdictions. On bankruptcy, X's title to all of his property will pass to his trustee in bankruptcy. The key point is that in all of these cases of succession, Y, whether transferee, heir, personal representative or trustee in bankruptcy, is conceived to take the *very same* right that X himself had. So what we are concerned with is the idea of a *transmissible* right, a right whose identity persists despite the fact that it passes from one person to another.

---

[1] This is one way of understanding acquisition of ownership by prescription.
[2] Inheritance has been abolished in England except for titles of nobility.

2. The Argument against Transfer or Transmissibility Stated: The Hohfeldian[3] Individuation Argument

Hohfeldians have a problem with the idea that Y can succeed, by transfer or otherwise, to X's property rights. The reasoning goes as follows: rights are inherently relational. There is a right bearer, A, and a duty ower, C. Assuming the existence of this right–duty relation between A and C, it is not clear what it would mean to replace A with B, such that B could simply step into the shoes of A whilst at the same time preserving the identity of the very right that obtained between A and C. To put the point technically, perhaps fussily, this is a question of the *individuation* of rights. At first glance, we might naturally think that the parties to a normative relationship are essential elements of the normative relationship itself. If rights are individuated by their right bearers and duty owers essentially, then it trivially follows that any right held by A cannot be the 'same' right when held by B (and the same would apply *mutatis mutandis* when the identity of the duty ower(s) changes). For Hohfeld, the idea that there are no true transfers of rights would appear to be a necessary result of his analysis (perhaps one of its motivations). As Hohfeld understood his jural relations,[4] right holders and duty bearers relate under two schemes: the paucital and the multital. A paucital jural relation obtains between two persons,[5] and a multital jural relation, such as a right *in rem*, which at first glance appears to obtain between one right holder and a numerous class of duty bearers, is actually a chimera. Properly analysed, it is just a group of *similar* personal relations. So Albert's claim-right to his copy of *Leviathan* really consists of a right that Tom not interfere with his right to immediate, exclusive possession of it, plus his right that Dick not interfere with his right to immediate, exclusive possession of it, plus his right that Mary not do so, and so on and on covering all the people within the jurisdiction. If Albert gives his *Leviathan* to Beatrix, then she now has an entirely new battery of claim-rights against all others not to interfere with her possession of the thing, including of course one against Albert himself. Whilst Albert may have a power to give his copy of the book to Beatrix, she having (in Hohfeldian terminology) a correlative 'liability' to be made owner of it, this is not really a power to transfer his set of jural relations to her, but rather a power to inaugurate an entirely new (though similar) set.

Whilst this power to inaugurate a new paucital right in the case of a novation is clear enough—this is simply the power to enter into contractual relations—it is not entirely clear how one ought to regard such a power in the case of tangible property. A kind of 'directional abandonment' route may be one possibility. In respect of tangibles like land or chattels, the notion of directional abandonment does appear to provide a 'functional' equivalent to the transfer of ownership. On a directional

---

[3] Hohfeld 1919.   [4] Hohfeld 1919.

[5] Hohfeld 1919 (Part II), 72. Note 18 indicates that strictly speaking, such a right is 'unital' if it is unique, and paucital if there are only a few similar rights obtaining between the right bearer and others, but Hohfeld is happy for 'paucital' to serve as a cover term for rights *in personam*.

abandonment conception of transfer, A relinquishes his possession of a chattel in circumstances where his transferee, B, is likely or guaranteed[6] to take possession next; when A does so and B takes possession, this, it might be said, operates, functionally at least, as a transfer.[7]

These 'functional' conceptions of transfer, the novation route to explaining the transfer of an assignable personal right, like a debt or share, and the directional abandonment route to explaining the transfer of a tangible appear completely straightforward (as indeed they are); whilst 'technically' the rights in issue prior to and after the transactions are distinct, we have a kind of 'functional' transfer of the rights in question. Though it remains the case that the rights prior to the transactions are not identical to the rights subsequent insofar as the identity of the relata is an essential feature of the right–duty relation—they are at best 'faux' transfers of rights if a transfer requires the transferee to have the identical right that the transferor has—this is not a problem because it makes no sense to say that B could have the same right vis-à-vis C that A had. On this score, the novation and directional abandonment routes *illuminate the true nature of the 'transfer of a right'*, which is that this is merely a functional notion in which the transferee acquires a *similar* right to that held by the transferor, but not truly the very *same* right.

Two points must now be made about the possibility of 'functional' analyses of this kind. Consider a change in the factual possession of a copy of *Leviathan*. If I hand my copy to you, then you are now in factual possession, but your factual possession is simply that—it is not as if you have assumed *my* factual possession. As regards the fact of possession, the same result would obtain whatever events led to my loss of possession and your assumption of it. The idea of *transfer*, on the other hand, is inherently intentional, involving my putting you in factual possession with the intention that you will assume possession as a consequence of my doing so, and your taking possession with an intention to do so. Such a transaction may not, strictly speaking, bespeak a power on my part to transfer, but it identifies a particular way in which we understand that my factual possession is relinquished and yours realized. In the absence of such an understanding of this particular way of effecting the change in possession from me to you, we would not *conceive* of any other way of doing so as functionally equivalent to a transfer. So, the directional abandonment conception of transfer is only conceived of *as a transfer* by analogy with the real thing. To my mind, the order of explanation really must go in that order. By reversing the reasoning, we could conceive of transfers as functional equivalents of directional abandonments. But we don't. This should bolster our sense that the distinction between transfer and either directional abandonment or novation is robust, and that our understanding of the former is prior to our understanding of the latter. The point can be made in another way: whilst empirically I can manage to put you in possession of a thing I possessed by way of directional abandonment, conceptually this cannot really amount to a transfer;

---

[6] For example, A puts B in possession of a book by handing it to him, and then says 'I abandon this'. This assumes that A has a power to abandon.

[7] See Penner 1997, 84–5.

in theory, something always might go wrong, and a third party intervene to take possession before you, my intended recipient manages to do so—you might for example fumble the handoff so you never acquire possession before the third party does—and no one thinks that because, as a matter of fact in this situation the third party acquires title by his taking possession following my relinquishing my possession, I have transferred the title to him, for that was never my intention. Nevertheless, the same mechanism of abandonment and taking possession occurred. The upshot is that however much empirically abandonment can work directionally, as a conceptual matter abandonment does not determine what follows in the way of any person, and which person, or no one, actually acquiring a new title by possession.

Treating directional abandonment as the legal mechanism of transfer also brings into play the nature and justification of acquiring rights by appropriating unowned things.[8] Whatever we think about that,[9] it seems out of place, surely, to regard the justice of transfer per se as having a conceptually necessary dependency upon the justice of original acquisition in each case; the intuitive view is surely that whilst the validity or legitimacy of B's right to the property transferred to him by A might well turn on the legitimacy of A's prior right to it (i.e. B's right may be heir to the same infirmities as was A's right because B acquired the title to the property from A), the question regarding transfers is one about whether, and with what validity or legitimacy, B acquired his title by transfer from A. Indeed, the latter question would need to be determined prior to asking how any deficiencies in A's prior right affected B; for *only* if B's title *is* the title A had, i.e. only if A effectively transferred A's right to B, should B be concerned with any deficiencies in A's prior right. If B's title was not A's, B should not be concerned with anything about it; rather he should be concerned only about the legitimacy of his own 'first' appropriation.

The foregoing is, I fear, a rather long-winded exposition of a fairly intuitive claim, viz. that whilst it may look like an easy way out, the ideas of directional abandonment and novation do not capture what we want to capture when we seek to understand the nature of the transfer of a right. We are therefore led to try to meet the Hohfeldian individuation argument, i.e. that rights are individuated necessarily by the identity of their right bearers and duty owers, head on.

3. Why the Hohfeldian Individuation Argument is Wrong

To show why the Hohfeldian individuation argument is wrong, we must proceed in steps, considering in turn the case of transmissible personal rights like the right to

---

[8] Parallel considerations arise in the case of novations—transfer now implicitly requires agreement between the duty ower, the right bearer, and the intended 'transferee'. It turns the transaction from one of a two-party transfer to one of a three-party contract. Thus it implicates our justification of contractual agreement, whereas transfers, e.g. gifts, are not necessarily contractual in nature.

[9] I am of the same mind as a few other scholars on this point, who do not regard the justification of first appropriation as particularly difficult. See Penner 2006, 172–3; Gaus and Lomasky 1990; Feser 2005; Sage 2012.

be paid £10 by C, and then what seems to be the more difficult case of the transmissible right *in rem*, like a fee simple estate in Blackacre.

There is a perfectly clear sense in which A's right to be paid £10 by C can be transferred or assigned to B, or is transmitted to B by inheritance, A's bankruptcy, and so on, such that B acquires the very same right that A had. All we need to show is that A, B, and any further successors, can benefit in the very same way when C discharges his duty. The payment of £10, this performance, is one that is capable of being performed, in principle, to the benefit of anyone, or at least to anyone who is entitled to receive payments. Picture a case in which C is entitled to make payment by placing a £10 note at the base of Nelson's column in Trafalgar Square. Prior to A's assignment to B, A had the right to pick up the note, and afterwards B has. How is B's right any different from A's right, conceived of as the right to pick up the note? Or take a case where C's duty is to do something that doesn't involve another person at all. Let us assume C has the duty to walk to Manchester, and that this right is assignable. The duty, let us say, arose under a contract with A, who assigns the benefit of this contract to B. B now has the legal right to C's performance, but I take it no one thinks C's duty to perform is any different whoever has the correlative right. These examples are not intended to restrict our sense of the identity of A's and B's rights to physical transactions, but only to make vivid the point that C's duty to deposit the note or walk to Manchester can only be distinguished as different duties on the basis that any duty must be individuated (in part) by the identity of the right bearer, and A and B have different identities. But this dogmatic assertion does no work here, for what we are trying to make sense of at this point is how a conception of a duty and its performance may not turn on the identity of the correlative right bearer, and these examples make it clear that we can, and routinely do, conceive of duties in this way. Moreover, these cases also provide the sense in which it is inherent to C's duty (it being assumed that it is a transmissible personal right—nothing I have said here would imply that any or all personal rights are in fact transmissible) that it correlates *both* to A's and to B's right (though not, of course, at the same time): C's duty to pay £10 is not a duty just to pay A; it is a duty to pay A or any successor of A; that is just what is involved in conceiving of a right as transmissible. To deny this way of conceiving C's duty is to deny that C's duty can be subject to a succession of correlative right bearers in respect of the duty he owes. But to deny that is simply to deny that the concept of succession makes sense in the case of rights, and again, we have just seen that that is false by showing that A's and B's rights clearly relate to the same duty of C's.

Now the clever Hohfeldian has a reply at this point, one which turns on the notion of title. The idea is that A's title to this intangible right is more complex than simply his right to C's performance, and this is perfectly right. A's title to the debt consists of the following elements, at least:[10]

---

[10] There will almost certainly be other elements, such as A's power to waive his right or release C from the debt, a power to declare a trust over the right, a liability to account for the payment for tax purposes, etc.

1. A's right to C's payment of £10;

2. The incident of this relation that payment by C of £10 discharges C's duty and extinguishes A's right;

3. A's power to enforce this right by legal action (hence its being a '*chose* or thing in action');

4. The incident that this title is transmissible by operation of law on death, insolvency, and so on;

5. A's power to transfer this title by assignment.

The clever Hohfeldian is apt to pounce on 4 and 5. Whilst elements 1 to 3 seem to be identical for both A and B—these are the right-like incidents of A's title which seem to correlate with identical duties or liabilities of C, the same cannot be said for 4 and 5. In the case of 4, different persons, for example, will inherit from A than from B if they were to die, and in the case of 5, we know for a certainty that there will be one person to whom A can transfer the right that B cannot: B himself of course, and likewise when B acquires title, A will be a possible object of B's power to transfer, while that was simply not true when A held that power. Call this the 'switched places' argument. It generalizes in a broader way when we deal with rights *in rem*, to which we will turn in a few sentences.

Our examples allow us to say that we have made some headway in meeting the Hohfeldian individuation argument. It seems plain that at least some elements of A's title to the right to be paid £10 by C can be shown to be identical whoever has title, elements 1 to 3. But at this point, we have not shown that every element of the title can escape the argument, because of the 'switched places' challenge.

The case of rights *in rem* seems to be more susceptible to the individuation argument, because the argument operates along two dimensions. Consider the following basic elements[11] of A's fee simple in Blackacre:

1. A's liberty to enter onto Blackacre, build upon it, dig up the soil, etc.;

2. The incident of title that A benefits from the observance by all others of their duty not to interfere with property that is not their own; this incident can also be described as A's right to immediate, exclusive, possession of Blackacre;

3. A's power to bring a claim for trespass when the duty in 2 is breached by a trespass on Blackacre;

4. The incident that this title is transmissible by operation of law on death, insolvency, and so on;

5. A's power to transfer this title.

It is obvious that from a Hohfeldian perspective the jural relations comprised by 1, 2, and 3 are impossible exhaustively to specify at any one time, because as people

---

[11] There are of course many more; the powers to license, create leases, mortgage Blackacre, grant easements and restrictive covenants, declare a trust over Blackacre, and the liability to property tax, are a few examples.

die and are born, the constellation of duties not to interfere with an owner's right to possession is constantly in flux. Indeed, on this strict Hohfeldian analysis, no owner just *has* a fee simple in Blackacre—as we have seen, he merely has a constantly fluctuating set of personal jural relations (which may for ease of exposition be bundled into one 'multital' right). In consequence, it is an error to regard A's fee simple as a right that persists through time, even for A himself. And it makes plain why A can never transfer 'his fee simple' to B. He never has the same fee simple himself from moment to moment, so how could there be any identity of his rights with any subsequently acquired by B? Call this the 'fluctuation' argument.

The second dimension is just the 'switched places' argument applied to rights *in rem*. When A transfers his fee simple in Blackacre to B, the one thing we know for certain is that, in the constellation of jural relations which, for a Hohfeldian, define the right as the right that it is, A previously owed no duty not to trespass on Blackacre and B did, whereas afterward B owes no such duty whilst A now does. So even in the unlikely case that A's fee simple is stable for the moment, because no one recently has died or been born to change the constellation of third-party duty owers, there will necessarily be a difference in the constellation of duty owers in A's case and B's case, as they have switched places. As was true of the case of A's title to the right to be paid £10 by C, the same argument applies to elements 4 and 5 in this case, too.

As to the fluctuation argument, I think the answer is straightforward, so let us tackle that first. In a paper written half a century ago,[12] Honoré gave us the clue to defeating the fluctuation argument. Consider this modified version of one of his examples.[13] One of the incidents of title to a fee simple is the power to license others to enter one's property. When that power is exercised, it alters the relations between the owner and at least one other that would alter the constellation of rights and duties that the owner has against others in respect of Blackacre; a licensee now has no duty not to enter Blackacre. But no one thinks that this means the owner has *a different fee simple* now from the one he had prior to the exercise of this power. It is part and parcel of the fee simple title that one can license others to enter one's land. The jural relations that result from the exercise of a power that is conceptually an aspect of that title cannot themselves be ones whose being brought into existence by the exercise of that power entail that the owner must lose that very fee simple and acquire some other one. Perhaps one might argue that this is a special case, involving the exercise of an owner's power to alter the constellation of correlative duty owers, and doesn't meet the more basic point about new duty owers arising by birth and others passing away on death. It is not clear to me whether or how a Hohfeldian might try to explain this example as an anomalous case, but it doesn't really matter, since the whole picture which animates the fluctuation argument is wrong-headed.

A right may persist, that is, its identity may remain unchanged, though the various normative incidents which go with having that right do not remain constant.[14] One of the things that Honoré's example indicates is that the Hohfeldian

[12] Honoré 1960.   [13] Honoré 1960, 454–5.

[14] I said something similar myself regarding the way that certain legal interests remain the same despite their incidents changing; see Penner 2010, 257–66. I should have cited Honoré there, but to my regret failed to do so.

'analysis' of rights like property rights into an ever-changing tangle of jural relations between the owner and others is unmotivated, philosophically speaking. Whatever one makes of the distinction between the essential and the accidental as regards the properties or features that make a thing what it is, clearly we rely upon some such distinction all the time when we make use of the concepts that we have. This is why we can step into the same river twice, why you are the same person you were yesterday despite the fact that many of the molecules of your body are different and that you are in a bad mood today but were in a good mood yesterday, why the steak that I cooked and ate was the same steak I bought raw at the butcher's. There is no sort of a priori reason, or at least none provided by Hohfeld or his supporters that I can see, that things are different in the realm of legal concepts. So there is nothing in principle obviously wrong in saying that a legal concept, a *technical* legal concept like the fee simple estate in Blackacre, has the content it has even though that concept continues to apply through time despite the fact that the configuration of jural relations between the owner and everyone else constantly changes. Consider: if legislation was passed tomorrow which changed the limitation period for bringing actions for breach of contract, a Hohfeldian would have to say that by operation of law all the extant legally valid contracts had been abolished by legislation and replaced with other, similar though not identical, contracts. I see no reason at all to accede to this preposterous conceptual fiat. I am not, of course, saying that there could not be a case of legislation that might produce this sort of effect. If, for example, legislation retrospectively made certain contracts illegal or unenforceable, or abolished the right to transfer a fee simple to anyone other than the Crown, then I might well *judge* that the contracts and fees simple in question were now, whatever we called them, different creatures. But it would be a matter of judgment which would not be foreclosed by the Hohfeldian's claim that there is no matter to be judged here since all of our rights are subject to this sort of fluctuation all the time.

Now to the switched places argument: here we can draw a genuine distinction between rights *in rem* and rights *in personam*. As we saw above with the case of C's duty to pay A £10, upon A's assignment, the right becomes B's, and the transfer has only this effect of moving the right from A to B. It is not the case that as a result of the assignment A comes under a duty he did not have before, nor is B is relieved of any duty he previously had.[15] But this is exactly what happens when A transfers his fee simple in Blackacre to B. Not only, it seems, is there a 'transfer' of the right, but there is also a corresponding 'transfer' of the duty not to trespass. Prior to the transfer, A had no duty not to trespass on Blackacre—he was its owner—whereas

---

[15] I am, clearly, simplifying here, for if we assume a duty not to induce another to breach of contract or some such duty, A does come under a duty and B is relieved of one; but all this shows is that rights *in personam* can have *in rem* effects. My purpose here is to distinguish transfers of rights *in personam* from transfers of rights *in rem*; whilst we can imagine a general duty such as a duty not to induce another to breach a right *in personam*, we don't have to; regarding the right to the payment of £10 itself, A acquires no duty and B loses none because the same duty ower C has that obligation throughout; B never had a duty to pay £10 and A doesn't acquire any. But it is, from this Hohfeldian perspective on rights *in rem*, impossible not to see the transfer of A's fee simple to B as resulting in A's acquiring the duty not to trespass and B's being relieved of that duty.

now he has, and of course vice versa for B. In this case, then, not only the right bearer changes, but so also does the duty ower. In a world where there are just A and B, a transfer results in a complete revolution in rights: whereas A was owed a duty by B in respect of Blackacre, B is now owed a duty by A in respect of Blackacre. In such a case, in order to identify B's right to Blackacre as the same right to Blackacre that A had, i.e. to say that A *transferred* his fee simple to B, we seem to be put in the position of having to say that we can individuate rights in a way that not only makes them invariant through changes of the right bearer, but also through changes in the duty ower.

As I see it, the only way to show why the Hohfeldian is led astray here is to reveal and explain the *impersonal* nature of the rights and duties at issue, and show why that allows us to see the rights (and the correlative duties) as persisting through both changes in right bearers and duty owers. That is, of course, easier said than done, and in order to show this, we have to work through the different jural relations which give a transmissible right such as a fee simple the shape that it has. We can begin with the power to transfer.

We start with the point that the fluctuation argument, as we have just seen, is flawed. The power to transfer the fee simple estate is not to be understood to fluctuate with the number of possible recipients, as some are born and some die. The power to transfer is conceived as a power to tranfer *to someone*, not a power to transfer to named individual X, named individual Y, and so on. Of course when a transfer is made only an identified individual or individuals will take, but that doesn't undermine the impersonal conception of the power. And it is worthwhile pointing out that this is the view of the common law, as shown by the way in which the law regards those who may take under a power of appointment pursuant to the terms of a trust, or those who are presumptive heirs, or those who are named beneficiaries of a will. In each of these cases, the law regards these individuals not as having any interest in the property in question, but rather as having a mere *spes*, or hope, of receiving. The trustee may in the end not appoint to anyone, the heir may die before his predecessor, the estate may have no property in it at the time of the testator's death for distribution to the beneficiaries under his will. These are cases where we *can actually identify* a list smaller than everyone alive as possible recipients, sometimes only a single individual, and yet the law does not regard the potential recipient(s) as being in a jural relation with respect to any property they might receive. At most they may be entitled to standing to ensure, for example, that the trustee does not make a purported appointment to someone outside the group of persons to whom he is entitled validly to appoint. In consequence, in the same way as we can conceive of a right to be paid £10 by C as persisting through its transfer from A to B, we can conceive of A's power to transfer the fee simple to Blackacre *to someone* as persisting through the transaction in which A exercises that power in favour of B; B, now with the fee simple, has the self-same power to transfer it to someone. The fact that now A is one of the individuals who might receive now that B, not A, has the power, is immaterial to our conception of the power, because the fact that A is a 'new' possible recipient because he is now no longer owner is no more material to the conception of the power than is the fact that D is a new possible recipient, having just been born.

Another way of putting this is that A, as former owner of Blackacre, has no special standing under the property norm as a new possible recipient by way of transfer; he is now just one of the multitude who come into being and pass away, through which comings into being and passings away the title to Blackacre, with its power to transfer, persists.

The same story can be told in respect of the right to immediate, exclusive, possession of Blackacre, but before addressing that directly, I want to provide one (rather gruesome) example where even a Hohfeldian who accepts the story I have told above about transmissible personal rights would, I think, be obliged to say that a right *in rem*, the very same right *in rem*, is transmitted from A to B. Here it is: assume one of the incidents of title to Blackacre is that property passes by way of inheritance, which was the old English rule for land. Now consider the case where A dies giving birth to her first (and obviously, only) child, B. At the moment A dies, B is born and inherits A's fee simple in Blackacre. Assume also that no one else is born or dies at the same moment. If we can individuate rights according to the identity of the performances or forbearances correlatively owed by the duty ower(s), as we established in our discussion of the transmissible right *in personam*, then in this case B succeeds to exactly the same right that A had, for B's right correlates exactly to all the same duties that A's right did, *for all the duty owers are third parties*. The case is structurally identical to the case of A's right to be paid £10 by C passing to B. That is, in this case, unlike the case in which A transfers title to Blackacre to B, A *does not* come under a duty to B not to trespass on Blackacre upon B's acquisition of the right—A *dies* at the very moment the right becomes B's. And B is not released from any duty not to trespass on Blackacre when he acquires the right, for his right comes into existence simultaneously with his birth, so there was never a duty he owed to A not to trespass on Blackacre prior to his acquisition of the right. So the exact same constellation of duty owers correlate with both A's and B's right, and thus this is a case of the transmission of the same right from A to B.

If this is right, then a Hohfeldian must acknowledge that in principle there can be a transmission of a right *in rem*, and all that he now has to turn to to deny that we should regard rights *in rem* as transmissible generally (by transfer, inheritance, and so on) is something along the following lines: 'Whilst, admittedly, for the reasons canvassed above, a right may persist through the change of some of its incidents, and this may be so even as regards the identity of its duty-owers (so the fact that some are born and some die does not mean that the owner of a fee-simple has a right which is itself continually changing its identity), there is something special about the fact that, upon "transfer", the former right-bearer is now one of the duty-owers, and one of the former duty-owers, is now the right-bearer.' Now, finally, I think we can see why isolating this particular 'revolution' in the rights of A and B is no longer a compelling reason to deny the transmissibility of rights, and again we turn to the impersonal nature of this right–duty correlation.

The mistake in this picture is to accord overdue significance to the change in A's and B's duties, and neglect both the power of transfer (or the other modes of succession which apply to transmissible rights) and the resultant change in A's and B's rights. It is to conceive the power to transfer not as something positive that the law facilitates, but rather as a way of imposing a duty upon oneself and, correspondingly, to treat the right to receive by way of transfer (or by inheritance, etc.)[16] as a way of escaping one. But the right to property is not simply the absence of a duty not to interfere with some tangible, for that would make me, you, and everyone else, an owner of any unowned chattel or piece of land, which is nonsense. To have a right to tangible property, that is, to have title in a tangible, is not merely to be free from a duty not to trespass, but to have the powers that go with that title, and to be subject to the incidents (the liability that it will pass to one's trustee in bankruptcy, and so on) that go with title. I am not denying that the incidents that go with title could be spelt out in exhaustive Hohfeldian fashion, but rather making the same point made above in regard to the duty of C to pay A a debt of £10, now assigned to B. We have already seen, in defeating the fluctuation argument, that on no sensible legal view would the right of a fee simple of A vary with every change in the exhaustive Hohfeldian list of jural relations which, for a Hohfeldian, would give the 'right' the identity it has. We now see that the 'switched places' problem, properly understood, is just a variant of the fluctuation problem, essentially a non-problem for just the same reason. It is, of course, true that those who are involved in the actual transaction whereby their property passes to another have a historical connection to the property that was once theirs that any old third party does not. And people may feel keenly the loss of their property, not only, for example, on insolvency, but when they transfer it themselves by contract or as a gift, depending upon the circumstances, but the juridical significance of this, if we want to accord it any, lies in the way we conceive of that loss; we do not conceive of that *loss* as a matter of their *acquiring* a duty not to interfere with it, i.e. they now are just one of the multitude of non-owners. Rather, what depicts their change of a position as a loss is the loss of their title, with all of its incidents, in particular those that concern its transmissibility. To repeat, former owners have no special status as duty owers once their property is no longer theirs. Their addition to the body of duty owers is no more significant to the right than is the birth of a new person, now under a duty not to interfere with the property.

These considerations can be sharpened.[17] In the first place, both the Hohfeldian and I agree that when A falls under a duty not to trespass on Blackacre after he sells it to B, it is not *B's* duty not to trespass that A acquires. There is a transfer of the title to B, not a transfer of B's duty not to trespass to A. If, for example, B was A's licensee prior to the transfer, there would be no duty of B's to transfer. Similarly, if A only transfers to B on condition that B grant A an immediate licence to enter Blackacre, A will acquire no duty upon the transfer. So we can see an asymmetry between A's loss of his title and his acquisition of the duty not to trespass; the former is a *result* of the transfer—a transfer is not a transfer if title doesn't pass—but the acquisition by A of a duty is just the usual *consequence* or *effect* of A's losing his title.

---

[16] On Hohfeld's idiosyncratic terminology, such a right to receive is a kind of 'liability'.
[17] Rob Chambers suggested the examples in this paragraph and the next to me.

This can also be shown by considering A's making B a co-owner. Let us say that, pursuant to the power granted in s. 72 of the Law of Property Act 1925, A transfers title to Blackacre to himself and B[18] as tenants in common. A's right to possession of the land is not altered by this transaction; he acquires no duty not to enter; what changes is that, not only has B no longer a duty not to trespass, but he acquires title to his undivided share of Blackacre. So again, the result of this transaction is A's having to share his title with B, but nothing about A's right to possession flows as a consequence.

The last example could, indeed, be generalized without a different result. Say a statute was passed that entitled any former owner, like A, to a licence for a year over land that he transferred, to B in our example. Could it seriously be maintained that A's transfer was ineffective as a transfer for the duration of that year, that during this time A hadn't given up his title, or that B didn't acquire title even though immediately following the transaction he became entitled to license others, transfer the property on (according himself the same year-long licence), and so on? Transfers and the acquisition of a duty not to trespass simply do not go together as a matter of conceptual necessity.

We must, as well, acknowledge that all of this is, so to speak, native to the very idea of transmissible rights. In the same way that in the case of an assignable debt, the duty of C correlates from time to time with the right of whomever is the beneficiary of that duty, the duty owed by any individual in the throng of those who have a duty not to trespass on Blackacre is owed to anyone, from time to time, who will come to be its owner. The very idea of transmissability is related to this idea of contingency—what is yours might as well be, and might come to be, not only mine, but his, hers, theirs, and so on. The fact that something you own might come to be mine, in which case I will typically no longer owe a duty not to trespass upon it and you typically will, is no reason not to think that the right that you had is precisely the right that I may acquire, rather the opposite. What I ought to conclude from this fact is that my duty amongst the myriad other duties owed by nameless others is precisely *not* to be elevated to some sort of special status, the extinction of which turns a fee simple title in Blackacre, for example, into the kind of right where *my* owing a duty not to trespass is an earth-shakingly important element of its continuing identity. To borrow again from the modified example of Honoré's, if I were licensed by you to enter onto Blackacre so that I had no such duty, it would not by one whit alter the normative significance of your then transferring the title in Blackacre to me even though vis-à-vis any duty I had (or not) not to trespass on Blackacre was unchanged. Or say I am some potentate of the realm who simply has no duty not to trespass on anyone's land. I have, one might say, an unlimited right to roam. Does that put me in a position whereby I own all the property in the realm, or cannot have property transferred to me? Of course not. Whilst I might have an unlimited right to roam, I have no power to license the property to others

[18] Whilst transferring one's title to *oneself* and another is how creating a co-ownership between oneself and another is conceived under the statute, the same transaction could be characterized differently, that is, simply as a power to make another a co-owner directly.

and no power to transfer it; the property will not go to my heirs on my death, nor will it go to my trustee in bankruptcy for the benefit of my creditors should I go insolvent.[19]

Our conclusion is the following: rights, one of whose incidents is that of succession, are those rights whose identity is independent of the right bearer, and this can be made sense of both for transmissible personal rights and transmissible rights *in rem*. In the case of assignable personal rights like debts or shares, the identity of the right *is* dependent on the identity of the duty ower: the right to be paid £10 by C is individuated both by the duty to pay £10, and by its being C that has to pay it. In the case of property rights in tangibles, the right is independent in both directions; the fact that the class of duty owers who have the duty not to interfere with the tangible property of others fluctuates (as does the class of persons who might receive the property by way of transfer, inheritance, and so on) does not mean that the right does not persist.

I must now deal with a recent objection to this way of looking at things, which has been raised both by Avihay Dorfman and Christopher Essert. I have claimed that the duty not to trespass on Blackacre is a general, impersonal duty, owed by everyone to whomever happens to be the owner of Blackacre at a given time. In consequence, I have claimed that the title to the fee simple in Blackacre persists as the same title, as it passes from owner to owner, since the correlative duty to the owner's right to immediate, exclusive possession remains the same through those transfers. Both Dorfman[20] and Essert[21] claim that under this conception, the title holder of property is reduced to a mere beneficiary of a general duty not to interfere with the property of others. And if that is so, there is no basis, at least no obvious basis, for the title holder's having any particular standing to bring a claim against a trespasser. The injury committed by a trespasser, on this account, is an injury to the practice as a whole, or a general reduction of the good provided by people observing such a general duty, not an injury that is, normatively speaking, done *to* the title holder. Another way of putting the point is that my conception denies the *bilateral* normativity, or *bilateral* relationality, that exists between the trespasser and the title holder. Not only does the absence of this bilaterality make it mysterious why the title holder is entitled to bring the claim in trespass, this absence also seems to take property rights out of the realm of private law in which, founded as it is on a notion of corrective justice, the bilateral relationship of claimant and defendant is an essential feature.

I think this argument, just like the Hohfeldian individuation argument, needs to be met head on. We all agree that being the beneficiary of someone's observing their duty does not entitle one to bring a claim when that duty is breached. Non-party beneficiaries of contracts who suffer as a result of a breach normally have no

---

[19] Rob Chambers points out to me that *Re Ellenborough Park* 1956 has something of a similar structure to my roaming potentate example. In that case the owner of the fee simple and those to whom he granted easements had a right to use a park as a pleasure ground. The fee simple owner and the easement holders are equally without a duty not to enter the park, but only the fee simple owner has the powers of title, to bring a claim against trespassers, for example, or to grant new easements or licences to use the park.

[20] Dorfman 2012, 579.   [21] Essert 2013, 6–12.

claim, nor do non-title holders who suffer as a consequence of a trespass to land. But there is nothing in any theory of rights of which I am aware that says that being a beneficiary of a duty *cannot* be a ground for having a correlative right, in particular a correlative power to make a claim when (1) a duty is breached, and (2) one suffers as a consequence of that breach. From the fact that *everyone* who suffers as the consequence of a breach of a duty, whether general or special, has not *ipso facto* had their rights violated, so that they are entitled to bring a claim against the wrongdoer, it does not follow that *no one* who suffers from a breach has had their rights violated, and is therefore entitled to make a claim. Another way of putting this is to say that a right bearer is the beneficiary of a duty which was imposed in his interest. It does not follow that the duty was imposed *only* in his interest. It is just to say that *the duty* (singular) was imposed in his interest, amongst others'. That there are particular beneficiaries of a general duty not to trespass who, in virtue of their title to individual properties, are the correlative right holders and entitled to bring claims for trespass is, I claim, the very structure of the normative situation between title holders and those with a duty not to trespass.

We can sharpen the sense of this normative structure by, once more, focusing on the impersonal nature of the duty. Dorfman says that I confuse the 'generality' of the duty with its 'impersonality', and thus mistakenly deny the relationality of the duty to the right, i.e. that the duty is owed by every individual to every property owner in respect of each of his tangible properties.[22] But in my view the relationship between generality and impersonality is explanatory; they are not categories of rights to be opposed. It is because a duty is impersonal, that is, can be conceived of and complied with in the absence of any facts about both the identity of the beneficiary (the title holder), and whose goods are which,[23] that it can be general, i.e. that everyone can have it. But the fact that a duty is impersonal and general of course does not mean that when it is violated an individual will not be the particular person to suffer from the violation. The duty not to trespass is in this respect no different from the duty not to injure others.

Now this leads us to consider the intuitive, or rhetorical, force of the idea that I owe each individual a bilaterally structured duty not to violate his right to his person, and to each individual a bilaterally structured duty not to trespass against each of his tangible properties. Let me deal with the rhetorical aspect first. It seems to me that there are two cases in which we would frame the normative situation as a bilateral relation. The first is when we are trying to impress upon someone the *generality* of the duty, that is, that one is not entitled to pick and choose the individuals that benefit from it. So whilst we all learn the duty not to violate the persons and property of others as a general duty, we may say, for example, to someone who has violated such a duty, injuring X, 'You owe a duty to X not to trespass on X's property', or 'You owe *that* duty as much to X as you do to anyone else'. But this is just a way of emphasizing that the duty is imposed in the interest of

[22] Dorfman 2012, at 570. At 570 Dorfman also says that I conceive the duties to 'run from duty holders to the *legal practice as a whole*' (his italics), but I've never said that.
[23] See the 'car park' example; Penner 1997 at 75.

everyone, not select individuals. It does not follow that *the* duty is merely a series of duties owed to individuals' bodily and property rights one by one. The other situation is when a breach has occurred. It is natural to say that by committing a trespass, one has violated X's rights, as indeed one has. But, I claim, it does not follow from this that the duty one has breached was one owed *specifically* to X and only to X.

The easiest way to see this[24] is to compare this impersonal, general duty to the nature of a rule; we do not conceive of rules as being the sum of the occasions for their application. The arithmetic rule of addition is positively *misconceived* if thought of as some sort of infinite normative entity simply because the occasions for its application are infinite. Something similar, I argue, is true of our duty not to trespass, either against persons or against their property. One way of elaborating the similarity is the idea of being normatively 'stretched' or burdened. Having got the rule of addition down, one should not feel 'burdened' when one is introduced to negative integers—negative integers may make life more complicated, but they do not make the rule a 'bigger rule'. One has simply been brought to understand that the rule of addition has wider application than one understood it to have before.

Similarly, note the difference between typical duties *in personam*, like contractual duties, and the duty *in rem* not to trespass against the body or tangible property of others. The more promissory or contractual obligations I have, the more I *am* truly normatively burdened.[25] Each paper I promise to get in by a certain deadline imposes another such burden. But do I feel the same way when a person is born? True it is that, as a matter of fact, there is one more person around whom I might injure by committing a trespass to the person, but it seems to me just intuitively false to say that my normative situation has changed. There is just another possible instance in which my duty not to trespass against the person might be engaged. There might be many reasons to worry about overpopulation, but to worry about it because one feels that it imposes an intolerable burden on one not to trespass against others seems crazy. Or take the case where A uses his paint to paint his car, so that the paint accedes to the car, thus extinguishing the property right in the paint. Should I think 'Phew—what a relief, one less duty not to trespass to worry about'? That seems to me also to be a crazy perspective to take.

It is wrong to think that these considerations only have intuitive force because we are discussing duties 'not to do', so that multiplying these negative duties cannot, in principle, be regarded as burdensome; the intuition I am exploring applies just as much to powers. Every time someone is born, and every time someone appropriates an unowned thing, one might regard that as an increase in one's normative opportunities—I can contract with another person that I couldn't before, I can offer to buy that property (rather than go appropriate some similar one myself), etc. Should I now feel that my normative power to enter contracts is *enhanced* by these

[24] I was much helped by Nick Sage in clarifying my thoughts on this point.
[25] I should say this is true of duties which correlate with *general* rights *in personam* as well, the most clear case being the right to the care of one's parents. As a parent, I am normatively burdened by each additional child I have.

and other like events? We must distinguish between the normative and the empirical.[26] As a matter of fact, my interests might be implicated in various ways when the world is overpopulated, when a catastrophe causes the loss of many lives, when someone else appropriates property or destroys property, and so on. But that does not mean my general duties and general normative powers are diminished or enlarged. But that is exactly what the Essert and Dorfman objection would seem to entail. In other words, the insistence on bilaterality they propose would require this counter-intuitive notion of normative fluctuation, another version of the Hohfeldian fluctuation problem which we have already shown to be misconceived.

In view of this, what *is* the consideration that picks out the individual whose body it is as the relevant beneficiary of the duty not to trespass against the person, and the property owner as the relevant beneficiary of the duty not to trespass against tangible things? To answer this fully would be to give a complete theory of private right, but the following, I suggest, will do for our purposes here: the beneficiary is the one whose purposive agency is most centrally implicated by the breach of the duty. In the case of a person and his body this seems perfectly obvious, though it is worthwhile remembering that it is not conceptually truistic. Where there is an institution of slavery in place, the legally recognized beneficiary of the duty would not be the individual whose body it is. The example of slavery makes us see that the concept of title has work to do even in the case of the right to bodily security. It is the person who has all the normative powers to enter into relations with others in respect of this body, or in respect of this thing, whose purposive agency is most implicated when a trespass occurs. It is the person who can consent to others touching this body, who can obligate this body to carry out a contract of personal service, who is liable when this body causes injury to another, who is the obvious beneficiary of the general duty not to commit trespass to the person. *Mutatis mutandis* with title to property and the general duty not to trespass on the tangible property of others: the person who is identified as the right-bearing, power-holding beneficiary of the duty not to trespass is the person in whom all the incidents, not just the possessory incidents, of the property reside, i.e. the one who has title: the person with the powers to license entry and transfer the property, the person in respect of whom other transmitting events will apply (inheritance on death, transfer to a trustee in bankruptcy on insolvency, etc.), the person in respect of whom other incidents, such as liability to property tax, will arise.

Dorfman also argues[27] that on the general, impersonal characterization of the duty not to trespass, property owners are conceived of as mere 'patients of the practice of property', not the agents that they are. Well, insofar as an owner's rights correlate with the duty not to trespass, the owner *is* conceived passively. Dorfman seems to want us to conceive owners as active agents as regards every incident of their title. He says:[28]

The duty (not to trespass) is *not* a mere restriction on using another's means, *tout court*. Instead, the duty would more accurately be described as prohibiting the *unauthorized* use of

---

[26] Here I pursue a line of thought that originates in Sage 2012.
[27] Dorfman 2012, 573–5.   [28] Dorfman 2012, 574, his italics.

another's means. And, therefore, the existence of a restriction in every given case is the *conclusion* of a prior process of inferring whether, and in what ways and to what extent, the means in question are, in fact, restricted—it all comes down to the (relational) question of authorization as given *by* the right holder.

Indeed, the giving of permission to enter one's property—the authority to fix the normative standings of others in relation to an object—does not merely serve to *excuse* duty holders from liability for trespass; for it is more accurately constitutive of whether there is a duty not to commit trespass to begin with. . . . [T]he very existence of the duty [not to trespass] depends on the judgment of each and every right holder with respect to the normative standing of each and every duty holder in relation to each and every piece of owned property.

But, with respect, this, surely, is just false. There is no general legal duty to infer what a title holder intends about what access he would authorize if asked. And 'the authority to fix the normative standings of others', in this context, is simply the power to license what would otherwise be a trespass. We could take away the power to license and that wouldn't change the character of the duty not to trespass. The duty not to trespass is conceptually prior, and it is a duty of which the title holder is a passive recipient.[29] That's a good thing—otherwise every owner would have to fix the boundary of his property with every other individual. If that were the case, then Dorfman would be right, and such duties not to trespass would be just the bilateral, personal duties he seeks to find; but it would be a normative nightmare, happily one unrealized by any extant legal system.

Dorfman also argues[30] that, as a matter of fact, the impersonality of the situation of the title holder vis-à-vis everyone else who has the duty not to trespass varies—in many cases, Dorfman claims, the duty ower knows precisely who the right bearer is. I myself claimed that when there is just 'one owner of everything', the duty not to trespass will be seen as being *in personam*,[31] and Dorfman takes the significance of this to be that, on my view, a duty not to trespass will in one case be impersonal, and another personal, depending on the circumstances, and this makes my account of the general duty not to trespass a matter of empirical factors, essentially the transaction costs of getting to know title holders and the extent of their stuff. This is misconceived. The example I gave of someone who owned everything was not intended to show that if it were easy to find out who the owner is, then the duty would be *in personam*. The aim of that example was to suggest that, where there was only one person who had the benefit of a general duty not to trespass, it would make sense in that case to conceive of his corresponding right on the Hohfeldian multital model, not because he was easily identified as an empirical matter, but because in principle there was no possibility that the duty could be owed to anyone else. Dorfman appears to believe, or appears to believe that I must accept, that where Y, the holder of the duty not to trespass, knows X, the holder of the title to

---

[29] The person in a coma, or the person who has no interest in dealing with others, is just as much the rightful beneficiary of the duty not to trespass on the property of others irrespective of the fact that they cannot or will not engage with others over their property boundaries.

[30] Dorfman 2012, 575–8.   [31] Penner 1997, 27, cited by Dorfman 2012, 577.

Blackacre, Y has a duty to X, a duty *in personam*, not to trespass on Blackacre. But this is wrong as a matter of principle. The duty, such as it is, is owed by Y *to X* contingently; it is in fact owed to X and any successor to X. That's the thing about transmissible rights—as a matter of principle, you can never tell for certain whose ox is being gored. X might have expired after being hit by a bolt of lightning just as you set foot on Blackacre, and his successor might be someone you know nothing about, who lives in another jurisdiction, perhaps, someone about whose intentions regarding restrictions on access you could infer precisely nothing. It is that feature of property rights which sets the 'single owner' case apart. In that case, there is no possibility of successors in title. If any of this has to do with information costs, it would have nothing to do with finding out about the here and now; it would be a matter of predicting the future.

One last point. The claim that bilaterality and private law go hand in hand, such that any duty conceived as a general, impersonal duty, such as the duty not to interfere with the property of others, must be regarded as a duty of public law, or at least not as a duty of private law, is, I would suggest, misconceived. Private law in the first instance concerns the rights, duties, powers, and liabilities we have in respect of other persons and they have in respect of us just because we are persons. Corrective justice, on the other hand, is that part of private law which concerns cases where things have gone wrong, where those rights have been violated, where those powers are purportedly validly exercised but in fact are not, and so on, *and* where the appropriate legal response is one which can be pursued by granting claims to individuals, rather than to the community at large or to the state. The ideal world would be one in which there was no corrective justice, because nothing had gone wrong; such a world would still contain *private law*, that is all the norms whose observance, in the case of rights and duties, and whose rightful exercise, in the case of powers, would protect and facilitate the interests of people acting as purposeful agents. It should be perfectly obvious that corrective justice, however we understand it, is parasitic upon the primary structure of rights, duties, powers, and so on which exist prior to any violations, invalid purported exercises of powers, and so on. If it turns out, as I claim, that title to property has a non-bilateral structure, then so be it. Corrective justice will just have to live with that.

Here I have proposed a solution to what some have seen to be a problem about the transmissibility of rights; at this point I am not in a position to deny that there may be other solutions. Two others have recently been proposed. Christopher Essert[32] argues that we should conceive of ownership as an office, and the transmission of property as a succession of office holders. In this volume Lisa Austin proposes a new notion of correlativity between the right to possess and the duty not to trespass, as a relation of omnilaterality, in which all are both owners and non-owners and a transfer is pictured as the moving from one status to the other on the part of the parties to it. It is beyond the scope of this already long chapter to interrogate these views in detail, but I would point out one difference between my

---

[32] Essert 2013.

account and both of theirs. Both Essert's and Austin's views of property depend upon the institution of conventional rules of trespass to make sense of the nature of a property right;[33] my account does not. I have not had to cite any conventions, or even rules of law, to elaborate my impersonal characterization of the rights, powers, and duties, which make the idea that a right is transmissible a plausible one. I think that is an advantage, for it would at least allow us to pursue the idea that transmissible rights may be justified as natural or universal rights, that is, rights which do not depend upon the institution of a legal system or state. As I shall claim in Section 4, property rights can be justified as rights of this kind, and it would be unfortunate if the very possibility of justifying property rights as natural rights were foreclosed by the kind of theoretical elaboration that Essert and Austin give them.

4. Justifying Transmissible Rights

I now turn to the second of the questions with which we began, whether and how transmissible rights can be justified.

The first issue to consider, given that a right to immediate, exclusive possession of a tangible is one thing, and the power to transfer title to it another, is whether these norms have different grounding justifications, and it would seem fairly clear that they might. Consider our old friend the contractual debt to be paid £10 by C. I think it would surprise most contract theorists if you told them that, in order to justify how C might have the power to bind himself to pay A £10 by agreeing to do so, they would also, at the same time, and necessarily so as a matter of the logic of personal rights generated by agreements, have to justify A's power to assign the debt to B. On the other hand, we do tend to see the link as more essential in the case of tangibles. I think the reason why is fairly obvious on a moment's reflection. Unlike purely personal claim-rights, as a matter of the nature of things tangibles and persons are not so intimately linked. Blackacre will be around forever, so if it is always owned, necessarily it will be owned by more than one person. Chattels may outlast their owners as well. In the case of tangibles, what is mine might well have been, or might well be yours, so the idea of transmissibility is, in that sense, native. But as far as I can see justifying the institution of the claim-right to immediate, exclusive possession is distinct from, indeed logically prior to, justifying any rules of succession, including of course the power of an incumbent to transfer it. Before one can justify a power to transfer, one must know *what* is to be transferred, and whether having that 'what' is justified in the first place. The same, of course, applies to the question of transferring intangible rights; there is no point in working out the details of assigning the rights under a hit man's contract if it turns out (as happens to be the case) that no one has the power to create such contracts in the first place.

The key to my non-conventional justification of the right to transfer property is the idea, which typifies the work of Raz and Gardner,[34] that humans, as part of

---

[33] Essert 2013, 15–20; in contrast to Essert's account, I would say that an owner occupies not an office, but what he would call a 'role'; Austin this volume.

[34] Raz 1975; Raz 2011; Gardner 2007.

their cognitive endowment, are able to respond to facts *as reasons*. That is, humans regard features of the world[35] as giving them reasons for acting in various ways, and to understand rational human behaviour is to understand how they operate with respect to reasons. Raz famously distinguished between the case where one is not subject to an exclusionary reason, where rationality requires that one weigh up all the various reasons for acting in one way rather than another and then decide to act in the way indicated by the balance of reasons, and the case where one is subject to an exclusionary reason. The most important and interesting kind of exclusionary reason is a moral reason. A moral reason is one which prevails over (at least some of) those reasons which are one's current personal goals. Though my (perfectly rational and acceptable) current personal goal is to finish this chapter, if you stumbled through my door requiring immediate medical attention I would be under a moral obligation to stop writing and help you get it. Our question here, then, is whether in light of this ability of human beings to respond to reasons, and respond in particular to exclusionary, moral, reasons, we can explain the transmissibility of property rights, in particular the power to transfer, without making reference to conventions. I think we can. To get the sense of this non-conventional approach to powers, let us first consider Shiffrin's non-conventional justification of the power to authorize what would otherwise be a battery.

4.1 The power to authorize what would otherwise be a battery

Shiffrin states:[36]

One could imagine a conception of autonomy without consent in which an agent exercised complete sovereignty over her body and other personal spaces, such as the home, but had no ability to share or transfer these powers to others. That is, the agent could not grant consent to others to exercise these powers in lieu of or alongside herself. Such a structure is imaginable but so impoverished as to be utterly implausible. As Joseph Raz has argued, the development and realization of our central autonomous capacities requires a diverse and rich set of meaningful options. Rights of autonomous control that were inalienable to this degree would render (morally) impossible real forms of meaningful human relationships and the full definition and recognition of the self (not to mention making medical and dental care cumbersome, dangerous, and awfully painful). To forge meaningful relationships, embodied human beings must have the ability to interact within the same physical space, to share the use of property, and to touch one another. They must therefore be able to empower particular people. A plausible account of autonomy would have to reject the isolation the constricted model of self-sovereignty would enforce as inconsistent with affording opportunities to lead a decent life and realize one's central capacities. It would have to include the power of consent to share at least some of the powers associated with self-sovereignty.

This passage is a most compelling statement of what might be called the 'social thesis', the thesis that the 'default' characterization of human existence for the purposes of exploring interpersonal morality is not that of a hermit in some state of

---

[35] Entities, properties, events, causal and other relations, the lot.
[36] Shiffrin 2008, 501–2.

nature who shares no interests with others, but one in which interpersonal relations of real significance are native or natural to human existence. As such, those normative means, like the power to consent to be touched by another or to make agreements, which make those interpersonal relations possible, are not some cultural achievement which we could plausibly be without, but are part and parcel of our natural endowments, in the same way as our basic responsiveness to reasons makes us (in part) the kind of creatures that we are.

I am not sure how much weight Shiffrin wishes to place on the Razian considerations of autonomy she cites; I would not place much. It seems to me that, considerations of the value of autonomy to one side, what her characterization of the importance of the power to consent makes plain is the ability of different individuals to respond to the same reason, not only when the interest is one they might share (forming a meaningful relationship), but even where the reason in question is an interest of only one of them (to have some dental work done). If this is right, then in order to explain the norms of property, all we have to do is make plausible that these norms are exclusionary reasons to which we would naturally respond in the appropriate social context. I take it that the preceding passage more than makes plausible the case for the power to consent to what would otherwise be a battery, so we can move on.

4.2 The right to immediate, exclusive possession of property

Imagine coming out of the woods and finding some fish neatly piled on the riverbank, or a basket of apples. I take it that you would not regard the fish or the apples just being there in that state as the result of some natural process, or, more precisely, since humans are part of nature, some process in which human agency was not involved. You would assume the fish to have been caught, and the apples gathered, by some person or persons. My sense is that you would understand that to grab the fish or the apples would be to interfere with some other human agent's purposive activity and that, understanding the interest people have in the success of their purposive activity, you would understand it to be wrong to take the fish or the apples, i.e. you would understand yourself to have a duty not to interfere with them. The duty would not be an absolute one, of course, but that is not the issue. Rather, respect for the interest that others have in the fulfilment of their purposes and the fish's and apples' contribution to that in this case could be cognitively assimilated, that is, understood by you, as a reason not to interfere which would prevail over your current, personal, goals, such that it would be both rational and reasonable to regard yourself to be under a duty not to interfere. Again, the point is not at this stage to determine the stringency of the duty, just its possibility. No convention is required here, just an understanding of human nature and the nature of the world in which we operate (it has fish, it has apples, they are edible, the former need to be caught and the latter need to be gathered, and so on). Much the same could be said about other appropriations, such as fencing off land to keep one's cattle in, planting a field, building a dwelling, and so on, although the judgments here require greater subtlety, and the reason for this greater subtlety is just that land, conceived of as a location, or space, can be used in different, and non-competitive ways. Moreover, this respect of the agency of others extends beyond the case of humans. Imagine you observe a bird laboriously constructing a nest over the course of several hours. I am not sure whether birds have rights, but I do think the bird's interest in the success of this project is a reason for you to forbear from smashing the nest just for the hell of it. A child who did so would quite properly be scolded.

Seeing the right to immediate exclusive possession as not requiring a convention deepens our appreciation of the way that the duty *in rem* not to interfere with the tangibles of others is general. Again, the key is responsiveness to reasons. The reason why the duty is general—and this is the systematic element of the duty not to interfere with property which can be mistaken for conventional—is that the responsiveness to reasons that gives rise to a right of possession are not personal to the individual appropriator; we deceive ourselves on this point when we think of coming across the caught fish lying on the bank or the apples gathered in the basket and naturally appreciate that it was a particular person or group of persons who did the fishing or gathering. But the reason is not personal to them; it reflects the way that human agency gives rise to reasons. We have a duty not to grab the fish or dump the apples out of the basket not because of 'fish exploitation reasons' or 'apple valuation reasons' that are relative to the particular appropriator, any more than we think the reason not to smash the bird's nest is a reason which applies only to that particular bird. We have that duty because of our reasons for respecting purposive human agency generally insofar as that involves engagement with the tangible resources of the world. We are not concerned with the particular uses or goals that the right holder has for the tangibles which he appropriates, just *that they are appropriated*.

At this stage of the argument I must emphasize that I am only justifying the right to immediate exclusive possession, not 'full-blown' title, with the power to transfer, and so on. I set out to justify those further incidents below. Nor am I, as I said at the outset of this section, saying that this right is absolute. Not all appropriations ought to be respected, any more than every agreement (e.g. to murder someone) ought to be respected. Nor am I saying that any engagement with the material world should be respected *as an appropriation giving rise to a right to immediate exclusive possession*. Consider the case of arrows marked in chalk dust on wilderness trails helping people find their bearings.[37] I should regard it as wrong of me to rub them out for no reason, but at the same time it is not because anyone has an immediate right to exclusive possession of these marks.

In the case of genuine appropriations, it is important to see that no compact or convention is needed to understand how this responsiveness to the reasons that the presence of human agency brings to the table is *reciprocal*, working just as much for the individual duty ower as for the right bearer whose right is respected. A particularly misleading rhetorical trope that arises in discussions of the justification of property needs to be addressed here. In looking at justifications of property, one often hears that the right to immediate exclusive possession needs to be justified by the right

---

[37] I owe the example to Rob Chambers.

bearers to the duty owers, or that property requires that 'non-owners' have a duty to respect the rights of owners. I think it should be obvious, but I shall say it anyway, that this gives arguments against the justifiability of property an unwarranted rhetorical advantage, assuming as it does that there is a class of owners on the one hand, and a class of non-owners on the other. That is clearly false. Non-owners are themselves just other owners, in *exactly* the same way as all bearers of the duty not to batter others are also, reciprocally, each bearers of the right not to be battered. Now, what is obviously lurking behind this rhetorical trope is a concern that the distribution of property rights might well be unjust, and so it is. But for reasons I have laboured elsewhere,[38] this question is distinct, and logically subsequent, to determining the justice of a right to immediate exclusive possession per se. Let me try to put the point, on this occasion, by considering the justification of the power to enter binding contracts, and the bindingness of the duties to which its exercise gives rise.

The power to enter binding contracts has just as many (perhaps more) implications for distributive injustice as the power to appropriate the tangibles of the earth does. I take this to be straightforwardly true. Yet contract theorists do not regard the 'distributive justice' problem which, let me insist, *essentially* arises as a consequence of empowering people to enter into binding contracts, as their first priority in determining the justification of a power to enter into contracts. What contract theorists ask, and quite rightly, is what moral considerations would support A's and B's being able to undertake voluntary obligations to each other just by agreeing to do so. Only having got that justification under their belts could they then proceed if they wanted to, and many do not, to see whether the distributive implications of acknowledging a power to enter into binding agreements, which from first principles seems to be acceptable, are so disastrous that this prima facie acceptability is eclipsed. By the way, I take the distributive infelicities of the general power to enter into binding agreements more seriously than I do the distributive infelicities of the power to appropriate unowned tangibles and the rights to immediate, exclusive possession to which its exercise gives rise. Leaving state action aside and sticking to private actions 'within the law', surely far more people have been screwed because of the systemic inequalities in the market economy, that is, of the systemic inequalities concerning information asymmetries, bargaining power, and so on, that bedevil the justice of contract formation and enforcement, than have been screwed by the actions of first appropriators, who are often feckless and sell their newly minted appropriations for a song to those who are 'good' at bargains. Consider the mythic sod-busting first appropriators of the 19th-century United States west. No one can seriously contend that *they* were the economic victors as opposed to the robber baron railway owners who controlled the markets for their produce.

4.3 The power to license and to give property away

I have discussed this at length elsewhere[39] and it also follows from Shiffrin's point above: ownership does not impose a condition of isolation. The 'wall' provided by

---

[38] Penner 1997, 2009.   [39] Penner 1996b; 1997, 74–5; 2006.

the right to immediate, exclusive possession has a 'gate'. We share property, for obvious reasons, and the most extensive 'licence to share' is the power to give, for only by having the power to give may I have the power to serve my interests in a thing where my interest lies in someone else's flourishing (my interest in their best interests).

4.4 The power to sell or transfer pursuant to an agreement

The question here is whether the appreciation of the interests of others, which I take to be necessary for the formation of agreements, as reasons that can be exclusionary reasons for oneself, is available in the absence of conventions for individuals to be able to enter binding agreements.

Elsewhere[40] I have described bargain agreements as agreements between strangers, which I explained to be cases where the parties did not share interests in each other's welfare or in some shared joint project (though I did question, given that there are all sorts of contracts where this is not the case, such as contracts of employment, long-term supply contracts, and relational contracts of various kinds, whether the bargain between strangers should be the paradigm it seems to be in contract law theory).[41] Nor in the case of bargains are parties usually in a position to help shape or reveal the interests of the other (the patter of certain sales people notwithstanding). Nevertheless, it would be a mistake to characterize bargains purely in terms of self-interest, narrowly conceived:[42]

It is often assumed that in a true bargain, one is supposed to disregard the interests of the other party, paying attention only to one's own. As a practical matter, in the limiting case of some simple transaction, such as the purchase of an umbrella, the interests of the other party hardly rise to consciousness; one simply goes through with the transaction. But generally, not only is this a poor bargaining strategy, it involves a misconception of the relationship bargainers have to each other's interests. In a bargain, parties do serve the interests of another, by acting in accordance with the normative character of the transaction (e.g. selling only what one has title or power to sell) or by performing executory undertakings. Each party therefore must 'take on board' the interests of the other—as defined by the agreement—by treating the agreement as an exclusionary reason guiding his or her behaviour. The value of bargains, indeed their nobility, is that this relationship of obligation and trust permits strangers voluntarily to treat the interests of each other as reasons guiding their behaviour.

Given the possibility of interactions between strangers, is the absence of conventions for agreeing fatal to their ability to enter into binding agreements because they cannot give the necessary commitments?

Consider Scanlon's example[43] of two hunters in a state of nature. They are on facing river banks, and one has thrown his spear to the opposite bank, the other his boomerang. Can they cooperate, promise each other, agree to return their weapons to each other? I want first to say that I am a little put off by the set-up to this story.

---

[40] Penner 1996b, 337–9.   [41] Penner 1996b, 341–3.
[42] Penner 1996b, 338.   [43] Scanlon 1998, 296–7.

Why not start (surely more plausibly) with the case where A, standing on his side of the river with his spear, sees B's boomerang sail over the river and land on his side. Now B appears, seeking his boomerang. It seems obvious to me that what A should and would do is just toss it back to him. Humans are responsive to reasons, and this includes the interests which others have.[44] Whilst on occasion one might have reasons for not doing this (B is a warrior intent on harming A, A simply hasn't the time, etc.), it is implausible that A would, as a constitutive matter of his stranger-hood vis-à-vis B, be *unable to appreciate* the interest of B, and thus not be able to take it on board as a reason for his action. Similarly, A would be able to realize his mistake if, after throwing it over to B, a third hunter, C, turned up beside him and jumped up and down, mimicking that he had thrown it, and thus that it was his (at which stage A sheepishly recalls that a boomerang tends to return in an arc). None of this requires any convention.

Now, consider another case. Child minder A is walking along the river past B, a stranger, when A's child falls into the water. If hunters can appreciate the interests that strange hunters have in their weapons, then I take it that B, a human, can recognize another human's interest in retrieving his child, stranger or not. Now let us assume that the only way A can retrieve the child is with the cooperation of B; say A needs B to hold onto a branch on the river bank and hold his hand out to A so he can reach the child. I don't see how we could doubt the possibility of this cooperation taking place. It seems like the most natural thing in the world, this cooperation forced by circumstances. Assuming that it is not perverse for B to consider the interests of the child and A as sufficiently motivating B to act the way he does, what motivation is there for denying B the facility of assuring A that he can trust him? If there is such a facility we can easily account for the intuition that B would do wrong if, just when A was about to reach the child, B wrested his hand from A's grasp, sending A into the river himself. In keeping with the preceding reliance upon the human responsiveness to reasons, it is just implausible to deny that we have an ability to respond to those reasons such that we could act in a coordinated fashion, *in concert* as it were.

If this is right, then cooperative activity in which people can be assured that others will play their part is no mystery, since it only turns on being responsive to reasons concerning the interests of others and their purposive activities that may be significant enough to serve as exclusionary reasons. The most obvious applications of such responsiveness to reasons generating the norms of cooperative activity is a division of labour and the trading of property. The fact that the division of labour is all too readily instantiated by conventional relations of status and domination does not undermine this—consider all the task-specific coordinations of behaviour that no conventional division of labour could possibly provide for.[45] As for the trading

---

[44] I am assuming there is no obvious hostile intent in this situation, but Scanlon assumes this as well.

[45] The fact that in a particular society women are the gatherers and men the hunters does not mean that within those broad divisions, women will not need to coordinate their gathering behaviour through agreements amongst themselves, and the same goes for the male hunters; furthermore, the gatherers and hunters as groups are likely to have to enter into task-specific coordination agreements.

of property, the power to enter into an agreement under which one transfers one's property to another, again the rationale in terms of fulfilling our interests is obvious. At its most basic level the trade of goods is simply the reification of the division of labour, turning it into the exchange of things. Marx made us see that this can have very deleterious ideological consequences, but the point here is that if any sort of division of labour that operates by way of agreement makes sense in the absence of convention, it is difficult to see how one could draw a line between that and the agreement to exchange goods, insisting the latter to depend upon conventions. So, on the basis of these considerations, it would seem that the power to exchange goods, a 'power to sell', is just as natural and not reliant upon convention as any of the other norms of ownership we have looked at.

4.5 The liability to execution

I only want to say a little here. When I speak of the liability to execution I do not mean to conjure up the idea of statutory insolvency regimes. The idea is that, on the basis, again, of simple human responsiveness to reasons, we can appreciate that we might come under obligations to dispose of our property that arise 'by operation of morality'. I am, of course, transposing the notion 'by operation of law' to morality, but that is perfectly licit, since all I am claiming is that we might come under moral obligations that arise, not because of the exercise of any normative power (such as the power to undertake obligations voluntarily), but because of various events that might occur. The obvious case is that of my wrongfully injuring another. This may give rise to any number of obligations on my part—to apologize, to help you overcome the injury, and so on—but take the simplest case of my wrongfully, say negligently, injuring some of your goods; say I eat your pineapple, mistaking it for my own. The most obvious remedial response here would be for me to give you my pineapple, the one I thought I was eating. More generally, I might have more abstract duties to compensate you in some way, and the best way of doing so might be by transferring you some of my property. Again, no conventions are necessary for me to respond to your interest in having the loss I caused you remedied by doing what I can to mitigate that loss, and that may involve requiring me to transfer my property to you in some cases. Indeed, all of us in the vicinity may come under a duty to transfer property to you where your interests are severely affected, even if not caused by any wrong committed by anyone. If your larder is swept away by a tornado outside the hunting and gathering season, the only reasonable and rational response to the reasons in play may be that we all fall under an exclusionary reason to contribute some of our stored food.

There is a sense, therefore, in which everyone is personally interested in the 'wherewithal' of others, all the economic assets at their disposal. This is broader than one's property, of course, for remedial assistance can also be rendered by human action, but it certainly includes the property one owns.

5. A Last Word on Conventions and Social Contexts

Throughout Section 4, I aimed to show that conventions are unnecessary for the justifications of some of the central norms of ownership, in particular the power to transfer. Let me say now what I think prompts the conventionalist's thoughts in this neck of the normative woods. It is a confusion between convention and social context, with all the local, cultural, and historical dimensions that social context makes us notice. It roughly matches Hart's confusion of, and thus his failure to distinguish between, rule-governed practices and cases where people merely act in accordance with generally accepted reasons.[46] That a way of behaving necessarily arises in a social context and does so because people respond to reasons to which they are all, in general, capable of responding, does not mean that such a way of behaving is conventional. Such behaviours, akin to the behaviour of tool-use, may become conventional, but are not inherently a matter of adopting conventions. The conventionalist will find his worries assuaged if he just regards consent, promises, and property rights and powers as responses to reasons, responses which humans are generally capable of having. And on that happy note, we may conclude.

[46] Raz 1975, 53–7.

12

Psychologies of Property (and Why Property is not a Hawk/Dove Game)

Carol M. Rose

Writers on property have generated an array of viewpoints about the psychological states associated with the institution. The bulk of these views take the perspective of the person who owns something, and they theorize or speculate on why it matters to people to be able to claim ownership.[1] In this chapter, I will designate this perspective the view from the 'inside'—that is, the property owner's perspective on his or her own situation—and I will briefly describe a range of the reasons that writers have given for the importance of owning things.

But my more serious interest is in what I will designate the 'outside' perspective, the psychological state of the *non*-owner, who is confronted regularly with things that belong to others. By the non-owner, I do not necessarily mean to signify persons who own little or nothing themselves, but I rather use this term more situationally, to designate those who in any particular instance observe but do not own the thing observed. It is this outside perspective that is of greatest interest in this chapter—that is, the non-owner's recognition of and heed to the ownership claims of others. I will argue that the outside perspective is critically important to the success or failure of property regimes, but that the non-owner's psychological state is not well understood.

One theory in particular identifies the non-owner as a 'dove' in a Hawk/Dove game, but I will argue that the hawk/dove analysis of property has serious flaws—not the least of which is the psychological state suggested by the dove role. A more promising avenue might be to note the relationship of the non-owner to a cooperative first mover in a tit-for-tat game, but here too the ultimate psychology remains somewhat mysterious, or as Jon Elster calls it, magical.[2]

But I will begin with the inside perspective, focusing on some psychological states that have been said to accompany property ownership. While there is considerably more to be said on the subject,[3] the following pages give a very rough summary of that topic.

---

[1] See e.g. a very interesting survey of psychological aspects of property, almost entirely focused on the perspective of the owner or claimant: Blumenthal 2009.
[2] Elster 1989, 194–202.   [3] See e.g. Blumenthal 2009.

1. The Inside Perspective

How does an owner feel about owning her things? Quite good, according to most writers on the subject, so good that she is thought to be considerably more reluctant to give up what she has than to try to get something of equal or greater value that is merely in prospect.[4] Indeed, although there are a few spoilsport dissenters, most attribute a larger social good to the good feelings that property gives to owners. Some of the theories on the topic overlap, but they can still be divided into several categories, on the understanding that these are not airtight.

1.1 Identity formation

Among legal theorists of property, the one who is probably most associated with this psychological view of ownership is Margaret Radin, due to her authorship in 1980 of a now very well-known article, 'Property and Personhood'.[5] In that article, the dominant psychological picture was that property enables persons to establish and develop a sense of self. Radin did not include all property in this category, however, but rather distinguished what she called 'personhood property' from 'fungible property'. In her depiction, only the former type of property has special significance for the property holder, whereas the latter type is interchangeable and impersonal. Nor does the category of 'personhood property' define any specific objects that carry those links by their nature. Instead, in Radin's presentation, a given object can shift categories in different contexts, depending on the object's history and the emotional freight that this history gives it for a particular individual.[6] In her example, a wedding ring is personhood property in the hands of the spouse, but it is fungible property in the hands of a pawnbroker.

In the original article, many of Radin's examples concerned people's homes. A home, like a highly personal object like a wedding ring, is a thing into which one pours ones memories, affiliations, personal projects—in short, the control of these kinds of objects helps one to construct a kind of personal saga and indeed to understand one's self *as* a self.

Radin's article generated an enormous follow-up literature by other authors, much of it treating the 'personhood' analysis very positively. But it has also drawn a certain modicum of criticism. For example, it has been difficult to see what legal consequences flow from the category of personhood property, since any given object can slip in and out of that category. The article's stress on homes has attracted some hostile fire as well. Recent empirical scholarship has argued that people do not actually see their homes as central to who they are; they are more likely to cite family, friends, and professions as the dominant features of their

---

[4] For the 'endowment effect', see e.g. Kahneman, Knetsch, and Thaler 1990; Knetsch 1989.
[5] Radin 1982.
[6] Radin 1982, 959–60. For a similar depiction, see Kopytoff 1986, 64–9, describing objects as moving in and out of commodity form.

identity.[7] Perhaps not surprisingly, Radin's own scholarship has moved beyond the personhood approach to property, first in exploring the phenomenon of commodification, and later in taking up issues of intellectual property and internet commerce.[8]

Nevertheless, the idea that property plays a role in identity formation continues to have considerable resonance, perhaps as much in literature and drama as anywhere else. The examples are legion: In the book and movie *The House of Sand and Fog*, the house in question clearly has a personal significance far beyond dollar value for the characters who claim to own it.[9] Ralph Ellison's *Invisible Man* defines himself at the beginning and the end of the novel by his brightly lit subterranean space.[10] The recent Masterpiece Theatre series, *Downton Abbey*, shows characters that are desperate to maintain their connection with the ancestral home.[11] And on it goes. From the inside point of view, then, it is unwise to dismiss identity formation as a significant category.

1.2 Identity fashioning

A second inside perspective in the psychology of property is closely related to identity formation, even overlapping it; but it suggests an outer-directed rather than an inner-directed aspect of the uses of property. On this perspective, property enables the holder to undertake projects and especially to project a chosen image of him- or herself out into the world. The perspective is not so much how one understands one's own self, but rather how one can interact with an external world and get others to understand who one is. Property is essential to those interactions. A particularly striking example—albeit a sad one—was given in Erving Goffman's book on asylums, dating back to the early 1960s, in which the author described the entry of patients into an institution.[12] At this juncture, they lost their personal clothing, their make-up, and their dressing accessories; that is, they lost the ability to present themselves to others in the ways that they thought best. The dismay of the new entrant, seeing herself unadorned in ill-fitting institutional garb, was poignant indeed. Goffman's book went on to describe the patients' relentless quest for the most miniscule forms of property: a particular chair, a customary seat in a particular place, a hidden stash somewhere on the grounds, best of all a kind of office space—all gave the patient what Goffman described as a 'personal territory' to maintain his or her own projects.[13] At an entirely different level, Thorstein Veblen's discussion of 'conspicuous consumption' too is a form of identity fashioning through property.[14]

Taken together the identity-forming and identity-fashioning categories paint a picture in which ownership of property creates a psychological state whereby one can construct a self, first for one's own self, then for others—or perhaps the other

[7] Stern 2009, 1099–120; see also Barros 2006, 277–82 (challenging personal importance of home).
[8] E.g. Radin 1987; Radin 1996a; Radin 1996b.   [9] Dubus III 1999; Perelman 2003.
[10] Ellison 1952; see also Brown forthcoming.   [11] Fellowes 2010.
[12] Goffman 1961, 18–21.   [13] Goffman 1961, 243–54.   [14] Veblen 1899.

way around. Notice that the self that one creates for others may be something of an artifice, with clothing and cosmetics and hairpieces, not to speak of muscle cars and pricey McMansions. But it is a protective artifice, which brings us to another psychological state.

1.3 Refuge

A third variant on these insider psychological perspectives on property is one that builds on the ability of property to exclude, more or less for the purpose of getting the breathing room one needs for other projects. A well-known example is Virginia Woolf's praise of *A Room of One's Own*.[15] A person needs space and security for the sake of privacy, calm, thought; in other words, one needs property for the sake of doing the things that one wants to do in the world. Libertarian thinking builds on this protective quality of property, albeit in a somewhat more truculent vein. But here too property is seen as giving the owner the privacy and refuge to do whatever he or she likes, free from the demands of nosy neighbours. On her own property, the owner may grow an apple, eat an apple, paint an apple, throw an apple, crush an apple. Property gives her the ability to say to the world, just get out of my hair, and let me do what I want so long as I do not intrude on *your* property.[16] The most striking examples of this strand of the psychology of property describe physical property—land, space, a room. Nevertheless, owning assets of a less tangible form can serve the same purpose. Woolf's main concern, after all, was an annual income.

1.4 Empowerment

Still another psychological state associated with property refers to a political dimension. A widely known example comes from the work of the economist Milton Friedman, who argued that dictatorship is well-nigh impossible where people can freely acquire and keep property.[17] Widely dispersed property ownership creates many alternative sources of power and implicitly gives people the confidence to speak their minds without fear of reprisal. Central capital ownership and a centralized direction of the economy, on the other hand, may make political engagement dangerous for the ordinary citizen: speak up and you lose your job, or your ability to travel, or the possibility to get your children into a good school. Individual property, on the other hand, is said to bolster the courage of owners, who have less to fear from those in political power.[18]

Moreover, property arguably gives people the sense that they have 'skin in the game' in the political order, with something to say about the political activities that

---

[15] Woolf 1929. [16] Purdy 2010, 19–20. [17] Friedman 1962, 7–32.

[18] Note the pedigree of this line of thinking, going back at least to early American small-r republican thinking, where the importance of 'independence' was paramount and often focused on ownership of one's own property. See, e.g. Federal Farmer 1787–8, 253.

may affect their property.[19] In this sense, legal scholar Bernadette Atuahene argues that titling programmes in less developed countries can 'deepen democracy'.[20] One might give an example from contemporary China: private individuals have only relatively recently been allowed to own their own residences, but China's newly minted owners of condominiums have organized themselves into local, regional, and even national associations to pursue common interests, and some have been able to raise objections when governments have acted arbitrarily toward their property.[21]

In these two somewhat different senses—independence on the one hand and a stake on the other—one could see property ownership as a psychological backdrop to political engagement.

1.5. Generosity

A fifth view of the psychology of property is that property enables the owner to be generous toward others. Indeed, the encouragement of this virtue was one of Aristotle's justifications for property.[22] There is of course plenty of evidence that poor people can be very generous indeed, and there is even a theory to explain this evidence (i.e. that high-risk situations encourage sharing).[23] But at the same time, grinding penury can narrow the mind's focus to one's own immediate necessities. Having more means having more to give away; the psychological security of having assets arguably allows one to pay attention to the needs and wants of others.

1.6 Economic incentives

A sixth and very widely cited psychological state associated with property links property to economic activity. Jeremy Bentham was the great exemplar of this version of the psychology of ownership: when one feels secure in one's ownership, he argued, one is encouraged to invest time, effort, and money on the things that one owns.[24] The reason is that the secure owner will take the gains from her own prudent investments; and of course if she lazes about, failing to plan and to work, she is very likely to suffer losses. Property thus acts as a psychological carrot as well as a stick, incentivizing each owner to improve what she has; moreover, if she can safely trade with others, she and everyone else will have even more reason to improve their belongings and make them even more valuable, for circulation in a larger market.

---

[19] This is also an old idea, propounded by some who thought that enlightened monarchs would assist commercial classes for the sake of increasing tax revenue, but then would find their own control challenged by the new classes. See Rose 1989, 80–2, and sources cited therein.

[20] Atuahene 2006.   [21] Kaufman 2004, A1.

[22] Aristotle 350bc, at 1120b (liberal person pays attention to property in order to be able to give to others).

[23] Ellickson 1993, 1332–44 (communal ownership described as a version of insurance in high-risk situations).

[24] Bentham 1789, chs. 7–11, 109–22.

On Bentham's picture, then, secure ownership encourages a psychological state of optimism in which an economy thrives and capitalism flourishes. On the other side of the coin, so to speak, insecurity of property takes a psychological toll: insecurity creates worries for owners about the possibility of their own potential losses and rouses their anxious sympathy for their neighbours' losses. What is worse, widespread and repeated incursions on property, according to Bentham, cause people to become mistrustful and lethargic. This pattern causes 'the deadening of industry', with terrible consequences for the overall economic well-being of a society.[25] Many years after Bentham wrote, Harvard Law School professor Frank Michelman famously used Bentham's analysis to create a formula for calculating the damage caused by governmental takings of property, notably weighing Benthamite 'demoralization costs' against the transaction costs of compensation.[26]

1.7 An admonitory postscript

Having noted all these positive emotions flowing from property, one should observe that there are some other less attractive psychological states that have been attributed to property ownership. One pithy example was written by British novelist E. M. Forster, in a brief satiric essay entitled 'My Wood'.[27] In the essay, Forster described his state of mind when he bought a forested lot out in the country. His first reaction was that the purchase made him feel vain and, more interestingly, physically *fat*: he was now a freeholder, a person of substance. He also found that he had become anxious and rather stingy, jealous of the boundaries of his property and dismayed at the hikers who strolled through on country paths. Moreover, he felt falsely proud. A bird landed on a shrub in his wood. 'My bird', thought Forster to himself. But then he was irked when 'his' bird flew off to sample other territories. To put it in a nutshell, Forster found that property ownership made him feel possessive and self-centred—or perhaps had simply awakened these unattractive character traits that he would have preferred to leave dormant.

Views like Forster's no doubt have played a role with religious institutions that require their most serious members to renounce individual property. Monks and nuns have had to give up their individual possessions, for example. Why? because property induces people to think and behave in ways that may detract from a spiritual mission. Owning and the associated getting and spending—and simply *thinking about* owning, getting, and spending—are distractions from the major pursuits of religious orders.[28] In a pattern that presents, roughly speaking, the flip side of Radin's famous article on property as a foundation for self-definition, a religious order might consider it undesirable that the members think at all about themselves and their personal projects. There is a trace of this view—that is, of individual property's effect on the mind—in the requirement that soldiers wear standard military uniforms rather than their own chosen clothing, and even in the effort to require children to wear school uniforms. To be sure, school uniforms can

---

[25] Bentham 1789, 115–19.   [26] Michelman 1967, 1214.   [27] Forster 1936.
[28] Goffman 1961, 19–20, related monastery life to the life of inmates in an asylum.

serve a variety of purposes, for example, reducing obvious signals of class difference in the schoolroom. But one idea may be that uniforms reduce personal distractions, and help children to focus on common goals of learning. In short, insofar as property encourages people to define and develop themselves as individuals, the range of choices normally associated with individual property may be out of place where some common project takes precedence. For those kinds of projects, the task may be to reduce the importance of individualized personal property, and to constrain the choices that property usually permits.

Some have asserted that this kind of thinking was a motivation for the limitations on private property in the old Soviet Union, particularly in the days of Stalin. Supposedly the Stalinist idea was to curtail private ownership as a part of an effort to create the 'new Soviet man', the person who would not be distracted by private concerns but who would rather be devoted to the well-being of the state as a whole.[29] Utopian communities more generally have often curtailed private property ownership.[30] Here too the thought is that common projects should take precedence over individual ones, and that private property threatens to introduce attitudes of individualism that threaten the communal well-being.

Richard Pipes, a respected historian of Soviet Russia, has argued that these constraints on private property have not worked well for most people.[31] (Indeed, Pipes became so soured on the idea that he wrote an entire book in praise of private property.)[32] Pipes regards the Soviet experience as a warning about the psychological evils that may fester when people are not allowed to have or control their own property: they suffer from lassitude, apathy, cynicism, hopelessness. Economic malaise follows this spiritual malaise, of course. In short, Bentham was right after all.

In spite of Pipes's warning, however, many have experienced a kind of euphoria in giving up property, at least for some periods of time. Severe crises in particular can bring on orgies of sharing that would seem to have very little to do with the calculations of risk or insurance. Rebecca Solnit has published a book recounting a number of these experiences, interestingly titled *A Paradise Built in Hell*.[33] One of her early chapters concerns the reaction of San Francisco residents to the 1906 earthquake. Merchants opened their stores, simply giving away everything to all comers, and they were only among the more visible of the persons who gave away whatever they had to fellow survivors.[34] No doubt these experiences of joyous altruism cannot last indefinitely, but while they do, they evidently create indelible memories and great nostalgia among those who take part in them. By contrast, the psychological pleasures and payoffs of property are the stuff of more prosaic and ordinary circumstances.

2. The Outside Perspective

So far, I have been discussing the psychology of property from what I have called the inside perspective, that is, the perspective of the property holder and the

---

[29] McNeal 1963, 114.   [30] Ellickson 1993, 1344–52; Rose 2007, 1897–9.
[31] Pipes 1996.   [32] Pipes 1999.   [33] Solnit 2009.   [34] Solnit 2009, 23–9.

psychological states that have been attributed to ownership. At this point I want to go to the other side, and to consider the psychology of property from the *outside* point of view; that is to say, from the perspective of the one who takes note of the property of others.

So how does it feel to be one who is confronted with the property of others? Certainly there are many literary and folk-tale accounts of the feelings of those who observe the belongings of others. Many of these accounts paint a rather miserable or gloomy picture of the mental states at issue: in the case of the poverty-stricken, wistful noses pressed against shop windows; in the case of others who may or may not have belongings of their own (but not exactly what they want), obsequiousness and scheming, covetousness, jealousy, rage, outrage. On the other hand, some stories depict more attractive sensibilities—although perhaps they are more boring because they are more common—like honour in the face of temptation, or disgust with thievery.

As opposed to literature's not-infrequent accounts of the sensibilities of characters who observe the property of others, however, legal scholarship to date has not shown much interest in these psychological states. But a few straws in the wind nevertheless bear on the topic.

2.1. The picture from *in rem*

In legal scholarship, one such straw about the outside perspective derives from the work of Henry Smith and Thomas Merrill and their discussion of the '*in rem*' character of property, a discussion that builds on the work of British philosopher James Penner.[35] '*In rem*' is a Latin phrase denoting a kind of legal procedure, in which the action is formally directed against a thing rather than against a particular person. Property claims are often said to be *in rem*, particularly in older treatises and texts. For example, in admiralty law, one 'libels' a vessel, an *in rem* action by which one claims ownership to it against all other potential claimants. To say that the *in rem* action is against the thing itself, rather than against other persons, is thus something of a fiction, but what it means is that property rights are good against every possible claimant—'the world'—as opposed to rights like those embodied in a contract. The latter are '*in personam*', and only binding against particular individuals, i.e. the parties to the contract.

The psychological question embedded in all this Latin is this: if property rights are rights against the world at large, how do people out there in the world think about the property rights that are 'good against' them? This is where Penner's work gives us a beginning point. Penner uses the very down-to-earth example of a person strolling through a parking lot ('car park' in Britain), to illustrate what most of us expect from the non-owner in an *in rem* world.[36] So, you take this stroll, and you may or may not have a car of your own in the lot, but you know nothing about who owns all these other automobiles. The only thing you know about them is that

---

[35] Merrill and Smith 2000; Merrill and Smith 2001b; Penner 1997.
[36] Penner 1997, 75–6. Penner's example is elaborated in Merrill and Smith 2012, 17–20.

whoever owns them, *you* don't. This knowledge gives you the minimal duty to keep off, a duty that applies to all the autos in the lot except the one (if any) that you do own.

The first point, then, is that in the role of non-owner, the observer *knows* that the observed things belong to someone else—making the non-owner a kind of audience for the rights of others.[37] A second point suggested by Penner's stroller is that for the most part, even if the metaphoric stroller owns a car in the lot, she is completely surrounded by the ownership claims of others—like most of us, afloat, as it were, in a small boat of her own property in an ocean of other people's property. Still, neither Penner nor Merrill and Smith give us much more information about how the non-owning stroller processes any information about her own state of non-ownership, and in particular, how she reacts to the knowledge that someone else owns the things that she observes. But there is another straw in the wind about the psychology of the non-owner, coming from law and economics, or rather more specifically, from a branch of game theory.

2.2 Hawks and Doves

In recent years, some scholars have taken to likening property to a 'Chicken Game', or sometimes a 'Hawk/Dove' game. The main scholar in this line is the Australian political economist Robert Sugden, a very inventive thinker.[38] The Chicken game supposedly originated in a crazed contest among teenagers in the 1950s, a variation of which was famously depicted in the 1955 movie, *Rebel without a Cause*.[39] In the classic form of this contest, two teenagers (or groups of teenagers) get into their automobiles at some distance apart, and then drive straight at each other. The first to flinch and to steer away is a Chicken, obviously the loser. If both flinch, both are chickens, but neither gets to lord it over the other. If neither flinches, of course, they are very likely to kill each other.

Considered as a matter of joint maximization, the best outcome of the Chicken game is for one contestant to flinch and the other not to do so. The shares are not equally distributed, to be sure, but at least one gets to play the hero, and neither gets killed.

The outcome analysis is the same under the very similar but slightly differently named game of Hawk/Dove, a set of strategies originally described by students of animal behaviour.[40] Like Chicken, Hawk/Dove describes a game in which the best outcome is for one player to defer while the other gets the prize: one plays hawk, the other dove. If both defer, i.e. dove/dove, the prize is split, or it may simply go to waste (more on this momentarily). If both claim the prize, they get into a fight.

---

[37] For the role of audience in property, see Rose 1985, 78–80; Smith 2003, 1117.

[38] Sugden 1986, 89–91; see also Zerbe and Anderson 2001, 133–4 (analysing property as Chicken/Hawk game).

[39] Ray 1955. In the movie variation, the contestants raced stolen cars toward a cliff. The first to jump out lost, as the 'chicken'.

[40] Krier 2009, 152, noting that the game is usually attributed to biologist Maynard Smith 1982 as well as Smith's earlier work.

That is likely to be wasteful for a different reason: they may hurt each other, and they may damage whatever the thing is that they are fighting about. Once again, the jointly maximizing outcome is for one to play hawk while the other plays dove.

Now, what does all this have to do with property? In property, supposedly, the hawk is the owner, and the dove is the non-owner. I want to stress here that I do not think that either Chicken or Hawk/Dove is a very good way to understand property relationships most of the time, but before I take up my main reasons, let me address a lesser reason that appears in many descriptions of the hawk/dove payoff matrix. In that description, the dove/dove quadrant merely splits the resource in two, with each party getting half.[41] But if that is the case, there is no particular advantage of property—that is to say, the parties taking opposite strategies of hawk and dove—over simply sharing. The sharing solution of one-half for Row plus one-half for Column adds up to the same joint payoff as complementary strategy in Hawk/Dove, where the split is one for Row plus zero for Column (or one for Column and zero for Row). That is to say, three of the quadrants have the same joint payoff (one), and the only exception is hawk/hawk, where the parties clash and damage each other in trying to take charge of the resource in question (one minus the conflict costs).

But at least from the utilitarian perspective, hawk/dove (or dove/hawk) should be better solutions than dove/dove. The great social advantage in property occurs because the resource in question falls under unitary and exclusive management. Especially when viewed over a longer period, the unitary owner is predicted to make better use of the resource than the several owners do when the resource is shared. The sharing scenario represented by dove/dove runs into transactions costs, common pool problems, free riders, and diminished incentives for investment—all the bugbears of the economic analysis of property.

Of course, all that is a matter of numbers and the ways in which one fills in the numbers in the matrix. My more serious objection to the Hawk/Dove characterization, however, harks back to the psychology of property from the outside perspective, that of the non-owner. In my view, the Hawk/Dove characterization misses a central feature of property.

To begin with the question of motivations: it is fairly easy to understand why any given player would want to play hawk. All players want the prize. But why would anyone play dove? The answer, of course, is the same in Hawk/Dove as it is in Chicken: the Dove's motivation is fear, and more specifically, fear of getting hurt. On this account, fear is the psychological state that defines the dove.

The importance of fear becomes clear in some of the expositions of property as a Hawk/Dove game, notably Sugden's. Sugden has been interested in signals that are salient to players, enabling them to coordinate their strategies. This is a matter that is particularly important in Hawk/Dove, where the players ideally take up opposite strategies. Where Sugden depicts property as a version of Hawk/Dove, the dominating signal for coordination is possession. The party in possession gets to play hawk, whereas the party out of possession takes the dove role.[42]

---

[41] Krier 2009, 152.   [42] Sugden 1986, 89–90; see also Stake 2004, 1764.

The next question is why possession might act as the critical signal for coordinating the roles of hawks and doves. The answer that Sugden gives is that possession itself generally gives the possessor some advantages: the possessor has the interior lines of defence and is usually in a superior position to defend control over the object in question. Moreover, by arriving first, the possessor has gone at least some distance to demonstrate that he or she is the one who most wants the object in question, and is thus likely to defend it more fiercely.[43] What follows is that the non-possessor defers to the possessor, based on the rational assessment that he or she is in the weaker position—in other words, he or she has a well-grounded fear of failure, and of injury to boot.

According to this theory, then, what motivates possessors to advertise their possessory status is the hoped-for emotion of fear in the potentially rivalrous non-possessors. Since the Hawk/Dove game originated in animal behaviour studies, it is not surprising that sociobiologists refer us to the behaviour of animals. Many animals try to signal that they are in possession of some territory, particularly at critical times in their breeding cycles, when there is competition for habitat. Birds sing in bushes, wolves urinate around their den areas, even domestic dogs bark around the fenced-in areas. All this signalling functions as a warning to other creatures, so that they will be fearful or at least cautious about intruding.[44]

To give the Hawk/Dove description its due, it may be a reasonably accurate view of the superiority of possession over non-possession as a means to retain some resource or object. It may also be a reasonably accurate view of the associated motivations and psychological states of the participants.

But here is the rub: possession is not *property*. The critical point about property is that the non-owner shows respect for the owner's property even when the non-owner has little reason to fear the owner's defence—that is, when the owner is not actually in possession, or when the owner is an obviously weaker party who could not repel invasion. When a non-owner defers to the owner under those circumstances, something other than fear is keeping her from moving in and stealing the car or the bicycle or whatever. And as to the property owner, when property is securely in the mind of the relevant non-owners, she need not remain in possession of the things she claims. She can feel at ease about leaving the car in the car park and going shopping in the mall. She may not bother to lock the car. She may even leave the keys in the car. Carrying the point further, the shop owner need not fear the car owner either, when the latter enters the shop. With respect to the items in the shop, the car owner is situationally a non-owner, but if she is a non-owner who respects property, she will not filch the soft drink or the box of stationery from the shelf.

Obviously, not all non-owners behave as owners wish they would. But for the strolling non-owner simply to pass by the unlocked car, the one with the keys in the ignition—this is the critical psychological state for non-owners that makes a system of property work. On this point, sociobiologists misunderstand the character of property when they conflate *property* with *possession*. To be sure, it is true that

---

[43] Sugden 1986, 90.   [44] Pipes 1996.

animals behave in such a way as to hold possession, or at least many of them do; and to be sure, it is true, at least insofar as we can tell, that the dominating emotion of the non-possessing rival animals is fear and a desire to avoid a damaging and fruitless conflict. But it is also true that animals have no respect for undefended claims. They constantly test one another, and with the exception of caring for the young (and not always then), they pounce on weakness. The basic attitude of the wolf or coyote appears to be that of the larcenist or opportunist, ranging from the sneak thief to the armed robber. Even sweet little songbirds invade the nests of others to engage in flagrant adultery.

But the core attribute of property is precisely that the non-owner respects the owner's claim even when it is *not* defended. There is no question but that for some non-owners, rational fear is the only impediment to larceny. But that is not what makes a property regime work. By and large, in a functioning property regime, most non-owners are not larcenists, and they do not like larcenists. That set of sensibilities is what makes property regimes function: you do not have to guard your things all the time, because the 'world' of non-owners respects your ownership.

The distinction between possession and property has been well known by legal writers for hundreds of years. Blackstone's discussion is a notable example, distinguishing possession (or mere occupancy) from property, the latter being a claim that endures beyond mere possession or occupancy.[45] Why does the distinction matter? It matters for several reasons. First, it matters because the owner's confidence about her property frees her actually to do something with it, without having to expend time and resources on securing what she has. With confidence about her property, she can also leave the property undefended, in order to assemble the other things she needs for whatever project she has in mind, be it a project that defines her personhood or one that makes her wealthy or one that she simply enjoys. Moreover, as James Krier has pointed out, any forms of property beyond simple physical objects are necessarily abstract, and these do not admit of possession in anything other than a metaphoric way. A modern economy depends on property of this sort—partnership interests, mortgages, stocks, options, derivatives. We could have none of this if property did not extend beyond possession.[46] But fundamentally, we could not have property, as distinct from possession, without the cooperation of the non-owner, the stroller through the car park who leaves the other owners' cars alone. That goes as well for the cashier at the movie theater, or the computer whizz who would not think of hacking into someone else's accounts—and who helps us to find those who do.

2.3 The virtues of non-ownership

American history gives some very striking examples of the sensibilities that respect property, in settings in which fear of retaliation or punishment was virtually non-existent. John Phillip Reid's study of cross-continental emigrants, perhaps

---

[45] Blackstone 1776, 2: 4–5.   [46] Krier 2009, 155–7.

infelicitously titled *Law for the Elephant*, describes an almost unbelievably robust respect for property among the migrants along the trails to California and Oregon.[47] These were persons who were far from organized law and order—families in covered wagons, making exceedingly difficult journeys in which wheel axles broke, pack animals escaped, or belongings were taken in Indian raids or lost in fording rivers. Numerous migrants were left with little or nothing after these misfortunes. Yet as Reid's book illustrates, they would not take other settlers' belongings without consent, even at the point of starvation. If there was fear of retaliation at some times, at many times there was not, yet unilateral taking was simply not done.

There were similar stories about Gold Rush miners, massive numbers of men thrown together pell-mell in the California foothills where they hoped to strike it rich. The miners too held very strong norms about property claims—or at least about the miners' own claims, given that all of them at the time were trespassers on the public lands of the United States. But among themselves, the gold rush miners quickly developed norms of respect for their respective mining 'stakes' and for the tools that they used to exploit them. Thieves were despised, and quickly dispatched.[48]

Where did these norms of respect for property come from, both on the part of individuals who respected others' claims, and on the part of the relevant collectivity that insists that non-owners respect the claims of recognized owners? Robert Ellickson has made the useful typology of first-party, second-party, and third-party constraints on behaviour. First-party constraints are those that one puts on one's self, deriving from such matters as conscience, honour, a sense of justice, or pride in being a certain kind of person. Second-party constraints are those that come from concern about the other party in a transaction, particularly that the second party may cease dealing or in a more extreme case may even retaliate. Third-party constraints are those imposed by outsiders to any given transaction— anything from the disapprobation of the neighbours to legal constraints.[49]

Fear of course can be a part of deference to owners' claims. The Hawk/Dove version of property-as-possession is essentially a story about second-party constraints, where the non-possessor fears confrontation with an owner in possession. Even when property is undefended by the owner, so that there will be no second-party retaliation, fear can enter into a non-owner's concern; third parties might play the enforcement role—the cops, the neighbours, the bystanders who might observe and punish larceny.

But fear is not the only psychological state involved. While fear of second parties is a relatively straightforward matter, fear does not explain first-party constraints on violating the property of others. Nor is fear a complete explanation of third-party constraints.[50] In a way, third-party enforcement only kicks the question upstairs,

[47] Reid 1980, 350–5.
[48] Zerbe and Anderson 2001, 128–35; McDowell 2002, 20; cf. Umbeck 1981 (arguing that the threat of violence enforced miners' property claims) 9, 98–132.
[49] Ellickson 1998, 547; Ellickson 1991, 123–36; Ellickson 1989, 43–6.
[50] Note the disagreement between Zerbe and Anderson 2001 and McDowell 2002 on the one side, and Umbeck 1981 on the other, concerning the reasons why gold rush miners obeyed property rules:

posing the question why the respect for ownership affects third parties at all, and indeed affects them so strongly that outsiders will stand behind individual owners and take the trouble to punish what they regard as malfeasance. But they do. Juries are notoriously hard on behaviour that they regard as forceful or fraudulent property invasion.[51]

One explanation suggests that the reason why non-owners respect property is, so to speak, 'third parties all the way down': each person's willingness to defer to property claims depends on the customary practices of the other people who share the same culture. In describing the Gold Rush norms, Richard Zerbe and Leigh Anderson argue that the miners brought a common culture with them, and that this culture explained (among other things) their view that individual miners' property rights were to be respected according to shared cultural norms of fairness. No doubt there is something to this view, and it could help to explain a phenomenon that Zerbe and Anderson mention: that for Europeans and Americans, the culture in question privileged themselves alone, but not others; they rejected Chinese, Latinos, and African-Americans as equal members of their mining communities and clashed repeatedly with different ethnic groups over mining practices.[52]

In any event, a cultural explanation for non-owners' respect for property raises the question of the origin of the culture itself. Might possession lurk at the root of property after all? David Hume suggested that it did, with an assist of customary practice. Like Sugden, who has admired and relied on Hume's work, Hume thought that property claims evolved from possession. The possessor of Stake A was of course non-possessor of Stakes B–Z, but all these possessors tacitly agreed to play dove with respect to the possessions of others, since all feared the disorder and destruction that would accompany any disruption in the initially fragile equilibrium, and presumably all shared common knowledge of this generally held fear. Jeremy Waldron in this volume develops the Hume thesis, with an evolutionary story in which property emerged from the situation in which each possessor was essentially in a standoff with each other possessor.

But, *pace* Waldron, there was a critical next move in the Hume story: that is, over time, in their roles as non-possessors, all these players—and everyone else—*got used to* deferring to possessors, so that they carried that deference over to situations where the one-time possessor was no longer on location or defending the possession.[53] Well, perhaps, but then, the 'getting used to' needs explanation. In Hawk/ Dove, deference to *possession* rests on rational fear, that is, calculations about

---

Umbeck attributes compliance to fear of second-party retaliation and third-party enforcement, whereas the other authors describe compliance as coming from first-party norms together with third-party enforcement. For a different perspective, arguing that the miners' rules actually destabilized security by favouring claim-jumpers, see Clay and Wright 2005, 162–78.

[51] See e.g. *Jacque v Steenberg Homes Inc.* 1997; Helmholz 1983, 356–8 (noting judges' and juries' hostility to claims based on knowing trespass).

[52] Zerbe and Anderson 2001, 135–7. Zerbe and Anderson barely mention the miners' treatment of local Native Americans, or the total lack of respect for the latter's fishing claims or even in some instances for their lives. See McEvoy 1986, 47–8, 53–5.

[53] Hume 1739–40b, *A Treatise of Human Nature*, vol. 2: Book 3, Part 2, s. 203, at 484–513.

expected harm from fights with the possessor. But fear would only lead the non-possessor to defer in situations where he expected resistance, and superior resistance at that. Predators are very likely to be on the lookout for any weakness in current possessors, and some are even likely to gain from the disruption of any temporary equilibrium among possessors. The chances for 'getting used to' are slim to non-existent in any scenario based simply on fear of reprisal or disorder. One might think that Hume himself had doubts about the standoff thesis, given the hortatory tone of the paragraphs in which he proposed it, and given the unusually copious supplementary footnotes that he added to these paragraphs.[54]

Deference to *property*, as opposed to deference to possession alone, depends on the entirely different mind-set of respect—respect even when rational calculations would advise grabbing from a weaker party, or grabbing and running from a momentarily absent or distracted stronger one. Making the leap from one mental state to the other, from rational fear to non-rational respect, is something of a mystery for rational actors. To be sure, one might say that the getting-used-to story has some explanatory power, particularly from the example of women. Until the later part of the 19th century, married women were not recognized as capable of property ownership, and it would be easy to see in this customary practice a pattern in which property ownership would be denied to those who had always been considered too weak to defend possession. On the other hand, the denial of property to women did not extend to widows, who could own some property even in the absence of male defenders. That pattern suggests that something else was driving the convention, and that the reasons for denying married women the right to property had less to do with their assumed weakness, and more to do with assuring women's deference to males as heads of household.[55]

Hume's discussion of property of course incorporated another idea about the psychology of respect for property, and indeed an idea that is much discussed in modern game theory, namely, the expectation of reciprocity.[56] That is, I expect that if I respect your property, you will respect mine, and we will both be better off. Or, put in an n-person context, if I respect everybody else's property, all of them will respect mine. This is the well-known strategy of Tit for Tat as a solution to Prisoners' Dilemmas, and this theory too has some explanatory power, though it is incomplete, perhaps even more so than Hume's version, which added custom to reciprocity. First is the well-known theoretical problem that in Tit-for-Tat games, someone has to make the first trusting move, at a time when no history has been established among the players—when it would be rational to suppose that every potential counterpart is simply waiting to play hawk.[57] As a matter of experience,

---

[54] Readers of Hume's *Treatise of Human Nature* will note the unusual number and length of footnotes in vol. 2, Book 3, Part 2, s. 3, 'Of the Rules Which Determine Property'. One long footnote discusses the uncertainty of the meaning of 'possession' itself. Another (5) explores a number of ways in which property depends on 'imagination'.

[55] Dubler 2003 (extensive study of 19th-century widows' property, which Dubler describes as circumscribed by widows' once-married state ever after the death of the husband).

[56] Hume 1739–40a, vol. 2: Book 3, Part 2, ss. 2–3.

[57] For the early description of tit-for-tat as a game, Axelrod 1984, 13–14, but see De Jasay 1989, 45–6 (noting first mover problem) and 67, n. 17 (noting endgame problem that may cause earlier cooperative inclination to self-destruct).

too, it is hard to imagine that respect for the property of others always depends on reciprocity. During the many centuries in which married women in western nations could not own property, many if not most still undoubtedly respected the property claims of men.

This is not to say that the reciprocity view is without merit, at least insofar as the absence of reciprocity has accompanied the absence of respect for property. As to property-denied married women, we cannot easily tell what resentments may have seethed behind their overt acceptance of their husbands', fathers', and brothers' rights of ownership.[58] In the American south, slaves constituted another class of people who could not own their own property, at least legally. Many no doubt would have respected their owners' claims even without the sting of fear. But slave owners often complained about slaves' pilferage—giving some support, at least negatively, to the idea that a willingness to play the dove role about other peoples' property depends on expectations of reciprocity about one's own.[59] The obverse is that if others do not respect your claims to ownership, you may not respect theirs either. It does seem fairly clear that those who do not own much property, or whose claims are disparaged and denied, as with slaves, do not always see owners' claims as just or otherwise worthy of respect. Insofar as the expectation of reciprocity explains the willingness to play dove and to respect the claims of owners, the key issue could be something other than direct reciprocity. It could rather be an optimism that property is attainable, and once attained, that it will be respected by others.[60]

But these are only speculations. For example, let us suppose that the respect for property is based on optimism about attainment, and let us suppose that I have nothing now of much value, but I expect that I may be able to acquire property and that others will respect what I acquire in future, just as I respect the property of others now. This optimism would seem to be unfounded in a world of rational actors, where every potential counterpart would be a hawk just waiting to seize on one's trust. Jon Elster, a political scientist who is interested in the phenomenon of socially useful behaviour, sees this kind of optimism not as rational but as an example of magical thinking: if I do X, others will do the same. This is not to discount the value of magical thinking; quite the contrary, Elster sees it as a foundation for solving the ubiquitous Prisoners' Dilemma problem.[61]

Nor does the centrality of magical thinking—or of sympathy, righteousness, mimesis, playfulness, generosity or other non-rational 'moral sentiments'—negate the value of rational actor models for mapping out human interactions. Rational behaviour, even rationality that is narrowly understood as self-interest, is necessarily

---

[58] See e.g. Murray 2007, 137–9 (describing Elizabeth Cady Stanton's comparison of marriage to slavery because of women's inability to hold property, contract, and have custody of children).

[59] Gross 1995, 275–6 (describing trial descriptions of vices of 'bad slaves', including stealing and running away).

[60] McDowell 2002, 64–5 gives an example in her explanation of the gold rush miners' acceptance of certain kinds of limitations on claims; she argues that they were uncertain about their luck in any one spot, and that the limiting rules would allow them other opportunities elsewhere if a present claim did not work out.

[61] Elster 1989, 186.

part of the mix in successful institutions like property, and thus rational actor models are clearly a powerful aid in understanding much of the logic of strategic situations.[62] But they are not complete. The example of property shows that these models need a supplement, an attention to emotional elements that do not fall into a conventionally narrow version of what rationality is.

That incompleteness should at least induce some humility in rational actor models, along with a willingness to investigate the emotional sources of successful institutions—and unsuccessful ones too. David Hume had that kind of humility, with his references to customary practice and to the importance of imagination, sympathy, and affection in ideas of property, as well as with his remark that human beings are not so relentlessly self-seeking as some of his contemporaries seemed to believe. It is one of the sources of his appeal.[63]

In the end, just as thoroughgoing rational actors would confront a certain fundamental mystery in solving PDs—who takes the first step? why does not backward induction unravel every solution?[64]—so they also would confront a certain mystery about why anyone respects the property of others. Clearly the non-owning actors are not all weak doves avoiding ferocious hawks. Where no hawks threaten, the doves may still have the view that the owner's claim is just, or that the owner will magically reciprocate toward property acquired by the current non-owner. Even then, this cooperative psychological state must at some times be threatened not only by the well-known and conventional dictates of self-seeking, but also by the sheer *frisson* of transgression. As Jean Genet famously remarked about the thrill of stealing, 'you feel yourself living.'[65]

One could concoct an evolutionary story in which a cooperative and non-transgressive psychological propensity—a kind of bourgeois virtue—once derived from a random genetic mutation among some class of persons, must have led to success at the group level. Or one could concoct a religious story, in which God gave Adam and Eve a break at the expulsion from the Garden, conceding them an angelic glimmer of cooperation, so that at least some of the time they could refrain from snatching the products that others created by the biblical sweat of the brow. Both stories have a just-so quality that makes them something less than convincing.[66] And yet, the mysterious, subtle, and not entirely universal psychological state of the cooperative non-owner functions critically to make property regimes function. To return to those sunny psychological states on the inside perspective on property, in which owners enjoy everything from self-definition to incentives to labour: those states build on outside psychology of *not* owning, of respecting the things that *others* own, even when the owners are not around.

---

[62] See Rose 2007, 1898–9 (describing property law's expectation of subject with sensible regard for self as well as others).

[63] Hume 1739–40b, vol. 2: Book 3, Part 2, ss. 2–4. The quotation criticizing 'certain philosophers' for their 'delight' in exaggerating human selfishness is in s. 2.

[64] De Jasay 1989, 63–6.

[65] Genet 1949, 30. See also the movie *The Grifters* (Frears 1990) depicting the perpetrators' glee at the successful conclusion of a long confidence game.

[66] See Mithen 2012 (criticizing Wilson's theory of group evolution). For the tendency of rational actor models to lapse into storytelling about the evolution of property, see Rose 1990.

13

Property and Disagreement

*Stephen R. Munzer**

For most of the 20th century, the idea that property is a bundle of sticks—more precisely, a set of normative relations between persons with respect to things—dominated the legal and philosophical landscape. Recently, some legal philosophers and property scholars have challenged this idea. I argue that these challenges, which typically see the right to exclude as the essence of property, are unsuccessful.

The challenges of interest potentially involve disagreements of three different sorts: disagreements over the definition or meaning of the word 'property', disagreements over the concept of property, and disagreements over the nature of property. A major figure behind these challenges is James Penner. His two landmark works are couched in terms of the definition of property, which suggests that he is concerned with the meaning of 'property', and in terms of the concept of property.[1] Penner has since published other books and articles on property, and he has advised me that he no longer holds all of the views advanced earlier in his career. But because his first two works have achieved iconic status, I cannot do justice to his writings without examining the central claims of his initial publications, which have greatly influenced the views of Thomas W. Merrill and Henry E. Smith in the United States.

In this chapter I first address the disagreements over the last quarter-century by looking at the phenomenon of disagreement and making use of recent philosophical literature on verbal disagreement and on concepts. I look at some actual disagreements in property theory to explore possible ways to clarify, dissolve, or resolve them. Clarification is laying bare the nature of the disagreement. Dissolution is showing that upon examination all or almost all of the disagreement turns out to be largely or totally insignificant. Resolution is showing that one side is right and the other wrong or, in some cases, that neither side is right or that both sides are

* For help with this project I thank David J. Chalmers, Paul Daniell, Simon Douglas, David Frydrych, Joshua Getzler, Mark Greenberg, Carrie Holmes, Rob Hughes, Robert Lawner, Harvey Lederman, Ben McFarlane, Arthur Ripstein, Luke Rostill, Brian Sawers, Henry Smith, Alexander Stremitzer, and Douglas Wolfe. I am indebted to Peter Hacker for a long conversation on Wittgenstein and the nature of concepts and to Sheldon Smith for access to some of his unpublished work. Special thanks go to James Penner. His constructive comments on two drafts of this chapter constitute the highest form of scholarly engagement, and I am deeply grateful to him.
[1] Penner 1996a; Penner 1997.

right in different respects. I next consider the possibility that, despite Penner's language to the contrary, the disagreement between us ultimately concerns the nature of property. Here I show that almost all of my arguments relating to substantive disagreements that seem either partly verbal or partly conceptual can be transposed into the key of disagreements over the nature of property.[2]

Rather different theoretical views fall under the heading of 'a theory of property'. For present purposes, the two most important views are these. View 1, to which I subscribe, presupposes that one is talking about existing institutions of property law and suggests a particular way of analysing property in institutional, especially legal, contexts. Those who harness Hohfeld's vocabulary to Honoré's account of ownership represent various ways of performing this task.[3] For them, property is a set of legal relations between persons with respect to things. The relations are right (claim-right)—duty, liberty-right (privilege)—no-right, power—liability (suscepti-bility to change of legal position), and immunity—disability (no-power) *plus* a thing that is the subject of these relations. The terminal ends of each of these relations are *normative modalities*. View 2 attempts to construct an institution of property law on the basis of building blocks that illuminate key doctrines of existing property institutions, such as *nemo dat quod non habet* and the *ad coelum* rule. Henry Smith pursues this modular enterprise. In certain respect he adapts Penner's work for his own purposes.[4]

Allow me to elaborate on these respective views. My version of the bundle theory of property exemplifies View 1. It is an arrangement of points made by other scholars. My version starts with existing legal systems and their associated laws of property. The chief objective of the theory is analytical clarity. To attain this objective it does the following: marks out a set of relations between persons with respect to things; shows how to use these relations in analysing cases and legislation; exposes confused thinking, such as the failure to discriminate between a claim-right and a liberty-right, between a claim-right and a correlative duty, between a claim-right and a power, between a power and a correlative liability, between a claim-right and an immunity, and so on; uncovers ambiguity, such as the multiple uses of the word 'right'; clarifies the policy issues that judges and legislatures face, e.g. whether a court should recognize a duty of non-interference with the land of another or only a penumbra of protection that falls short of a duty not to interfere; maps out different incidents of property such as possession, use, management, transferability, excludability, and others; identifies the relative functional importance of these different incidents in particular legal systems; isolates different property holders

---

[2] Penner's views have changed somewhat over the years, and his most recent essay on this topic—not addressed here—is Penner 2011.

[3] E.g. Becker 1977, ch. 2, and Munzer 1990, ch. 2, both invoke Hohfeld 1919 and Honoré 1961. The American Law Institute 1944 relied heavily on Hohfeld's analysis. Penner 1996a and Penner 1997 offer a different way of making use of, but also partly rejecting, some views of Hohfeld and Honoré, and in that respect are partly competitors with bundle theories of property. These two works by Penner differ, I think, from the modular enterprise conducted in terms of information costs that is character-istic of Smith's recent work.

[4] Smith 2012a; Smith 2012b; Smith this volume.

such as natural persons, married couples, cotenants, corporations, limited partnerships, cities, counties, and the state; and applies these tools to a wide range of different systems of property, from early, relatively undeveloped arrangements to complicated contemporary institutions of property law in industrialized nations. Worthy of note are specific illustrations of the usefulness of the bundle approach: its employment to good effect by the US Supreme Court,[5] a stimulating account of the importance of a privilege (liberty-right) in American legal history,[6] and an explanation of property transfers in terms of a network of claim-rights, powers, duties, and liberty-rights.[7] This list is sizeable but incomplete.

Smith's recent work exemplifies View 2. Its object is to conduct a modular enterprise that, with low information costs, can build up from scratch a legal institution of property and that explains salient rules and doctrines of property law. Smith's central insight is that it can be efficient to construct a set of property rules and institutions by using basic building blocks ('modules') and stacking them together in various ways. Mind you, Smith is very good at parsing and criticizing existing rules of property law. That is evident from his many articles, most written from the perspective of law and economics, which illuminate the advantages and disadvantages of various property rules. His background in linguistics aids him in expertly remapping property law. It is, then, his most recent work that goes in a new direction.

Near the end of this chapter I argue that my version of the bundle theory and Smith's recent modular work are rather different enterprises with rather different objectives. There is a slight area of competition between these two views, chiefly because Smith may have different positions on concepts and 'things' from mine and he values Albert Kocourek's analysis of rights *in rem* more highly than I.[8] To the extent that there seems to be a greater area of competition, it exists partly because Smith claims that the allegedly high information costs of a bundle theory make it unattractive. Still, bundle theorists can use context and heuristics to hold down information costs. Applying a bundle theory need not be computationally intensive.

Otherwise, my principal conclusions are these. Verbal disagreements differ from verbal misunderstandings and from substantive disagreements. There are many kinds of verbal disagreements, and I do not try to classify them. Instead, I concentrate on what David J. Chalmers calls disagreements that are both partly verbal and partly substantive.[9] An illustration is the disagreement between Penner

---

[5] E.g. *United States v Craft* 2002; *Hodel v Irving* 1987. These cases remind us that some disagreements over property involve practical legal problems.

[6] Horwitz 1992, 155–6, 164. However, I disagree with much of what Horwitz says about 'the dephysicalization of property' because he does not distinguish clearly and consistently between 'a bundle of legal relations' and 'a bundle of legal relations between persons with respect to things'. Horwitz 1992, 156, 162 and *passim*.

[7] Munzer 2011, 267–8.

[8] E.g. Smith 2012b, 1696; Kocourek 1920. Insofar as Smith would reiterate the centrality of the right to exclude based on James Penner's work, the discussion of Penner below would also cover Smith.

[9] Chalmers 2011 actually speaks of 'verbal disputes'. My use of 'disagreements' tallies with his use of 'disputes'. For brevity, I elide his distinction between 'broadly' and 'narrowly' verbal disagreements, as my concern is with the former.

and me on whether property is the right to exclude (his view), or whether property is better understood as a set of relations between persons with respect to things (my view). Our partly substantive, partly verbal disagreement has analytical and meta-physical dimensions. I clarify the nature of this disagreement and resolve at least part of it.

Some disagreements about property turn on the nature of concepts, their individuation, or the possibility of using concepts without fully understanding them. I suggest that some academic lawyers might either have different concepts of property or, if they use the same concept of property, have incomplete understandings of that concept. I examine two illustrations of this possibility. One is a disagreement between Jim Harris and Tony Honoré on the one side and me on the other regarding the relations involved in property. I suggest that once the logic of relations is correctly understood, the disagreement between us is of minor significance. This disagreement is clarified in one respect and dissolved in another. Of considerably greater philosophical interest is the disagreement between Penner and me, partly because it shows that some disagreements can have both verbal and conceptual aspects, and partly because the Wittgensteinian theory of family-resemblance concepts he uses is incompatible with Penner's effort to mark out the essence of property, and in fact supports a bundle approach to property. I clarify our disagreement in some respects and resolve it in others.

The final section of this chapter entertains the possibility that, despite appearances, all substantive disagreements discussed here concern, deep down, the nature of property. I suggest that most of the substantive arguments presented earlier in the chapter can be redeployed to clarify the nature of property.

1. Disagreements Substantive and Verbal

Verbal disagreement is not the same as verbal misunderstanding. In the many times I have taught the basic course in contract law, I have often asked students to discuss the example of Samuel Williston's tramp. In the example a benevolent man tells a tramp, 'If you go around the corner to the clothing shop there, you may purchase an overcoat on my credit.' The tramp then walks to the store and the legal question is whether, in so doing, the tramp has offered consideration.[10] One time, a student argued earnestly that the tramp could well have given consideration, and that her sexual behaviour and reputation were irrelevant to the issue of consideration. I replied, as gently as possible, that he and Williston were using the word 'tramp' in different senses. The student was not verbally disagreeing with Williston. He misunderstood what Williston meant by 'tramp'.

---

[10] Williston 2008, 412–15.

1.1 Verbal disagreements

Perhaps the best-known illustration of verbal disagreement comes from William James's case in which a man and a squirrel move rapidly around a tree, always with the tree being between them and with both facing the tree, and a dispute erupts over whether the man 'goes round' the squirrel.

'Which party is right', I said, 'depends on what you *practically mean* by "going round" the squirrel. If you mean passing from the north of him to the east, then to the south, then to the west, and then to the north of him again, obviously the man does go round him, for he occupies these successive positions. But if on the contrary you mean being first in front of him, then on the right of him, then behind him, then on his left, and finally in front again, it is quite obvious that the man fails to go round him .... Make the distinction, and there is no occasion for any farther dispute.'[11]

Chalmers offers a taxonomy of verbal disagreements. The kind of disagreement that is most important for my purposes is both broad and partial. As to breadth, his characterization is:

A dispute over [a sentence] *S* is (broadly) verbal when, for some expression *T* in *S*, the parties disagree about the meaning of *T*, and the dispute over *S* arises wholly in virtue of this disagreement regarding *T*.[12]

He then relaxes the foregoing characterization by replacing 'wholly' with 'partly'. Relaxing it makes the disagreement partly verbal and partly substantive. More precisely, it gives us 'an apparent first-order dispute [that] arises partly in virtue of a metalinguistic disagreement and partly in virtue of a substantive nonmetalinguistic disagreement'.[13]

Here is a non-property example of this kind of disagreement for the term 'chef' in the following sentence *S*: 'Lazarus is a chef'. Mary believes that the word 'chef' applies to a person who consistently cooks meals that are pleasing to the palate. Martha believes that the word 'chef' applies to a person who has gone through professional training at a culinary institute. If both Mary and Martha believe that *S* is true, their agreement would be only apparent if Lazarus both consistently cooks meals that are pleasing to the palate and has been professionally trained at a culinary institute. If only Mary or only Martha believes *S* is true, the *verbal* aspect of their disagreement stems from the fact that they mean different things by the word 'chef'. Yet Mary and Martha also have a *substantive* non-metalinguistic disagreement over what has to go on in the world in order for Lazarus to qualify as a chef.[14] By comparison, James's example of the squirrel and 'going round' might be dismissed as trivial or as a 'merely' verbal disagreement. That is not true of the partly verbal and partly substantive disagreement between Mary and Martha, for

[11] James 1907, 44 (italics in original). James's dissolution does not consider whether the dispute involves different linguistic communities or whether the disputants are all competent users of the expression 'going round'.
[12] Chalmers 2011, 522. I have benefited from his article but do not follow it in all respects.
[13] Chalmers 2011, 526.   [14] Chalmers 2011, 525–6.

their dispute goes both to the meaning of 'chef' and to the question of what makes someone a chef.

1.2 Disagreement that is partly substantive and partly verbal

I turn to the work of James Penner for a disagreement over property that is both partly substantive and partly verbal. Penner is a well-known opponent of the claim that property is a bundle of rights.[15] Insofar as this claim is a slogan, Penner is not concerned to refute it, because he regards a slogan as 'an expression that conjures up an image, but which does not represent any clear thesis or set of propositions'.[16] *Pace* Penner, I claim that at least my version of the bundle theory is a theory because it sees property as a set of relations between persons with respect to things. In making this claim, I have to confront his insistence that it is 'quite mistaken' to see this claim 'as any kind of *analysis* or substantial *thesis*' because that would take property to be 'a structural composite, *i.e.,* that its nature is that of an aggregate of fundamentally distinct norms'.[17] A chapter of a book I wrote is a conspicuous target of his critique.[18]

a) Clarifying the disagreement

It is not easy to get clear on what Penner's alternative position is, for he states his position, or perhaps positions, in different ways. The three most prominent ways are:

> W_1—Property is the right to exclude (or, sometimes, the right of exclusive use).
>
> W_2—The right to property is the right to exclude.
>
> W_3—The right to (or of) property is the right of exclusive use.

It is not so much that one of these ways dominates Penner's writing as that he oscillates among them. As an example of W_1, under such headings as 'the definition of property' and 'an alternative definition of property',[19] he writes:

> The foregoing analysis of property as the right of exclusive use implicitly undermines the substantive bundle of rights thesis .... Property qua the right of exclusive use stands for the proposition that property is not by its nature some bundled together aggregate or complex of norms, but a single, coherent right.[20]

Because of his definitional aspirations I take him to be partly concerned with the meaning of 'property' and hence with a partly verbal disagreement. Many passages exemplify W_2. For instance, he states his 'exclusion thesis' as follows: 'the right to

---

[15] Penner 1996a; Penner 1997.

[16] Penner 1996a, 714. Cf. Penner 1996a, 767, 769, 778, 819–20.

[17] Penner 1996a, 741 (italics in original).   [18] Penner 1996a, 774–7; Munzer 1990, ch. 2.

[19] Penner 1997, 152 (bold type and initial capital letters omitted) and Penner 1996a, 742 (initial capital letters omitted), respectively. The emphasis on the word 'property' and the concept for which it stands is most evident in Penner 1996a, 767–99.

[20] Penner 1996a, 754.

property is a right to exclude others from things which is grounded by the interest we have in the use of things'.[21] He adds: 'On this formulation use serves as a justificatory role for the right, while exclusion is the formal essence of the right.'[22] As to W_3 he writes, 'We can now reformulate the right of property, or the right of exclusive use, to take account of the element of alienability . . . '[23]

This tripartite classification clarifies the nature of the disagreement. These three ways of formulating an alternative position are not equivalent, and they propose three different jurisprudential projects. W_1 is a clear competitor with a bundle approach to property in a way that W_2 and W_3 are not. W_1 is about property. According to W_1 property consists of only one normative modality, whereas under my version of the bundle theory property consists of many normative modalities with respect to things. W_2 presupposes that there is a unique right that one can point to as *the* right to property. Possible competitors with W_2 are the claims that the right to property is the right to possess or the right to use. W_3 is something of a compromise proposal compared to W_2, for one could easily break down W_3 into two rights, the right to exclude and the right to use. A possible competitor with W_3 is the claim that the right to property is the set of the rights to exclude, possess, use, abandon, and destroy. As indicated below, my version of the bundle theory is somewhat, though not entirely, orthogonal to W_2 and W_3.

I concentrate on W_1: that property is the right to exclude.[24] If the disagreement between us is partly verbal, one could say that by 'property' he means 'property$_1$' whereas I mean 'property$_2$'. This move might clarify any partly verbal aspect of our disagreement but it would not resolve it. Yet the main point of interest would still lie in a partly substantive disagreement between us, which has at least two different dimensions: analytical and metaphysical. I explain each in turn, point out how each is also partly verbal, and try to resolve some of the points in dispute. Only at the end do I tackle W_2 and W_3. What I say in this section clarifies some aspects of our dispute and resolves others.

To launch the investigation, let us confirm that W_1 and my version of the bundle theory meet the test for the pertinent kind of disagreement over the term 'property'. I give both a practical legal example and a more theoretical example. Both examples also illustrate Chalmers's method of elimination.[25] The method's purpose is to give a sufficient condition for determining whether a dispute over S is wholly or partly verbal with respect to some term T. The method is first to bar use of the term T and then to try to find another sentence S' over which two parties disagree partly substantively such that the disagreement over S' is part of the disagreement over S.

Consider the following sentence S: 'Crosswinds, a large, stately home suitable for use as a quadruplex or as a bed-and-breakfast, is the property of four sisters—Amy, Beth, Cathy, and Donna—as tenants in common'. Suppose the term T is 'property'. Now consider the sentence S' which does not contain the term T: 'Amy has

---

[21] Penner 1997, 71 (italics omitted).   [22] Penner 1997, 71.   [23] Penner 1997, 103.
[24] For brevity I use the short form 'right to exclude' rather than 'right to exclude (or, sometimes, right of exclusive use)'.
[25] Chalmers 2011, 526–30.

the right to exclude others from setting foot on Crosswinds'. The acute lawyer will immediately pick out an ambiguity in S'—namely whether Amy has a right to exclude all other persons from Crosswinds, which would be the case for rights *in rem*, or only a right to exclude some persons from Crosswinds. The uncautious lawyer might answer that of course Amy has a right to exclude everyone else. But the acute lawyer will answer that if Crosswinds is used as a quadruplex, then Amy cannot exclude her sister cotenants because of a legal rule in the United States that all cotenants are 'entitled to possession of all parts of the land at all times'.[26] If, instead, Crosswinds is used as a bed-and-breakfast, then it is a public accommodation in the United States and the cotenants may not exclude any potential customers on account of race, natural origin, religion, sexual orientation, disability, or marital status.[27] Thus, a partly substantive disagreement exists over S' such that the disagreement over S' is part of the disagreement over S, for the extent of the right to exclude is part of the dispute over what property is. So the disagreement over S is partly verbal and partly substantive.

My second property example belongs to the realm of legal theory. Consider the following sentence S: 'A salient feature of the definition of property is whether it is legally permissible to sell whatever items of property one owns.' Suppose that the term T in S is 'the definition of property'. Is S true? Suppose Abercrombie says yes and Fitch says no. We can use the method of elimination to determine whether the disagreement is wholly or partly verbal with respect to T by barring that term from the following sentence S': 'A woman has the legal right to sell land that she owns in fee simple absolute.' Is S' true? Again Abercrombie says yes and Fitch says no. Abercrombie follows most thinkers who write about the theory of property by saying, as to S', that the woman most assuredly has the right to sell the land. Fitch follows Penner, who says that 'property entails a right to give, but not to sell'.[28] Penner adds that 'the definition of property I have proposed is completely neutral on the question of whether one should be able to sell one's property; that concerns the limit and extent of the justification of a very different interest, the interest in undertaking voluntary obligations by way of a particular kind of agreement, *i.e.*, the bargain'.[29] Consequently, a partly substantive disagreement over S' is part of the disagreement over S, since the existence of the right to sell land held in fee simple absolute is part of the dispute over what property is. The disagreement over S is therefore partly verbal and partly substantive.

---

[26] Stoebuck and Whitman 2000, 203 (case citations omitted). This rule sometimes leads to amusing classroom discussions about the impenetrability of matter at the macro level.

[27] The limits on whom the cotenants may exclude vary from state to state. Singer 1996.

[28] Penner 1996a, 746 (footnote omitted). My example follows Penner in using the term 'right' to sell rather than, as I would prefer, the legal 'power' to sell. The right/power distinction is a side issue in our dispute. Most legal systems contain both a right and a power to exclude. Later, when Penner refers to a right to give, that would involve a correlative duty to accept. That is odd because in most legal systems a donee can refuse the gift. It would be better to say that donor has a power to give, and the donee has both a liberty-right and a power to accept or refuse the gift.

[29] Penner 1996a, 746–7.

b) The analysis of property

With this spadework done, I turn to the first dimension in which Penner and I disagree in relation to W_1—namely, the analysis of property. I maintain that property is a set of relations between the owner and other persons with respect to things, and that a good many normative modalities are involved in property besides the right to exclude. I regard this right as salient but consider other normative modalities, such as the owner's rights to use and possess and her power to transfer, to be important, too. In addition, the owner has other claim-rights, liberty-rights, powers, and immunities as well as a duty not to use the thing in certain ways that harm others. Recently I gave reasons for preferring my view to a view like Penner's.[30] I remain unrepentant.

By contrast, Penner contends that the right to exclude is not merely the core of property but its 'formal essence'.[31] True, he makes room for the rights to use and to abandon. He allows the right holder to give the thing to someone else. But he makes some startling claims in mapping out what property or the right to property does not encompass. Chief among them is that his definition of property takes no position on 'whether one should be able to sell one's property'.[32] Here Penner moves what is commonly regarded as a salient topic in the theory of property to the theory of contract.[33] Moreover, in partial opposition to Honoré, Penner maintains that liability of property to execution and an owner's duty not to use her property harmfully are not incidents of property.[34] Finally, Penner's explication of the right to exclude is itself somewhat unusual. He stresses the duty on all others (in the case of property rights *in rem*) 'to exclude themselves' from the owner's property.[35] It would, he writes, be 'a serious misconception' to understand the 'right to exclude' as a right or power on the part of an owner to physically boot others off her land or to order others off or even to put up a fence so as actually to exclude others.[36] To a degree, these remarks are common sense. Others have duties not to interfere, and the law limits what an owner can do to keep others off her land. Yet to some scholars, Penner might seem not to give due weight to the owner's claim-rights and liberty-rights, and her powers, to exclude interlopers. For instance, the owner can exercise her liberty-right to erect a fence provided that doing so violates no governmental or private restrictions. Again, if someone damages her land by repeatedly crossing over it, she can exercise her power to bring an action for trespass in order to obtain damages and an injunction.

Alas, resolving the substantive dimension of this disagreement regarding the analysis of property would require more ink that I am allowed to spill here. I would have to answer all objections he lodges against my view in the works under discussion.[37] Perhaps not even Penner and I could sustain interest in such a fine mincing.

---

[30] Munzer 2011. [31] Penner 1997, 71. [32] Penner 1996a, 746.
[33] Penner 1996a, 747. [34] Penner 1996a, 761–5. [35] Penner 1997, 71.
[36] Penner 1997, 71–2; Penner 1997, 743–4. [37] Penner 1996a; Penner 1997.

Nevertheless, deference to community usage might help to resolve the verbal aspect of our disagreement with respect to W_1.[38] Here the relevant linguistic community is all speakers of English who talk and write about property in a given legal system. These speakers include not only judges, lawyers, and law teachers but also homeowners and tenants, real estate agents, land-use experts, state condemnation authorities, licensors of copyrights and patents, and financiers of the purchase and leasing of land, office buildings, and aircraft. In the United States, the bundle approach to property dominates, and not just as a slogan.

Of course, Penner and others are free to make a proposal that is partly linguistic: that 'property' is the right to exclude. I doubt that the proposal will enjoy much support in the United States once members of the pertinent community learn that, so far as the legal theory of property goes, for Penner property does not include a power to sell, a liability to attachment in bankruptcy or to execution to satisfy a court judgment, a duty to refrain from certain harmful uses, a power to sue others for trespass or nuisance, or, apparently, an immunity against government expropriation for public use unless it pays the owner just compensation.[39]

His proposal, or some other, might jibe better with community usage in some other legal system, but it does not seem to work any better in England than it does in the United States. Boiling down the meaning of 'property' in English law to the right to exclude is closer to a linguistic recommendation than it is to a faithful report on usage in British English within the relevant linguistic community, namely English judges, lawyers, law teachers, and others. For example, Gray and Gray's treatise on English land law observes:

> 'Property' in land means no more and no less than what the state actually permits an individual to do with 'his' or 'her' land.... On this analysis, each individuated element of utility within the bundle of rights (or 'bundle of sticks') which comprises an estate or interest can itself be characterised as a species of 'property'.[40]

Although this treatise notices the importance of the right to exclude, it also sees property as 'a socially constructed concept' that includes a bundle of limitations as well as a bundle of rights, and points out that the state can augment or curtail the bundle of rights.[41] Judges, too, point out the partly offsetting 'sticks' in the bundle. 'The [defendants'] liability is simply an incident of the ownership of the land which gives rise to it. The peaceful enjoyment of land involves the discharge of burdens which are attached to it as well as the enjoyment of its rights and privileges.'[42]

---

[38] This dispute could be explicitly verbal or implicitly verbal under a refinement introduced by Chalmers 2011, 525 n. 8.

[39] Penner 1996a, 746, 761–4, 815; US Constitution, amendment V.

[40] Gray and Gray 2009, 111 (footnote omitted). '[C]asual lay concepts of "ownership" [sometimes] dissolve into differently constituted aggregations or bundles of power exercisable over land.' Gray and Gray 2009, 93.

[41] Gray and Gray 2009, 91, 102, 111.

[42] *Aston Cantlow and Wilmcote with Billesley Parochial Church Council v Wallbank* 2004, 572 (per Lord Hope of Craighead), cited by Gray and Gray 2009, 92 n. 3. Here land is the thing with respect to which the owner and other persons have various relations.

Of course, arguments based on community usage have limitations. Even if such arguments can sometimes uncover errors in accurately grasping the usage of different linguistic communities, they can also stymie intellectual progress. Penner has an important insight: if one stripped the right to exclude from the other normative modalities associated with property, what remains would be vastly impoverished. Still, this insight should not blind us to the fact that if one stripped out either the right to use, or the power to transfer, from the other modalities (including the right to exclude) associated with property, what remains would also be vastly poorer.

c) The metaphysics of property

A second dimension of our disagreement in relation to W_1 is distantly linked to the metaphysical problem of the one and the many.[43] Penner's preferred view is that 'exclusion frames the practical essence of the right' to property.[44] Later, he puts what seems to be the same point by saying that exclusion is the 'formal essence' of that right.[45] I do not know what either 'practical' or 'formal' means in this context, or what distinction, if any, exists between practical essence and formal essence. So let us use 'essence' without any adjectival qualification, and regard the essence of something as that which makes it what it is. For Penner, the essence of both property and the right to property is the right to exclude. He is for the one.[46]

Now, Penner also holds that the right to property includes, among other normative modalities, the right to possess, the rights to use, manage, and receive income, and the power to give.[47] These are included only because he apparently considers them derivable from or already encompassed by the right to exclude. But I am not willing to grant him this step in his argument. The right to exclude others is one thing. That right does not, so far as I can see, entail the rights to use, manage, and receive income. Surely it does not entail the power to give; a power is a distinct normative modality from a right. Further, he pays little attention to exceptions to and limitations on the right to exclude arising from necessity, custom, circumscribed self-help, antidiscrimination laws, and public policy as well as public accommodations law.[48] These exceptions and limitations become even more complicated in the case of what some call 'entity property' such as leases, condominiums, cooperatives, trusts, corporations, and partnerships.[49] Accordingly, Penner's right to exclude is a good deal less robust than he believes.

---

[43] The classic form of the problem lies in the difference between the hylomorphism of Aristotle and Plato's mature account of how all things called by a common name, say 'bed', partake of the Form of the Bed. The 'one over many' argument appears in *Republic* 596a–b, but there is more sophisticated discussion in *Parmenides*, *Sophist*, and *Philebus*. It is doubtful that Plato's works contain just one problem of the one and the many. Cresswell 1972.

[44] Penner 1996a, 743.   [45] Penner 1997, 71.

[46] The distant link to Plato is not that Penner believes that a Form of Property exists but that he claims property has something that makes it what it is: its essence is the right to exclude.

[47] Penner 1996a, 746, 755–64.   [48] E.g. Merrill and Smith 2012, 387–94, 399–49.

[49] Merrill and Smith 2012, 646–806.

Here it is worth attending to a point made over a century ago by William James: the 'Oneness' or 'union' in the world 'may be enormous, colossal; but absolute monism is shattered if, along with all the union, there has to be granted the slightest modicum, the most incipient nascency, or the most residual trace, of a separation that is not "overcome".'[50] James's rhetoric is overblown. My point is more limited: if Penner's insistence that property has an essence which is the right to exclude amounts to a property-monism, then his position will be hard to sustain, for he will need some other means to make room for rights to use, manage, and receive income and the power to give.

Moreover, a strong independent case can be made for the many. Recall that Penner writes that it is a mistake to regard property as a 'structural composite, *i.e.*, that its nature is that of an aggregate of fundamentally distinct norms'.[51] Why is this position a mistake? We don't think it is a mistake that other fields of inquiry include composites. In chemistry, for example, we study suspensions, emulsions, solutions, and compounds, and the different isotopes characteristic of most elements. In the law of contract, measures of monetary recovery for breach can be based, at least in the United States, on fundamentally different norms coming from contract damages, restitution, and tort-like non-economic damages.[52]

Here it is useful to remind ourselves of the historical contingency of property arrangements and property law. To illustrate, the tenurial system that evolved after the Norman Conquest was a pyramidal structure that had the King at the top, mesne lords below him, and tenants who held of the mesne lords. The set of rights attached to mesne lords, known as a seignory, was, though an abstraction, nonetheless conceived of materially. The lord who had the seignory of Blackacre was 'seised in service of Blackacre'. The tenant who had actual possession of the land was 'seised *in demesne* of Blackacre'.[53] This division of rights was such that both the holder of the seignory and the tenant could be said to be the 'owners' of Blackacre. In that respect, the situation was quite different from the modern liberal idea of ownership so capably explicated by Honoré, especially in allodial systems of property. Much later, in the late nineteenth century, when the idea of property as a bundle of rights began to dominate judicial and academic thinking, in many quarters it was thought to give greater constitutional protection to property rights and to be in that respect 'anti-statist'.[54] The point of this abbreviated survey is that the ways in which people think of property vary across time and place, and often legal systems have seen property in ways that are plural and aggregated. It is no defect to think of property in terms of the many.

The foregoing considerations affect this second dimension of our substantive disagreement in relation to W_1 as follows. First, as to substance, many of the subjects of other fields of inquiry are composites. Some of these subjects are also

---

[50] James 1907, 152, 160.–1.   [51] Penner 1996a, 741.

[52] Farnsworth 2004, ch. 12; *Decker v Browning-Ferris Industries of Colorado, Inc.* 1997.

[53] Simpson 1986, 47–8.

[54] Banner 2011, ch. 3; Epstein 2011. My sympathy for the bundle approach to property has never turned on whether it is anti-statist or pro-statist. I just think the approach is analytically useful. E.g. Munzer 2009 illustrates its analytical utility.

historically contingent. They are also partly the product of human artifice in the context of specific socioeconomic conditions. As varied as these conditions are, it is understandable that property might turn out to be a structural composite. Seeing property as a set of relations among persons with respect to things fits well here. Second, as to partly verbal disagreement, the foregoing considerations help to explain why most versions of the bundle theory tally nicely with relevant community usage in the United States and, I believe, in England, and why Penner's linguistic proposal does not.

d) What about W_2 and W_3?

Penner's positions W_2 and W_3 merit a brief treatment. They are not direct competitors with my version of the bundle theory, because my version addresses property rather than the so-called right to property. A salient difficulty with both W_2 and W_3 is why *any* single right should be considered *the* right to property. No doubt one can pick out some rights that are more important than others in the functioning of a system of property. One might acknowledge that the right to exclude is functionally more important than, say, the right to pledge. But there are many rights—such as the rights to use and to possess—that are almost as functionally important as the right to exclude. Other highly functionally important rights include the rights to receive income, to abandon, and to destroy. For these reasons, Penner's search for the essence of the right to property in W_2 and W_3 is misguided.

Penner could try to skirt this criticism by weakening his claims in at least two ways. First, he could say that 'the' right to property is the *set* of the rights to exclude, use, possess, receive income, abandon, and destroy—call this position W_4. Second, he could map out layers of 'the' right to property based on the functional importance of various rights. This second move—call it W_5—would take Penner farthest from W_1 and W_2. Clearly, either W_4 or W_5 would cede the distinctive features of Penner's approach to property.

2. Concepts, their Individuation, and the Incomplete Understanding of Concepts

I shift now to disagreements that turn on the nature of concepts. Word meanings and concepts differ partly because word meanings are often conventional in a Humean sense and concepts are not ordinarily conventional in that or any other sense. Philosophers of mind and language will object to some of my remarks on concepts, if only because they often object to one another's writings. They are unlikely to find anything here that is both sound and novel. There is no current philosophical consensus on concepts, but the following quite tentative account may have some promise. If this account proves defective, Wittgenstein's family-resemblance account of concepts will enable my argument to go through. Concepts, as types, are abstract objects. Concepts, as tokens of those types, are mental representations.[55] The particularity of the concept of property, as a mental-representation token of that type, helps to explain how each person can think and express thoughts about property. The abstractness of the concept of property as a type helps to explain how people can understand each other when they talk or write about property. In my view, all or almost all concepts as types are mind-dependent abstract objects— that is, they did not exist until some thinking entity first used them.[56] Concepts qua types are causally inefficacious.[57] Some philosophers and some cognitive scientists hold that concepts qua tokens are causally inefficacious and others do not. I leave the matter open.

The extension of a concept qua type is the set of all items that fall under that concept. For classical ('crisp') sets, each item in a universe of discourse either falls under a given concept or it does not. 'Fuzzy' sets are a generalization of classical sets, and in fact classical sets are thought of as a special case of fuzzy sets. In the universe of discourse, any item that is neither fully within nor fully outside a fuzzy set is typically given a grade of membership value between 0 and 1.[58] Following a current philosophical convention, I will sometimes write 'the concept PROPERTY' as well as 'the concept of property'.

Even though concepts as tokens are mental representations, it is unnecessary for present purposes to subscribe to any position of the exact nature of these representations. It is doubtful that all or even some representations are mental images, as the classical empiricist philosophers believed.[59] It is unknown whether mental representations have some semantic or syntactic or other structure. Perhaps some complicated concepts qua tokens, such as that of a vested remainder subject to partial divestment, have a structure. Yet simple concepts qua tokens, like that of water, might not. Neither is it evident that the concept of property has the same, i.e. qualitatively identical, mental-representation tokens across all persons, or within each given person over time.[60] I take no position on the ontological status of concepts as tokens.

Sometimes it is difficult to tell whether two scholars who use a concept qua type, such as the concept of property, are using the same concept as type, or are using two different concepts of property as type. Difficulties of this sort raise issues about the individuation of concepts. One can find these difficulties in many fields of inquiry.

---

[55] Fodor 1983, 260, 331. For the type/token distinction, see Wetzel 2009. The species *Ursus arctos horribilis* (grizzly bear) is a type. Members of that species are tokens of that type. Wetzel 2009, xi. For an excellent discussion of abstract objects of various sorts, see Hale 1987.

[56] Cf. Raz 2009, 23: 'The fact that for the most part concepts are there independently of any one of us does not mean of course that they are independent of us collectively.' Perhaps, as Frege 1884, 105 held, numbers are mind-independent abstract objects. Still, one must distinguish the number 1 from the concept of the number 1.

[57] Rosen 2012, s. 3.2.   [58] Ross 2010, 25–47.

[59] Prinz 2002 surveys the philosophical landscape from classical empiricism to radical concept nativism.

[60] This statement is sympathetic to the scientific project of some psychologists, e.g. Carey 2009, but one should not suppose that contemporary philosophers interested in concepts have the same project.

Does the history of biology, for example, contain a single concept of a gene, or does it have two or more such concepts in light of the progress between Gregor Mendel and contemporary molecular and cell biology? In the history of philosophy, is there a single concept of weakness of will, or two or more such concepts?

I distinguish between two propositions. P1: the concept of property is incomplete. P2: the understanding of the concept of property is incomplete. I take no position on the truth value of P1. However, I assert that P2 is sometimes true. Thus, I am ascribing incompleteness not to the concept of property itself but to some understandings of that concept.

This preamble is important for the discussion of Harris and Honoré in Section 3. It plays a significant role in the examination of Penner's views on concepts in Section 4. It requires, in each setting, further elaboration. The elaboration is partly metaphysical and partly epistemic.[61]

3. A Minor Disagreement that is both Substantive and Conceptual

Applying this view of concepts facilitates a new approach to a disagreement between Harris and Honoré on the one hand and me on the other. Harris writes that the items we call property, which he labels 'items on the ownership spectrum', all 'involve a juridical relation between a person (or group) and a resource'.[62] Citing Harris, Honoré says: 'Property relations all involve a juridical relation between a person or group and a resource, in law a "thing".'[63] He continues:

[P]roperty interests are not to be analysed merely as consisting in relations between people, but as relations between people and things, protected by rules that impose restraints on others....

The contrary view, that property is always concerned with relations between people as to the use or exploitation of things is attributed, I am glad to say, to *illegitimate* inferences drawn from treatments of the topic by Hohfeld and myself.[64]

I shall argue that there is little substantive or conceptual difference between their view and mine, and that Honoré's comment on which relations are primary and which are secondary is open to another interpretation. In short, I clarify this dispute in some respects and dissolve it in another.

The first point is that the view espoused by Harris and Honoré is truth-functionally equivalent to the view that I hold, even though there is some difference in verbal formulation and perhaps also in meaning.[65] On my view, the concept of property involves a set of three-place relations among a person, other persons (all

---

[61] Raz 2009, 18–24, 53–87, avoids most metaphysical issues but attends more than I to epistemic issues.

[62] Harris 1996, 5.   [63] Honoré 2006, 131 (footnote omitted).

[64] Honoré 2006, (italics in original, footnote omitted).

[65] In this chapter I use 'truth-functional equivalence' to include first-order equivalence in predicate logic.

other persons if the right is *in rem*), and a thing. On their view, the concept of property involves a set of three-place relations among a person, a thing or 'resource', and trespassory rules (Harris) or 'rules that impose restraints on others' (Honoré).[66]

These two sets of three-place relations are different ways of saying basically the same thing, for the various normative modalities imposed on others (my view) seem not to differ from the restraints imposed by certain rules (their view). If that is correct, then the concept of property has the same extension for all three of us. Accordingly, propositions of property law on my view are truth-functionally equivalent to counterpart propositions of property law on their view. Obviously, the term 'counterpart propositions' has to be explained so as not to beg the question. But here is a straightforward example: the proposition that a fee simple absolute in Blackacre is protected in part by duties on others to the owner not to trespass or create a nuisance on Blackacre (my view) is truth-functionally equivalent to the proposition that a fee simple absolute in Blackacre is protected in part by rules that impose restraints on others in favour of the owner pertaining to trespass and nuisance on Blackacre (their view).

A possible reply to the argument that their view and my view are truth-functionally equivalent is that it takes into account only the extension of the concept of property. It does not include the intension of that concept. But debate exists over the nature of the intension of concepts. A current position is to characterize intension as a function from a possible world to an extension. This position will cut no ice with those who see possible worlds metaphysics as misguided. Even those who have no difficulty with possible worlds have various intensional and modal logics from which to choose. Thus, to make the reply stick anyone offering it will have to do some preliminary work on intension for the counter-argument to get off the ground.[67] In contrast, there is general philosophical consensus that the extension of a concept is all of the things that fall under it (with appropriate adjustments for fuzzy concepts).

So much for the first point. The second is that Honoré adds a comment that is separate from the extension of the concept of property and that does not contradict anything that I have written:

Indeed, Harris could argue that the relation of the holder of the interest to the thing is primary, since the main task of the law of property is to regulate the use of resources. The relation of the holder of the interest to other people, though a necessary element in a property relationship, is secondary in the sense that it presupposes and serves to uphold the relation of the holder to the thing.[68]

---

[66] Honoré puts the point a bit differently when he says that 'property interests require that there should be legal relations of various sorts between the holder of the interest and others'. Honoré 2006, 131 n. 10.

[67] It is unclear to me whether Smith this volume is attracted to a possible worlds approach as he characterizes intensions in various non-equivalent ways. In intensional and modal logic, the distinction between 'intension' and 'extension'—the words Smith employs most often—was first powerfully developed by Carnap (1956) but earlier and later logicians contributed to the enterprise. Carnap does not speak of possible worlds.

[68] Honoré 2006, 131.

Honoré's comment concerns the primacy of *things* in the analysis of property.[69] In my version of the bundle theory, property always has to do with relations between persons with respect to things, so it would be incorrect to say that I fail to give attention to things. Beyond that, I believe that I am free to accept or reject what Honoré adds. Still, whether I accept or reject his appended comment, there is another sense in which the first relation in the passage quoted is secondary (because the holder is an agent and the thing or resource is rarely an agent) and the second relation is primary (because a central aim of property law is to regulate behaviour between persons with respect to things).[70] By parity of reasoning, Honoré would be free to accept or reject what I just wrote. The underlying reason for this intellectual freedom on each side is that 'primary' and 'secondary' are being used in two different ways.[71]

A possible objection is that I have misattributed a set of three-place relations to Harris and Honoré, for they couch their theory in terms of a set of two two-place relations that are tied to each other. This objection is unsound. Using capital letters for relations, and omitting lower case letters for relata, let us characterize my position as RST, whereas their position would be either $(RS)T$ or $R(ST)$. However, under the associative law of the composition of relations, $(RS)T = R(ST) = RST$.[72] Elsewhere I allow that the concept of property is imprecise at the margins.[73] For example, some might debate whether a licence coupled with an interest counted as property under the original Restatement.[74] Given this allowance, some might complain that my version of the bundle theory leaves the limits of property inadequately defined. I disagree with the complaint.[75] But even if the complaint were well taken, it would pose no obstacle to my argument against this objection. Just as there are crisp sets and fuzzy sets, there are classical ('crisp') relations and 'fuzzy' relations—with the latter commonly indicated by a squiggle under a capital letter.[76] The associative law for the composition of relations also holds for fuzzy relations.[77] Hence, $(\underset{\sim}{R}\,\underset{\sim}{S})\,\underset{\sim}{T} = \underset{\sim}{R}(\underset{\sim}{S}\,\underset{\sim}{T}) = \underset{\sim}{R}\,\underset{\sim}{S}\,\underset{\sim}{T}$.[78]

There seem to be no differences between Harris and Honoré and me on the extension of the concept of property. Only minor differences survive between us on the best way to articulate or explain the concept of property. To that extent, any tempest here appears to belong in a very small cup.[79] The analysis offered here

---

[69] See also Penner 1997, 105–27; Smith 2012b. Penner's separability thesis requires 'things' that are property to be 'contingently associated with any particular owner'. Penner 1997, 111. But if people have any property rights in parts of their own bodies, these body parts are rarely only contingently associated with them. Body parts acquired from others, e.g. a transplanted kidney, are an exception.

[70] I say 'rarely an agent' because slavery is outlawed almost everywhere and informed opinions differ over which non-human animals, if any, are agents.

[71] The same point applies to Smith this volume.   [72] Ross 2010, 52.

[73] Munzer 1990, 24.   [74] American Law Institute 1944, s. 513, Illustration 3.

[75] Munzer 2011, 271.   [76] Ross 2010, 48–88.   [77] Ross 2010, 55.

[78] The Appendix gives a slightly more formal treatment of the objection in the text.

[79] I do not know whether Honoré had me in mind when he spoke of illegitimate inferences from the work of Hohfeld and himself. From my perspective, I *inferred* nothing—validly or invalidly, legitimately or illegitimately—from their work. I merely *adapted* Hohfeld's vocabulary to the analysis of property and *conjoined* it with Honoré's work on ownership. Munzer 1990, 22.

almost entirely dissolves the disagreement between us, and otherwise it resolves the dispute in my favour.

4. Penner Redux: A Major Disagreement that is both Substantive and Conceptual

Penner is one of the few lawyer-philosophers to devote sustained attention to the nature of concepts. In a major article he separates a Classical view of concepts from a Criterial view.[80] Under the Classical view, concepts are tied to a rigorous semantics. In a rigorous semantics, the word 'property' has a definite meaning if, and only if, one can give necessary and sufficient conditions for its application. In turn, the Classical concept of property must have a correspondingly definite extension: each item of property falls under the concept of property, and each item that is not property is outside its extension. Though Penner makes little mention of sets, evidently his précis of the Classical view of concepts rests on classical set theory. This section is concerned with Penner's positions earlier labelled W_1 and to a lesser extent W_2 and W_3. I clarify the nature of our conceptual disagreement and resolve it in favour of a tentative account of concepts that addresses their individuation and incomplete understanding. I also show that Wittgensteinian family-resemblance concepts favour my position over Penner's.

Penner believes that what he calls the Classical concept of property does not tally at all well with bundle theories of property as he understands them. Bundle theories offered by Christman, Grey, Hoffmaster, Honoré, Waldron, and A. Weinrib are, despite their differences, all found wanting to a greater or lesser extent.[81] They come up short because they leave indefinite the metes and bounds of the concept of property. I am in the dock with the others, though charitably Penner finds it more difficult to detect a fixed position in my book.[82] I acknowledge, with thanks, his charity and caution. I agree with him, if on different grounds, that it is not possible to supply necessary and sufficient conditions for the concept of property.

Furthermore, Penner is right to be unsatisfied by the concept/conception distinction that Waldron borrows from Dworkin and employs in Waldron's book on property. Penner seems to hold that the distinction just allows Waldron to avoid issues about which 'things' can be property.[83] Reasons exist to think that Dworkin's distinction, at least as drawn as late as 1977, suffers from considerable infirmities.[84] It is, moreover, difficult to figure out how it is possible even in principle to distinguish concepts from conceptions. How can I tell, in writing this sentence, whether my thought involves the concept of property rather than

---

[80] Penner 1996a, 767–98. Penner 1997 replicates little of his earlier discussion, and talks more about the idea rather than the concept of property—e.g. at 1–3, 169–86.

[81] Penner 1996a, 770–9.

[82] Penner 1996a, 774–7. In 1990, I had no well-considered view on concepts.

[83] Penner 1996a, 778. Cf. Waldron 1988, 52 and n. 53; Dworkin 1978, 103, 134–6. Dworkin in turn seems to get the distinction from Rawls 1955, 3–4, 19, 24–30, 32; Rawls 1971, 5–11.

[84] Munzer and Nickel 1977, 1037–41.

some conception of that concept, or somehow both of them? For the moment I lay to one side whether Dworkin's later work, in *Law's Empire* and *Justice for Hedge-hogs*, solves or sidesteps these problems.[85]

Penner turns to the Criterial view of concepts for a congenial analysis of the concept of property.[86] This view, he says, rests largely 'on Wittgenstein's later writings on language and rule-following in the *Philosophical Investigations*'.[87] As to the concept of property, the chief value of the Criterial view, he writes, is that 'it allows us to outline a theory of terms on which the absence of Classical definition [through necessary and sufficient conditions] is not to be regarded as a sign that a term has a diminished, much less no, meaning'.[88] The thrust of his argument is that the Criterial view helps to 'explain the determinate character of concepts . . . while recognizing the real diversity of phenomena which, in a real diversity of circum-stances, satisfy complex concepts underpinning terms like "property"'.[89] Just as Wittgenstein's notion of family resemblance arguably enables us to elucidate the concept of a game, so, Penner reasons, that notion arguably helps us to explain the concept of property—in terms not only of criteria but also of the circumstances in which the concept and the term for that concept are correctly applied.[90] The concept of property and related concepts such as that of ownership are useful because, Penner holds, similarities illuminated by family resemblance give those concepts, within limits, a determinateness unblemished by rigidity.[91] So the Criterial view, Penner suggests, explains why the concept of property has a unitary content whose essence is the right to exclude rather than dissolving into the composite fluidity of, he believes, a bundle theory.

4.1 Reservations: of Wittgenstein and Dworkin

A significant worry about Penner's account of the Criterial view is his heavy reliance on Wittgenstein in arguing for W_1. The relevant section of his article is headed 'The Criterial View of Concepts'.[92] Throughout that section he frequently refers to concepts generally and to particular concepts, such as those of property and games. He peppers these reflections with discussions of meaning, sense, Wittgenstein's philosophy of language and rule following, Criterial semantics, the defeasibility of the correct use of terms and expressions, and internal relations of grammar.[93] Penner's heavy reliance on Wittgenstein's notion of family resemblance, I think, undoes his project W_1. Games may exhibit a family resemblance, but they do not have an essence. It is baffling how Penner can think that property has an essence if a family resemblance is in play.[94]

---

85 Dworkin 1986; Dworkin 2011.   86 Penner 1996a, 779–98.
87 Penner 1996a, 779–80 (footnote omitted).   88 Penner 1996a, 780.
89 Penner 1996a, 780.   90 Penner 1996a, 783–5.   91 Penner 1996a, 787–9.
92 Penner 1996a, 779.
93 Penner 1996a, 779–98. Penner does not mention work on concepts done by cognitive scientists such as Fodor 1975 and Fodor 1983.
94 Penner 1996a, 798–818.

I offer a stronger claim: a Wittgensteinian view of concepts in terms of family resemblance actually favours, not Penner's position W_1, but the idea that property is a set of relations among persons with respect to things. Wittgenstein explains family resemblance in various passages of the *Philosophical Investigations* and other works.[95] 'I *can* give the concept of number rigid boundaries... but I can also use it so that the extension of the concept is *not* closed by a boundary. And this is how we use the word "game".'[96] In response to the objection that a 'blurred concept' is not a concept at all, Wittgenstein points out we do not always need a sharp photograph and that sometimes 'one that isn't sharp [is] just what we need'.[97] We see similarities and affinities, 'a complicated network of similarities overlapping and criss-crossing'.[98] Baker and Hacker's masterful exposition of Wittgenstein on concepts and family resemblance simultaneously gives an overall picture and attends to detail.[99] They observe that his idea of 'family resemblance concepts' performs, among other jobs, 'the negative task of shaking us free from the illusions of real definitions, of the mythology of analysis as disclosing the essences of things'.[100]

I do not consider myself a follower of Wittgenstein, but if for the moment I occupy that role it is easy to see why a family resemblance concept would do quite nicely as an explanation of the concept of property, including its blurriness at the edges. The place to start is not with some definition of property or with an analysis that tries to identify its essence. Rather, one should start by looking at particular legal systems and taking note of what those working within the system mark out as 'property' (or 'Eigentum' or 'propriété' etc.). One is likely to see that the region marked out varies somewhat from one legal system to another, but that there are many similarities and affinities. One is also likely to see that within any given legal system the region identified as property includes a welter of different rules and subsidiary concepts that vary a good deal in their functional importance. Consider this remark of Wittgenstein's:

> Frege compares a concept to a region, and says that a region without clear boundaries can't be called a region at all. This presumably means that we can't do anything with it.—But is it senseless to say 'Stay roughly here'? Imagine that I were standing with someone in a city square and said that.[101]

The blurriness of Wittgenstein's family resemblance concepts is something that I would prefer to think of in terms of fuzzy sets, fuzzy concepts, and fuzzy relations. It is hard to know whether Wittgentstein would have been receptive to such an idea. He died in 1951. Lofti Zadeh's influential article on fuzzy sets did not appear until 1965.[102]

---

[95] E.g. Wittgenstein 1953, ss. 67–77; cf. Wittgenstein 1967, ss. 326, 373–81, 441.
[96] Wittgenstein 1953, s. 68 (italics in original).   [97] Wittgenstein 1953, s. 71.
[98] Wittgenstein 1953, s. 66.
[99] Baker and Hacker 2009, vol. 1, part 1, 201–26, and part 2, 153–71; vol. 2, 48 n. 1, 91.
[100] Baker and Hacker 2009, vol. 1, part 1, 226.   [101] Wittgenstein 1953, s. 38.
[102] Zadeh 1965.

It is important to get clear on two different though connected strands of inquiry: the theory of concepts and the theory of language. As brought out at the beginning of Section 2, concepts qua types are abstract objects whereas concepts qua tokens are mental representations. Concepts qua types are not conventional. But the relation between words and their meanings is conventional. These theories are no longer the sole domain of philosophers. Psychology, linguistics, and cognitive science have made many contributions of their own.

One way to connect these strands of inquiry is to clarify an issue about words and reference. Modifying Strawson, one can say that people can use certain words to refer.[103] Take the word 'dog'. People can use this word to refer to the set of all dogs. Differently, they can also use it to refer to the concept DOG. The first use refers to the extension of the concept whereas the second refers to the concept itself. There are many natural languages. People can use the words 'Hund' and 'chien' to refer to all dogs or to the concept DOG, and use the words 'Eigentum' and 'propriété' to refer to all items of property or to the concept PROPERTY.

The options for explicating the concept of property are fewer once we reject the Classical view and the Criterial view. There remain Ronald Dworkin's interpretive account of concepts and an account of the individuation of concepts and the incomplete understanding of them. I look first at Dworkin's most recent work.

With *Law's Empire*, Dworkin's work took an interpretive turn; that turn included a chapter on interpretive concepts.[104] A quarter-century later, in *Justice for Hedgehogs*, he returned to interpretation in earnest.[105] The latter work devotes an entire chapter to conceptual interpretation and interpretive concepts.[106] My exposition rests on his account in *Justice for Hedgehogs* as his final view, and I ignore minor differences between the two books.

Dworkin's taxonomy recognizes criterial (small 'c') concepts, natural-kind concepts, and interpretive concepts. Although Dworkin holds that not all concepts have necessary and sufficient conditions for their application, he does not use the term 'criterial concepts' in the same way as Penner. Penner regards Criterial (capital 'C') concepts as definite enough, while Dworkin admits of both precise criterial concepts, e.g. of an equilateral triangle, and vague criterial concepts, e.g. of baldness.[107] Dworkin pays little attention to natural-kind concepts, such as those of a chemical compound or an animal species; these seem almost entirely irrelevant

---

[103] Strawson 1950. Strawson was concerned, not with all words or even all nouns, but with referring expressions such as demonstrative pronouns, proper names, and phrases beginning with 'the' followed by a noun or noun phrase.

[104] Dworkin 1986, 45–86.   [105] Dworkin 2011, 97–188.

[106] Dworkin 2011, 157–88. The concept/conception distinction pops up from time to time, e.g. at 161, but it is on the fringe of the inquiry. Some literature on concepts and conceptions in the philosophy of mind distinguishes between having a concept and mastering it. E.g. Villanueva 1998, 149–96. Dworkin does not cite this literature and it may not be relevant to his project. It may, however, be pertinent to the incomplete understanding of concepts, which I consider later in this section.

[107] Dworkin 2011, 158–9.

to his project.[108] His attention centres on interpretive concepts, such as the concepts we find in morality, politics, and law, including the concept of property.[109] A concept is interpretive if we (1) 'share [it] in spite of not agreeing about a decisive test', (2) regard the best way of understanding it to be justifying its operation in our shared value-practices, and (3) use the concept 'as interpreting the practices in which [it] figure[s]'.[110]

Property counts as an interpretive concept under Dworkin's account of interpretation. It would be inappropriate to list him as a supporter of a bundle theory of property, because though he writes in this way he does not mention, let alone consider, any alternative to a bundle theory.[111] Still, one can deploy his view of interpretive concepts in favour of a bundle theory. The way that the concept of property functions and is understood in contemporary legal systems outstrips the right to exclude with a correlative duty not to trespass on or harm the owner's land. Lawyers today recognize that zoning and covenants, land transfer and finance, defence against government intrusion, appropriate use of eminent domain, and many other practice areas are within the repertoire of property lawyers. Intellectual property is a booming area. One could hardly make sense of these features of legal systems and law practice without recourse to powers to transfer, lease and licence, immunities against expropriation without compensation, and a vast array of other rights, powers, liberty-rights, immunities, and disabilities. Even if disagreement exists on the exact contours of property, conceptual interpretation helps in understanding these disagreements while pointing out the huge domain of property on which our practices and justifications for inclusion agree.

This argument should not be thought of in terms of linguistic deference. Deference of that sort might help to reduce, if not dissolve, the partly verbal disagreement between Penner and me treated in Section 1. In this conceptual context, however, the intellectual work is done by justificatory arguments for interpreting our practices regarding property and the concept of property along the lines of my version of the bundle theory. Even if Penner were minded to appeal to Dworkin on interpretive concepts, it would aid Penner hardly at all. Dworkin's interpretive concepts and the legal and social practices they illuminate are far richer than Penner's insistence on the right to exclude.

At the same time, I am not comfortable with relying on Dworkin's account of conceptual interpretation and interpretive concepts in responding to Penner. First, I do not accept Dworkin's claim that conceptual 'interpretation is interpretive all the way down', unless of course that claim is tautological.[112] He is willing to travel down Friedrichstrasse farther than I am. Second, I do not accept the 'overall theme

---

[108] Dworkin 2011, 159–60.

[109] Dworkin 2011, 160–3, 166–70, 180–8, 327–415. He mentions property on 374–5, where he seems to assume that some version of the bundle theory is sound.

[110] Dworkin 2011, 160, 162, 164.

[111] Dworkin 2011, 375. At 374–5 he is more concerned with libertarian versus non-libertarian concepts of property.

[112] Dworkin 2011, 162.

of [his] book: the unity of value'.[113] For me, value is sometimes discontinuous or fragmented. Third, though Dworkin does not conflate the theory of concepts and the theory of language, he once says that conceptual disagreements that seem to be merely apparent are 'only verbal', 'spurious', or 'illusory'.[114] Indeed, the sole verbal disagreements he seems to recognize are ones labelled 'only' or 'merely' verbal.

4.2 Individuation and incomplete understanding

To see whether another account of concepts besides Wittgenstein's can shed light on the disagreement between Penner and me on the concept of property, let us incorporate here my remarks at the beginning of Section 2. Two main topics will occupy our attention: the individuation of concepts and the incomplete understanding of concepts. I suggest provisionally that either Penner and I use different concepts of property or that, if we share a single concept of property, possibly neither of us has mastered it. This suggestion, I believe, helps to resolve part of our conceptual dispute.

Anyone who surveys the history of different disciplines is likely to conclude that at one time people used a certain word for one concept and at a later time used the same word for a different though related concept.[115] In psychoanalysis, various analysts have different concepts of identification. Even within a given historical period and culture, libertarians have a different concept of freedom from left-wing liberals. Perhaps not all stem cell biologists share the same concept of stemness.[116]

One's view of concepts has a part to play in their individuation. In regard to the individuation of concepts as types, it might seem appealing to do so by their extensions. But this proposal is vulnerable to undesirable results. For instance, the concept UNICORN and the concept PHLOGISTON have the same extension—the null set—but are different concepts, because the former concerns a mythical animal and the latter a bogus explanation of fire. Or, to use a familiar example, the concept WELL-FORMED CREATURE WITH A HEART and the concept WELL-FORMED CREATURE WITH A KIDNEY are extensionally equivalent but they are plainly two different concepts. In these examples as with the concept PROPERTY, it is crucial to pay heed to both the intension and the extension of a concept.

Given my view that concepts as types are mind-dependent abstract entities, one can say: two concepts C_1 and C_2 are distinct if, and only if, there are two distinct propositions in which C_2 has been substituted for C_1 and the two propositions are not informationally equivalent. The proposition that the morning star is the morning star and the proposition that the morning star is the evening star are not informationally equivalent propositions.[117] As to the individuation of concepts

---

[113] Dworkin 2011, 1–2, 163.　　[114] Dworkin 2011, 158.

[115] I do not believe that concepts themselves, as types, change.

[116] Leychkis, Munzer, and Richardson 2009.

[117] My account is superior to the view that concepts are individuated by their roles in inferences, for the reasons given in Fodor 1994. If Raz has an account of the individuation of concepts, I do not understand it. Sometimes he seems to think of individuation in terms of possession conditions. Raz 2009, 22, 55–6. Cf. Peacocke 1992; Peacocke 2004, and the criticisms

as tokens, given my view that these are mental representations, these representations are distinct so long as they belong to different individuals, or to the same individual at different times. This criterion for concepts as tokens gives a sufficient but not necessary condition for individuation.

Penner and I seem to have two different concepts of property qua type because his is narrower than mine. For him, the concept of property applies only to the right to exclude.[118] To my mind, he takes a central feature of property and idealizes it into the only feature of property. He might prefer to say that he has discerned the central organizing norm of property, though I think that formulation fits W_1 less well than mine. In any case, W_2 and W_3 make different claims from W_1. For me, the concept of property includes a great deal besides the right to exclude, or even the right to exclusive use. It also includes powers to sell, devise/bequeath, mortgage/pledge, and lease to others; liberties to consume and, within some limits, to destroy; immunities against expropriation; and some duties not to use one's property to harm others.

Now to incomplete understanding: understanding a concept as type is a matter of degree. Consider the concept of glaucoma. Some laypersons in the United States could tell you that glaucoma is an eye disease that can cause blindness. Other laypersons could tell you that glaucoma has something to do with pressure inside the eyeball. Neither lay group has mastered the concept of glaucoma; the understanding of both groups is incomplete. If, however, someone else said that glaucoma is an eye disease in which high intraocular pressure damages the optic nerve and can thereby cause blindness, his or her understanding reveals mastery of the concept.[119] Generally, what makes an understanding of a concept incomplete is that the understanding is underinclusive or overinclusive, or fails to assemble properly the components of a complex concept such as that of a vested remainder subject to partial divestment.

An incomplete understanding of concepts might seem to be just the sort of thing that leads people to talk past each other. To some observers they might seem not really to disagree with each other at all. That would be a mistake. Consider the concept of property, and lay to one side for the moment my earlier suggestion that Penner and I have two different concepts of property. Suppose that Penner and I disagree about the concept of property because neither of us understands the concept completely. This supposition might seem bizarre. Penner knows pretty well how I understand the concept of property; he just thinks I am partly wrong. I reckon that I know less about property law than he does. But I believe that I know pretty well how he understands the concept of property; I just think he is partly

in Davis 2005. At other times Raz suggests that the 'identity' of a concept turns on 'idealizations' of conceptual practices. Raz 2009, 23.

[118] I do not know whether Penner 1997, 111, takes the separability thesis to be part of the concept of property, or an observation about that concept. Cf. my n. 69.

[119] Philosophers draw the line between incomplete understanding and mastery in different places. E.g. Greenberg 2000; Raz 2009.

wrong. Sometimes it is hard to tell whether (1) incomplete understandings of the same concept, or (2) complete or incomplete understandings of two or more concepts, are in play.

So how is the debate over the concept of property to move forward? Deference to experts is not the answer.[120] No party to this debate is in the position of a lay patient asking his physician to explain more thoroughly what glaucoma is. Of course, a scholar might come along whose understanding of the concept of property is far deeper than that of either of us. Such a scholar might conclude that Penner and I are each partly right and partly wrong. Thus, our conceptual disagreement is not spurious, and we are not just talking past each other. Yet this imagined scholar is not infallible and cannot just make pronouncements about the concept of property. She has to supply arguments for them, and others might spot flaws in those arguments.

A first step forward is to isolate some varieties of indeterminacy that pertain to incomplete understanding.[121] Metaphysical Extensional Indeterminacy (MEI) holds that the concept-type PROPERTY is extensionally fuzzy because some items fall under it only to a matter of degree. MEI is compatible with the view that some items can be categorically outside and others categorically inside the extension of the concept-type PROPERTY. MEI involves cases where there is no matter of fact as to whether a particular individual falls under the concept—e.g. the concept BALD in the proposition that Joe Biden is bald, despite the fact that one can determine how many hairs he has on his head. Metaphysical Intensional Indeterminacy (MII) holds that the concept-type PROPERTY does not have an essence. MII involves cases where a concept has no unproblematic essentialist or conceptual reductions—e.g. if one reduced the concept GAME to the proposition that a game is a strategic interaction between multiple players, then it is hard to see how solitaire fulfils this condition. Epistemic Conceptual Indeterminacy (ECI) holds that some concept-tokens of PROPERTY do not fully capture the concept-type PROPERTY. Mark Green-berg has suggested to me that even if the concept FUNNY is metaphysically determinate extensionally and intensionally, there might be a limit on human cognitive faculties to understanding this concept: either to grasp completely what falls under the concept or to give a reductive explanation of what makes funny things funny.

As to the concept PROPERTY, I subscribe to MEI and MII. Either is enough to entail ECI if an understanding of the concept-type PROPERTY is incomplete. Penner would reject MII. Perhaps his texts do not commit him to any position regarding MEI or ECI. Even if some understandings of the concept-type PROPERTY are incomplete, ECI would not entail either MEI or MII. However, ECI would be evidence for MEI and MII. Once these different positions and their interrelations are out in the open, a move in the right direction is to shift from metaphysical analysis to an epistemic inquiry regarding incomplete understandings of the concept of property.

---

[120] Rey 1998, 98, suggests such a move. [121] Paul Daniell prompted these remarks.

The next step is to see that argument can reduce or eliminate incomplete understandings of the concept of property. But the most promising appeal to argument is not, I suggest, the Dworkinian method of arguments about interpreting the concept of property. Neither is it the Hegelian dialectical method of a never-ending sequence of thesis-antithesis-synthesis, with each synthesis giving rise to the next thesis.[122] Something more down to earth is preferable: a Peircean method of inquiry that explicates concepts. We owe to Cheryl Misak a remarkably patient and insightful stitching together of Peircean—not necessarily Peirce's—views on inquiry, truth, and the fixation of belief.[123] For her, Peirce does not have either a correspondence or a coherence theory of truth; nor does he offer a definition of truth. Rather, for Peirce truth (T) applies to a hypothesis (H) that one believes to be true at the end of inquiry (I) and deliberation. More precisely, there are two different theses here, and even both together yield only a 'practical', not a 'transcendental', truth:

(T-I): If H is true, then, if inquiry relevant to H were pursued as far as it could fruitfully go, H would be believed;

and

(I-T): If, if inquiry were pursued as far as it could go, H would be believed, then H is true.[124]

We have beliefs about many things. Among them are beliefs about concepts qua types. To my knowledge, nowhere in Peirce's sprawling corpus does he discuss the concept of property. But we can adapt what he says about the elucidation of other concepts, such as the concept of truth, to the concept of property. To paraphrase a Peircean position that Misak adopts from Christopher Hookway, if we commit ourselves to a belief about the concept of property, we expect our practical experience to jibe with this belief or 'with some successor of it', i.e. that the belief 'in some form will survive future inquiry', even if the content of our belief is 'indeterminate'.[125]

Some might object that anyone who adopts a Peircean, practical view of the concept of truth is committed to adopting analyses of all concepts that have the most fruitful practical consequences. I am not sure that such a broad commitment follows. But even if it did, no problem results so far as the concept of property is concerned. Property law is a practical enterprise. It creates no difficulty to have a concept of property that serves the practical objective of analytical clarity claimed in the introduction for my version of the bundle theory.

---

[122] Hegel 1820a, 40–57, does, however, contribute insightfully to our understanding of property. Munzer 1990, 67–74, 80–3, 150–7; Waldron 1988, 343–89. Those who ignore Hegel's contributions do so at their peril.
[123] Misak 2004.   [124] Misak 2004, 125 (initial capital letters added); cf. Misak 2004, 43.
[125] Misak 2004, x; Hookway 2000, 57.

5. The Nature of Property

To this point I have stuck to the letter of Penner's treatment of the concept of property and the definition of 'property'. Only by doing so could I be faithful to his texts. I want now to address the possibility that we do not disagree about either of these. Instead, we disagree about the nature of property. Approaching the disagreement in this fashion will also help to clarify the extent to which Smith's recent 'architectural' or 'modular' discussion of property differs from my version of the bundle theory. Throughout I understand the nature of property broadly to include the essence of property (if it has one), the indispensable characteristics of property (if it has any), and the explication of property.[126] As to essence, some philosophers do not think that mastery of a concept requires knowledge of the essence of the things to which the concept applies. They might say, for instance, that mastery of the concept of water does not require knowing that according to the best current theory water is H_20 with two hydrogen atoms covalently bonded to one oxygen atom. Thus, insofar as Penner's conceptual inquiry considers the essence of property, it could be that the essence of property (if it has one) actually belongs to an inquiry into the nature of property. In some cases, inquiries into the nature of property brush up against inquiries into the meaning of 'property' or the concept of property. I do not claim that a rigid trichotomy exists.

5.1 Penner: definition, concept, and nature

Sometimes when philosophers write about definition they are not concerned with the definition of a word, such as the word 'property'. If that is correct, then they might not be proposing that, say, the word 'property' has a different meaning from what other philosophers mean by that word. So what are they proposing? A somewhat technical possibility is that they are proposing what philosophers call a 'real' definition—that is, an account that gives the essence of something. It could be that Penner is attempting to do so in the case of property, because he does talk about the 'formal essence' and the 'practical essence' of property, which for him centre on the right to exclude. Another possibility is that Penner is using the word 'definition' loosely and that he aims only to give an account of the nature of property: its indispensable characteristics, and an explication of property. Both philosophers and non-philosophers sometimes use the word 'definition' in this loose fashion.

On these possibilities, one could conclude that Penner and I are not giving different meanings to the word 'property' and hence that no verbal disagreement exists between us. We would, however, still have some substantive disagreements: whether property has an essence, whether the right to exclude is an indispensable characteristic of property, and whether the best way to explicate property is in terms

---

[126] Mark Greenberg has helped me with this inquiry but at times I have, no doubt rashly, gone my own way.

of a right to exclude. We would also have some subordinate substantive disagreements: whether the justification of a right or power to sell belongs to the theory of property or the theory of contract, and whether property is as historically contingent an institution as I claim. For that reason, the substantive dimensions of my arguments against Penner remain at the heart of the disagreements between us.

One can perform a partly similar manoeuvre in the case of the concept of property. The question is: are the differences between Penner and me disagreements over the concept of property? Some of them once were. Penner's invocation of Wittgensteinian family-resemblance concepts as a foundation for his conceptual arguments is the leading case in point. As argued in Section 4, Wittgenstein's view of concepts actually supports the bundle theory, not Penner's essentialism about property. But that is ancient history, for in commenting on a draft of this chapter Penner advised me that he is not now an adherent of many of the conceptual views that he espoused in his 1996 article on the 'bundle of rights' picture of property. In addition, Penner could take or leave my musings about concepts qua types and concepts qua tokens, about fuzzy concepts and fuzzy relations, and about seeking any help from Dworkin's interpretive concepts. Penner has let me know that he does not think that we are using different concepts of property. Whether one or both of us have incomplete understandings of the concept is perhaps a closer question.

Here, too, Penner could say that our substantive disagreements go to the nature of property. Our dispute is over the matters listed two paragraphs ago. I remain sceptical that property has an essence. If it has any indispensable characteristics, then both the right to use and the right and power to transfer are every bit as indispensable as the right to exclude. And one can usefully explicate property as a set of normative relations with respect to things such that some relations are functionally much more important than others.

5.2 Smith and the architecture of property

Henry Smith's most recent work, mentioned in the introduction, takes the inquiry into property in a new direction. This work is daring, insightful, and creative. It has considerable explanatory power and illuminates many purposes of property law. It is certain to be the subject of close study in coming years.

This work is not definitional. Part of it is conceptual, or at least Smith writes as if it is. He makes much of the distinction between the intensions and extensions of concepts. He flirts with Frege's views on *Sinn*, or 'sense', which Smith usually cashes out as intension. Smith's ruminations on concepts and their intensions are insufficiently clear for me to say whether we have any conceptual disagreements over property. His flirtation with Frege's views leaves undecided whether concepts are mind independent or mind dependent.[127] As noted, it is not clear whether his recent work has just one consistent account of intensions.[128]

---

[127] Smith this volume.   [128] See my n. 67.

Smith and I may disagree on whether property has indispensable characteristics. I believe that various normative relations with respect to things are objective characteristics of particular systems of property law. I also believe that if a system of property law lacked a right and power to exclude, a power to transfer, and a right to use, then it would be so etiolated that one would be hard put to regard it as property at all. It is unclear to me whether Smith would hold that if a property system were not modular, then it could not be property at all. Perhaps he would say only that such a system would be hugely defective. Whichever position Smith takes on this matter, it might not mark out a difference between us. Smith finds bundle theories of little use, but that is different from saying that a subset of normative relations with respect to things would be indispensable. In my view, modularity is a quite useful feature of systems of property law.

We are more likely to disagree on the usefulness of modular theories and bundle theories regarding the explication of property. I find the underpinnings of Smith's modular theory puzzling. At times his theory appears to rest on parsimony.[129] But without canvassing the options one cannot say whether it is the most parsimonious theory, or whether the most parsimonious theory is the likeliest to be true, or the likeliest to be useful. At other times his theory seems to rest on tractability, i.e. ease of use as a matter of human psychology.[130] Yet it is not obvious that the modular theory is the most tractable theory, or that the most tractable theory has the best chance of being true, or the best chance of being useful. Neither is it obvious that his modular theory is both the most parsimonious and the most tractable. Smith could say that his modular theory need not be the best such theory from the standpoint of either parsimony, tractability, truth, or usefulness let alone all of these. However, his modular theory would be especially appealing if he could show that it is in fact the best such theory from all of these standpoints.

As regards bundle theories, to think of property in terms of the many is not to suppose that all elements of the set of relations with respect to things are equally important, malleable at will, or closely tied to legal realism. This supposition, or something close to it, mars Smith's 'Property as the Law of Things'.[131] Most contemporary defenders of a bundle theory would agree that the rights to use and exclude and the power to transfer are functionally much more important than, say, the right to pledge or the duty to observe a conservation easement. There is plenty of middle ground between Penner's essentialism on the one hand and the disintegrative view of Thomas Grey and the conclusory labelling of Edward Rubin on the other.[132]

As to bundle theorists and their connection to Hohfeld and legal realism, Smith highlights the role of the legal realists, and largely ignores the much more astringent and unpoliticized use of Hohfeld by philosophers.[133] Like many philosophers

---

[129] Smith 2012b, 1694–5, 1726.   [130] Smith 2012b, 1704; Smith 2012a, 2107–20.

[131] Smith 2012b.

[132] Smith 2012b, 1692, 1697. Cf. Grey 1980, discussed in Munzer 1990, 31–6; Rubin 1984, 1086.

[133] Philosophers influenced by Hohfeld, who are often drawn to some version of the bundle theory, include Becker 1977, 7–23; Stoljar 1984a; Thomson 1990, 37–78, 322–47; Upton 2000; Wellman

influenced by Hohfeld's work, I find his analytical vocabulary useful but have never been much impressed by legal realism. When Smith writes 'property is a bundle of rights and other legal relations between persons', he is referring to the legal realist Felix Cohen.[134] Smith ignores the fact that other thinkers concerned with property could add, as I do, 'with respect to things'. For Smith to have an effective argument against better versions of a bundle theory, he might reconsider his intense focus on legal realism. Once that is done, he will find that a perceptive bundle theory need not regard his modular theory as a competitor. Moreover, even if a Hohfeldian analysis supports the modularity of property law, it also shows that Hohfeld's legal relations unveil the distinct role of property rights in legal systems.[135] As to the centrality of things to property law, my dissolution of the two-place relations versus three-place relations disagreement with Harris and Honoré in Section 3 should largely lay this dispute to rest. Beyond that, Smith and I just have two rather different projects with rather different objectives.

6. Conclusion

It requires patience to determine whether recent disagreements in the theory of property, though in part certainly substantive, are also verbal or conceptual, or perhaps concern the nature of property. Penner makes a case for the idea that the right to exclude is the essence of property. The case crumbles for many reasons. But all who think about property are indebted to his boldness, even if at day's end we must conclude that the right to use and the power to transfer are as central to property as the right to exclude. Smith's modular theory of property breaks new ground. However, its aims and accomplishments are quite different from those of a well-crafted bundle theory of property. The two theories illuminate different features of property law and are not, save at the margin, competitors with each other. They certainly do not exhaust the many issues that confront the moral, political, and legal theory of property.

Appendix

For simplicity's sake, my response in Section 3 to a possible objection on behalf of Harris and Honoré omitted lower case letters for the relata. I now include them. Let the individual variables x, y, and z range over an owner, a thing or resource, and another person or group of persons who does not own the thing or resource, respectively. Let the letter C stand for the two-place relation 'is owner of' between x and y and the letter D for the two-place relation 'can exclude' between x and z. In a common notation, we have $C(x, y)$ and $D(x, z)$,

---

1985; Wellman 1995. Many philosophers, myself included, are critical of some features of Hohfeld's fundamental legal conceptions. For example, Hart 1972 argues that Bentham has a deeper analysis of legal powers than Hohfeld.

[134] Smith 2012b, 1691 n. 2.   [135] Douglas and McFarlane this volume so argue.

respectively.[136] These two two-place relations, it is said on behalf of Harris and Honoré, suffice to explain some of the rudiments of the concept of property. For if x has a right of exclusion with respect to y, and if x can exclude z, then we have a central piece of the concept of property, viz. the right to exclude. However, the objection to my argument depends on a connection between the two relations just specified; the connection is, as Honoré says, a 'necessary element in a property relationship'.[137] There is no reasonable way to understand D other than by making it relative to a thing or resource. We can express this connection by the following three-place relation: x has the right to exclude z from y. Let the letter E stand for the relation '… is owner of… and can exclude….' So the hitching of $C(x, y)$ and $D(x, z)$ yields $E(x, z, y)$. The argument thus far applies just to the relation of exclusion. Yet it can easily be extended to all of the three-place relations that make up my account of the bundle theory, be those relations crisp or fuzzy. Of course, a defender of Harris and Honoré could say that one could just as easily decompose my set of three-place relations into a set of connected two-place relations. True. But that just supports my point that, owing to the argument above and the associative law of the composition of relations, little difference if any exists between their view and mine from the standpoint of truth-functional equivalence.

---

[136] Swart 1998, 79–82, uses this simple notation. Set-theoretic notations are more complicated, as is evident from Barker-Plummer, Barwise, and Etchemendy 2011, 431–6, and, especially, Whitehead and Russell 1927, 1: 187–326.

[137] Honoré 2006, 131.

14

Emergent Property

*Henry E. Smith**

Property theory suffers from a peculiar kind of reductionism. Commentators pay great attention to the various purposes of property, while rarely leaving the stratosphere of abstraction. As a result, property theory always teeters on the brink of reducing property to its purposes or to the interests it serves—and thereby effacing what is special about the law of property itself. This chapter will show that reductionism is surprisingly widespread in property theory because a wide range of theories fail to take sufficiently seriously the difference between legal concepts and their consequences. Without delving too deeply into the nature of concepts themselves, I will show how it is useful to think of law as having both an *intensional* and an *extensional* aspect: we might attain the same set of real-world consequences by a variety of conceptual routes. Even when these routes lead to the same consequences in terms of who owes duties to whom, and so forth—the intensions have the same extension—the concepts or intensions may be very different in terms of information costs. General legal concepts—like general concepts generally—serve as shortcuts that lower the cost of handling complex information. In the case of property, this information is the system of actors and their actions that affect each other through their use of things.

To see how concepts serve to economize on information costs, it is useful to perform a Coasean thought experiment on the extreme case of the frictionless world of zero transaction costs.[1] Compare the full property afforded by fee simple ownership, and the collection of rights (and other legal relations) that make up the bundle. The two may (but typically do not) carry with them the same consequences in terms of who can sue whom, but even if a particular bundle were engineered to replicate traditional property, the fee simple (or full ownership of personal property) and the maximally articulated bundle of rights could not be more different in terms of how easy it would be actually to employ them to set up and operate a property system. Delineating a thing and protecting it through an

* I would like to thank Andrew Gold, Michael Kenneally, Stephen Munzer, James Penner, and participants at the Conference on the Philosophical Foundations of Property Law, the Property Works in Progress Conference, and faculty workshops at the University of Toronto Faculty of Law and the University of San Diego School of Law for their helpful comments on an earlier draft of this chapter. All errors are mine.

[1] Coase 1960; see also Lee and Smith 2012; Merrill and Smith 2011.

exclusion strategy backed up with governance of particular uses is a far cry from—and much less costly than—specifying each legal relation between the owner and each other member of society with respect to each use of each aspect of a resource. In a zero transaction cost world, we could afford to define property by defining each Hohfeldian relation individually. In the real world where delineation costs something, however, the stick-by-stick method is a complete non-starter. In our world, concepts—and which concepts we employ in property law—matter a great deal.

Nevertheless, the analytical impulse started by Hohfeld and his contemporaries morphed into an extreme version of reductionism in the hands of the legal realists and their successors. The realists and their successors were aggressive anti-conceptualists. They could not do away with concepts altogether, but they did repudiate traditional general concepts in the law, which they saw as impeding progress in the form of enlightened policy making. To clear the way for re-engineering property, the realists sought to bring legal concepts as close as possible to sets of consequences. Very specific and malleable concepts relating to finely sliced problems—who gets which stick for what—would substitute for notions like title, *ad coelum*, and property itself. And the realists have not been alone in this attempt to reduce property to the vanishing point. Even non-realist theories that seek to explain property in terms of uses and interests can wind up focusing on the purposes of property and downplaying the substantive contribution that property's structure makes to the shape of the institution. Despite being very anti-realist in their friendliness to conceptualism, many non-realist theories dwell on the purposes that property serves and thereby pay insufficient attention to the reasons why concepts and other constituents of property law might not directly reflect property's purposes. Property theory winds up being a contest of purposes working at cross-purposes.

There is a way out of this circle. In this chapter, I will argue that general legal concepts play a crucial role of lowering information costs, and that recognizing this economizing role of property concepts allows us to reconcile various positions on some of the key issues in property theory. These include, in addition to conceptualism itself, the proper role of formalism in property, the relation of functionalism and interpretivism, and the way in which property theory must in practice be holistic. I then apply the information cost perspective to the perennial problem in property theory of the nature of *in rem* rights. If we keep distinct how property law delineates rights, how duty holders process their duties, and what the consequences are of the legal relations making up property, then we can give an account that preserves the right-duty structure while explaining its coarse-grainedness relative to its purposes.

1. Intensions and Conceptualism in Property Law

In controversies over property theory, as in private law more generally, accusations fly back and forth that this or that theory suffers from excessive or insufficient conceptualism, formalism, functionalism—and reductionism. In this chapter I argue that the root of these ills can be located in a reduction of property's conceptual structure to its effects. Or, put differently, the approach to legal concepts in property is too oriented to extensions and seeks—unsuccessfully—to efface the intensional level consisting at least in part of legal concepts. It is with conceptualism that we must begin.

A central problem with property theory is its failure to draw a distinction between legal concepts and the categories they pick out. Much theorizing about property seeks to reduce the former to the latter, and self-consciously pursues anti-conceptualism. Modern conceptualists on the other hand resist this excessive reductionism by being somewhat sceptical of efforts to evaluate and alter legal doctrine in light of its consequences.[2] But even other non-realist theories, which emphasize the right to use as the core of property, typically reduce the structure of legal concepts to the use-based purposes they are meant to serve. Whether in the hands of the realists or latter-day conceptualists, seeing property as based on a bundle of rights closely tied to interests in use tends to efface the structure of the property right in favour of its purposes.

Concepts and categories are not the same thing. In this chapter I will for practical purposes assume that concepts are modes of presentation. They thus mediate between language and the world. In doing so, I do not rule out that concepts may be instead—or in addition—mental representations.[3] If concepts are mental representations, much remains to be discovered about their nature. Even on the representational view of concepts, the mental representations may have different structure, different acquisition conditions, and different means by which they in turn refer to the outside world. What is important in what follows is that the externals of the world can be organized differently, and in a way that often goes under the heading of 'concept'. These modes of presentation are more fine-grained than the sets of externals they correspond to—which is easily captured by noting that intensions (like Fregean senses, Frege 1892/1997) are more discriminating than extensions (referents). Moreover, as we will see, some modes of presentation are more economical than others, which is a point that legal realism has done much to obscure.

Concepts pick out categories and so organize a mass of particulars. Two concepts might pick out the same set but that does not make them the same concept. This can be illustrated with the famous examples of the morning star and the evening star in the philosophy of language. Word meaning is sometimes identified with the 'extension' or external referent of the word. In the case of 'morning star' and 'evening star', that external referent is the planet Venus. But if extensions were all there was to word meaning, then we would expect the terms to be interchangeable. In epistemic contexts (relating to belief and the like), however, the two words are not interchangeable, because the referent of the words in epistemic contexts is its intension. 'John believes that the morning star is Venus' does not entail 'John

---

[2] Weinrib 1995; Ripstein 2009.
[3] Compare Fodor 1998 with Dennett 1987 and Peacocke 1992. See generally Margolis and Laurence 2012.

believes that the evening star is Venus'—nor vice versa. A word is associated with a sense or intension, which is a mode of presenting the referent or extension. Thus, 'morning star' and 'evening star' have the same extension but are associated with different ways of getting there.[4] (Sometimes intensions are analysed as functions from possible worlds to extensions.[5]) Crucial for my purposes is that these modes of presentation may present the same referent but not be equally costly. Consider another example: both 'the administration of the 32nd President of the United States' and 'FDR's administration' have the same extension, but different intensions, and for most people the latter is much easier to use.

The role that intensional meaning plays in epistemic contexts is highly suggestive of the part it plays in the law. Concepts are what the mind works with (whether or not we accept the representational theory of the mind) in order to navigate the world of particulars, and one's beliefs depend on which concepts one uses. Moreover concepts prove their worth in how cost-effectively they allow one to pick out useful categories. They are shortcuts over an enumeration of every element of every category.[6] No one thinks about the world in terms of every particular of a set: rather, a general concept allows one to grasp an important referential category: intensions are functions from the world to extensions.

Importantly, some of these intensional functions will be easier to use than others. For one thing, the usefulness of concepts reflects a familiar trade-off between generality and accuracy. (General categories suppress some referential detail, which makes them formal, as we shall see.) But for the limits of the human mind, it would not matter so much how we organize externals into categories or how we delineate such categories via concepts. In the world of zero transaction costs,[7] one could costlessly move between the world and any set of particulars, and the intension-extension distinction would not be so significant. John would know all about Venus. Furthermore, in the positive-transaction cost world (ours), even two concepts that pick out the same category may yield the same benefit (lead to the same extension) but differ in the costliness of the function to get there (intension). Thus, for an early riser 'morning star' might be an easier concept. And certainly it is easier to have a concept that picks out the planet Venus rather than one that makes reference to every molecule making up Venus. And, likewise, the concept 'FDR's administration' is usually easier to employ than the concept 'the administration of the 32nd President of the United States'.

---

[4] This example goes back to Frege who provided the philosophical roots of intensional logic. See Frege 1892, 156.

[5] For examples of sources in linguistics and philosophy discussing intensionality, see Chierchia and McConnell-Ginet 2000, 257–328; Dowty, Wall, and Peters 1981, 141–78; Montague 1973, 228–32; Stalnaker 1976. For present purposes, I am interested in distinguishing concepts and categories, intensions and extensions, rather than insisting on a particular version of concepts. For a discussion of different types of concepts in property, see Penner 1996a.

[6] Intensions are shortcuts, but are sometimes said to be more fine-grained than extensions in a different sense: for any extension there are many corresponding intensions. Not all such intensions would be equally useful.

[7] Coase 1960; Lee and Smith 2012; Merrill and Smith 2011.

These considerations of cost in concepts have their direct parallel in law, and in the theory of property in particular. Consider the bundle of rights as a concept of property. If transaction costs were zero, we might expect any bundle to be as cost-effective as any other. In particular, any two bundles with the same 'bottom line'— they can receive the same Hohfeldian analysis—would be totally equivalent. But not in our world of positive transaction costs. From an extensional point of view we might, in the Hohfeldian spirit, ask what the smallest unit of a complex of legal relations like property is. If we label as C the set of all the possible claimants in the world, as D the set of all the possible duty bearers, as A the set of all the possible actions, and as R the set of all the possible resource attributes, then the domain of an initial assignment of entitlements would be the set P of all the quadruples: $P = C \times D \times A \times R$.[8] Now consider the assignment of entitlements from an intensional and extensional point of view. The extension would be a set of 4-tuples. The intension would be the function from the domain P to the set $\{0, 1\}$, which would assign 1 to those 4-tuples in the category and 0 otherwise. In other words, extensionally we find out who controls which action with respect to whom and who has control over which feature of a resource.

Crucially, the possible intensions for reaching a given extension are not equally cost-effective. The intension could be a gigantic list of 4-tuples with the associated 1 or 0 (in or out). Or the intension could assign 4-tuples to the category in a wholesale fashion. If A has property in Blackacre, a cost-effective intension would require the *in rem* aspect of property to specify the duty bearers largely at one stroke, and would rely on the definition of a thing to deal with many resource features at once. The exclusion strategy will also allow many uses to be protected (indirectly) without the need to spell out most uses individually; only in especially important contexts does the law focus in on particular uses, through 'off-the-shelf' law (e.g. nuisance, zoning) or parties' contracting.[9] Actual property delineation in terms of things and exclusion is a huge short cut over the fully articulated stick-by-stick method of elimination and many less economic intermediate versions as well. Same extension, vastly different intension.

Unfortunately, the realists did their best to obscure precisely this point. The legal realists defined themselves in part as anti-conceptualists. This is not to say that they never used legal concepts of any sort, which would be hard to imagine. Nevertheless, the legal realists were deeply sceptical of the value of general concepts in private law, and in property in particular. They believed, incorrectly,[10] that traditional property concepts stood as an unjustified barrier to needed reform and were a means for entrenched owner interests to resist incursions on their power and wealth. On a theoretical level, they saw no point in legal concepts that did not respond fully to considerations of policy, and what mattered from a policy point of view were the external facts—consequences—of the legal system.

If we want to see how intension and extension work in property, and how the realists tended to obscure the former in favour of the latter, a good place to start is

---

[8] Lee and Smith 2012.   [9] Smith 2002; Smith 2004, 1023–4.
[10] Merrill and Smith 2001b; Smith 2009.

with the bundle of rights. The bundle often builds off Hohfeld's scheme of jural relations.[11] Hohfeld was a reductionist, in that he wanted to break down the law into its smallest constituents—its 'lowest common denominators'. Hohfeld analysed property (and other legal concepts) in two ways. First, he developed a system of jural correlatives and opposites: rights correlate to duties, privileges to no-rights, powers to liabilities, and immunities to disabilities.[12] Property would be an aggregate of a claim-right and a variety of privileges of use, an immunity against certain changes of legal position, and so on. Each of these more fine-grained relations holds between persons—not between a person and a thing. To capture the '*in rem*' aspect of property (and certain other rights such as those of bodily integrity and reputation), he reduced an *in rem* right to a collection of similar rights availing between the owner and each individual duty holder. So, instead of a right availing against the world, or against people in general, a 'multital' right is a congeries of similar 'unital' rights holding between the owner and *A, B, C,* and so on. By contrast a contract right is 'paucital' because it is a collection of few such 'unital rights'.[13]

In the hands of the realists this reductionism became 'greedy'. Daniel Dennett coined the term 'greedy reductionism' for situations in which 'in their eagerness for a bargain, in their zeal to explain too much too fast, scientists and philosophers . . . underestimate the complexities, trying to skip whole layers or levels of theory in their rush to fasten everything securely and neatly to the foundation'.[14] The realists were greedy in trying to reduce concepts (intensions) to consequences (extensions).

The realists' version of Hohfeld's scheme is highly extensional. There was little left over that the aggregate of the Hohfeldian atoms did not capture, on their view. I have argued elsewhere that realists like Corbin and Radin took a highly over-extensional view of Hohfeld.[15] In the process they resisted critiques by legal theorists like Albert Kocourek over the nature of *in rem* rights, a subject to which I return in Section 5.

As another example of the realist impulse against a significant role for intensionalism in law, take Jerome Frank's violent reaction against Roscoe Pound's suggestion that areas of law need to be differentiated as to their appropriate degree of formalism. A forerunner of the realists, Pound eventually came to the view that context could not be available all the time but instead 'rules of law . . . which are applied mechanically are more adapted to property and to business transactions; standards where application proceeds upon intuition are more adapted to human conduct and to the conduct of enterprises'.[16] He considered it a matter of 'wise social engineering' that '[i]n matters of property and commercial law, where the economic forms of the social interest in the general security—security of acquisitions and security of transactions—are controlling, mechanical application of fixed, detailed rules or of rigid deductions from fixed conceptions is a wise social engineering. . . . Individualization of application and standards that regard the individual circumstances of

---

[11] Gregory Alexander has traced the first known use of the bundle-picture metaphor to a late 19th-century treatise on eminent domain. Alexander 1997, 455 n. 40—citing Lewis 1888, 43.

[12] Hohfeld 1913, 30.   [13] Hohfeld 1917b, 718–23.   [14] Dennett 1995, 82.

[15] Smith 2012a.   [16] Pound 1923b, 951.

each case are out of place here.'[17] Frank criticized this view as being too unrealistically rule-bound when it comes to property:

Pound errs, that is, in too sharply differentiating between (a) one department of law which requires the application of abstract rules and (b) another department which calls for the just and painstaking study of the novel facts of the particular case. This is, as we have seen, an unreal dichotomy. Every case presents the question of the extent to which the judge should adhere to settled precedents as against flexible modification of the precedents. There must be gradations and degrees of fixity and flexibility.[18]

Frank grants that in the economic sphere there may be reason to stick to precedent more often but denies the value of using rigid rules.

More importantly for our purposes and in keeping with the rest of his oeuvre, Frank thought that consequences should be always kept closely in view and legal 'rules' are to be kept provisional, responsive to context, and readily revisable. Moreover, Frank preferred law to emphasize what I am identifying as the extensional over the intensional. He approvingly read Holmes as in agreement:

Pound view[s] property and commercial transactions as if they were divorced from human relations, as if they were inert . . . But surely property and commercial transactions are not lifeless entities which of their own motion come into court. They are brought there by human needs and hopes and fears and desires.

There seems to be in this differentiation [by Pound of property and commercial transactions from other areas of law] what Holmes would call 'delusive exactness.' Or, to quote him perhaps more appositely, there is here a need 'to think things instead of words.'[19]

In a 'personalized and intense' 'attack' on Pound,[20] Frank accuses Pound of having 'never completely freed himself of rule-fetishism',[21] and of being 'reluctant to relinquish the age-old legal myths'[22] because:

Not only does he try to preserve one portion of the law for mechanical jurisprudence, but he over-emphasizes, now and again, even in the realm of discretion, the importance of the generalized aspect of decisions. Where rules do no work, such things as 'standards' are nevertheless in order, he believes, But 'standards', as he defines them are little more than 'safety-valve' concepts, so vague as to be meaningless.[23]

By contrast, Frank believed that lawyers and judges should be 'experimentalists' taking consequences first and working back to concepts and premisses.[24] According to Frank, adherence to old principles amounted to little short of devil worship (really) as the 'high priests of the Old Deal' did.[25] Extensions should lead, for policy reasons only, back to tentative and functionally transparent intensions.

Nor (at least in this respect) was Frank an outlier among the realists. Felix Cohen's attack on conceptualism was only atypical in its detail and philosophical trappings. Cohen exhibits both the anti-intensionalism of realism and explicitly

---

[17] Pound 1923a, 154.   [18] Frank 1930, 227. See also Cohen 1933, 1–40.
[19] Frank 1930, 226.   [20] White 1972, 1021.   [21] Frank 1930, 228 n. 8.
[22] Frank 1930, 215.   [23] Frank 1930, 228 n. 8.   [24] Frank 1934, 1064–7.
[25] Frank 1934, 1064.

draws out its consequences for property. For Cohen, property was characterized by a thin notion of the right to exclude emanating from the state.[26] But as such the state could always withdraw or alter its endorsement of an owner's decisional power. For Cohen, traditional notions of property are worse than useless in this regard, especially because of their specious presumptive force that draws on everyday notions of 'things' and traditional morality.[27] Here Cohen explicitly invokes a (curious) combination of pragmatist and logical-positivist currents in philosophy to dismiss the traditional views as metaphysical, meaningless, and superstitious.[28] Externals are everything, and the intensional level must conform and closely hew to the extensions which alone matter. Echoing Bentham's critique of natural rights as 'nonsense on stilts', Cohen's essay 'Transcendental Nonsense and the Functional Approach'[29] dismisses what I am calling an independent intensional level of the law as overly metaphysical and supernatural,[30] and cannot resist snide references to scholastic theologians and medieval popes,[31] angels on needles,[32] myths,[33] 'true believers in orthodox legal theology',[34] 'moral faiths and prejudices',[35] and 'otherworldy morality'.[36] In this broad-gauged attack and in the course of a discussion of trade names, Cohen draws out the implications for the concept of property itself:

> The circularity of legal reasoning in the whole field of unfair competition is veiled by the 'thingification' of *property*. Legal language portrays courts as examining commercial words and finding, somewhere inhering in them, *property rights*. It is by virtue of the property right which the plaintiff has acquired in the word that he is entitled to an injunction or an award of damages. According to the recognized authorities on the law of unfair competition, courts are not *creating* property, but are merely *recognizing* a pre-existent Something.[37]

In my terms, the intension of property is being reduced to a highly malleable something close to its extension.

Anti-conceptualism that reduces intension to something close to extension has a long pedigree in realist and pre-realist thought. As noted earlier, Holmes was invoked by the realists as an anti-conceptualist. And his emphasis on real world consequences and prediction as well as his de-emphasis on mental states are consistent with an orientation toward extensions rather than a robust intensional level. Interestingly,

---

[26] Cohen 1954, 374.   [27] Cohen 1935, 815–17.   [28] Cohen 1935.

[29] Cohen 1935, 848 ('Since the brilliant achievements of Bentham, descriptive legal science has made almost no progress in determining the consequences of legal rules') (footnote omitted).

[30] Cohen 1935, 810, 811, 816, 821, 822, 826, 828, 831. Jeremy Waldron defends the role of concepts against Cohen's critique, by arguing that Cohen overlooked the role that concepts play in supporting the systematicity of the law. Waldron 2000.

[31] Cohen 1935, 810, 813.

[32] Cohen 1935, 810, 813.

[33] Cohen 1935, 812.

[34] Cohen 1935, 818; see also Cohen 1935, 821, 831.

[35] Cohen 1935, 816; see also Cohen 1935, 841.

[36] Cohen 1935, 840; see also Cohen 1935, 837, 839–40. Cohen advocates a functional approach to religion itself. See Cohen 1935, 830.

[37] Cohen 1935, 815. The pairing of disdain for the imaginary and 'old ways of thinking' versus advocacy of 'scientific' social engineering was quite common. See e.g. Robinson 1934, 235–6.

Holmes's famous 'bad man' can be regarded as a thought experiment designed to get at the extensional level:

The confusion with which I am dealing besets confessedly legal conceptions. Take the fundamental question, What constitutes the law? You will find some text writers telling you that it is something different from what is decided by the courts of Massachusetts or England, that it is a system of reason, that it is a deduction from principles of ethics or admitted axioms or what not, which may or may not coincide with the decisions. But if we take the view of our friend the bad man we shall find that he does not care two straws for the axioms or deductions, but that he does want to know what the Massachusetts or English courts are likely to do in fact. I am much of his mind. The prophecies of what the courts will do in fact, and nothing more pretentious, are what I mean by the law.[38]

Also as for the realists, for Holmes extensions are important because they are closer to the aims of the law, taken, in reductive fashion, individually:

Still it is true that a body of law is more rational and more civilized when every rule it contains is referred articulately and definitely to an end which it subserves, and when the grounds for desiring that end are stated or are ready to be stated in words.[39]

Anti-conceptualism, functionalism, reductionism, and inattention to the holistic emergence of property's institutional features are characteristic of later realism.

Holmes was not the only pre-realist to emphasize extensions over intensions, in my terms. In perhaps the first realist writings, 'What Is the Law', and 'The Nature of Legal Rights and Duties', Joseph Bingham begins with the relation of concepts and externals (roughly, our intension and extension).[40] Anticipating the later realists' interest in the psychology of judging, Bingham states that concepts in the law are purely private and can never be shared by more than one person. Concepts are useful for thinking but are not externally real and only serve to ease thought about the externals that matter. He emphasizes extension over intension:

My main theme has been that the law—i.e., the thing which is the object of our professional knowledge,—is not a set of rules and principles; that not even the common law should be studied as is a dead language; that the law is an external field of concrete phenomena; that it should be studied with such intense and careful attention as is devoted to other fields of scientific investigation; and that the rules and principles which may be endorsed as part of a science of law are not authoritative promulgations, but are mental generalizations evolved in a manner similar to those of any science. I have attempted to clarify this theme by indicating briefly the interrelations of some of the principal sorts of elements operating in the concrete field of law and by explaining, criticising and reconciling with my theory various modes of thought and speech current in the profession. The words right and duty are so frequent in legal discussion that there would be a noticeable gap in my article, fragmentary though it is, unless I gave some account of the nature of the things denoted by these terms.[41]

---

[38] Holmes 1897, 460–1.   [39] Holmes 1897, 469.

[40] Whether Bingham was an extremely early realist or a pre-realist is open to dispute. See DiMatteo 2004, 406 and n. 22 (noting importance of Bingham to the realists and discussing Pound's and Fuller's views).

[41] Bingham 1913, 26 n. 24.

Like the later realists, Bingham did not see much of an independent role for morality as a grounding of legal concepts or judicial decision making; rather, policy-oriented public consensus should always carry the day.[42] Bingham believed that 'morality' is too uncertain and 'the law consists of the flux of concrete occurrences and their legal consequences brought about through the operation of authoritative governmental law-determining machinery and that the essential field of legal study consists of such actual sequences and the potentialities of similar future sequences'.[43] It turns out that the distinction between what I am calling the extensional versus intensional views of law plays out in the realm of legal rights and duties, and the rights and duties that constitute property in particular. I return to rights and duties in Section 5.

Where the realists differed was in the strength of their anti-conceptualism. If anything, what might be termed 'moderate conceptualism' in the legal realist era shows even more clearly how—and why—the intensional level of law is important. In keeping with the orientation of realists towards extensions, Karl Llewellyn believed that concepts had to prove their worth in terms of real world usefulness.[44] Realists 'want to check ideas, and rules, and formulas by facts, to keep them close to facts'.[45] As is well known, he approached the concept of 'title' and its pervasive use under the older sales act and case law quite sceptically. For Llewellyn, merely asking which transactor had title (for a wide range of purposes such as default risk allocation and remedies) was unjustified over-conceptualism.[46] Nevertheless, in drafting the Uniform Commercial Code, Llewellyn found the notion of title somewhat useful, for reasons that this chapter argues is the function of intensions: it turns out to be useful to have a concept that can be plugged in simply in many contexts, so that 'it should be made to serve merely as the general residuary clause'.[47] As I have argued elsewhere, in their generality and less than fully tailored quality, concepts like title are modular and have a complexity-managing effect.[48]

The oft-noted nominalism of the realists depends crucially on clearing away any important role for the intensional level of law.[49] Walton Hamilton and Irene Till famously declared that property is nothing more than 'a euphonious collection of letters which serves as a general term for the miscellany of equities that persons hold in the commonwealth'.[50] As noted earlier, this is exactly Jerome Frank's model of legal reasoning and development. The idea is to work back from the desired set of

---

[42] Bingham 1913, 3.   [43] Bingham 1913, 3, citing Bingham 1912, 9–12.

[44] See e.g. Llewellyn 1930, 438–51 (distinguishing between abstract legal verbalisms and concrete empirical facts).

[45] Llewellyn 1931, 1223. He continues, 'They view rules, they view law, as means to ends; as only means to ends; as having meaning only insofar as they are means to ends.'

[46] See Llewellyn 1938, 169 ('[Title] remains, in the Sales field, an alien lump, undigested').

[47] Llewellyn 1938, 170.   [48] Smith 2012a.

[49] Merrill (1998, 737) notes that '[a]lthough traces of the nominalist conception can be found in the Nineteenth Century, it is basically a product of the Legal Realist movement of the Twentieth.' One such trace noted by Merrill is Henry Clay's pronouncement: 'That is property which the law declares to be property.' *The Works of Henry Clay*, 8: 152 (ed. C. Colton, 1904), quoted in Hylton et al. 1998, 68.

[50] Hamilton and Till 1937, 528. See also American Law Institute 1936 § 10 ('The word "owner," as it is used in this Restatement, means the person who has one or more interests').

extensions—policy-oriented conclusions about consequences—to a convenient but highly tentative and plastic set of shallow and transparent concepts, thereby making the intensional level a mere afterthought.

The realists are not alone in paying insufficient attention to the distinction between concepts and categories. Even theories that for reasons of natural law or natural rights hark back to the traditional 'trilogy' or 'trinity' of rights to possess, use, and dispose, also bring the formal content of rights closer to the purposes they are supposed to serve.[51] If exclusion is the formal core of the right it is not because it reflects an interest: there is no interest per se in excluding.[52] Our interest in dealing with things is in using them (taken broadly to include non-consumptive uses like aesthetic enjoyment and existence value). The right to exclude—or exclusion-based strategies—indirectly protect many Hohfeldian privileges of use.[53] In some contexts, we may single out uses for robust protection, which makes the privilege appear more like a claim-right. Thus, in nuisance and easements, protection of the entitlement holder may give enough control over the use and sufficient protection from interference that it is easy to speak of a right to use.

However, making property a generalized right to use—or, on one tradition, to invoke the trinity of rights, to possess, use, and dispose of—is only partly helpful. Possession, use, and disposition are closer to the interests served by property but the question still remains whether we delineate property this way. I argue that we do not: the law does not usually involve delineating these three rights individually. The moderate version of the bundle that seeks a kind of stability in the traditional trinity of rights to possess, use, and dispose of still pays insufficient attention to the intensional level of property. How is it that we pick out the consequences that can indeed be organized (at least partly) under these three headings? Property law proceeds by delineating things and using strategies of protection that start with the rough and approximate exclusion strategies and fine tune with governance of use.[54]

---

[51] See e.g. *United States v General Motors Corp.* 1945, 377–8 (stating that a more accurate conception of property rights is an individual's right to possess, use, and dispose); Blackstone 1765, 134 (discussing an individual's right of property as 'free use, enjoyment, and disposal'); Epstein 1985, 22 (citing Blackstone's conception of property); Epstein 2007, 490 ('The standard definitions of property that have worked from Roman times forward always stressed a trinity of rights that included exclusive possession, use, and disposition'); Claeys 2006, 442 (discussing Richard Epstein's book and its idea of property rights as 'possession, use, and control'); Mossoff 2009, 2007–19 (discussing the bundle metaphor and exclusion conceptions of property).

[52] See e.g. Penner 1997; Smith 2009, 2012b.

[53] See e.g. Penner 1997; Smith 2004, 2009; McFarlane and Douglas this volume. For a defence of the view that there is an interest in exclusion, see Ripstein this volume. To decide between theories of property sounding in use or exclusion, much will depend on the nature of the shift from exclusion strategies to use-governance, as in the law of nuisance. For starters, the protection to rights of exclusion are much weaker in the case of trespass to land (a fortiori in the case of personal property) than they are in the law of assault, which protects exclusion rights in the person. One might say on Ripstein's approach that the interest in exclusion is stronger in the case of the person, or on the view adopted in the text it might be that the interest-in-exclusion model is more appropriate for persons as opposed to property. The difficulty in prising the two models apart stems in part from the fact that exclusion can be thought of as a broad and robust method of picking out use. In many contexts, 'exclusion' and 'use' may differ intensionally but not extensionally.

[54] See Smith 2002, 2004, 2009.

These strategies are an important part of the intensional level of the law and what distinguishes exclusion from governance is the specificity with which uses are picked out in the process of delineation (and processing by duty bearers). The 'right to exclude' protects uses but without doing much to mention them. One could say that exclusion is like use-neutral governance, and governance is use-based exclusion.

2. Formalism versus Contextualism

When reductionism effaces the intensional level of legal concepts, it is natural to regard resistance to this way of thinking as formalistic. Or to take things the other way around, the anti-formalists' attempt to make context always available in principle tends to lead to an overemphasis on extensions.

Concepts as intensions are often identified with formalism. Formalism comes in several varieties. The anti-formalists who are the most sceptical of formalism in property see concepts as part of an approach to law that is overly autonomous. The anti-formalist holds that if concepts were allowed to play an essential role in legal reasoning, they would gloss over important parts of the real world context and get in the way of making policy through legal reasoning. The Holmesian aphorism 'The life of the law has not been logic: it has been experience'[55] is the rallying cry for those who see concepts as getting in the way of policy-oriented pragmatism. Further, the traditional concepts of the law were regarded by the realists and their successors as building in an inherent bias for the status quo and entrenched interests. Ownership itself and the formulation of property in terms of rights serve merely as barriers to overcome in tailoring property to particular types of situations and achieving policy goals.

The opposition of contextualism and formalism is a gross oversimplification that nevertheless contains a kernel of truth. To begin with, there is some question as to whether pre-realist law was as formalistic as the realists claimed it was.[56] The realists found it convenient to define their opponents. It may well have been rhetorically effective to oppose traditional property concepts in order to take a decisive new direction, but it was not strictly necessary. To this day, progressive courts sometimes achieve results that could have been reached employing traditional property concepts, but they go out of their way to disparage concepts themselves. The most famous recent and emblematic example is *State v Shack*.[57] In that case, the New Jersey Supreme Court held that the landowner could not prevent migrant agricultural workers living on his land from receiving aid workers as guests. The court held that the aid workers had not violated the criminal trespass statute. The court could have grounded the result in the right of tenants to receive guests, and at least one other court took exactly this route.[58] But the New Jersey court disdained this

---

[55] Holmes 1881, 1.   [56] Compare Tamanaha 2009 with Leiter 2010.
[57] 1971, 374–5.
[58] See e.g. *State v DeCoster* 1995, 894 (holding that farmworkers living on housing provided by a farmer are 'tenants', and as such 'have a right to quiet enjoyment, which includes a right to receive visitors in their homes'). See Smith 2009, 982–4.

approach, by declaring that '[p]roperty rights serve human values' and that '[t]hey are recognized to that end, and are limited by it'.[59] Moreover, in the court's view concepts are confining and merely get in the way:

We see no profit in trying to decide upon a conventional category and then forcing the present subject into it. That approach would be artificial and distorting. The quest is for a fair adjustment of the competing needs of the parties, in the light of the realities of the relationship between the migrant worker and the operator of the housing facility.[60]

Shack is in a long line of New Jersey cases that engage in relatively low-level balancing to decide whether other interests overcome the owner's right to exclude[61]—culminating in the court's balancing act extending to the question of card counters in casinos.[62] This approach is open to the objection that it is less simple and stable than the traditional approach.[63] The alternative would be to see how many of the results, like the rights of migrant workers, can be achieved through the traditional categories (such as landlord–tenant).

Relatedly, approaches that advocate the most direct and transparent role for property in promoting policy, whether of efficiency, fairness or human flourishing, tend to dismiss the notion of exclusion as being too formalistic. Recent work on human flourishing is distinguished by impatience with property's lack of fit with notions of flourishing in various situations, leading to a variety of anti-formalism.[64] Elsewhere, Merrill and I have shown how Coase-inspired law and economics likewise downplays traditional notions of exclusion in property in favour of the bundle of sticks tailored to individual resource conflicts.[65]

Again, property uses a combination of more and less direct means to promote human flourishing, and the problem with this recent work is its tendency, like the realism out of which it grows, to flatten property out and reduce it to its consequences. Even those who profess to be pluralists are reductionists in this sense: they reduce property to a level very close to extensions.

By contrast, elsewhere in private law theory, formalism is taken very seriously indeed, to the extent that the intensional level of property might really be quite immune from revision in light of our views about the extensional consequences of the current set of rules.[66] Thus it appears to many that formalism is a matter of all or nothing and calls for simply taking one's pick between logical coherence and congruence with policy.

---

[59] *State v Shack* 1971, 372.   [60] *State v Shack* 1971, 374.
[61] See e.g. *State v Schmid* 1980; Alexander 2009; Smith 2009.
[62] *Uston v Resorts International Hotel, Inc.* 1982. The court declared that 'when property owners open their premises to the general public in the pursuit of their own property interests, they have no right to exclude people unreasonably.' *Uston v Resorts International Hotel, Inc.* 1982, 375. In a possible sign that the New Jersey Supreme Court's balancing approach to the law of trespass should not be taken too literally, the court dismissed much of the expansive discussion in *Uston* as '*dicta*' and fell back on an unelaborated 'public policy' limit on trespass, in the course of an opinion the very next year upholding the right of a racetrack owner to eject a horse racer. *Marzocca v Ferone* 1983, 1137; Kenneally ms.
[63] Smith 2009, 982–5.   [64] Alexander 2009; Peñalver 2009.
[65] Merrill and Smith 2001b; 2011.   [66] Weinrib 1995; Ripstein 2009.

There is a way out of this dilemma, and again it derives from paying attention both to the intension-extension distinction and to why it matters—in a functionally motivated formalism. The idea that conceptualism in property is formal is not entirely wrong, but we need a better definition of formalism and a new account of why it is desirable.

Formalism can be defined as relative invariance to context, which makes property concepts formal.[67] The functions from worlds to categories are formal in the sense of not being fully responsive to context. The functions are not conditioned on every fact of the world: some are ruled out. And categories are not as narrow as they could be (in the limit they would replicate the complexity of all the particulars). In this sense concepts are formal in picking out general categories. Recall that the realists were not in favour of general or abstract concepts like property and title.

Contrary to the tenor of much of the debate between formalists and contextualists, formalism comes in degrees. The exclusion strategy is not the last word but it has some presumptive force. Exceptions to the exclusion strategy are many and various. Airplane overflights clearly call for an exception (or clarification) of the right to exclude, whereas the interests of card counters—which the New Jersey Supreme Court apparently see as outweighing the traditional rule that businesses can exclude patrons for any reason or no reason—clearly do not. Once antidiscrimination statutes and a variety of regulations are in place, the benefits from abrogating the traditional exclusion right across the board or balancing it on an ongoing basis look strained at best.[68]

Use of context at the intensional of level of law is costly. Particularly where large numbers of duty bearers must process rights, it makes sense to lower information costs by employing formal concepts. The concept of property itself relies on separation and exclusion to make the things through which rights and duties are mediated simpler and easier to use. I return to the right-duty structure of law in Section 5.

This view of formalism versus contextualism is, in fact, consistent with the actual natural rights and natural law tradition, or the 'Grand Style', which was targeted at discouraging evasion and opportunism.[69] Realists see this earlier tradition as free-wheeling 'situation sense' and modern natural rights theorists see it as more formalistic. It is actually a hybrid with a modular architecture.

---

[67] Heylighen 1999, 49–53.

[68] See Smith 2009, 984 and n. 137. The leading case for the right of business owners to exclude patrons is *Wood v Leadbitter* 1845, which was largely overturned in a convoluted opinion in *Hurst v Picture Theatres, Limited* 1915 (Ct. App. (UK) 1914).

[69] See Clinton 2000, 948 (discussing Carl Dibble's identification of a 'moderate Enlightenment' tradition of legal interpretation associated with Grotius, Blackstone, and Marshall, that emphasized the role of equity and located the need for interpreting laws not in the ambiguity of language but in the possibility 'that corrupt, duplicitous persons will "treat the law in a sophisticated manner" in order to advance their own individual interests'), quoting Dibble 1994, 5.

3. Functionalism

The functionalist justification of formalism I just presented can be generalized. The account here is functionalist at a meta level, allowing us to take both the intensional and extensional levels of the law, and their relation, seriously. There is no need to reduce the former to the functions of the latter.

Functionalism is thought to be closely connected to reductive anti-conceptualism. As Ben Zipursky points out, the main contention between corrective justice theorists and legal economists is not about deontology versus utilitarianism; instead, disagreement centres on whether to capture the law's function is to capture the law.[70] In Zipursky's view, economic analysis fails just as all purely functional accounts of the law do, because they do not give an account of law's concepts: they reduce legal concepts purely to their functions.[71]

But functionalism need not be purely reductive. The information cost account does not suffer from the explanatory defects of pure (or greedy) reductionism. Functionalism here holds true at a meta level. Concepts themselves can be (partially) explained in terms of their function of managing complexity.

Indeed, if we keep the functional justification at the level of the system and bring information costs into the picture, it turns out that a functional economic account of private law, and property in particular, overlaps to a great extent with private law theory based on a variety of moral theories and corrective justice. Both tort law and property law employ concepts that keep the law modular: not all information is available all the time. Thus, tort law's bilateral structure, duty, and causation are among the many devices for keeping its informational demands manageable.[72] Property is even more straightforwardly simple and standardized in its most *in rem* aspects, and achieves simplicity—or, more accurately, allows for overall complexity through local simplicity—by defining things.[73] Importantly in both torts and property, the employment of widely shared moral concepts reduces the costs of coordinating and communicating information about rights, duties, and other legal relations.[74] Overall, then, moral and economic accounts of the law converge more than is usually thought. Disagreement can be left for foundational theories, but the scope and structure of the intensional level and its relation to the extensional, are susceptible of a multiplicity of explanations, including a non-greedy functional one based on information costs.

Keeping in mind that the functional justification here is not supposed to be an exhaustive explanation and is certainly not supposed to substitute for the concepts themselves, we can avoid the perils of a reductive functionalism.

---

[70] Zipursky 2000, 482.   [71] Zipursky 2000, 465, 474–5.   [72] Smith 2011a.
[73] See e.g. Merrill and Smith 2000, 2001a; Smith 2003, 2012b.
[74] Merrill and Smith 2007a; Smith 2011a.

4. Holism and Emergence

By separating out our interests in using things and the devices that legally protect those interests, the desirable features of property emerge out of their interaction. Property's effectiveness cannot be associated with interests alone (or in the main) as the modern natural rights thinkers would have it, and they cannot be associated with mechanism alone as the bundle theorists believe. Otherwise, property is an uneasy blend of the intensional and the extensional, whether this blend is more chunky as in natural rights or more detailed and contingent as it is in realism and post-realism.

Not distinguishing what property does from how it does it—roughly extension versus intension—tends to lead to the fallacy of division. On the conventional approach, concepts and rules are expected to track closely their desired consequences. But if property in all its parts should reflect the purposes of property, we wind up expecting each of the concepts and rules to reflect them as well. To expect this generally is to commit the fallacy of division: just as water is wet without water molecules being wet, property may serve a purpose or be just or efficient without entailing that the constituents of property law, or each occasion it is invoked, will do the same.[75]

Some rules and concepts may, as intensions, be closer to extensions justifiable in terms of fairness, and other intensions may track efficiency-oriented extensions. For example, the Implied Warranty of Habitability is easier to see as based on fairness, whereas the operation of the law of trespass with its deference to owners may be seen as implementing a policy of promoting efficiency, liberty, or autonomy.

Closely related to the moderate functionalism of the information cost theory is its ability to capture emergent properties of property. The purposes of property law might well be served by the institution as a whole—through its overall architecture. Rather than individual rules or concepts taken in isolation serving these purposes, they may work in tandem to produce them. As Herbert Simon noted a long time ago, complex systems and their frequent reliance on modular architecture allows one to be an 'in principle' reductionist and a 'pragmatic' holist.[76] Because I am not arguing for a particular foundational theory, let it suffice that the type of reductionism and holism that the information cost theory employs is fully consistent with respecting the holistic nature of the institution of property.

---

[75] Smith 2012b. Hart made a similar point about morality and law: after noting that the connection between law and sanctioning or between law and efficacy might hold at the level of a legal system without doing so at the level of individual laws or rules taken separately, he has this to say: 'Perhaps the differences with respect to laws taken separately and a legal system as a whole are also true of the connection between moral (or other) conceptions of what the law ought to be and law in this wider sense.'

[76] Simon 1981, 195.

5. An Application to *in Rem* Rights and Duties

Keeping concepts and categories—intensions and extensions—distinct in property theory allows us to untangle a perennial problem at the heart of property: the nature of *in rem* rights and duties.

Let's start with a deceptively simple question: to whom do duty bearers owe their duties in the law of property? James Penner points out that a duty bearer need not know much about the owner of a thing and that this is true of owners in general.[77] He concludes that the duty is owed not to individual owners but is what might be termed 'reverse *in rem*'—owed to a large and indefinite class of owners. So, according to Penner, property is two-way *in rem*.

Some lack of personalization is indeed at the heart of property. It can help explain the *numerus clausus* principle.[78] Large numbers of far-flung and impersonal duty bearers cannot be expected to keep track of large amounts of idiosyncratic information.

More generally, property manages complexity through modularity, which hides much personal information from other parts of the system. Duty bearers do not need to know much about the identity of owners, as in Penner's example of someone in a parking lot not needing to know the identity of the owners of cars in order to know not to take or damage them.[79] Rules about good faith purchase and *nemo dat* (and even more so negotiability) make certain information about past transactions less relevant to current holders and would-be holders of property rights. Interactions between actors with respect to the use of resources are broken into components containing much purely internal interaction, and between these components interactions are limited to those consistent with defined interfaces.[80] This modularization begins with defining things and employing exclusion strategies to protect them as a first pass.

That the intensional level lowers information cost by suppressing some information helps explain one of the controversies between the realists and Albert Kocourek over the Hohfeldian system of legal relations. As we have seen, Corbin and the realists insisted that *in rem* rights were really a collection of numerous 'unital' rights. The two sides argued about situations that were not necessarily different extensionally, but the approaches clearly differed at the intensional level, with Corbin and the realists downplaying the role of concepts and insisting that they track closely the articulated Hohfeldian lowest common denominator-style, externally oriented relations.[81] By contrast, Kocourek, building on the indefiniteness of *in rem* rights, argued that the key characteristic of *in rem* rights was based on delineation: 'a right in rem is one of which the essential investitive facts do not serve directly to identify the person who owes the incident duty'.[82] Kocourek gave the example of an owner *A* who gave an easement to everyone except *B*.[83] Is *A*'s right

---

[77] Penner 1997.   [78] Merrill and Smith 2000; Smith 2011b.   [79] Penner 1997, 75–6.
[80] Smith 2012b.   [81] Smith 2012a.   [82] Kocourek 1920, 335 (emphasis omitted).
[83] Kocourek 1920, 33.

against *B in rem* or *in personam*? In terms of numerosity it is *in personam*, but Kocourek insisted it is *in rem*, over the objection of Corbin. Corbin thought that in such an example *B* was directly identified,[84] but here Corbin is relying on some combination of the extension and what someone is likely to know in that scenario by isolating *B* in that fashion.

Again, the intensional level helps untangle the nature of *in rem* rights. As Kocourek argued, an *in rem* right is not delineated in terms of the identity of the duty bearer—or, as we shall see, in terms of the identity of the owner—so whether one knows more than is needed is beside the point. Kocourek's example of the near-universal easement is unrealistic, precisely because delineation costs in giving an easement to everyone except *B* would be virtually as high as if one created *in rem* rights duty holder by duty holder in a literally Hohfeldian fashion. Kocourek's investitive facts relate to the intensional level, or, as he termed it, the level of '*internal, substantial qualities*'.[85]

In Kocourek's terms, the 'investitive' facts of property are in the first instance relatively free from information about use. Kocourek drew inspiration from the civilians and may have been inspired by Austin's civilian-style declaration that the essence of property is its indefiniteness.[86] When delineation in terms of investitive facts suppresses information and allows property rights to be indefinite (in terms of duty bearers, the residual claim, and the like), the intensional level affords an opportunity to save on information costs.

A similar story can be told about a duty bearer's knowledge about owners. Christopher Essert argues that one can owe duties without knowing much about the right holder.[87] He notes that Penner has pointed out a serious problem with the Hohfeldian analysis of rights and duties. If an *in rem* right consists of a series of *in personam* right-duty relations between *A* and *B*, *A* and *C*, *A* and *D*, etc., then after the transfer to *B*, the relations between *A* and *B* are reversed, but also *C*, *D*, etc. now owe a duty to *B*, not *A*. How can the transfer from *A* to *B* affect the content of the duties owed by these many others, i.e. everyone else? Most of these others are probably unaware of and need not know about the transfer. Penner considers this massive shift in the content of duties to be absurd, and Essert dubs this 'Penner's Problem'. Essert agrees with Penner that this is indeed a problem, and that the right-duty relationship in property is depersonalized in both directions, at least before any violation has occurred. He disagrees with Penner's solution of two-way *in-rem*-ness, in which the duty of non-owners is not owed to individual owners, but is to respect ownership of Blackacre, Whitacre, etc. generally. Essert wants to maintain that duties are owed to individual owners, but impersonally: his solution is to posit an office of owner: the duty bearer owes the duty to the owner qua owner. One owner can be substituted for another by assuming the office. Thus, the

---

[84] Corbin 1921, 232 n. 4.   [85] Kocourek 1921, 133.
[86] Austin 1885, 799 ('[I]ndefiniteness is of the very essence of the right; and implies that the right...cannot be determined by exact and positive circumscription').
[87] Essert 2013.

duty bearer need not know anything about the owner, as Penner requires, even though the duty is to the owner (qua owner, as the office holder).

Distinguishing concepts from categories, or intensions from extensions, permits another solution to Penner's Problem, without any extra machinery. The use of things to mediate the right-duty relationship facilitates two-way depersonalization. But this depersonalization relates to delineation and Kocourek's investitive facts—at the intensional level—which is consistent with the rights and duties availing between individuals at the extensional level. So one can owe an extensional duty to an owner that is delineated using an intensional mode of presentation (with investitive facts) that makes no reference whatever to the personal characteristics of the owner. Moreover, the mode of presentation, at the level of concepts, economizes on information costs, precisely because it does not make reference to personal information of owners—or of duty bearers. Duty bearers need not know anything about owners and vice versa, most of the time. As with the controversy between Corbin and Kocourek, what serves to identify an owner and what a duty bearer needs to know are easier to account for when we keep intensions (where this information matters) distinct from extensions (where it generally does not). Thus, the Hohfeldian multital right—a conglomeration of paucital or unital rights—is extensionally accurate in capturing *in rem* rights but does not capture the mode of presentation, the concept or intension. Thus, one can be an extensional Hohfeldian (as is Essert) but an intensional Pennerite. To do so, we need not conflate the structure of rights and duties with the psychological states of right holders and duty bearers. Nor do we need a new device of an office of ownership (at least for these purposes), because the concept, or mode of presentation, serves to depersonalize the relation where it counts for information cost purposes. Again, it is essential to distinguish the intensional from the extensional in property law.

6. Conclusion

In this chapter I have argued that identifying the important role that concepts play as intensions—modes of presenting particulars in the world—explains some dilemmas in property theory and paves the way for a better type of theory that combines the best of conceptualism and realism, formalism and contextualism, functionalism and moralism, and even reductionism and holism. Most accounts must veer to one pole or the other because they do not allow the intensional level to do all the work it can do. In particular, isolating the intensional level brings the costs of delineating property back into the picture, which is an essential factor in shaping the contours of actual property law.

References

American Law Institute (1936) *Restatement of the Law of Property* (St Paul, MN: American Law Institute)

American Law Institute (1944) *Restatement of the Law of Property* (St Paul, MN: American Law Institute)

American Law Institute (1965) *Restatement of the Law, Second: Torts 2d* (St Paul, MN: American Law Institute)

American Law Institute (1979) *Restatement of the Law, Second: Torts 4d* (St Paul, MN: American Law Institute)

Alexander, G. S. (1997) *Commodity & Propriety: Competing Visions of Property in American Legal Thought, 1776–1970* (Chicago: University of Chicago Press)

Alexander, G. S. (2009) 'The Social-Obligation Norm in American Property Law' 94 *Cornell Law Review* 745

Alexander, G. S. and E. M. Peñalver (2012) *An Introduction to Property Theory* (Cambridge: Cambridge University Press)

Aquinas, T. (1265–74) *Summa Theologica* Fathers of the English Dominican Province trans. (London: Blackfriars, 1913–42)

Aristotle (350 BC) '4 Nicomachean Ethics' in J. Barnes ed. *The Complete Works of Aristotle*, vol. 2 (Princeton: Princeton University Press, 1984) 1768

Arnold, E. C. (1922) 'The Law of Accession of Personal Property' 22 *Columbia Law Review* 103

Ash, S. H. (1941) 'Water Problem in the Pennsylvania Anthracite Mining Region' *United States Department of the Interior Information Circular I. C. 7175* (Washington, DC: United States Department of the Interior, Bureau of Mines)

Ashcraft, R. (1986) *Revolutionary Politics and Locke's Two Treatises of Government* (Princeton: Princeton University Press)

Atuahene, B. (2006) 'Land Titling: A Mode of Privatization with the Potential to Deepen Democracy' 50 *St. Louis University Law Review* 761

Austin, J. (1885) *Lectures on Jurisprudence: or, The Philosophy of Positive Law*, vol. 2 (London: John Murray)

Austin, L. M. (2013) 'Pluralism, Context and the Internal Life of Property: A Response to Hanoch Dagan' 63 *University of Toronto Law Journal* 22

Austin, L. M. (forthcoming) 'Property and the Rule of Law' *Legal Theory*

Axelrod, R. (1984) *The Evolution of Cooperation* (New York: Basic Books)

Bacon, M. and H. Gwillim (1798) *A New Abridgment of the Law* (London: A Strahan)

Bagshaw, R. (2012) 'The Edges of Tort Law's Rights' in D. Nolan and A. Robertson eds. *Rights and Private Law* (Oxford: Hart Publishing)

Baker, G. P. and P. M. S. Hacker (2009) *Analytical Commentary on the Philosophical Investigations*, vols. 1–4, 2nd edn. (Oxford: Wiley-Blackwell)

Ballantine, H. W. (1919) 'Claim of Title in Adverse Possession' 28 *Yale Law Journal* 219

Banner, S. (2011) *American Property: A History of How, Why, and What We Own* (Cambridge, MA: Harvard University Press)

Barker-Plummer, D., J. Barwise, and J. Etchemendy (2011) *Language, Proof, and Logic* (Stanford, CA: CSLI Publications)

Barros, B. (2006) 'Home as a Legal Concept' 46 *Santa Clara Law Review* 255

Baudouin, J. and A. M. Linden (2010) *Tort Law in Canada* (Dordrecht: Kluwer)

Bebchuk, L. A. and O. Ben-Shahar (2001) 'Precontractual Reliance' 30 *Journal of Legal Studies* 423

Becker, L. C. (1977) *Property Rights: Philosophical Foundations* (London: Routledge & Kegan Paul)

Becker, L. C. (1992) 'Too Much Property' 21 *Philosophy & Public Affairs* 196

Bell, A. (2009) 'Should Decreases in Property Value Caused by Regulations be Compensated?' in G. K. Ingram and H. Yu-Hung eds. *Property Rights and Land Policies* (Cambridge, MA: Lincoln Institute of Land Policy)

Ben-Shahar, O. (2004) 'Contracts without Consent: Exploring a New Basis for Contractual Liability' 152 *University of Pennsylvania Law Review* 1829

Benson, P. (2001) 'The Unity of Contract Law' in P. Benson ed. *The Theory of Contract Law: New Essays* (Cambridge: Cambridge University Press) 175

Bentham, J. (1789) 'Principles of the Civil Code' in C. K. Ogden ed. *Theory of Legislation* (Littleton, CO: Fred B. Rothman & Co., 1987) 88

Bentham, J. (1843) 'Principles of Penal Law' in J. Bowring ed. *The Works of Jeremy Bentham* (New York: Russell & Russell, 1962) 557

Bingham, J. (1912) 'What Is the Law?' 11 *Michigan Law Review* 1

Bingham, J. (1913) 'The Nature of Legal Rights and Duties' 12 *Michigan Law Review* 1

Birks, P. (1995) 'Concept of a Civil Wrong' in D. Owen ed. *Philosophical Foundations of Tort Law* (Oxford: Clarendon Press)

Birks, P. (1996) 'Equity in the Modern Law: An Exercise in Taxonomy' 26 *University of Western Australia Law Review* 1

Blackburn, S. (2008) *How to Read Hume* (London: Granta Books)

Blackman, J. (2011) 'Outfoxed: Pierson v Post and the Natural Law' 51 *American Journal of Legal History* 417

Blackstone, W. (1765) *Commentaries on the Laws of England*, A. W. B. Simpson introd. and ed. (Chicago: University of Chicago Press, 1979)

Blumenthal, J. A. (2009) 'To Be Human: A Psychological Perspective on Property Law' 83 *Tulane Law Review* 609

Bohlen, F. (1926) 'Incomplete Privilege to Inflict Intentional Invasions of Interests of Property and Personality' 39 *Harvard Law Review* 307

Brantly, W. T. (1890) *Principles of the Law of Personal Property* (Charleston, SC: Bancroft-Whitney, 2010)

Bright, S. and B. McFarlane (2005a) 'Personal Liability in Proprietary Estoppel' 69 *Conveyancer and Property Lawyer* 14

Bright, S. and B. McFarlane (2005b) 'Proprietary Estoppel and Property Rights' 64 *Cambridge Law Journal* 449

Brown, A. (forthcoming) 'My Hole is Warm and Full of Light: The Sub-Urban Real Estate of Invisible Man'

Brown, R. A. (1975) *The Law of Personal Property*, 3rd edn. (Chicago: Callaghan & Co.)

Brudner, A. (1993) 'Editor's Introduction' 6 *Canadian Journal of Law & Jurisprudence* 183–4

Brudner, A. (1995) *The Unity of the Common Law: Studies in Hegelian Jurisprudence* (Berkeley: University of California Press)

Buchanan, J. (1975) *The Limits of Liberty* (Chicago: University of Chicago Press)

Buckle, S. (1991) *Natural Law and the Theory of Property: Grotius to Hume* (Oxford: Clarendon Press)

Calabresi, G. (1997) 'Remarks: The Simple Virtues of the Cathedral' 106 *Yale Law Journal* 2201

Calabresi, G. and A. D. Melamed (1972) 'Property Rules, Liability Rules, and Inalienability: One View of the Cathedral' 85 *Harvard Law Review* 1089

Carey, S. (2009) *The Origin of Concepts* (New York: Oxford University Press)

Carnap, R. (1956) *Meaning and Necessity: A Study in Semantics and Modal Logic*, 2nd edn. (Chicago: University of Chicago Press)

Chalmers, D. J. (2011) 'Verbal Disputes' 120 *Philosophical Review* 515

Chierchia, G. and S. McConnell-Ginet (2000) *Meaning and Grammar: An Introduction to Semantics* (Cambridge, MA: MIT Press)

Chitty, J. (1844) *Treatise on Pleading*, 7th edn. (Dublin: Law Booksellers & Publishers)

Chitty, J. (1883) *Treatise on Pleading*, 16th edn. (Springfield, MA: Merriam & Co.)

Christman, John (1994) *The Myth of Property: Toward an Egalitarian Theory of Ownership* (New York: Oxford University Press)

Claeys, E. R. (2006) 'Takings: An Appreciative Retrospective' 15 *William and Mary Bill of Rights Journal* 439

Claeys, E. R. (2008) 'The Private Society and Public Good in John Locke's Thought' 21 *Social Philosophy & Policy* 201

Claeys, E. R. (2009a) 'Property 101: Is Property a Thing or a Bundle?' 32 *Seattle University Law Review* 617

Claeys, E. R. (2009b) 'Virtue and Rights in American Property Law' 94 *Cornell Law Review* 889

Claeys, E. R. (2010a) 'Jefferson Meets Coase: Land-Use Torts, Law and Economics, and Natural Property Rights' 85 *Notre Dame Law Review* 1379

Claeys, E. R. (2010b) 'The Right to Exclude and the Shadow of the Cathedral: A Response to Parchomovsky and Stein' 104 *Northwestern University Law Review* 391

Claeys, E. R. (2012) 'Exclusion and Legal Theory: A Comment on *Property As the Law of Things*' 125 *Harvard Law Review Forum* 133

Claeys, E. R. (2013) 'Intellectual Usufructs: Trade Secrets, Hot News, and the Usufructuary Paradigm at Common Law' in S. Balganesh ed. *Intellectual Property and the Common Law* (Cambridge: Cambridge University Press) 404

Claeys, E. R. (forthcoming) 'Locke Unlocked: Productive Use in Encroachment, Adverse Possession and Labor Theory'

Clarke, A. (2005) 'Use, Time and Entitlement' 57 *Current Legal Problems* 239

Clashfern, L. M. O. (2008) *Halsbury's Laws of England* (London: LexisNexis)

Clay, K. and G. Wright (2005) 'Order Without Law? Property Rights During the California Gold Rush' 42 *Explorations in Economic History* 155

Clerk, J. F. (1891) 'Title to Chattels by Possession' 7 *Law Quarterly Review* 236

Clinton, F. S. (2000) 'Classical Legal Naturalism and the Politics of John Marshall's Constitutional Jurisprudence' 33 *John Marshall Law Review* 935

Coase, R. H. (1960) 'The Problem of Social Cost' 3 *Journal of Law & Economics* 1

Coase, R. H. (1988) *The Firm, the Market, and the Law* (Chicago: University of Chicago Press)

Cohen, F. S. (1933) *Ethical Systems and Legal Ideals* (New York: Falcon Press)

Cohen, F. S. (1935) 'Transcendental Nonsense and the Functional Approach' 35 *Columbia Law Review* 809

Cohen, F. S. (1954) 'Dialogue on Private Property' 9 *Rutgers Law Review* 357

Cohen, G. A. (1995) *Self-Ownership, Freedom, and Equality* (Cambridge: Cambridge University Press)

Coke, E. (1628) *The First Part of the Institutes of the Laws of England: or, A Commentary Upon Littleton*, C. Butler and F. Hargrave eds. (London: E. & R. Brooke, 1794)

Coleman, J. L. (2002) *Risks and Wrongs* (Oxford: Oxford University Press)

Coleman, J. L. and J. Kraus (1986) 'Rethinking the Theory of Legal Rights' 95 *Yale Law Journal* 1335

Coletta, R. (1990) 'Reciprocity of Advantage and Regulatory Takings: Toward a New Theory of Takings Jurisprudence' 40 *American University Law Review* 297

Cooke, E. (2000) *The Modern Law of Estoppel* (Oxford: Oxford University Press)

Cooke, J. H. S. and R. R. Cornah (2008) *Lowndes and Rudolf: The Law of General Average and the York-Antwerp Rules*, 13th edn. (London: Sweet & Maxwell)

Corbin, A. L. (1921) 'Jural Relations and their Classification' 30 *Yale Law Journal* 226

Corbin, A. L. (1922) 'Taxation of Seats on the Stock Exchange' 31 *Yale Law Journal* 429

Craft, R. L. (1995) 'Of Reservoir Hogs and Pelt Fiction: Defending the Ferae Naturae Analogy between Petroleum and Wildlife' 44 *Emory Law Journal* 697

Craswell, R. (1996) 'Offer, Acceptance, and Efficient Reliance' 48 *Stanford Law Review* 481

Cresswell, M. J. (1972) 'Is There One or Are There Many One and Many Problems in Plato?' 22 *Philosophical Quarterly* 149

Dagan, H. (1999) 'Takings and Distributive Justice' 85 *Virginia Law Review* 741

Dagan, H. (2013) 'The Public Dimension of Private Property' 24 *King's Law Journal* 260

Davidson, N. M. (2008) 'Standardization and Pluralism in Property Law' 61 *Vanderbilt Law Review* 1597

Davis, W. A. (2005) 'Concept Individuation, Possession Conditions, and Propositional Attitudes' 39 *Noûs* 140

De Bracton, H. (1250) *On the Law and Customs of England*, G. E. Woodbine ed. and S. E. Thorne trans. (Cambridge, MA: Harvard University Press, 1977)

Deigh, J. (2002) 'Promises under Fire' 112 *Ethics* 483

De Jasay, A. (1989) *Social Contract, Free Ride: A Study of the Public Goods Problem* (New York: Oxford University Press)

Dennett, D. (1987) *The International Stance* (Cambridge, MA: MIT Press)

Dennett, D. (1995) *Darwin's Dangerous Idea: Evolution and the Meanings of Life* (New York: Simon & Schuster)

Dias, R. W. M. (1956) 'A Reconsideration of Possessio' 14 *Cambridge Law Journal* 235

Dibble, C. M. (1994) 'The Lost Tradition of Modern Legal Interpretation' (unpublished essay prepared for delivery at the 1994 Annual Meeting of the American Political Science Association)

DiMatteo, L. A. (2004) 'Reason and Context: A Dual Track Theory of Interpretation' 109 *Penn State Environmental Law Review* 397

Dixon, M. (2008) *Modern Land Law*, 6th edn. (Abingdon: Routledge-Cavendish)

Dorfman, A. (2010) 'Private Ownership' 16 *Legal Theory* 1

Dorfman, A. (2012) 'The Society of Property' 62 *University of Toronto Law Journal* 563

Douglas, S. (2008) 'The Abolition of Detinue' *Conveyancer and Property Lawyer* 30

Douglas, S. (2009) 'The Nature of Conversion' 68 *Cambridge Law Journal* 198

Douglas, S. (2011a) *Liability for Wrongful Interferences with Chattels* (Oxford: Hart Publishing)

Douglas, S. (2011b) 'The Scope of Conversion: Property and Contract' 74 *Modern Law Review* 329

Dowty, D., R. Wall, and S. Peters (1981) *Introduction to Montague Semantics* (Dordrecht: D. Reidel)

Drassinower, A. (2006) 'Capturing Ideas: Copyright and the Law of First Possession' 54 *Cleveland State Law Review* 191

Dubler, A. (2003) 'In the Shadow of Marriage: Single Women and the Legal Construction of the Family and the State' 112 *Yale Law Journal* 1641

Dubus III, A. (1999) *House of Sand and Fog* (New York: W. W. Norton & Co.)

Dukeminier, J. and J. E. Krier eds. (2002) *Property*, 5th edn. (New York: Aspen Publishers)

Dworkin, R. (1978) *Taking Rights Seriously* (Cambridge, MA: Harvard University Press)

Dworkin, R. (1986) *Law's Empire* (Cambridge, MA: Belknap Press of Harvard University Press)

Dworkin, R. (2004) 'Hart's Postscript and the Character of Political Philosophy' 24 *Oxford Journal of Legal Studies* 1

Dworkin, R. (2011) *Justice for Hedgehogs* (Cambridge, MA: Belknap Press of Harvard University Press)

Edelman, J. (2013) 'Two Fundamental Questions for the Law of Trusts' 129 *Law Quarterly Review* 66

Ellickson, R.C. (1989) 'Bringing Culture and Human Frailty to Rational Actors: A Critique of Classical Law and Economics' 65 *Chicago-Kent Law Review* 23

Ellickson, R. C. (1989) 'A Hypothesis of Wealth-Maximizing Norms: Evidence From the Whaling Industry' 5 *Journal of Law, Economics & Organization* 83

Ellickson, R. C. (1991) *Order Without Law: How Neighbors Settle Disputes* (Cambridge, MA: Harvard University Press)

Ellickson, R. C. (1993) 'Property in Land' 102 *Yale Law Journal* 1315

Ellickson, R. C. (1998) 'Law and Economics Discovers Social Norms' 27 *Journal of Legal Studies* 537

Ellison, R. (1952) *Invisible Man* (New York: Random House)

Elster, J. (1989) *The Cement of Society: A Study of Social Order* (Cambridge: Cambridge University Press)

Epstein, R. A. (1979) 'Possession As the Root of Title' 13 *Georgia Law Review* 1221

Epstein, R. A. (1985) *Takings: Private Property and the Power of Eminent Domain* (Cambridge, MA: Harvard University Press)

Epstein, R. A. (1998) *Principles for a Free Society: Reconciling Individual Liberty with the Common Good* (Reading, MA: Perseus Books)

Epstein, R. A. (2007) 'David Josiah Brewer Addresses Yale Law School' 10 *Green Bag 2d* 483

Epstein, R. A. (2011) *Design for Liberty: Private Property, Public Administration, and the Rule of Law* (Cambridge, MA: Harvard University Press)

Essert, C. (2013) 'The Office of Ownership' 63 *University of Toronto Law Journal* 418

Etherton, T. (2009) 'Constructive Trusts and Proprietary Estoppel: The Search for Clarity and Principle' *Conveyancer and Property Lawyer* 104

Farber, D. A. and J. O'Connell eds. (2010) *Research Handbook on Public Choice and Public Law* (Northampton, MA: Edward Elgar Publishing)

Farnsworth, E. A. (2004) *Contracts*, 4th edn. (New York: Aspen Publishers)

Federal Farmer (1787–8) 'Letters from the Federal Farmer to the Republican' in H. J. Storing and M. Dry eds. *The Complete Anti-Federalist*, vol. 2 (Chicago: University of Chicago Press, 1981) 214

Feinberg, J. (1970) 'The Nature and Value of Rights' 4 *Journal of Value Inquiry* 243

Feinberg, J. (1973) *Social Philosophy* (Englewood Cliffs, NJ: Prentice-Hall)

Feinberg, J. (1984) *The Moral Limits to the Criminal Law*, vol. 1: *Harm to Others* (New York: Oxford University Press)

Fellowes, J. (2010–) *Downton Abbey* (Carnival Films)

Fennell, L. A. (2004) 'Taking Eminent Domain Apart' *Michigan State Law Review* 957

Feser, E. (2005) 'There is No Such Thing as an Unjust Initial Acquisition' 22 *Social Philosophy & Policy* 56

Finnis, J. (1972) 'Some Professorial Fallacies about Rights' 4 *Adelaide Law Review* 377

Fodor, J. A. (1975) *The Language of Thought* (New York: Thomas Crowell)

Fodor, J. A. (1983) *Representations: Philosophical Essays on the Foundations of Cognitive Science* (Cambridge, MA: MIT Press)

Fodor, J. A. (1994) 'Concepts: A Potboiler' 50 *Cognition* 95

Fodor, J. A. (1998) *Concepts: Where Cognitive Science Went Wrong* (New York: Oxford University Press)

Forster, E. M. (1936) 'My Wood' in *Abinger Harvest* (London: Edward Arnold & Co.)

Fox, D. (2006) 'Relativity of Title at Law and in Equity' 65 *Cambridge Law Journal* 330

Frank, J. (1930) *Law and the Modern Mind* (New York: Brentano's)

Frank, J. (1934) 'Realism in Jurisprudence' 7 *American Law School Review* 1063

Frears, S. (1990) *The Grifters* (Miramax)

Frege, G. (1884) *The Foundations of Arithmetic: A Logico-Mathematical Enquiry into the Concept of Number*, 2nd edn. J. L. Austin trans. (Oxford: Basil Blackwell, 1953)

Frege, G. (1892) 'On Sinn and Bedeutung' in M. Beaney ed. *The Frege Reader* (Oxford: Blackwell, 1997) 151

Fried, C. (1981) *Contract as Promise: A Theory of Contractual Obligations* (Cambridge, MA: Harvard University Press)

Friedman, M. (1962) *Capitalism and Freedom* (Chicago: University of Chicago Press)

Fuller, L. L. (1969) *The Morality of Law* (New Haven: Yale University Press)

Fuller, L. L. and W. R. Perdue Jr. (1936) 'Reliance Interest in Contract Damages: 1' 46 *Yale Law Journal* 52

Gardner, J. (2007) 'Nearly Natural Law' 52 *American Journal of Jurisprudence* 1

Garnett, N. S. (2006) 'The Neglected Political Economy of Eminent Domain' 105 *Michigan Law Review* 101

Gaus, G. F. and L. E. Lomasky (1990) 'Are Property Rights Problematic?' 73 *The Monist* 483

Genet, J. (1949) *The Thief's Journal*, B. Frechtman trans. (New York: Grove Press, 1964)

Getzler, J. S. (2005) 'Use of Force in Protecting Property' 7 *Theoretical Inquiries in Law* 243

Goetz, C. and R. Scott (1980) 'Enforcing Promises: An Examination of the Basis of Contract' 89 *Yale Law Journal* 1261

Goffman, E. (1961) *Asylums: Essays on the Social Situation of Mental Patients and Other Inmates* (New York: Doubleday)

Gray, K. and S. F. Gray (2009) *Elements of Land Law*, 5th edn. (Oxford: Oxford University Press)

Green, S. and J. Randall (2009) *The Tort of Conversion* (Oxford: Hart Publishing)

Greenberg, M. (2000) 'Thoughts without Masters: Incomplete Understanding and the Content of Mind' (D.Phil. Thesis: Oxford University) <http://ssrn.com/abstract=1726547>

Gregor, M. ed. (1996) *Immanuel Kant: Practical Philosophy* (Cambridge: Cambridge University Press)

Gretton, G. (2007) 'Ownership and its Objects' 71 *Rabels Zeitschrift* 802

Grey, T. C. (1980) 'The Disintegration of Property' in J. R. Pennock and J. W. Chapman eds. *Nomos XXII: Property* (New York: New York University Press) 69

Gross, A. (1995) 'Pandora's Box: Slave Character on Trial in the Antebellum Deep South' 7 *Yale Journal of Law and the Humanities* 267

Grotius, H. (1604) *Commentary on the Law of Prize and Booty* (Indianapolis: Liberty Fund, 2006)

Grotius, H. (1609) *The Free Sea*, D. Armitage ed. (Indianapolis: Liberty Fund, 2004)

Grotius, H. (1625) *Grotius on the Rights of War and Peace: An Abridged Translation*, W. Whewell ed. and trans. (Cambridge: Cambridge University Press, 1853)

Hale, B. (1987) *Abstract Objects* (Oxford: Basil Blackwell)

Hamilton, W. H. and I. Till (1937) 'Property' 12 *Encyclopaedia of the Social Sciences* 528

Harris, J. W. (1996) *Property and Justice* (Oxford: Oxford University Press)

Harris, J. W. (2004) 'Human Rights and Mythical Beasts' 120 *Law Quarterly Review* 428

Hart, H. L. A. (1961) *The Concept of Law* (Oxford: Clarendon Press)

Hart, H. L. A. (1968) *Punishment and Responsibility* (Oxford: Oxford University Press)

Hart, H. L. A. (1972) 'Bentham on Legal Powers' 81 *Yale Law Journal* 799

Hart, H. L. A. (1983) *Essays in Jurisprudence and Philosophy* (Oxford: Oxford University Press)

Hegel, G. W. F. (1807) *Phenomenology of Spirit*, A. V. Miller trans. (Oxford: Oxford University Press, 1977)

Hegel, G. W. F. (1820a) *Hegel's Philosophy of Right*, T. M. Knox trans. (Oxford: Clarendon Press, 1952)

Hegel, G. W. F. (1820b) *Outlines of the Philosophy of Right*, S. Houlgate ed. and T. M. Knox trans. (Oxford: Oxford University Press, 2008)

Helmholz, R. (1983) 'Adverse Possession and Subjective Intent' 61 *Washington University Law Quarterly* 331

Heylighen, F. (1999) 'Advantages and Limitations of Formal Expression' 4 *Foundations of Science* 25

Hickey, R. (2010) *Property and the Law of Finders* (Oxford: Hart Publishing)

Hill, C. ed. (1983) *Winstanley: 'The Law of Freedom' and Other Writings* (Cambridge: Cambridge University Press)

Hill, C. (1991) *The World Turned Upside Down* (London: Penguin Books)

Hobbes, T. (1640) *The Elements of Law, Natural and Political* (Oxford: Oxford University Press, 1994)

Hobbes, T. (1642) 'De Cive' in B. Gert ed. *Man and Citizen* (Gloucester, MA: Peter Smith, 1978)

Hobbes, T. (1651a) *Leviathan*, M. Oakeshott ed. (Oxford: Basil Blackwell, 1957)

Hobbes, T. (1651b) *Leviathan: With Selected Variants from the Latin Edition of 1868*, E. Curley ed. (Indianapolis: Hackett, 1994)

Hohfeld, W. N. (1913) 'Some Fundamental Conceptions as Applied in Legal Reasoning' 23 *Yale Law Journal* 16

Hohfeld, W. N. (1917a) 'Faulty Analysis in Easement and License Cases' 27 *Yale Law Journal* 66

Hohfeld, W. N. (1917b) 'Fundamental Legal Conceptions as Applied in Judicial Reasoning' 26 *Yale Law Journal* 710

Hohfeld, W. N. (1919) *Fundamental Legal Conceptions as Applied in Judicial Reasoning and Other Legal Essays*, W. W. Cook ed. (New Haven: Yale University Press)

Holmes, O. W. (1872) 'Arrangement of the Law: Privity' 7 *American Law Review* 46

Holmes, O. W. (1881) *The Common Law*, M. Howe ed. (Cambridge, MA: Belknap Press, 1963)

Holmes, O. W. (1897) 'The Path of the Law' 10 *Harvard Law Review* 457

Honoré, A. M. (1960) 'Rights of Exclusion and Immunities against Divesting' 34 *Tulane Law Review* 453

Honoré, A. M. (1961) 'Ownership' in A. G. Guest ed. *Oxford Essays in Jurisprudence* (Oxford: Clarendon Press) 104

Honoré, A. M. (2006) 'Property and Ownership: Marginal Comments' in T. Endicott, J. Getzler, and E. Peel eds. *Properties of Law: Essays in Honour of Jim Harris* (Oxford: Oxford University Press)

Hookway, C. (2000) *Truth, Rationality, and Pragmatism: Themes from Peirce* (Oxford: Clarendon Press)

Horwitz, M. J. (1992) *The Transformation of American Law, 1870–1960: The Crisis of Legal Orthodoxy* (New York: Oxford University Press)

Hume, D. (1739–40a) *A Treatise on Human Nature*, L. A. Selby-Bigge ed. (Oxford: Clarendon Press, 1888)

Hume, D. (1739–40b) *A Treatise on Human Nature*, L. A. Selby-Bigge ed. (Oxford: Clarendon Press, 1896)

Hume, D. (1739–40c) *A Treatise on Human Nature*, 2nd rev. edn. L. A. Selby-Bigge ed. and P. Nidditch rev. (Oxford: Clarendon Press, 1978)

Hume, D. (1777) *Enquiries Concerning Human Understanding and Concerning the Principles of Morals*, P. Nidditch ed. (Oxford: Oxford University Press, 1975)

Hylton, J. G., et al. (1998) *Property Law and the Public Interest* (Charlottesville, VA: Lexis Law Publishing)

James, W. (1907) *Pragmatism: A New Name for Some Old Ways of Thinking* (New York: Longmans, Green & Co., 1931)

Jones, N. (1998) 'Trusts in England after the Statute of Uses: A View from the 16th Century' in R. Helmholz and R. Zimmerman eds. *Itinera Fiduciae: Trust and Treuhand in Historical Perspective* (Berlin: Duncker & Humblot)

Kahneman, D., J. Knetsch, and R. H. Thaler (1990) 'Experimental Tests of the Endowment Effect and the Coase Theorem' 98 *Journal of Political Economy* 1325

Kant, I. (1797) *The Metaphysics of Morals*, M. Gregor ed. and trans. (Cambridge: Cambridge University Press, 1991)

Kaplow, L. and S. Shavell (2002) *Fairness versus Welfare* (Cambridge, MA: Harvard University Press, 2006)

Katz, A. (1996) 'When Should an Offer Stick? The Economics of Promissory Estoppel in Preliminary Negotiations' 105 *Yale Law Journal* 1249

Katz, L. (2008) 'Exclusion and Exclusivity in Property Law' 58 *University of Toronto Law Journal* 275

Katz, L. (2010a) 'The Moral Paradox of Adverse Possession: Sovereignty and Revolution in Property Law' 55 *McGill Law Journal* 47

Katz, L. (2011a) 'Regulative Function of Property Rights' 8 *Econ Journal Watch* 236

Katz, L. (2011b) 'Ownership and Social Solidarity' 17 *Legal Theory* 119

Katz, L. (2012) ' "Governing through Owners": How and Why Formal Private Property Rights Enhance State Power' 160 *Pennsylvania Law Review* 2030

Kaufman, J. (2004) 'New Crop of Protesters in Tiananmen Square: Restive Homeowners' *Wall Street Journal* 9 June

Keenan, C. M. (1963) *Historical Documentation of Major Coal-Mine Disasters in the United States not Classified as Explosions of Gas or Dust: 1846–1962—Bureau of Mines Bulletin 616* (Washington, DC: United States Department of the Interior)

Keeton, W. P. et al. eds. (1984) *Prosser and Keeton on the Law of Torts*, 5th edn. (St Paul, MN: West Publishing)

Kendrick, L. (2011) 'The Lockean Rights of Bequest and Inheritance' 17 *Legal Theory* 145

Kenneally, M. (MS) 'Directed Duties, Conventional Wrongs, and the Right to Exclude'

Kent, J. (1826–30) *Commentaries on American Law* (New York: Da Capo Press, 1971)

Kimel, D. (2003) *From Promise to Contract: Towards a Liberal Theory of Contract* (Oxford: Hart Publishing)

Klimchuk, D. (2001) 'Necessity and Restitution' 7 *Legal Theory* 59

Klimchuk, D. (forthcoming) 'Equity and the Rule of Law' in Lisa Austin and Dennis Klimchuk eds. *Private Law and the Rule of Law* (Oxford: Oxford University Press)

Klimchuk, D. (MS) 'Grotius on the Right of Necessity'

Knetsch, J. (1989) 'The Endowment Effect and Evidence of Non-Reversible Indifference Curves' 79 *American Economic Review* 1277

Kocourek, A. (1920) 'Rights in Rem' 68 *University of Pennsylvania Law Review* 322

Kocourek, A. (1921) 'Polarized and Unpolarized Legal Relations' 9 *Kentucky Law Journal* 131

Kopytoff, I. (1986) 'The Cultural Biography of Things' in A. Appadurai ed. *The Social Life of Things: Commodities in Cultural Perspective* (Cambridge: Cambridge University Press)

Kramer, M. (1997) *John Locke and the Origins of Private Property: Philosophical Explorations of Individualism, Community, and Equality* (Cambridge: Cambridge University Press)

Krier, J. E. (2009) 'Evolutionary Theory and the Origin of Property Rights' 95 *Cornell Law Review* 139

Krier, J. E. and C. Serkin (2004) 'Public Ruses' *Michigan State Law Review* 859

La Forest, A. W. ed. (2006) *Anger and Honsberger: Law of Real Property*, 3rd edn. (Toronto: Canada Law Book)

Lee, B. A. (2013) 'Just Undercompensation: The Idiosyncratic Premium in Eminent Domain' 113 *Columbia Law Review* 593

Lee, B. A. and H. E. Smith (2012) 'The Nature of Coasean Property' 59 *International Review of Economics* 145

Leiter, B. (2010) 'Legal Formalism and Legal Realism: What Is the Issue?' 16 *Legal Theory* 111

Lewis, J. (1888) *A Treatise on the Law of Eminent Domain in the United States* (Chicago: Callaghan and Co.)

Leychkis, Y., S. R. Munzer, and J. L. Richardson (2009) 'What Is Stemness?' 40 *Studies in the History and Philosophy of Biological and Biomedical Sciences* 312

Llewellyn, K. N. (1930) 'A Realistic Jurisprudence—The Next Step' 30 *Columbia Law Review* 431

Llewellyn, K. N. (1931) 'Some Realism about Realism—Responding to Dean Pound' 44 *Harvard Law Review* 1222

Llewellyn, K. N. (1938) 'Through Title to Contract and a Bit Beyond' 15 *New York University Law Quarterly Review* 159

Locke, J. (1689a) 'Epistola de Tolerantia ad Clarissimum Virum' in R. Klibansky ed. and J. W. Gough trans. *John Locke, Epistola de Tolerantia: A Letter on Toleration* (Oxford: Clarendon Press, 1968)

Locke, J. (1689b) *Two Treatises of Government*, P. Laslett ed. (Cambridge: Cambridge University Press, 1988)

Locke, J. (1693) 'Some Thoughts Concerning Education' in R. W. Grant and N. Tarcov eds. *Some Thoughts Concerning Education: and, Of the Conduct of the Understanding* (Indianapolis: Hackett Publishing, 1996)

Locke, J. (1695) *The Reasonableness of Christianity*, G. W. Ewing ed. (Washington, DC: Regnery Gateway, 1965)

Locke, J. (1700) *An Essay Concerning Human Understanding*, 4th edn., P. Nidditch ed. (Oxford: Clarendon Press, 1979)

Low, K. (2010) 'Equitable Title and Economic Loss' 126 *Law Quarterly Review* 507

Lueck, D. (1995) 'The Rule of First Possession and the Design of the Law' 38 *Journal of Law & Economics* 393

Lueck, D. (2003) 'First Possession as the Basis of Property' in T. L. Anderson and F. S. McChesney eds. *Property Rights: Cooperation, Conflict and Law* (Princeton: Princeton University Press)

MacCormick, N. (1972) 'Voluntary Obligations and Normative Powers' 46 *Proceedings of the Aristotelian Society, Supplementary Volumes* 59

McDowell, A. (2002) 'From Commons to Claims: Property Rights in the California Gold Rush' 14 *Yale Journal of Law & the Humanities* 1

McDowell, A. (2007) 'Legal Fictions in Pierson v. Post' 105 *Michigan Law Review* 735

McEvoy, A. (1986) *The Fisherman's Problem: Ecology and Law in the California Fisheries* (Cambridge: Cambridge University Press)

McFarlane, B. (2008) *The Structure of Property Law* (Oxford: Hart Publishing)

McFarlane, B. (2010) 'The Protection of Pre-Contractual Reliance: A Way Forward' 10 *Oxford University Commonwealth Law Journal* 95

McFarlane, B. (2011) 'The Numerus Clausus Principle and Covenants Relating to Land' in S. Bright ed. *Modern Studies in Property Law*, vol. 6 (Oxford: Hart Publishing)

McFarlane, B. (2012) 'Tulk v Moxhay (1848)' in C. Mitchell and P. Mitchell eds. *Landmark Cases in Equity* (Oxford: Hart Publishing) 203

McFarlane, B. (2013) 'Keppell v Bailey (1834); Hill v Tupper (1863): The Numerus Clausus and the Common Law' in N. Gravells ed. *Landmark Cases in Land Law* (Oxford: Hart Publishing)

McFarlane, B. and A. Robertson (2009) 'Apocalypse Averted: Proprietary Estoppel in the House of Lords' 125 *Law Quarterly Review* 535

McFarlane, B. and R. Stevens (2010) 'The Nature of Equitable Property' 4 *Journal of Equity* 1

MacIntyre, A. (1984) 'Hume on the "Is" and the "Ought"' in *Against the Self-Images of the Age*, 2nd edn. (South Bend, IN: University of Notre Dame Press)

McKenna, M. (2007) 'The Normative Foundations of Trademark Law' 82 *Notre Dame Law Review* 1839

McNeal, R. H. (1963) *The Bolshevik Tradition* (Englewood Cliffs, NJ: Prentice Hall)

Macpherson, C. B. (1962) *The Political Theory of Possessive Individualism: Hobbes to Locke* (Oxford: Oxford University Press)

Macpherson, C. B. (1978) 'The Meaning of Property' in *Property: Mainstream and Critical Positions* (Toronto: University of Toronto Press) 3

Mäkinen, V. (2011) 'Poverty' in H. Lagerlund ed. *Encyclopedia of Medieval Philosophy* (Dordrecht: Springer) 1066

Margolis, E. and S. Laurence (2012) 'Concepts' in E. N. Zalta ed. *The Stanford Encyclopedia of Philosophy, Fall 2012* <http://plato.stanford.edu/archives/fall2012/entries/concepts>

Markovits, D. (2004) 'The No-Retraction Principle and the Morality of Negotiations' 152 *The University of Pennsylvania Law Review* 1903

Marx, K. (1867) *Capital*, vol. 1, B. Fowkes trans. (London: Penguin Classics, 1990)

Matthews, P. (2010) 'The Words Which Are Not There: A Partial History of the Constructive Trust' in C. Mitchell ed. *Constructive and Resulting Trusts* (Oxford: Hart Publishing) 3

Mee, J. (2011) 'Proprietary Estoppel, Promises and Mistaken Belief' 6 *Modern Studies in Property Law* 171

Merrill, T. W. (1985) 'Trespass, Nuisance, and the Costs of Determining Property Rights' 14 *Journal of Legal Studies* 13

Merrill, T. W. (1986) 'The Economics of Public Use' 72 *Cornell Law Review* 61

Merrill, T. W. (1998) 'Property and the Right to Exclude' 77 *Nebraska Law Review* 730

Merrill, T. W. (2010) 'Accession and Original Ownership' 1 *Journal of Legal Analysis* 459

Merrill, T. W. (2012) 'The Property Strategy' 160 *University of Pennsylvania Law Review* 2061

Merrill, T. W. and H. E. Smith (2000) 'Optimal Standardization in the Law of Property: The *Numerus Clausus* Principle' 110 *Yale Law Journal* 1

Merrill, T. W. and H. E. Smith (2001a) 'The Property/Contract Interface' 101 *Columbia Law Review* 773

Merrill, T. W. and H. E. Smith (2001b) 'What Happened to Property in Law and Economics?' 111 *Yale Law Journal* 357

Merrill, T. W. and H. E. Smith (2007a) 'The Morality of Property' 48 *William and Mary Law Review* 1849

Merrill, T. W. and H. E. Smith (2007b) *Property: Principles and Policies* (New York: Foundation Press)

Merrill, T. W. and H. E. Smith (2011) 'Making Coasean Property More Coasean' 54 *Journal of Law & Economics* S77

Merrill, T. W. and H. E. Smith (2012) *Property: Principles and Policies*, 2nd edn. (New York: Foundation Press)

Michelman, F. I. (1967) 'Property, Utility, and Fairness: Comments on the Ethical Foundations of "Just Compensation" Law' 80 *Harvard Law Review* 1165

Mill, J. S. (1993) *Utilitarianism: On Liberty; Considerations on Representative Government; Remarks on Bentham's Philosophy*, G. Williams ed. (London: J. M. Dent & Sons)

Misak, C. J. (2004) *Truth and the End of Inquiry: A Peircean Account of Truth* (Oxford: Clarendon Press)

Mithen, S. (2012) 'How Fit is E. O. Wilson's Evolution?' *New York Review of Books* 21 June

Montague, R. (1973) 'The Proper Treatment of Quantification in Ordinary English' in K. J. J. Hintikaa, J. M. E. Moravcsik, and P. Suppes eds. *Approaches to Natural Language: Proceedings of the 1970 Stanford Workshop on Grammar and Semantics* (Dordrecht: D. Reidel) 221

Mossoff, A. (2002) 'Locke's Labor Lost' 9 *University of Chicago Law School Roundtable* 155

Mossoff, A. (2003) 'What Is Property? Putting the Pieces Back Together' 45 *Arizona Law Review* 371

Mossoff, A. (2009) 'The Use and Abuse of IP at the Birth of the Administrative State' 157 *University of Pennsylvania Law Review* 2001

Mulligan, C. (2013) 'A Numerus Clausus Principle for Intellectual Property' 80 *Tennessee Law Review* 235

Munzer, S. R. (1990) *A Theory of Property* (Cambridge: Cambridge University Press)

Munzer, S. R. (2009) 'Commons, Anticommons, and Community in Biotechnological Assets' 10 *Theoretical Inquiries in Law* 271

Munzer, S. R. (2011) 'A Bundle Theorist Holds On to his Collection of Sticks' 8 *Econ Journal Watch* 265

Munzer, S. R. and J. W. Nickel (1977) 'Does the Constitution Mean What It Always Meant?' 77 *Columbia Law Review* 1029

Murray, A. (2007) 'Marriage—The Peculiar Institution: An Exploration of Marriage and the Women's Rights Movement in the 19th Century' 16 *UCLA Women's Law Journal* 137

Myers, P. C. (1999) *Our Only Star and Compass: Locke and the Struggle for Political Rationality* (Lanham, MD: Rowman & Littlefield)

Myers, P. C. (2005) 'On Michael Zuckert's Launching Liberalism' 32 *Interpretation: A Journal of Political Philosophy* 231

Nagel, T. (1995) 'Personal Rights and Public Space' 24 *Philosophy & Public Affairs* 83

Neuberger, D. (2009) 'The Stuffing of Minerva's Owl? Taxonomy and Taxidermy in Equity' 68 *Cambridge Law Journal* 537

Newman, C. M. (2011) 'Transformation in Property and Copyright' 56 *Villanova Law Review* 251

Neyers, J. (2003) 'Towards a Coherent Theory of Estoppel' 25 *Journal of Obligations and Remedies* 45

Nicholls, F. M. ed. (1865) *Britton* (Oxford: Oxford University Press, 1983)

Nolan, D. (2012) 'A Tort against Land' in D. Nolan and A. Robertson eds. *Rights and Private Law* (Oxford: Hart Publishing)

Nolan, R. C. (2006) 'Equitable Property' 122 *Law Quarterly Review* 232

Nozick, R. (1974a) *Anarchy, State, and Utopia* (Oxford: Basil Blackwell)

Nozick, R. (1974b) *Anarchy, State, and Utopia* (New York: Basic Books)

Oakeshott, M. (1983) 'The Rule of Law' in *On History and Other Essays* (Oxford: Basil Blackwell) 119

Olivecrona, K. (1974) 'Locke's Theory of Appropriation' 24 *Philosophical Quarterly* 220

Oosterhoff, A. H. and W. B. Rayner eds. (1985) *Anger and Honsberger: Law of Real Property*, 2nd edn., vol. 2 (Toronto: Canada Law Book)

Oswald, L. J. (1997) 'The Role of the "Harm/Benefit" and "Average Reciprocity of Advantage" Rules in a Comprehensive Takings Analysis' 50 *Vanderbilt Law Review* 1449

Palmer, N. (2000) 'Finding, Bailment and the Fruits of Crime' in F. Meisel and P. J. Cook eds. *Property and Protection: Legal Rights and Restrictions: Essays in Honour of Brian W. Harvey* (Oxford: Hart Publishing)

Palmer, N. (2009) *Palmer on Bailment*, 3rd edn. (London: Sweet & Maxwell)

Palmer, V. V. (1992) *Paths to Privity of Contract: The History of the Third Party Beneficiary Contract at English Law* (Clark, NJ: The Lawbook Exchange, 2006)

Peacocke, C. (1992) *A Study of Concepts* (Cambridge, MA: MIT Press)

Peacocke, C. (2004) 'Interrelations: Concepts, Knowledge, Reference and Structure' 19 *Mind & Language* 85

Peñalver, E. M. (2009) 'Land Virtues' 94 *Cornell Law Review* 821

Penner, J. E. (1996a) 'The "Bundle of Rights" Picture of Property' 43 *UCLA Law Review* 711

Penner, J. E. (1996b) 'Voluntary Obligations and the Scope of the Law of Contract' 2 *Legal Theory* 325

Penner, J. E. (1997) *The Idea of Property in Law* (Oxford: Clarendon Press)

Penner, J. E. (2006) 'Ownership, Co-ownership, and the Justification of Property Rights' in T. Endicott, J. Getzler, and E. Peel eds. *Properties of Law: Essays in Honour of Jim Harris* (Oxford: Oxford University Press) 166

Penner, J. E. (2009) 'Property, Community, and the Problem of Distributive Justice' 10 *Theoretical Inquiries in Law* 193

Penner, J. E. (2010) 'Resulting Trusts and Unjust Enrichment: Three Controversies' in C. Mitchell ed. *Constructive and Resulting Trusts* (Oxford: Hart Publishing) 237

Penner, J. E. (2011) 'Potentiality, Actuality, and "Stick"-Theory' 8 *Econ Journal Watch* 274

Perelman, V. (2003) *House of Sand and Fog* (Dreamworks)

Pipes, R. (1996) 'Human Nature and the Fall of Communism' 49 *Bulletin of the American Academy of Arts & Sciences* 38

Pipes, R. (1999) *Property and Freedom* (New York: Alfred A. Knopf)

Pollock, F. and F. W. Maitland (1898), *History of English Law before the Time of Edward I*, vol. 2, 2nd edn. (Cambridge: Cambridge University Press)

Pollock, F. and R. S. Wright (1888) *An Essay on Possession in the Common Law* (Oxford: Clarendon Press)

Posner, R. A. (1995) 'Wealth Maximization and Tort Law' in D. G. Owen ed. *Philosophical Foundations of Tort Law* (Oxford: Oxford University Press)

Pound, R. (1923a) *Interpretations of Legal History* (New York: Macmillan)

Pound, R. (1923b) 'The Theory of Judicial Decision III: A Theory of Judicial Decision for Today' 36 *Harvard Law Review* 940

Pratt, M. (1999) 'Identifying the Harm Done: A Critique of the Reliance Theory of Estoppel' 21 *Adelaide Law Review* 209

Pratt, M. (2002) 'Promises and Perlocutions' 5 *Critical Review of International Social & Political Philosophy* 93

Pratt, M. (2007) 'Promises, Contracts, and Voluntary Obligations' 26 *Law & Philosophy* 531

Prinz, J. J. (2002) *Furnishing the Mind: Concepts and their Perceptual Basis* (Cambridge, MA: MIT Press)

Purdy, J. (2010) *The Meaning of Property: Freedom, Community, and the Legal Imagination* (New Haven: Yale University Press)

Radin, M. (1923) 'Disseisin of Chattels: The Title of a Thief' 11 *California Law Review* 259

Radin, M. J. (1982) 'Property and Personhood' 34 *Stanford Law Review* 957

Radin, M. J. (1987) 'Market-Inalienability' 100 *Harvard Law Review* 1849

Radin, M. J. (1988) 'The Liberal Conception of Property: Cross Currents in the Jurisprudence of Takings' 88 *Columbia Law Review* 1667

Radin, M. J. (1996a) *Contested Commodities* (Cambridge, MA: Harvard University Press)

Radin, M. J. (1996b) 'Property Evolving in Cyberspace' 15 *Journal of Law & Commerce* 509

Rastell, J. (1721) *Les Termes de la ley; or, Certain Difficult and Obscure Words and Terms of the Common and Statute Laws of England, Now in Use, Expounded and Explained* (Littleton, CO: F. B. Rothman, 1933)

Rawls, J. (1955) 'Two Concepts of Rules' 64 *The Philosophical Review* 3

Rawls, J. (1971) *A Theory Of Justice* (Cambridge, MA: Harvard University Press)

Rawls, J. (1993) *Political Liberalism* (New York: Columbia University Press)

Rawls, J. (1999) *A Theory of Justice*, revised edn. (Cambridge, MA: Harvard University Press)

Ray, N. (1955) *Rebel without a Cause* (Warner Bros)

Raz, J. (1972) 'Reply to MacCormick' 46 *Proceedings of the Aristotelian Society (Supplement)* 80

Raz, J. (1975) *Practical Reason and Norms* (Princeton: Princeton University Press, 1990)

Raz, J. (1977a) 'Promises and Obligations' in P. M. S. Hacker and J. Raz eds. *Law, Morality, and Society: Essays in Honour of H. L. A. Hart* (Oxford: Clarendon Press) 210

Raz, J. (1977b) 'The Rule of Law and its Virtue' 93 *Law Quarterly Review* 195

Raz, J. (1982) 'Promises in Morality and Law' 95 *Harvard Law Review* 916

Raz, J. (1985) 'Authority and Justification' 14 *Philosophy and Public Affairs* 3

Raz, J. (1986) *The Morality of Freedom* (Oxford: Oxford University Press)

Raz, J. (1990) 'Introduction' in J. Raz ed. *Authority* (New York: New York University Press)

Raz, J. (2009) *Between Authority and Interpretation* (Oxford: Oxford University Press)

Raz, J. (2011) *From Normativity to Responsibility* (Oxford: Oxford University Press)

Reich, C. (1964) 'The New Property' 73 *Yale Law Journal* 733

Reid, J. P. (1980) *Law for the Elephant: Property and Social Behavior on the Overland Trail* (San Marino, CA: The Huntington Library)

Rey, G. (1998) 'What Implicit Conceptions are Unlikely to Do' in E. Villanueva ed. *Concepts: Philosophical Issues*, vol. 9 (Atascadero, CA: Ridgeview Publishing Co.) 93

Ripstein, A. (2007) 'As If It Had Never Happened' 48 *William and Mary Law Review* 1957

Ripstein, A. (2009) *Force and Freedom: Kant's Legal and Political Philosophy* (Cambridge, MA: Harvard University Press)

Ripstein, A. (forthcoming) 'The Rule of Law and Time's Arrow' in Lisa Austin and Dennis Klimchuk (eds.), *Private Law and the Rule of Law* (Oxford: Oxford University Press)

Robertson, A. (2000) 'Reasonable Reliance in Estoppel by Conduct' 23 *University of New South Wales Law Journal* 87

Robertson, A. (2008) 'The Reliance Basis of Proprietary Estoppel Remedies' 72 *Conveyancer and Property Lawyer* 295

Robertson, A. (2010) 'Unconscionability and Proprietary Estoppel Remedies' in E. Bant and M. Harding eds. *Exploring Private Law* (Cambridge: Cambridge University Press) 402

Robinson, E. S. (1934) 'Law—An Unscientific Science' 44 *Yale Law Journal* 235

Rose, C. M. (1985) 'Possession as the Origin of Property' 52 *University of Chicago Law Review* 73

Rose, C. M. (1989) 'The Ancient Constitution vs. the Federalist Empire: Anti-Federalism from the Attack on "Monarchism" to Modern Localism' 84 *Northwestern University Law Review* 74

Rose, C. M. (1990) 'Property as Storytelling: Perspectives from Game Theory, Narrative Theory, Feminist Theory' 2 *Yale Journal of Law and the Humanities* 37

Rose, C. M. (2007) 'The Moral Subject of Property' 48 *William and Mary Law Review* 1897

Rose, F. (2005) *General Average: Law and Practice*, 2nd edn. (London: LLP)

Rosen, G. (2012) 'Abstract Objects' *Stanford Encyclopedia of Philosophy*

Ross, T. J. (2010) *Fuzzy Logic with Engineering Applications*, 3rd edn. (Chichester, West Sussex: John Wiley & Sons Ltd)

Rotherham, C. (2002) *Proprietary Remedies in Context: A Study in the Judicial Redistribution of Property Rights* (Oxford: Hart Publishing)

Rousseau, J. (1762) 'The Social Contract' in *The Social Contract and the Discourses* (New York: Alfred A. Knopf Inc., 1973) 197

Rubin, E. L. (1984) 'Due Process and the Administrative State' 72 *California Law Review* 1044

Rudden, B. (1987) 'Economic Theory v Property Law: The *Numerus Clausus* Problem' in J. Eekelaar and J. Bell eds. *Oxford Essays in Jurisprudence, Third Series* (Oxford: Clarendon Press)

Rushworth, A. and A. Scott 'Total Chaos?' (2010) *Lloyd's Maritime and Commercial Law Quarterly* 536

Sackman, J. L. et al. (2012) *Nichols on Eminent Domain*, 3rd edn. (New York: Matthew Bender)

Sage, N. W. (2012) 'Original Acquisition and Unilateralism: Kant, Hegel, and Corrective Justice' 25 *Canadian Journal of Law & Jurisprudence* 119

Salkowski, C. (1886) *Institutes and History of Roman Private Law with Catena of Texts*, E. E. Whitfield ed. and trans. (London: Stevens & Hayes)

Samet, I. (2012) 'What Conscience Can Do for Equity' 3 *Jurisprudence* 13

Samet, I. (forthcoming) 'Proprietary Estoppel and Responsibility for Omissions'

Scanlon, T. M. (1998) *What We Owe to Each Other* (Cambridge, MA: Belknap Press of Harvard University Press)

Scanlon, T. M. (2001) 'Promises and Contracts' in P. Benson ed. *The Theory of Contract Law: New Essays* (Cambridge: Cambridge University Press) 86

Schroeder, Jeanne (1994) 'Chix Nix Bundle-O-Stix: A Feminist Critique of the Disaggregation of Property' 93 *Michigan Law Review* 239

Schwartz, A. and R. Scott (2007) 'Precontractual Liability and Preliminary Agreements' 120 *Harvard Law Review* 661

Sheehan, D. (2011) *The Principles of Personal Property Law* (Portland, OR: Hart Publishing)

Shiffrin, S. V. (2008) 'Promising, Intimate Relationships, and Conventionalism' 117 *Philosophical Review* 481

Simmons, A. J. (1992) *The Lockean Theory of Rights* (Princeton: Princeton University Press)

Simmons, A. J. (1994) 'Original-Acquisition Justifications of Private Property' 11 *Social Philosophy & Policy* 63

Simmons, A. J. (1998) 'Makers' Rights' 2 *Journal of Ethics* 197

Simon, H. A. (1981) *The Sciences of the Artificial* (Cambridge, MA: MIT Press)

Simpson, A. W. B. (1986) *A History of the Land Law*, 2nd edn. (Oxford: Clarendon Press)

Singer, J. W. (1996) 'No Right to Exclude: Public Accommodations and Private Property' 90 *Northwestern Law Review* 1283

Singer, J. W. (2011) 'Original Acquisition of Property: From Conquest & Possession to Democracy & Equal Opportunity' 86 *Indiana Law Journal* 1

Smith, H. E. (2002) 'Exclusion versus Governance: Two Strategies for Delineating Property Rights' 31 *Journal of Legal Studies* S453

Smith, H. E. (2003) 'The Language of Property: Form, Context, and Audience' 55 *Stanford Law Review* 1105

Smith, H. E. (2004) 'Exclusion and Property Rules in the Law of Nuisance' 90 *Virginia Law Review* 965

Smith, H. E. (2007) 'Intellectual Property as Property: Delineating Entitlements in Information' 116 *Yale Law Journal* 1742

Smith, H. E. (2009) 'Mind the Gap: The Indirect Relation between Ends and Means in American Property Law' 94 *Cornell Law Review* 959

Smith, H. E. (2011a) 'Modularity and Morality in the Law of Torts' 4 *Journal of Tort Law* Article 5

Smith, H. E. (2011b) 'Standardization in Property Law' in K. Ayotte and H. E. Smith eds. *Research Handbook on the Economics of Property Law* (Cheltenham: Edward Elgar) 148

Smith, H. E. (2012a) 'On the Economy of Concepts in Property' 160 *Pennsylvania Law Review* 2097

Smith, H. E. (2012b) 'Property as the Law of Things' 125 *Harvard Law Review* 1691

Smith, H. E. (forthcoming) 'Property, Equity, and the Rule of Law' in Lisa Austin and Dennis Klimchuk eds. *Private Law and the Rule of Law* (Oxford: Oxford University Press)

Smith, M. J. (1982) *Evolution and the Theory of Games* (Cambridge: Cambridge University Press)

Solly, A. R. (1949) 'Edmund Hickeringill: Eccentric' 58 *Essex Review* 127

Solnit, R. (2009) *A Paradise Built in Hell: The Extraordinary Communities That Arise in Disaster* (New York: Viking Press)

Southwood, N. and D. Friedrich (2009) 'Promises beyond Assurance' 144 *Philosophical Studies* 261

Spence, M. (1999) *Protecting Reliance: The Emergent Doctrine of Equitable Estoppel* (Oxford: Hart Publishing)

Sreedhar, S. (2010) *Hobbes on Resistance: Defying the Leviathan* (Cambridge: Cambridge University Press)

Sreenivasan, G. (1995) *The Limits of Lockean Rights in Property* (New York: Oxford University Press)

Stake, J. E. (2004) 'The Property "Instinct"' 359 *Philosophical Transactions of the Royal Society* 1763

Stalnaker, R. (1976) 'Propositions' in A. F. MacKay and D. D. Merrill eds. *Issues in the Philosophy of Language: Proceedings of the 1972 Oberlin Colloquium in Philosophy* (New Haven: Yale University Press) 79

Stern, S. M. (2009) 'Residential Protectionism and the Legal Mythology of the Home' 107 *Michigan Law Review* 1093

Stevens, R. (2007) *Torts and Rights* (Oxford: Oxford University Press)

Stigler, G. J. (1971) 'The Theory of Economic Regulation' 2 *Bell Journal of Economics and Management Science* 3

Stoebuck, W. B. and D. A. Whitman (2000) *The Law of Property*, 3rd edn. (St Paul, MN: West Group)

Stoljar, S. (1984a) *An Analysis of Rights* (New York: St Martin's Press)

Stoljar, S. (1984b) 'Possession in the Civil Codes' 33 *International & Comparative Law Quarterly* 1026

Strawson, P. F. (1950) 'On Referring' 59 *Mind* 320

Sugden, R. (1986) *The Economics of Rights, Cooperation and Welfare* (Basingstoke: Palgrave Macmillan, 2004)

Swart, H. D. (1998) *Introduction to Natural Language Semantics* (Stanford, CA: CSLI Publications)

Tamanaha, B. Z. (2009) *Beyond the Formalist–Realist Divide: The Role of Politics in Judging* (Princeton: Princeton University Press)

Tettenborn, A. (1982) 'Covenants, Privity of Contract, and the Purchaser of Personal Property' 41 *Cambridge Law Journal* 58

Thompson, E. P. (1975) *Whigs and Hunters: The Origin of the Black Act* (London: Allen Lane)

Thomson, J. J. (1990) *The Realm of Rights* (Cambridge, MA: Harvard University Press)

Treanor, W. (1997) 'The Armstrong Principle, the Narratives of Takings, and Compensation Statutes' 38 *William and Mary Law Review* 1151

Tully, J. (1980) *A Discourse on Property: Locke and his Adversaries* (Cambridge: Cambridge University Press)

Tully, J. (1993) *An Approach to Political Philosophy: Locke in Contexts* (Cambridge: Cambridge University Press)

Turner, P. (2010) 'Consequential Economic Loss and the Trust Beneficiary' 69 *Cambridge Law Journal* 445

Umbeck, J. (1981) *A Theory of Property Rights: With Application to the Californian Gold Rush* (Iowa City: Iowa State University Press)

Upton, H. (2000) 'Right-Based Morality and Hohfeld's Relations' 4 *Journal of Ethics* 237

Veblen, T. (1899) *The Theory of the Leisure Class: An Economic Study of Institutions* (Oxford: Oxford University Press, 2007)

Villanueva, E. ed. (1998) *Concepts: Philosophical Issues*, vol. 9 (Atascadero, CA: Ridgeview Publishing Co.)

Viner, J. (1742) *A General Abridgement of Law & Equity: Alphabetically Digested Under Proper Titles with Notes and References to the Whole*, vol. 16 (London: G. G. J. and J. Robinson)

Von Pufendorf, S. (1672) *De Jure Naturae et Gentium Libri Octo*, C. H. Oldfather and W. A. Oldfather trans. (New York: Oceana, 1964)

Von Pufendorf, S. (1673) *The Whole Duty of Man According to the Law of Nature* (Indianapolis: Liberty Fund, 2003)

Waldron, J. (1981) 'Locke's Account of Inheritance and Bequest' 19 *Journal of the History of Philosophy* 39

Waldron, J. (1982) 'The Turfs my Servant Has Cut' 13 *The Locke Newsletter* 9

Waldron, J. (1983) 'Two Worries about Mixing one's Labour' 33 *The Philosophical Quarterly* 37

Waldron, J. (1984) 'Locke, Tully and the Regulation of Property' 32 *Political Studies* 98

Waldron, J. (1988) *The Right to Private Property* (Oxford: Clarendon Press)

Waldron, J. (1994) 'The Advantages and Difficulties of the Humean Theory of Property' 11 *Social Philosophy & Policy* 85

Waldron, J. (2000) '"Transcendental Nonsense" and System in the Law' 100 *Columbia Law Review* 16

Waldron, J. (2002) *God, Locke, and Equality: Christian Foundations in Locke's Political Thought* (Cambridge: Cambridge University Press)

Waldron, J. (2003) 'Indigeneity? First Peoples and Last Occupancy' 1 *New Zealand Journal of Public and International Law Review* 55

Waldron, J. (2005) 'Nozick and Locke: Filling the Space of Rights' 22 *Social Philosophy & Policy* 81

Waldron, J. (2008) 'The Concept and the Rule of Law' 43 *Georgia Law Review* 1

Waldron, J. (2009) 'Community and Property—For Those Who Have Neither' 10 *Theoretical Inquiries in Law* 161

Weinrib, E. J. (1976) 'Illegality as a Tort Defence' 26 *University of Toronto Law Journal* 28

Weinrib, E. J. (1995) *The Idea of Private Law* (Cambridge, MA: Harvard University Press)

Weinrib, E. J. (2011) 'Private Law and Public Right' 61 *University of Toronto Law Journal* 191

Wellman, C. (1985) *A Theory of Rights: Persons under Laws, Institutions, and Morals* (Totowa, NJ: Rowman & Allanheld)

Wellman, C. (1995) *Real Rights* (New York: Oxford University Press)

West, T. G. (2012) 'The Grounds of Locke's Law of Nature' 29 *Social Philosophy & Policy* 1

Wetzel, L. (2009) *Types and Tokens: On Abstract Objects* (Cambridge, MA: MIT Press)

White, G. E. (1972) 'From Sociological Jurisprudence to Realism: Jurisprudence and Social Change in Early Twentieth-Century America' 58 *Virginia Law Review* 999

Whitehead, A. N. and B. Russell (1927) *Principia Mathematica* (Cambridge: Cambridge University Press)

Williston, S. (2008) *Williston on Contracts*, 4th edn. R. A. Lord ed. (Eagan, MN: Thomson Reuters)

Wingate, E. (1658) *Maximes of Reason: or, The Reason of the Common Law of England* (Charleston, SC: Nabu Press, 2010)

Wittgenstein, L. (1953) *Philosophical Investigations*, 4th edn. P. M. S. Hacker and J. Schulte ed. and G. E. M. Anscombe, P. M. S. Hacker, and J. Schulte trans. (Chichester, West Sussex: Blackwell, 2009)

Wittgenstein, L. (1967) *Zettel*, 2nd edn. (Berkeley: University of California Press, 1981)

Woolf, V. (1929) *A Room of One's Own* (London: Hogarth Press, 1974)

Zadeh, L. A. (1965) 'Fuzzy Sets' 8 *Information and Control* 338

Zerbe, R. O. and C. L. Anderson (2001) 'Culture and Fairness in the Development of Institutions in the California Gold Fields' 61 *Journal of Economic History* 114

Zipursky, B. C. (2000) 'Pragmatic Conceptualism' 6 *Legal Theory* 457

Zuckert, M. (2005) 'Reconsidering Lockean Rights Theory: A Reply to my Critics' 32 *Interpretation: A Journal of Political Philosophy* 257

Index